CHARLES R. SWINDOLL

SWINDOLL'S
LIVING
INSIGHTS

NEW TESTAMENT COMMENTARY

ACTS

Tyndale House Publishers
Carol Stream, Illinois

Swindoll's Living Insights New Testament Commentary, Volume 5

Visit Tyndale online at www.tyndale.com.

Insights on Acts copyright © 2016 by Charles R. Swindoll, Inc.

Cover photograph copyright © Paolo Cipriani/Getty Images. All rights reserved.

Photograph of notebook copyright © jcsmilly/Shutterstock. All rights reserved.

Unless otherwise noted, all artwork copyright © Tyndale House Publishers. All rights reserved.

All images are the property of their respective copyright holders and all rights are reserved.

Maps copyright © 2016 by Tyndale House Publishers. All rights reserved.

Designed by Nicole Grimes

Published in association with Yates & Yates, LLP (www.yates2.com).

ISBN 978-1-4143-9375-9   Hardcover

Previously published by Zondervan under ISBN 978-0-310-28440-6

Printed in China

28   27   26   25   24
10   9   8   7   6

CONTENTS

AUTHOR'S PREFACE

For more than sixty years I have loved the Bible. It was that love for the Scriptures, mixed with a clear call into the gospel ministry during my tour of duty in the Marine Corps, that resulted in my going to Dallas Theological Seminary to prepare for a lifetime of ministry. During those four great years I had the privilege of studying under outstanding men of God, who also loved God's Word. They not only held the inerrant Word of God in high esteem, they taught it carefully, preached it passionately, and modeled it consistently. A week never passes without my giving thanks to God for the grand heritage that has been mine to claim! I am forever indebted to those fine theologians and mentors, who cultivated in me a strong commitment to the understanding, exposition, and application of God's truth.

For more than fifty years I have been engaged in doing just that—*and how I love it!* I confess without hesitation that I am addicted to the examination and the proclamation of the Scriptures. Because of this, books have played a major role in my life for as long as I have been in ministry—especially those volumes that explain the truths and enhance my understanding of what God has written. Through these many years I have collected a large personal library, which has proven invaluable as I have sought to remain a faithful student of the Bible. To the end of my days, my major goal in life is to communicate the Word with accuracy, insight, clarity, and practicality. Without informative and reliable books to turn to, I would have "run dry" decades ago.

Among my favorite and most well-worn volumes are those that have enabled me to get a better grasp of the biblical text. Like most expositors, I am forever searching for literary tools that I can use to hone my gifts and sharpen my skills. For me, that means finding resources that make the complicated simple and easy to understand, that offer insightful comments and word pictures that enable me to see the relevance of sacred truth in light of my twenty-first-century world, and that drive those truths home to my heart in ways I do not easily forget. When I come across such books, they wind up in my hands as I devour them and then place them in my library for further reference . . . and, believe me, I often return to them. What a relief it is to have these resources to turn to when I lack fresh insight, or when I need just the right story or illustration, or when I get stuck in the tangled text and cannot find my way out. For the serious expositor, a library is essential. As a mentor of mine once said, "Where else can you have ten thousand professors at your fingertips?"

In recent years I have discovered there are not nearly enough resources like those I just described. It was such a discovery that prompted me to consider becoming a part of the answer instead of lamenting the problem. But the solution would result in a huge undertaking. A writing project that covers all of the books and letters of the New Testament seemed overwhelming and intimidating. A rush of relief came when I realized that during the past fifty-plus years I've taught and preached through most of the New Testament. In my files were folders filled with notes from those messages that were just lying there, waiting to be brought out of hiding, given a fresh and relevant touch in light of today's needs, and applied to fit into the lives of men and women who long for a fresh word from the Lord. *That did it!* I began to work on plans to turn all of those notes into this commentary on the New Testament.

I must express my gratitude to both Mark Gaither and Mike Svigel for their tireless and devoted efforts, serving as my hands-on, day-to-day editors. They have done superb work as we have walked our way through the verses and chapters of all twenty-seven New Testament books. It has been a pleasure to see how they have taken my original material and helped me shape it into a style that remains true to the text of the Scriptures, at the same time interestingly and creatively developed, and all the while allowing my voice to come through in a natural and easy-to-read manner.

I need to add sincere words of appreciation to the congregations I have served in various parts of these United States for more than five decades. It has been my good fortune to be the recipient of their love, support, encouragement, patience, and frequent words of affirmation as I have fulfilled my calling to stand and deliver God's message year after year. The sheep from all those flocks have endeared themselves to this shepherd in more ways than I can put into words . . . and none more than those I currently serve with delight at Stonebriar Community Church in Frisco, Texas.

Finally, I must thank my wife, Cynthia, for her understanding of my addiction to studying, to preaching, and to writing. Never has she discouraged me from staying at it. Never has she failed to urge me in the pursuit of doing my very best. On the contrary, her affectionate support personally, and her own commitment to excellence in leading Insight for Living for more than three and a half decades, have combined to keep me faithful to my calling "in season and out of season." Without her devotion to me and apart from our mutual partnership throughout our lifetime of ministry together, Swindoll's Living Insights would never have been undertaken.

I am grateful that it has now found its way into your hands and, ultimately, onto the shelves of your library. My continued hope and prayer is that you will find these volumes helpful in your own study and personal application of the Bible. May they help you come to realize, as I have over these many years, that God's Word is as timeless as it is true.

> The grass withers, the flower fades,
>> But the word of our God stands forever. (Isa. 40:8)

Chuck Swindoll
Frisco, Texas

THE STRONG'S NUMBERING SYSTEM

Swindoll's Living Insights New Testament Commentary uses the Strong's word-study numbering system to give both newer and more advanced Bible students alike quicker, more convenient access to helpful original-language tools (e.g., concordances, lexicons, and theological dictionaries). The Strong's numbering system, made popular by the *Strong's Exhaustive Concordance of the Bible*, is used with the majority of biblical Greek and Hebrew reference works. Those who are unfamiliar with the ancient Hebrew, Aramaic, and Greek alphabets can quickly find information on a given word by looking up the appropriate index number. Advanced students will find the system helpful because it allows them to quickly find the lexical form of obscure conjugations and inflections.

When a Greek word is mentioned in the text, the Strong's number is included in square brackets after the Greek word. So in the example of the Greek word *agapē* [26], "love," the number is used with Greek tools keyed to the Strong's system.

On occasion, a Hebrew word is mentioned in the text. The Strong's Hebrew numbers are completely separate from the Greek numbers, so Hebrew numbers are prefixed with a letter "H." So, for example, the Hebrew word *kapporet* [H3727], "mercy seat," comes from *kopher* [H3722], "to ransom," "to secure favor through a gift."

INSIGHTS ON ACTS

Throughout this narrative, Luke shows the

church challenged, the church guided by

the Holy Spirit, and the church triumphant.

Therefore, I would state Luke's purpose this way:

to demonstrate, from the facts of history, that

the church has become God's instrument

for stewarding the new covenant, that the

church is guided by His Spirit, and that nothing

can prevent Christ from building His church.

The book of Acts opens with a question about

the kingdom of God and Christ's commissioning

and empowering of the church, and it closes

with the assurance that, even under arrest in

Rome, Paul continued "preaching the kingdom

of God . . . unhindered" (28:31).

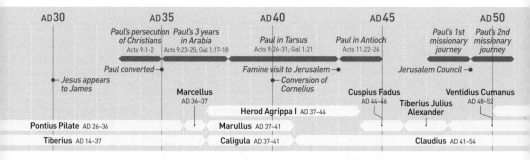

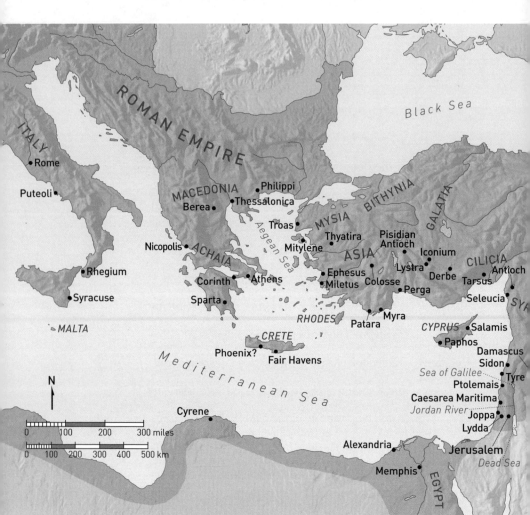

The Roman World in the Time of the Apostles. The Roman Empire spanned the entire Mediterranean world, from Syria to Spain and from Egypt to Macedonia. Acts tells the story of how, following the Day of Pentecost (2:1–47), the apostles and their associates carried the good news of salvation by grace through faith in Jesus throughout the entire Roman world.

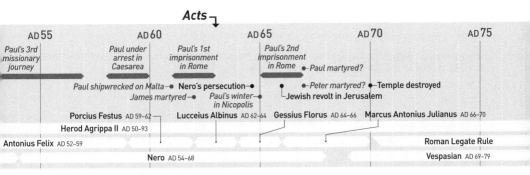

Acts

| AD 55 | AD 60 | AD 65 | AD 70 | AD 75 |

Paul's 3rd
missionary
journey

Paul under
arrest in
Caesarea

Paul's 1st
imprisonment
in Rome

Paul's 2nd
imprisonment
in Rome ●—Paul martyred?

Paul shipwrecked on Malta —● Nero's persecution—● ●—Peter martyred? ●—Temple destroyed
James martyred—● Paul's winter—● └─Jewish revolt in Jerusalem
in Nicopolis

Porcius Festus AD 59–62 ─┐ Lucceius Albinus AD 62–64 Gessius Florus AD 64–66 Marcus Antonius Julianus AD 66–70
Herod Agrippa II AD 50–93

Antonius Felix AD 52–59 Roman Legate Rule

Nero AD 54–68 Vespasian AD 69–79

ACTS

INTRODUCTION

"Unhindered." That's the very last word in the book of Acts. "Unhindered" is a fitting final word because it perfectly describes the central theme of Luke's historical account of the first-century church. That's not to say that the movement established by Jesus Christ and carried forward by His followers didn't meet with opposition. On the contrary, Acts describes opposition so ferocious and so deadly that any other organization would have folded immediately. "Unhindered" doesn't suggest that the first believers didn't experience challenges. They did, in fact, meet challenges so insidious, so unique, and so frequent that following conventional wisdom would have hastened their doom. "Unhindered" simply indicates that nothing would keep the church from fulfilling its divine purpose.

While Luke provides an accurate, detailed account of the first-century church and its spread across much of the known world, his book really does not focus on ideas or events, or even the people who served and led the church. In fact, the usual title, Acts of the Apostles, could mislead readers; the book primarily recounts the actions of two key apostles—Peter and Paul—though both were always in close cooperation with numerous gifted associates and ministry assistants. Perhaps a more apt title might be "Acts of the Holy Spirit." One of these Spirit-filled ministry associates, the physician Luke, has assembled a grand mosaic using facts like colored bits of broken pottery to display the work of God as He carries out His plan to redeem and transform the world.

Because Acts tells part of the story about God and His relationship with the world, it's helpful to see where this book fits in the grand scheme of redemptive history. The late evangelist Billy Sunday

THE BOOK OF ACTS AT A GLANCE

SECTION	THE BIRTH OF THE CHURCH	THE RISE OF THE CHURCH
PASSAGE	1:1–7:60	8:1–12:25
THEMES	The Church Is: Born Tested Purified Strengthened Empowered	The Gospel Is: Spreading Multiplying Changing Lives Breaking Traditions
KEY TERMS	Apostle Be Amazed Witness Sign Wonder	Preach/Proclaim Evangelize Disciple Repent Circumcision

THE EXPANSION OF THE CHURCH	THE CHALLENGES OF THE CHURCH
13:1–20:2	20:3–28:31
The Witness Is: Extended Received and Rejected Changing Lives Unifying Jews and Gentiles	The Movement Is: Tested Persecuted Defended Unhindered
Reason With/Discuss Make Known Widely/Proclaim Exhort/Encourage Suddenly/At Once Faith	Persecute Solemnly Testify Immediately Accuse Command

described his experience of the Scriptures in a poignant first-person word picture:

> Twenty-two years ago, with the Holy Spirit as my guide, I entered the wonderful temple of Christianity. I entered at the portico of Genesis, walked down through the Old Testament art galleries, where the pictures of Noah, Abraham, Moses, Joseph, Isaac, Jacob and Daniel hang on the wall.
>
> I passed into the music room of Psalms, where the Spirit swept the keyboard of nature, until it seemed that every reed and pipe in God's great organ responded to the tuneful harp of David, the sweet singer of Israel. I entered the chamber of Ecclesiastes, where the voice of the preacher was heard, and into the conservatory of Sharon, and the lily of the valley's sweet-scented spices filled and perfumed my life. I entered the business office of Proverbs, and then into the observatory of the Prophets, where I saw telescopes of various sizes, pointed to far-off events, but all concentrated upon the bright and Morning Star, which was to rise above the moon-lit hills of Judea for our salvation.
>
> I entered the audience room of the King of kings, and caught a vision of His glory, from the standpoint of Matthew, Mark, Luke and John; passed into the Acts of the Apostles, where the Holy Spirit was doing His work in the formation of the infant Church. Then into the correspondence room, where sat Paul, Peter, James and John, penning their Epistles. I stepped into the throne room of Revelation, where towered the glittering peaks, and I got a vision of the King sitting upon the throne, in all His glory, and I cried:
>
>> All hail the power of Jesus's name,
>> Let angels prostrate fall;
>> Bring forth the royal diadem,
>> And crown Him Lord of all.[1]

Acts is a pivotal book in the great narrative of God's redemptive plan. The Old Testament introduces God to humanity and establishes His covenants with Israel, all in anticipation of Jesus Christ. The Gospels—Matthew, Mark, Luke, and John—tell the story of how the God-man, Jesus, came to fulfill the Old Testament covenants and to establish a new covenant with humanity. God summarized this new covenant through the prophet Jeremiah:

"Behold, days are coming," declares the LORD, "when I will make a new covenant with the house of Israel and with the house of Judah, not like the covenant which I made with their fathers in the day I took them by the hand to bring them out of the land of Egypt, My covenant which they broke, although I was a husband to them," declares the LORD. "But this is the covenant which I will make with the house of Israel after those days," declares the LORD, "I will put My law within them and on their heart I will write it; and I will be their God, and they shall be My people. They will not teach again, each man his neighbor and each man his brother, saying, 'Know the LORD,' for they will all know Me, from the least of them to the greatest of them," declares the LORD, "for I will forgive their iniquity, and their sin I will remember no more." (Jer. 31:31-34)

Acts documents the launch of the new covenant and traces the new-covenant community's phenomenal growth in the first three decades after Jesus' death and resurrection.

The Place of Acts in the Bible

└─ *The Book of Acts*

1. **Pentateuch** *(5 books)*
2. **History** *(12 books)*
3. **Poetry** *(5 books)*
4. **Major Prophets** *(5 books)*
5. **Minor Prophets** *(12 books)*

39 books in the Old Testament

6. **History** *(5 books)*
7. **Pauline Epistles** *(13 books)*
8. **General Epistles** *(8 books)*
9. **Prophecy** *(1 book)*

27 books in the New Testament

THE PURPOSE OF ACTS

Today, the books of the New Testament appear in a standardized order—Matthew, Mark, Luke, John, Acts, Romans, and so on—that separates Luke and Acts. But the book of Acts was never intended to be read as a stand-alone document; rather, it is the second volume of Luke's two-volume work, which began with his historical account of Christ's life, the Gospel of Luke.

Nevertheless, the book of Acts is well placed after the Gospels. It is a book of transitions, documenting the period after the earthly ministry of Jesus when the church began receiving the written treasures of the apostles. Consequently, it comes after the Gospels and before the Epistles in the New Testament. Luke's second volume narrates an era like no other in history, a time when God had much to say but spoke less through individual prophets and more through a growing, Spirit-filled community.

As with the first volume of his work, Luke dedicated the second volume to "Theophilus," whose identity remains a mystery (Luke 1:3; Acts 1:1). The name means "one who loves God," which could be the nickname of Luke's patron. In ancient times, wealthy people typically commissioned histories, usually for self-serving reasons. The head of a family might want to establish a credible family line in order to claim a title or give the family name a higher standing. Or he might commission a history to vindicate the actions of his ancestors or to glorify his family's achievements. In other words, the patron would have had a specific reason for paying a historian to compile a history that others would read. In the case of the first volume, Luke states his purpose, which likely reflects that of his patron: "so that you may know the exact truth about the things you have been taught [concerning Jesus]" (Luke 1:4). We can therefore say with reasonable certainty that Theophilus commissioned Luke to research the life of Jesus and to meticulously set down the facts to undergird the faith of the church.

The purpose of the second volume most likely follows that of the first, with a slight variation in emphasis. Perhaps prompted by the recent challenges the church was facing, Theophilus may have commissioned Luke to chronicle the rise and expansion of Christ's body by focusing on a recurring theme: "unhindered" growth despite overwhelming opposition, with special emphasis given to the role of the Holy Spirit.

Several fine expositors have offered credible suggestions about the purpose of Acts. On the one hand, F. F. Bruce sees Luke as a pioneer apologist, defending Christians against misinformation and misunderstanding spread by their unbelieving critics.[2] He arrives at this opinion because so much of Acts depicts the church as unfairly accused and unjustly treated, and Paul's appearances before secular authorities are given special attention. On the other hand, William Barclay claims that "Luke's great aim was to show the expansion of Christianity, to show how that religion which began in a little corner of Palestine had in a little more than 30 years reached Rome."[3] A few commentators point to Luke's stated purpose for his Gospel, saying that persecution shook the faith of many in the church and that the book of Acts assured them Christ would not let His church fail.

I have difficulty with these suggestions because they give too much attention to the issue of persecution, only one of *many* trials threatening the first-century church. Throughout this narrative, Luke shows the church challenged, the church guided by the Holy Spirit, and the church triumphant. Therefore, I would state Luke's purpose this way: *to demonstrate, from the facts of history, that the church has become God's instrument for stewarding the new covenant, that the church is guided by His Spirit, and that nothing can prevent Christ from building His church.* The book of Acts opens with a question about the kingdom of God and Christ's commissioning and empowering of the church (Acts 1:6-8), and it closes with the assurance that, even under arrest in Rome, Paul continued "preaching the kingdom of God . . . unhindered" (28:31).

THE AUTHOR OF ACTS

Luke is a small figure in the story of the early church, but he looms large in its history.[4] Some identify him as Lucius of Cyrene (13:1), one of the leading elders in Syrian Antioch who commissioned Paul and Barnabas for the first missionary journey. Some church traditions place Luke in Antioch during these early days of the church, but we have little hard evidence to support the theory. If we take the book of Acts at face value, Luke appears to be a late addition to Paul's evangelistic team instead of a top-ranking voice in the most influential Gentile church at that time. (For an extended discussion of Luke's identity, see my introduction to *Insights on Luke*.[5])

LUKE IN THE NEW TESTAMENT
Acts 16:10-17[6]
Acts 20:5–21:18
Acts 27:1–28:16
Colossians 4:14
2 Timothy 4:11
Philemon 1:24

In three extended passages in Acts, Luke uses the pronoun "we." Presumably, when Luke uses "they" and "them," he means that he wasn't personally present at the time. Based on that assumption, we

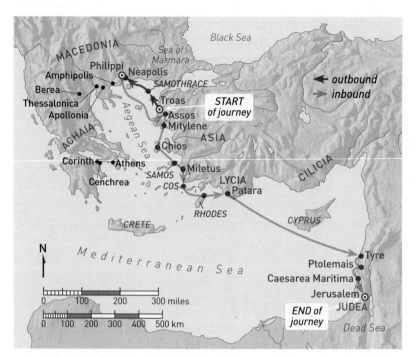

Luke's Travels with Paul. Luke met Paul on the course of Paul's second missionary journey. Paul left him to work in Philippi, and then Luke rejoined him for the journey back to Jerusalem.

find that Luke encountered Paul for a period during the first missionary journey but didn't meet him again until the end of the third missionary journey. Luke later traveled with Paul from Jerusalem to Rome.

Luke apparently met Paul and his entourage during the second missionary journey as the men lingered in Troas. When the Holy Spirit prevented them from penetrating the Roman provinces of Bithynia, Asia, and Mysia with the gospel, the team remained in this port city for an extended time, pondering their next move (16:6-8). Luke may have been a believer when he encountered Paul, or perhaps Paul led him to faith while in Troas. Luke doesn't say. We know only that when Paul and the members of his team decided to alter their course for Macedonia and Greece, Luke traveled with them on the first leg of the journey, from Troas to Philippi. He witnessed the beating and imprisonment of Paul and Silas (16:22-40), and as a physician (Col. 4:14), undoubtedly took the lead in treating the men's wounds. When the team continued on to Thessalonica and then Greece, Luke remained in Philippi, because it is possible he had lived there before meeting Paul.

On the third missionary journey, Paul and his entourage passed through Philippi on their way to Greece, again without adding Luke to their number. After several months of ministry in Greece, Paul intended to sail directly home from Cenchrea, a port city near Corinth, but a plot to kill him changed his plans. To distract any would-be assassins, he instructed his team to board a ship in Cenchrea as originally planned, but to sail for Troas, where he would rendezvous with them. Meanwhile, he retraced his steps through Philippi (Acts 20:2-5), where he evidently invited Luke to join him. According to the second "we" passage, Luke accompanied Paul to Troas. We know this was not Luke's last journey with Paul. It is possible that Luke remained at Paul's side for the rest of the apostle's life.

The third "we" passage (27:1–28:16) follows Paul from his arrest in Jerusalem to confinement in the palace of Herod Agrippa, along the journey to Rome, and through his two years of house arrest awaiting trial. No one knows for certain where Paul traveled after his release, but within a couple of years, he was back in Rome and again in prison. As he penned his final letter to Timothy and prepared for the end, he mentioned that only Luke remained at his side (2 Tim. 4:11).

THE STRUCTURE OF ACTS

Luke's Gospel followed Jesus' earthly ministry in ever-narrowing circles from Nazareth and Galilee (Luke 4:14–9:50), through Samaria and Judea (Luke 9:51–19:27), and ultimately to Jerusalem (Luke 19:28–24:12). The book of Acts, however, radiates from Jerusalem outward in ever-expanding circles. When the risen Lord met with His disciples for the last time, they asked, "Is it at this time You are restoring the kingdom to Israel?" (Acts 1:6). They still expected Jesus to seize the reins of religious and political power and become the leader of a worldwide Jewish empire, through which God would rule the earth. But Jesus corrected their understanding of the plan. He said, "It is not for you to know times or epochs which the Father has fixed by His own authority; but you will receive power when the Holy Spirit has come upon you; and you shall be My witnesses both in Jerusalem, and in all Judea and Samaria, and even to the remotest part of the earth" (1:7-8).

Note the emphasis on geography: "Jerusalem, and in all Judea and Samaria, and even to the remotest part of the earth." This becomes an "inspired outline" for the book of Acts: "Jerusalem" (Acts 1–7), "all Judea and Samaria" (Acts 8–12), "the remotest part of the earth" (Acts 13–28).

THE UNFINISHED STORY

In His last appearance in the Gospel of Luke, Jesus summarized His earthly ministry using the Old Testament Scriptures as a guide (Luke 24:44-49). He demonstrated from the Scriptures that God's plan had *always* been for the Messiah to suffer on behalf of His people and conquer death on the third day. His plan had *always* been to call the nations to repent of sin, receive His forgiveness, and trust that His grace is sufficient to save. The city of Jerusalem had *always* been the Lord's intended light on a hill (see Ps. 43:3; Matt. 5:14) and would finally become the starting point of world evangelism (Isa. 43:10; 44:8; Acts 1:8).

The Lord's final proclamation (Luke 24:36-49), densely packed with meaningful terms and expressions, foreshadows many of the key themes and events in the book of Acts. For example, the term for "witness" (*martys* [3144], Luke 24:48; Acts 1:8; 2:32) is the term from which we derive the English word "martyr." Above all, the apostles were witnesses to the Lord's resurrection (1:22). The English meaning of the word "martyr" developed from the fact that some of the witnesses to Jesus' death and resurrection were willing to readily die rather than recant the gospel message (7:59-60; 12:1-2).

The verb meaning "send forth" (*apostellō* [649], Luke 24:49; Acts 3:20, 26) is related to the term from which we get "apostle." Jesus had been sent from God, and He had sent the Holy Spirit (Luke 24:49) so that the apostles could be sent forth even to the Gentiles (Acts 26:17; 28:28).

The "promise of My Father" (Luke 24:49; cf. Acts 1:4-5, 8) is a reference to the Holy Spirit, who would soon "[clothe them] with power." This word picture is taken from the commissioning ceremony of a government official. The phrase "from on high" declares the source of their commissioning and power, God Himself (cf. 4:13-20).

As the book of Acts opens, the power of the Holy Spirit falls like lightning on the newly commissioned witnesses, who begin teaching and preaching the good news with boldness in the temple. The Jesus movement then emanates from Jerusalem to the surrounding territory, then to neighboring Samaria, up to the Gentile lands just north of Galilee, and from there all across the eastern Roman Empire.

We don't find a nice, tidy conclusion at the end of Luke's second volume; instead, the last lines describe the apostle Paul's two years of house arrest in Rome, where against all odds, he was "preaching the kingdom of God and teaching concerning the Lord Jesus Christ with all openness, unhindered" (28:31). This feels very much like the soft ending of volume one, after which Luke clearly intended to continue the story. We do not know whether he intended to write a volume three. Paul had hoped to say a final farewell to his mission east of Rome and then embark for the western frontier as far as Spain (Rom. 15:23-28). Luke undoubtedly expected to go with him and document every step. But that was not to be.

Regardless of Luke's literary plans, the Holy Spirit intended the narrative to end with volume two. I don't see this open-ended conclusion as an accident. Luke didn't foresee Nero's persecution, which led to Paul's second imprisonment and execution, but God was not surprised by it. Could the Lord have left the narrative open intentionally for others to complete—not in writing, but by continuing the commission Jesus gave His first one hundred or so witnesses in Jerusalem? When you think about it, there's no good place to conclude a history of the church. For two millennia, each generation of believers has met challenges, responded through the power of the Holy Spirit, and perpetuated the gospel. They have continued to "write" the history of the church—and now that duty falls to us. Throughout the twenty centuries of church narrative, nothing could stop its inevitable expansion, and it continues today—unhindered.

THE BIRTH OF THE CHURCH (ACTS 1:1–7:60)

The book of Acts documents a span of time unlike any other era in history. Like the Exodus of the Hebrews from Egypt—with its plagues, Red Sea parting, glowing shekinah pillars, and manna from heaven—the early days of the church saw supernatural events that will never be repeated. As Luke's second volume opens, the church doesn't exist; the Holy Spirit has not yet come to reside in Christ's followers; the apostles possess no power, no courage, no authority, no direction. Yet by the last verse, the church will span the Roman Empire from Jerusalem to Rome. In the first few months of church history, recorded in Acts 1:1–7:60, a glorious explosion of divine power energized a group of ordinary men and women to carry out a God-sized mission using supernatural abilities.

Just as Jesus had said (Luke 24:47; Acts 1:8), the disciples would begin their mission in Jerusalem, declaring the new covenant message of redemption in the presence of the very religious leaders and temple authorities who had handed Jesus over to Pilate. In this first stage of the divine plan for the church's growth (1:8), the believers would learn to trust in God's plan and power to overcome all obstacles, including persecution from without (4:1-31), failures and tension within (5:1-11; 6:1), and even the loss of important leaders to martyrdom (6:8–7:60). Jesus' miraculous power and message would be manifest through the suffering of His followers.

Within days of His ascension, the believers received the first part of His promise: The Holy Spirit filled every believer, granting each one the power to fulfill his or her role in God's redemptive plan. At Pentecost, the first believers stunned their peers with supernatural, miraculous abilities, prompting thousands of Jews to embrace Jesus as their Messiah. They, in turn, also received power from the Holy Spirit to be witnesses, preaching in the temple and evangelizing Jerusalem. In time, the church of Jerusalem grew strong and vibrant while Peter and John provided solid leadership, guiding the congregation despite constant pressure from the Sanhedrin. Even persecution by Saul did little to curb the church's growth—until the martyrdom of Stephen dealt the community of believers its first significant blow.

apostolos (ἀπόστολος) [652] "apostle," "sent one," "official envoy," "commissioner"

The noun form of the verb *apostellō* [649] ("to send," "to send with a commission or with authority") described an official government envoy, who might carry official news or read proclamations publicly across the empire. Greek religion and philosophy later used the term to refer to divinely sent teachers. In Christianity, it came to describe both the function and official capacity of certain men; to be called an "apostle," one must have personally encountered Jesus Christ after His resurrection and received His commission to bear the good news to others.

existēmi (ἐξίστημι) [1839] "to be amazed," "to be separated from something," "to be beside oneself," "to be out of one's senses"

Literally, this word means "to be displaced." Figuratively, it refers to a psychological state of mind in which one no longer has control over oneself. By the time of Jesus, this had become hyperbole, in the same way we might say someone "lost his mind" with excitement. Another, milder term used often by Luke is *thaumazō* [2296], which simply means "astonished" or "filled with wonder." *Existēmi* is decidedly more colorful, used to characterize someone as animated in his or her astonishment.

thaumazō (θαυμάζω) [2296] "to wonder," "to be amazed," "to marvel," "to be in awe"

This term describes being extraordinarily impressed, awed, or even disturbed by something, especially when confronted with some form of divine revelation. In the Septuagint it indicates worship, honor, and admiration, generally referring to "religious experience face to face with what transcends human possibilities."[1]

martyria (μαρτυρία) [3141] "witness," "testimony," "evidence"

This term refers to "confirmation or attestation on the basis of personal knowledge or belief"[2] and was commonly used in connection with legal proceedings. In ancient courts, the corroborating testimony of independent witnesses was considered virtually irrefutable.

sēmeion (σημεῖον) [4592] "sign," "authenticating mark," "token," "miracle"

The most basic meaning of this word is "something that gives a true indication of something else." A road sign accurately indicates what lies ahead for the traveler. The Greeks gave the term special attention as a physical indication of divine will or supernatural omens. Lightning, for example, indicated the will of Zeus, and thunder was considered a foreboding indication that he was about to speak through a sign. For the Jews, a "sign" provided visual confirmation that a prophet was authentically from God or was a physical manifestation of God's glory.

teras (τέρας) [5059] "wonder," "portent," "omen," "miracle"
Never used alone and frequently appearing in tandem with *sēmeion*, this word refers to something that astonishes or causes people to wonder. The term often denotes an extraordinary event that suggests something much deeper or more important has occurred or will occur soon. For example, Augustus claimed that the wonder of a bright comet was, in fact, the spirit of his adopted father, Julius Caesar, entering heaven.

Operation Revolution
ACTS 1:1-14

NASB

¹The first account I ᵃcomposed, Theophilus, about all that Jesus began to do and teach, ²until the day when He was taken up *to heaven*, after He had ᵃby the Holy Spirit given orders to the apostles whom He had chosen. ³To ᵃthese He also presented Himself alive after His suffering, by many convincing proofs, appearing to them over *a period of* forty days and speaking of the things concerning the kingdom of God. ⁴ᵃGathering them together, He commanded them not to leave Jerusalem, but to wait for ᵇwhat the Father had promised, "Which," *He said,* "you heard of from Me; ⁵for John baptized with water, but you will be baptized ᵃwith the Holy Spirit ᵇnot many days from now."

⁶So when they had come together, they were asking Him, saying, "Lord, is it at this time You are restoring the kingdom to Israel?" ⁷He said to them, "It is not for you to know times or epochs which the Father has fixed by His own authority; ⁸but you will receive power when the Holy Spirit has come upon you; and you shall be

NLT

¹In my first book* I told you, Theophilus, about everything Jesus began to do and teach ²until the day he was taken up to heaven after giving his chosen apostles further instructions through the Holy Spirit. ³During the forty days after he suffered and died, he appeared to the apostles from time to time, and he proved to them in many ways that he was actually alive. And he talked to them about the Kingdom of God.

⁴Once when he was eating with them, he commanded them, "Do not leave Jerusalem until the Father sends you the gift he promised, as I told you before. ⁵John baptized with* water, but in just a few days you will be baptized with the Holy Spirit."

⁶So when the apostles were with Jesus, they kept asking him, "Lord, has the time come for you to free Israel and restore our kingdom?"

⁷He replied, "The Father alone has the authority to set those dates and times, and they are not for you to know. ⁸But you will receive power when the Holy Spirit comes upon you. And you will be my witnesses,

My witnesses both in Jerusalem, and in all Judea and Samaria, and even to the remotest part of the earth."

⁹And after He had said these things, He was lifted up while they were looking on, and a cloud received Him out of their sight. ¹⁰And as they were gazing intently into ᵃthe sky while He was going, behold, two men in white clothing stood beside them. ¹¹They also said, "Men of Galilee, why do you stand looking into ᵃthe sky? This Jesus, who has been taken up from you into heaven, will come in just the same way as you have watched Him go into heaven."

¹²Then they returned to Jerusalem from the ᵃmount called ᵇOlivet, which is near Jerusalem, a ᶜSabbath day's journey away. ¹³When they had entered the city, they went up to the upper room where they were staying; that is, Peter and John and ᵃJames and Andrew, Philip and Thomas, Bartholomew and Matthew, ᵃJames the son of Alphaeus, and Simon the Zealot, and Judas the ᵇson of ᵃJames. ¹⁴These all with one mind were continually devoting themselves to prayer, along with the women, and Mary the mother of Jesus, and with His brothers.

1:1 ᵃLit made 1:2 ᵃOr through 1:3 ᵃLit whom 1:4 ᵃOr eating with; or lodging with ᵇLit the promise of the Father 1:5 ᵃOr in ᵇLit not long after these many days 1:10 ᵃOr heaven 1:11 ᵃOr heaven 1:12 ᵃOr hill ᵇOr Olive Grove ᶜI.e. 2K cubits, or approx 3/5 mile 1:13 ᵃOr Jacob ᵇOr brother

telling people about me everywhere—in Jerusalem, throughout Judea, in Samaria, and to the ends of the earth."

⁹After saying this, he was taken up into a cloud while they were watching, and they could no longer see him. ¹⁰As they strained to see him rising into heaven, two white-robed men suddenly stood among them. ¹¹"Men of Galilee," they said, "why are you standing here staring into heaven? Jesus has been taken from you into heaven, but someday he will return from heaven in the same way you saw him go!"

¹²Then the apostles returned to Jerusalem from the Mount of Olives, a distance of half a mile.* ¹³When they arrived, they went to the upstairs room of the house where they were staying.

Here are the names of those who were present: Peter, John, James, Andrew, Philip, Thomas, Bartholomew, Matthew, James (son of Alphaeus), Simon (the zealot), and Judas (son of James). ¹⁴They all met together and were constantly united in prayer, along with Mary the mother of Jesus, several other women, and the brothers of Jesus.

1:1 The reference is to the Gospel of Luke. 1:5 Or in; also in 1:5b. 1:12 Greek a Sabbath day's journey.

Ours is a world in motion—high speed, perpetual progress, nonstop change. Hundreds of years used to separate scientific revolutions; now we expect them every couple of decades. Most don't even make the news; they simply shift our scientific paradigms—and shift us right along with them. A few decades ago, one good technological advance was enough to propel a new company straight to Fortune 500 status. Now, if your company isn't changing its industry every couple of years, you won't have a company for long.

Given our rapid-fire-change culture, I am encouraged to see the church not only surviving but thriving! This amazing venture enjoys a strong grasp on tradition yet continues to affect every culture it touches. Furthermore, the church remains relevant despite two thousand years of cultural evolution. The late Steve Jobs once said, "Innovation distinguishes between a leader and a follower."[3] We have the most creative, forward-thinking, adaptive, innovative, progressive Leader the world has ever known, and He has been with the organization from the beginning. In fact, He started this global enterprise and has served as its Leader through countless challenges and changes.

— 1:1-2 —

Luke begins with a quick glance back to his Gospel account. This indicates a definite break in his narrative, but not one so large he had to bridge a chasm. He assumes the life of Jesus remains fresh in the reader's mind. After all, Luke had gone to great lengths to show that the man Jesus is not only the Messiah but that He came to earth as God in human flesh. God sent His message to humanity wrapped in the blood, bone, sinew, and muscle of someone like us. He walked among people for thirty-plus years, preaching, teaching, healing, casting out demons, and raising the dead. Ultimately, He was crucified, buried, and then raised to a new kind of life. That's what Luke means by "all that Jesus began to do and teach" (1:1).

Take note of the word "began." The work isn't finished. There's more to do. Yet the next phrase tells us that Jesus was taken up to heaven. We won't see Jesus face to face until either we die or He returns in the same way He departed—in the clouds (1:11). So how would Jesus complete the work He "began"? The answer is foreshadowed in the phrase, "had by the Holy Spirit given orders to the apostles whom He had chosen" (1:2).

— 1:3-5 —

After rising from the dead, Jesus spent forty days consoling His followers, who had endured a gut-wrenching ordeal of their own. In the dark hours leading up to His crucifixion, they abandoned their Lord (Mark 14:50). Then they watched in horror as the unthinkable occurred: The Messiah—their Master and Lord—died! Upon His return from the grave, He first had to prove the authenticity of His resurrection. Myth and folklore had taught them to believe in ghosts. Common views of resurrection among the doctrinally influential Pharisees taught them to believe in a future mass resurrection of both the righteous and the

BAPTISM

ACTS 1:5

A literal translation of the Lord's promise in Acts 1:5 reads, "You will be baptized *into* the Holy Spirit." People of ancient cultures understood the significance of this symbolic rite of baptism; we need the help of some cultural and historical context.

The ritual of baptism in ancient cultures symbolized identification. An organization or society initiated a new member by immersing him or her in a liquid of some kind—usually water, or in the case of many pagan rituals, the blood of sacrificed animals.[4] So, when one was "baptized into" a community, he or she became one with it and, therefore, identified with it. After an initiate had been immersed into something and surrounded by it, he or she emerged from the pool soaked and dripping—covered, as it were, in the same substance as all the other members. After being "baptized into" a society, the initiate was considered both a member and a representative of the community's beliefs. A person "baptized into" a society, therefore, received everything that goes along with membership: rights, benefits, powers, and responsibilities.

In Judaism, a new convert was ceremonially immersed in pure water after attending classes to learn the Hebrew language, study Hebrew history and culture, and most importantly, learn the Law of Moses. After passing an examination, the males were circumcised, and all converts were baptized. The symbol of baptism became a figurative once-for-all cleansing from sin before entering the Hebrew covenant community. To be "baptized into" Judaism was to become a "son of the covenant" along with natural-born Jews.[5]

John the Baptizer then gave the rite of Gentile baptism a new application. He called Jews to a baptism of repentance, saying, in effect, "Because of your sin, you are outside of Abraham's covenant with God—*unclean*! You must repent like a Gentile and come to God as if for the first time." According to Jesus, the water baptism administered by John would eventually be followed by a supernatural baptism from above. The disciples understood the concept of "baptism into" the Holy Spirit, but they could not have made sense of all its implications. At least, not yet. To be "baptized into the Spirit of God" means to be made a member of God's supernatural society and taking on all the rights, benefits, powers, and responsibilities shared within the Trinity.

wicked. But a miraculous resurrection of the Messiah alone prior to the resurrection of the rest of humanity? That required a reworking of their understanding of end-times events.

Accepting the fact of Christ's miraculous bodily resurrection, however, would be only the first of *many* significant paradigm changes.

Jesus spent those forty days meeting with His followers, deconstructing their false notions about the kingdom of God, and then setting them on the right course. By the time He ascended to heaven, the disciples had been well provisioned with the truth. Unfortunately, they had no power. And truth without power accomplishes little in a world dominated by evil. As it happens, the Lord never intended to send them out powerless. Therefore, He told them to wait for a special event, describing it in terms that must have stunned and amazed the disciples. Luke's Gospel had mentioned "what the Father had promised" many times (Acts 1:4):

- John the Baptizer said Jesus would "baptize . . . with the Holy Spirit and fire" (Luke 3:16).
- Jesus, when speaking of the good gifts human fathers like to give their children, asked, "If you then, being evil, know how to give good gifts to your children, how much more will your heavenly Father give the Holy Spirit to those who ask Him?" (Luke 11:13).
- Jesus assured His disciples that they would suffer persecution, but He also promised, "When they bring you before the synagogues and the rulers and the authorities, do not worry about how or what you are to speak in your defense, or what you are to say; for the Holy Spirit will teach you in that very hour what you ought to say" (Luke 12:11-12; cf. Luke 21:15).

"Not many days from now" (Acts 1:5), the disciples would receive the fulfillment of God's promise.

— 1:6 —

When I studied at Dallas Theological Seminary, a course taught by Dr. Howard Hendricks called "Bible Study Methods" forever changed my life. In one of those unforgettable classes, "Prof" challenged us to examine Acts 1:8 and record fifty observations. Many classes of students before me had completed this assignment, as well as every graduate of that seminary since. I stared at that verse for hours. Then, I saw a detail I had overlooked for years: the tiny, incredibly significant three-letter word "but." There it sat at the head of the verse, begging me to discover what contrast this conjunction indicated.

I traced Luke's river of thought to its source and found a question: "Lord, is it at this time You are restoring the kingdom to Israel?" (1:6).

All of the Lord's followers, even the inner circle of disciples that He had trained for leadership, struggled to understand His agenda. All their lives, they had been taught that the kingdom of God was Israel. They had been taught to expect a Messiah who would revive the broken nation of Hebrews—now whittled down to the tribe of Judah—and return it to the kind of glory they hadn't known since David and Solomon. They anticipated a religious and political leader who would wear both the king's crown and the high priest's robe.

God is not done with Israel. Jesus will, of course, fulfill all those Old Testament promises. He owns the king's crown *and* the priestly robes, and He will wear them—literally, not just figuratively—in the future. But He hadn't planned to build the kingdom of God in the time or manner anyone expected. When God fulfills His promises, He always exceeds our expectations.

— 1:7-8 —

Jesus answered the disciples' question (1:6) with gentle admonishment to be patient. He said, in effect, "Relax. God's plan will unfold on His schedule, and nothing can stop it." Note that He didn't refute or correct their understanding of the coming kingdom, only its timing and method. No, He would not assemble an army for a march on Jerusalem—at least, not yet (see Rev. 19:11-21; 20:4). He wouldn't take control of the nation by diplomacy or intrigue. He wouldn't expand His kingdom in the manner of Nebuchadnezzar or Alexander or Augustus. "But . . ."

The Messiah is destined to receive the power and authority to rule the whole world (Dan. 7:13-14; Rev. 11:15), "but," He said, "*you* will receive power when the Holy Spirit has come upon you" (Acts 1:8, emphasis mine).

In the Old Testament, the power of the Holy Spirit was reserved for kings and prophets, and occasionally for regular folk when the Lord wanted to accomplish something extraordinary. The filling of the Holy Spirit was a rare gift and almost always temporary. He filled and empowered certain individuals for a brief time for a specific purpose and then departed. Exceptionally few individuals were granted the indwelling presence of the Holy Spirit for life, among them John the Baptizer (Luke 1:15). So, the announcement that the Spirit of God would indwell each believer seemed unthinkable—an unbelievable extravagance the followers of Jesus could barely comprehend.

The filling and empowerment of the Holy Spirit for every believer was not a brand-new concept. Hundreds of years earlier, God had revealed that a new kind of kingdom would emerge from the new covenant, which required every citizen to have the mind of God (Jer. 31:31-34; Ezek. 37:14; Joel 2:28-32). From the beginning of time, He planned to give His people the power to carry out His commands as citizens of His kingdom.

Note, however, that He granted them power. He didn't outline a program. He didn't give them a detailed strategy. Such a thing wouldn't stand the test of time, as we observe in the business world. Rather than set down a specific business model, God gave each member of the organization the mind of the CEO, in a manner of speaking. Instead of laying out a concrete battle plan, the Lord gave each soldier a brain that thinks in synchronization with the mission and values of the General. God, having baptized individuals into His kingdom, gives each citizen power.

The Greek term for "power" (*dynamis* [1411]) refers to one's ability or capacity; it suggests "being able" or "being capable of" something. The specific ability or capability in question depends upon the context. If the task is to lift a great weight, the "ability" is physical strength. If the task is to defeat an army, the "capacity" is that of a seasoned general. The Lord's promise leaves the *dynamis* indefinite. In other words, whatever is required, we will receive the power to do what God asks.

This *dynamis* yields results. In Matthew 28:19-20, the Lord issued a command to "go . . . and make disciples of all the nations." But that was another day and another mountaintop conference. Here on the Mount of Olives, the spot of His eventual return, Jesus instead made a prediction: "You shall be My witnesses" (Acts 1:8). The term for "witness" is *martys* [3144], from which we derive the English term "martyr," although back then it didn't have a strong religious connotation. First-century Greek writers understood *martys* as a legal term describing one who testified in court about something he or she had personally seen.

As noted earlier, Jesus' prediction foreshadows the unfolding of the story of the church. Luke calls special attention to the Lord's promise, because the rest of this narrative stands as a witness to its fulfillment: "Jerusalem" (Acts 1–7), "all Judea and Samaria" (Acts 8–12), "the remotest part of the earth" (Acts 13–28).

Volume one of Luke's work explains how the truth of God became flesh, how the good news became incarnate. Volume two demonstrates how, after Jesus physically departed the earth, the truth of God remained among flesh. He sent His Spirit to indwell His people. The good news of "God with us" continues with people who incarnate His message and are enabled by His power.

— 1:9-11 —

These verses overlap Luke's description of the Lord's final moments before ascending to heaven at the end of volume one. He led His followers to a spot on the Mount of Olives, probably over the ridge from Jerusalem, somewhere down the eastern slope. It's a deeply meaningful place in the Old Testament. When the light of God's presence departed the forsaken temple, never to be seen there again, "the glory of the LORD went up from the midst of the city and stood over the mountain which is east of the city" (Ezek. 11:23). According to the prophet Zechariah, the Lord will come to this mount before taking control of Jerusalem. Only the all-powerful King won't climb and then descend the mountain; the mountain will miraculously move out of His way, parting like a curtain before Him (Zech. 14:4).

This is where Jesus ascended. He rose up through the clouds and then passed from our earthly dimension to the heavenly realm. Two angels announced that Jesus—the Savior of the world and its future King—will return in this same manner. He will not again be born as a baby. He will not appear in another form or take another identity. He will not be reincarnated or channel His personality through another individual. He will not return in spirit form—He's already here in the person of the Holy Spirit! He will descend through the clouds in His own human body. Physically. Literally. Dramatically. Unmistakably.

— 1:12-14 —

The Lord's followers did exactly as He commanded; they walked the short distance back across the Kidron Valley to Jerusalem, most likely to the same room where they had earlier been hiding out (Luke 24:33-36; John 20:19). And they waited. Though they didn't know exactly when the Spirit would arrive, God knew that "not many days from now" (Acts 1:5) meant the Feast of Weeks (Pentecost)—fifty days from the end of Passover and therefore ten days from Christ's ascension. During this holiday Jews from all over gathered in Jerusalem to make an offering to God during the time of harvesting the first fruits (Exod. 34:22; Deut. 16:9-12). Fittingly, God was about to offer His own "first fruits" of the Spirit as a faithful remnant of Jews became the first initiates into the new community of the Spirit: the church.

Meanwhile, those dedicated disciples maintained a season of constant prayer. As the late expositor Harry Ironside once stated,

> When God is going to do some great thing He moves the hearts of people to pray. He stirs them up to pray in view of that which

He is about to do so that they might be prepared for it. The disciples needed the self-examination that comes through prayer and supplication, that they might be ready for the tremendous event which was about to take place, the coming to earth of God the Holy Spirit to dwell in believers and empower them to witness for Him.[6]

Luke makes special note of the people present. During His earthly ministry, Jesus had chosen twelve men to receive concentrated spiritual instruction and leadership training. Judas Iscariot had betrayed Jesus to the temple officials in exchange for money and then, in unrepentant regret, hanged himself. The remaining eleven banded together. Several women had faithfully met the practical needs of ministry and were considered devoted learners of the Master. They, along with Mary, the mother of Jesus, joined the eleven in prayer. And surprisingly, the Lord's half brothers accompanied them. Originally hostile to the teaching of Jesus (Mark 3:21), they were affected by His crucifixion and then convinced by His resurrection.

Luke specifically mentions these people, but they were not the only disciples involved in this season of continual prayer. In the quiet between the promise of the Holy Spirit and its fulfillment, 120 believers joined in prayerful anticipation. This band of ordinary men and women would become the nucleus around which the worldwide, twenty-century (and counting), multicultural, multiethnic kingdom of God would grow. Their world was about to change, and they were about to become the agents of this change.

APPLICATION: ACTS 1:1-14

His Plan, His People, His Power

God has a plan for redeeming the world. It's not a new plan; it existed in the mind of the Creator before the first humans committed the first sin. None of what's happening surprises Him. He established a covenant with Abraham and his descendants, the Hebrews, calling them to teach the Scriptures, model obedience to the Law, and become an example of living faith in God. He strategically placed the nation of Israel on a narrow land bridge, through which the great civilizations of the region had to pass when conducting trade or making war with each other, so that all could see the shalom (peace and wellbeing) of Israel and learn of their God. The plan of God had *always* been to send His Son, who would succeed where Israel had failed, suffer on behalf of His people, and conquer death on the third day. Remember, God had *always* called people to repent of sin, receive His forgiveness, and trust that His grace is sufficient to save. The city of Jerusalem had *always* been the Lord's intended light on a hill (see Ps. 43:3; Matt. 5:14), and in the days of the apostles, it would finally become the starting point of world evangelism (Isa. 43:10; 44:8; Acts 1:8).

Now we are a part of His plan. We, like the disciples, do not know when the kingdom will come (1:6-8). At the present time, we know only that God has called us to join Him in reclaiming creation from evil by our witness to the resurrected Messiah. He's given us a genuine stake in the plan's fulfillment, and there is no "Plan B." As I consider what the Lord is doing and how He has involved us, I have two observations.

First, *to carry out the plan, people must be infused.* You'll never advance the healing power of Christianity in a sick, dying world if you stay away from those infected with sin and error. Christ made consistent contact with His disciples, those disciples made consistent contact with their generation, and the world was infused with the antidote to sin and death. To implement an effective plan, we must infuse people with the cure of the gospel. Remember, this is about truth incarnated, divine truth in human flesh. It's not theoretical truth floating around on the pages of books that saves people. It's one life affecting another.

Second, *to impact a rapidly changing world, the power of the Holy Spirit must be released.* I am amazed at how few Christians really know the dynamics of the Holy Spirit. Truly amazed. All the power it took to raise Christ from the dead—not loud power but silent, effective, dynamic power—has been given to us. But we know so little about the potential energy of having the presence of God within, how to let Him fill and control us, and how to transform that power into positive change in the world.

Many years ago, I gave the closing message at a conference. Just as soon as the last words of my prayer slipped out of my mouth and we had a little music, a couple came right down front. "You talked about the Holy Ghost today," they said. (They used the archaic expression "Holy Ghost," which made me curious.)

"Yes," I said, "I mentioned the Spirit."

"We read that in the Bible and we don't know about that. What is it like?" This told me right away they had never been taught about the

Holy Spirit. So I gave an impromptu lesson that took about twenty minutes, and their mouths literally stayed open as they heard for the first time the truth concerning how the power of God, in the control of the Holy Spirit, can literally take them through life. They had never heard it, yet they had been Christians for many years.

Unfortunately, most believers don't really know much more—we have good theology, but no practical wisdom. If we pay attention, the book of Acts will fill in some deep gaps in our understanding of the Holy Spirit. I urge you to make the Holy Spirit a subject of intense study, not only to gain theological knowledge, but to discover how to release the incredible power of God residing within you.

Dice in the Prayer Meeting
ACTS 1:15-26

NASB

15aAt this time Peter stood up in the midst of the brethren (a gathering of about one hundred and twenty bpersons was there together), and said, 16"Brethren, the Scripture had to be fulfilled, which the Holy Spirit foretold by the mouth of David concerning Judas, who became a guide to those who arrested Jesus. 17For he was counted among us and received his share in this ministry." 18(Now this man acquired a field with the price of his wickedness, and falling headlong, he burst open in the middle and all his intestines gushed out. 19And it became known to all who were living in Jerusalem; so that in their own language that field was called Hakeldama, that is, Field of Blood.) 20"For it is written in the book of Psalms,

'LET HIS HOMESTEAD BE MADE
    DESOLATE,
AND LET NO ONE DWELL IN IT';

and,

'LET ANOTHER MAN TAKE HIS
    aOFFICE.'

NLT

15During this time, when about 120 believers* were together in one place, Peter stood up and addressed them. 16"Brothers," he said, "the Scriptures had to be fulfilled concerning Judas, who guided those who arrested Jesus. This was predicted long ago by the Holy Spirit, speaking through King David. 17Judas was one of us and shared in the ministry with us."

18(Judas had bought a field with the money he received for his treachery. Falling headfirst there, his body split open, spilling out all his intestines. 19The news of his death spread to all the people of Jerusalem, and they gave the place the Aramaic name *Akeldama,* which means "Field of Blood.")

20Peter continued, "This was written in the book of Psalms, where it says, 'Let his home become desolate, with no one living in it.' It also says, 'Let someone else take his position.'*

21Therefore it is necessary that of the men who have accompanied us all the time that the Lord Jesus went in and out ᵃamong us— 22beginning ᵃwith the baptism of John until the day that He was taken up from us— one of these *must* become a witness with us of His resurrection." 23So they put forward two men, Joseph called Barsabbas (who was also called Justus), and Matthias. 24And they prayed and said, "You, Lord, who know the hearts of all men, show which one of these two You have chosen 25to ᵃoccupy this ministry and apostleship from which Judas turned aside to go to his own place." 26And they ᵃdrew lots for them, and the lot fell ᵇto Matthias; and he was ᶜadded to the eleven apostles.

1:15 ᵃLit *In these days* ᵇLit *names* 1:20 ᵃLit *position as overseer* 1:21 ᵃLit *to us* 1:22 ᵃLit *from* 1:25 ᵃLit *take the place of* 1:26 ᵃLit *gave* ᵇOr *upon* ᶜLit *voted together with*

21"So now we must choose a replacement for Judas from among the men who were with us the entire time we were traveling with the Lord Jesus—22from the time he was baptized by John until the day he was taken from us. Whoever is chosen will join us as a witness of Jesus' resurrection."
23So they nominated two men: Joseph called Barsabbas (also known as Justus) and Matthias. 24Then they all prayed, "O Lord, you know every heart. Show us which of these men you have chosen 25as an apostle to replace Judas in this ministry, for he has deserted us and gone where he belongs." 26Then they cast lots, and Matthias was selected to become an apostle with the other eleven.

1:15 Greek *brothers.* 1:20 Pss 69:25; 109:8.

I have been married to Cynthia for a very long time. As of this writing, I have been married to her twice as long as I was single. She has been my lover, friend, confidant, companion, advisor, comforter, and partner for so much of my life that I have a hard time remembering what life was like without her. Thinking through major decisions with her is as natural as breathing; I can't imagine not discussing important matters with her.

The church should be like that. We can barely imagine the church operating apart from the Holy Spirit. For more than two thousand years, the gathering of God's people has had the Holy Spirit as its guide. That's because each person who trusts in Jesus Christ for redemption from the eternal consequences of sin receives the Holy Spirit as a gift. The very presence of God immediately takes up residence in that individual, and a supernatural transformation begins. Now, instead of thinking with a spiritually darkened mind—making self-serving decisions as a slave to sin—the new believer has the mind of God to guide, teach, convict, comfort, and encourage. Because the church is composed of gathered believers, the church has enjoyed the leadership of God's Spirit from the very beginning.

Actually, to be precise, I should say *almost* from the very beginning.

As I stated earlier, the book of Acts is a book of transitions. And the first transition Luke describes is, without question, the most dramatic the world has ever known. Acts 1:12-26 paints a curious picture of the fellowship of believers before the church was launched—an almost forgotten image of the cowering congregation prior to the arrival of the Holy Spirit. Luke offers a timid, fearful, almost pathetic rendering of uncertain believers groping for direction just a few days before the Holy Spirit took over. The apostles remained huddled in a room, waiting for marching orders from the Lord, unable to make a decision without specific physical indicators of His will. Then the events of Acts 2:1-4 change everything—literally *everything*. They go from drawing lots to discern God's will (1:26) to speaking forth the "mighty deeds of God" by the power of the indwelling Spirit (2:11)—from having trouble hearing God's word to unhesitatingly speaking it with power!

— 1:15-17 —

As Luke's Gospel closes and the book of Acts resumes the story, we find 120 of the Lord's followers waiting in Jerusalem, just as He had commanded (1:13-15; see Luke 24:49; Acts 1:4). We tend to think of them as larger-than-life heroes of history, idealized marble figures without blemish or defect . . . but no one in that scene wears a halo. Luke names Peter, who denied knowing Jesus three times, calling down curses to make his lies sound more credible. We see among them John and James, the tempestuous "Sons of Thunder" (Mark 3:17). Philip, the facts-and-figures disciple (Mark 6:37; John 6:7), could look across the room at Thomas, the melancholy "show me" man (John 11:16; 20:25). Also among them are the mother and half siblings of Jesus, who once believed the Lord had lost His mind and who therefore wanted to curtail His ministry (Mark 3:21). Evidently, Christ's crucifixion and resurrection changed their minds. Each of the disciples fled when the Lord was arrested, tried, and crucified. The others failed to stand with Jesus throughout His ordeal. Consequently, all of them had been restored from some kind of failure after the Lord's resurrection.

They gathered to pray and to wait for the Lord's promise to be fulfilled. Leading the prayer meeting were the eleven disciples whom the Lord had personally trained. *Eleven.* But hadn't Jesus made a promise about *twelve*? Hadn't he said, "In the regeneration when the Son of Man will sit on His glorious throne, you also shall sit upon twelve thrones, judging the twelve tribes of Israel" (Matt. 19:28)?

Twelve tribes, twelve thrones . . . eleven disciples. Maybe it was because Peter did the math and saw the problem that he decided to take action. He stood up and reminded the other followers that the Old Testament had predicted the fate of Judas (Pss. 69:25; 109:8) yet that the Lord anticipated twelve apostles.

— 1:18-19 —

At this point, it appears that Luke inserted a parenthetical historical note concerning the fate of Judas in the middle of Peter's speech. Many commentators have noted that Luke's facts and those offered by Matthew 27:3-10 imply an apparent contradiction. However, a reasonable explanation emerges when we combine Luke's facts with Matthew's account. Putting all the information together, I suggest the following sequence of events.

In his fit of remorse, Judas cast the thirty pieces of silver onto the temple floor and then hanged himself in a remote field. No one found him until his body had decayed, become bloated, fallen from the noose, landed face down, and burst open, and his organs had spilled onto the ground. The Greek word translated "headlong" is *prēnēs* [4248], which doesn't have the meaning "headfirst" in other Greek literature but simply "level," "prostrate," or "face down."[7]

Ancient people considered this gruesome scene the most shameful way to die and an unthinkable way for a body to decay. In the Jewish mind, a hanged man was "accursed of God," and if the corpse was not buried the same day, the land was considered defiled (Deut. 21:23). Moreover, Jews avoided cadavers and blood at all costs. This was cursed ground.

The priests didn't want the money and no one wanted the land, so the landowner was compensated for his loss and the field reviled as "the blood field."

— 1:20-22 —

Luke's narrative resumes Peter's speech, in which he quoted two royal psalms, songs of David that foreshadow the Messiah. In these ancient poems, the enemies of David prefigure the enemies of the Messiah; in this case, the psalms predict his demise of one in particular. With twelve thrones, twelve tribes, Judas gone, and eleven apostles remaining, Peter reasoned from Scripture that they needed a replacement. But not just any man—only a man with the right qualifications could bear the title of "apostle."

Peter established two primary criteria for potential replacements: Like the eleven, the candidate must have been a follower of Jesus from the beginning and must have personally interacted with the resurrected Lord. Peter had good reasons for those two requirements. First, the primary means of teaching and leading the growing numbers of believers would be verbal and personal; the apostles would serve as the church's source of theological truth for the next few decades (2 Pet. 3:2). Today, we have the New Testament to teach, reprove, correct, and train (2 Tim. 3:16), but the first-century believers depended upon the authority of the apostles. Therefore, these men had to have been personally trained by the Son of God—divine truth in human flesh.

Remember, this was a time of transition; it would not always be this way. When the apostles eventually died, they didn't hand their authority to another generation of apostles in a policy some call *apostolic succession*. By the time all of the original apostles died, the New Testament had been completed and was being circulated—writings that Peter acknowledged as the authoritative Word of God (2 Pet. 1:20-21), not the least of which were Paul's letters (2 Pet. 3:15-16).

A second reason for Peter's requirements was that if the men had not been firsthand eyewitnesses to the Resurrection, then their testimony would not have been admissible in court, the minimum standard of credibility in Roman culture.

Third, without firsthand training from the Lord and the assurance of having seen the resurrected Jesus with their own eyes, apostles who were not eye witnesses would have been more easily tempted to backtrack on their confession in the midst of pressure. Torture is a powerful instrument of mind control; people have been known to deny their own names under intense duress. The apostles were about to face the same men who provoked Roman authorities to torture and crucify Jesus, and those corrupt temple leaders needed Jesus' followers to recant, not merely stay quiet. The apostles' conviction of the truth had to be unassailable—something only firsthand, eyewitness assurance could provide (the Holy Spirit notwithstanding, of course).

— 1:23-26 —

The apostles "put forward two men" who met the two criteria (1:23). We can assume that if other men qualified, they would have been included. Joseph also went by the nickname Barsabbas, which means "son of the Sabbath." No one knows the significance. The name of the second man was Matthias, a shortened version of Mattathias. Everyone knew of an earlier Mattathias, the heroic priest who sparked the Maccabean Revolt that eventually led to Judea's independence.[8] To this day, Jews celebrate their victory and God's provision as Hanukkah, the Feast of Lights/Dedication (cf. John 10:22).

Having identified the individuals bearing the necessary qualifications, the gathering of believers prayed, seeking God's mind on the matter. In this short passage, Luke offers a glimpse of church leadership before the Holy Spirit filled believers. The people of God did not have divine discernment living within; they had to use a time-honored Old Testament method of determining the will of God. Believing in the power of prayer and rejecting the notion of random chance, they "drew lots"—a method not unlike drawing straws or rolling dice—and expected God to direct the outcome (Prov. 16:33; see Lev. 16:8; Josh. 14:2; 1 Sam. 14:41-42; Neh. 10:34; 11:1).

It was a safe bet—in a manner of speaking. This method of discerning God's will may seem strange to us. Few mature Christians would consider making important decisions—especially church-leadership decisions—by rolling dice. But the apostles had already used their best "sanctified" reasoning to narrow the candidates down to two, so they weren't choosing between right and wrong. Both men were of excellent character and eminently qualified for the role. So, all things being equal, the disciples trusted in the sovereignty of God, and the lot fell to Matthias, who became one of "the Twelve."

As this chapter closes, the church looks ready for action. The people stand ready. The best available men fill positions of leadership. Nothing remains to be done. And so they wait, anticipating the day their heavenly Leader makes divine truth incarnate again. They have no idea what they are about to witness and experience!

APPLICATION: ACTS 1:15-26

I try, I fail; I trust, He succeeds.

In his penetrating book *Your Churning Place*, Robert Wise tells the story of how Burt Lancaster, one of Hollywood's biggest stars of yesteryear, got into show business. Most people don't know he began as a circus performer.

> [At an audition] he was asked to perform on the parallel bars, so he leaped on the bars and began his routine. Because he was nervous, his timing was off, and he spun over the bar, falling

flat on his face some ten feet below. He was so humiliated that he immediately leaped back on the bar. As he spun again at the same point, he flipped off and smashed to the ground once more!

Burt's tights were torn, he was cut and bleeding, and he was fiercely upset! He leaped back again, but the third time was even worse, for this time he fell on his back. The agent came over, picked him up, and said, "Son, if you won't do that again, you've got the job!"[9]

I think that's exactly the way we approach the Christian life. We start out determined to do it, even if it kills us. We keep trying and trying in our own strength, throwing ourselves at the task with ruthless abandon, often landing flat on our backs over and over again. We try, we fail.

Perhaps that's you. You've given your best routine time after time, and you keep coming back bloodied and torn and bruised and broken.

You might feel encouraged to know that the people described in the first chapter of Acts had abysmal track records: broken people, imperfect people, bruised, failing, unsuccessful, weak, fearful, insecure men and women secretly cowering in an upper room, hoping to escape the notice of their enemies. They had done their routine, and God said, "You stay right there. Don't do that anymore. Stop trying. Start trusting." As they continued to trust and wait, He would do something marvelous: He would send His Spirit to dwell within them.

Let me draw two principles from this portrait of helpless believers.

First, *the people God chooses to empower are not perfect performers but dependent followers*. Isn't that a relief? If you learn anything from this passage, I hope you discover that God isn't looking for perfect performers to execute flawless routines in their own strength. These men and women had faulty and frayed track records.

Our world, however, wants you to believe that it's wrong to ever be wrong and inexcusable to ever fail. We're living under an incredible man-made standard called "perfection"! While we say we embrace grace, in practice we *really* uphold a performance-based standard of worth in the Christian life. The fact is, however, you don't always have to be right. You don't need to be a "tryer"; you need to be a "truster."

Second, *the plan God honors is not complicated but simple*. Essentially, He commanded His followers, "Go to Jerusalem and wait." They went to Jerusalem and waited. And He basically assured them, "Trust Me to send the power." They trusted Him to send the power. And He did just that! But we don't like plans that require us to release control. We don't operate like that.

We ask, "God, what's Your plan for me?"

God says, "Plan A." And He unveils a path that requires trust and obedience.

We say, "Do you have a Plan B?"

Why? Because Plan A reminds us that we're helpless. Plan A requires trusting in God, and let's face it—we don't always want to trust God!

So, what's the solution? It comes down to a decision based on the realization that when I try, I fail, but when I trust, He succeeds. The solution is simple—not at all easy, but uncomplicated: *Stop trying; start trusting.*

Supernatural Churchbirth
ACTS 2:1-13

NASB

¹When the day of Pentecost ᵃhad come, they were all together in one place. ²And suddenly there came from heaven a noise like a violent rushing wind, and it filled the whole house where they were sitting. ³And there appeared to them tongues as of fire ᵃdistributing themselves, and ᵇthey ᶜrested on each one of them. ⁴And they were all filled with the Holy Spirit and began to speak with other ᵃtongues, as the Spirit was giving them ᵇutterance.

⁵Now there were Jews living in Jerusalem, devout men from every nation under heaven. ⁶And when this sound occurred, the crowd came together, and were bewildered because each one of them was hearing them speak in his own ᵃlanguage. ⁷They were amazed and astonished, saying, "ᵃWhy, are not all these who are speaking Galileans? ⁸And how is it that we each hear *them* in our own ᵃlanguage ᵇto which we were born? ⁹Parthians and Medes and Elamites, and residents of Mesopotamia, Judea and Cappadocia, Pontus and ᵃAsia,

NLT

¹On the day of Pentecost* all the believers were meeting together in one place. ²Suddenly, there was a sound from heaven like the roaring of a mighty windstorm, and it filled the house where they were sitting. ³Then, what looked like flames or tongues of fire appeared and settled on each of them. ⁴And everyone present was filled with the Holy Spirit and began speaking in other languages,* as the Holy Spirit gave them this ability.

⁵At that time there were devout Jews from every nation living in Jerusalem. ⁶When they heard the loud noise, everyone came running, and they were bewildered to hear their own languages being spoken by the believers.

⁷They were completely amazed. "How can this be?" they exclaimed. "These people are all from Galilee, ⁸and yet we hear them speaking in our own native languages! ⁹Here we are—Parthians, Medes, Elamites, people from Mesopotamia, Judea, Cappadocia, Pontus, the province of

NASB

¹⁰Phrygia and Pamphylia, Egypt and the districts of Libya around Cyrene, and ᵃvisitors from Rome, both Jews and ᵇproselytes, ¹¹Cretans and Arabs—we hear them in our *own* tongues speaking of the mighty deeds of God." ¹²And they all continued in amazement and great perplexity, saying to one another, "What does this mean?" ¹³But others were mocking and saying, "They are full of ᵃsweet wine."

2:1 ᵃLit *was being fulfilled*   **2:3** ᵃOr *being distributed*   ᵇLit *it*   ᶜOr *sat*   **2:4** ᵃOr *languages*   ᵇOr *ability to speak out*   **2:6** ᵃOr *dialect*   **2:7** ᵃLit *Behold*   **2:8** ᵃOr *dialect*   ᵇLit *in*   **2:9** ᵃI.e. west coast province of Asia Minor   **2:10** ᵃLit *the sojourning Romans*   ᵇI.e. Gentile converts to Judaism   **2:13** ᵃI.e. new wine

NLT

Asia, ¹⁰Phrygia, Pamphylia, Egypt, and the areas of Libya around Cyrene, visitors from Rome ¹¹(both Jews and converts to Judaism), Cretans, and Arabs. And we all hear these people speaking in our own languages about the wonderful things God has done!" ¹²They stood there amazed and perplexed. "What can this mean?" they asked each other.

¹³But others in the crowd ridiculed them, saying, "They're just drunk, that's all!"

2:1 The Festival of Pentecost came 50 days after Passover (when Jesus was crucified).   **2:4** Or *in other tongues.*

Back in the 1970s, I was watching the eleven o'clock news when the cameras cut to the scene of a banquet. A governor rose to address the audience, and instead of looking calm and distinguished, he appeared flustered and disheveled. He began with an apology: "I have something that I would like to say that might cost me votes in the months ahead. But I nevertheless must tell the truth as to why I was delayed. My wife and I were delayed by a UFO that stopped our car on the way to the banquet. I cannot explain fully what transpired, but it was . . . it was supernatural."

He didn't succeed in his bid for the election.

I don't think it's a stretch to say that the experiences of Acts 2 would have been something like reporting a close encounter with a UFO. Nothing like this event had ever occurred. Anyone not present in that room had great difficulty believing it had happened. The people who experienced the events were hard pressed to explain what they saw, heard, and felt during this supernatural phenomenon, and those who tried were written off as kooks.

As unbelievable as it seemed, however, John the Baptizer had told them, "As for me, I baptize you with water; but One is coming who is mightier than I, and I am not fit to untie the thong of His sandals; He will baptize you with the Holy Spirit and fire" (Luke 3:16; cf. Matt. 3:11; Mark 1:8; John 1:33). Jesus had also told His disciples what to expect (John 14:16-17, 26; 15:26; 16:7; Acts 1:5). But let's face it—no one could have anticipated what occurred on that particular day, known forevermore as "*the* day of Pentecost" (see 2:1).

The word "Pentecost" is a transliteration of the Greek word *pentēkostē* [4005], which means "fiftieth." Hellenistic Jews used this name to denote the Jewish Feast of Weeks (Shavuot), also called the Feast of the Harvest, which begins fifty days after the Passover meal (Lev. 23:15-16; Deut. 16:9-10). For centuries, this time between the two feasts has been a period of great anticipation for devout Jews, who mark the time by the "Counting of the Omer." Scripture commanded that on the day after Passover, a sheaf of the first grain stalks should be cut and brought to the temple as an offering (see Lev. 23:10-11). Later generations determined that a sheaf of grain yielded one *omer*, a dry measure of about 2 quarts. Families then begin counting down the days from that first omer of grain to Pentecost, which commences the Feast of the Harvest. During the Counting of the Omer, they maintain a mild state of mourning by avoiding weddings, banquets, and parties.

Clearly, the Lord took full advantage of the symbolism surrounding Passover, the Counting of the Omer, Pentecost, and the weeklong harvest celebration. Jesus Christ is the first fruits from the dead (Acts 26:23; 1 Cor. 15:20-23), having been the first to be raised from the dead. He spent forty days on earth (Acts 1:3) and then ascended. On the fiftieth day, Pentecost, the Spirit of God came precisely as Jesus had predicted, coinciding with the great national harvest celebration.

On that day, about 120 believers had gathered in one place. Luke doesn't say where, but it probably wasn't the upper room where they had been praying, for they could be seen by a very large number of devout Jews living in Jerusalem (2:5). Perhaps they had decided to celebrate together in the courtyard of a private home near the center of town.

— 2:1-3 —

Suddenly, unexpectedly, abruptly—not like a flood, where the river rises and slowly leaves its banks; not like a hurricane building strength over the waters; but like a sudden, jolting earthquake—a noise shook the house. It was "like a violent rushing wind" (2:2), a sound we might compare with standing next to a 747 at takeoff. Luke doesn't say "a wind blew through"; he describes a *noise*. The curtains didn't blow. They felt no current or movement of air. In the ordinary environment of a house, a deafening roar came from above. Luke identifies the source as heaven.

An amazing sight accompanied the sound: "Tongues as of fire" peeled off to form individual ribbons of blazing . . . what? Flames, perhaps? Who knows? Luke had seen lightning before, so he could have referred to that (*astrapē* [796], cf. Luke 10:18; 17:24), but he chose "fire" (*pyr* [4442]) instead. Perhaps it looked like the ethereal light of God's fiery glory, which later Judaism came to call the shekinah. This "fire" always appeared when God wanted His presence known. He caused a bush in the Midian wilderness to burst into flames, yet the fire did not consume it as a normal blaze would have (Exod. 3:1-3). This fiery glow led the Israelites as a pillar (Exod. 13:21-22). The shekinah covered the summit of Mount Sinai before the people of Israel (Exod. 19:18; 24:17). And behind the thick tapestry partition in the temple, this "fire" resided above the ark of the covenant in the most holy place (Exod. 25:22; Lev. 16:2). Jews familiar with the Scriptures would have identified the "fire" as the holy light of God's presence.

Luke describes the energy as coming from "tongues" (plural) like fire, a blazing substance dividing and distributing itself into one stream per individual. Unlike a lightning strike, the flames came to rest on each person. I suggest the image remained in place long enough for each person to look around and see that *everyone* in the group received the same flaming power, the same gift of the Holy Spirit. Each received the same empowerment. No one was left out.

— 2:4 —

The gathered believers *heard* something, they *saw* something, and— now the most familiar and misunderstood phenomenon—they *said* something. Just as they had been promised by John the Baptizer, their water baptism had been followed by their baptism with "the Holy Spirit and fire" (Matt. 3:11; Luke 3:16). They received divine power, and that power accomplished the impossible. The believers had been told they would "receive power when the Holy Spirit [had] come upon" them, resulting in their becoming Jesus' witnesses (Acts 1:8). They began to speak in other languages as the Spirit gave them ability.

The NASB rendering of this key phrase is "began to speak with other tongues, as the Spirit was giving them utterance," which we need to analyze in detail.

"Began to speak" indicates that the believers received an ability that would continue after this event. Luke uses this phrase in much the same way we might say a small child "began to walk": not only at that moment, but from then on.

"With other tongues" refers to other languages. Some claim these followers spoke in a "heavenly language" known only to God and angels,

a kind of supernatural communication that sounds like gibberish to human ears yet holds meaning in the spirit realm. Charismatic groups practice this today and call it "speaking in tongues." Several factors in the text, however, do not point to a "heavenly language" but rather to human languages.

First, the Greek words for "other" and "tongues" are plural. Moreover, the term rendered "other" is *heteros* [2087], indicating that the languages were different from one another. The word "various" would be appropriate. The phrase indicates that the people spoke in more than one actual language, not one "heavenly language." And let's face it—the idea of heaven having more than one language simply doesn't make sense. Long before this, God had confounded human communication on earth (Gen. 11:7), not among the angels in the spirit realm.

Second, the practice of incomprehensible ecstatic speech known today as "speaking in tongues" has a long history in pagan religion. Various sects and cults had practiced a form of "ecstatic utterance" for centuries, both as a frenzied emotional expression and a seemingly rational form of communication. If these Christians had "spoken in tongues" in the ecstatic manner seen today, their behavior would not have been regarded by onlookers as a special, unique, miraculous gift of God.

Third, the following verses clearly indicate the ability of spectators to hear their native languages spoken. The term translated "language" in Acts 2:6 is *dialektos* [1258], from which we derive our term "dialect."

"As the Spirit was giving them utterance" indicates that the disciples didn't instantaneously acquire another language, suddenly becoming bilingual. This was a supernatural ability given by the Spirit, presumably to empower the believers to fulfill the Lord's promise that they would be His witnesses (1:8). The Greek term translated "utterance" (*apophthengomai* [669]) means "to speak out loudly and clearly, or with emphasis (of philosophers, ecstatics . . . singers, and prophets)."[10] This strongly suggests that each person was able not only to speak in another language, but was also given the thoughts to express the message eloquently.

— 2:5-6 —

Pentecost was the second of three festivals that required Jewish men to visit Jerusalem for at least a week (Exod. 23:14, 17; 34:23; Deut. 16:16). So "devout men" from all around the Roman Empire and beyond had converged on the city (Acts 2:5). Jerusalem, of course, also had a permanent population of both devout and non-devout Jews. The loud noise (2:2) captured the attention of this mixed group, and the sound of people talking in various dialects drew them in for a closer look. The gathered followers of Christ, now filled with the Holy Spirit and empowered to witness, didn't speak in order to be noticed; they were "speaking of the mighty deeds of God" (2:11). The Jews from out of town, however, could hear their own languages being spoken by the witnesses. Their reaction is described as "bewildered" (*syncheō* [4797]), which could also be translated as "dismayed," "disturbed," "confused," or "stirred up."

— 2:7-11 —

Two familiar terms from Luke's Gospel appear again in Acts. Throughout Luke's account of Jesus' ministry of healing and casting out demons, the people continually felt "amazed" and "astonished." Now the *disciples* have been empowered to amaze and astonish.

The remarkable linguistic feat of the disciples surprised the crowd for more than one reason. Not only were the out-of-towners able to hear their own languages spoken, but the words came from *Galileans*! That doesn't mean anything to us, but it meant a lot in that day. Most Jews in first-century Palestine lived in one of two sections. The northern section, Galilee, was what we might call the hick section, the home of country bumpkins. Despite their relatively significant literacy rate, Galileans were considered uneducated by their more cosmopolitan cousins to the south, in Judea. According to one expositor, "Galileans had difficulty pronouncing gutturals and had the habit of swallowing syllables when speaking; so they were looked down upon by the people of Jerusalem as being provincial."[11]

While Galilean Jews received an education in the synagogues, their training couldn't compare to that of the well-educated Judeans. Those in Jerusalem spoke Aramaic and Koine Greek (the common Greek of the empire), and perhaps a few would have had training in classical Greek and Latin. The Jews from other parts of the world felt stunned to hear uneducated Galileans speaking so many languages with such eloquence.

The Jews living around the world were known as the Diaspora, that is, "the dispersed" or "the scattered ones" (cf. Jas. 1:1; 1 Pet. 1:1). Luke names fifteen of the places from which the visitors had traveled, which covered much of the known world, including lands outside of Roman control. The places didn't represent physical distance as much

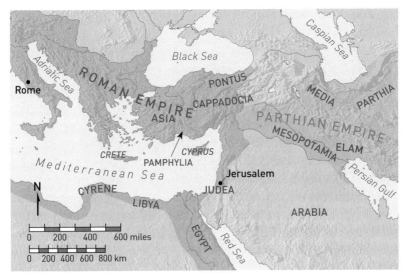

The Jewish Diaspora at Pentecost (Acts 2:9-11).

as variation in language, a much more difficult obstacle to evangelism. On this day, however, the Holy Spirit proved His ability and intent to overcome any obstacle to communicate God's truth and carry out God's plan of redemption.

— 2:12-13 —

"They" in 2:12 refers to the same people in 2:7 who exclaimed, "Why, are not all these who are speaking Galileans?" The term rendered "amazement" here is a form of *existēmi* [1839], which brings to mind a colorful word picture of a person "out of his senses" with surprise. "Great perplexity" (*diaporeō* [1280]) can also be translated "at a loss." The onlookers had no ordinary explanation for what they witnessed; it was clearly supernatural, something they would have a difficult time explaining to the folks back home.

They couldn't explain how these ordinary people could do something so extraordinary, so they stopped to consider the implications. "What does this mean?" (2:12) was more than a rhetorical question; many of the spectators were discerning enough to see that something of great significance was happening. "What does this mean?" looked to the future.

A number of others were "mocking" (*diachleuazō* [1315b]). The same term is also translated "to laugh in scorn" or "to jeer" in other Greek literature. Clearly unable—or unwilling—to see the significance of the disciples' speaking about God's mighty deeds in other languages, they dismissed the event with a put-down, suggesting the followers of Christ were drunk on "sweet wine" (2:13).

"Sweet wine" (*gleukos* [1098]) cannot refer to "new wine," as some suggest; Pentecost occurs in April or May, too early for fresh grapes. More likely, it refers to a winemaking process now called *chaptalization*, whereby honey is added to unfermented grape mash, which produces a higher alcohol content during the fermentation process. The end product doesn't taste sweet, but it sure packs a bigger punch!

We shouldn't imagine that the put-down implies the 120 disciples behaved like drunks. Far from appearing inebriated, they spoke in other languages with such eloquence that out-of-towners marveled at their level of education. While there certainly was a commotion after the sound of violent wind, the flash of shekinah light, and the noise of people shouting praises to God in a multitude of languages, this was no frenzied spectacle. It was the beginning of a new movement—with God Himself as the organizer.

While people today struggle with the idea of UFO encounters and alien contact, the first-century Christians didn't have a problem telling their supernatural story. Some people scoffed. Many others rejected it. But a great number of people believed, received the Holy Spirit personally, and then played significant roles in the supernatural birth of the church. The scoffing of people didn't bother Peter; he merely used their skepticism as an opportunity to deliver the very first sermon ever preached in the church. And my, what a difference the Holy Spirit made!

APPLICATION: ACTS 2:1-13

Let the Holy Spirit Do the Talking

A lot of churches place a great burden on their members to repeat the experience of Pentecost, at least in part. According to some leaders in certain circles, the ability to speak in tongues is a necessary indication that a person is a genuine follower of Christ. Many correctly understand that the Holy Spirit immediately takes up residence in a believer at the very moment of salvation, but they think it happens only on a temporary basis. Taking Acts 2 as their example, they conclude that speaking in tongues is a necessary outward sign of the Holy Spirit's presence.

Therefore, no speaking in tongues means no Holy Spirit within, and no Holy Spirit within means no salvation.

Others call the Holy Spirit a "second blessing," noting that Acts reports at least one case in which people received salvation and then received the Holy Spirit sometime later (8:14-17).[12] They conclude that the Holy Spirit and His attendant gifts are an additional blessing for which one must pray earnestly. According to this view, speaking in tongues doesn't indicate salvation as much as measure piety. Consequently, genuine believers who do not speak in tongues are considered underdeveloped or incomplete as Christians.

Both views have significant biblical and theological flaws.

The fact is, we are *never* commanded to experience Pentecost or even to seek it. *We can't!* That's like telling someone to experience the parting of the Red Sea or the feeding of the five thousand. Those were unique works of God, done by Him through His own initiative at a specific point in history to teach unbelieving bystanders something about Himself. He used believers as instruments to accomplish a specific purpose; therefore, to expect a person to repeat the experience of Pentecost would be like asking a screwdriver to be picked up by its owner.

In addition, these miraculous events brought glory to God alone. The giving of the Holy Spirit in Acts 2 was a onetime event, marking the beginning of a brand-new era. It didn't bring glory to the people; the coming of the Holy Spirit and their subsequent speaking in other languages put the Lord at center stage. Their speaking in tongues didn't prove their incredible piety as Christians, because none of them were very mature Christians at all!

Finally, we must remember, the "speaking in tongues" described in Acts 2 produced a number of human languages that could be understood by people from other nations; it was an effective evangelistic tool, not some kind of heavenly language unintelligible on earth. Therefore, if we want to use speaking in tongues as an indicator of salvation or a measure of godliness, no one today passes the test!

Never are we commanded to be *baptized* in the Spirit or to produce supernatural evidence of the Spirit. God gives His Spirit immediately, fully, and permanently to believers when we receive His gift of salvation. And anything He does—miraculous or otherwise—is His prerogative, subject to His sovereign authority, irrespective of what anyone else does, desires, or expects. W. E. Vine writes,

There is no evidence of the continuance of this gift after apostolic times nor indeed in the later times of the apostles themselves; this provides confirmation of the fulfillment in this way of 1 Cor. 13:8, that this gift would cease in the churches, just as would "prophecies" and "knowledge" in the sense of knowledge received by immediate supernatural power (cf. 1 Cor. 14:6). The completion of the Holy Scriptures has provided the churches with all that is necessary for individual and collective guidance, instruction, and edification.[13]

As I consider the issue of speaking in tongues while reflecting on this passage in Acts 2, two truths emerge that help guide me through these troubled waters.

First, *when God does a work, no one can duplicate it or ignore it.* When God does something miraculous, it's obviously of God, and no doubt remains. People might reject it—think of the scoffers who accused the believers of drunkenness—but they cannot deny the unmistakable hand of God. "Supernatural," by definition, refers to something God alone can do. When people try, the response is doubt, skepticism, questioning. People analyze it like a magician's illusion. But when God does something truly miraculous, no one can duplicate it or ignore it.

Second, *when the Spirit gives power, God receives the credit, not people.* When a surgeon performs a lifesaving procedure in the operating room, no one later praises the scalpel. It didn't do anything on its own. Similarly, we are incapable of supernatural activity—on our own. Furthermore, the surgeon didn't choose that particular scalpel because it had made itself useful for the job; it was made by someone, sharpened by someone, sterilized by someone, and then finally put to use by someone. We are no different. People cannot make themselves either capable or worthy of supernatural power.

When God works supernaturally, any thought of human recognition is absurd, especially to the people involved.

The next time you see something that claims to be the supernatural work of God, ask yourself two questions, in this order:

If this is genuine, for whom do I feel admiration right now? (If it's anyone but God, beware.)

Is it possible to duplicate this feat or accomplish the appearance of it through human means? (If so, beware.)

Peter's First (and Best) Sermon
ACTS 2:14-36

NASB

¹⁴But Peter, ᵃtaking his stand with the eleven, raised his voice and declared to them: "Men of Judea and all you who live in Jerusalem, let this be known to you and give heed to my words. ¹⁵For these men are not drunk, as you suppose, for it is *only* the ᵃthird hour of the day; ¹⁶but this is what was spoken of through the prophet Joel:

¹⁷ 'AND IT SHALL BE IN THE LAST
  DAYS,' God says,
'THAT I WILL POUR FORTH OF MY
  SPIRIT ON ALL ᵃMANKIND;
AND YOUR SONS AND YOUR
  DAUGHTERS SHALL PROPHESY,
AND YOUR YOUNG MEN SHALL SEE
  VISIONS,
AND YOUR OLD MEN SHALL DREAM
  DREAMS;
¹⁸ EVEN ON MY BONDSLAVES, BOTH
  MEN AND WOMEN,
I WILL IN THOSE DAYS POUR FORTH
  OF MY SPIRIT
And they shall prophesy.
¹⁹ 'AND I WILL GRANT WONDERS IN
  THE SKY ABOVE
AND SIGNS ON THE EARTH BELOW,
BLOOD, AND FIRE, AND VAPOR OF
  SMOKE.
²⁰ 'THE SUN WILL BE TURNED INTO
  DARKNESS
AND THE MOON INTO BLOOD,
BEFORE THE GREAT AND GLORIOUS
  DAY OF THE LORD SHALL
  COME.
²¹ 'AND IT SHALL BE THAT EVERYONE
  WHO CALLS ON THE NAME OF
  THE LORD WILL BE SAVED.'

²²"Men of Israel, listen to these words: Jesus the Nazarene, a man ᵃattested to you by God with ᵇmiracles and wonders and ᶜsigns which God performed through Him in your midst, just as you yourselves

NLT

¹⁴Then Peter stepped forward with the eleven other apostles and shouted to the crowd, "Listen carefully, all of you, fellow Jews and residents of Jerusalem! Make no mistake about this. ¹⁵These people are not drunk, as some of you are assuming. Nine o'clock in the morning is much too early for that. ¹⁶No, what you see was predicted long ago by the prophet Joel:

¹⁷ 'In the last days,' God says,
  'I will pour out my Spirit upon
    all people.
  Your sons and daughters will
    prophesy.
  Your young men will see
    visions,
  and your old men will dream
    dreams.
¹⁸ In those days I will pour out my
    Spirit
  even on my servants—men and
    women alike—
  and they will prophesy.
¹⁹ And I will cause wonders in the
    heavens above
  and signs on the earth below—
  blood and fire and clouds of
    smoke.
²⁰ The sun will become dark,
  and the moon will turn blood
    red
  before that great and glorious
    day of the LORD arrives.
²¹ But everyone who calls on the
    name of the LORD
  will be saved.'*

²²"People of Israel, listen! God publicly endorsed Jesus the Nazarene* by doing powerful miracles, wonders, and signs through him,

43

NASB

know— ²³this *Man,* delivered over by the predetermined plan and foreknowledge of God, you nailed to a cross by the hands of ^agodless men and put *Him* to death. ^{24a}But God raised Him up again, putting an end to the ^bagony of death, since it was impossible for Him to be held ^cin its power. ²⁵For David says of Him,

'I SAW THE LORD ALWAYS IN MY
  PRESENCE;
FOR HE IS AT MY RIGHT HAND, SO
  THAT I WILL NOT BE SHAKEN.
²⁶ 'THEREFORE MY HEART WAS GLAD
  AND MY TONGUE EXULTED;
MOREOVER MY FLESH ALSO WILL
  LIVE IN HOPE;
²⁷ BECAUSE YOU WILL NOT ABANDON
  MY SOUL TO HADES,
NOR ^aALLOW YOUR ^bHOLY ONE TO
  ^cUNDERGO DECAY.
²⁸ 'YOU HAVE MADE KNOWN TO ME
  THE WAYS OF LIFE;
YOU WILL MAKE ME FULL OF
  GLADNESS WITH YOUR
  PRESENCE.'

²⁹"^aBrethren, I may confidently say to you regarding the patriarch David that he both died and was buried, and his tomb is ^bwith us to this day. ³⁰And so, because he was a prophet and knew that GOD HAD SWORN TO HIM WITH AN OATH TO SEAT *one* ^aOF HIS DESCENDANTS ON HIS THRONE, ³¹he looked ahead and spoke of the resurrection of ^athe Christ, that HE WAS NEITHER ABANDONED TO HADES, NOR DID His flesh ^bSUFFER DECAY. ³²This Jesus God raised up again, to which we are all witnesses. ³³Therefore having been exalted ^ato the right hand of God, and having received from the Father the promise of the Holy Spirit, He has poured forth this which you both see and hear. ³⁴For it was not David who ascended into ^aheaven, but he himself says:

NLT

as you well know. ²³But God knew what would happen, and his prearranged plan was carried out when Jesus was betrayed. With the help of lawless Gentiles, you nailed him to a cross and killed him. ²⁴But God released him from the horrors of death and raised him back to life, for death could not keep him in its grip. ²⁵King David said this about him:

'I see that the LORD is always
  with me.
I will not be shaken, for he is
  right beside me.
²⁶ No wonder my heart is glad,
  and my tongue shouts his
  praises!
My body rests in hope.
²⁷ For you will not leave my soul
  among the dead*
  or allow your Holy One to rot
  in the grave.
²⁸ You have shown me the way
  of life,
  and you will fill me with the
  joy of your presence.'*

²⁹"Dear brothers, think about this! You can be sure that the patriarch David wasn't referring to himself, for he died and was buried, and his tomb is still here among us. ³⁰But he was a prophet, and he knew God had promised with an oath that one of David's own descendants would sit on his throne. ³¹David was looking into the future and speaking of the Messiah's resurrection. He was saying that God would not leave him among the dead or allow his body to rot in the grave.

³²"God raised Jesus from the dead, and we are all witnesses of this. ³³Now he is exalted to the place of highest honor in heaven, at God's right hand. And the Father, as he had promised, gave him the Holy Spirit to pour out upon us, just as you see and hear today. ³⁴For David himself never ascended into heaven, yet he said,

'THE LORD SAID TO MY LORD,
"SIT AT MY RIGHT HAND,
35 UNTIL I MAKE YOUR ENEMIES A
    FOOTSTOOL FOR YOUR FEET."'

36 Therefore let all the house of Israel know for certain that God has made Him both Lord and ᵃChrist—this Jesus whom you crucified."

2:14 ᵃOr *being put forward* as spokesman **2:15** ᵃI.e. 9 a.m. **2:17** ᵃLit *flesh* **2:22** ᵃOr *exhibited* or *accredited* ᵇOr *works of power* ᶜOr *attesting miracles* **2:23** ᵃLit *men without the Law;* i.e. pagan **2:24** ᵃLit *Whom God raised up* ᵇLit *birth pains* ᶜLit *by it* **2:27** ᵃLit *give* ᵇOr *devout* or *pious* ᶜLit *see corruption* **2:29** ᵃLit *Men brothers* ᵇLit *among* **2:30** ᵃLit *of the fruit of his loins* **2:31** ᵃI.e. the Messiah ᵇLit *see corruption* **2:33** ᵃOr *by* **2:34** ᵃLit *the heavens* **2:36** ᵃI.e. Messiah

'The LORD said to my Lord,
"Sit in the place of honor at my
    right hand
35 until I humble your enemies,
making them a footstool under
    your feet."'*

36 "So let everyone in Israel know for certain that God has made this Jesus, whom you crucified, to be both Lord and Messiah!"

2:17-21 Joel 2:28-32. **2:22** Or *Jesus of Nazareth.* **2:27** Greek *in Hades;* also in 2:31. **2:25-28** Ps 16:8-11 (Greek version). **2:34-35** Ps 110:1.

If you ever want to embarrass a preacher, ask him about his first sermon. Very few of us want to remember the first time we stood before a congregation, and most of us hope no one else *can* remember that embarrassing time!

One of my professors in seminary told the story of his first sermon, which he gave in a church far out in the country. As he stood up to preach, he opened his Bible, and at that very moment, the back door of the church flew open. In came a herd of goats. He said, "I tried to go on. And they were clattering and clanging around, jumping over the little country pews. And finally, I just stepped out of the pulpit, rolled up my sleeves, and with twenty or so other country folks, grabbed hold of those goats and pushed them back out the door." During the scuffle, one of them butted him in the nose. For the rest of the sermon, he wiped blood from his face while he preached.

Another friend said he felt scared to death preparing for his first sermon, so he typed up page after page of notes, fourteen or fifteen in all. He stacked them in order and stuffed them into his Bible right where he planned to preach. He had been taught that immediate eye contact with the audience is crucial; don't look at your notes, look at the people. He got up from the bench on the platform, walked to the pulpit, and on the way, dropped his stack of notes. But he didn't know it, because he was looking at the people. When he finished his introduction, he looked down to find his notes strung all across the platform—out of order, of course. To make matters worse, he had forgotten to number the pages.

He spent the next several minutes picking them up and putting them back in the proper order.

On the Day of Pentecost, the Holy Spirit came down with the roaring sound of a violent wind and a flash of shekinah light and gave the otherwise hesitant Peter a miraculous ability to communicate the gospel. Unbelieving spectators marveled at what they saw. Some rejected the tongues event and ridiculed these followers of Christ as drunks (2:13, 15). Others couldn't dismiss what they had seen, but neither could they understand the implications. Deeply troubled, they asked, "What does this mean?" (2:12).

A new age had begun, and the world would need to know. Peter stood to preach his very first sermon in public.

— 2:14 —

The phrase "taking his stand" is translated from the passive verb meaning "to stand," which could suggest the rendering "being put forward." The connected phrase "with the eleven" makes it possible they looked around at one another and agreed that Peter was the man for the occasion. As Henry Jacobsen writes, "He had no sermon notes, but he had two things that were infinitely more important. He had something to say, and he had the power of the Spirit."[14] Even without notes or the benefit of preparation, Peter's sermon appears very well organized; it was uncomplicated, direct, scriptural, and Christ-centered—what I would hope could be said of every sermon, especially mine.

He divided his message into two parts that precede his call to repentance in 2:38. Each part is prefaced with a direct address ("Men of Judea" and "Men of Israel," respectively). Here's an outline:

A. An explanation of the phenomenon (2:15-21)
 1. Not drunk (2:15)
 2. Fulfilling prophecy (2:16-21)
B. A declaration of Jesus Christ (2:22-35)
 1. Authenticated (2:22)
 2. Crucified (2:23)
 3. Resurrected (2:24-32)
 4. Ascended (2:33-34)
 5. Glorified (2:35)

The two sections roughly correspond to the two statements uttered by the crowd: "They are full of sweet wine" and "What does this mean?" The first section answers the false charge of the scoffers while preparing the "devout men" for the second section, which proclaims Jesus Christ as the long-anticipated Messiah.

Peter addressed the onlookers as "Men of Judea" and "all you who live in Jerusalem," descriptions that correspond to the two groups present: permanent residents of Judea and those housed in Jerusalem for the Feast of the Harvest (or the Feast of Weeks). This was a very Jewish gospel message. He was about to appeal to the Old Testament as the foundation of his argument, which unbelieving Gentiles would not have found convincing. The Greek phrase translated "give heed" is used only here in all of the New Testament, but it appears thirty-two times in the Septuagint (the Greek translation of the Old Testament), generally introducing something of grave importance. The prophet Joel, for example, opened his oracle with, "Hear this, O elders, and listen, all inhabitants of the land" (Joel 1:2).

— 2:15-16 —

Peter answered the false charge that the disciples were drunk on "sweet wine," an especially potent form of wine. He noted the time as "the third hour of the day," which would be nine o'clock in the morning when reckoned with the Jewish timekeeping method. According to one historian, "Scrupulous Jews drank wine only with flesh, and, on the authority of [Exod. 16:8], ate bread in the morning and flesh only in the evening. Hence wine could be drunk only in the evening."[15] The charge of drunkenness was not a light one; it carried implications of complete moral neglect. Peter replied, in effect, "We are as devout as any Jew in Jerusalem."

Koine Greek has two contrasting conjunctions we render as "but." The first is a small, almost casual contrast. But the one that follows Peter's denial of drunkenness is *alla* [235], which indicates a sharp distinction. So Peter's declaration could be rendered, *"On the contrary, this is what was spoken of through the prophet Joel."* Peter struck down the accusation of ungodliness and asserted instead that the unusual event was the work of God.

— 2:17-21 —

Peter quoted Joel 2:28-32 from memory (Acts 2:17-21). In that Old Testament prophecy, God promised to "pour out My Spirit on all mankind" (Joel 2:28; cf. Acts 2:17). "All mankind"—that is, every living person—will be filled with the Holy Spirit *only* when the kingdom of God has come to earth in its literal, physical form. For Joel's prophecy to be completely fulfilled, all unbelievers must be saved—or *gone*! Jews correctly understood that a fulfillment of Joel 2:28-29 would mark the beginning of the end of the world and the establishment of God's kingdom, described in Joel 2:30-31. But they expected the outpouring of the Holy Spirit to be an *event* of the end times, not a *process* leading to the "day of the LORD" (Joel 2:31).

According to their understanding,

Peter introduced a new idea—at least new to Jewish theology at the time. According to his sermon,

Old Testament Era → Interim Era Joel 2:28-29 HOLY SPIRIT → Kingdom of God Joel 2:30-31

It's important to note that on Pentecost, only about 120 people initially received the Holy Spirit, a far cry from "all mankind." Peter pointed to the *beginning* of an outpouring, not its completion. Peter claimed that this particular Pentecost marked the beginning of a new era that would *ultimately* lead to all living people receiving the Holy Spirit.

He concluded his quotation of Joel's prophecy with the reassuring line, "Everyone who calls on the name of the Lord will be saved" (Acts 2:21; Joel 2:32). That gave him the opportunity to transition into the second part of his sermon and explain how anyone can be saved. Between Pentecost and the day of the Lord exists an era of grace made possible by the Messiah.

— 2:22-23 —

Peter addressed the audience as "Men of Israel," recalling their national identity as the covenant people of God, people He had promised to make into the kingdom of God. Peter declared Jesus of Nazareth to be the King of that kingdom, the Messiah. His sermon then covered five points:

1. Authenticated (2:22)

God authenticated Jesus as uniquely from above, having the ability to do what no other human had ever done or ever could do without divine power. The Greek word translated "attested" literally means "to put forward for public recognition or appointment" or "to show forth the quality" (*apodeiknymi* [584]). For example, the Septuagint uses the term to describe Daniel's promotion as a provincial ruler in Babylon (Dan. 2:48). In Jesus' case, His "miracles" (*dynamis* [1411], "works of power"), "wonders" (*teras* [5059]), and "signs" (*sēmeion* [4592]) validated Him as heaven-sent.

"Wonders" describes acts or events that have deeper, supernatural implications. For example, a healing was more than the reversal of injury or disease; healing told witnesses something about the healer, the person being healed, and God's mind on the matter.

"Signs" denotes something that gives a true indication of something else, a physical indication of divine will or supernatural activity. For the Jews, a "sign" was a visual confirmation that a prophet was authentically from God.

Peter reminded his audience that Jesus had performed these works of power, wonders, and signs in the presence of many witnesses.

2. Crucified (2:23)

By this time, the people undoubtedly were nodding and saying to one another, "Yes, I remember that. Do you remember when Jesus . . . ?" Then Peter brought up a painful memory, still fresh in the minds of everyone after only fifty days. They had followed the lead of the Sanhedrin in killing Jesus. Some of the men present had done more than lend their silent approval; they had participated in crucifying Him. Many—if not most—of them had demanded His execution in Pilate's courtyard (Luke 23:18).

Peter acknowledged that while Jesus was authentically from God, His divine destiny had led Him to the cross. "Predetermined" doesn't capture the personal nature of the Greek word (*horizō* [3724]), which means "appointed" or "designated." Jesus wasn't merely *fated* to be crucified; God appointed Him, assigned His Son the mission. During His earthly ministry, Jesus said, "Indeed, the Son of Man is going [to the cross] as it has been determined; but woe to that man by whom He is betrayed!" (Luke 22:22).

As the audience squirmed at the reminder of their treachery, Peter pressed against the wound. He stacked up words of indictment end to end: "delivered over," "nailed to a cross," "by the hands of godless men," "put . . . to death"—by *you*. He held nothing back. In the Hebrew mind, to be "godless" (*anomos* [459]) was to be without the Law (*a + nomos* [3551]), outside the covenant, pagan, estranged from God. This indictment linked his audience to the *anomos* men who crucified Jesus.

— 2:24-32 —

The Greek text has no break between 2:23 and 2:24. While many English versions begin a new sentence with "but," the Greek text has the relative pronoun "whom," referring to Jesus: "whom God raised up again."

3. Resurrected (2:24-32)

Peter's declaration places God in the active role. God foreknew and appointed Jesus to die on the cross, and God raised Him up again, "putting an end to the agony of death"—or literally, "destroying the birth pains of death" (2:24). Of course, no one could imagine a more painful experience than giving birth—or one more impossible to escape. Peter gave God the credit for accomplishing the Resurrection, but he linked the Father's power with the power of Jesus. The NASB translates the Greek conjunction (*kathoti* [2530]) as "since," meaning "because" or "in view of the fact." God raised Jesus in view of the fact that nothing was capable of holding Him back (2:24).

This is important because it establishes a link between the power of God and the power of the man Jesus. Their power works in concert *because it is the same power.* Imagine me saying, "God empowered me to climb the mountain because nothing could keep me from reaching the top." That's a bold statement for someone who isn't God! That statement essentially puts me on a par with God. Sacrilegious for Chuck, a statement of fact for Jesus.

Peter upheld this bold claim by quoting—again from memory and without preparation—Psalm 16:8-11. It's a song written by David about his own death and his hope of resurrection through "Your Holy One" (an Old Testament title for the Messiah), who would not decay in a grave. In other words, David pinned his hope of resurrection on the resurrection of the Messiah. David could not have been talking about himself as "Your Holy One" because he died and was buried; Peter's contemporaries could go to the cemetery to visit his remains (Acts 2:29).

The sermon also recalls God's prediction that the Messiah would come from David's lineage (Pss. 89:3-4; 132:11; 2 Sam. 7:12-13). Jesus could trace His lineage back to David through His natural mother, Mary (asserting a genetic right to the throne), and His adoptive father, Joseph (asserting a legal right to the throne). No one would have disputed the lineage of Jesus; keeping track of one's genealogy was a sacred duty of every Jew.

Based on these facts, Peter reasoned that if the Messiah was to be resurrected, then a resurrected man must be the Messiah.[16] He declared that Jesus had risen from the dead, and at least 120 eyewitnesses (*martys* [3144]) could testify to that fact. Just as Jesus had predicted, the disciples received power to be His witnesses (Acts 1:8).

— 2:33-35 —

Peter's sermon didn't stop with resurrection. He claimed to have further confirmation of Jesus' identity as the Messiah.

4. Ascended (2:33-34)

Peter and the other followers of Jesus had personally seen Jesus stand in their presence. They heard Him speak. They saw Him eat. They touched His physical body. For more than a month, they were taught by Him. And then they saw Him do what only the Son of Man (Dan. 7:13-14) could do: He ascended to heaven. During His trial before the Sanhedrin, Jesus had said He would ascend and "be seated at the right hand of the power of God," a clear messianic image (Luke 22:67-70). The Sanhedrin felt justified in killing Jesus because of this claim (Luke 22:71). But if He *was* raised from the dead, then there was no reason to doubt His prediction.

Peter again appealed to the prophecies of David, this time from Psalm 110:1, the very passage Jesus quoted in His dialogue with the religious experts (Luke 20:41-44). Peter made the same point that Jesus had: David could not have been talking about himself sitting at the right hand of the Father, since his grave was still occupied.

5. Glorified (2:35)

In John's narrative, Jesus spoke of a coming "hour" in which the Son of God would be "glorified" (John 12:23). Jesus repeatedly spoke of this event using the Greek term *doxazō* [1392], which means "to have splendid greatness," "to be clothed in splendor," or "to be glorified." To be glorified meant to receive supreme vindication in the eyes of all witnesses. For Jesus, it meant that the truth He had been teaching and the truth of His identity would be vindicated in the eyes of all humanity by a stupendous display of His greatness. His identity as the Messiah would be confirmed by His rising from the dead and ascending to heaven.

The fact that He sits at the right hand of the Father vindicates all of Jesus' claims. As the Father promised, all those who denied the Messiah, rejected the Messiah, disparaged the Messiah, and tried to destroy the Messiah would be made His "footstool," a graphic image of involuntary servitude.

— 2:36 —

Peter summed up his speech with an appeal to "all the house of Israel," that is, all the descendants of Abraham, Isaac, and Jacob—whose name God had changed to "Israel." Based on the proofs of Scripture and the eyewitness testimonies of Jesus' resurrection, they should have been ready to accept the fact of His identity. He is "Lord" (*kyrios* [2962]), a title that combines the ideas of power and authority—God's own authority. Most likely it is a direct reference to the Hebrew label *adonai*, God's title. He is the *christos* [5547] (Christ), the Greek term that translated the Hebrew messianic title *mashiyach* [H4899], which referred to the "Anointed One" or "Messiah."

With a final flourish, Peter accused his audience of crucifying their own Messiah.

Amazing, isn't it? Just a few weeks earlier, Peter had denied being one of the Twelve and disowned Jesus with curses. His denial would have driven him out of ministry altogether if Jesus hadn't intervened to restore him. Just days earlier, he cowered in a dark room, fearing the power of the religious authorities in the temple. Now that the Holy Spirit had arrived, look at the effect!

Peter witnessed with remarkable power. He had become a transformed man.

APPLICATION: ACTS 2:14-36

Preaching 101

As a preacher, I can't hear or read a sermon without some degree of analysis. Not criticism—*analysis*. It's part of my nature now to consider what makes a sermon hit the target or veer off. I learn from other accomplished speakers and preachers, and I scrutinize my own preaching to determine how I can make the connection between Scripture and people. As I analyze Peter's sermon, I find three essential qualities that made it great.

Quality #1: *It was simple.* Peter spoke in simple, understandable terms that the people in his audience, who shared his culture and language, could understand without having to spend time in contemplation. They didn't have to guess at his meaning. If you are engaged as a communicator—if you teach a Bible class or you pastor a church, if you're on the radio or produce a podcast, if you write books—whatever your form of communication, make it simple. Simplicity is hard work. Some mistake a confusing delivery for depth. Sometimes a speaker will communicate poorly and then convince the audience that it was *their* fault for not fathoming what he or she was saying. When you communicate, teenagers should be able to understand you without difficulty.

Quality #2: *It was scriptural.* Peter quoted Scripture and alluded to passages throughout his message. He expertly wove his points around God's Word. He didn't rely upon his own insights, his man-made doctrinal conclusions, or his own human perspectives. He stood on the authority of divine truth revealed to all and available to all for inspection.

If you want to have a message that God will use to impact people's lives, simply tell them what the Bible says. God will honor His Word. If you're going to communicate, show how scriptural principles apply. People are starving for a clear presentation of the relevance of Scripture. They'll love your sermon, they'll love you for opening the Word, and they'll love their Lord more. I have yet to speak to an audience that doesn't thank me for helping them understand Scripture with greater clarity.

Quality #3: *It was Christ centered.* Peter repeatedly turned every point in his sermon back to Christ. Consequently, the people responded as though the crucified and risen Lord Jesus stood before them: "They were pierced to the heart, and said to Peter and the rest of the apostles, 'Brethren, what shall we do?'" (2:37).

Peter must have felt overwhelmed with affirmation. What an encouragement to this first-time preacher of the gospel! Fresh off of failure, preaching his heart out, only to be interrupted by three thousand people asking, "What shall we do [in response to this truth]?" They started by asking, "What does this mean?" and Peter's Christ-centered message prompted a better question: "What shall we do?"

That's not a bad way to structure a Bible lesson. Start by asking, "What does it mean? What is God saying?" Start where they are and help them see the meaning. Then, when they understand, be sure they know what to do about God's message.

Regardless, never forget that God will faithfully use your best effort, even if your ability pales in comparison to other, more experienced communicators. Please don't think you have to be a pro to get the job done! The professionals can never get in where you work and live. You're already there. You already have an audience. Just give the truth to them as you know it. Stumble through it if you have to, but get it out. Then model what you believe. Become an example of the message.

The Birth of Three Thousand "Babies"
ACTS 2:37-47

NASB

[37] Now when they heard *this*, they were [a]pierced to the heart, and said to Peter and the rest of the apostles, "[b]Brethren, [c]what shall we do?" [38] Peter *said* to them, "Repent, and each of you be baptized in the name of Jesus Christ for the forgiveness of your sins; and you will receive the gift of the Holy Spirit. [39] For the promise is for you and your children and for all who are far off, as many as the Lord our God will call to Himself." [40] And with many other words he solemnly testified and kept on exhorting them, saying, "[a]Be saved from this perverse generation!" [41] So then, those who had received his word were baptized; and that day there were added about three thousand [a]souls. [42] They were continually devoting themselves to the apostles' teaching and to fellowship, to the breaking of bread and [a]to prayer. [43] [a]Everyone kept feeling a sense of awe; and many wonders and [b]signs were taking place through the apostles. [44] And all those who had believed [a]were together and had all things in common; [45] and they *began* selling their property and possessions and were sharing them with all, as anyone might have need. [46] Day by day continuing with one mind in the temple, and breaking bread [a]from house to house, they were taking

NLT

[37] Peter's words pierced their hearts, and they said to him and to the other apostles, "Brothers, what should we do?" [38] Peter replied, "Each of you must repent of your sins and turn to God, and be baptized in the name of Jesus Christ for the forgiveness of your sins. Then you will receive the gift of the Holy Spirit. [39] This promise is to you, to your children, and to those far away*—all who have been called by the Lord our God." [40] Then Peter continued preaching for a long time, strongly urging all his listeners, "Save yourselves from this crooked generation!" [41] Those who believed what Peter said were baptized and added to the church that day—about 3,000 in all. [42] All the believers devoted themselves to the apostles' teaching, and to fellowship, and to sharing in meals (including the Lord's Supper*), and to prayer. [43] A deep sense of awe came over them all, and the apostles performed many miraculous signs and wonders. [44] And all the believers met together in one place and shared everything they had. [45] They sold their property and possessions and shared the money with those in need. [46] They worshiped together at the Temple each day, met in homes for the Lord's

their [b]meals together with gladness and [c]sincerity of heart, [47]praising God and having favor with all the people. And the Lord was adding [a]to their number day by day those who were being saved.

Supper, and shared their meals with great joy and generosity*—[47]all the while praising God and enjoying the goodwill of all the people. And each day the Lord added to their fellowship those who were being saved.

2:37 [a]Or *wounded in conscience* [b]Lit *Men brothers* [c]Or *what are we to do* 2:40 [a]Or *Escape* 2:41 [a]I.e. persons 2:42 [a]Lit *the prayers* 2:43 [a]Lit *fear was occurring to every soul* [b]Or *attesting miracles* 2:44 [a]One early ms does not contain *were* and *and* 2:46 [a]Or *in the various private homes* [b]Lit *food* [c]Or *simplicity* 2:47 [a]Lit *together*

2:39 Or *and to people far in the future,* or *and to the Gentiles.* 2:42 Greek *the breaking of bread;* also in 2:46. 2:46 Or *and sincere hearts.*

The Bible was written to be a blessing. Unfortunately, people frequently turn the Scriptures into a battleground. Acts 2 happens to be one of the hotter skirmish lines. I can think of at least four major denominations that find their theological distinctiveness in this passage. These are large segments of the Protestant church; in addition, countless splinter factions have unique interpretations, and not all of them are sound. Some of their interpretations are so convoluted that the people belonging to these groups don't even understand their own theology. Others oversimplify the text and draw ludicrous, almost comical, conclusions.

In this chapter we must come to terms with three major issues: (1) Pentecostal theologians find here a basis for speaking in tongues (which I discussed in the comments on Acts 2:1-13), the gift of prophecy, and certain other supernatural gifts of the Spirit. (2) Then there is the whole question of how Pentecost, the kingdom of God, and the end times are related. (I hope my position on this last issue is clear from the preceding section.) (3) Finally, the Church of Christ and a few Baptist denominations find justification for a doctrine called baptismal regeneration, which touches on other issues, such as the role of faith, grace, salvation, and perseverance—for starters! In the comments on this section, I will address this important issue.

After the Holy Spirit filled the believers at Pentecost, Peter stood to preach in response to two statements: a question and an insult (2:12-14). In response to seeing the Holy Spirit fill the followers of Christ and hearing them speak in multiple languages and dialects from around the world, some asked, "What does this mean?" Others scoffed, saying, "They are full of sweet wine." His sermon silenced the cynics and captured the attention of the "devout men" who had come to Jerusalem for the Feast of the Harvest.

By the end of Peter's sermon, a significant number of people in the audience moved from apathy to anxiety (2:37). He had success-fully demonstrated that they had killed their Messiah and that now the Messiah had been raised from the dead and would establish His kingdom. The gravity of their earlier choice to hand Jesus over for cru-cifixion was a tragic, erroneous decision—a grave sin for which they would be held accountable.

— 2:37 —

In response to Peter's sermon, many of the people were "pierced to the heart." This expression describes what might be called conviction, or God-given guilt. The Greek word for this (*katanyssomai* [2660]) means "to be pierced or stabbed," and by extension, "to feel sharp pain." Like a well-honed blade, this truth from God penetrated all their protective layers and brought emotional pain to their hearts. This prompted their question, one that was pitiable but that would be encouraging to any evangelist: "Brethren, what shall we do?" It's the same question asked by the Philippian jailer (16:30), and by Paul when confronted by Jesus on the road to Damascus (22:10).

— 2:38-39 —

Peter responded to their desperate question with a forthright, uncom-plicated answer. Somehow over the past twenty centuries, however, we have managed to give Acts 2:38 more twists than a roller coaster. As we examine the verse closely, I will attempt to follow a common rule of thumb of biblical interpretation: "If the plain sense makes good sense, then seek no other sense."

We don't use the word "repent" much today. The New Testament idea reflects the Old Testament prophetic call to "turn around"— presumably to go in the opposite direction. This same description was also applied to conversion by ancient rabbis.[17] Repentance requires a change of mind *and* a turning away from everything God has declared wrong; it means reversing course and seeking God's help in doing what He says is right.

Repentance is not mere remorse, a *feeling* of strong regret that may or may not lead to the necessary decision to change direction. Judas felt deep remorse for betraying Jesus, but instead of seeking God's forgive-ness, he hanged himself.

Peter's use of "each of you" emphasizes the individual nature of salvation. We all stand individually before God to give an answer for ourselves. A father cannot save other members of his household by repenting and submitting to baptism. One cannot be saved by being in a saved family or inherit salvation from a previous generation.

The word "baptize" is a transliteration of the Greek word *baptizō* [907], which means "to dip under," "immerse," "sink," "bathe," or "wash." Ritual immersion was used by various societies—including pagan religious communities—to symbolize a new member's identification with the group. To be "baptized into" a community was to become identified with the collective group, to share the benefits of membership, and to help shoulder its responsibilities.

By the time of Jesus, Jews used ritual immersion to welcome Gentile converts into God's covenant with Abraham. After rigorous study and a thorough examination to demonstrate competence in the Law of Moses, plus circumcision for the men, converts were baptized, thus becoming "sons of the covenant" along with natural-born Jews. Their baptism also represented complete cleansing from moral impurity.

John the Baptizer gave the Jewish ritual a prophetic twist, calling natural-born Jews to a "baptism of repentance," implying that their bloodline had no power to save them. They should instead recognize that sin had broken their relationship with God, that Israel had broken all its covenants with God, and that all Jews should approach Him as though for the first time, just like Gentile converts.

As a ritual connected with the new covenant, with the kingdom of God under Christ, Peter called for baptism in water for the same reasons John the Baptizer did. For John, baptism was an outward symbol of an inward change. New Testament baptism is the same—and more. Conditioned upon repentance, it's also an initiation into the new covenant, into the kingdom of God—which makes the next phrase crucial.

"In the name of Jesus Christ" means "on the authority of Jesus Christ" or "by the authorization of Jesus Christ." Imagine some of your friends allowing you to attend a concert using their season tickets. The tickets are in their names, but they can assign their privileges to you. They merely inform the ticket office that you have their authorization to attend, and you will be granted all the privileges of a season-ticket holder.

Your admittance is not based on your authority but on the ticket holders'. As an initiation into the new covenant, a symbol of your admittance to the kingdom of God, baptism is not validated by your authority but by the Ticket Holder's! You can enter only if He has assigned His privileges to you. Any baptism not on His authority—that is, not "in the name of Jesus Christ"—stands for nothing.

"For the forgiveness of your sins" is a notoriously difficult phrase.

The key word is the tiny Greek preposition *eis* [1519], rendered "for." In similar grammatical contexts, *eis* has eight basic uses in Greek literature,[18] only three of which are relevant to our verse. It can indicate any of these:

> Purpose: "for," "in order to," "to"
> Result: "so that," "with the result that"
> Respect/Reference: "with respect to," "with reference to"

Earlier, I stated that we would follow the Bible interpreter's motto: "If the plain sense makes good sense, seek no other sense." Now is a good opportunity to introduce two more interpretive guidelines. First, *always interpret unclear passages in the light of clearly understood passages.* And second, *never base your doctrine on unclear passages.* In this case, the interpretation "be baptized *in order to* receive forgiveness" contradicts *everything* the New Testament teaches about salvation by grace alone through faith alone in Christ alone. As A. T. Robertson writes,

> My view is decidedly against the idea that Peter, Paul, or anyone in the New Testament taught baptism as essential to the remission of sins or the means of securing such remission. So I understand Peter to be urging baptism on each of them who had already turned (repented) and for it to be done in the name of Jesus Christ on the basis of the forgiveness of sins which they had already received.[19]

While we might disagree over the precise meaning of this phrase, we know what it *can't* be. It cannot be option one, "purpose." It's also very doubtful that option two, "result," is correct. That, too, would contradict the gospel of grace as taught throughout the New Testament. Option three is the best; *eis* frequently means "with respect to" or "with reference to." In this case, I would paraphrase the verse this way: "Repent, and each of you be baptized in the name of Jesus Christ *in view of* the forgiveness of your sins."

Peter then states the result of repenting: "You will receive the gift of the Holy Spirit." This is another way of saying, "You will receive the Holy Spirit as a gift." This represented hope to the anxious audience. The promise of the Holy Spirit upon repenting was great news!

We should not see in this verse a set pattern required in salvation. In this case, the order is repentance, baptism, Holy Spirit. In other places, such as 10:44-48, the order is repentance, Holy Spirit, baptism. In 8:38, there is repentance and baptism but no mention of the Holy Spirit. In 8:12-17, there's a significant delay between baptism and the Holy Spirit. And in 19:5-6, people had been baptized by John before hearing the complete story of Jesus' atoning death. They were then rebaptized, and at that moment they received the Holy Spirit.

We must be careful not to see the narrative of Acts as normative. In other words, just because something happened a certain way in Acts doesn't mean it should occur that way for everyone. Always remember this: Acts describes *a period of transition* from the old covenant to the new covenant.

That said, however, Peter's sermon most definitely established a necessary link between repentance and baptism. For Peter, the apostles, and the early church, baptism had no meaning apart from a new believer's decision to turn away from sin and begin following Christ. Unfortunately, some denominations apply this sacred rite of the church to infants, who haven't the cognitive capacity to choose, believe, or repent.

By their reckoning, infant baptism serves a similar purpose to the Old Testament rite of circumcision, which occurred on the eighth day of life for Hebrew boys. As biblical Jews understood circumcision, the ritual committed the community of faith to teaching the young boy to become a man "circumcised of heart" (see Deut. 30:6; Rom. 2:29), that is, a true follower of God, a willing participant in God's covenant with Abraham, not merely by ethnicity but by choice. The analogy between circumcision and baptism, however, breaks down on two points. First, God established the old covenant—and the corresponding symbol of circumcision—with a specific ethnic group, irrespective of any individual's personal choice. The early church, on the other hand, reserved baptism for those who repented and believed in Christ, irrespective of any other factor. Second, the old covenant was not a means of spiritual salvation; Abraham, like all who are saved from sin, was declared righteous by grace through faith (Gen. 15:6; Rom. 4:3, 9, 22). The early church viewed baptism as a de facto symbol of spiritual salvation with strong implications about a person's eternal destiny.

— 2:40-41 —

We don't know how long Peter preached—certainly longer than the three minutes it takes to read his sermon. Throughout his Gospel account, Luke boiled speeches down to their essence and occasionally summarized the events of several months in a single sentence. After completing his first sermon, Peter continued "with many other words" as he "solemnly testified" (*diamartyromai* [1263]), an expression for exhorting, urging, or giving an earnest warning. He also was also "exhorting" them (*parakaleō* [3870]), a word for issuing a strong appeal or encouragement (2:40). In this case, Peter was warning and exhorting them to accept the Lord's gift of salvation.

His preaching produced astounding results. By day's end, the church had grown from about 120 all the way to three thousand people. As any minister of the gospel will tell you, however, the work of making disciples doesn't end with conversion; that's when the real work begins.

Think of it: Three thousand new babies were born on that remarkable Day of Pentecost—three thousand untrained, untaught, ignorant, brand-new believers with no church handbook, no guidelines, and no building to meet in. Add to that a hostile society that had taken an active part in the crucifixion of Christ and you've got the makings of a superhuman task. When Jesus ascended, he left to Peter and his eleven colleagues this demanding and exhausting work of spiritual infant care (cf. Matt. 28:19-20; John 21:15-17).

The first responsibility? Baptize them. The three thousand were immersed in water. Luke doesn't tell us how, where, or by whom. The details are unimportant. He offers only three relevant facts. First, they had "received his word"; that is, they accepted Peter's preaching as truth, believed what he said, heeded his admonition to repent, and began following the Messiah. Second, they "were baptized." This identified them publicly as followers of Jesus Christ and gave them a strong sense of belonging. And third, they "were added." In a single day, the movement grew by three thousand souls.

— 2:42 —

Luke's next line begins with "They were," and it is an encouraging and exciting "they." "*They,*" not just the original 120. Not just the three thousand new people. "They" refers to one body with no distinctions between old and new.

Literally rendered, Luke says, "They were being in a state of constant engagement in the teaching of the apostles. . . ." This is the first example in Acts of Luke's habit of summarizing a time period. Throughout his Gospel, he uses the imperfect verb tense to describe ongoing, recurring, or habitual activities over a period of weeks or months. Because he blends these so smoothly with discrete events, we can easily mistake these summary passages for isolated events.

Over an extended period of time, they all devoted themselves to four priorities: *teaching, fellowship, worship*, and *prayer.*

Teaching. The text clearly states that the apostles did the teaching. These twelve men were trained by Jesus from the very beginning (1:21-22), and they had personally interacted with the resurrected Savior. Of course, they didn't have a building dedicated to meeting together. No one had a home large enough for three thousand people! Later, we will discover that they broke into smaller groups to meet in multiple homes throughout the week and then met as one body in a public area of the temple.

They did not yet have the completed New Testament. The instruction was based on the Old Testament and the teaching of Jesus gleaned and remembered by the apostles from their time with Him. Instead of writing a body of work, Jesus poured His divine knowledge into these people, and then He gave them His Holy Spirit to guide their interpretation of Old Testament Scripture to keep them right and true in their teaching.

Fellowship. The Greek term is *koinōnia* [2842], referring to "a close association involving mutual interests and sharing."[20] Secular Greek writers used the term to describe the unique bond shared by a husband and wife. For a group, the word denotes a mutual personal investment of the members with one another.

Anne Ortlund, in her delightful book *Up with Worship*, compares two kinds of communities commonly found in churches. One she describes as a bag of marbles. The people come together for fellowship, they clack and clatter, they glitter and throw off light beautifully, and they scratch each other. They connect, but they don't mingle. That's not *koinōnia*. The other kind of community she describes as a bag of grapes. Shake the bag around a little, and it starts to drip. Look inside and it's not a pretty sight, but they're mingling. Each life bleeds into the others. That's *koinōnia*. That's authentic, Spirit-empowered fellowship.

Worship. The phrase is "the breaking of bread," which originally mingled the ideas of *koinōnia* and the communion ceremony (cf. 2:46-47; 20:7; 1 Cor. 10:16-17; Jude 1:12). The custom of "the Lord's Supper" comes from the time Jesus shared a worshipful Passover meal with His disciples, at which time He recast the image of the traditional cup and bread to represent His blood and body (Matt. 26:26-29; Mark 14:22-25; Luke 22:17-20). The first believers continued this practice, making communion a part of what came to be known as "love feasts." They met in homes to enjoy a banquet, sing hymns, read Scripture, and hear teaching. Later, Paul would admonish some for allowing the meal to overshadow communion (1 Cor. 11:17-22).

The phrase "the breaking of bread" has in mind "a meal which had the double purpose of satisfying hunger and thirst and giving expression to the sense of Christian brotherhood. At the end of this feast, bread and wine were taken according to the Lord's command, and after thanksgiving to God were eaten and drunk in remembrance of Christ and as a special means of communion with the Lord Himself and through Him with one another."[21]

Prayer. These little cells that began meeting in the city of Jerusalem began to grow and ignite with excitement and enthusiasm. They most often met in homes around the city for the purpose of prayer.

Observing these priorities led to some great results (Acts 2:47). The next several verses appear to coincide with the four priorities listed in 2:42: teaching (2:43), fellowship (2:44-45), worship (2:46), and prayer (2:47).

— 2:43 —

The new believers were receiving instruction from qualified, trustworthy men who had supernatural ability and divine power to affirm their teaching through "many wonders and signs." As a result of this teaching, "everyone kept feeling a sense of awe" (*phobos* [5401])—not a terrified-for-your-life kind of fear, but a reverential wonderment (cf. Mark 4:41; Luke 7:16; 1 Pet. 1:17).

— 2:44-45 —

The remarkable fellowship of the followers of Christ was such that they lost their sense of personal entitlement; wealth and possessions became a means of meeting the needs of fellow believers. This doesn't mean they lived communally together in a compound like one large household. It means their unique fellowship produced extraordinary unity and generosity. People became more important to them than things or their own comfort.

— 2:46 —

This verse amplifies the phrase "breaking bread" by describing worship. The first believers were, like Jesus, Jews, so they continued to participate in the temple sacrificial worship prescribed by the Old Testament. They never lost their sense of Jewishness. And why should they? The teaching of Jesus was and is entirely compatible with biblical

Hebrew theology. They worshiped the one true God who had made a covenant with Abraham and his descendants, made them into a nation, and promised them a Messiah. Christianity, therefore, became the fulfillment of true Hebrew worship and practice.

These followers of the Messiah worshiped in the house of God as well as in their homes for heartfelt *koinōnia* [2842] worship. Luke characterizes their worship with two Greek words that mean "joy" (*agalliasis* [20]) and "simplicity" (*aphelotēs* [858]).

— 2:47 —

Following these verses' pattern of expanding on 2:42, the words of 2:47 can be understood to amplify "prayer." Joy, simplicity, and prayer produced a people with a satisfying vertical relationship and great horizontal relationships—the way a group of believers ought to be. Well-taught, authentic followers of Jesus praise God and encourage people. And they look to the Lord in prayer to add to their number. The Lord worked, and as their friends and peers examined their manner of life, the first community of believers grew exponentially.

APPLICATION: ACTS 2:37-47

The Good WIFE

As Christians, we have a commitment to one another, regardless of our positions, our levels of maturity, or how long we've been believers. We are mutually bound by a duty to help one another grow toward greater maturity. The church—not the building, but the community—is how we accomplish that. Every congregation must commit to godly priorities that further this purpose, just like the first body of Christ's followers. Above, we saw how Luke described the early church's priorities (2:42-47).

The church is called the "bride" of Christ (Rev. 19:7; cf. Eph. 5:23), and if you'll allow me some leeway, I'd like to present the church's four essential responsibilities using the acronym "WIFE"—*Worship, Instruction, Fellowship, Expression*.

Worship

The first-century followers of Christ continued to meet in the temple, not only because it provided a large venue for their growing numbers, but because it seemed like a natural meeting place. As good Jews, they continued to participate in temple worship. They also met in homes, where they sang together and observed communion.

The purpose of salvation is to bring into God's presence a body of worshipers. In Ephesians, Paul says God foreordained us "to the praise of the glory of His grace" (Eph. 1:6). In Philippians, he says that Jesus came to earth and suffered as He did and was raised "so that at the name of Jesus every knee will bow, of those who are in heaven and on earth and under the earth, and that every tongue will confess that Jesus Christ is Lord, to the glory of God the Father" (Phil. 2:10-11). We were created for worship, we were redeemed for worship, and we will enjoy worship for eternity. Therefore, a church must make worship a priority.

Instruction

The first Christians couldn't get enough teaching. As we'll discover later in Acts, they met in the temple for instruction. They also met in homes where teaching took place. They wanted to know everything that Jesus had taught the apostles. They remained hungry for spiritual nourishment.

Paul says transformation begins with the mind (Rom. 12:2). Although we mustn't mistake biblical and theological knowledge for maturity, growth cannot occur without it. Instruction gives the mind the building material with which the Holy Spirit renovates the old person into a new, Christlike person. If new Christians are like hungry babies needing nourishment, then a church must provide quality biblical and theological teaching, or it will forever remain a nursery.

Fellowship

I examined the four priorities in Acts 2:42-47 as individual elements, but in the early church they were interconnected. The people gathered for worship. Instruction was part of their love feasts. Baptism gave them a sense of identity with one another. They prayed individually and communally. Sharing the bread and cup of communion reminded them of their interconnectedness, and that prompted them to be extraordinarily generous with one another. Like coals in a fire, people grow cold and die when separated; however, they produce light and warmth when connected, sharing joyfully and generously with each other.

Expression

Acts 2:42 specifically lists prayer as the driving force behind everything the church does: satisfying worship, nourishing instruction, life-sustaining fellowship, meaningful outreach, and effective evangelism. That's why Luke amplifies the idea of prayer in the phrase "praising God and having favor with all the people." The result? "The Lord was adding to their number day by day those who were being saved" (2:47).

Churches can become overly inward focused, adopting an "us four and no more" mentality. Worship, instruction, and fellowship serve the needs of the body, while visitors feel like outsiders looking in. Meanwhile, no one gives any thought to impacting the culture and community beyond the church property line. Expression in the biblical sense cannot be contained; it naturally affects everyone the members encounter, wherever they may be.

Churches can also become overly outward focused, so that every function of the church becomes evangelistic. While evangelism is an essential function of the church, it must not come at the expense of other priorities: worship, instruction, and fellowship. If all four priorities are upheld with prayer and maintained in balance, evangelism naturally occurs. People don't have to be cajoled or coerced to tell others about Christ; their spiritual growth will become an easy topic of most conversations. As the first Christians devoted themselves to worship, instruction, fellowship, and prayer, they became bold witnesses of the gospel to the world outside. As Millard Erickson states,

> In biblical times the church gathered for worship and instruction. *Then* they went out to evangelize. In worship, the members of the church focus upon God; in instruction and fellowship, they focus upon themselves and fellow Christians; in evangelism, they turn their attention to non-Christians. It is well for the church to keep some separation between these several activities. If this is not done, one or more may be crowded out. . . . For example, worship of God will suffer if the gathering of the body becomes oriented primarily to the interaction among Christians, or if the service is aimed exclusively at evangelizing the unbelievers who happen to be present. This was not the pattern of the church in the Book of Acts. Rather, believers gathered to praise God and be edified; then they went forth to reach the lost in the world without.[22]

Is your church a healthy bride of Christ?

The Beggar Who Danced in Church
ACTS 3:1-26

NASB

¹Now Peter and John were going up to the temple at the ªninth *hour,* the hour of prayer. ²And a man who had been lame from his mother's womb was being carried along, whom they used to set down every day at the gate of the temple which is called Beautiful, in order to beg ªalms of those who were entering the temple. ³When he saw Peter and John about to go into the temple, he *began* asking to receive alms. ⁴But Peter, along with John, fixed his gaze on him and said, "Look at us!" ⁵And he *began* to give them his attention, expecting to receive something from them. ⁶But Peter said, "I do not possess silver and gold, but what I do have I give to you: In the name of Jesus Christ the Nazarene—walk!" ⁷And seizing him by the right hand, he raised him up; and immediately his feet and his ankles were strengthened. ⁸ªWith a leap he stood upright and *began* to walk; and he entered the temple with them, walking and leaping and praising God. ⁹And all the people saw him walking and praising God; ¹⁰and they were taking note of him as being the one who used to sit at the Beautiful Gate of the temple to *beg* alms, and they were filled with wonder and amazement at what had happened to him.

¹¹While he was clinging to Peter and John, all the people ran together to them at the so-called ªportico of Solomon, full of amazement. ¹²But when Peter saw *this,* he replied to the people, "Men of Israel, why are you amazed at this, or why do you gaze at us, as if by our own power or piety we had made him walk? ¹³The God of Abraham, Isaac and Jacob, the God of our fathers, has glorified

NLT

¹Peter and John went to the Temple one afternoon to take part in the three o'clock prayer service. ²As they approached the Temple, a man lame from birth was being carried in. Each day he was put beside the Temple gate, the one called the Beautiful Gate, so he could beg from the people going into the Temple. ³When he saw Peter and John about to enter, he asked them for some money.

⁴Peter and John looked at him intently, and Peter said, "Look at us!" ⁵The lame man looked at them eagerly, expecting some money. ⁶But Peter said, "I don't have any silver or gold for you. But I'll give you what I have. In the name of Jesus Christ the Nazarene,* get up and* walk!"

⁷Then Peter took the lame man by the right hand and helped him up. And as he did, the man's feet and ankles were instantly healed and strengthened. ⁸He jumped up, stood on his feet, and began to walk! Then, walking, leaping, and praising God, he went into the Temple with them.

⁹All the people saw him walking and heard him praising God. ¹⁰When they realized he was the lame beggar they had seen so often at the Beautiful Gate, they were absolutely astounded! ¹¹They all rushed out in amazement to Solomon's Colonnade, where the man was holding tightly to Peter and John.

¹²Peter saw his opportunity and addressed the crowd. "People of Israel," he said, "what is so surprising about this? And why stare at us as though we had made this man walk by our own power or godliness? ¹³For it is the God of Abraham, Isaac, and Jacob—the God of all our ancestors—who has brought glory to his servant

His ªservant Jesus, *the one* whom you delivered and disowned in the presence of Pilate, when he had decided to release Him. ¹⁴But you disowned the Holy and Righteous One and asked for a murderer to be granted to you, ¹⁵but put to death the ªPrince of life, *the one* whom God raised from the dead, *a fact* to which we are witnesses. ¹⁶And on the basis of faith in His name, *it is* ªthe name of Jesus which has strengthened this man whom you see and know; and the faith which *comes* through Him has given him this perfect health in the presence of you all.

¹⁷"And now, brethren, I know that you acted in ignorance, just as your rulers did also. ¹⁸But the things which God announced beforehand by the mouth of all the prophets, that His ªChrist would suffer, He has thus fulfilled. ¹⁹Therefore repent and return, so that your sins may be wiped away, in order that times of refreshing may come from the presence of the Lord; ²⁰and that He may send Jesus, the ªChrist appointed for you, ²¹whom heaven must receive until *the* ªperiod of restoration of all things about which God spoke by the mouth of His holy prophets from ancient time. ²²Moses said, 'THE LORD GOD WILL RAISE UP FOR YOU A PROPHET ªLIKE ME FROM YOUR BRETHREN; TO HIM YOU SHALL GIVE HEED to everything He says to you. ²³And it will be that every soul that does not heed that prophet shall be utterly destroyed from among the people.' ²⁴And likewise, all the prophets who have spoken, from Samuel and *his* successors onward, also announced these days. ²⁵It is you who are the sons of the prophets and of the covenant which God ªmade with your fathers, saying to Abraham, 'AND IN YOUR SEED ALL THE FAMILIES OF THE EARTH SHALL

Jesus by doing this. This is the same Jesus whom you handed over and rejected before Pilate, despite Pilate's decision to release him. ¹⁴You rejected this holy, righteous one and instead demanded the release of a murderer. ¹⁵You killed the author of life, but God raised him from the dead. And we are witnesses of this fact!

¹⁶"Through faith in the name of Jesus, this man was healed—and you know how crippled he was before. Faith in Jesus' name has healed him before your very eyes.

¹⁷"Friends,* I realize that what you and your leaders did to Jesus was done in ignorance. ¹⁸But God was fulfilling what all the prophets had foretold about the Messiah—that he must suffer these things. ¹⁹Now repent of your sins and turn to God, so that your sins may be wiped away. ²⁰Then times of refreshment will come from the presence of the Lord, and he will again send you Jesus, your appointed Messiah. ²¹For he must remain in heaven until the time for the final restoration of all things, as God promised long ago through his holy prophets. ²²Moses said, 'The LORD your God will raise up for you a Prophet like me from among your own people. Listen carefully to everything he tells you.'* ²³Then Moses said, 'Anyone who will not listen to that Prophet will be completely cut off from God's people.'*

²⁴"Starting with Samuel, every prophet spoke about what is happening today. ²⁵You are the children of those prophets, and you are included in the covenant God promised to your ancestors. For God said to Abraham, 'Through your descendants* all the families on earth will

NASB

BE BLESSED.' 26For you first, God raised up His aServant and sent Him to bless you by turning every one *of you* from your wicked ways."

3:1 aI.e. 3 p.m.   3:2 aOr *a gift of charity*   3:8 aLit *Leaping up*   3:11 aOr *colonnade*   3:13 aOr *Son*   3:15 aOr *Author*   3:16 aLit *His name*   3:18 aOr *Anointed One;* i.e. Messiah   3:20 aOr *Anointed One;* i.e. Messiah   3:21 aLit *periods, times*   3:22 aOr *as* He raised up *me*   3:25 aLit *covenanted*   3:26 aOr *Son*

NLT

be blessed.' 26When God raised up his servant, Jesus, he sent him first to you people of Israel, to bless you by turning each of you back from your sinful ways."

3:6a Or *Jesus Christ of Nazareth.*   3:6b Some manuscripts do not include *get up and.*   3:17 Greek *Brothers.*   3:22 Deut 18:15.   3:23 Deut 18:19; Lev 23:29.   3:25 Greek *your seed;* see Gen 12:3; 22:18.

Everyone has faced adversity, some more than others; all of us have encountered difficulties that have challenged our faith and tested our limits. We can overcome some adversities and disadvantages with hard work; we dig deep and find a strength we didn't know we had. Some struggles require creativity, forcing a change in perspective that helps us survive the adversity and even thrive like never before. There are, however, some adversities that no amount of work or creativity can overcome; nothing short of an act of God will suffice.

Acts 3 is a story about adversity. Or, more precisely, about the power of God to turn adversity into opportunity. Luke chose to fast-forward through church history several weeks or months to focus on a remarkable incident in the temple, not only because of the extraordinary events themselves, but to introduce a major theme for this section of Acts (1:1–7:60). The next crucial months would bring the leaders of the growing church face to face with insurmountable difficulties, challenges for which no amount of work, creativity, money, or fortitude could suffice. Beginning with this story of a man disabled from birth, Luke reveals the power of God to overcome any adversity, and—more importantly—how every difficulty, when given to God, becomes His means of accomplishing His sovereign will and perfect plan.

As God's power becomes evident in tackling the adversities in the lives of believers, those nearby have a fresh opportunity to turn to God as well. In the present passage, we'll see this as Peter preaches on the heels of God's healing of the disabled man.

— 3:1-2 —

The "ninth hour" (3:1) refers to the ninth hour of daylight. This would have been about three o' clock in the afternoon by our reckoning and marked a time that the Jews had set aside as one of three times for prayer in the temple: 9:00 a.m., 12:00 p.m., and 3:00 p.m. (cf. 10:9, 30; Ps. 55:17; Dan. 6:10; 9:21). Peter and John, two of the Twelve, went to the temple to join other devout Jews in prayer. On their way, they encountered a man who had been disabled since birth. We will later discover that the problem existed in his feet and ankles (Acts 3:7), which apparently had not developed properly. Everywhere the man went, someone had to carry him. He never knew the joy of standing erect, to say nothing of walking or running, abilities most of us take for granted. He never knew a healthy day. He never knew a day that his legs were not as limp as a dishrag—no feeling, no movement, nothing but the prospect of another day begging for alms.

He was "being carried along" (3:2), which suggests his friends were moving toward the temple along with Peter, John, and scores of other devout Jews. Luke describes the man as one "whom they used to set down every day," quite probably because many first-century Jewish Christians remembered the man. For as long as history records, right up to today, it has been the custom of disabled people to line roads leading to a temple or shrine in the hope of receiving compassion in the form of money. How long had he occupied his customary place "at the gate of the temple which is called Beautiful"? His friends placed him there daily, but we don't know how long this had been his regular spot. If it was a year, Jesus must have seen him on more than one occasion.

"Beautiful Gate" was a colloquial name, not an official one, so we can't determine exactly which entrance Luke had in mind. The temple was a massive complex, covering more than 35 acres according to some

Courts of the Temple in Jerusalem

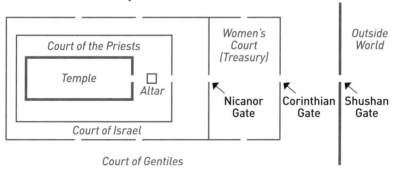

Courts of the Temple in Jerusalem. Besides the eastern gate, two other gates offer strong possibilities for the location of the healing of the crippled man: the Corinthian Gate, through which only Jewish men and women could pass, and the Nicanor Gate, through which only Jewish men could enter. Josephus stated that the gate separating Jews from Gentiles "was of Corinthian brass, and greatly excelled those that were only covered over with silver and gold."[24] No doubt, the crippled man had the best opportunity to receive alms from the greatest number of Jews while sitting at the Corinthian Gate.

calculations,[23] and arranged in a series of nested courts, each surrounded by a wall and accessed through gates. Anyone, Jew or Gentile, could visit the public areas of the temple, entering the complex through any one of several doors.

— 3:3-5 —

Regardless of where he *normally* sat, it appears from the narrative that the disabled man and the apostles encountered one another outside the temple complex, among the throngs of people coming for evening prayer. Luke presents the scene with a subtle hint of happenstance, as though their encounter occurred at random. Of course, his literary irony points to the greater truth that God had ordained their meeting.

The man asked Peter and John for money, perhaps while scanning the crowd for other prospects. Anyone who regularly walks through the downtown area of a large city knows that eye contact with a panhandler amounts to an invitation for begging, so most people avert their eyes. Peter, however, saw opportunity rather than potential nuisance. He locked eyes with the man and commanded his full attention.

— 3:6-7 —

The disabled man expected a touchable, tangible answer to his most immediate need: money for food, clothing, and shelter. Quite reasonably, he didn't expect a solution to his deeper problem, the inability to use his feet. Peter spoke for both John and himself, saying what the man heard dozens of times each day: "We don't have any money . . ."

What a cruel statement—apart from the rest of the sentence! Peter's declaration illustrates the mind-set of the church and should serve as a guide for all Christian service. You can't give what you don't have, but you do have something—so give that! In this case, Peter and John knew they had received supernatural power through the Holy Spirit, and guided by the Spirit, they felt prompted to heal the man. "In the name of Jesus Christ" (3:6) declares the authority by which Peter was able to perform this miracle. Not in his own power, but by the power of Jesus Christ, he took the man by his begging hand and lifted him to his feet (3:7).

The details of Luke's description are important. Peter "seiz[ed] him by the right hand," the hand extended for alms. He "raised him up," pulling the man upward. "Immediately," not over time, not gradually— no physical therapy sessions required—immediately, a surge of life filled a formerly dead part of the body. His feet and his ankles became normal. The phrase "were strengthened" is a divine passive, implying that God accomplished the miracle—just in time to support the man's body weight.

— 3:8-10 —

We later learn that the man was more than forty years old (4:22). As a child, he could only watch his friends run, leap, and play. As a Jew, he would have been stigmatized as a recipient of divine punishment for his wrongdoing in the womb or as retribution for his parents' sin (cf. Ps. 51:5; Luke 13:2; John 9:2). As a crippled man, he was shunned from the inner courts where other Jewish men found a warm welcome, and he did not have the opportunity to work,[25] a key factor of identity for men.

So it should not surprise us that when he suddenly found himself standing on his own two feet, he did first what he could never do before. He walked, leaped, and undoubtedly ran!

To the phrase "entered the temple" (Acts 3:8), Luke adds three participles. The man didn't merely enter; he was walking, springing, and praising God, and he drew the attention of "all the people," that is, everyone arriving for prayer. They immediately recognized him as a fixture of the temple, the beggar man everyone knew. According to Luke, they were filled with wonder (*thambos* [2285]) and amazement (*ekstasis* [1611]). Today, we might say they were "blown away."

— 3:11-12 —

The "portico of Solomon" (3:11) was a long, colonnaded area running the length of the eastern side of the temple complex. Covered by a roof, it had become a common place for congregations to hear teaching (John 10:23; Acts 5:12). As Peter, John, and the ecstatic beggar entered through the eastern gate, people already inside the temple rushed over to see what had happened. Seeing the disabled man completely healed and dancing around the courtyard filled them with "amazement."

Peter recognized this as another opportunity to preach. In fact, that may have been his intention from the beginning. Regardless, it was clearly God's plan to turn the man's disability into an opportunity for His witnesses to fulfill their mandate. Peter began his message the same way as on the Day of Pentecost, by addressing the "Men of Israel" (3:12; cf. 2:22). He did not intend to omit women but rather to establish himself as one of their kindred. And before going any further, he deflected credit for the healing away from himself and John, giving God all the glory for the beggar's healing: "Why do you gaze at us, as if by our own power or piety we had made him walk?" (3:12).

commons.wikimedia.org

A model of the **Herodian temple complex** in Jerusalem viewed from the northeast corner, looking to the southwest. The portico of Solomon appears in the upper left of this photo.

— 3:13-15 —

Peter continued his sermon by interpreting the miraculous sign for all those present. Peter named "the God of Abraham, Isaac and Jacob" to distinguish Him as the God of the Hebrew Scriptures and God of their covenant and went on to declare the power at work in this miraculous healing: God had "glorified His servant Jesus"—that is, vindicated Him as the Messiah through resurrection. Peter boldly reminded the people in the temple that they had participated in the murder of their Messiah by asking for Barabbas when Pilate gave them the opportunity to release Jesus (3:13; see Matt. 27:20; Mark 15:11; Luke 23:18). To drive the point home, Peter called Jesus by three different titles that identify Him as both the Messiah and God:

1. "His servant" recalls the title given to the Messiah in several of Isaiah's songs about the "Suffering Servant" who dies on behalf of His people (Acts 3:13; see Isa. 42:1-9; 49:1-13; 50:1-11; 52:13–53:12).

2. "The Holy and Righteous One" points to the Messiah (Acts 3:14; see Ps. 16:10; Mark 1:24; Luke 1:35; 4:34; John 6:69) and in the Old Testament was used only of God (2 Kgs. 19:22; Job 6:10; Ps. 71:22; Isa. 1:4; 60:9, 14; Jer. 51:5; Ezek. 39:7; Hos. 11:9, 12; Hab. 1:12; 3:3) or His supernatural creatures (Deut. 33:3; Job 5:1; 15:15; Ps. 89:5; Dan. 4:17, 23).

3. "The Prince of life" (Acts 3:15) is the term *archēgos* [747], which referred to the hero of a city, that is, its founder and ruler. It also carried the idea of an originator. The original Greek city-states didn't have kings like other civilizations; they emerged from obscurity when a leader with a vision originated a new administrative idea and then rallied people behind him. He was, therefore, the founder and first example of his new way. The "*archēgos* of life" has established a new city called life and reigns as its king.

Just as he did in his sermon at Pentecost, Peter indicts the people for murdering their Messiah and then declares His resurrection. This would undoubtedly frighten those who believed Peter's message.

— 3:16-21 —

Peter's call for repentance looks very similar to the sermon at Pentecost, which should not surprise us. Everything occurred by the foreknowledge and plan of God. The Messiah had to suffer in fulfillment of Old Testament Scripture. He was raised from the dead and offers forgiveness to those who repent. We see an interesting difference at one point, however. While he had declared that Jesus was "exalted to the right hand of God" in the earlier sermon (2:33), this time Peter emphasizes His end-time return, implying that Jesus sits by the right hand of the Father now but will return to earth in the future to fulfill all the Old Testament promises of God's kingdom on earth (3:19-21).

Peter calls for repentance, not only for the sake of the people's personal salvation, but to hasten the return of Christ. Note how he characterizes the unfolding of God's plan: "Repent and return, so that your sins may be wiped away, in order that": (1) "times of refreshing may come from the presence of the Lord [now]," and (2) "[God] may send Jesus, the Christ appointed for you" (3:19-20).

Furthermore, Christ will remain above until "the period of restoration of all things" (3:21). This refers to the time when Christ restores the world to the order God first created in Genesis (Rom. 8:20-21), a world without sin, disease, disabilities, suffering, disasters, or death. It refers to the Messiah's physical reign on earth, the literal establishment of His kingdom.

— 3:22-26 —

Peter briefly reminded the audience of their prophetic heritage, beginning with their human founder, Moses. All the prophets pointed to the same Messiah and declared the penalty for rejecting or disobeying this Prophet-King (3:22-25a). Peter also reminded them that God had chosen them to inherit the covenant He had established with Abraham and that through repentance, the Messiah—Jesus—would make them worthy of the blessings God had promised their patriarch (3:25b-26).

Peter preached this sermon to all the people in the temple, but let us not forget the man most impacted that day, the man who had been healed. After receiving the use of his feet for the first time, he heard about the grace of God, the mercy offered him through the atonement of Jesus Christ, and the forgiveness of sins made possible through repentance.

Who knows what happened to that formerly disabled man? Scripture says nothing more about him. He could have become a prominent figure in the growing Jerusalem church. We do know that God used the man's adversity to further His agenda—a pattern that will repeat several times in the next few chapters, beginning in Acts 4:1.

APPLICATION: ACTS 3:1-26

Time to Dance

I am intrigued that the disabled beggar had been lying at the gate called Beautiful long enough for everyone to know him, probably long enough to have been there during Jesus' ministry on earth. We don't know for certain the man was around when Jesus visited the temple, but to me it seems like a strong possibility. Yet Jesus never healed him. It seems that, like the blind man of John 9:1-3, the man's healing awaited a foreordained time when God's work would be manifest in a new way.

When Peter and John healed the man, it set off a remarkable chain of events, beginning with Peter's second great sermon. As we'll discover in later chapters, this healing became a pivotal moment in the history of the church, triggering events that would not have occurred otherwise. So, the disabled man lay at the intersection of the world's affliction and God's design for the future, waiting for Peter and John to turn his adversity into an occasion for rejoicing; he lay waiting for the preordained moment when the apostles would "happen by" and then do as they had been commanded—make disciples.

I see two principles at work in this passage, each with an implied response.

First, *your impossibility is God's opportunity; turn to Him.* The disabled beggar couldn't work to overcome his adversity, and creativity would do nothing to help. He needed help beyond the realm of human ability. He needed God to do what no one else could do. He had no way of knowing what his day would bring at the beginning of his pilgrimage that morning when the sun rose and friends carried him to the temple. He sought nothing more from the day than a few coins to keep him fed, clothed, and sheltered. But God had something supernatural—something personally wonderful—planned.

The man's impossible circumstances had always been God's opportunity to accomplish His plan. While we don't know the precise cause of the man's disability, we do know that the Lord had given the man's affliction a divine purpose before anything had been created. The same is true of your adversities.

I'm not suggesting that you will get what you want or that you will receive a miraculous reversal of misfortune like this man. I know too many wonderful people who have gone bald from chemotherapy or who hobble through life with physical challenges or who are confined to wheelchairs. I never want to presume upon God's sovereign design and make promises I have no business making. But I can say that God will not ignore you. Rather, He will do what is best for you and everyone connected with you. Therefore, turn to Him. Tell Him what you desire, but leave your expectations behind. Surrender to His will, accept His way, and trust His timing.

He will hear, and He will respond as He chooses; that's His sovereign right.

Second, *God's mercy is your opportunity; return to Him.* The Lord used the disabled man's healing and his joyful dance around the temple to give Peter an opportunity to preach. Peter then proclaimed a message for first-century Jews—and for people of all races throughout all time. It's a message of mercy, inviting all who have sinned to repent, turn toward God, and receive forgiveness.

Take this opportunity if you have not already. When you do, it will be your turn to dance.

Religion vs. Christianity
ACTS 4:1-22

NASB

¹As they were speaking to the people, the priests and the captain of the temple *guard* and the Sadducees came up to them, ²being greatly disturbed because they were teaching the people and proclaiming ᵃin Jesus the resurrection from the dead. ³And they laid hands on them and put them in jail until the next day, for it was already evening. ⁴But many of those who had heard the ᵃmessage believed; and the number of the men came to be about five thousand.

⁵On the next day, their rulers and elders and scribes were gathered together in Jerusalem; ⁶and Annas the high priest *was there,* and Caiaphas and John and Alexander, and all who were of high-priestly descent. ⁷When they had placed them in the center, they *began to* inquire, "By what power, or in what name, have you done this?" ⁸Then Peter, ᵃfilled with the Holy Spirit, said to them, "ᵇRulers and elders of the people, ⁹if we are ᵃon trial today for a benefit done to a sick man, ᵇas to how this man has been made well, ¹⁰let it be known to all of you and to all the people of Israel, that ᵃby the name of Jesus Christ the Nazarene, whom you crucified, whom God raised from the dead—ᵃby ᵇthis *name* this man stands here before you in good health. ¹¹ᵃHe is the STONE WHICH WAS REJECTED by you, THE BUILDERS, *but* WHICH BECAME THE CHIEF CORNER *stone.* ¹²And there is salvation in no one else; for there is no other name under heaven that has been given among men by which we must be saved."

NLT

¹While Peter and John were speaking to the people, they were confronted by the priests, the captain of the Temple guard, and some of the Sadducees. ²These leaders were very disturbed that Peter and John were teaching the people that through Jesus there is a resurrection of the dead. ³They arrested them and, since it was already evening, put them in jail until morning. ⁴But many of the people who heard their message believed it, so the number of men who believed now totaled about 5,000.

⁵The next day the council of all the rulers and elders and teachers of religious law met in Jerusalem. ⁶Annas the high priest was there, along with Caiaphas, John, Alexander, and other relatives of the high priest. ⁷They brought in the two disciples and demanded, "By what power, or in whose name, have you done this?"

⁸Then Peter, filled with the Holy Spirit, said to them, "Rulers and elders of our people, ⁹are we being questioned today because we've done a good deed for a crippled man? Do you want to know how he was healed? ¹⁰Let me clearly state to all of you and to all the people of Israel that he was healed by the powerful name of Jesus Christ the Nazarene,* the man you crucified but whom God raised from the dead. ¹¹For Jesus is the one referred to in the Scriptures, where it says,

'The stone that you builders rejected
has now become the cornerstone.'*

¹²There is salvation in no one else! God has given no other name under heaven by which we must be saved."

[13] Now as they observed the confidence of Peter and John and understood that they were uneducated and untrained men, they were amazed, and *began* to recognize them [a]as having been with Jesus. [14] And seeing the man who had been healed standing with them, they had nothing to say in reply. [15] But when they had ordered them to leave the [a]Council, they *began* to confer with one another, [16] saying, "What shall we do with these men? For the fact that a noteworthy [a]miracle has taken place through them is apparent to all who live in Jerusalem, and we cannot deny it. [17] But so that it will not spread any further among the people, let us warn them to speak no longer to any man in this name." [18] And when they had summoned them, they commanded them not to speak or teach at all [a]in the name of Jesus. [19] But Peter and John answered and said to them, "Whether it is right in the sight of God to give heed to you rather than to God, you be the judge; [20] for we cannot stop speaking about what we have seen and heard." [21] When they had threatened them further, they let them go (finding no basis on which to punish them) on account of the people, because they were all glorifying God for what had happened; [22] for the man was more than forty years old on whom this [a]miracle of healing had been performed.

[13] The members of the council were amazed when they saw the boldness of Peter and John, for they could see that they were ordinary men with no special training in the Scriptures. They also recognized them as men who had been with Jesus. [14] But since they could see the man who had been healed standing right there among them, there was nothing the council could say. [15] So they ordered Peter and John out of the council chamber* and conferred among themselves.

[16] "What should we do with these men?" they asked each other. "We can't deny that they have performed a miraculous sign, and everybody in Jerusalem knows about it. [17] But to keep them from spreading their propaganda any further, we must warn them not to speak to anyone in Jesus' name again." [18] So they called the apostles back in and commanded them never again to speak or teach in the name of Jesus.

[19] But Peter and John replied, "Do you think God wants us to obey you rather than him? [20] We cannot stop telling about everything we have seen and heard."

[21] The council then threatened them further, but they finally let them go because they didn't know how to punish them without starting a riot. For everyone was praising God [22] for this miraculous sign—the healing of a man who had been lame for more than forty years.

4:2 [a]Or *in the case of* 4:4 [a]Lit *word* 4:8 [a]Or *having just been filled* [b]Lit *Rulers of the people and elders* 4:9 [a]Lit *answering* [b]Or *by whom* 4:10 [a]Or *in* [b]Or *Him* 4:11 [a]Lit *This One* 4:13 [a]Lit *that they had been* 4:15 [a]Or *Sanhedrin* 4:16 [a]Or *sign* 4:18 [a]Or *on the basis of* 4:22 [a]Or *sign*

4:10 Or *Jesus Christ of Nazareth*. 4:11 Ps 118:22. 4:15 Greek *the Sanhedrin*.

In the early sixties, a transforming work of God took place on Greenville Avenue in Dallas, Texas. It happened in a church that had never experienced anything like it. They had no pastor at the time and struggled for existence. They had only one adult class; it numbered four on average— five when everybody showed up. Those four or five people got their heads together and thought, *There's got to be a better way than this.*

They dipped into the student body of an evangelical seminary not far away and found a young, first-year student named Harold. They had never met him. Though he struggled to get his head together in Greek and Hebrew and theology and church history, he agreed to teach the class on Sundays. He took the Bible as his only text, opened it, and began to teach—chapter by chapter, verse by verse—through a book of the Bible, something that had never been done in this church before. These people had been exceedingly religious, but most had not been born again. How they loved discovering what God had to say through that young teacher!

By and by, the class doubled. And then doubled again—and then again.

As that school year came to an end, this first-year student decided that he should look into the ministry of Campus Crusade for Christ, which required training in San Bernardino, California, that summer. He asked another young man if he would teach the class in his place. He did. Through the summer, the class grew even larger—fifty, sixty . . . seventy. In fact, the room would seat only about sixty-five uncomfortably, so people stood along the back and side walls of this adult class. Meanwhile, the search for a pastor continued.

Fall and winter came, and the class approached one hundred. By that time, they had been through several books of the Bible and were studying the book of Jonah. The members began to learn how to study the Bible on their own, to see the truth of God for themselves and all the relevance of authentic Christianity. Numerous people came to know Christ.

Before long, the church called a pastor, who told the young seminary student that he could no longer stay and teach the class. The new (liberal) minister complained that the people were becoming too serious about the Bible, talking too much about Jesus rather than talking about how to grow the church.

In the place of the seminary student, the pastor's wife began to teach. She began with a series on great Americans. Within a matter of weeks, the class dwindled back to five.

My friend, Harold, was the first teacher; I was the second. And that was my first blunt encounter with religion and its destructive power. I never forgot that experience; in fact, I made a point to keep those memories alive. Not out of bitterness, but so I would forever remain on guard against its intrusion, both in my own life and in any ministry I would serve.

Karl Marx once wrote, "Religion is the sigh of the oppressed creature, the heart of a heartless world and the soul of soulless conditions. It is the opium of the people."[26] Not Christianity—which is what he thought he meant. *Religion*. Religion has a deadening, dulling effect. Religion puts structure in place of the Savior. Religion tells the individual that denomination holds the answers to the big questions of life and that more religious involvement will feed a hungry soul. Religion says, "Fit into the system rather than turn your life over to Christ." Religion says, "Work hard, appease God's anger, gain His favor, and God will be impressed with you and one day will allow you to enter heaven." But it's a deadly lie. Biblical Christianity means God is finding us and meeting our needs, knowing that we could never meet our needs on our own.

After God healed the disabled man, Peter and John had taken the opportunity to preach. Peter's sermon affected many who heard (4:4), and it also captured the attention of the religious authorities in the temple. In the confrontation that followed, the church faced its first great challenge: religion.

— 4:1-3 —

While Peter and John addressed the gathered crowd in the portico of Solomon, men representing three groups approached.

- *Priests*: The priests were charged with observing the Law of Moses in the temple by officiating worship services and carrying out the rites mandated by the Pentateuch. They had very little political power, but they retained immense influence among the Jews.
- *The Temple Guard*: The temple had treasures to protect and order to keep. These armed guards kept Gentiles from going past the Corinthian Gate. They were also among those who seized Jesus in Gethsemane and kept Him under watch between trials. The captain of the guard accompanied the priests and Sadducees. His presence was like that of the chief of police showing up with a warrant.
- *Sadducees*: Mostly aristocratic and holding positions of political power, which included authority over Herod's magnificent temple, these men were the deists of their day—vehemently skeptical of anything supernatural and fatalistic to the core. While the Sadducees controlled the temple, they did so only at the pleasure of Rome.

THE SADDUCEES

ACTS 4:1

The Sadducees were a peculiar breed. While Hebrew blood coursed through their veins, they lived and behaved like Greeks. Wealthy, aristocratic, and politically ambitious, these men chose a theological perspective that best served their earthly motivations. They adopted a theologically conservative stance, accepting no teaching or tradition beyond what could be found in the Pentateuch, the first five books of the Old Testament. Accepting only the writings of Moses could appear noble at first glance, but in fact, it was the doctrine most convenient to their personal goals. The prophets had condemned Israel's cooperating with foreign powers, so the Sadducees discredited those writings as later tradition.

Based on their reading of the Pentateuch, the Sadducees rejected all notions of life after death, resurrection, angels, and eternal punishment or reward. They believed God to be utterly remote, leaving each person free to craft his or her own fate—a kind of divine hands-off policy. The Sadducees resembled the deists of the eighteenth century, vehemently rejecting the possibility of supernatural activity and therefore being fatalistic to the core. They believed each person had free will and therefore was responsible for the events of his or her life, including sickness, poverty, misfortune, and even manner of death. Moreover, they thought punishment for sin was the duty of people and should be merciless and severe.[27]

With God uninvolved in human affairs and people in charge of the world, the Sadducees seized religious and political power as their birthright, finding all the theological justification they needed to have the ultimate power of God among men.

The religious authorities had three problems with Peter and John. First, these followers of the man they had killed were teaching the people. Second, they were teaching in the name of this same man. Third, they were claiming this murdered man had risen from the dead and that people who believe in Him can be resurrected too.

They would have questioned Peter and John, but sundown had nearly arrived, and nighttime trials violated their law. Of course, that didn't prevent their trying Jesus at night; but in this case, time was on their side. They thought a night in jail might rattle the two apostles, making them more pliable when questioned in the morning. The Fortress of Antonia would have been the most logical place to hold the two men. Both Jewish and Roman forces kept watch over the temple grounds from this garrison adjacent to the temple; no place in Jerusalem would have been more secure.

No doubt the two apostles had a difficult night, physically at least. The next morning the Sanhedrin would learn an important lesson about the gospel: You can lock up the messengers, but you can't contain or restrain the message.

— 4:4-6 —

The temple authorities undoubtedly knew they had a serious public-relations problem to manage. They had to squelch these rogue teachers, but their preaching had already won at least five thousand converts—"five thousand men," not including their families (4:4)! These five thousand men represented a significant political force on the side of Peter and John. Therefore, simply killing the apostles would only cause more problems; the temple elite needed them to recant so that their following would disintegrate. Religious people are easily threatened.

"Rulers and elders and scribes" (4:5) refers to the constituent members of the Sanhedrin. This governing body of seventy Jewish statesmen was, for Israel, the equivalent of a parliament and supreme court combined into one institution. A presiding elder, called the *nasi,* worked closely with the high priest to set the council's agenda, which included making laws, setting the official Jewish ritual calendar, deciding national policy, regulating the temple, and ruling on serious court cases. According to Jewish tradition, the *nasi* during this time was Gamaliel, the grandson of the great rabbi Hillel and teacher of a young Pharisee named Saul of Tarsus (22:3).

The following day, as the Sanhedrin gathered for the hearing, four men, who on most occasions would not have been present, joined the proceedings.

- *Annas:* Although Caiaphas officially held the office of high priest, many recognized his father-in-law, Annas, as the true power ruling the temple. Annas was originally appointed high priest in AD 6 by Quirinius but later was deposed by Valerius Gratus (in AD 15). Nevertheless, he remained the head of a vast empire of organized corruption in Jerusalem. One writer notes, "He and his family were proverbial for their rapacity and greed."[28] After his removal from office, he wielded power through his son Eleazar and then his son-in-law, Caiaphas. A good mental image of Annas? Think of him as the "godfather" of their religious group.

- *Caiaphas*: This son-in-law of Annas filled the post of high priest from AD 18 to 36, at which time Vitellius deposed him. Though he was only a puppet of Annas, it had been his idea to kill Jesus as a means of solving the political dilemma He posed. Normally, the high priest would not attend hearings, leaving administration of the Sanhedrin in the hands of the *nasi*.
- *John*: Most likely the son of Annas and future high priest (AD 36–37 and 44). He was apparently groomed for the position along with three other brothers and a grandson of Annas.
- *Alexander*: This man was related to Annas, though not as a son or grandson. Luke mentions him undoubtedly because his readers knew him. He has since been covered over by the dust of history.

Luke mentions Annas and his relatives because their presence adds a sinister element to an already-dark scene. The Sanhedrin wielded the visible power of Jerusalem; Annas controlled the invisible elements, the dark world of organized crime clothed in religious garb. In contemporary terms, Peter and John had been brought before a joint session of Congress and the Mafia.

This is a remarkable display of how power operates in the absence of truth. People in power (especially religious power) who have no concern for truth will follow a predictable pattern when challenged by their constituents:

- *Intimidation*: Use authority to strike fear into the hearts of those holding opposing views (4:1-6).
- *Tradition*: Invoke the long history of believing something and doing something a certain way. Don't conduct a genuine investigation, and refuse to hear opposing arguments (4:7).
- *Coercion*: Manipulate the behavior of opponents using any means necessary: threats, bribes, blackmail, flattery . . . and if necessary, eliminate them altogether (4:13-18).

Some things never change.

— 4:7 —

The Sanhedrin met in an area of the temple where elders could rule on cases and make community decisions. The petitioner or the accused, depending upon the case, stood in the center, surrounded by the members of the council. To appreciate the pressure Peter and John faced, imagine two American, high-school-educated, working-class, regular Joes hauled before a joint session of Congress and the Supreme Court without the benefit of legal representation. Keep in mind that this is where Jesus stood not long before to face a mock trial, His fate already decided by two nighttime trials with Annas and Caiaphas officiating in different areas of their large home. (I believe they shared the same large palace.)

Religion finds security in numbers, in formalism, in rank, in protocol, in status, in class, in what is "proper." Religion doesn't think creatively; it emphasizes precedent. And religious people use all of that to intimidate.

Model by Alec Garrard; photo © Leen Ritmeyer

At the east end of the Royal Portico in the temple, seventy-one elders sat in semicircular rows around an area resembling a threshing floor. The Sanhedrin officially met here to set national and religious policy and to rule on civil and criminal cases. All of their deliberations and decisions were open to the public.

It is noteworthy that the first question the council asked did not probe the men for truth but challenged their authority. They didn't ask Peter and John to offer a defense for their views, to back up their preaching with Scripture or factual evidence; they asked for their résumés and credentials. Bear in mind that Peter and John had healed a man paralyzed from birth, an *undeniable* miracle witnessed by literally hundreds of people! Despite this irrefutable proof of the power of Jesus' name, Israel's religious and political officials were determined to silence the men.

— 4:8 —

As Peter stood and responded, he didn't have to rely on his own wisdom and courage; he was "filled with the Holy Spirit." The word "filled" here is another example of a divine passive, indicating that God did the filling. Peter simply yielded to the Spirit, and the Spirit empowered Peter, guiding his decisions and words.

Peter's defense addresses two key points: authority (4:9-10) and truth (4:11-12).

— 4:9-10 —

Peter understood, of course, that the question of authority wasn't a genuine question but a charge: *You don't have the authority to preach or teach because we have not authorized you.* The apostle reminded the leaders of the man's miraculous healing. If the Sanhedrin was genuinely worried about the question of authority, they need only consider the fact that a forty-year-old man, disabled from birth, was now dancing somewhere in Jerusalem while Peter and John languished in a jail cell. Their authority came directly from the resurrected Messiah, to whom the Sanhedrin should have rendered complete submission and obedience.

— 4:11-12 —

Peter boldly and shrewdly turned the Sadducees' accusation of insurrection around to show that *they*—not he and John—were the treasonous ones. His cryptic reference to "the stone which was rejected" points back to Jesus' words when these same men had challenged Jesus' authority:

> When [Jesus] entered the temple, the chief priests and the elders of the people came to Him while He was teaching, and said, "By what authority are You doing these things, and who gave You this authority?" . . .
>
> Jesus said to them, "Did you never read in the Scriptures,

'THE STONE WHICH THE BUILDERS REJECTED,
THIS BECAME THE CHIEF CORNER stone;
THIS CAME ABOUT FROM THE LORD,
AND IT IS MARVELOUS IN OUR EYES'?

Therefore I say to you, the kingdom of God will be taken away from you and given to a people, producing the fruit of it. And he who falls on this stone will be broken to pieces; but on whomever it falls, it will scatter him like dust."

When the chief priests and the Pharisees heard His parables, they understood that He was speaking about them. When they sought to seize Him, they feared the people, because [the people] considered Him to be a prophet. (Matt. 21:23, 42-46)

In the Lord's reply to the religious authorities, He drew upon a metaphor in Psalm 118:22 to declare Himself the Messiah. The Jewish scholars understood His claim. The Messiah is the chief cornerstone in the building called the kingdom of God. But these very men had schemed to arrest Jesus, try Him illegally, and hand Him over to the Romans for execution so they could retain political and religious power for themselves. By killing their Messiah, the Sanhedrin had subverted the rightful government of the kingdom of God.

Far from shrinking back because of intimidation, Peter and John used this earlier memory to turn the accusation of sedition around. Then Peter drove home the final point in his countercharge, saying, in effect, "The King you killed is alive again, He is God, and you must come to Him—and no other—for salvation." Peter spoke with invincible confidence.

— 4:13-16 —

The reaction of the Sanhedrin would be comical if this were a work of fiction. It surprised them to find that their intimidation had no effect on the two men. Most of them were probably used to seeing results from good old-fashioned bullying. After all, they were the *Sanhedrin*! But they had just gone head to head—seventy-four against two—with "uneducated and untrained" fishermen from rural Galilee (4:13)—and *lost*.

Peter and John were not "uneducated" in the same sense as the majority of Gentiles at the time; as Jews, they had learned how to read and write Hebrew in the synagogues, memorized Scripture, and knew the history of Israel as well as anyone. But they were not formally trained in higher education to debate theology and discuss philosophy, like the Sadducees, scribes, and wealthy Gentiles. They couldn't quote Rabbi

So-and-So to defend their point of view. The apostles stood on Christ's authority, not their own.

Another huge factor in the Sanhedrin's defeat: "Seeing the man who had been healed standing with them, they had nothing to say in reply" (4:14). Ah, but they weren't about to let a simple, undeniable miracle stand in their way. The word translated "miracle" (sēmeion [4592]) could also mean "sign." Luke highlights it to make it plain that the Sanhedrin didn't reject the testimony of Peter and John because they *couldn't* believe but because they *wouldn't* believe. Their response was a matter of the will, not of intellect or evidence. They acted to preserve their power irrespective of the truth. Religious authorities operate the same way to this day.

— 4:17-22 —

The council sent the two men out in order to confer. Not to determine the truth, but to stifle the two men and thereby preserve their hold on religious and political power—the ability to control the people of Israel. When intimidation didn't work and their appeal to tradition failed, the council resorted to coercion. But they failed to understand their opponents. Peter and John would not succumb to the threats of power or the suppression of truth because the apostles had both—the truth of Christ and the power of the Holy Spirit!

The two "uneducated and untrained men" (4:13) could have remained quiet in the trial, left the chamber, and simply resumed their preaching. Instead, they openly rejected the Sanhedrin's gag order, stating their intention to continue proclaiming the risen Jesus as Messiah. I detect no hint of arrogance or insolence, just the humble declaration of two confident men with news too good to keep quiet.

Eventually, the Sanhedrin backed down for fear of the people—the power of public opinion. But it was only a tactical retreat. The campaign to crush the church had only begun.

APPLICATION: ACTS 4:1-22

Three Qualities of Godly Courage

Careful examination of this passage reveals no fewer than three qualities that distinguish a godly person courageously choosing to do what is right. Each quality points to a principle that can help us imitate Peter and John in the face of intimidation and coercion.

First, observe the *confidence* of Peter and John. This is not arrogance. When the Holy Spirit fills someone, humility displaces arrogance. Arrogance comes from insecurity; these two men spoke with confidence because they found security in the Lord, not in themselves.

Second, consider the *authority* of Peter and John. They never received formal training to debate theology and philosophy like the powerful and intelligent temple leaders. They had only the basic education given to all Jewish children in Galilee. The apostles stood on Christ's authority, not their own. They possessed a direct line to absolute truth: Jesus Christ, the living Word of God.

Third, see the *effectiveness* of Peter and John. By yielding to the control of the Holy Spirit, the men became instruments of God's will. Doing what is right in the face of intimidation and coercion produces results. The price might be high, even the sacrifice of one's life. But the Lord will honor obedience. The undeniable effect of the apostles' obedience stood beside them—a formerly paralyzed man restored to perfect health.

When you choose to do what is right, you can walk and speak with secure, humble confidence. Your thoughts and actions proceed from a clear understanding of truth. Though perhaps misunderstood, maligned, or even persecuted, you can still walk with steadfast peace deep within, knowing that the Lord understands, approves, and rewards those who remain faithful.

Pioneer Christians
ACTS 4:23-37

NASB

23 When they had been released, they went to their own *companions* and reported all that the chief priests and the elders had said to them. 24 And when they heard *this,* they lifted their voices to God with one accord and said, "O ªLord, it is You who MADE THE HEAVEN AND THE EARTH AND THE SEA, AND ALL THAT IS IN THEM, 25 who by the Holy Spirit, *through* the mouth of our father David Your servant, said,

NLT

23 As soon as they were freed, Peter and John returned to the other believers and told them what the leading priests and elders had said. 24 When they heard the report, all the believers lifted their voices together in prayer to God: "O Sovereign Lord, Creator of heaven and earth, the sea, and everything in them—25 you spoke long ago by the Holy Spirit through our ancestor David, your servant, saying,

'WHY DID THE ᵃGENTILES RAGE,
AND THE PEOPLES DEVISE FUTILE
THINGS?
²⁶ 'THE KINGS OF THE EARTH ᵃTOOK
THEIR STAND,
AND THE RULERS WERE GATHERED
TOGETHER
AGAINST THE LORD AND AGAINST
HIS ᵇCHRIST.'

²⁷For truly in this city there were gathered together against Your holy ᵃservant Jesus, whom You anointed, both Herod and Pontius Pilate, along with the ᵇGentiles and the peoples of Israel, ²⁸to do whatever Your hand and Your purpose predestined to occur. ²⁹And ᵃnow, Lord, take note of their threats, and grant that Your bond-servants may speak Your word with all confidence, ³⁰while You extend Your hand to heal, and ᵃsigns and wonders take place through the name of Your holy ᵇservant Jesus." ³¹And when they had prayed, the place where they had gathered together was shaken, and they were all filled with the Holy Spirit and *began* to speak the word of God with boldness.

³²And the ᵃcongregation of those who believed were of one heart and soul; and not one *of them* ᵇclaimed that anything belonging to him was his own, but all things were common property to them. ³³And with great power the apostles were giving testimony to the resurrection of the Lord Jesus, and abundant grace was upon them all. ³⁴For there was not a needy person among them, for all who were owners of land or houses would sell them and bring the ᵃproceeds of the sales ³⁵and lay them at the apostles' feet, and they would be distributed to each as any had need.

³⁶Now Joseph, a Levite of Cyprian birth, who was also called Barnabas by the apostles (which translated means Son of ᵃEncouragement),

'Why were the nations so angry?
Why did they waste their time
with futile plans?
²⁶ The kings of the earth prepared
for battle;
the rulers gathered together
against the LORD
and against his Messiah.'*

²⁷"In fact, this has happened here in this very city! For Herod Antipas, Pontius Pilate the governor, the Gentiles, and the people of Israel were all united against Jesus, your holy servant, whom you anointed. ²⁸But everything they did was determined beforehand according to your will. ²⁹And now, O Lord, hear their threats, and give us, your servants, great boldness in preaching your word. ³⁰Stretch out your hand with healing power; may miraculous signs and wonders be done through the name of your holy servant Jesus." ³¹After this prayer, the meeting place shook, and they were all filled with the Holy Spirit. Then they preached the word of God with boldness.

³²All the believers were united in heart and mind. And they felt that what they owned was not their own, so they shared everything they had. ³³The apostles testified powerfully to the resurrection of the Lord Jesus, and God's great blessing was upon them all. ³⁴There were no needy people among them, because those who owned land or houses would sell them ³⁵and bring the money to the apostles to give to those in need.

³⁶For instance, there was Joseph, the one the apostles nicknamed Barnabas (which means "Son of Encouragement"). He was from the tribe of Levi and came from the

³⁷and who owned a tract of land, sold it and brought the money and laid it at the apostles' feet.

island of Cyprus. ³⁷He sold a field he owned and brought the money to the apostles.

4:24 ªOr *Master*   **4:25** ªOr *nations*   **4:26** ªOr *approached*   ᵇOr *Anointed One;* i.e. Messiah   **4:27** ªOr *Son*   ᵇOr *nations*   **4:29** ªOr *as for the present situation*   **4:30** ªOr *attesting miracles*   ᵇOr *Son*   **4:32** ªOr *multitude*   ᵇLit *was saying*   **4:34** ªLit *the prices of the things being sold*   **4:36** ªOr *Exhortation* or *Consolation*

4:25-26 Or *his anointed one;* or *his Christ.* Ps 2:1-2.

There's something incomparable about a pioneer. Without having the course charted, without the benefit of a predecessor, a pioneer moves ahead and blazes a new trail, prepared for danger yet with little knowledge of what obstacles or challenges lie ahead. Undeterred by hardship, the pioneer forges ahead to reach the goal. If you've ever had the opportunity to meet an authentic pioneer, it's like time stands still as the whole value system of your life goes through a realignment. You can't help but reevaluate your lifestyle, your schedule, your goals, your spending, and your priorities.

My maternal grandfather was a pioneer in the literal sense of the term. L. O. Lundy traveled to the plains of Texas in a covered wagon. He settled there, met and married my grandmother, and the two of them reared a family of four in a small town in south Texas. Until the day of his death, Granddaddy Lundy was respected for his strength of character, his unerring integrity, his keen mind, and more than any other quality, his sensitive heart for God.

Pioneer missionaries are the same sort of people. They go where others haven't or wouldn't. They endure hardships that would send most people packing for home by the end of the first week. They accomplish tasks without the benefit of forerunners because they *are* the forerunners.

If I were to identify the distinctive qualities of a pioneer Christian, two come to mind. First, *they are tough outside.* They're resilient, determined, disciplined, mentally rugged people who don't know the word "quit." They are unintimidated. They pursue and perform, regardless of the elements or obstacles pushing them back.

Second, *they are tender inside.* They hear when God speaks. They're sensitive to His voice. They care very much that they are in the center of His plan.

If somehow we could step into a time machine and travel back twenty centuries, we would find ourselves surrounded by pioneers: the early Christians. They were tough yet tender people whose vision came directly from Jesus Christ, whose direction came from the Holy Spirit within, and who endured challenges, obstacles, and enemies we can barely imagine. Johannes Weiss describes the five simple characteristics of these pioneer Christians: They had "a tempestuous enthusiasm, an overwhelming intensity of feeling, an immediate awareness of the presence of God, an incomparable sense of power, and an irresistible control over the will and inner spirit and even the physical condition of other men—these are the ineradicable features of the historical picture of early Christianity."[29]

This becomes prominent in the fourth chapter of Acts, where we learn about the first organized persecution of the church, when Peter and John were slammed into prison overnight and then brought before the court. That was when the first followers of Jesus Christ began to show their true colors.

— 4:23 —

The Sanhedrin had released Peter and John from custody with a strong warning: "Do not speak or teach at all in the name of Jesus" (see 4:18). The apostles' respect for the religious leaders didn't blind them to their duty before the Lord, so they humbly promised to do exactly the opposite (4:19-20). The Sanhedrin feared public reprisal, so they had to let the men go—for now (4:21-22).

Immediately after their release, Peter and John "went to their own" (4:23, literally rendered). They came to their own people, their own kind, those with a kindred spirit who would listen and seek to understand. Peter and John were pioneers, but they weren't lone rangers. They didn't deny their need for their community. They recognized the reason God gave His people one another, and they made a beeline for their brothers and sisters in Christ.

— 4:24-28 —

When the community of believers heard the apostles' report, they broke out in spontaneous prayer. No one announced, "Okay, let's break up into small groups and spend the next twelve minutes praying for Peter and John. Then join us in the Family Life Center for refreshments." They immediately and spontaneously engaged in prevailing prayer. Their prayer has two main sections:

- Celebrating the sovereignty of God (4:24-28)
- Requesting the encouragement of God (4:29-30)

Their celebration of God's sovereignty begins by addressing Him as "Lord" (4:24). In this case, the Greek word is not *kyrios* [2962], but *despotēs* [1203]. We derive our word "despot" from this, but the proper translation is "owner" or "master," one who owns a property either by inheritance or by purchase and therefore has the right to do whatever he desires with that land or anything on it. Peter and John used the language of servants. The prayer continues with a quotation from Psalm 146:6. Affirming God as Creator carries with it an acknowledgment of His supreme authority to rule His creation and His supreme power to control what He has made. Then they quote a well-known messianic text, Psalm 2:1-2. In this taunt, the composer chides the enemies of God for their vain attempts to defeat the Lord's "Anointed" (4:26; *mashiyach* [H4899]), the Messiah.

The church found in these recent events a parallel to Psalm 2. The powers of the earth vainly thought they could destroy the Messiah, rebel against God, and retain sovereignty for themselves. Don't forget—the Sanhedrin couldn't deny the authenticity of the miracle; they simply had no way to suppress the news of it or disregard its relevance. Nevertheless, they could not overcome the predetermined plan of God, who moves the greatest powers on earth like pawns.

— 4:29-35 —

Having declared the Lord's sovereign control over the challenges outside their community, they acknowledged their own fear. I love that they didn't apologize for feeling afraid; they simply admitted their weakness and called on their Master for help: "Grant us confidence" (see 4:29). They could just as easily have prayed, "Get us out of here" or "Kill off the Sanhedrin." Instead they said, in effect, "Keep it going. Don't stop, Lord. And when this happens again, let us speak again plainly without reservation."

Their prayer continued with a statement of faith: "while You extend Your hand to heal, and signs and wonders take place through the name of Your holy servant Jesus" (4:30). They took for granted that the Lord would accomplish what He said—no doubt about that. So their personal safety took second place to the fulfillment of His plan. They said, as it were, "While You're getting the job done, Lord, we want to be a part of what You're doing."

Luke closes this episode in the history of the church with a description of God's answer to their prayer. They experienced events similar to Pentecost, but with some significant differences. When these believers finished their prayer, "the place where they had gathered together was shaken" (4:31). At Pentecost, you'll recall, the power of God came down manifested as light and flowed into each believer. But in this case, the building trembled with the power of God as it flowed *outward* from their prayers and into the world. They had asked for His power—healing, signs, and wonders—to create opportunities for them to witness. The answer to their petition rolled out of that place and into the world to prepare it for their confident proclamation of the gospel.

Luke also says that "they were all filled with the Holy Spirit" (4:31). They already had received the *gift* of the Holy Spirit (2:1-4), His indwelling presence. He didn't leave and then return. This is different. To be "filled" with something means to be overtaken and then controlled by it. You can be "filled" with emotion, meaning it exerts a strong, almost overwhelming, influence. You can be filled with knowledge, which guides your decisions. Paul warned believers not to be filled with alcohol, which takes control of the mind, robbing it of judgment. He called instead for us to be filled with the Holy Spirit—that is, controlled by the Holy Spirit in an especially profound way. We do that by submitting to His influence, yielding control to Him. How? These believers were filled as a result of their prayer.

Two results flowed from their spontaneous prayer and their subsequent filling. First, they "began to speak the word of God with boldness" (4:31), giving powerful "testimony to the resurrection of the Lord Jesus" (4:33). Obviously, Luke meant they had boldness in the days and weeks that followed, not just there in the room together. It's easy to speak boldly among kindred spirits; that doesn't require courage. Acts 4:31 creates a transition from a discrete event to one of Luke's many summary passages. The building rumbled with the surging power of God, and the people were changed within. The impact of that transforming change continued, causing the believers to be bold and un-hesitating in their preaching.

Second, the church became extraordinarily generous. As we saw in 2:43-45, the individuals became selfless and shared their abundance with the church so none of their community would be without the necessities of life. None of the members claimed ownership of their possessions; these belonged to the Lord and, therefore, to one another (4:32). The church followed through with action; they made it their practice to sell off their abundance and then share it with the community (4:34-35).

All of this occurred over an extended period of time, perhaps months.

— 4:36-37 —

Luke transitions from the summary passage (4:31b-35) to introduce a pivotal man in church history. A man named Joseph was a Levite, a descendant of the patriarch Levi, whose family God had designated to serve in the temple (Num. 8:24-26). They fulfilled the routine duties of the temple as paid clergy, much like ministers are supported in modern times. Levites were not supposed to own property (Num. 18:20, 24), but this rule applied only to land in Israel. Joseph came from the island of Cyprus, where he owned property.

The apostles gave Joseph the nickname Barnabas, which means "Son of Encouragement" (4:36).[30] The reason for his renaming will become clearer as the story of Acts unfolds. For now, Luke gives us a glimpse into his character. He was one of those who sold off his property and brought the proceeds to the apostles to use in the ministry of the church.

Some today point to the church described in Acts as the ideal model of how a church should exist. I am one of them. This is the goal. Regardless of the organizational structure and what programs a church adopts, this is what we hope to see. Nevertheless, even the bold and generous members of the first church struggled with sin. Luke's example of Barnabas's generosity introduces a dark episode in the life of the church. While the Holy Spirit filled and transformed the great majority of believers, some in their midst refused to yield.

APPLICATION: ACTS 4:23-37

How to Be a Spiritual Pioneer

Not everyone can be a pioneer. Very few are called to be pioneer missionaries. But nothing keeps you from adopting a pioneer Christian mind-set. I find in Acts 4:23-37 three qualities worthy of every believer and available for the asking. As the first Christians asked for confidence in the face of persecution, you can ask the Lord for these pioneer qualities to be more effective in whatever circumstances you face.

First, ask for *compassion*. I don't mean compassion for yourself. Ask the Lord to give you compassion for others. The Bible distinguishes between the emotions of compassion and pity. Pity feels sorry for someone less fortunate but remains passive. Given time and distance, pity fades away. Compassion, on the other hand, remains unsatisfied until you follow through with tangible help.

What have you done for someone else in the past week? What did you do for the sheer purpose of helping another person, prompted by nothing but compassion? What have you given? If you struggle to answer, pray for compassion. I will warn you, however. When you ask for compassion, you're asking for an itch not easily scratched. But I can think of no better way to make your faith real. James writes searching, convicting words:

> If a brother or sister is without clothing and in need of daily food, and one of you says to them, "Go in peace, be warmed and be filled," and yet you do not give them what is necessary for their body, what use is that? Even so faith, if it has no works, is dead, being by itself. (Jas. 2:15-17)

Second, ask for *initiative*. Pioneers don't sit in one place waiting for opportunities to come to them; they go where the opportunities exist. If you desire to tell unbelievers about Christ, you must go where unbelievers live. That takes initiative, a willingness to leave your comfort zone and to insert yourself where you might not be expected. It's not comfortable. It's not convenient. The risks can feel overwhelming. But that's the frontier of faith. Initiative is the "want to" that overcomes inertia and puts faith into action.

Third, ask for *vulnerability*. Ask for the courage to admit your own inadequacies and needs as you seek help from others. To get anything done in the kingdom of God, each person needs help from others within the community of Christ. Recognizing our need isn't enough; we must make ourselves vulnerable enough to seek assistance and then to accept it.

When you put those three qualities together—when you integrate them and live them out—you're a pioneer Christian. Regardless of your place of service or your circumstances, you will become like members of the first church: tough outside and tender inside.

A Deadly Deception
ACTS 5:1-11

NASB

¹But a man named Ananias, with his wife Sapphira, sold a piece of property, ²and kept back *some* of the price for himself, with his wife's ᵃfull knowledge, and bringing a portion of it, he laid it at the apostles' feet. ³But Peter said, "Ananias, why has Satan filled your heart to lie to the Holy Spirit and to keep back *some* of the price of the land? ⁴While it remained *unsold,* did it not remain your own? And after it was sold, was it not ᵃunder your control? Why is it that you have ᵇconceived this deed in your heart? You have not lied to men but to God." ⁵And as he heard these words, Ananias fell down and breathed his last; and great fear came over all who heard of it. ⁶The young men got up and covered him up, and after carrying him out, they buried him.

⁷Now there elapsed an interval of about three hours, and his wife came in, not knowing what had happened. ⁸And Peter responded to her, "Tell me whether you sold the land ᵃfor such and such a price?" And she said, "Yes, ᵃthat was the price." ⁹Then Peter *said* to her, "Why is it that you have agreed together to put the Spirit of the Lord to the test? Behold, the feet of those who have buried your husband are at the door, and they will carry you out *as well.*" ¹⁰And immediately she fell at his feet and breathed her last, and the young men came in and found her dead, and they carried her out and buried her beside her husband. ¹¹And great fear came over the whole church, and over all who heard of these things.

5:2 ᵃOr *collusion* 5:4 ᵃOr *in your authority* ᵇLit *placed* 5:8 ᵃLit *for so much*

NLT

¹But there was a certain man named Ananias who, with his wife, Sapphira, sold some property. ²He brought part of the money to the apostles, claiming it was the full amount. With his wife's consent, he kept the rest.

³Then Peter said, "Ananias, why have you let Satan fill your heart? You lied to the Holy Spirit, and you kept some of the money for yourself. ⁴The property was yours to sell or not sell, as you wished. And after selling it, the money was also yours to give away. How could you do a thing like this? You weren't lying to us but to God!"

⁵As soon as Ananias heard these words, he fell to the floor and died. Everyone who heard about it was terrified. ⁶Then some young men got up, wrapped him in a sheet, and took him out and buried him.

⁷About three hours later his wife came in, not knowing what had happened. ⁸Peter asked her, "Was this the price you and your husband received for your land?"

"Yes," she replied, "that was the price."

⁹And Peter said, "How could the two of you even think of conspiring to test the Spirit of the Lord like this? The young men who buried your husband are just outside the door, and they will carry you out, too."

¹⁰Instantly, she fell to the floor and died. When the young men came in and saw that she was dead, they carried her out and buried her beside her husband. ¹¹Great fear gripped the entire church and everyone else who heard what had happened.

Every once in a while, we need something to shock us into reality. When things are going well, it's easy to coast along without a worry as good fortune creates a false sense of security. If we're not careful, we can drift off course or fail to see the warning signs of disaster ahead.

In the fall of 1973, I received a shock like that. At about seven o' clock on a foggy morning, I arrived at my study in the church with my arms full of books and my mind crowded with routine details. I unlocked the door, swung it open, shut it with my heel, plopped the books down on my desk, turned around, and came face to face with a casket, covered with a spray of wilted flowers and topped with a large picture of me!

I checked the second hand of my watch. (Still moving.)

I felt my pulse. (Strong and rapid.)

I puffed into my hands. (Something came out.)

Reassured that I was the victim of a practical joke and very much alive, I praised God and then plotted my revenge! In the quiet moments after that initial shock, however, I found myself the recipient of a unique gift. Very few people get to see a preview of their own funeral. My glimpse of the future caused me to take stock of my life—my priorities, my direction, my strengths, my weaknesses, and potential dangers.

As the fledgling church in Jerusalem overcame its first great challenge—the arrest, trial, and attempted intimidation by the Sanhedrin—people responded to the apostles' witness in droves. Peter's first sermon brought three thousand new believers into the kingdom; his second sermon brought another five thousand. These new Christians were filled with the Holy Spirit, bold in their proclamation of Jesus Christ, and supernaturally generous with their material wealth. The church became a little taste of heaven on earth. Then, something shocked every member of the movement, snapping them back into reality.

— 5:1-2 —

This portion of the narrative begins with the ominous word "but." Why the contrast? A quick glance back just a few verses reminds us of the glory days of *koinōnia* [2842]. Members of the Jerusalem church were filled with the Spirit of God, bursting at the seams with the good news, worshiping together, eating together, learning together, growing together, and sharing their material possessions. In fact, it had become commonplace for landowners to sell off their property and donate all of the proceeds to the church (4:34-35).

Luke names one of these extraordinary Christians (4:36-37), probably for two reasons. First, to introduce the remarkable man named

Joseph, a Levite from Cyprus. Nicknamed Barnabas, "Son of Encouragement," he became well known for the grace he displayed toward others. Second, to provide a suitable backdrop for the story of Ananias and Sapphira. With Acts 5:1, the story turns from simple, transparent generosity to dark, deceitful hypocrisy.

The husband and wife went through the same external motions as Barnabas. They sold a piece of land and brought money to the apostles to help meet the needs of less fortunate people in the church. That, in itself, was a wonderful act of generosity. They would have been thanked for their display of grace—except that they lied (5:2-4).

— 5:3-4 —

The husband and wife didn't arrive together. Ananias came first with the money. Peter's indictment highlights an important contrast. While the Holy Spirit filled Barnabas and the other believers, Satan filled the hearts of Ananias and Sapphira (5:3). Instead of wisdom driving their actions, foolishness told them they could lie to an omniscient God. The apostle clarified two points of misconception.

First, *Ananias and Sapphira were not required to do anything* (5:4). They could have kept the land to produce more wealth for themselves. They could have invested the proceeds in another business venture. They could have spent the money on something nice for their family or used it to pay for a luxurious vacation. Nothing in the teaching of Christ declares material wealth sinful. Furthermore, He doesn't command a specific amount of charitable giving. Rather than requiring sacrifices, instead of mandating offerings in a temple, far from demanding a 10 percent tax (a tithe), God fills His people with His Spirit and transforms their hearts. As a result of this filling, His people respond with spontaneous generosity (4:32-35).

Their freewill gift of money to the church would have been received gratefully if they had not lied. The man and his wife presented a partial sum of money to the apostles, claiming that it represented *all* of the proceeds (cf. 5:8). They could have said, "Brothers, we sold a piece of property, and we have brought a portion of the proceeds to you today; we have need of the other part." Nothing wrong with that. But they pretended they were sacrificing like Barnabas, moved by the Spirit to give all.

Second, *Christians aren't morally accountable to apostles, church leaders, or any other humans.* Because our actions affect one another, we are mutually accountable. Because church leaders must act in the best interest of the church, they must confront unrepentant sin. But we answer directly to God for our actions. Ananias and Sapphira thought pleasing the apostles counted for something, but Peter set them straight. He said, in effect, "You gain nothing spiritually by fooling us."

— 5:5-6 —

We're not told exactly what caused the man's death. Heart attack? Brain aneurysm? Stroke? Luke's grammar strongly implies divine activity without saying so outright. Regardless, we see a definite cause-and-effect relationship between the man's deception and his sudden death.

Jewish Law called for quick handling of cadavers. If a death occurred close to sundown, the body would have been wrapped hastily in linen strips soaked with spices and resin and then placed in a cave. Preparation for permanent burial would have been completed the next day, followed by an extended period of mourning by the family.

— 5:7-10 —

Three hours later, Ananias's wife, Sapphira, came to the apostles. For what reason, we can only surmise. Perhaps she hoped to receive the same accolades as Barnabas. Upon her arrival, Peter questioned the woman, giving her ample opportunity to be honest. He could not have been more direct in his question: "Tell me whether you sold the land for such and such a price?" (5:8). Tragically, she lied as well: "Yes, that was the price" (5:8).

Peter's indictment of the woman parallels that of her husband. "Lie to the Holy Spirit" (5:3) parallels "put the Spirit of the Lord to the test" (5:9). The Greek word for the latter, *peirazō* [3985], describes the process of discovering the true nature of something by means of experiment. Think of a man biting on a gold coin to see if it's genuine, and you have the right idea. The term also carries the idea of entrapment: "to entice to improper behavior."

Ananias and Sapphira didn't set out to test God's character or to draw Him into sin; nevertheless, that would have been the outcome if God had not responded the way He did. Peter implied that their actions backed God into a corner, so that allowing them to get away with their fraud would have made Him a silent accomplice.

Within moments, the woman joined her husband in eternity (5:9-10). Before the sun went down, her body lay beside her husband's in the family tomb. What a tragedy for their family! What a sad day for the church! Hypocrisy brought two lives to their ends.

— 5:11 —

Acts 5:11 repeats the last half of 5:5. A respectful awe for the holiness and power of God filled the church. This terrible incident served as a wake-up call for the church, a sobering shock back to reality. Everything within the church had been going smoothly—almost ideally, in fact. The sin of Ananias and Sapphira reminded the church that Christians aren't immune to sin. People can receive the Holy Spirit in salvation without yielding to His power in sanctification. They can appear one way on the outside while harboring sin on the inside. The church also learned that God's grace doesn't make Him soft on sin. He's still the holy, righteous God who deals harshly with rebellion.

APPLICATION: ACTS 5:1-11

Christian Responsibilities

As I reflect on the sin of Ananias and Sapphira, two observations emerge. First, *the act was premeditated.* It wasn't a mistake. They didn't simply do a poor financial accounting of the transaction. They colluded to perpetrate a fraud in the name of the Holy Spirit.

Second, *their sin was motivated by pride.* Plain and simple. They wanted to appear generous like their peers. They weren't willing to say, "Peter, as we bring this sum of money, we bring it for the glory of God, for His purpose only. We want you to know that we received more than this, but we've kept the rest for our own needs. We don't want to give you the impression that we're in any way in the same league as Barnabas. But here's a portion of the money; use it as you like." That's honesty. That's humility.

Bear in mind that this is in the context of a church moved to generosity by the Holy Spirit. This would be the equivalent of a few people on the Day of Pentecost speaking in a fake foreign language to appear Spirit filled like the rest. As true representatives of the Holy Spirit, we have three significant responsibilities.

First, *we have a responsibility to maintain personal integrity.* We must make truth a priority in every aspect of life. We must cultivate a lifestyle of transparency and authenticity—the opposite of hypocrisy. Ananias and Sapphira failed here. We are responsible to examine our motives, and if we don't like what we see, present them to the Lord. As David wrote,

> Search me, O God, and know my heart;
> Try me and know my anxious thoughts;
> And see if there be any hurtful way in me,
> And lead me in the everlasting way. (Ps. 139:23-24)

and

> Create in me a clean heart, O God,
> And renew a steadfast spirit within me. (Ps. 51:10)

All through my four years in seminary, a little hand-painted sign hung in front of me at the desk where I sat. Every time I looked up from my studies, I faced the words, "What is your motive?" Today, more than fifty years later, when I look up from my desk in my study at home, those words hang before me in my mind's eye.

What is your motive? Why do you do what you do?

Second, *we have a responsibility to maintain a clear conscience*. In Psalm 32, David reflects on the trap of deception:

> How blessed is the man to whom the LORD does not impute
> iniquity,
> And in whose spirit there is no deceit!
> When I kept silent about my sin, my body wasted away
> Through my groaning all day long.
> For day and night Your hand was heavy upon me;
> My vitality was drained away as with the fever heat of summer.
> (Ps. 32:2-4)

The king's tortured conscience made him physically ill. The Lord held him responsible to maintain a clear conscience, not only as a man of God, but in his role as judge. With his sin unconfessed, he could not be a fair and impartial judge of right and wrong in the cases brought before him. Finally, when Nathan penetrated his veil of secrecy, pointed his finger, and said, "You are the man," the king admitted his guilt—and found relief (2 Sam. 12:1-14). Only then could he fulfill his duties as God's representative, the Lord's embodiment of right in a world gone wrong.

That's our responsibility as well. As bearers of God's Spirit, we have a duty to represent the voice of right in a world dominated by evil.

Third, *we have a responsibility to be authentic*. Ananias and

Sapphira might have benefited from the words Paul would pen a couple of decades later: "None of us lives to himself, and none of us dies to himself" (Rom. 14:7, ESV). (I would add, "None of us sins to himself.") But Ananias and Sapphira should have known better even without Paul's words in front of them. The sin of hypocrisy always involves somebody else; in fact, it's a sin committed against everyone. The Lord places us in a community so that we might encourage one another. That requires honesty!

I'm encouraged when another believer admits to having struggles. I feel less alone. It gives me an opportunity to share my own struggles. I learn how to face my temptations and weaknesses when I see someone else face similar difficulties and overcome them. God designed this community called the church to be a system of mutual support. So when one decides to put on a mask and pretends to have it all together, we all suffer.

We Overwhelmingly Conquer
ACTS 5:12-42

NASB

12a At the hands of the apostles many signs and wonders were taking place among the people; and they were all with one accord in Solomon's portico. 13 But none of the rest dared to associate with them; however, the people held them in high esteem. 14 And all the more believers in the Lord, multitudes of men and women, were constantly added to *their number,* 15 to such an extent that they even carried the sick out into the streets and laid them on cots and pallets, so that when Peter came by at least his shadow might fall on any one of them. 16 Also the ᵃpeople from the cities in the vicinity of Jerusalem were coming together, bringing people who were sick ᵇor afflicted with unclean spirits, and they were all being healed.

17 But the high priest rose up, along with all his associates (that is

NLT

12 The apostles were performing many miraculous signs and wonders among the people. And all the believers were meeting regularly at the Temple in the area known as Solomon's Colonnade. 13 But no one else dared to join them, even though all the people had high regard for them. 14 Yet more and more people believed and were brought to the Lord—crowds of both men and women. 15 As a result of the apostles' work, sick people were brought out into the streets on beds and mats so that Peter's shadow might fall across some of them as he went by. 16 Crowds came from the villages around Jerusalem, bringing their sick and those possessed by evil* spirits, and they were all healed.

17 The high priest and his officials, who were Sadducees, were filled

NASB

the sect of the Sadducees), and they were filled with jealousy. [18] They laid hands on the apostles and put them in a public jail. [19] But during the night an angel of the Lord opened the gates of the prison, and taking them out he said, [20] "Go, stand and [a]speak to the people in the temple [b]the whole message of this Life." [21] Upon hearing *this,* they entered into the temple about daybreak and *began* to teach.

Now when the high priest and his associates came, they called the [a]Council together, even all the Senate of the sons of Israel, and sent *orders* to the prison house for them to be brought. [22] But the officers who came did not find them in the prison; and they returned and reported back, [23] saying, "We found the prison house locked quite securely and the guards standing at the doors; but when we had opened up, we found no one inside." [24] Now when the captain of the temple *guard* and the chief priests heard these words, they were greatly perplexed about them as to what [a]would come of this. [25] But someone came and reported to them, "The men whom you put in prison are standing in the temple and teaching the people!" [26] Then the captain went along with the officers and *proceeded* to bring them *back* without violence (for they were afraid of the people, that they might be stoned).

[27] When they had brought them, they stood them [a]before the Council. The high priest questioned them, [28] saying, "We gave you strict orders not to continue teaching in this name, and [a]yet, you have filled Jerusalem with your teaching and intend to bring this man's blood upon us." [29] But Peter and the apostles answered, "We must obey God rather than men. [30] The God of our fathers

NLT

with jealousy. [18] They arrested the apostles and put them in the public jail. [19] But an angel of the Lord came at night, opened the gates of the jail, and brought them out. Then he told them, [20] "Go to the Temple and give the people this message of life!"

[21] So at daybreak the apostles entered the Temple, as they were told, and immediately began teaching.

When the high priest and his officials arrived, they convened the high council*—the full assembly of the elders of Israel. Then they sent for the apostles to be brought from the jail for trial. [22] But when the Temple guards went to the jail, the men were gone. So they returned to the council and reported, [23] "The jail was securely locked, with the guards standing outside, but when we opened the gates, no one was there!"

[24] When the captain of the Temple guard and the leading priests heard this, they were perplexed, wondering where it would all end. [25] Then someone arrived with startling news: "The men you put in jail are standing in the Temple, teaching the people!"

[26] The captain went with his Temple guards and arrested the apostles, but without violence, for they were afraid the people would stone them. [27] Then they brought the apostles before the high council, where the high priest confronted them. [28] "We gave you strict orders never again to teach in this man's name!" he said. "Instead, you have filled all Jerusalem with your teaching about him, and you want to make us responsible for his death!"

[29] But Peter and the apostles replied, "We must obey God rather than any human authority. [30] The God of

raised up Jesus, ªwhom you had put to death by hanging Him on a ᵇcross. ³¹He is the one whom God exalted ªto His right hand as a ᵇPrince and a Savior, to grant repentance to Israel, and forgiveness of sins. ³²And we are witnesses ªof these things; and *so is* the Holy Spirit, whom God has given to those who obey Him."

³³But when they heard this, they were cut ªto the quick and intended to kill them. ³⁴But a Pharisee named Gamaliel, a teacher of the Law, respected by all the people, stood up in the Council and gave orders to put the men outside for a short time. ³⁵And he said to them, "Men of Israel, take care what you propose to do with these men. ³⁶For some time ago Theudas rose up, claiming to be somebody, and a group of about four hundred men joined up with him. ªBut he was killed, and all who ᵇfollowed him were dispersed and came to nothing. ³⁷After this man, Judas of Galilee rose up in the days of the census and drew away *some* people after him; he too perished, and all those who ªfollowed him were scattered. ³⁸So in the present case, I say to you, stay away from these men and let them alone, for if this plan or ªaction is of men, it will be overthrown; ³⁹but if it is of God, you will not be able to overthrow them; or else you may even be found fighting against God."

⁴⁰They ªtook his advice; and after calling the apostles in, they flogged them and ordered them not to ᵇspeak in the name of Jesus, and *then* released them. ⁴¹So they went on their way from the presence of the ªCouncil, rejoicing that they had been considered worthy to suffer shame for *His* name. ⁴²And every day, in the

our ancestors raised Jesus from the dead after you killed him by hanging him on a cross.* ³¹Then God put him in the place of honor at his right hand as Prince and Savior. He did this so the people of Israel would repent of their sins and be forgiven. ³²We are witnesses of these things and so is the Holy Spirit, who is given by God to those who obey him."

³³When they heard this, the high council was furious and decided to kill them. ³⁴But one member, a Pharisee named Gamaliel, who was an expert in religious law and respected by all the people, stood up and ordered that the men be sent outside the council chamber for a while. ³⁵Then he said to his colleagues, "Men of Israel, take care what you are planning to do to these men! ³⁶Some time ago there was that fellow Theudas, who pretended to be someone great. About 400 others joined him, but he was killed, and all his followers went their various ways. The whole movement came to nothing. ³⁷After him, at the time of the census, there was Judas of Galilee. He got people to follow him, but he was killed, too, and all his followers were scattered.

³⁸"So my advice is, leave these men alone. Let them go. If they are planning and doing these things merely on their own, it will soon be overthrown. ³⁹But if it is from God, you will not be able to overthrow them. You may even find yourselves fighting against God!"

⁴⁰The others accepted his advice. They called in the apostles and had them flogged. Then they ordered them never again to speak in the name of Jesus, and they let them go. ⁴¹The apostles left the high council rejoicing that God had counted them worthy to suffer disgrace for the name of Jesus.* ⁴²And every day,

NASB

temple and ªfrom house to house, they ᵇkept right on teaching and ᶜpreaching Jesus *as* the ᵈChrist.

5:12 ªLit *Through*   5:16 ªLit *multitude* ᵇLit *and*
5:20 ªOr *continue to speak* ᵇLit *all the words*
5:21 ªOr *Sanhedrin*   5:24 ªLit *this would become*
5:27 ªLit *in*   5:28 ªLit *behold*   5:30 ªOr *on whom you had laid violent hands* ᵇLit *wood*   5:31 ªOr *by* ᵇOr *Leader*   5:32 ªOne early ms adds *in Him*
5:33 ªOr *in their hearts*   5:36 ªLit *Who was killed* ᵇLit *were obeying*   5:37 ªLit *were obeying*
5:38 ªOr *work*   5:40 ªLit *were persuaded by him* ᵇLit *be speaking*   5:41 ªOr *Sanhedrin*   5:42 ªOr *in the various private homes* ᵇLit *were not ceasing to* ᶜLit *telling the good news of* ᵈI.e. Messiah

NLT

in the Temple and from house to house, they continued to teach and preach this message: "Jesus is the Messiah."

5:16 Greek *unclean.*   5:21 Greek *Sanhedrin;* also in 5:27, 41.   5:30 Greek *on a tree.*   5:41 Greek *for the name.*

In Romans 8, Paul offers a striking image of Christians living in a hostile world: "'We were considered as sheep to be slaughtered.' But in all these things we overwhelmingly conquer through Him who loved us" (Rom. 8:36-37). I find that image both terrifying and comforting. We are powerless, yet we cannot be defeated. We face fearsome opposition, yet we should not fear. We could have been "slaughtered," yet we overwhelmingly conquer. If that tension seems impossible to maintain, that's because it is! As far as human ability goes, anyway.

The Lord doesn't require us to have superhuman strength or genius-level intelligence or heroic bravery. He merely calls us to be faithful and obedient and to leave the business of conquering to Him. This was the lesson God taught the first Christians as they faced their next major challenge.

— 5:12-16 —

This segment of Luke's narrative opens with a summary statement describing the rise of the church over a period of several weeks or months. Through the power of the Holy Spirit and in defiance of the Sanhedrin's warning, the apostles continued to heal the sick and proclaim the resurrection of Jesus. These first Christians were Jewish, of course, so they continued to meet in the temple. In fact, they made it their custom to use the portico of Solomon, where Peter and John had earlier been taken into custody.

The believers had prayed for confidence (4:29); clearly, the Lord granted their request!

As Jews came and went, they could not have missed the large meetings taking place in the main courtyard. Many Jews lived in Jerusalem and the surrounding areas, but many others traveled from distant lands to sacrifice and to worship. Before leaving, however, they heard about Jesus, the Old Testament proofs about Him being the Messiah, and the eyewitness testimony of His rising from the dead. The number of Christians grew steadily as people responded in belief. Still, a great number feared the power of the religious officials and kept their distance. But no one could ignore the movement of God in the temple.

Not everyone understood what they saw. Superstition and rumor prompted people to line the streets with their infirm relatives, hoping that Peter's shadow might bring healing. Luke doesn't say Peter's shadow healed anyone, only that people thought it possible. They could have approached any one of the apostles in the temple courtyard, but they feared retribution. The Sanhedrin didn't approve of this growing sect of Jesus followers.

— 5:17-18 —

The teaching of the apostles challenged not only the religious power of the Sanhedrin—the growing movement also threatened to upset the fragile political balance the religious leaders were struggling to maintain. For decades, the Sadducees and Pharisees had successfully maintained a delicate balance of power between nationalistic Jews and Rome. They used the threat of Roman cruelty to discourage insurrection among the commoners, and they convinced Rome that keeping its distance would minimize the possibility of revolution. This arrangement gave the temple rulers incredible power and extreme wealth. As the popularity of the church continued to grow, however, the temple officials could do nothing but watch helplessly as their political power gradually slipped away with each new convert.

The religious leaders' attempted shakedown of Peter and John (4:3-22) had failed to accomplish anything. In fact, the two men found themselves joined by ten more, and the evangelistic meetings continued right at the spot of the men's arrest. So, the high priest decided to increase the pressure by arresting all twelve of the apostles and holding them in a "public jail" overnight before questioning (5:18). The Greek adjective translated "public" (*dēmosios* [1219]) has two primary meanings: "belonging to the state" and "open or visible to the public." All jails belonged to the state; therefore, this must have been a jail where prisoners were put on display as a warning to others. The high priest hoped a night in jail would cause at least some to weaken or perhaps even split the group into factions. Then, a hearing the next morning might capitalize on their failing solidarity.

THE POLITICS OF RELIGION

ACTS 5:17, 34

Religion has always been a favorite tool of kings and governments. All you need is a visible institution to embody the beliefs of the people you want to control and the credibility to determine who can be in and who should remain out. If people believe that you hold their eternal destinies in your hands, you can make them believe almost anything, want almost anything, and most significantly, *do* almost anything. Some of the world's greatest evils have been perpetrated by people who believed that their actions—however horrific or inhuman—were good and right because of their religion. A classic example is September 11, 2001.

In first-century Israel, two primary groups vied for religious control, which kept them locked in a symbiotic, love-hate relationship with each other. The aristocratic Sadducees occupied the official positions of power, which included authority over Herod's magnificent temple, Israel's most visible institution. But their open collaboration with Rome made them very unpopular with the Jewish population, who wanted nothing less than a free nation. The nationalistic Pharisees maintained control over the Jewish masses by becoming conspicuously Jewish. And if obedience to the Law of Moses made someone Jewish, they would remain kings of the moral hill at any cost.

The Sadducees controlled the temple only at the pleasure of Rome, and they needed the religious clout of the Pharisees to control the Jewish people. Although the Pharisees wielded heavy influence over the people, their pugnacious attitude toward Rome and lack of military might have kept them from doing much more than chanting slogans. Rome needed the Sadducees to keep Roman interference to a minimum. Of the two things needed to manipulate people—a religious institution and religious authority—neither party had both. So they jealously guarded what they did control.[31]

In the past, the tactic had probably worked well for the high priest. Who knows how many upstarts and rabble-rousers he had silenced? Only this time, he failed to take a critical factor into account—the power of God.

— 5:19-20 —

During the night, the Lord undermined the temple leaders. They were planning to humiliate the apostles by placing them in a public jail, so the Lord freed the men in a public declaration of His support. He sent an angel to miraculously open the locked doors and gates and march them past the guards and out into the street without being noticed. There was no natural way for them to escape without detection.

Notice, however, that instead of fleeing the city, they returned to the temple to resume their proclamation of Christ's resurrection. A simple jailbreak would have proven nothing. As fugitives, the men would attract dissenters while compromising their standing among devout Jews. By resuming their activities with God's blessing, they sent an altogether different message to potential believers.

The apostles returned to the very spot of their earlier arrest and resumed their ministry of preaching, teaching, and healing.

— 5:21-25 —

When the council convened later in the morning, they sent for the prisoners. Again, they hoped to intimidate the apostles because they needed them to recant their testimony. By now, many thousands of people had heard them declare Jesus resurrected. The Sanhedrin had already killed Jesus; now they had an enemy they couldn't destroy—except by discrediting His witnesses.

When the report came back that the apostles had disappeared from their cell, the temple leaders were "greatly perplexed" (5:24; *diaporeō* [1280]). The word could also be translated "at a loss," not only to comprehend or explain what had occurred, but also as to what might happen next. When they heard the news, they expected the men to be long gone, which created two potential outcomes. First, the men could begin an underground movement against them, not unlike the secret campaigns of the Zealots. Second, the men could flee to Galilee or further north and resume their ministry there. Either way, the Sanhedrin would have to respond in the same way: discredit the apostles as fugitive enemies of God's temple.

Of course, the religious authorities didn't expect these men to be teaching openly in the portico of Solomon, exactly where they had been taken into custody!

— 5:26-32 —

The captain of the temple guard and a contingent of soldiers *politely* requested the apostles to join the Sanhedrin for a meeting. The crowd undoubtedly knew what had occurred the day before; after all, the apostles had been thrown into a public prison. The temple guard, commissioned to keep the peace in the temple precincts, feared the potential reaction of the crowd gathered to hear the apostles (5:26).

When Caiaphas the high priest indicted the apostles, he carefully avoided speaking the name of Jesus. Instead, he used "this name" and "this man" (5:28). (Even today, the name of Jesus makes people uncomfortable.) All the same, everyone knew whom he had in mind.

The expression "bring this man's blood upon us" refers to imputed guilt (5:28). The council had undoubtedly rationalized their conspiracy against Jesus, perhaps convincing themselves that His own words condemned Him or that Pilate was to blame. Regardless, they worried about the public blaming them for an innocent—even righteous—man's execution. They feared the loss of power, not moral guilt or what the truth might be.

The apostles responded with words we would all do well to memorize: "We must obey God rather than men" (5:29). Peter didn't avoid the issues that caused the Sanhedrin discomfort. He went on to overwhelm the indictment with a coun025charge layered with messianic language. He said, in effect, "You're worried about being blamed for crucifying the Messiah because you are, in fact, *guilty* of crucifying the Messiah!" But this same Jesus, Peter testified, had been raised from the dead by the power of God and had received all the power and authority promised to the Messiah in the Scriptures (5:30-31).

Peter didn't offer any theological reasoning; he didn't need to. The professional theologians understood the implications better than anyone. Peter and the apostles presented as evidence their personal experience, what they had witnessed firsthand. Jesus told them He would be arrested, tortured, and sacrificed for the sins of His people, and He predicted His resurrection. Jesus then fulfilled everything He promised (5:32).

Clearly the men would not back down.

— 5:33-39 —

The temple leaders almost decided to dispose of the believers as they had done with Jesus, but a highly respected teacher named Gamaliel intervened. Beginning with a short history of other failed movements, he reminded the men that their noninterference policy had served them well in the past. As each would-be messiah or populist movement had surfaced, the Sanhedrin had refused to lend its support for fear of Rome's wrath. But they had also avoided taking sides with Rome to avoid angering the people. In each case, the deceptive leader was killed, his movement fell apart, and the crisis passed without the Sanhedrin's involvement (5:35-37). Gamaliel therefore reasoned that if this movement didn't have God behind it, the crisis would resolve itself. If, on the other hand, these Jesus followers had God on their side, the council would be wise to stay out of the Lord's way (5:38-39).

While Gamaliel acted in the interests of communal self-preservation, he uttered more truth than he realized. As a leader of Israel, he was admitting that only divine power could help a group of simple, uneducated, unarmed civilians expand under the suffocating domination of Rome. Because the council wanted to remain free of Roman dominion as much as anyone, they saw no reason to quash any movement that might prove successful—that is, so long as Rome didn't blame the Sanhedrin for failing to keep the peace. So far, this troublesome movement had remained politically peaceful.

— 5:40-42 —

The council accepted Gamaliel's reasoning. Besides, their murder of Jesus had not only failed to destroy His following, but it had fueled deeper devotion and accelerated growth. They couldn't imagine what *twelve* murders would do. So, they flogged the apostles and released them with another warning to stop teaching in the name of Jesus (5:40).

The word translated "flogged" (*derō* [1194]) means literally "to skin," but it's a general term for striking, beating, or whipping. It could have been as simple as a symbolic punishment, such as a few lashes with a leather whip, or as severe as the scourging Jesus received prior to crucifixion. Many references in classical Greek literature convey the idea of flaying or parting the skin. Taking all things into consideration, the apostles were probably whipped until they were bloody but were not subjected to the halfway-to-death scourging Jesus endured. The punishment undoubtedly left permanent scars.

Upon leaving the council chambers, the church leaders *rejoiced* (5:41)! They considered their ordeal a fulfillment of the Lord's many predictions during His earthly ministry (Matt. 10:17, 22; 23:34; 24:9; Mark 13:9-13; Luke 12:11; 21:12, 17; John 15:19-21). And what did they do next? They returned to the temple courts—most likely the portico of Solomon where they had been arrested twice before—and continued their ministry of healing and proclaiming the resurrection of the Messiah, Jesus.

As we examine the history of the church, it's easy to think of the first Christians as larger than life, even superhuman, especially when you consider the disadvantages they faced compared to our circumstances in the United States today. They had no building in which to meet. They had no governmental protection. In fact, their governments very much wanted them dead. They had no guarantee of privacy, no freedom of speech, no assurance of due process or fair hearings. They had little in the way of tangible resources. No political power. No impressive education. Not even a complete Bible—none of the New Testament had been written yet.

They had so much more working against them than we do today—yet they literally changed the world. Still, let us not forget that these were ordinary men and women not much different from us. These first Christians would not have been equal to the challenges they faced were it not for the Holy Spirit. They conquered because they relied upon the same power God has given us today.

APPLICATION: ACTS 5:12-42

Attention, Soldiers of the Cross!

Jesus didn't fit the theological mold of the Messiah in first-century Israel. The ancient experts in Old Testament prophecy expected a larger-than-life political mogul, a muscular military commander, economic guru, prophetic sage, and moral champion, all rolled into one magnificent package. They expected this man to make life good again, to restore Israel's military power, economic prosperity, and religious order. So, when a peaceful carpenter from the boonies of Galilee presented Himself as the long-awaited King announcing a very different kind of agenda, the religious leaders of Israel frowned, jeered, and rejected Him.

Even those who accepted Him as the Messiah didn't understand His mission, regardless of how many times Jesus promised the exact opposite of health and wealth, comfort and ease. Even after His resurrection, they had wondered, "Is it at this time You are restoring the kingdom to Israel?" (1:6).

After receiving the Holy Spirit, with His power and wisdom, the followers of Jesus gained a very different view of the Messiah and His mission. They now had the transforming mind of God. Consequently, as I observe Acts 5:12-42, I see twelve men emerging from persecution bearing the scars of injustice not with curses or questions but with *rejoicing*. They considered their ordeal an indication of God's favor! This suggests two principles for all those who suffer for the cause of Christ today. First, *opposition may mean you're in the will of God, not out of it.* Second, *the will of God may set you against popular opinion, not with it.*

Difficult as it is to understand, Jesus never promised His followers—then or now—that living in a fallen world would be easy or bring popularity. Yet for some reason, we think that good fortune indicates God's pleasure or confirms that we are in His will. And we continue to suspect that painful circumstances indicate God's displeasure or that we have wandered outside His sovereign design. The fact is, God may will for His people to live as poor as dirt, to suffer rejection and sorrow, to endure outrageous injustice and then die painfully—just like His own Son and the apostles who followed Him. Isaac Watts expressed this well in one of his great hymns, first published about three centuries ago.

Am I a soldier of the cross,
A follower of the Lamb,
And shall I fear to own His cause,
Or blush to speak His Name?

Must I be carried to the skies
On flowery beds of ease,
While others fought to win the prize,
And sailed through bloody seas? . . .

Sure I must fight if I would reign;
Increase my courage, Lord!
I'll bear the toil, endure the pain,
Supported by Thy Word.

Remain faithful in season and out of season. Don't forget that—ultimately—we overwhelmingly conquer.

Growing Pains
ACTS 6:1-7

NASB

[1] Now ᵃat this time while the disciples were increasing *in number,* a complaint arose on the part of the ᵇHellenistic *Jews* against the *native* Hebrews, because their widows were being overlooked in the daily serving

NLT

[1] But as the believers* rapidly multiplied, there were rumblings of discontent. The Greek-speaking believers complained about the Hebrew-speaking believers, saying that their widows were being

NASB

of food. ²So the twelve summoned the ªcongregation of the disciples and said, "It is not desirable for us to neglect the word of God in order to serve tables. ³Therefore, brethren, select from among you seven men of good reputation, full of the Spirit and of wisdom, whom we may put in charge of this task. ⁴But we will devote ourselves to prayer and to the ªministry of the word." ⁵The statement found approval with the whole ªcongregation; and they chose Stephen, a man full of faith and of the Holy Spirit, and Philip, Prochorus, Nicanor, Timon, Parmenas and ᵇNicolas, a ᶜproselyte from Antioch. ⁶And these they brought before the apostles; and after praying, they laid their hands on them.

⁷The word of God kept on spreading; and the number of the disciples continued to increase greatly in Jerusalem, and a great many of the priests were becoming obedient to the faith.

6:1 ªLit *in these days* ᵇJews who adopted the Gr language and much of Gr culture through acculturation 6:2 ªLit *multitude* 6:4 ªOr *service* 6:5 ªLit *multitude* ᵇGr *Nikolaos* ᶜI.e. a Gentile convert to Judaism

NLT

discriminated against in the daily distribution of food.

²So the Twelve called a meeting of all the believers. They said, "We apostles should spend our time teaching the word of God, not running a food program. ³And so, brothers, select seven men who are well respected and are full of the Spirit and wisdom. We will give them this responsibility. ⁴Then we apostles can spend our time in prayer and teaching the word."

⁵Everyone liked this idea, and they chose the following: Stephen (a man full of faith and the Holy Spirit), Philip, Procorus, Nicanor, Timon, Parmenas, and Nicolas of Antioch (an earlier convert to the Jewish faith). ⁶These seven were presented to the apostles, who prayed for them as they laid their hands on them.

⁷So God's message continued to spread. The number of believers greatly increased in Jerusalem, and many of the Jewish priests were converted, too.

6:1 Greek *disciples;* also in 6:2, 7.

During the 1970s, I witnessed a rebirth of sorts. The previous two decades had been a dismal time for the church in America as every pundit and radical took potshots at what they termed "God's frozen people" who remained icily immobile in their "suburban captivity." Then something curious happened. A period of affirmation, experimentation, and revitalization took hold of some congregations, while most mainline denominations continued to suffer steady decline. As these large, traditional organizations lost attendance and funding, many other sanctuaries were bursting at the seams.

Books and seminars tried to explain why some churches flourished while others wilted: bus ministries, expository preaching, contemporary worship, aggressive evangelism, social action, community consciousness. Many had good things to say. But as I witnessed such rapid growth in the church where I served as senior pastor and in others nearby, I observed a common denominator not mentioned in most books. I saw churches grow rapidly for one reason or another, only to fizzle or fracture just as quickly. The churches that continued to grow were those with wise, adaptable leaders who were guided by tradition but not constrained by tradition.

In the first several months after Pentecost, the church in Jerusalem faced a number of challenges. The people met the challenge of public scorn with sound preaching. They met the challenge of intimidation with prayers for boldness. They met the challenge of hypocrisy with uncompromising integrity. They met the challenge of persecution with rejoicing and continued faithfulness. After three thousand members joined the disciples at Pentecost and five thousand more embraced Jesus as the Messiah in the temple—along with unknown numbers that came into the family of God daily throughout this time—the apostles faced one of the greatest challenges of all: success.

Elton Trueblood calls this early church an "incendiary fellowship."[32] F.F. Bruce calls it the "spreading flame."[33] This first-century phenomenon had no constitution, no organizational plan—nothing but the indwelling Holy Spirit to keep it cohesive and heading in the right direction. While the church remained relatively small, this worked just fine. Eventually, however, the Jerusalem church encountered the perils that accompany rapid growth.

— 6:1 —

"The disciples" refers to the entire local assembly in Jerusalem—all of the Christians, regardless of culture, language, background, or when they joined the congregation. While Jesus called twelve men to join an inner circle of students for the sake of leadership training, He had many followers—hundreds, and at times, thousands—during His earthly ministry. Luke calls all of the followers of Christ "disciples."

At this time the entire body of believers was Jewish, but they represented two groups from two very different backgrounds. You'll notice that in the NASB the words "Jews" and "native" are in italics. The editors inserted those words for clarity, but they don't appear in the Greek text. The Greek terms could be rendered "Hellenists" and "Hebrews," which have colloquial meanings.

The "Hellenists" were no less Hebrew than the "Hebrews," at least by birth and bloodline. While Jewish by birth, they had adopted many customs from their Gentile neighbors and assimilated into their local communities in many ways. Many Hellenists rejected pagan religions, worshiped God exclusively, came to the temple for sacrifices and festivals, and generally obeyed the Law of Moses. Even so, they dressed like Gentiles, socialized with Gentiles, and embraced the Roman government as their own. They were known as Hellenists because, like much of the Roman world, they had adopted Greek as their primary language.

The "Hebrews," on the other hand, were more traditionally Jewish in their manner of life, dress, and customs. They obeyed the Law of Moses in the Pentateuch, and they followed the traditions of the rabbis. The latter consisted of the strict, Pharisaic code of conduct that dictated every aspect of life: how they dressed, how they washed, what they ate, how they conducted business, what they touched, and with whom they socialized. Whereas most Hellenists attempted to accommodate Greek culture without completely abandoning their Jewish identity, the Hebrews scrupulously insulated themselves from anything Gentile. They also tended to be very nationalistic. Consequently, they spoke colloquial Hebrew or Aramaic as much as possible and Greek only when necessary.

These two vastly different groups filled the church in Jerusalem and mingled quite well because of their common bond in Jesus Christ and their mutual filling of the Holy Spirit. Still, from a purely human perspective, friction was inevitable.

In those days, many destitute people joined the church. To care for their basic needs, the church, through the generosity of men like Barnabas (4:36-37), purchased food, prepared it, and served it in baskets or on tables to those in need. And no one needed more help than widows. The core idea behind the Greek word for widow (*chēra* [5503]) is "forsaken." Unfortunately, for much of history, a woman left without a man could not expect to survive long; indeed, many died from hunger, exposure, or assault. Many ancient cultures valued people to the extent they served the community. Old women could neither bear children nor bear hard labor; consequently, life became a bleak existence for old women with no family. (We might be reminded of the plight of Naomi in the book of Ruth.)

Widows fared much better in Hebrew culture, which valued kindness to widows and orphans as honoring to God; naturally, the church continued this Jewish tradition. Some Hellenists, however, complained that Hellenistic widows had been overlooked in the distribution of food, subtly suggesting cultural bias was to blame.

The Perils of Success

ACTS 6:1

The Jerusalem church encountered the perils that accompany rapid growth. I can identify four.

A first major peril in a rapidly growing church is an uncertain purpose. What was very clear in the early days becomes less clear as rapid growth kicks into high gear. Rapid growth has a way of erasing memories. Before long, the principles and priorities that once gave the church purpose and direction get forgotten.

According to Howard Ball, the founder of Churches Alive, the leaders of most churches in America (including pastors) cannot answer the questions "Where are you going as a church?" and "How will you get there?" That's quite an indictment. There's a missing purpose, a lack of definition, when church leaders cannot articulate the direction and purpose of their ministry. That's part of the fallout of a rapidly growing assembly.

Second, vague priorities. Something highly important yesterday may lose significance tomorrow in a rapidly growing church. The tyranny of the immediate can take over when facilities need expanding, the parking lot overflows, nursery volunteers feel overwhelmed, and multiple services begin to tax resources. In that kind of chaos, the priorities that gave the church early success become casualties of the "squeaky-wheel syndrome."

Third, professionalism, where we hire people to carry burdens the congregation should voluntarily bear together. I don't mean things like custodial work and grounds keeping. I mean ministries like missions, evangelism, social work, and caregiving. An attitude of professionalism prefers to send money rather than people to the mission field. It's easier to hire an evangelism pastor and then expect him to do all the evangelizing. If someone is hired to be on staff, it should be to equip and lead volunteers in the work of ministry.

Fourth, diminished individual significance. In a large church,

(continued on next page)

people can begin to lose significance as individuals. As one among thousands, a person might think, "Who really cares if my son has run away? Who really cares if my spouse left me? Who in that great big church down there even knows me well enough to realize I'm dying on the inside? Who will help me now that I've lost my job and have no food to eat? Does anybody care? Maybe they just don't want me to rock the boat."

If a rapidly growing church doesn't watch for these four perils of success and take action, it can become like the machine in a joke I once heard. A man sat in the office of a patent attorney playing with his invention. He pushed a button and it jumped to life. Lights flashed, gears turned, pulleys spun, and belts rolled as a little symphony of fascinating mechanical noises drew everyone's attention. The person next to him said, "My, that's impressive! What does it do?" The inventor replied, "Do? It doesn't do anything. But doesn't it run beautifully?"

A big church can run beautifully yet accomplish very little.

— 6:2-4 —

The apostles could not be everywhere at once. Moreover, God had called the twelve men to teach, preach, and lead, not to minister to every individual need in person. They quickly recognized the need for an organizational structure. They needed people of godly character to meet the legitimate needs of individuals so that the church did not lose focus. The church had to take care of its members without failing in its primary mission: to "be My witnesses both in Jerusalem, and in all Judea and Samaria, and even to the remotest part of the earth" (1:8). Its members had not yet extended ministry beyond the walls of Jerusalem; they couldn't afford to get bogged down by details—even the important detail of caring for widows.

To accommodate their growth and to keep their focus on the Lord's mandate, the apostles charged the congregation with the task of selecting seven men to oversee the distribution of food to widows (6:3). The word translated "select" here (*episkeptomai* [1980a]) means "to observe by inspection and examination." These individuals selected for service were not to be the first seven who expressed an interest or who had the spare time. The church was to look at the responsibilities required and then find gifted men who could fulfill those responsibilities.

The apostles initially named only two criteria in selecting these men. They were to have a good reputation and have evidence of the Holy Spirit's filling. The apostles wanted men they could trust to do the job with the same integrity that they would.

What an ingenious plan! The apostles didn't appoint the deacons themselves; they had the congregation make the selections. While a popular vote isn't generally the best policy in churches, it was the best way for the Twelve to deal with the suspicious implication of favoritism. The complaint of the Hellenists suggested that the "Hebrews" discriminated in their distribution of food to widows. All twelve apostles belonged to the suspected faction. Having the congregation determine who served them precluded any future accusation.

— 6:5-6 —

The congregation chose seven men, all with Greek names, suggesting a Greek orientation (6:5). Nicolas wasn't even Jewish by birth; he had become a Jew by conversion (*prosēlytos* [4339]) prior to responding to the gospel. Stephen would soon become a key figure in Luke's narrative, as would Philip, but Scripture says nothing more about the other five.

Then the congregation brought those they had chosen to the apostles, who "laid their hands on them" (6:6). The practice of "laying on of hands" dates back to the earliest days of the Hebrew people. The gesture symbolizes passing something intangible from one person to another, such as blessing (Gen. 48:14; Matt. 19:14-15), guilt (Exod. 29:10), judgment (Lev. 24:14), authority (Num. 27:18-20), or the Holy Spirit (Acts 8:17-20). The New Testament church adopted the practice as a means of commissioning someone to carry out a specific task (9:17; 13:3).

Eventually, these men would come to be known as the first "deacons" (*diakonos* [1249]), a title based on the verb translated "serve tables" in 6:2. In its most literal sense, the term *diakonos* means "one who serves at table." By extension, it carries the idea of serving obediently and willingly, offering service with a submissive attitude. Although the duties of a deacon would be expanded, the people serving in this capacity were never to forget their table-waiting roots.

— 6:7 —

Luke's summary statement here[34] confirms that the apostles made the right decision. They met the challenge of success wisely. The church continued to address the needs of current members without neglecting its ministry to people outside the congregation.

The additional comment that "a great many of the priests were becoming obedient to the faith" may be significant because this administrative decision appealed to the priests working in the temple. These priests were socially and economically different from the high priest and chief priests, who were Sadducees in their politics and theology. These men were middle class and devout, and they usually carried the responsibility of practical care in the temple. For them, the gospel message became convincing when the church gave it practical relevance.

APPLICATION: ACTS 6:1-7

Principles for Growing

The challenges faced by the rapidly growing church in Jerusalem suggest four principles that still apply today.

First, *strong leadership doesn't guarantee an absence of problems.* You may have strong, capable leaders who are filled and led by the Holy Spirit, but in a growing church you're still going to have some problems. Remember those who led the Jerusalem church in those early days? Twelve apostles trained by Jesus for years, eleven of them under the close, personal supervision of the Messiah! Yet problems still challenged the church.

Don't blame leaders when difficulties arise. Blaming is easier than participating in the solution, but it does nothing to eliminate the problem.

Second, *rapid growth doesn't excuse unmet needs.* Now, that's a lesson for today's leadership to remember. These men in leadership listened to a legitimate complaint and then did something about it. They didn't defend themselves against the accusation of favoritism. They didn't ignore the problem as something beneath their level of concern. They didn't dismiss or minimize the need, and they certainly didn't discredit the people complaining. They listened to the criticism and then saw it as an opportunity to address an unmet need.

Third, *concerned involvement doesn't require losing priorities.* The apostles found a way to meet the congregation's needs and solve the problem without sacrificing their top priorities. That's a tough balance to maintain! It takes creative thinking, willingness to flex, courage to delegate, and the wisdom to risk failure. Welcome to Leadership 101.

Fourth, *a large church can have an effective ministry.* In fact, smaller churches cannot manage some ministries. I'm not saying one is better than another. I simply maintain that both small and large churches have their advantages. Smaller churches don't struggle with many of the dangers affecting larger churches (see "The Perils of Success" on pages 115–116). Nevertheless, if the leaders of a large church can steer around those perils, they can minister to people who would otherwise lack what they need. A large church can minister to special-needs children, brain-injured veterans, and people who are deaf, blind, or disabled using resources unavailable to churches with a small budget.

When God gives increase to a congregation, He doesn't leave it without direction. If the church's leadership, through prayer and sensitivity to the Holy Spirit, takes care to avoid the perils of success and diligently applies these principles, its leaders can keep the church strong *and* maintain a pattern of growth.

The First Martyr's Last Stand
ACTS 6:8-7:60

NASB

[8]And Stephen, full of grace and power, was performing great wonders and ªsigns among the people. [9]But some men from what was called the Synagogue of the Freedmen, *including* both Cyrenians and Alexandrians, and some from Cilicia and ªAsia, rose up and argued with Stephen. [10]But they were unable to cope with the wisdom and the Spirit with which he was speaking.

NLT

[8]Stephen, a man full of God's grace and power, performed amazing miracles and signs among the people. [9]But one day some men from the Synagogue of Freed Slaves, as it was called, started to debate with him. They were Jews from Cyrene, Alexandria, Cilicia, and the province of Asia. [10]None of them could stand against the wisdom and the Spirit with which Stephen spoke.

¹¹Then they secretly induced men to say, "We have heard him speak blasphemous words against Moses and *against* God." ¹²And they stirred up the people, the elders and the scribes, and they came up to him and dragged him away and brought him ªbefore the ᵇCouncil. ¹³They put forward false witnesses who said, "This man incessantly speaks against this holy place and the Law; ¹⁴for we have heard him say that this Nazarene, Jesus, will destroy this place and alter the customs which Moses handed down to us." ¹⁵And fixing their gaze on him, all who were sitting in the ªCouncil saw his face like the face of an angel.

⁷:¹The high priest said, "Are these things so?"

²And he said, "Hear me, brethren and fathers! The God of glory appeared to our father Abraham when he was in Mesopotamia, before he lived in ªHaran, ³and said to him, 'LEAVE YOUR COUNTRY AND YOUR RELATIVES, AND COME INTO THE LAND THAT I WILL SHOW YOU.' ⁴Then he left the land of the Chaldeans and settled in ªHaran. From there, after his father died, *God* had him move to this country in which you are now living. ⁵But He gave him no inheritance in it, not even a foot of ground, and *yet,* even when he had no child, He promised that HE WOULD GIVE IT TO HIM AS A POSSESSION, AND TO HIS DESCENDANTS AFTER HIM. ⁶But God spoke to this effect, that his DESCENDANTS WOULD BE ALIENS IN A FOREIGN LAND, AND THAT THEY WOULD ªBE ENSLAVED AND MISTREATED FOR FOUR HUNDRED YEARS. ⁷ 'AND WHATEVER NATION TO WHICH THEY WILL BE IN BONDAGE I MYSELF WILL JUDGE,' said God, 'AND AFTER THAT THEY WILL COME OUT AND ªSERVE ME IN THIS PLACE.' ⁸And He gave him ªthe covenant of circumcision; and

¹¹So they persuaded some men to lie about Stephen, saying, "We heard him blaspheme Moses, and even God." ¹²This roused the people, the elders, and the teachers of religious law. So they arrested Stephen and brought him before the high council.*

¹³The lying witnesses said, "This man is always speaking against the holy Temple and against the law of Moses. ¹⁴We have heard him say that this Jesus of Nazareth* will destroy the Temple and change the customs Moses handed down to us."

¹⁵At this point everyone in the high council stared at Stephen, because his face became as bright as an angel's.

⁷:¹Then the high priest asked Stephen, "Are these accusations true?"

²This was Stephen's reply: "Brothers and fathers, listen to me. Our glorious God appeared to our ancestor Abraham in Mesopotamia before he settled in Haran.* ³God told him, 'Leave your native land and your relatives, and come into the land that I will show you.'* ⁴So Abraham left the land of the Chaldeans and lived in Haran until his father died. Then God brought him here to the land where you now live.

⁵"But God gave him no inheritance here, not even one square foot of land. God did promise, however, that eventually the whole land would belong to Abraham and his descendants—even though he had no children yet. ⁶God also told him that his descendants would live in a foreign land, where they would be oppressed as slaves for 400 years. ⁷'But I will punish the nation that enslaves them,' God said, 'and in the end they will come out and worship me here in this place.'*

⁸"God also gave Abraham the covenant of circumcision at that time. So when Abraham became the

so *Abraham* became the father of Isaac, and circumcised him on the eighth day; and Isaac *became the father of* Jacob, and Jacob *of* the twelve patriarchs.

⁹ "The patriarchs became jealous of Joseph and sold him into Egypt. *Yet* God was with him, ¹⁰ and rescued him from all his afflictions, and granted him favor and wisdom in the sight of Pharaoh, king of Egypt, and he made him governor over Egypt and all his household.

¹¹ "Now a famine came over all Egypt and Canaan, and great affliction *with it,* and our fathers ᵃcould find no food. ¹² But when Jacob heard that there was grain in Egypt, he sent our fathers *there* the first time. ¹³ On the second *visit* Joseph ᵃmade himself known to his brothers, and Joseph's family was disclosed to Pharaoh. ¹⁴ Then Joseph sent *word* and invited Jacob his father and all his relatives to come to him, seventy-five ᵃpersons *in all.* ¹⁵ And Jacob went down to Egypt and *there* he and our fathers died. ¹⁶ *From there* they were removed to ᵃShechem and laid in the tomb which Abraham had purchased for a sum of money from the sons of ᵇHamor in ᵃShechem.

¹⁷ "But as the time of the promise was approaching which God had assured to Abraham, the people increased and multiplied in Egypt, ¹⁸ until THERE AROSE ANOTHER KING OVER EGYPT WHO KNEW NOTHING ABOUT JOSEPH. ¹⁹ It was he who took shrewd advantage of our race and mistreated our fathers so that they would ᵃexpose their infants and they would not survive. ²⁰ It was at this time that Moses was born; and he was lovely ᵃin the sight of God, and he was nurtured three months in his father's home. ²¹ And after he had been set outside, Pharaoh's daughter

father of Isaac, he circumcised him on the eighth day. And the practice was continued when Isaac became the father of Jacob, and when Jacob became the father of the twelve patriarchs of the Israelite nation.

⁹ "These patriarchs were jealous of their brother Joseph, and they sold him to be a slave in Egypt. But God was with him ¹⁰ and rescued him from all his troubles. And God gave him favor before Pharaoh, king of Egypt. God also gave Joseph unusual wisdom, so that Pharaoh appointed him governor over all of Egypt and put him in charge of the palace.

¹¹ "But a famine came upon Egypt and Canaan. There was great misery, and our ancestors ran out of food. ¹² Jacob heard that there was still grain in Egypt, so he sent his sons—our ancestors—to buy some. ¹³ The second time they went, Joseph revealed his identity to his brothers,* and they were introduced to Pharaoh. ¹⁴ Then Joseph sent for his father, Jacob, and all his relatives to come to Egypt, seventy-five persons in all. ¹⁵ So Jacob went to Egypt. He died there, as did our ancestors. ¹⁶ Their bodies were taken to Shechem and buried in the tomb Abraham had bought for a certain price from Hamor's sons in Shechem.

¹⁷ "As the time drew near when God would fulfill his promise to Abraham, the number of our people in Egypt greatly increased. ¹⁸ But then a new king came to the throne of Egypt who knew nothing about Joseph. ¹⁹ This king exploited our people and oppressed them, forcing parents to abandon their newborn babies so they would die.

²⁰ "At that time Moses was born—a beautiful child in God's eyes. His parents cared for him at home for three months. ²¹ When they had to abandon him, Pharaoh's daughter

NASB

[a]took him away and nurtured him as her own son. 22 Moses was educated in all the learning of the Egyptians, and he was a man of power in words and deeds. 23 But when he was approaching the age of forty, it entered his [a]mind to visit his brethren, the sons of Israel. 24 And when he saw one *of them* being treated unjustly, he defended him and took vengeance for the oppressed by striking down the Egyptian. 25 And he supposed that his brethren understood that God was granting them [a]deliverance [b]through him, but they did not understand. 26 On the following day he appeared to them as they were fighting together, and he tried to reconcile them in peace, saying, 'Men, you are brethren, why do you injure one another?' 27 But the one who was injuring his neighbor pushed him away, saying, 'WHO MADE YOU A RULER AND JUDGE OVER US? 28 YOU DO NOT MEAN TO KILL ME AS YOU KILLED THE EGYPTIAN YESTERDAY, DO YOU?' 29 At this remark, MOSES FLED AND BECAME AN ALIEN IN THE LAND OF [a]MIDIAN, where he became the father of two sons.

30 "After forty years had passed, AN ANGEL APPEARED TO HIM IN THE WILDERNESS OF MOUNT Sinai, IN THE FLAME OF A BURNING THORN BUSH. 31 When Moses saw it, he marveled at the sight; and as he approached to look *more* closely, there came the voice of the Lord: 32 'I AM THE GOD OF YOUR FATHERS, THE GOD OF ABRAHAM AND ISAAC AND JACOB.' Moses shook with fear and would not venture to look. 33 BUT THE LORD SAID TO HIM, 'TAKE OFF THE SANDALS FROM YOUR FEET, FOR THE PLACE ON WHICH YOU ARE STANDING IS HOLY GROUND. 34 I HAVE CERTAINLY SEEN THE OPPRESSION OF MY PEOPLE IN EGYPT AND HAVE HEARD THEIR GROANS, AND I HAVE COME DOWN TO RESCUE

NLT

adopted him and raised him as her own son. 22 Moses was taught all the wisdom of the Egyptians, and he was powerful in both speech and action.

23 "One day when Moses was forty years old, he decided to visit his relatives, the people of Israel. 24 He saw an Egyptian mistreating an Israelite. So Moses came to the man's defense and avenged him, killing the Egyptian. 25 Moses assumed his fellow Israelites would realize that God had sent him to rescue them, but they didn't.

26 "The next day he visited them again and saw two men of Israel fighting. He tried to be a peacemaker. 'Men,' he said, 'you are brothers. Why are you fighting each other?'

27 "But the man in the wrong pushed Moses aside. 'Who made you a ruler and judge over us?' he asked. 28 'Are you going to kill me as you killed that Egyptian yesterday?' 29 When Moses heard that, he fled the country and lived as a foreigner in the land of Midian. There his two sons were born.

30 "Forty years later, in the desert near Mount Sinai, an angel appeared to Moses in the flame of a burning bush. 31 When Moses saw it, he was amazed at the sight. As he went to take a closer look, the voice of the LORD called out to him, 32 'I am the God of your ancestors—the God of Abraham, Isaac, and Jacob.' Moses shook with terror and did not dare to look.

33 "Then the LORD said to him, 'Take off your sandals, for you are standing on holy ground. 34 I have certainly seen the oppression of my people in Egypt. I have heard their groans and have come down to

THEM; ᵃCOME NOW, AND I WILL SEND YOU TO EGYPT.'

35 "This Moses whom they disowned, saying, 'WHO MADE YOU A RULER AND A JUDGE?' is the one whom God ᵃsent *to be* both a ruler and a deliverer with the ᵇhelp of the angel who appeared to him in the thorn bush. 36 This man led them out, performing wonders and ᵃsigns in the land of Egypt and in the Red Sea and in the wilderness for forty years. 37 This is the Moses who said to the sons of Israel, 'GOD WILL RAISE UP FOR YOU A PROPHET ᵃLIKE ME FROM YOUR BRETHREN.' 38 This is the one who was in the ᵃcongregation in the wilderness together with the angel who was speaking to him on Mount Sinai, and *who was* with our fathers; and he received living oracles to pass on to you. 39 Our fathers were unwilling to be obedient to him, but repudiated him and in their hearts turned back to Egypt, 40 SAYING TO AARON, 'MAKE FOR US GODS WHO WILL GO BEFORE US; FOR THIS MOSES WHO LED US OUT OF THE LAND OF EGYPT—WE DO NOT KNOW WHAT HAPPENED TO HIM.' 41 ᵃAt that time they made a ᵇcalf and brought a sacrifice to the idol, and were rejoicing in the works of their hands. 42 But God turned away and delivered them up to ᵃserve the ᵇhost of heaven; as it is written in the book of the prophets, 'IT WAS NOT TO ME THAT YOU OFFERED VICTIMS AND SACRIFICES FORTY YEARS IN THE WILDERNESS, WAS IT, O HOUSE OF ISRAEL? 43 YOU ALSO TOOK ALONG THE TABERNACLE OF MOLOCH AND THE STAR OF THE GOD ᵃROMPHA, THE IMAGES WHICH YOU MADE TO WORSHIP. I ALSO WILL REMOVE YOU BEYOND BABYLON.'

rescue them. Now go, for I am sending you back to Egypt.'*

35 "So God sent back the same man his people had previously rejected when they demanded, 'Who made you a ruler and judge over us?' Through the angel who appeared to him in the burning bush, God sent Moses to be their ruler and savior. 36 And by means of many wonders and miraculous signs, he led them out of Egypt, through the Red Sea, and through the wilderness for forty years.

37 "Moses himself told the people of Israel, 'God will raise up for you a Prophet like me from among your own people.'* 38 Moses was with our ancestors, the assembly of God's people in the wilderness, when the angel spoke to him at Mount Sinai. And there Moses received life-giving words to pass on to us.*

39 "But our ancestors refused to listen to Moses. They rejected him and wanted to return to Egypt. 40 They told Aaron, 'Make us some gods who can lead us, for we don't know what has become of this Moses, who brought us out of Egypt.' 41 So they made an idol shaped like a calf, and they sacrificed to it and celebrated over this thing they had made. 42 Then God turned away from them and abandoned them to serve the stars of heaven as their gods! In the book of the prophets it is written,

'Was it to me you were bringing
    sacrifices and offerings
  during those forty years in the
    wilderness, Israel?
43 No, you carried your pagan
    gods—
  the shrine of Molech,
  the star of your god Rephan,
  and the images you made to
    worship them.
So I will send you into exile
  as far away as Babylon.'*

⁴⁴"Our fathers had the tabernacle of testimony in the wilderness, just as He who spoke to Moses directed *him* to make it according to the pattern which he had seen. ⁴⁵And having received it in their turn, our fathers brought it in with ªJoshua upon dispossessing the ᵇnations whom God drove out before our fathers, until the time of David. ⁴⁶*David* found favor in God's sight, and asked that he might find a dwelling place for the ªGod of Jacob. ⁴⁷But it was Solomon who built a house for Him. ⁴⁸However, the Most High does not dwell in *houses* made by *human* hands; as the prophet says:

⁴⁹ 'HEAVEN IS MY THRONE,
AND EARTH IS THE FOOTSTOOL OF
MY FEET;
WHAT KIND OF HOUSE WILL YOU
BUILD FOR ME?' says the
Lord,
'OR WHAT PLACE IS THERE FOR MY
REPOSE?
⁵⁰ 'WAS IT NOT MY HAND WHICH
MADE ALL THESE THINGS?'

⁵¹"You men who are stiff-necked and uncircumcised in heart and ears are always resisting the Holy Spirit; you are doing just as your fathers did. ⁵²Which one of the prophets did your fathers not persecute? They killed those who had previously announced the coming of the Righteous One, whose betrayers and murderers you have now become; ⁵³you who received the law as ordained by angels, and *yet* did not keep it."

⁵⁴Now when they heard this, they were cut to the quick, and they *began* gnashing their teeth at him. ⁵⁵But being full of the Holy Spirit, he gazed intently into heaven and saw the glory of God, and Jesus standing at the right hand of God; ⁵⁶and he said, "Behold, I see the heavens opened

⁴⁴"Our ancestors carried the Tabernacle* with them through the wilderness. It was constructed according to the plan God had shown to Moses. ⁴⁵Years later, when Joshua led our ancestors in battle against the nations that God drove out of this land, the Tabernacle was taken with them into their new territory. And it stayed there until the time of King David. ⁴⁶"David found favor with God and asked for the privilege of building a permanent Temple for the God of Jacob.* ⁴⁷But it was Solomon who actually built it. ⁴⁸However, the Most High doesn't live in temples made by human hands. As the prophet says,

⁴⁹ 'Heaven is my throne,
and the earth is my footstool.
Could you build me a temple as
good as that?'
asks the LORD.
'Could you build me such a
resting place?
⁵⁰ Didn't my hands make both
heaven and earth?'*

⁵¹"You stubborn people! You are heathen* at heart and deaf to the truth. Must you forever resist the Holy Spirit? That's what your ancestors did, and so do you! ⁵²Name one prophet your ancestors didn't persecute! They even killed the ones who predicted the coming of the Righteous One—the Messiah whom you betrayed and murdered. ⁵³You deliberately disobeyed God's law, even though you received it from the hands of angels."

⁵⁴The Jewish leaders were infuriated by Stephen's accusation, and they shook their fists at him in rage.* ⁵⁵But Stephen, full of the Holy Spirit, gazed steadily into heaven and saw the glory of God, and he saw Jesus standing in the place of honor at God's right hand. ⁵⁶And he told them, "Look, I see the heavens opened and

up and the Son of Man standing at the right hand of God." ⁵⁷But they cried out with a loud voice, and covered their ears and rushed at him with one impulse. ⁵⁸When they had driven him out of the city, they *began* stoning *him;* and the witnesses laid aside their robes at the feet of a young man named Saul. ⁵⁹They went on stoning Stephen as he called on *the Lord* and said, "Lord Jesus, receive my spirit!" ⁶⁰Then falling on his knees, he cried out with a loud voice, "Lord, do not hold this sin against them!" Having said this, he ᵃfell asleep.

the Son of Man standing in the place of honor at God's right hand!"

⁵⁷Then they put their hands over their ears and began shouting. They rushed at him ⁵⁸and dragged him out of the city and began to stone him. His accusers took off their coats and laid them at the feet of a young man named Saul.*

⁵⁹As they stoned him, Stephen prayed, "Lord Jesus, receive my spirit." ⁶⁰He fell to his knees, shouting, "Lord, don't charge them with this sin!" And with that, he died.

6:8 ᵃOr *attesting miracles* 6:9 ᵃI.e. west coast province of Asia Minor 6:12 ᵃLit *into* ᵇOr *Sanhedrin* 6:15 ᵃOr *Sanhedrin* 7:2 ᵃGr *Charran* 7:4 ᵃGr *Charran* 7:6 ᵃLit *enslave them and mistreat them* 7:7 ᵃOr *worship* 7:8 ᵃOr *a* 7:11 ᵃLit *were not finding* 7:13 ᵃOr *was made known* 7:14 ᵃLit *souls* 7:16 ᵃGr *Sychem* ᵇGr *Emmor* 7:19 ᵃOr *put out to die* 7:20 ᵃLit *to God* 7:21 ᵃOr *adopted him* 7:23 ᵃLit *heart* 7:25 ᵃOr *salvation* ᵇLit *through his hand* 7:29 ᵃGr *Madiam* 7:34 ᵃLit *and now come!* 7:35 ᵃLit *has sent* ᵇLit *hand* 7:36 ᵃOr *attesting miracles* 7:37 ᵃOr *as* He raised up *me* 7:38 ᵃGr *ekklesia* 7:41 ᵃLit *in those days* ᵇOr *young bull* 7:42 ᵃOr *worship* ᵇI.e. heavenly bodies 7:43 ᵃOther mss spell it: *Romphan*, or *Rempham*, or *Raiphan*, or *Rephan* 7:45 ᵃGr *Jesus* ᵇOr *Gentiles* 7:46 ᵃThe earliest mss read *house* instead of *God;* the Septuagint reads *God* 7:60 ᵃI.e. died

6:12 Greek *Sanhedrin;* also in 6:15. 6:14 Or *Jesus the Nazarene.* 7:2 *Mesopotamia* was the region now called Iraq. *Haran* was a city in what is now called Syria. 7:3 Gen 12:1. 7:5-7 Gen 12:7; 15:13-14; Exod 3:12. 7:13 Other manuscripts read *Joseph was recognized by his brothers.* 7:31-34 Exod 3:5-10. 7:37 Deut 18:15. 7:38 Some manuscripts read *to you.* 7:42-43 Amos 5:25-27 (Greek version). 7:44 Greek *the tent of witness.* 7:46 Some manuscripts read *the house of Jacob.* 7:49-50 Isa 66:1-2. 7:51 Greek *uncircumcised.* 7:54 Greek *they were grinding their teeth against him.* 7:58 *Saul* is later called Paul; see 13:9.

Reading this segment of Scripture is like standing on hallowed ground before a fallen hero's monument. As I read about the first martyr's last stand, I can see the entire tragic scene in my mind's eye. I see a man looking death in the face yet humbly submitted to truths he refuses to deny. I hear the shouting of enraged religious leaders against the calm reasoning of a man constrained and upheld by truth. I can feel the rumble of pent-up pride and hatred ready to roll down on a man simply for holding his own in a debate.

This is not just any inquisition by any tribunal, however. History records the final words of many brave souls facing certain death for their convictions. Luke includes this trial in his record of church history because this moment will mark a turning point. Perpetrated by evil men yet foreordained by God, this tragedy established a pattern that would define church growth for centuries to come.

— 6:8-10 —

To read the entire story of Stephen, which begins in Acts 6:5, you would think he came from a long line of great preachers. We don't actually know a lot about his background. But we do know that he was a part of the seven men chosen to serve the believers so the apostles could focus on teaching. In faith, Stephen submitted himself to the direction of the Holy Spirit and worked to serve the church. This is exactly the kind of faithful Christian God loves to use to do big things. Stephen took his faith seriously, and he yielded to the Holy Spirit's control. That's what it means to be "full" in this way. Consequently, he was able to perform supernatural feats—"wonders and signs" (*teras* [5059] and *sēmeion* [4592])—to validate his preaching as authentically from God (6:8).

According to the Jerusalem Talmud, 480 synagogues existed in and around Jerusalem before being destroyed by Vespasian along with the temple in the first century.[35] Of course, that number could be an exaggeration.[36] In any case, among the various synagogues that were in Jerusalem was one called "the Synagogue of the Freedmen," whose members began to oppose Stephen (6:9). "Freedmen" (*Libertinos* [3032]) were former slaves who had purchased their freedom or were set free. The Roman general Pompey had taken many Jews as prisoners of war and turned them into slaves, only to release them later. They may have returned to Judea and established a synagogue for mutual support.[37] According to Luke, the "freedmen" came from three very different parts of the empire, all along the arc of the Mediterranean. Cyrene and Alexandria were on the Mediterranean coast of North Africa; Cilicia lay just north of Syrian Antioch; and moving west from there, the province of Asia lay between the Mediterranean, the Aegean, and the Black Seas (see 6:9).

Synagogues not only held services for worship and teaching, but they also served as community centers where people met socially.[38] This made them ideal locations to discuss theology. Stephen and the other believers regularly frequented synagogues, looking for opportunities to testify about Jesus the Messiah and His resurrection from the dead. Stephen quickly demonstrated a remarkable ability to debate, which infuriated these freedmen (6:10).

— 6:11-15 —

Unable to refute Stephen's wisdom in theological debate, the Jewish freedmen urged their peers to break the ninth commandment, "You shall not bear false witness against your neighbor" (Exod. 20:16). The

Greek term rendered "secretly induced" (Acts 6:11; *hypoballō* [5260]) appears only here in the New Testament. The expression implies a coercion that occurs by way of money or favors. We might say, "They paid off a few guys to falsify their testimony."

They charged Stephen with blasphemy (6:11; *blasphēmos* [989]), a term that means "cursing," "slandering," or "treating someone with contempt." Blasphemy is any manner of speech that disregards or disrespects the value of someone. Earlier, the religious leaders used the same claim to charge Jesus (Matt. 26:59-65; Mark 14:55-64). In the end, however, they couldn't trap Jesus with lies; they eventually convicted Him with the truth: He claimed to be the Son of God (Matt. 26:63-65; Mark 14:61-64). That pattern was about to repeat itself.

Stephen's enemies engaged in a deliberate, sustained campaign of slander, working from the bottom of the religious hierarchy up (Acts 6:12): "the people . . . the elders . . . the scribes . . . the Council" (i.e., the Sanhedrin). The specific charge said Stephen spoke against the temple ("this holy place"), the same initial charge brought against Jesus. In addition, Stephen's opponents tacked on a charge of blasphemy against the Law of Moses (Acts 6:11). At Jesus' trial, the testimony about the temple was a half-truth, which deliberately twisted the context of a lesson Jesus had given in the temple after one of His many confrontations with Annas's illegal racket involving the money changers (Luke 19:45-47). The religious authorities—puppets of the powerful godfather of Jerusalem—challenged Jesus, asking, "What sign do You show us as your authority for doing these things?" (John 2:18). In other words, "We have the authority of the high priest; who authorizes *your* actions?" Jesus answered the question with a prediction that claimed both authority and superiority over the temple.

> Jesus answered them, "Destroy this temple, and in three days I will raise it up." The Jews then said, "It took forty-six years to build this temple, and will You raise it up in three days?" But He was speaking of the temple of His body. (John 2:19-21)

Apparently, this same issue came up during one of Stephen's many discussions in the synagogue. Just like before, the enemies of Christ twisted the testimony to support a charge of blasphemy. Nestled in their web of lies, however, lay one element of truth. Jesus did indeed come to "alter the customs which Moses handed down to us" (Acts 6:14). That much was true—but not in the way these men characterized His mission.

Luke describes Stephen's face as "like the face of an angel" (6:15). Unfortunately, we have no way of knowing what this means. The phrase may describe something supernaturally literal, like the unsettling glow Moses wore after his encounter with God (Exod. 34:29-35). Or perhaps Luke meant that Stephen had a look of serene confidence. Similar descriptions appear in the accounts of notable martyrs, such as the story of Polycarp: "He was inspired with courage and joy, and his face was filled with grace, so that not only did he not collapse in fright at the things that were said to him, but on the contrary the proconsul was astonished."[39] Regardless, Stephen didn't show anxiety or guilt, what the religious leaders typically saw on the faces of indicted men.

— 7:1 —

The high priest was Caiaphas, the son-in-law of Annas. His question, "Are these things so?" could be seen as improper; the rules clearly stated that no defendant could be compelled to testify against himself[40] and that he had a right to representation.[41] Indeed, the question would have been pointless if they had followed the rules of testimony, which required that the testimony of two or three witnesses be in perfect alignment (Deut. 17:6; 19:15). Furthermore, witnesses for the prosecution were to be examined and cross-examined extensively (Deut. 19:16-20; cf. Mishnah *Sanhedrin* 4:1), leaving no room for doubt.

On the other hand, the high priest might simply have used the question to give Stephen an opportunity to speak on his own behalf.

Imagine yourself standing before the most powerful and influential officials in your country's government. Evidence has been presented that makes you appear guilty of a capital crime, for which the sentence of death will be carried out before sundown. These officials have the power to decide whether you live or die, and if you die, how quick or how painful your death will be. Your next words will determine what happens next. Do you feel the pressure of Stephen's situation?

Stephen looked at his circumstances and, instead of feeling the pressure to save his own life, saw a once-in-a-lifetime opportunity. For a few precious moments, he was given the undivided attention of the most powerful and influential men in Jerusalem. Rather than waste those critical moments pleading for his life or refuting the false testimonies of Christ's enemies, he chose to say what Israel's leaders needed to hear. He preached a sermon that established three points simultaneously:

- The apex of God's progressive plan is not the temple; Christ and His kingdom is.
- God has blessed Israel throughout its history, regardless of whether it had a temple.
- Israel has a long history of attempting to frustrate God's plan and has *always* consisted of two groups: the righteous and the rebellious.

Keep these points in mind as Stephen traces the history of Israel from Abraham to the moment he delivered his sermon.

— 7:2-8 —

Abraham

Even though Stephen was a Hellenist—Jew by birth but Greek by culture—he addressed the Sanhedrin as "brethren and fathers" (7:2). He then began rehearsing their shared history, repeatedly calling the biblical patriarchs "our fathers." In fact, he used a version of this phrase just under a dozen times.[42] But in his indictment of the leaders, he would call the *apostate* men of history "*your* fathers" (7:52).

In this first section (7:2-8), Stephen demonstrates that God initiated the relationship with Israel when He chose Abraham. He told this patriarch to leave his country and his relatives for a land yet to be revealed (7:3; cf. Gen. 12:1). Abraham initially traveled only as far as Haran, a city on the northern edge of his country, taking his father along with him. We also know he took his nephew Lot. Eventually, however, Abraham made it to Canaan, which God revealed as the "land of promise" (Heb. 11:9). The Lord didn't give the land to Abraham right away; that promise would be fulfilled in time, to be received by his descendants. In the meantime, as a token of the covenant, the Lord instituted the rite of circumcision—an outward symbol of His covenant with Abraham.

Abraham fathered Isaac. Isaac fathered Jacob, who was renamed Israel. Jacob fathered twelve sons, who would become the forebears of the twelve tribes of Israel.

— 7:9-16 —

Joseph

Ten of the patriarchs sold their brother into slavery, so he was carried off to Egypt and forgotten, maligned, and mistreated. But Joseph waited on God to deliver him, and eventually God used the evil intentions of Joseph's brothers to fulfill His own plan for Israel. God protected the forebears of the Hebrew nation by elevating Joseph to the position of prime minister in Egypt, just under Pharaoh, so that he could provide shelter for his people during a severe famine. For the next four hundred years, the nation of Israel mushroomed in a protected and fertile region of Egypt.

Note the sovereign grace of God to fulfill His covenant with Abraham despite the rebellion of the majority.

— 7:17-35 —

Moses

The Lord gave such prosperity and protection to the Israelites in Egypt that the Egyptians began to fear them, and their hosts became their captors. But God raised up a deliverer named Moses and used the Egyptians to equip the boy for leadership. In other words, the Lord used the Egyptians to prepare the man who would eventually confront their sin, warn them of God's wrath, exhort them to obey, and then liberate God's people. But Moses only obeyed in part; he tried to become the liberator of Israel apart from the power or direction of God. Meanwhile, the people of Israel rejected their savior.

Note the partial obedience, the obstinacy of the people, and the progressive fulfillment of God's plan.

— 7:36-45 —

Exodus

After forty years, the Lord commissioned Moses to liberate the people of Israel from their captors and lead them to the land He had promised to Abraham. But the Israelites left captivity dragging their feet, carrying along the idols they had worshiped in Egypt, bickering with their savior, Moses, and even constructing new idols along the way. Even so, the Lord continued to protect and provide for His people, leading them to the land He had originally promised to Abraham. Eventually, God led the Israelites into Canaan, gave them the ability to conquer the inhabitants, and helped them establish themselves. This included giving them specific instructions on how to build the tabernacle for worshiping the true God who had delivered them from Egypt. During this time, Moses promised Israel a prophet (Deut. 18:15), a man from among them who would be God's spokesman and representative—the Messiah.

Note the partial obedience, the rebellion of the majority, God's grace despite the Israelites' sin, and the progressive fulfillment of His covenant with Abraham.

— 7:46-50 —

David and Solomon

Though they never fully possessed the land God had promised to Abraham, Israel's glory peaked with King David and his son Solomon. Until Solomon's reign, Israel worshiped in the tabernacle. Now, through the greatness and prosperity of Solomon's kingdom, a permanent temple was established in Jerusalem. Nevertheless, after a split between the northern kingdom (Israel) and the southern kingdom (Judah), disobedience led to the destruction of Solomon's temple.

The Hebrews survived the Exile without a temple, and the temple built after their return suffered desecration, plunder, and the abuse of war over the next four hundred years. The magnificent temple Herod had constructed was fewer than fifty years old by the time of Stephen's sermon.

Even though Stephen's history barely touches on Solomon's temple, the Sanhedrin would have called to mind the history of the temple mount and the reason two previous buildings had suffered so terribly—Israel's rebellion. His quotation of Isaiah 66:1-2 in Acts 7:49-50 demonstrates that the Sanhedrin's reverence for a mere building was dramatically out of step with God's historic priorities and had caused them to rebel against God's leadership, embodied in Jesus the Messiah. God cares less about *where* His people worship than *how* they worship—"in spirit and truth" (John 4:23).

— 7:51-53 —

Indictment

Finally, Stephen's sermon comes to the real issue at hand. The next couple of lines in Isaiah's oracle read, "But to this one I will look, to him who is humble and contrite of spirit, and who trembles at My word" (Isa. 66:2). The religious leaders had elevated the temple building to almost idol status, yet they continued to rebel against the God they claimed to worship. Stephen's description, "stiff-necked and uncircumcised in heart and ears" (Acts 7:51) used familiar imagery to invalidate their identity as Jews.[43] He declared their outward religion a sinister form of rebellion that aligned them with the rebellious factions that had opposed God's plan throughout Israel's history.

Note Stephen's switch from "our fathers" to "your fathers" (7:51).[44] At the mention of the Messiah, he no longer identified them as brothers. They killed their Messiah to preserve the temple, from which they derived their power. Stephen and the other believers, on the other hand,

131

embraced Jesus as their Messiah and drew their power from the Holy Spirit, not a temporal building or a corrupt institution.

— 7:54 —

When confronted with sin, the guilty sometimes repent; more often, however, they respond with rage. And if you want to enrage the heart of a religious person, talk about his or her sin.

"Cut to the quick" represents a Greek term that literally means "to saw through" (*diapriō* [1282]). Figuratively, this refers to their visceral fury at being cut to the heart, emphasizing the depth of their rage. Indeed, Stephen's opponents were so infuriated that they ground their teeth at him.

— 7:55-56 —

For a fourth time, Luke describes Stephen as completely yielded to the control of God's Spirit (cf. 6:3, 5, 8). In response to the seething fury of the Sanhedrin, Stephen calmly focused on his Savior and narrated the vision he witnessed. His claiming to see Jesus "standing at the right hand of God" recalls Psalm 110:1: "The LORD says to my Lord: 'Sit at My right hand until I make Your enemies a footstool for Your feet.'" Caiaphas and his cronies would have recognized the phrase not only as a messianic psalm, but it may have even rekindled in their minds the similar words Jesus had quoted at His own trial before the same Sanhedrin:

> The high priest said to Him, "I adjure You by the living God, that You tell us whether You are the Christ, the Son of God." Jesus said to him, "You have said it yourself; nevertheless I tell you, hereafter you will see THE SON OF MAN SITTING AT THE RIGHT HAND OF POWER, and COMING ON THE CLOUDS OF HEAVEN."
>
> Then the high priest tore his robes and said, "He has blasphemed! What further need do we have of witnesses? Behold, you have now heard the blasphemy; what do you think?" They answered, "He deserves death!" (Matt. 26:63-66; cf. Dan. 7:13-14)

— 7:57-58 —

When danger rises up against righteousness, the Lord offers courage, not necessarily escape. The Sanhedrin had already broken several of its rules of jurisprudence (according to Mishnah *Sanhedrin* 4.1-2):[45]

- Capital cases were to follow a strict order, with arguments by the defense followed by arguments for conviction.

- All Sanhedrin judges could argue for acquittal, but not all could argue for conviction.
- Voting for conviction and sentencing in a capital case was to be conducted individually, beginning with the youngest so that younger members would not be influenced by the voting of the elder members.
- The members of the Sanhedrin were to meet in pairs all night, discuss the case, and reconvene for the purpose of confirming the final verdict and imposing the sentence.
- Sentencing in a capital case was not to occur until the following day.

The august assembly of Israel's finest minds and most respected statesmen turned into a lynch mob. They rushed Stephen, swept him to the outskirts of town—in strict keeping with Jewish law, of course (Lev. 24:14-16)—and executed him as a heretic.

At this point, Luke introduces a new figure to the narrative—Saul, a Pharisee from Tarsus, the star pupil of Gamaliel, and possibly even the clandestine instigator of the trial. This is just a theory, but I think it is more than plausible. Luke's narrative implies that Saul led a conspiracy from the shadows, acting on behalf of the high priest, who in turn answered to Annas, the godfather of Jerusalem. The corrupt temple officials and religious hard-liners shared a common enemy: the church. When they couldn't intimidate the apostles, they set out to discredit the followers of Jesus as enemies of Judaism. Saul didn't play an official role in the case—neither as prosecutor nor as witness—yet Luke underscores the young Pharisee's presence during the events. According to Jewish law, the witnesses against the accused were to cast the first stones (Deut. 17:7). Before taking up their stones, these witnesses laid their outer garments at the feet of Saul (Acts 7:58).

— 7:59-60 —

Stoning was the traditional form of execution in Israel. Stoning is, by its very nature, a communal form of capital punishment because no one can be assigned blame or credit for dealing the death blow. It's also a slow form of death. During his agonizing last moments, Stephen responded to his tormentors as Jesus did on the cross (Luke 23:34, 46); he asked the Lord to receive his spirit, and he forgave his executioners. The text speaks with a view to resurrection when it says that Stephen "fell asleep" (Acts 7:60). Once separated from life on earth, the Christian receives an immediate welcome in heaven.

Tertullian, an early church theologian, said that the blood of the martyrs is the seed of the church.[46] The Sanhedrin's attempt to stamp out the church failed to do anything but spread the gospel farther. Like the wind carrying seeds, the fury of the Sanhedrin scattered the disciples of the risen Messiah. Far from exterminating Christianity, the council merely prompted the fulfillment of Christ's prediction. Jesus had promised His followers, "You shall be My witnesses both in Jerusalem [stage 1], and in all Judea and Samaria [stage 2], and even to the remotest part of the earth [stage 3]" (1:8).

Stephen's stoning became the defining moment in the church as the second stage of the Lord's plan went into effect.

APPLICATION: ACTS 6:8–7:60

The Godly under Pressure

Acts 7 records for posterity the testimony of the first Christian martyr. Stephen may have been the first documented instance of a believer dying for his total devotion to Christ, but he wouldn't be the last. Since that time, history has been punctuated with periods of persecution in which men and women have given their lives for their faith. Stephen's example of a godly man under extreme pressure by the authorities leads me to a couple of practical reminders as we face our own pressures for living godly lives in a world increasingly hostile to God's standards of truth and righteousness.

First, *when you walk with Christ, the world will usually resent it, not support it.* We have unrealistic expectations if we think the secular school or college we attend is going to rejoice that we're walking with the Lord. And those in your workplace, family, or circle of friends who are offended by the positions you take on issues of faith or morality will often oppose you, not politely disagree with you.

You see, when confronted with the reality of their sinfulness by seeing it in the mirror of a testimony of righteousness, the world will be enraged, not receptive. Acts 7:54 says, "When [the Jewish leaders] heard this, they were cut to the quick." They were riddled with conviction. Their reaction was visceral and audible—they began gnashing their teeth at him!

Why do we so often expect to be applauded, respected, or at least politely disagreed with when it comes to our countercultural Christian convictions? Let the warning of Christ prepare you to persevere under increasing pressure from the world around you: "If the world hates you, you know that it has hated Me before it hated you. If you were of the world, the world would love its own; but because you are not of the world, but I chose you out of the world, because of this the world hates you" (John 15:18-19).

Second, *when you respond with truth, the pressure will increase, not decrease.* After the Sanhedrin gnashed their teeth at Stephen, our hero of the faith didn't seek the best legal representation to defend his personal religious rights, fight back with either physical or rhetorical weapons, or back down from his convictions to keep the peace. Instead, he proved to be personally empowered by and devoted to the triune God: "But being full of the Holy Spirit, he gazed intently into heaven and saw the glory of God, and Jesus standing at the right hand of God; and he said, 'Behold, I see the heavens opened up and the Son of Man standing at the right hand of God'" (Acts 7:55-56).

How did the rulers respond? They screamed, covered their ears, and rushed upon Stephen with an impulse to kill (7:57). In fact, they drove him out of the city and proceeded to stone him. Think of that! Those executioners were seemingly good, righteous people, but they nevertheless picked up stones to stone him. They dragged him out of the city and began pummeling his body with stones. And these were the *religious* leaders . . . those who had been taught from early on "Thou shalt not kill!" If those who claimed to be devoted to God were treating His witnesses this way, imagine what the enemies of God and all that's good will do.

Actually, we don't have to imagine. We have countless examples throughout history of the godly being put under pressure and keeping the faith.

So be ready! We must always be prepared to respond with godliness to the ungodly, even when it means losing comfort, reputation, friends, family, freedom, or even our very lives!

THE RISE OF THE CHURCH (ACTS 8:1-12:25)

Human nature abhors change, yet we cannot live without it. The fact is, our bodies and brains need a certain amount of stress to keep us moving, growing, and adapting. Without something to inspire creativity and to challenge our survival instincts, our muscles would atrophy and our brains would turn to mush. Fortunately, the only constant in our world is change. The tension created between turbulence and our desperate need to restore equilibrium forces us to grow stronger and wiser. And sometimes coping with change requires a complete overhaul of our worldview, a dramatic exchange of one perspective for another.

In the early 1960s, Thomas Kuhn gave this drastic change of perspective a name. We now call it a "paradigm shift."[1] This occurs when a scientist or researcher cannot make sense of data using conventional perspectives. When scientists finally tire of stretching the old models to fit the new shape of information, a new way of thinking is born, and humanity takes a leap forward. But paradigm shifts are painful—like all significant changes. Those receiving the gift of a new worldview experience deep distress and often painful self-doubt: "Am I crazy for thinking this way?" They frequently endure the stinging rejection of peers as they take their tentative first steps toward a new frontier of thought. Theirs is a world of misunderstanding until other minds become receptive and a fresh generation begins to embrace the new paradigm.

The book of Acts documents the dramatic changes the first Christians faced. This particular section represents some of the most difficult and painful changes of all. The martyrdom of Stephen became a watershed moment in the life of the church—and in the progression of God's plan.

Instead of stifling the message of salvation, persecution dispersed the good news like pollen in the wind. As the believers spread from Jerusalem, the Lord's plan (1:8) entered its second stage, with Samaritans (8:15) and Gentiles (10:44-48) receiving the Holy Spirit. Peter thus came to embrace the new paradigm (11:1-18). Meanwhile, Saul, who had approved of Stephen's execution, was converted and commissioned to proclaim Christ to the Gentiles (9:1-31), for a time joining Christians in Antioch who had also begun telling Greeks the gospel message (11:19-26).

Until this time, all of Jesus' followers—numbering in the tens of thousands—were Jewish, and the epicenter of Christianity was the temple. These believers had inherited a covenant in which God selected Abraham, gave him and his descendants a piece of land, blessed them, and promised to make of them a great nation. He established Israel in that part of the world to be a light to other nations, a theocracy situated at the crossroads of civilization, ordained as a priestly nation whose purpose was to bring the world under the dominion of God as King. Furthermore, God promised the Hebrew people a Messiah, a supernatural King who would establish a kingdom that would grow to overtake the entire planet as nation after nation bent the knee to this King and became His citizens. The Jewish believers in Jerusalem had embraced Jesus as this celebrated monarch.

While these Jesus-following Hebrews fully expected to share the fellowship of the Holy Spirit with Gentiles, they *thought* they understood the process of expansion. In their minds, Gentiles would come into the church of the Messiah through the door of Judaism. Like the Gentile proselyte Nicolas (6:5), all non-Jewish individuals would embrace the Law of Moses, participate in the temple rites, submit to baptism and circumcision to become "sons of the covenant," accept Jesus as their Messiah, and receive the Holy Spirit. That is how everyone thus far had come into the fellowship of the saints. The coming months, however, would force them to see things differently. Stephen's death set the church on a path to a paradigm shift, led by the most devoutly steadfast Jew in the church, Peter.

The other first Christians were Jewish and couldn't imagine how ignorant, unclean, idolatrous people could become citizens of God's kingdom apart from His covenant with Abraham. Besides the theological issues, Jews had cultivated a generations-long disgust with all things Gentile: how they ate, what they touched, who they contacted, where they worked—every aspect of non-Jewish life prompted aversion. Then Peter became the Lord's anti-prejudice project.

After a disturbing vision, Peter was sent to preach in a quintessentially "unclean" home so he could personally observe the Lord's acceptance of Gentile believers. He saw a repeat of Pentecost in Caesarea. The Old Testament promise of the Holy Spirit was fulfilled in people the Jews considered outsiders. Now, however, God had spoken; His Spirit filled kosher and "unclean" equally and without prejudice. No one could deny the acceptance of Gentiles into the kingdom of God.

KEY TERMS IN ACTS 8:1–12:25

kēryssō (κηρύσσω) [2784] "to preach," "to proclaim," "to be a herald"

This word generally describes making official, public proclamations such as those announcing royal decrees, public festivals and fasts, and military actions. Such uses appear in the Septuagint (e.g., Exod. 32:5; 36:6; 2 Chr. 20:3), along with less frequent uses for proclamations of judgment (e.g., Jon. 3:2) and for the call of the lady wisdom (Prov. 1:21; 8:1; 9:3). Thus in the New Testament we often read of commissioned messengers proclaiming the good news of the Messiah's kingdom.

euangelizō (εὐαγγελίζω) [2097] "to evangelize," "to tell good news," "to announce," "to proclaim"

In the secular sphere, this verb was used for the action of an official messenger bringing good news, such as an update on the progress of battle, the birth of a royal, or the pending arrival of the king. The New Testament carries over the ideas of liberation and victory, applying this word specifically to preaching salvation in Jesus Christ. Of the fifty-four times this verb appears in the New Testament, almost half occur in Luke and Acts (ten times in Luke and fifteen in Acts). The majority of the other instances can be found in the letters of Luke's mentor, Paul (twenty-one times).

mathētēs (μαθητής) [3101] "disciple," "student," "follower"

A *mathētēs* is one who subjects him- or herself to a process of becoming familiarized with, experiencing, learning, or receiving direction about something. This usually implied the aid of another person, and as the term fully developed, it became inconceivable for one to be a learner without a guide or a master. The term is used to refer to the disciples of rabbis and of John the Baptizer, the Pharisees, and Moses (e.g., Mark 2:18; John 9:28). Throughout Acts, Luke uses the term for those following Jesus as their Master (e.g., Acts 6:1), though not all had yet heard the complete gospel (19:1-5).

metanoeō (μετανοέω) [3340] "to repent," "to change one's mind or purpose," "to regret," "to be converted"

A word with a well-known general meaning can take on a very specific, technical meaning within a particular community. In secular Greek, this verb means, "to change one's thinking," "to regret," or "to have remorse." Within the Gospels, however, it almost exclusively carries the idea of being reconciled to God after turning away from sin.[2] Therefore, in Luke and Acts, when one repents, one is saved, converted, and added to the ranks of genuine believers. In Acts, the related noun form *metanoia* [3341] usually describes an ongoing state of mind and indicates that someone is in right relationship with God.

> *peritomē* (περιτομή) [4061] "circumcision," "a circumcised one," "one among the circumcised"
>
> This Greek noun derives from the verb meaning "to cut around" and describes the Hebrew rite in which the foreskin of a male is cut away. As instituted by God (Gen. 17:10), this ritual identified the male as a participant in God's covenant with Abraham. In time, this distinguishing feature became symbolic of the people, the covenant, and the culture. Eventually, many Jews thought the circumcised state itself entitled one to blessings from God and salvation from divine judgment (Acts 15:1). In Acts, the place of this covenantal sign in the church becomes a point of tension as uncircumcised Gentiles come to faith in the Messiah (11:1-18; 15:1-35).

The Pure and the Phony
ACTS 8:1-24

NASB

¹Saul was in hearty agreement with putting him to death.

And on that day a great persecution ᵃbegan against the church in Jerusalem, and they were all scattered throughout the regions of Judea and Samaria, except the apostles. ²*Some* devout men buried Stephen, and made loud lamentation over him. ³But Saul *began* ravaging the church, entering house after house, and dragging off men and women, he would put them in prison.

⁴Therefore, those who had been scattered went about ᵃpreaching the word. ⁵Philip went down to the city of Samaria and *began* proclaiming ᵃChrist to them. ⁶The crowds with one accord were giving attention to what was said by Philip, as they heard and saw the ᵃsigns which he was performing. ⁷For *in the case of* many who had unclean spirits, they were coming out *of them* shouting with a loud voice; and many who had been paralyzed and lame were healed. ⁸So there was much rejoicing in that city.

⁹Now there was a man named Simon, who formerly was practicing

NLT

¹Saul was one of the witnesses, and he agreed completely with the killing of Stephen.

A great wave of persecution began that day, sweeping over the church in Jerusalem; and all the believers except the apostles were scattered through the regions of Judea and Samaria. ²(Some devout men came and buried Stephen with great mourning.) ³But Saul was going everywhere to destroy the church. He went from house to house, dragging out both men and women to throw them into prison.

⁴But the believers who were scattered preached the Good News about Jesus wherever they went. ⁵Philip, for example, went to the city of Samaria and told the people there about the Messiah. ⁶Crowds listened intently to Philip because they were eager to hear his message and see the miraculous signs he did. ⁷Many evil* spirits were cast out, screaming as they left their victims. And many who had been paralyzed or lame were healed. ⁸So there was great joy in that city.

⁹A man named Simon had been a sorcerer there for many years,

NASB

magic in the city and astonishing the people of Samaria, claiming to be someone great; [10]and they all, from smallest to greatest, were giving attention to him, saying, "This man is what is called the Great Power of God." [11]And they were giving him attention because he had for a long time astonished them with his magic arts. [12]But when they believed Philip preaching the good news about the kingdom of God and the name of Jesus Christ, they were being baptized, men and women alike. [13]Even Simon himself believed; and after being baptized, he continued on with Philip, and as he observed signs and great miracles taking place, he was constantly amazed.

[14]Now when the apostles in Jerusalem heard that Samaria had received the word of God, they sent them Peter and John, [15]who came down and prayed for them that they might receive the Holy Spirit. [16]For He had not yet fallen upon any of them; they had simply been baptized [a]in the name of the Lord Jesus. [17]Then they *began* laying their hands on them, and they were receiving the Holy Spirit. [18]Now when Simon saw that the Spirit was bestowed through the laying on of the apostles' hands, he offered them money, [19]saying, "Give this authority to me as well, so that everyone on whom I lay my hands may receive the Holy Spirit." [20]But Peter said to him, "May your silver perish with you, because you thought you could obtain the gift of God with money! [21]You have no part or portion in this [a]matter, for your heart is not right before God. [22]Therefore repent of this wickedness of yours, and pray the Lord that, if possible, the intention of your heart may be forgiven you. [23]For I see that you are in the gall of bitterness and in the [a]bondage of iniquity." [24]But

NLT

amazing the people of Samaria and claiming to be someone great. [10]Everyone, from the least to the greatest, often spoke of him as "the Great One—the Power of God." [11]They listened closely to him because for a long time he had astounded them with his magic.

[12]But now the people believed Philip's message of Good News concerning the Kingdom of God and the name of Jesus Christ. As a result, many men and women were baptized. [13]Then Simon himself believed and was baptized. He began following Philip wherever he went, and he was amazed by the signs and great miracles Philip performed.

[14]When the apostles in Jerusalem heard that the people of Samaria had accepted God's message, they sent Peter and John there. [15]As soon as they arrived, they prayed for these new believers to receive the Holy Spirit. [16]The Holy Spirit had not yet come upon any of them, for they had only been baptized in the name of the Lord Jesus. [17]Then Peter and John laid their hands upon these believers, and they received the Holy Spirit.

[18]When Simon saw that the Spirit was given when the apostles laid their hands on people, he offered them money to buy this power. [19]"Let me have this power, too," he exclaimed, "so that when I lay my hands on people, they will receive the Holy Spirit!"

[20]But Peter replied, "May your money be destroyed with you for thinking God's gift can be bought! [21]You can have no part in this, for your heart is not right with God. [22]Repent of your wickedness and pray to the Lord. Perhaps he will forgive your evil thoughts, [23]for I can see that you are full of bitter jealousy and are held captive by sin."

[24]"Pray to the Lord for me," Simon

Simon answered and said, "Pray to the Lord for me yourselves, so that nothing of what you have said may come upon me."

exclaimed, "that these terrible things you've said won't happen to me!"

8:7 Greek *unclean*.

8:1 ªLit *occurred* 8:4 ªOr *bringing the good news of* 8:5 ªI.e. the Messiah 8:6 ªOr *attesting miracles* 8:16 ªLit *into* 8:21 ªOr *teaching*; lit *word* 8:23 ªLit *bond*

Tracing the history of the church in the book of Acts is like following a wounded deer through freshly fallen snow; pools of blood mark the trail from the Sanhedrin in Jerusalem to Nero in Rome. As the previous section came to a close, we witnessed the martyrdom of Stephen, whose final words, "Lord, do not hold this sin against them!" (7:60), were crushed and suffocated under a pile of rocks. As the enemies of God turned from the gruesome memorial of a faithful man, the church lost a great deacon, the saints lost a beloved brother, and heaven received a genuine hero.

Shortly after the martyrdom of this authentic, Spirit-filled believer, the gospel flowed down from the mountaintop city of Jerusalem into the surrounding valleys of Judea and then northward into Samaria. While many heard the good news of the risen Messiah and responded in genuine belief, not everyone embraced the gospel with good intentions. In this next segment, Luke brings us face to face with a phony. The contrast of Simon Magus to Stephen could not be starker.

— 8:1-4 —

The statement "Saul was in hearty agreement with putting [Stephen] to death" (8:1) is a pivotal sentence. It forms a hinge between the story of the church's expansion in Jerusalem and the expansion of the church beyond the city walls. Luke also uses this opportunity to introduce a man who would play a critical role in that expansion. His comment that "the witnesses laid aside their robes at the feet of a young man named Saul" (7:58) might otherwise pass as a curious detail. Instead, the name Saul headlines the sobering declaration "And on that day a great persecution began against the church in Jerusalem."

This "Saul of Tarsus" is better known to us today as "Paul the apostle." At this point in the story, however, he was to the Christians what Adolf Eichmann would become to the Jews of 1930s Germany—the architect of a holocaust. Driven by religious zeal, Saul determined to exterminate the followers of Jesus.

Few people in the twenty-first-century West have ever experienced religious persecution. We may endure a little mockery at school, a sarcastic slam at the office, some ruffled feathers in the neighborhood, but little more. It would be exceedingly revealing if persecution put our modern-day churches to the test. One wonders how many would quickly defect. Though the early believers fled, they did not defect.

Luke's summary passage (8:1-4) reassures the reader that Saul's campaign failed. Instead of wiping out the church, his efforts facilitated the plan of God. Stage one of God's plan saw the arrival of the Holy Spirit and the evangelization of Jerusalem; the believers had become His witnesses (2:1–7:60). The persecution became the catalyst for stage two: "Judea and Samaria" (cf. 1:8). As the rank-and-file Christians fanned out into the surrounding region, called Judea by the Romans, and filtered into the region called Samaria, they continued to proclaim the resurrected Jesus as the Messiah of Israel.

— 8:5 —

Luke's summary statement in 8:4 introduces a series of notable examples that make up the second major section of his narrative:

- Philip witnesses in Samaria (8:5-24)
- An Ethiopian envoy becomes a believer (8:25-40)
- Saul is converted by Christ (9:1-19)
- Saul begins to preach Christ (9:20-31)
- Peter ministers throughout Judea (9:32-43)
- Peter preaches to Gentiles (10:1-48)
- The apostles accept Gentile Christians as brothers and sisters (11:1-18)
- Gentile Christians in Syrian Antioch form a church (11:19-30)
- God vindicates Peter's ministry among the Gentiles (12:1-25)

This first episode involves one of the seven original deacons (6:5), a man named Philip, who left the persecution in Jerusalem (where the apostles remained; 8:1) and then began to preach the gospel in the region called Samaria. Luke refers specifically to "the city of Samaria," the old capital of the northern kingdom (1 Kgs. 16:24) and a place long associated with religious compromise and bitter contention with Jerusalem. It would be no exaggeration to say that Jews hated Samaritans as idolatrous half-breeds—ethnically polluted, religiously confused, and morally debased. This prejudice ran deep. During a particularly dark period in Israel's history (glimpses of which are seen in Ezra 4),

A BRIEF HISTORY OF SAMARIA

ACTS 8:5

Originally, the Hebrew nation settled the Promised Land and thrived for several centuries as twelve tribes united by worship at one tabernacle, located in Shiloh, about 10 miles from Mount Gerizim. Eventually, Solomon, Israel's third king, constructed a permanent temple in Jerusalem.

Shortly after Solomon's death, the northern ten tribes rejected the legitimate successor to the throne, chose an idolatrous rebel general to lead them, formed a separate nation, and claimed the name Israel for themselves. The southern tribes of Benjamin and Judah remained loyal to Solomon's son and became known as Judah. North and South fought intermittently for the next two hundred years, until Israel was distracted by repeated assaults from the Assyrian kings Pul (2 Kgs. 15:19-20; 1 Chr. 5:26) and Tiglath-pileser (2 Kgs. 15:29; Isa. 9:1). Finally, Shalmaneser (2 Kgs. 17:3-6) and his successor, Sargon, finished off Israel by deporting the northern tribes and intermarrying them with other conquered nations, virtually breeding them out of existence. After 721 BC, only a small remnant of the Israelite tribes remained in the northern territory, and most of them had begun to intermarry with Gentiles.

After the people of Judah were exiled to Babylon (606–587 BC) and later returned under the leadership of Ezra and Nehemiah, they found the northern region inhabited by Samaritans, people of mixed Hebrew and Gentile heritage. The returning people of Judah by then had become known as Jews. Tensions mounted when the Samaritans opposed the rebuilding of Jerusalem and the temple, and the final breach occurred when the Samaritans built their own temple on Mount Gerizim, claiming it, not Jerusalem, to be the authentic place of worship. This temple was destroyed by the Jewish high priest John Hyrcanus in 128 BC,[3] and its location was, like that of the Jerusalem temple, further desecrated by Emperor Hadrian's erection of pagan shrines in the second century AD.

the Hebrew inhabitants of this region intermarried with Gentiles and established their own temple on Mount Gerizim to rival the one in Jerusalem (cf. John 4:20). This temple was destroyed by the Jewish high priest John Hyrcanus in 128 BC.[4] Most Jews would not risk uncleanness by setting foot on Samaritan soil and would not have expected a warm welcome there.

None of this deterred Philip. God has a missionary heart that beats for the whole world. He doesn't see half-breeds. He doesn't see Gentiles. He sees lost people in need of rescue. Sadly, none of the early believers entered Samaria with the gospel until persecution forced the church out of its comfort zone. Regardless, Philip decided to proclaim Christ to the people most despised in Jerusalem.

— 8:6-8 —

The central theme of true evangelism is the message of Jesus Christ. An authentically Christian ministry must have Christ as the sole object of worship and devotion. Philip didn't talk about the past, he didn't argue about the location of the temple (cf. John 4:20), and he didn't defend the superiority of Jewish theology. He preached Christ and ministered to the people. His message was accompanied by "signs" (miraculous evidence of authentic divine teaching) and recalled the earthly ministry of Jesus because the infirm were healed and demons were cast out (Acts 8:7). Many of the Samaritans must have remembered the ministry of Jesus (cf. John 4:39-42); in any case, they responded to Philip's ministry with rejoicing (Acts 8:8).

— 8:9-11 —

Like technology today, "the practice of magic was omnipresent in classical antiquity."[5] And like our near addiction to the convenience of smartphones and tablets, Wi-Fi devices and laptops, dependence on magicians and their magical props in the first century was epidemic. From superstitious curses to supernatural cures, people from every social class were exposed to the magic arts. One historian summarizes what most pagans believed about these practitioners: "Magicians had a direct link to the divine world, and magic was seen as a gift from the gods."[6] These peddlers of falsehood commonly gained fear, respect, admiration, and money through their sleight of hand and deceptive illusions.

Enter Simon the Samaritan, often called by Christian historians in the ancient church Simon Magus or Simon the Magician. He had become an expert in the magic arts. It's possible that Simon had purchased secrets and performed tricks that could easily have been repeated by a modern-day illusionist. However, given the context of Acts and the prevalence of conflict with spirits of wickedness, it's just as possible that Simon "astonished" people with supernatural power (8:9, 11)—not the power of God, but the power of demons. In either case, Simon didn't give God credit for the miracles; he claimed it for himself, allowing people to call him "the Great Power of God" (8:10). This curious phrase essentially calls Simon a visible manifestation of God, or at least a demigod. Regardless, he undoubtedly appeared humble and magnanimous when hailed as something more than mere human, but you can be certain he didn't object—unlike Paul and Barnabas (cf. 14:11-15).

— 8:12-13 —

When Philip arrived with the ability to "astonish" with power from the true God—not to create fear and respect for himself, but to demonstrate that God validated his teaching—people responded in droves. He preached the gospel and they believed; he pointed them toward the resurrected Jesus and they embraced Him as Messiah. As an outward symbol of their belief, the people submitted to water baptism.

Luke says plainly, "Simon himself believed" (8:13). He expects us to take that statement at face value; after all, Philip didn't doubt the man's authenticity. Simon was baptized in water and then followed Philip like a disciple, observing the deacon's ministry of preaching, healing, and casting out demons. Luke describes Simon as "constantly amazed," the imperfect tense of *existēmi* [1839]—he was "out of his senses."

It should be noted that Luke doesn't mention the Holy Spirit in conjunction with any of the conversions in Samaria. In itself, that isn't significant; Luke sometimes omits any mention of the Holy Spirit (2:37-41; 4:4; 5:14) even when the context implies that the believers were filled. In this case, the believers didn't receive the Holy Spirit right away (8:15-16), for reasons that will become clear shortly.

— 8:14-19 —

The apostles in Jerusalem were not present at the time of the Samaritans' conversion, so they sent Peter and John to join Philip. Upon their arrival, they prayed and laid their hands on the new believers, at which time they received the Holy Spirit (8:14-17). Luke depicts Simon as an observer, not a participant—which is notable—and he describes the magician's perspective. To Simon, it appeared that Peter and John had bestowed the Holy Spirit on them, a serious misunderstanding.[7] God didn't bring the apostles to Samaria to *bestow* the Holy Spirit but to *witness* the Samaritans receiving the Holy Spirit. The Lord delayed the falling of the Holy Spirit for the apostles' benefit, to assure them that He had accepted the Samaritans' belief and had made them full-fledged brothers and sisters in the kingdom.

At last, we see that Simon had not received the Holy Spirit because he had not genuinely believed. This becomes evident in his viewing the power of the Holy Spirit the same way he had used magic—real or illusion—for selfish gain. In fact, his understanding of the gospel was so far off, he actually asked to purchase the Holy Spirit's power!

— 8:20-23 —

Peter's response to Simon appears much harsher in the original Greek. The word for "perish" (8:20) refers to the total destruction of something, its utter ruin. He said, in effect, "May your money follow you into hell, because that's where you're headed!" But Peter didn't condemn Simon to hell or even wish his destruction. He merely expressed his contempt for Simon's offer while warning the man that eternal destruction lay in his future. The apostle urged Simon to repent—"if possible" (8:22).

The Greek phrase for "if possible" is *ei ara* [1488, 686], which is less tentative than the English rendering implies. "If possible" implies less than fifty-fifty odds, whereas *ei ara* implies near certainty if an effort is made. Then, in Acts 17:27, Paul told the Athenians that God created people for relationship with Himself so that "*if perhaps* they might grope for Him" they might "find Him, though He is not far from each one of us" (emphasis mine). The phrase here implies that seeking God almost certainly results in finding Him.

Peter's warning holds out the possibility that Simon's desire for God might have been smothered by his own envy and pride. The "gall of bitterness" (8:23) is a vivid metaphor for someone who is "deeply envious or resentful of someone." Being in the "bondage of iniquity" could be paraphrased "handcuffed to wrongdoing," implying that Simon's capacity for free choice had been so compromised by his dependence upon evil that he could not escape without help. In other words, if one seeks repentance, God will certainly grant it; the question is whether Simon actually wanted to repent.

— 8:24 —

Simon's reply appears genuine, at least on the surface. Peter called for Simon's repentance. Simon asked for Peter's intercession before God on his behalf, but he still didn't "get it." No one can do our repenting for us. We must repent all on our own. Our loved ones can pray for us, but they cannot pray us out of our destiny. Each of us will stand before God accountable for our own decision in response to His call for repentance.

According to Irenaeus (around AD 180), Simon became the father of "all sorts of heresies,"[8] not the least of which was a kind of proto-Gnosticism. According to Irenaeus and others, he also laid the intellectual foundation for the false teachings of Cerdo and Marcion.[9] His precise role in the formation of later false teachings is debatable, but this fact seems certain: He did not become a genuine believer in the Lord Jesus Christ.

Faith That Saves

ACTS 8:13

Simon the Magician believed and was baptized, yet his attitudes and actions demonstrate that he clearly was not born again. Obviously, God expects something more than mere intellectual assent in conversion. So what kind of faith is "saving faith"?

Saving faith—the kind of belief God accepts as genuine and for which He grants the gift of His Spirit—is more than accepting as fact the historical personage of Christ. To accept the fact that a man named Jesus lived at some point in time and later died on a cross is merely a starting point. Furthermore, genuine belief must do more than admire Jesus or emulate Him or follow His teachings. It's not even enough to venerate Jesus as more than human.

Those kinds of belief make for a good beginning. But the kind of belief to which we have been called encompasses much more. First, the Greek term pisteuō [4100] means "to believe," that is, to acknowledge the truthfulness of a claim—that it corresponds with reality. When I say that I believe the book of Luke, I mean to say that I accept its content as truth. To believe in Christ is, first, to accept what He says as truth. Second, and more importantly, pisteuō means "to trust," "to rely upon," or "to derive confidence in" something or someone. When I say I believe in Jesus Christ, I declare that I trust Him, I rely upon Him, I have placed my complete confidence in Him; everything I know about this life and whatever occurs after death depends upon His claims about Himself and my positive response to His offer of grace.

That is what God accepts as genuine faith, the kind that grants a person eternal life, fills him or her with the Holy Spirit, and begins an internal transformation.

APPLICATION: ACTS 8:1-24

How to Spot a Phony

Luke's chronicle of the early church has given us many examples of what genuine Christian ministry looks like. In this segment of his narrative, we have an opportunity to compare and contrast authentic ministry and phony religious scams.

In Philip's ministry, we see three qualities of genuine ministry flowing from the power of the Holy Spirit.

First, we see *the centrality of Jesus Christ in the message* (8:4-5). Not any other leader. Not a philosophical system or a regimen of activities. Not even a specific doctrine, regardless of how important or valid the teaching. The central focus of all worship, instruction, fellowship, and expression must be our living Leader and Lord, Jesus Christ. If the ministry continually points followers toward Christ, giving Him all the glory, you can rest assured that it's of God.

Second, *a dynamic of liberating power* (8:6-7). People find freedom from their bondage to sin. Philip healed and cast out demons with the power of God, not to create fear in the people or to establish himself as the village shaman, but to grant freedom. His power authenticated his message as divine in origin and pointed people toward God, not himself. As the people gained freedom from their illnesses, they accepted the message of freedom from the bondage of sin. Genuine Christian ministries create and encourage freedom for the followers of Christ.

Finally, *a contagious joy* (8:8). The city rejoiced as a result of Philip's preaching, teaching, and healing. They weren't saddled with a list of responsibilities or duties to perform. The new believers didn't become dour, dark, moody captives of a rigid system of thinking and behaving. They rejoiced in their freedom; they experienced a happiness and contentment like never before.

The activity of Simon Magus, on the other hand, illustrates several characteristics of a phony ministry. I see at least four.

1. *The ministry exalts a person rather than Christ.* You've got trouble when you're in a system (or a church) that exalts a person other than the person of Christ. Simon came on the scene and made exclusive claims to inspire devotion to himself. Spiritualists, magicians, and witch doctors have done this for millennia, creating fear in the community to

establish themselves as the sole intermediaries between the spiritual and physical realms. Even today, I see men and women putting on modern-day "magic healing shows," and while they pretend to give God the glory, they cleverly establish themselves as the "go-to people" for healing and instruction.

2. *The ministry draws a following with promises to solve temporal problems.* Watch out for any ministry that promises to solve your financial, physical, relational, and emotional problems. Authentic Christianity can certainly make life better all around; obedience to the Lord and His transforming Holy Spirit can work amazing wonders. But no particular ministry can make those hard-and-fast claims. God grants healing and blessings and wisdom and freedom directly. You have a direct line to Him through prayer, and He will deal with you personally. You don't need to send money. You don't have to purchase a cloth or oil or water or books or any other token. And you certainly don't need some particular person claiming great power to pray for you.

3. *The ministry exercises a counterfeit power.* Beware the magic shows of some television evangelists; they peddle their counterfeit power for donations. The "supernatural" exhibitions of faith healers convince no one but the gullible. They perform their illusions in very controlled environments, and either their "healings" are limited to mild improvements or they claim results difficult to verify.

The miracles of the Bible, like the healing of the beggar in Acts 3, had an immediate and visible impact; no one could deny their truth. The signs and wonders described in Scripture left no room for doubt by even the most ardent skeptics of the day. Nothing we see today fits this category of genuine miraculous activity.

4. *The ministry demonstrates a preoccupation with the material rather than the spiritual.* In phony ministries, you'll hear a lot of talk about money, material wealth, buildings, private planes, and special equipment, but very little about what purposes they serve. All ministries need certain things to accomplish their missions, but authentic Christian ministries keep spiritual matters primary; for them, physical things serve spiritual purposes. For example, a ministry might want to raise money to purchase a building. If it's a genuine ministry, the primary beneficiaries of the building will be the people the ministry serves.

Listen to the ministry leader carefully. Pay attention to what is said—and left unsaid. If the vast majority of his or her instruction concerns physical issues, such as health and money, beware!

A Divine Appointment
ACTS 8:25-40

NASB

[25] So, when they had solemnly testified and spoken the word of the Lord, they started back to Jerusalem, and were preaching the gospel to many villages of the Samaritans.

[26] But an angel of the Lord spoke to Philip saying, "Get up and go south to the road that descends from Jerusalem to Gaza." ([a]This is a desert *road.*) [27] So he got up and went; and there was an Ethiopian eunuch, a court official of Candace, queen of the Ethiopians, who was in charge of all her treasure; and he had come to Jerusalem to worship, [28] and he was returning and sitting in his [a]chariot, and was reading the prophet Isaiah. [29] Then the Spirit said to Philip, "Go up and join this [a]chariot." [30] Philip ran up and heard him reading Isaiah the prophet, and said, "Do you understand what you are reading?" [31] And he said, "Well, how could I, unless someone guides me?" And he invited Philip to come up and sit with him. [32] Now the passage of Scripture which he was reading was this:

> "HE WAS LED AS A SHEEP TO
> SLAUGHTER;
> AND AS A LAMB BEFORE ITS
> SHEARER IS SILENT,
> SO HE DOES NOT OPEN HIS
> MOUTH.
> [33] "IN HUMILIATION HIS JUDGMENT
> WAS TAKEN AWAY;
> WHO WILL [a]RELATE HIS
> [b]GENERATION?
> FOR HIS LIFE IS REMOVED FROM
> THE EARTH."

[34] The eunuch answered Philip and said, "Please *tell me,* of whom does the prophet say this? Of himself or of someone else?" [35] Then Philip opened his mouth, and beginning

NLT

[25] After testifying and preaching the word of the Lord in Samaria, Peter and John returned to Jerusalem. And they stopped in many Samaritan villages along the way to preach the Good News.

[26] As for Philip, an angel of the Lord said to him, "Go south* down the desert road that runs from Jerusalem to Gaza." [27] So he started out, and he met the treasurer of Ethiopia, a eunuch of great authority under the Kandake, the queen of Ethiopia. The eunuch had gone to Jerusalem to worship, [28] and he was now returning. Seated in his carriage, he was reading aloud from the book of the prophet Isaiah.

[29] The Holy Spirit said to Philip, "Go over and walk along beside the carriage."

[30] Philip ran over and heard the man reading from the prophet Isaiah. Philip asked, "Do you understand what you are reading?"

[31] The man replied, "How can I, unless someone instructs me?" And he urged Philip to come up into the carriage and sit with him. [32] The passage of Scripture he had been reading was this:

> "He was led like a sheep to the
> slaughter.
> And as a lamb is silent before
> the shearers,
> he did not open his mouth.
> [33] He was humiliated and received
> no justice.
> Who can speak of his
> descendants?
> For his life was taken from the
> earth."*

[34] The eunuch asked Philip, "Tell me, was the prophet talking about himself or someone else?" [35] So beginning with this same Scripture,

from this Scripture he preached Jesus to him. 36 As they went along the road they came to some water; and the eunuch said, "Look! Water! What prevents me from being baptized?" 37 [ªAnd Philip said, "If you believe with all your heart, you may." And he answered and said, "I believe that Jesus Christ is the Son of God."] 38 And he ordered the ªchariot to stop; and they both went down into the water, Philip as well as the eunuch, and he baptized him. 39 When they came up out of the water, the Spirit of the Lord snatched Philip away; and the eunuch no longer saw him, ªbut went on his way rejoicing. 40 But Philip ªfound himself at ᵇAzotus, and as he passed through he kept preaching the gospel to all the cities until he came to Caesarea.

8:26 ªOr This city is deserted 8:28 ªOr carriage
8:29 ªOr carriage 8:33 ªOr describe ᵇOr family
or origin 8:37 ªEarly mss do not contain this
v 8:38 ªOr carriage 8:39 ªLit for he was going
8:40 ªOr was found ᵇOT: Ashdod

Philip told him the Good News about Jesus.

36 As they rode along, they came to some water, and the eunuch said, "Look! There's some water! Why can't I be baptized?"* 38 He ordered the carriage to stop, and they went down into the water, and Philip baptized him.

39 When they came up out of the water, the Spirit of the Lord snatched Philip away. The eunuch never saw him again but went on his way rejoicing. 40 Meanwhile, Philip found himself farther north at the town of Azotus. He preached the Good News there and in every town along the way until he came to Caesarea.

8:26 Or Go at noon. 8:32-33 Isa 53:7-8 (Greek version). 8:36 Some manuscripts add verse 37, "You can," Philip answered, "if you believe with all your heart." And the eunuch replied, "I believe that Jesus Christ is the Son of God."

Being an effective witness for Christ is neither easy nor natural. God knows that. He understood the problem so well that He instructed the followers of Christ to remain still until they received divine power to help them achieve the difficult and to accomplish the supernatural. Only then could they become His witnesses at home, across town, and around the world (1:8).

Most of us struggle with our responsibility to be effective witnesses for Christ. We're hampered by fear, mostly of the unknown. We're discouraged by ignorance, worried that others will ask questions we can't answer or that we won't "get it right." And—let's face it—we're held back by indifference; we just don't care enough about others to tell them the most important news they'll ever hear. So, we ease our guilty consciences in all sorts of clever ways while avoiding the Lord's most direct command: "Be My witnesses" (1:8).

Philip the deacon is perhaps the finest example of personal, one-on-one evangelism we have in the book of Acts. We can learn a great deal from his encounter with an earnest traveler on a lonely road.

— 8:25-26 —

After Peter's ugly encounter with the phony Simon Magus, he and John returned to Jerusalem. On their way, the apostles took their time, stopping to preach and teach in Samaritan villages. Meanwhile, an angel appeared to Philip in Samaria and sent him to a road that led down from Jerusalem (2,500 feet above sea level) to the Mediterranean seaport of Gaza—a route that probably headed south from Jerusalem slightly before descending along a ridge toward the valley of Elah in the Judean hill country. Luke inserts a parenthetical comment that "this is a desert road" (8:26), meaning one unfrequented by people.

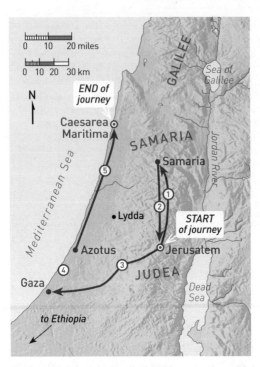

Bear in mind that the angel didn't tell Philip why. Furthermore, Philip didn't know whom he would meet. From a human perspective, the new orders didn't make sense. He was instructed to leave his extremely successful ministry among the many populated villages of Samaria for a lonely road in the remote hill country, a two-day journey south.

Philip's Ministry. God called Philip away from his ministry in Samaria to a road running southwest from Jerusalem, where he evangelized and baptized an Ethiopian official, probably before reaching Gaza. Philip was then "Spirited away" to continue preaching in Azotus, to the north.

— 8:27-28 —

Luke's simple, direct language reflects Philip's response: He obeyed immediately. Somewhere along the remote road, he saw an "Ethiopian eunuch" (8:27) from the country of ancient Nubia, which was also called Cush, north of present-day Ethiopia. The people of "Ethiopia" occupied the region between the Nile and the Red Sea, from Aswan in southern Egypt to Khartoum in present-day Sudan.

EXCURSUS: CAN I GET A WITNESS?

ACTS 8:35

I've seen a lot of evangelism methods used in my fifty-plus years of ministry. Some are better than others. I don't think there's any single method of sharing the gospel that works for all people at all times, but there are at least three models that everyone should *avoid*.

THE BOUNTY HUNTER

The bounty hunter wakes up in the morning all excited about explaining the basics of Christianity to anybody and everybody, regardless of the circumstances or people's interest level. Everybody he meets, he tells: the guy at the gas station, the woman in the grocery store, the delivery man at the office, the friend of a friend, the person in the next booth at the restaurant or sitting next to him on the plane. Ready or not, here he comes!

On the upside, the bounty hunter definitely gets results. By sheer force of numbers, a percentage does hear the gospel and respond. On the downside, how many are pushed away and become more resistant to the gospel as a result? That doesn't matter to the bounty hunter. He feels the end justifies the means and feels relieved of any guilt. In fact, many bounty hunters dismiss any concern for being offensive. They rationalize that "the message of Christ is offensive to an evil world," without stopping to think that *they* might be the offending element, not the gospel.

My friend Bob told me that the first person he ever saw witnessing was a girl he knew in high school. She wore out-of-date clothes—dark, long dresses, thick hose, and a little hat—and carried "a 4-ton Bible." She used to hide behind the lockers and, whenever someone would walk by, she'd jump out, shove a tract into their hands, and say, "Don't blame Jesus if you go to hell!"

Bob said, "I thought, *Fine, I won't blame Him!*"

Bounty hunters care more about decisions and numbers than changed lives and relationships.

THE EGGHEAD

Eggheads like what I call "the Ivy League approach." An egghead is the opposite of the bounty hunter in most ways. Rather than appear too eager or overly zealous, the intellectual witness says, "Let's discuss the world's religions." The egghead is an expert in apologetics but never gets to the bottom line: a decision to trust Christ.

The Ivy League approach has a few advantages. This method recognizes the broad spectrum of human opinions, seeks to understand other points of view, and cares to communicate the point through dialogue. It's educational. It's even stimulating to discover how one religion differs from another and how they're similar. Eggheads find more information to fill their already-crowded heads.

The disadvantage: It's reason-centered and rarely works. People don't generally come to know Christ because they lost a debate. The problem of sin isn't an intellectual problem; it's the result of rebellion against God. A decision for Christ is a crisis of the will. That's not to say apologetics doesn't have its place in evangelism. The effective use of reason helps demonstrate that Christianity is a reasonable faith.

(continued on next page)

That helps keep the entrance uncluttered. Then, once a person's heart becomes receptive to the gospel, apologetics can help clear away intellectual obstructions from the path to Christ.

THE SECRET AGENT

Truth be told, most of us are secret-agent Christians. These believers rationalize their lack of initiative by declaring themselves "silent witnesses for God." They hope their lifestyle will do all the talking. They're waiting for somebody to walk up and say, "Friend, I've been watching your life. And I'm interested in knowing how to receive Christ as my personal Savior. Do I receive Him by faith?" When that happens, the secret agent will tell the individual all about Christ and how to know Him personally. Problem is, that never happens.

I've heard people say, "Wait—which is more important to God, your life or your message?" That's like asking a pilot, "Which wing is more important, the left or the right?" A plane must have both, or it will never get off the ground.

The advantage of being a secret agent is that you never offend. This method also keeps you accountable to maintain a life of authenticity, integrity, kindness, and generosity. But this approach comes at the cost of a terrible disadvantage. It's a self-centered means of easing your conscience while shirking a solemn responsibility given by Christ.

Clearly, the best approach brings together the most effective elements of all three. Be transparent about your relationship with Jesus Christ and talk openly about your spiritual growth. Study other religions and engage people in thoughtful, respectful, and calm conversations, taking care to listen and to offer rational responses to questions. By all means, let your life do the talking—but not *all* the talking! At some point, once you have gained trust and have earned a fair hearing, get to the issue at hand: the need to repent of sin and to accept Christ's gift of eternal life.

A eunuch was a surgically castrated male. In some ancient Eastern civilizations, a man could volunteer for service in the palace on the condition that he surrender all or part of his genitals. Sometimes the procedure was quite brutal, and a significant number of volunteers didn't survive the trauma. In addition to demonstrating loyalty, castration also served a practical purpose: The surgery virtually eliminated the most common motives for treachery. Consequently, eunuchs became highly trusted servants of the court. In this case, the eunuch administered his nation's treasury.

Candace is not necessarily a personal name; it may have been a title, like Pharaoh, Dauphin, or Shah. According to some historians, the Nubians "regarded the sun as the father of their kings, and gave the title Candace to the mother."[10] Her authority was almost absolute, often greater than the king's. For what it's worth, her name might have been Amanitere, although the exact dates of her reign are in dispute.

Though the religion of the Nubians would have been just as pagan as that of their Egyptian neighbors, this eunuch had just worshiped in Jerusalem. Jewish law prevented eunuchs from becoming full-fledged "sons of the covenant" (cf. Deut. 23:1); nevertheless, this one was evidently quite committed and even owned a copy of the Scriptures. Hand-copied scrolls, meticulously produced by a Jewish scribe, cost a fortune. Everything about the man says he was a devout worshiper of the Hebrew God as well as a man of education and financial means.

On his way down the hill country in his carriage, he read from Isaiah 53. (The Greek term *harma* [716] indicates a two-wheeled vehicle pulled by horses, which came in two varieties, the military chariot and a traveler's carriage.) Other people may have been walking alongside the carriage, perhaps listening, when Philip ran to catch up.

— 8:29-31 —

It was not mere chance that the eunuch was there; the Holy Spirit had arranged a meeting. Luke doesn't tell us how the Holy Spirit spoke to Philip, but I lean toward his hearing an audible voice, not merely a thought in Philip's mind. Earlier an angel had instructed Philip (8:26). In addition, the events before and after the encounter display a distinctly supernatural character. Regardless, the Spirit directed Philip to approach the carriage. The eunuch had been reading aloud, as was the custom, so the deacon used this opportunity to open a conversation.

— 8:32-34 —

The portion of Isaiah read by the eunuch comes from the last of four "servant songs" (Isa. 42:1-4; 49:1-6; 50:4-9; 52:13–53:12), in which an anonymous servant of Yahweh acts on behalf of God's people. In this last song, the servant suffers punishment for the sins of his people, despite his personal innocence. The song suggests resurrection from the dead as a reward for his selfless sacrifice. The eunuch focuses on the climax of the servant's horrific suffering:

> He was oppressed and He was afflicted,
> Yet He did not open His mouth;
> Like a lamb that is led to slaughter,
> And like a sheep that is silent before its shearers,
> So He did not open His mouth.
> By oppression and judgment He was taken away;

And as for His generation, who considered
That He was cut off out of the land of the living
For the transgression of my people, to whom the stroke
was due? (Isa. 53:7-8)

The man asked an astute question: Who's the prophet describing? (Acts 8:34). Jewish theologians had been wrestling with the very same mystery for a long time. The Jews of Jesus' day thought of the Messiah as a warrior-king who would vanquish Israel's foes, lead them into prosperity, and rule from the throne of David forever. So they ruled out any thought of the Messiah being this Suffering Servant; after all, how could a dead man vanquish any foe or rule from any throne? No one in Jesus' day had considered the possibility that the Messiah might die to save His people and then rise from the dead apart from the general resurrection of the righteous to become their everlasting King.

— 8:35-37 —

Earlier, Jesus had identified the Suffering Servant as the Messiah and then claimed to be the fulfillment of this prophetic song (Luke 22:37; cf. Isa. 53:12). Like Peter, Philip "preached Jesus" (Acts 8:35; cf. 5:42). If he followed Peter's pattern, he showed that Jesus is the Christ, that He suffered the penalty of sin for the world, that He rose from the dead, and that He offers forgiveness to anyone who trusts in Him.

Luke's original manuscript almost certainly omits the details of the man's conversion. Acts 8:37 doesn't appear in any of the earliest manuscripts; it appears only in the "Western" family of manuscripts, so called because they originated in the Western Roman Empire. At some point, a scribe probably inserted the text because it seemed strange that the eunuch was baptized with no mention of his conversion.[11] Even though it's not original to Luke's text, the verse offers a glimpse of what the early church west of Rome thought about conversion. They clearly understood baptism to be a rite for believers only.[12] And the content of belief was relatively simple: that Jesus is the Christ, the Son of God.

— 8:38 —

Philip evidently took the eunuch's belief at face value. While they rode, the eunuch saw water and an opportunity for water baptism, and the deacon saw no objection. Luke's description strongly supports baptism by immersion in keeping with Jewish tradition; otherwise, there would have been no need for *both* of them to enter the water. Some suggest

EXCURSUS: TEXTUAL CRITICISM AND THE RELIABILITY OF THE SCRIPTURES

ACTS 8:37

I have always disliked the term "textual criticism." It suggests that experts in the field have dedicated their lives to criticizing the Bible until the text of Scripture is either meaningless or untrustworthy. Undoubtedly, some scholars have attempted to do just that. But many fine men and women pursue the true intent of textual criticism, which aims to ascertain which of the thousands of ancient manuscripts contain the original words the Bible's writers dutifully penned under the inspiration of the Holy Spirit.

As Paul, Luke, James, Peter, John, and other men in first-century Christianity wrote, the Holy Spirit prompted them to include all the information we would need to believe and obey God, and He kept them from error as they wrote. What emerged was divine truth, preserved in ink on papyrus. And because these words of the church's apostles and prophets were recognized as authoritative, prophetic truth, copyists made duplicates by hand for distribution to other churches. Then copies were made of these copies, and more copies were later produced from those copies. Before long, hundreds of copies circulated among the churches. Meanwhile, the papyrus of the original texts deteriorated.

The original scrolls are long gone now, and unfortunately, the process of copying was not perfect. An added word or phrase here, a dropped word there, some letters confused with others. Then those small errors in one manuscript became a part of every copy created from it. Occasionally, a scribe would inadvertently create an error by trying to correct an earlier mistake—or what he *thought* to be a mistake—thus propagating another "variant."

Many centuries later, we have uncovered more than five thousand manuscripts or fragments of manuscripts, all of them containing some portion of the original words of the New Testament.

A good example of this phenomenon recently showed up on bulletin boards all over the United States. Years ago, someone copied what I had written in a piece I titled "Attitudes." They typed it onto a sheet of paper in order to produce a rudimentary poster. Someone else liked it and copied it for a couple of friends, who displayed it on their bulletin boards. Later on, copies of those copies were handwritten and/or faxed and copied again. Before long, my original piece had been copied and faxed so many times that it was barely legible—the letters were blotched and smeared and faded. Yet very few people had difficulty reading the quote, even with missing letters and words.

Although there were of course no photocopiers, the original manuscripts went through a similar process and were treated with the greatest of care. Scribes were famously diligent; nevertheless, after hundreds of copies, some errors arose. While this manual copying system was less than perfect, it nevertheless preserved divine truth over the span of some two thousand years. The vast majority of errors are small and well known, so the meaning of the original text has not been affected. In cases where the meanings have been impacted, the sheer number of manuscripts makes it relatively easy to spot a mistake and correct it. And because most variants involve *additions* to the original text, the original wording is usually easy to determine.

(continued on next page)

Fortunately, we have the dedication and expertise of textual critics to analyze and compare thousands of ancient copies in order to recover the original text of Scripture. The Bibles we have today are extremely reliable copies of the original texts—as close to accurate as any church would have had back then—and all thanks to the efforts of diligent, godly scholars.

that the men could have entered the water where Philip could have poured or sprinkled the eunuch, but both men were familiar with the Jewish baptism of new converts, which required full immersion.

— 8:39-40 —

When the men emerged from the water, the Holy Spirit "snatched away" the deacon (8:39). The term used here, *harpazō* [726], means "to carry something away by force."[13] Luke leaves little room to see this in anything but literal terms. For reasons known only to the Holy Spirit, Philip disappeared from one place and then appeared somewhere else. Luke's choice of words implies that Philip's sudden removal came as a surprise to him; after getting his bearings, he realized that he had been taken 20 miles to Azotus.

From the eunuch's point of view, Philip simply vanished as soon as they emerged from the water (8:39). Nevertheless, he returned home "rejoicing," that is, in a state of happiness and well-being.

APPLICATION: ACTS 8:25-40
Guidelines for a Winning Witness

Philip's example offers several guidelines for how to avoid becoming an obnoxious witness, an ineffective witness, or an apathetic witness (the bounty hunter, the egghead, and the secret agent mentioned on pages 153–154). I find five helpful guidelines in the deacon's divinely appointed encounter with a stranger.

Guideline #1: Be sensitive.
Put yourself in Philip's sandals. Here he is in the midst of a super exciting ministry in Samaria, enjoying incredible success. Lives are being changed, families brought together, illnesses healed, and entire

villages turning to follow Jesus Christ. Suddenly, the Lord says, "Leave all of that and go to a lonely road in the middle of nowhere." Philip didn't argue or resist. He obeyed.

An effective witness maintains a sensitive heart, ready and willing to follow the Lord's prompting. Effective witnesses don't just suddenly arrive on the scene; they're led by the Holy Spirit, the same Lord who brings that other person alongside and creates an opportunity leading to an encounter.

Guideline #2: Be available.

Sensitivity has a twin named Availability. They always go together. You can't have one without the other. If you're sensitive to the leading of the Spirit, then you're available for obeying His prompting. Philip didn't question the Lord's decision to move him from large populations and great activity to a remote road; he simply obeyed. He recognized that kingdom building is God's enterprise; he was merely a laborer. Whether he worked in Samaria, Gaza, Azotus, or Caesarea, it didn't matter. He was available.

Guideline #3: Be proactive.

It takes initiative to break the silence barrier. We don't want to be obnoxious, but we can't always lie back and wait for people to ask us for help. They don't know what they don't know! Most are confused by the whole subject of religion and, therefore, tentative about beginning a conversation. So, connect on a personal level, looking for opportunities to address a need they might have. Answer questions or clear up misunderstandings while remaining transparent about your beliefs.

Philip saw an opportunity in the man's reading material. He asked a simple, unobtrusive, nonthreatening question: "Do you understand what you are reading?" (8:30).

Guideline #4: Be tactful.

D. James Kennedy illustrates the quality of tact this way:

> I once heard a man walk up to a woman and say, "How are your kidneys today?" That's the truth! I actually heard the man ask that question. Her response? Did she hit him with her purse? No, she said the following: "Oh, they're much better today, thank you, Doctor." I overheard those words in a hospital room. The doctor had earned the right to ask that personal question. If you doubt that, stop the next [woman] you meet on the street and ask it yourself, and see what happens.

All of which is to say, we need to earn the right to ask personal questions. We can do this by becoming a friend, by getting to know the people, by listening to what they have to say, by showing interest, by hearing them when they talk.[14]

Don't blame the lost person for being offended if you're offensive. That individual has every reason in the world to be offended. Earning the right to ask personal questions—and spiritual questions are among the most personal and sensitive of all—is the definition of tact.

Guideline #5: Be precise.

Beginning at that Scripture, Philip "preached Jesus to him" (8:35). Isn't that great? He didn't talk about comparative religion or evidence for intelligent design. He didn't discuss theological issues or social ills. There's a time and place for those discussions, but they are tangential to what is primary: Jesus Christ and how we are to respond to Him. While we must be tactful and address questions or objections, we must not talk around the central issue.

A Persecutor Turned Preacher
ACTS 9:1-22

NASB

[1] Now [a]Saul, still breathing [b]threats and murder against the disciples of the Lord, went to the high priest, [2] and asked for letters from him to the synagogues at Damascus, so that if he found any belonging to the Way, both men and women, he might bring them bound to Jerusalem. [3] As he was traveling, it happened that he was approaching Damascus, and suddenly a light from heaven flashed around him; [4] and he fell to the ground and heard a voice saying to him, "Saul, Saul, why are you persecuting Me?" [5] And he said, "Who are You, Lord?" And He *said,* "I am Jesus whom you are persecuting, [6] but get up and enter the city, and it

NLT

[1] Meanwhile, Saul was uttering threats with every breath and was eager to kill the Lord's followers.* So he went to the high priest. [2] He requested letters addressed to the synagogues in Damascus, asking for their cooperation in the arrest of any followers of the Way he found there. He wanted to bring them—both men and women—back to Jerusalem in chains.

[3] As he was approaching Damascus on this mission, a light from heaven suddenly shone down around him. [4] He fell to the ground and heard a voice saying to him, "Saul! Saul! Why are you persecuting me?"

[5] "Who are you, lord?" Saul asked.

And the voice replied, "I am Jesus, the one you are persecuting! [6] Now will be told you what you must do." [7] The men who traveled with him stood speechless, hearing the [a]voice but seeing no one. [8] Saul got up from the ground, and though his eyes were open, he [a]could see nothing; and leading him by the hand, they brought him into Damascus. [9] And he was three days without sight, and neither ate nor drank.

[10] Now there was a disciple at Damascus named Ananias; and the Lord said to him in a vision, "Ananias." And he said, "Here I am, Lord." [11] And the Lord *said* to him, "Get up and go to the street called Straight, and inquire at the house of Judas for a man from Tarsus named Saul, for he is praying, [12] and he has seen [a]in a vision a man named Ananias come in and lay his hands on him, so that he might regain his sight." [13] But Ananias answered, "Lord, I have heard from many about this man, how much harm he did to Your [a]saints at Jerusalem; [14] and here he has authority from the chief priests to bind all who call on Your name." [15] But the Lord said to him, "Go, for he is a chosen [a]instrument of Mine, to bear My name before the Gentiles and kings and the sons of Israel; [16] for I will show him how much he must suffer for My name's sake." [17] So Ananias departed and entered the house, and after laying his hands on him said, "Brother Saul, the Lord Jesus, who appeared to you on the road by which you were coming, has sent me so that you may regain your sight and be filled with the Holy Spirit." [18] And immediately there fell from his eyes something like scales, and he regained his sight, and he got up and was baptized; [19] and he took food and was strengthened.

Now for several days he was with the disciples who were at Damascus, [20] and immediately he *began* to

get up and go into the city, and you will be told what you must do."

[7] The men with Saul stood speechless, for they heard the sound of someone's voice but saw no one! [8] Saul picked himself up off the ground, but when he opened his eyes he was blind. So his companions led him by the hand to Damascus. [9] He remained there blind for three days and did not eat or drink.

[10] Now there was a believer* in Damascus named Ananias. The Lord spoke to him in a vision, calling, "Ananias!"

"Yes, Lord!" he replied.

[11] The Lord said, "Go over to Straight Street, to the house of Judas. When you get there, ask for a man from Tarsus named Saul. He is praying to me right now. [12] I have shown him a vision of a man named Ananias coming in and laying hands on him so he can see again."

[13] "But Lord," exclaimed Ananias, "I've heard many people talk about the terrible things this man has done to the believers* in Jerusalem! [14] And he is authorized by the leading priests to arrest everyone who calls upon your name."

[15] But the Lord said, "Go, for Saul is my chosen instrument to take my message to the Gentiles and to kings, as well as to the people of Israel. [16] And I will show him how much he must suffer for my name's sake."

[17] So Ananias went and found Saul. He laid his hands on him and said, "Brother Saul, the Lord Jesus, who appeared to you on the road, has sent me so that you might regain your sight and be filled with the Holy Spirit." [18] Instantly something like scales fell from Saul's eyes, and he regained his sight. Then he got up and was baptized. [19] Afterward he ate some food and regained his strength.

Saul stayed with the believers* in Damascus for a few days. [20] And proclaim Jesus in the synagogues, [a]saying, "He is the Son of God." 21 All those hearing him continued to be amazed, and were saying, "Is this not he who in Jerusalem destroyed those who called on this name, and *who* had come here for the purpose of bringing them bound before the chief priests?" 22 But Saul kept increasing in strength and confounding the Jews who lived at Damascus by proving that this *Jesus* is the [a]Christ.

9:1 [a]Later called Paul [b]Lit *threat* 9:7 [a]Or *sound* 9:8 [a]Lit *was seeing* 9:12 [a]A few early mss do not contain *in a vision* 9:13 [a]Or *holy ones* 9:15 [a]Or *vessel* 9:20 [a]Lit *that* 9:22 [a]I.e. Messiah

immediately he began preaching about Jesus in the synagogues, saying, "He is indeed the Son of God!" 21 All who heard him were amazed. "Isn't this the same man who caused such devastation among Jesus' followers in Jerusalem?" they asked. "And didn't he come here to arrest them and take them in chains to the leading priests?"

22 Saul's preaching became more and more powerful, and the Jews in Damascus couldn't refute his proofs that Jesus was indeed the Messiah.

9:1 Greek *disciples.* 9:10 Greek *disciple;* also in 9:26, 36. 9:13 Greek *God's holy people;* also in 9:32, 41. 9:19 Greek *disciples;* also in 9:26, 38.

There is no one more persistent than God when He decides to save someone. And few can appreciate God's persistent, pursuing love more than Francis Thompson. By almost any measure of success, Thompson was a failure. He failed to become a Roman Catholic priest. He failed to become a medical doctor. He lasted only two weeks as a surgical instrument maker and two months as an encyclopedia salesman—during which time he read the entire work and sold nothing. He lasted a short time in the military before failing the physical exam, most likely due to his severe addiction to opium.

Eventually, he left home to make his own way in London, hoping to become a successful writer. But, as one biographer put it, "It had been his habit to obey the command of the drug by the disposal of his books and medical instruments."[15] In a short time, he was destitute, wandering the streets of London in filthy rags and broken shoes, unable to keep work when fortunate enough to find it, and then reduced to selling matches to keep from starving. But within the shirtless vagabond beat a heart that God had claimed for Himself.

After reading Thompson's poetry, Wilfrid and Alice Meynell, editors of the magazine *Merrie England*, rescued Thompson from the streets. They gave him a place to live and brokered his first book deal, which made him an instant celebrity. He later wrote—in the words of many critics—the greatest English ode ever put in print: "The Hound of Heaven," a mystical poem about God's relentless pursuit of His beloved.

I fled Him, down the nights and down the days;
I fled Him, down the arches of the years;
I fled Him, down the labyrinthine ways
Of my own mind; and in the mist of tears
I hid from Him, and under running laughter.
Up vistaed hopes I sped;
And shot, precipitated,
Adown Titanic glooms of chasmèd fears,
From those strong Feet that followed, followed after.
But with unhurrying chase,
And unperturbèd pace,
Deliberate speed, majestic instancy,
They beat—and a Voice beat
More instant than the Feet—
"All things betray thee, who betrayest Me."[16]

Many can appreciate Francis Thompson's story because it mirrors their own desperate flights from the grace of God. Thanks to the Lord's persistent, pursuing love—and despite their own efforts to reject His gracious gift of freedom—they now enjoy the kind of life none could have imagined.

Seventeen centuries before Thompson lived, another man ran from God. He wasn't a vagrant, but a scholar. He wasn't a drug addict, but one of the most religious and devout men of his time. He wasn't a failure, but one of the keenest minds in all the Middle East—brilliant, persuasive, dogmatic, obnoxious—immensely successful by all the standards by which his peers measured achievement. Nevertheless, he was running. While Thompson consciously ran away from the Lord, this zealous Jew conscientiously ran toward God. At least he *thought* so.

Saul of Tarsus became a one-man army against what he considered to be the most dangerous heresy of his day—Christianity.

— 9:1-2 —

Luke's description of Saul's hatred for Christians drips with foreboding. Earlier, the narrative indicates that Saul had supported the plot to arrest, convict, and stone Stephen (7:58; 8:1). Saul then began a reign of terror in Jerusalem, "ravaging the church, entering house after house, and dragging off men and women, he would put them in prison" (8:3). Saul's persecution may have lasted as long as three years. But instead of destroying the church, his efforts sent the gospel farther, faster.

Some Christians fleeing Jerusalem found refuge in the desert villages east and south of the city. Others relocated to cities north of Galilee, in Syria, beyond Jewish political influence. Damascus would have been a popular location because it offered the protection and conveniences of a sizable city—not to mention plenty of opportunities for spreading the gospel in a major metropolitan area and its surroundings. Besides all this, the refugee Christians would be protected from the fires of persecution in Jerusalem . . . or so they thought.

When Saul discovered the community of Christians huddling in Damascus, he planned to expand his persecution, but because of the political climate he required help from the temple. The high priest wrote letters to the Jewish leaders in Damascus encouraging them to support Saul in his quest. He planned to extradite these Jewish followers of Jesus to face trial before the Sanhedrin. Luke used the term "the Way" to describe those who believed in Christ, most likely because Jesus called Himself "the way, and the truth, and the life" (John 14:6).

— 9:3-4 —

Damascus lay 140 miles to the northeast of Jerusalem, at least a six-day journey on foot. The context of the story suggests that Saul and his contingent of the temple guard were no more than a day's journey from Damascus when a bright light surrounded them (26:13). The adverb "suddenly" (9:3) indicates the event came upon them quickly and unexpectedly. The preposition rendered "from" is *ek* [1537], which usually has a spatial aspect when referring to something visible. In other words, *ek* indicates both source and direction; the light appeared like a beam or column "out from" heaven. The verb translated "flashed" suggests the idea of lightning; the intensity outshone the sun, illuminating everything in the area. According to Saul's later account, this occurred around noon (22:6).

The light that accompanied Jesus' appearance to Saul is an example of a theophany, a visible manifestation of God. Throughout the Old Testament, the Lord indicated His presence in the form of a supernatural light, later called the shekinah. This light appeared in a bush to Moses (Exod. 3:1-3), led the Israelites through the wilderness in a pillar (Exod. 13:21-22), and settled on Mount Sinai in front of the Israelites (Exod. 19:18; 24:17). When the tabernacle—and later the temple—was constructed, the shekinah hovered over the ark of the covenant behind a thick veil in the most holy place (Exod. 25:22; 40:35; Lev. 16:2). The Lord did this for the benefit of His people, to affirm His presence among them as their one and only God. Here, Saul benefits from this revelation.

Saul fell to the ground and heard a voice indicting him for persecuting "Me" (Acts 9:4)—not "them" or "the church" or even "My church," but "Me." Such an odd choice of pronoun might have confused Saul. He had earnestly pursued a course he thought righteous—he wanted to stamp out a heresy. Some of his Jewish brethren were calling a dead man the Messiah, which violated everything he knew about the Hebrew Scriptures.

From Christ's point of view, "the Way" wasn't a theological perspective, but a living part of Himself. The church is, to Christ, His own body. The people that Saul had been beating and killing? The Holy Spirit had been baptizing them into Christ, making them one with Christ, just as Christ is one with the Father and the Spirit (John 17:18-21). Collectively, we the church are the visible representation of Jesus Christ in the world! To persecute the church is to assault the Son of God.

— 9:5-6 —

Saul's question, "Who are You, Lord?" (9:5), does not itself imply that Paul regarded the voice he heard as belonging to God or Jesus. (The NASB capitalization reflects the reader's point of view, not Paul's.) His use of "lord" was respectful and could be understood as "sir" (e.g., Gen. 18:12; 19:2; Matt. 13:27; 27:63; John 4:11; Acts 10:4). However, given the supernatural aspect of the event, it seems evident that Saul thought the voice belonged to God or one of His angels. Imagine Saul's astonishment when the voice identified Himself as "Jesus whom you are persecuting" (9:5).

The Greek term for "persecute" (*diōkō* [1377]) carries the idea of "forcing," "pressing," "impelling," "pursuing," or "zealously engaging," usually for the sake of a particular cause. Unlike the English term "persecute," this Greek word (and the Hebrew or Aramaic wording it represents) has connotations that often correspond with "pursue vigorously" and are not strictly negative. For example, we find the Greek word *diōkō* translating the Hebrew *radap* [H7291] in the admonition of Psalm 34:14 to "seek peace and *pursue* it." And Saul would later write "I *press on* so that I may lay hold of that for which also I was laid hold of by Christ Jesus" (Phil. 3:12).

Therefore, Jesus' reference to "persecution" in His exchange with Saul was not an unreserved and unequivocal condemnation. While Saul's vigorous pursuit of Christians was clearly wrong in the eyes of God, he nevertheless pressed his cause with right motives, albeit

PAUL'S ENCOUNTER WITH THE RISEN CHRIST ON THE ROAD TO DAMASCUS

AS TOLD BY LUKE IN ACTS	PAUL'S DEFENSE BEFORE THE JEWS IN THE TEMPLE IN ACTS	PAUL'S TRIAL BEFORE AGRIPPA II IN CAESAREA IN ACTS
As he was traveling, it happened that he was approaching Damascus, and suddenly a light from heaven flashed around him; and he fell to the ground and heard a voice saying to him, "Saul, Saul, why are you persecuting Me?" (9:3-4)	"But it happened that as I was on my way, approaching Damascus about noontime, a very bright light suddenly flashed from heaven all around me, and I fell to the ground and heard a voice saying to me, 'Saul, Saul, why are you persecuting Me?'" (22:6-7)	"While so engaged as I was journeying to Damascus with the authority and commission of the chief priests, at midday, O King, I saw on the way a light from heaven, brighter than the sun, shining all around me and those who were journeying with me. And when we had all fallen to the ground, I heard a voice saying to me in the Hebrew dialect, 'Saul, Saul, why are you persecuting Me? It is hard for you to kick against the goads.'" (26:12-14)
And he said, "Who are You, Lord?" And He said, "I am Jesus whom you are persecuting." (9:5)	"And I answered, 'Who are You, Lord?' And He said to me, 'I am Jesus the Nazarene, whom you are persecuting.'" (22:8)	"And I said, 'Who are You, Lord?' And the Lord said, 'I am Jesus whom you are persecuting.'" (26:15)
"But get up and enter the city, and it will be told you what you must do." (9:6)	"And I said, 'What shall I do, Lord?' And the Lord said to me, 'Get up and go on into Damascus, and there you will be told of all that has been appointed for you to do.'" (22:10)	"But get up and stand on your feet; for this purpose I have appeared to you, to appoint you a minister and a witness not only to the things which you have seen, but also to the things in which I will appear to you; rescuing you from the Jewish people and from the Gentiles, to whom I am sending you, to open their eyes so that they may turn from darkness to light and from the dominion of Satan to God, that they may receive forgiveness of sins and an inheritance among those who have been sanctified by faith in Me." (26:16-18)
The men who traveled with him stood speechless, hearing the voice but seeing no one. (9:7)	"And those who were with me saw the light, to be sure, but did not understand the voice of the One who was speaking to me." (22:9)	
Saul got up from the ground, and though his eyes were open, he could see nothing; and leading him by the hand, they brought him into Damascus. (9:8)	"But since I could not see because of the brightness of that light, I was led by the hand by those who were with me and came into Damascus." (22:11)	

"ignorantly in unbelief" (1 Tim. 1:13). Saul earnestly opposed the Christians because he honestly thought they opposed God. Consequently, Saul "was shown mercy" (1 Tim. 1:13) in response to his sin. Rather than strike Saul dead or allow his own sin to consume him, the risen Christ *pursued* the unrighteous pursuer and confronted him with his sin.

Jesus instructed Saul to continue his journey to Damascus, but with a different agenda, which would be disclosed later. Many years later, when recalling this encounter before Agrippa (Acts 26:12-21), Saul would compress the events of the next several days to summarize everything he had heard from the Lord.

— 9:7-9 —

The men with Saul saw no one, but they saw the light and heard the sound of the voice without comprehending the exchange (9:7; 22:9). Saul, on the other hand, plainly understood the message from the risen Christ. During the encounter, he was literally blinded by the light, so his companions led him as he continued on to Damascus, where he sat in his own personal darkness for three days, fasting and refusing water (9:8-9).

According to Saul's recollection of this entire episode before Agrippa, he spent those three days in communication with the Lord. Saul summarized what he heard during those three days in Acts 26:16-18 (see chart on the facing page). During that time, he also received a vision reassuring him that he would regain his sight through the ministry of a Christian in Damascus (9:12).

— 9:10-16 —

Meanwhile, across town, the Lord prepared a "disciple at Damascus named Ananias" who was "devout by the standard of the Law, and well spoken of by all the Jews who lived there" (9:10; 22:12). The Lord gave Ananias the name and address of the house where Saul waited (9:11) and assured him that Saul knew he would be coming (9:12). All that was left was for Ananias to "get up and go" (9:11).

Of course, Ananias expressed concern, not only for his own safety, but also in the interest of justice. The Lord didn't reveal His entire plan or even that Saul might be on the cusp of conversion; He merely told the man to seek out Saul and lay hands on him. It probably seemed to Ananias that a blind Saul benefited the church. Restoring sight to an enemy of the Christians seemed counterproductive. It was a valid concern. Ananias didn't object or refuse to obey; he simply wanted to understand.

The Lord doesn't always explain Himself, and He's under no obligation to do so. Still, He honored the earnest response of His servant. The Lord revealed to Ananias what Saul discovered during his three-day fast: that He had pursued the proud, violent, zealous Pharisee from Tarsus to save him and to give him a critical role in His redemptive plan for the world (9:15). The Lord spoke in terms that emphasize His sovereign choice of Saul. "Chosen" means "[made] a special choice based upon significant preference, often implying a strongly favorable attitude toward what is chosen."[17] In other words, this was no dispassionate, pragmatic choice; God's choosing of Saul came from a place of love.

"Instrument" (*skeuos* [4632]) literally means "vessel." Vessels are generally crafted to serve specific functions. A vessel for storing wine looked very different from a vessel designed to contain household utensils. God had made Saul a certain way and had directed his steps for a purpose. Saul was a highly trained Jew with a first-class education under the great Gamaliel, and he had been reared near the famous Greek academy in Tarsus; he would thus be the ideal ambassador of a Jewish King to Gentile cultures. This Hebrew scholar with Roman citizenship could speak with authority in both worlds.

Saul of Tarsus, who would become Paul the apostle, had a destiny. He would become a witness to the Gentiles, to kings, and to his fellow Jews. Moreover, just in case anyone is worried about justice, Saul would suffer greatly for the sake of the gospel he once tried to stamp out (9:16).

— 9:17-19 —

Ananias wasted no time obeying. He departed his residence and entered the house where Saul lay blinded, the home of a man named Judas (9:11). He greeted Saul as "Brother Saul," showing no hesitation in embracing Saul as a genuine believer and co-worker in the cause of Christ (9:17). His greeting also demonstrated his complete knowledge of what Saul had experienced without first hearing it from him; the Lord who had appeared to Saul on the road had also appeared to Ananias in Damascus. Ananias's pronouncement implies that Saul received the Holy Spirit when he regained the use of his eyes (9:17).

Luke describes "something like scales" that fell from Saul's eyes (9:18). The Greek word *lepis* [3013] denotes something thin and flaky like the scales of fish or snakes. While a physical phenomenon accompanied Saul's restored sight, this was a supernatural healing. Scales fell from his eyes and the Spirit filled his body; his eyes received sight and his soul received vision. Even before Saul broke his fast, he submitted to water baptism (9:18). Then he ate (9:19).

— 9:20-22 —

Saul wasted no time; he "immediately" began declaring in the synagogues that Jesus is "the Son of God" (9:20). The Old Testament uses sonship language with respect to Israel as a nation (Exod. 4:22-23; Isa. 63:16; 64:8; Jer. 3:19; 31:9; Hos. 11:1), the anointed king of Israel (2 Sam. 7:14; 1 Chr. 22:10; Ps. 89:26-27), and the Messiah (Ps. 2:7).

Let's not forget that Saul had in his possession letters from the high priest to the leaders of these same synagogues authorizing the arrest and extradition of Christians. Saul had come to Damascus to seize any Jew who proclaimed Jesus as the Messiah; now he had become an enthusiastic Jesus follower. Saul would grow greatly in his understanding of the implications of the gospel in coming years, but even at this early stage he was skilled in debate and possessed unparalleled knowledge of the Hebrew Scriptures. This made him a formidable advocate for Christ among his Jewish brothers.

APPLICATION: ACTS 9:1-22

The Road from Here

Saul's conversion experience was like no other. Most people don't receive a supernatural, in-person encounter with the risen Christ! Even so, I find in his experience a paradigm that applies to the birth and nurturing of all new Christians. Take note of the events following Saul's conversion.

A Relationship

Immediately after Saul's encounter with Christ, the Lord sent a mature believer to minister to him. Ananias became his friend, advocate, and guide. Paul had questions; Ananias offered answers. Paul needed the companionship of someone who had experienced this transformation; Ananias became his first Christian companion. It's a jolting, sometimes overwhelming experience when the Holy Spirit first takes up residence in a new believer; he or she needs someone to help with those first halting steps as life begins from a completely new perspective.

A Community

Ananias didn't shoulder this burden alone; he quickly introduced Saul to the community of believers in Damascus. They, in turn, helped Paul determine what he should do next. They supported his convictions, they protected him from his enemies, and they nurtured his growth as a believer. The church helped Saul begin to rewrite his theology now that he had met the Messiah. Their support led to the next stage of Paul's transformation.

An Education

Though Paul jumped into evangelism and preaching immediately, his Damascus road experience and obvious call to ministry didn't mean he could circumvent doctrinal and practical preparation. Though we don't know exactly what he did there, Paul left Damascus to spend time in Arabia (Gal. 1:17). Perhaps he was studying, meditating, and communing with the Lord and even receiving special revelations from the Holy Spirit. After an unspecified time period, he returned to Damascus and then Jerusalem (see Gal. 1:17-18). Still his practical ministry preparation wasn't complete. Long before his call to work among Gentile converts in Antioch and his famous send-off with Barnabas on the first missionary journey, Paul relocated to his hometown of Tarsus (Acts 9:29-30), where he spent ten years studying and laboring in ministry. Only then, after much doctrinal and practical preparation, did God launch Paul into his role as an apostle.

A Reproduction

With his own spiritual development well underway, Saul the Pharisee was transformed into Paul the apostle, and he began to reproduce as a believer. His testimony became the basis of a worldwide evangelistic ministry whereby his faith brought others to faith in Jesus Christ. And that's what God intends for everyone who becomes a part of His kingdom: disciples making disciples, who make more disciples.

A Man in Need of a New Name
ACTS 9:23-31

NASB

23 When many days had elapsed, the Jews plotted together to do away with him, 24 but their plot became known

NLT

23 After a while some of the Jews plotted together to kill him. 24 They were watching for him day and night at

to Saul. They were also watching the gates day and night so that they might put him to death; 25but his disciples took him by night and let him down through *an opening in* the wall, lowering him in a large basket.

26When he came to Jerusalem, he was trying to associate with the disciples; ªbut they were all afraid of him, not believing that he was a disciple. 27But Barnabas took hold of him and brought him to the apostles and described to them how he had seen the Lord on the road, and that He had talked to him, and how at Damascus he had spoken out boldly in the name of Jesus. 28And he was with them, ªmoving about freely in Jerusalem, speaking out boldly in the name of the Lord. 29And he was talking and arguing with the ªHellenistic *Jews;* but they were attempting to put him to death. 30But when the brethren learned *of it,* they brought him down to Caesarea and sent him away to Tarsus.

31So the church throughout all Judea and Galilee and Samaria ªenjoyed peace, being built up; and going on in the fear of the Lord and in the comfort of the Holy Spirit, it continued to increase.

9:26 ªLit *and* 9:28 ªLit *going in and going out* 9:29 ªJews who adopted the Gr language and much of Gr culture through acculturation 9:31 ªLit *was having*

the city gate so they could murder him, but Saul was told about their plot. 25So during the night, some of the other believers* lowered him in a large basket through an opening in the city wall.

26When Saul arrived in Jerusalem, he tried to meet with the believers, but they were all afraid of him. They did not believe he had truly become a believer! 27Then Barnabas brought him to the apostles and told them how Saul had seen the Lord on the way to Damascus and how the Lord had spoken to Saul. He also told them that Saul had preached boldly in the name of Jesus in Damascus.

28So Saul stayed with the apostles and went all around Jerusalem with them, preaching boldly in the name of the Lord. 29He debated with some Greek-speaking Jews, but they tried to murder him. 30When the believers* heard about this, they took him down to Caesarea and sent him away to Tarsus, his hometown.

31The church then had peace throughout Judea, Galilee, and Samaria, and it became stronger as the believers lived in the fear of the Lord. And with the encouragement of the Holy Spirit, it also grew in numbers.

9:25 Greek *his disciples.* 9:30 Greek *brothers.*

I am convinced that all Christians must pass through three stages en route toward spiritual maturity.

While everyone must pass through each stage, no one experiences them in the same way. Some zip right through the first, only to get stuck in the second. Others spend most of their lives trudging through the third and never quite reach full maturity. Regardless, the stages of growth are common to all—including Saul of Tarsus, perhaps the most notable Christian in all of history. In Acts 9, we see a synopsis of his spiritual growth:

Stages En Route to Spiritual Maturity

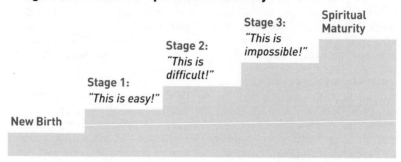

- *"This is easy!"* (9:19-22)—Saul had great success debating his Jewish brethren in the synagogues. His natural abilities, great intellect, and extensive knowledge equipped him to outwit the finest minds of his day.
- *"This is difficult!"* (9:23-25)—Saul became the target of assassination plots and had to flee the city. As Dr. Stanley Toussaint writes, "Saul's plans for persecuting Christians in Damascus took a strange turn; he had entered the city blind and left in a basket! Ironically *he* became the object of persecution."[18]
- *"This is impossible!"* (9:26-30)—Saul returns to Jerusalem to find no place among his old peers in the temple and no welcome in the understandably suspicious community of Christians.

This portion of Paul's spiritual journey took as long as four years to complete. Longer, if you include the decade he spent in his hometown of Tarsus. Eventually, he did reach that critical milestone of spiritual maturity at which point a believer not only accepts the "impossible" standards of the Christian life but learns how to thrive in his or her helplessness through the power of the Holy Spirit. It could be said that a Christian doesn't really begin to experience new life until he or she starts living by this all-important perspective.

As Luke continues his narrative of church history, Saul has just begun to grow. Up to this point, the Christian life has been easy for him, but he has a long way to travel, both geographically and spiritually.

— 9:23-25 —

Saul's encounter with the risen Lord on the road to Damascus left him completely blind, and for three days he fasted and prayed in the home of his friend Judas.[19] During that time, he received a rare and wonderful gift from the Lord: a preview of his greatness as a Christian witness to

Gentiles, kings, and Jews (9:15-16). When he received his sight again, he also received the Holy Spirit (9:17). And before he broke his fast, he submitted to water baptism as an outward symbol of his inner cleansing and as a public declaration of his belief in Jesus Christ as the Son of God, the Hebrew Messiah, the Savior of the world.

While still in Damascus, Saul began proclaiming the resurrection of Jesus, telling everyone about his encounter with the Messiah only days earlier. At first, ministry came easily. After all, he was a natural! He had studied Scripture and theology most of his life, so when he finally met the Messiah—to whom all of the Old Testament points—everything fell into place.

PAUL'S TRAVELS REFERENCED IN ACTS 9	
Jerusalem	(Acts 9:1-2)
Damascus	(Acts 9:3-22)
Arabia	(Gal. 1:17)
Damascus	(Acts 9:23-25; Gal. 1:17; 2 Cor. 11:32-33)
Jerusalem	(Acts 9:26-29; Gal. 1:18-20)
Caesarea	(Acts 9:30)
Tarsus	(Acts 9:30; Gal. 1:21-24)

He possessed an incredible leadership ability and excellent oratory skills. He had been a highly respected Pharisee among the temple elite. He undoubtedly had numerous contacts in Roman government; as a natural-born Roman citizen (22:28) from an important city (21:39), he enjoyed a rare and highly prized station in society. If God wanted to recruit a CEO-type individual to take the helm of the growing church, no one had a better résumé than Saul of Tarsus.

As Saul soon learned, however, God doesn't recruit leaders like a corporate headhunter. A solid résumé is only a good beginning. Becoming prepared for service in the kingdom of God requires the overhaul of one's character: a deconstruction followed by a fallow season and then, in time, a reconstruction.

"Many days had elapsed" with Saul trying to minister in Damascus when the synagogue leaders plotted to "do away with him" (9:23). This could have been a plot to arrest Saul and return him to Jerusalem to stand trial or one to kill him outright. Unable to locate him inside the city, they posted spies at the gates, hoping to seize him while he was entering or leaving (9:24). "His disciples" refers to the men and women Saul had won to Christ or had begun teaching while in Damascus. These helped him escape "through an opening in the wall" (9:25).

Many ancient cities were enclosed by two walls separated by a gap of approximately 15 feet. The bottom was filled with stone and rubble to make it more difficult for enemies to breach the city's defenses. Higher up, however, wooden beams spanned the gap between the inner and outer walls to form floor joists for living quarters. Most likely, Saul escaped through an apartment window facing outward. His disciples lowered him in a basket, allowing him to get clear of the city undetected.

According to his letter to the Galatian believers, written years later, Saul mentions a time of retreat in Arabia after his conversion:

> I did not immediately consult with flesh and blood, nor did I go up to Jerusalem to those who were apostles before me; but I went away to Arabia, and returned once more to Damascus.
>
> Then three years later I went up to Jerusalem to become acquainted with Cephas, and stayed with him fifteen days. (Gal. 1:16-18)

When this passage is placed alongside Acts 9, it's not entirely clear how long he spent in Arabia, at what point he departed, or to what specific period "three years" refers. Piecing the clues together from Acts 9 and Galatians 1 and arranging the events in chronological order, we have two main options.

Acts 9 Chronology: Option 1

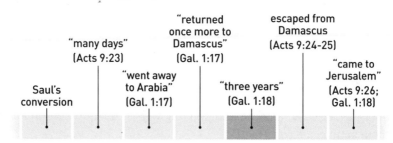

One option is that Saul ministered in Damascus "many days" (9:23) before departing for Arabia, perhaps for reading, study, and training. He returned and ministered in Damascus for three years, during which time a plot to kill him forced his escape. Upon leaving Damascus, he went up to Jerusalem.

This is certainly possible, and on the surface, it appears to make sense of the English adverb "then" in Galatians 1:18. After a closer look at how the Greek adverb is used, however, I'm not so sure. As I assemble all of the facts, I'm more inclined to accept the second option.

Acts 9 Chronology: Option 2

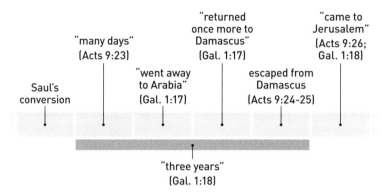

According to this chronology, Saul spent "many days" ministering in Damascus until he wore out his welcome in the synagogues. He then relocated to Arabia, spending two years getting better equipped for ministry. After he returned to Damascus and resumed his ministry there, the synagogue leaders plotted "to do away with him" (Acts 9:23), prompting his nighttime escape. He then traveled to Jerusalem.

In this arrangement, a total of three years separated his conversion and journey to Jerusalem. In other words, three years after his conversion, not after his return to Damascus, Saul visited Peter in Jerusalem. As Kenneth Wuest explains, "The words *after three years* do not merely refer to a lapse of time. They are argumentative. [That is, they build an argument.] Paul is showing all through this section, his entire independence of the Jerusalem apostles. Therefore, the three years have reference, not to the time after his return from Arabia, but to the period of time after his conversion."[20]

Saul had come a long way in his spiritual journey. After his conversion, he remained in the little incubator called Damascus, nurtured and accepted, encouraged and mentored, strengthened and protected by a little group of disciples who had witnessed his conversion. They had seen the Holy Spirit fall on him and watched as the Spirit transformed his character. He enjoyed a close-knit community and ministered regularly in the synagogues. For Saul, this portion of the Christian life was *easy*!

The next few years, however, were *difficult*. Rejected by the synagogue leaders, he disappeared into the wilderness to get his bearings. He then returned to an even more hostile climate. While his enemies had conspired against him, at least he had the fellowship of the believers in Damascus. In Jerusalem, life would be *impossible*.

— 9:26-27 —

Saul had passed through periods of ease and difficulty in his Christian life. Now in Jerusalem, life became *impossible*. By either reckoning (see charts on pages 174 and 175), Saul had been away for several years—time enough to erode his influence among his Jewish colleagues but not nearly enough to erase the memories of his earlier years of persecution (9:26). Enemies in the temple and fear in the church left Saul isolated, cut off from both communities—a man without a group to identify with, as it were. Saul could do nothing to help himself.

When the Christian life becomes impossible, the believer must learn the all-important concept of surrender. "Surrender" doesn't mean "quit." There's no bitterness or self-pity or blame or resentment in surrender. The surrendered spirit has no sense of entitlement. The surrendered Christian recognizes his or her own powerlessness. But that attitude comes hard for those who have enjoyed great success in the past and to those who naturally possess immense potential.

Saul began his spiritual journey as a self-sufficient, zealous, driven, highly capable religious leader with a clear sense of direction. His encounter with the risen Lord then put him on an entirely new path

Saul's (Paul's) Early Travels. In a zealous quest to persecute Christians, Saul journeyed from Jerusalem to Damascus. Once he converted to Christianity, his early travels included Arabia, Jerusalem, Caesarea Maritima, and Tarsus.

in life. Without a doubt, his conversion energized the most astute Christians; a man with obvious potential for the kingdom had just embraced the Messiah. One could only imagine what the great Saul of Tarsus could accomplish when filled with the Holy Spirit! But this self-willed man of God had a long way to go before he would reach his potential for the Lord.

A. W. Tozer once wrote, "It is doubtful whether God can bless a man greatly until He has hurt him deeply."[21] Alan Redpath once said something similar: "When God wants to do an impossible task, He takes an impossible man and crushes him."[22] That's not to suggest that God takes delight in hurting people; it's only to say that a painful recovery usually follows spiritual surgery. For people like Saul, the therapeutic rehabilitation of a strong will can take a very long time—in his particular case, almost fifteen years! When, at last, a strong will surrenders—when the individual finally comes to terms with the truth of his or her own helplessness—God has help waiting nearby.

Just three years into his journey, Saul spent the beginning of his time in Jerusalem on his own, being avoided by the believers (9:26).

Saul had no identity, no community, no direction, no hope. He could do nothing for himself to turn things around. Since life had become impossible, surrender was essential. That's when Barnabas came to his rescue (9:27; cf. 4:36). Earlier, Ananias had befriended Saul in Damascus; now Barnabas became his advocate in Jerusalem. We don't know how Barnabas knew the details of Saul's spiritual journey; it would be in perfect keeping with his nature to take Saul at his word. Regardless, Barnabas brought Saul together with "the apostles," who welcomed this former enemy into the fellowship of believers.

Although Luke writes that Saul visited with "the apostles," Galatians 1:18-19 indicates that the only apostles he saw were Peter and James. James, the brother of Christ, was not one of the Twelve, although the church in Jerusalem apparently recognized him as an apostle (Gal. 1:18; Acts 12:17; 15:13; 21:18). Therefore, Luke probably uses the term "apostles" in the broad sense of "leaders," those who gave functional leadership to the church under the guidance of the Twelve.

— 9:28-30 —

Again, we can't determine conclusively how long Saul lived in Jerusalem. According to his later recollection, he visited with Peter for fifteen days (Gal. 1:18), but he may have been in the city several weeks before Barnabas intervened on his behalf. Undoubtedly, he spent additional time actively engaged in ministry after his time with Peter. Much like he did in Damascus, Saul argued with the "Hellenistic Jews" (Acts 9:29; *Hellēnistēs* [1675]) in Jerusalem; ironically, this was the same group that instigated the slander campaign against Stephen—a plot Luke subtly attributes to Saul (7:58; 8:1). As a result of their interaction, this group tried to kill Saul. At the time, some probably considered this a stroke of cosmic justice; Saul reaped the harvest of seeds he had once sown against Stephen. And indeed Saul had helped to nurture the anti-Christian attitude that came back to bite him. But grace always abounds! Saul had been forgiven of his sins, regardless of the temporal consequences that remained.

When Saul's brothers and sisters in the church heard about this latest plot to kill him, they arranged his escape to Caesarea Maritima, where he would catch a ship for his hometown of Tarsus. He would spend the next decade learning, growing, and becoming ever more ready for leadership in the church. God had marked this brilliant Pharisee for ministry among the Gentiles, but the church was not yet ready for him. While God prepared Saul of Tarsus to become Paul the apostle, He also prepared the Jewish church in Jerusalem to welcome Gentiles as brothers and sisters.

— 9:31 —

With a brief summary statement, Luke transitions from the story of Saul's conversion to a description of Peter's ongoing ministry. The word rendered "so" by the NASB is a Greek conjunction (*oun* [3767]) that has different functions depending upon the context. When used in a narrative, it simply resumes the story after an interruption. In this case, we might insert the word "meanwhile." Luke's narrative took a brief detour to present the major events surrounding Paul's conversion; meanwhile, the church had continued its own spiritual journey. Peter's ministry would carry him, as well as the congregation he led, into uncharted waters.

APPLICATION: ACTS 9:23-31

Lessons on Surrender

As I examine the early days of Paul's spiritual journey as a Christian, two important lessons take shape.

Number one is this: *In our growth in Christ, God does everything possible to neutralize the flesh*. What I mean by "the flesh" is what Paul describes in Romans 7 as the part of the Christian's nature that is "sold into bondage to sin" (Rom. 7:14). It represents the part of the believer that continues to make decisions and to take actions consistent with his or her old, habitually sinful way of thinking. When "the flesh" drives decisions, this leads to self-sufficient, self-righteous, and self-interested attitudes and self-motivated outcomes. Spiritual growth requires the triumph of the Spirit of God within the believer over that old, sinful, self-oriented perspective.

Some of us are stubborn, however. We learn slowly. Because we're educated, experienced, energetic, driven people who have survived difficulties before, we sincerely believe we can accomplish anything; all we need is a little help from God. Meanwhile, the Holy Spirit works to put that perspective to death so we can truly experience His power. He doesn't take up residence in believers to help us carry out our agendas; He comes to make us a part of the Lord's plan. While we keep a white-knuckle grip on what we want, the Spirit gradually—and sometimes painfully—peels back each finger so He can replace what we *want* with what we *need*.

When that happens, when the Spirit neutralizes the flesh, a feeling of uncertainty can take over. It looks like the world has turned its back. You were so effective at one time, but no longer. That feels terrible—but in fact, it's a great sign of progress. Your Father in heaven, your Lord, knows exactly what it takes to strip away the energy of the flesh so that you become receptive to relying upon His power.

Here's the second lesson: *The work of ministry requires surrendered saints*. Surrendered believers take their orders from the same Spirit, so they accomplish the work of ministry as with one mind. Can you imagine what would happen if every Christian did his or her own thing with supernatural power? The church would become a supersized mess! This is *His* work. Ministry must carry out His agenda. Therefore, all servants of God must surrender their wills and accept the truth of their own powerlessness to allow the will and power of God to flow uninhibited.

Many years ago, an anonymous poet described the Lord's transforming of a soul this way:

When God wants to drill a man,
And thrill a man,
And skill a man

When God wants to mold a man
To play the noblest part;

When He yearns with all His heart
To create so great and bold a man
That all the world shall be amazed,
Watch His methods, watch His ways!

How He ruthlessly perfects
Whom He royally elects!
How He hammers him and hurts him,
And with mighty blows converts him

Into trial shapes of clay which
Only God understands;
While his tortured heart is crying
And he lifts beseeching hands!

How He bends but never breaks
When his good He undertakes;
How He uses whom He chooses,
And which every purpose fuses him;
By every act induces him
To try His splendor out—

God knows what He's about.

God knows what He's about. Never forget that! He will be faithful to
do His part. Our part is to surrender our wills to His will, to abandon
our ways for His way.

Supernatural Manifestations
ACTS 9:32-43

NASB

[32] Now as Peter was traveling through all *those regions,* he came down also to the [a]saints who lived at [b]Lydda. [33] There he found a man named Aeneas, who had been bedridden eight years, for he was paralyzed. [34] Peter said to him, "Aeneas, Jesus Christ

NLT

[32] Meanwhile, Peter traveled from place to place, and he came down to visit the believers in the town of Lydda. [33] There he met a man named Aeneas, who had been paralyzed and bedridden for eight years. [34] Peter said to him, "Aeneas, Jesus Christ

heals you; get up and make your bed." Immediately he got up. ³⁵And all who lived at ªLydda and Sharon saw him, and they turned to the Lord.

³⁶Now in Joppa there was a disciple named Tabitha (which translated *in Greek* is called ªDorcas); this woman was abounding with deeds of kindness and charity which she continually did. ³⁷And it happened ªat that time that she fell sick and died; and when they had washed her body, they laid it in an upper room. ³⁸Since Lydda was near Joppa, the disciples, having heard that Peter was there, sent two men to him, imploring him, "Do not delay in coming to us." ³⁹So Peter arose and went with them. When he arrived, they brought him into the upper room; and all the widows stood beside him, weeping and showing all the ªtunics and garments that Dorcas used to make while she was with them. ⁴⁰But Peter sent them all out and knelt down and prayed, and turning to the body, he said, "Tabitha, arise." And she opened her eyes, and when she saw Peter, she sat up. ⁴¹And he gave her his hand and raised her up; and calling the ªsaints and widows, he presented her alive. ⁴²It became known all over Joppa, and many believed in the Lord. ⁴³And Peter stayed many days in Joppa with a tanner *named* Simon.

heals you! Get up, and roll up your sleeping mat!" And he was healed instantly. ³⁵Then the whole population of Lydda and Sharon saw Aeneas walking around, and they turned to the Lord.

³⁶There was a believer in Joppa named Tabitha (which in Greek is Dorcas*). She was always doing kind things for others and helping the poor. ³⁷About this time she became ill and died. Her body was washed for burial and laid in an upstairs room. ³⁸But the believers had heard that Peter was nearby at Lydda, so they sent two men to beg him, "Please come as soon as possible!"

³⁹So Peter returned with them; and as soon as he arrived, they took him to the upstairs room. The room was filled with widows who were weeping and showing him the coats and other clothes Dorcas had made for them. ⁴⁰But Peter asked them all to leave the room; then he knelt and prayed. Turning to the body he said, "Get up, Tabitha." And she opened her eyes! When she saw Peter, she sat up! ⁴¹He gave her his hand and helped her up. Then he called in the widows and all the believers, and he presented her to them alive.

⁴²The news spread through the whole town, and many believed in the Lord. ⁴³And Peter stayed a long time in Joppa, living with Simon, a tanner of hides.

9:32 ªOr *holy ones* ᵇOT: Lod   9:35 ªOT: Lod
9:36 ªI.e. Gazelle   9:37 ªLit *in those days*
9:39 ªOr *inner garments*   9:41 ªOr *holy ones*

9:36 The names *Tabitha* in Aramaic and *Dorcas* in Greek both mean "gazelle."

Peter proclaimed the grace of God effectively because he needed grace more than most. Born to a devout, middle-class family, Peter grew up hauling nets on the Sea of Galilee, married, and perhaps raised a little family in the fishing village of Bethsaida. Then he met Jesus. Not long after that, he gave up his stake in what might have been a busting-at-the-seams fishing company to follow the Messiah and to become one of His most challenging disciples. Peter shared a certain affinity with the

Sea of Galilee, with its tempestuous, unpredictable nature. He spoke too quickly, acted without thinking, committed himself impulsively, and led with unflinching pride.

On the eve of His arrest, Jesus prepared His disciples for the difficult hours that would follow. He said, "You will all fall away because of Me this night, for it is written, 'I will strike down the shepherd, and the sheep of the flock shall be scattered.' But after I have been raised, I will go ahead of you to Galilee" (Matt. 26:31-32). But Peter would hear none of it. "Even though all may fall away because of You, I will never fall away. . . . Even if I have to die with You, I will not deny You" (Matt. 26:33, 35).

But Peter did deny His Lord—three times. He denied knowing Jesus, swearing oaths and calling down divine curses on himself in order to convince others of his lie. With the crow of the rooster and the light of day came the realization that he had not only abandoned his Lord, but he had sought the approval of those who wanted Jesus dead. The memory of Jesus' words and his response washed over Peter, scrubbing him clean of any pride.

For many days, tears were Peter's only companion until the risen Lord took him aside for a significant conversation. Having probed Peter's heart for any remaining traces of pride and finding none, Jesus commanded the fallen disciple, "Shepherd My sheep" (John 21:16). And shepherd them he did! It was Peter who first preached in the streets of Jerusalem, where he turned three thousand scoffers into disciples. It was Peter who first suffered persecution for his faith; beaten with John in the temple, he became one of the first to feel the scourge on his back. It was Peter who left the whipping post to preach again in the temple precincts and to win another five thousand followers for the cause of Christ. It was Peter who rebuked the duplicity of Ananias and Sapphira and, later, Simon Magus. The grace of Jesus Christ lifted Peter from the lowest of lows to give him the highest position of authority in the Jerusalem church. Even though Peter had once wanted to retreat into the shadows in shame, Christ made him the most prominent spokesman among the first Christians. Peter also became a man through whom God worked some of the greatest miracles of the apostolic era. As with Saul's conversion, grace abounds.

— 9:32-33 —

As Luke resumes his narrative of the Jerusalem church, we discover that Peter had expanded his personal mission to include all of Judea.

During his travels, he came to the town of Lydda, which was called Lod in the Old Testament (1 Chr. 8:12; Ezra 2:33; Neh. 7:37; 11:35). Originally founded by a Benjamite Hebrew during the conquest of Israel, the town presided over the intersection of the highway between Babylon and Egypt and the main road connecting Jerusalem and Joppa. It was, therefore, a major military and commercial center, famous for textiles and pottery. Today, it's the location of Ben Gurion Airport near Tel Aviv.

While in Lydda, Peter encountered a man named Aeneas, who had been paralyzed for eight years. He had faced the same dismal prospect day after day. Someone had to dress him. Someone had to sit him up. Someone had to feed him and help him with hygiene. Someone had to move him from one place to another. All day, every day, for eight long years.

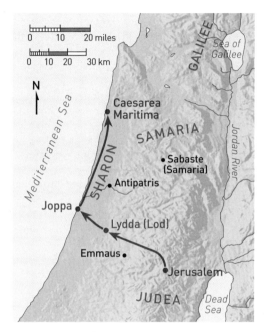

Peter's Ministry. Peter expanded his ministry beyond the church in Jerusalem by traveling throughout Judea, making stops in Lydda, Joppa, and Caesarea Maritima. When he returned, he brought the news that the Holy Spirit had fallen upon the Gentiles.

— 9:34-35 —

The apostle intended to use the miracle to attract attention—not to himself, but to the message he brought. Therefore, Peter didn't make a big spectacle of his own activity; he simply said, "Jesus Christ heals you" (9:34) and instructed the man to treat his bed like an able-bodied person would. The man's malady had forced him to lie on his bed through the day; now he should get up and tidy his bed like everyone else.

Luke uses the word "immediately" (*eutheōs* [2112]) to highlight the miraculous result. The man didn't experience a turnaround and then grow stronger with physical therapy. God instantaneously restored him to complete health.

The miracle accomplished its purpose. Lydda, as I mentioned, is

THE NATURE OF MIRACLES

ACTS 9:32-35

Miracles don't happen every day. "If they did," a colleague of mine once noted, "we'd call them 'regulars.'" Even though they appear common in the Bible, miracles are in fact extremely rare in history. God usually reserves them for brief, remarkable periods of time just prior to His making a big change in how He interacts with His creation. In fact, *most* miracles—though certainly not all miracles—in the Bible are limited to three relatively short, extremely remarkable eras:

1. The Exodus, Wanderings, and Conquest
   After four hundred years of silence, God astonished the Egyptians and the Hebrews with a series of miraculous events as He freed His covenant people from slavery in Egypt and then settled them in the Promised Land.

2. The Prophetic Ministries of Elijah and Elisha
   In the days of the kings, after many decades of repeated warnings, God sent these two prophets to turn Israel from idolatry. He then used miracles to validate their message as divine.

3. The Foundational Ministries of Christ and the Apostles
   After four hundred years of silence, God sent His Son with the ability to accomplish miraculous feats that rivaled the miraculous periods of the Old Testament. He then produced miracles through the apostles to validate the message of Jesus Christ as heaven-sent.

Miracles are rare, having occurred very infrequently throughout history; nevertheless, God always has been supernaturally at work in the world. But there's a difference between "supernatural" and "miraculous."

When God created all things out of nothing, He also devised laws of nature, such as the laws of gravity and thermodynamics, to give order to everything in the universe. For the most part, He allows the cosmos to work according to those laws of nature, and when He takes steps to advance His plan, He usually works *through* the laws of nature, not *against* them. In other words, when He interacts with His creation to accomplish His will, He doesn't always make a show of it. He very often directs history and shapes events without the people involved ever knowing they are being directed. For example, Peter told the crowd at Pentecost, "this Man [Jesus], delivered over by the predetermined plan and foreknowledge of God, you nailed to a cross by the hands of godless men and put Him to death" (2:23). The Lord shaped history and directed events to have the Son of God die on behalf of His people, just as prophecy had foretold.

The Creator interacts with His creation from outside nature—"supernaturally"—in all sorts of ways. He creates what appear to be coincidental circumstances, He alters otherwise normal patterns of events, He empowers people to accomplish what they otherwise could not, He heals people in ways that defy medical treatment or explanation. All of these are the supernatural activities of God.

Miracles, on the other hand, are a special brand of supernatural activity. A miracle occurs when God makes an obvious display of supernatural activity, usually to make a point. He dramatically defies the laws of nature in order to validate an event as divinely ordered. The purpose of the miracle is to make an undeniable display of divine power to draw everyone's attention and to authenticate the activity or message as God's. He parts the waters of a sea to make a dry path from one side to the other (Exod. 14:22). He causes a donkey to speak like a human (Num. 22:28). He causes an ax head to float (2 Kgs. 6:6). He allows three young men to enter a blazing fire and emerge without a hair being singed (Dan. 3:23-27).

These are authentic miracles—dramatic, undeniable acts of God in which He contravenes the laws of nature. They usually remedy problems that would be impossible within the normal framework of life.

The Lord never ceases to work supernaturally, but *miracles* are exceedingly rare.

the city. Sharon is the coastal plain on which the city is situated; it is roughly 10 miles wide and 50 miles long. The vast majority of the people in Lydda and the surrounding area accepted Peter's preaching as divinely authenticated. Luke uses the phrase "turned to the Lord" to mean that they became followers of Jesus (9:35; 11:21; 15:19), which would mean believing, being baptized, and receiving the Holy Spirit.

— 9:36-38 —

Another stop in Peter's itinerant ministry included Joppa, the harbor town to which Jonah had run many centuries earlier (Jon. 1:3). Throughout its history, Joppa became the possession of one conqueror after another until Caesar finally granted it to Herod. Unfortunately, Herod hated the people of Joppa, so he built a state-of-the-art seaport about 30 miles north and called it Caesarea Maritima. Consequently, Joppa enjoyed some sea trade, but none compared to its newer rival. Still, when people came via the sea to visit Jerusalem, they frequently used the Joppa port.

A follower of Christ lived in Joppa, a woman Luke describes as a "disciple" who was "full of good works and charitable giving" (literally rendered), noting that this was her habitual lifestyle (Acts 9:36). Her Aramaic name, Tabitha, and her Greek name, Dorcas, both mean "gazelle." Luke translated her name for the sake of his Greek readers, but we can surmise she was Jewish by birth. While Peter was ministering in the town of Lydda, just 12 miles up the main road leading to Jerusalem, the woman died of an illness.

Rather than bury her immediately, as would be in keeping with Jewish custom, her friends cleansed her corpse and placed it in the room above the main living quarters (9:37). This was highly unusual for a couple of reasons. First, they had no means of preserving the body from decay, so the normal procedure would have directed them to apply an initial coating of spiced resin to the body and then place it in a burial cave. A day or so later, they would complete the burial by wrapping the body in strips of linen soaked in as much as 100 pounds of spiced resin to contain the smell during decomposition. But they didn't even complete the first stage of burial preparation; instead, they merely washed the body. Second, they placed the body in a space normally reserved for dining or for housing special guests. Deliberately placing a dead body where people sleep or eat simply wasn't done!

If we were telling this story today, we would expect Tabitha's friends to follow the normal protocol following a death. They would call an emergency number to report the death. They would allow the coroner or a funeral home to take the body away, place it in cool storage, prepare it for viewing, hold a memorial service, and then have the body buried or cremated. Instead, her friends bathed the body, dressed the body, and placed it in the guest bedroom.

Luke's narrative thus sends a signal to the ancient reader. Tabitha's friends did *none* of the things people normally do in anticipation of a funeral. Instead, they seem to be preparing the woman for resurrection.[23] That's remarkable because Luke's narrative gives no indication that anyone had been raised from the dead since Jesus. So far as we know, these friends had no precedent to think that Peter could do anything other than officiate at Tabitha's memorial service. Nevertheless, they sent a messenger 12 miles up the Joppa–Jerusalem road to summon Peter. They pleaded for him to come without delay (9:38).

— 9:39-41 —

When Peter arrived, an unusual scene greeted him: a body not prepared for burial, lying in the guest quarters, surrounded by mourning widows. These were undoubtedly women Tabitha had helped through her sewing ministry. As Peter stood in that upper room, staring down at a lifeless body on the bed, I imagine he found the whole scene eerily familiar, almost a re-creation of at least two other episodes in biblical history, one ancient and one more recent.[24]

In 1 Kings 17:17-24, Elijah carried the dead body of a widow's son to the upper room where he was staying, laid him on the bed, and then prayed.

> He called to the LORD and said, "O LORD my God, have You also brought calamity to the widow with whom I am staying, by causing her son to die?" Then he stretched himself upon the child three times, and called to the LORD and said, "O LORD my God, I pray You, let this child's life return to him." The LORD heard the voice of Elijah, and the life of the child returned to him and he revived. Elijah took the child and brought him down from the upper room into the house and gave him to his mother; and Elijah said, "See, your son is alive." (1 Kgs. 17:20-23)

Then during Jesus' ministry, the Lord and His disciples came upon a funeral in Nain. The deceased was the only son of a widow.

> When the Lord saw her, He felt compassion for her, and said to her, "Do not weep." And He came up and touched the coffin; and the bearers came to a halt. And He said, "Young man, I say to you, arise!" The dead man sat up and began to speak. And Jesus gave him back to his mother. (Luke 7:13-15)

Peter sent out the grieving widows, most likely without telling them his intentions (Acts 9:40). Rather than claim any knowledge of God's will in the matter or presume upon the power of the Holy Spirit or make a great show of power, he prayed quietly in private. His command recalls the resurrection of Jairus's daughter by Jesus. The Lord had given the command "Talitha, arise" (see Mark 5:41; cf. Luke 8:51-56), and Peter's command was "Tabitha, arise."

In response to Peter's command and by the power of the Holy Spirit, the woman instantly revived. Peter then presented her to the people waiting outside (9:41).

— 9:42 —

The witnesses to the miracle and the town of Joppa at large responded in belief, much like those who saw God's power in Elijah and Jesus. In Elijah's case, the woman said, "Now I know that you are a man of God and that the word of the LORD in your mouth is truth" (1 Kgs. 17:24). After Jesus' miracle in Nain, "fear gripped them all, and they began glorifying God, saying, 'A great prophet has arisen among us!' and, 'God has visited His people!' This report concerning Him went out all over Judea and in all the surrounding district" (Luke 7:16-17). So it was with Peter's miracle in Joppa. The news quickly spread and "many believed in the Lord" (Acts 9:42).

During what we call the apostolic era—the time between the Lord's ascension and the death of John, the last of the twelve apostles—the Holy Spirit gave preachers and teachers miraculous abilities. The purpose was to validate the message of the gospel as authentically from God. As I have stated before, the book of Acts documents an unusual time of transition in history. The new covenant (Jer. 31:31-34) had come in sudden and dramatic power, and God spoke through apostles. But this time of transition came to an end. As John Walvoord writes in his helpful book *The Holy Spirit*,

> With the completion of the New Testament, and its almost universal acceptance by those true to God, the need for further unusual display of miraculous works ceased. The preacher of today does not need the outward evidence of ability to heal or speak with tongues to substantiate the validity of his gospel. Rather, the written Word speaks for itself, and is attended by the convicting power of the Spirit.[25]

— 9:43 —

Luke closes the episode with a statement that stitches this story to the next. Peter remained in Joppa to reap the harvest of new believers as a result of the miracle. He probably intended to turn south or east to continue his ministry in Judea, but as is often true, the Lord had other plans.

Many centuries earlier, the prophet Jonah came to Joppa to avoid the mission God had prepared for him. Rather than travel north to Nineveh in obedience to the Lord's command, he retreated to Joppa and caught a ship bound for Tarshish on the coast of modern-day Spain, the farthest a Phoenician ship would carry him.

While still in Joppa, Peter would soon receive his own challenging command from the Lord. What would his response be?

APPLICATION: ACTS 9:32-43

Miracle Work

The Bible says that we should expect another season of miracles. Sometime in the future, dramatic displays of supernatural activity—miraculous events—will signal the beginning of the end, the events described in Revelation. This suggests that the present era, the time after the apostles and before the Great Tribulation, will see few miracles, if any at all. Still, I don't rule out the possibility that God might choose to contravene the laws of nature in a great display of His power and that He might accomplish this through a person. If so, I will be looking for at least four indications of authentic, miraculous work, all of which are reflected in the miracle accounts involving Peter that we just looked at.

Number one: *The Lord alone is glorified, never a man or a woman.* If the supernatural activity exalts a person in any way, you can rest assured that it's not of God! My advice? Get out. Get away. Any activity that doesn't glorify God, regardless of how impressive, does God's people no good.

Number two: *There is no showmanship.* In the Bible, miracles rarely have a large audience, and the display of divine power is quiet, serene, dignified, and personal. None of the Old Testament prophets, none of the apostles, and not even Jesus Himself ever used miracles to impress, entertain, dazzle, or draw a crowd.

Number three: *Unbelievers are convinced to believe.* Throughout the Scriptures, God's miraculous activity gave people the opportunity to believe. Many responded in faith; others couldn't deny divine activity, yet they willfully rejected Him. Regardless, miracles reveal God's goodness and power so that those far away will approach Him.

Number four: *Biblical truth is validated.* When God works a miracle, you don't have to hide your Bible behind your back or defend against critics. Miracles create the opportunity to proclaim the truths of God boldly. Miracles remove doubt and then create a crisis of the will. Therefore, if someone witnesses a genuine miracle and then rejects Christ, the problem is not in the head but in the heart.

Facing the Prejudice *Sin*drome
ACTS 10:1-23

NASB

1 Now *there was* a man at Caesarea named Cornelius, a centurion of what was called the Italian ᵃcohort, 2 a devout man and one who feared God with all his household, and gave many ᵃalms to the *Jewish* people and prayed to God continually. 3 About the ᵃninth hour of the day he clearly saw in a vision an angel of God who had *just* come in and said to him, "Cornelius!" 4 And fixing his gaze on him and being much alarmed, he said, "What is it, Lord?" And he said to him, "Your prayers and ᵃalms have ascended as a memorial before God. 5 Now dispatch *some* men to Joppa and send for a man *named* Simon, who is also called Peter; 6 he is staying with a tanner *named* Simon, whose house is by the sea." 7 When the angel who was speaking to him had left, he summoned two of his ᵃservants and a devout soldier of those who were his personal attendants, 8 and after he had explained everything to them, he sent them to Joppa.

9 On the next day, as they were on their way and approaching the city, Peter went up on the housetop about the ᵃsixth hour to pray. 10 But he became hungry and was desiring to eat; but while they were making preparations, he fell into a trance; 11 and he saw the ᵃsky opened up, and an ᵇobject like a great sheet coming down, lowered by four corners to the ground, 12 and there were in it all *kinds of* four-footed animals and ᵃcrawling creatures of the earth and birds of the ᵇair. 13 A voice came to him, "Get up, Peter, ᵃkill and eat!" 14 But Peter said, "By no means, Lord, for I have never eaten anything ᵃunholy and unclean." 15 Again a voice *came* to him a second time, "What God has cleansed, no *longer*

NLT

1 In Caesarea there lived a Roman army officer* named Cornelius, who was a captain of the Italian Regiment. 2 He was a devout, God-fearing man, as was everyone in his household. He gave generously to the poor and prayed regularly to God. 3 One afternoon about three o'clock, he had a vision in which he saw an angel of God coming toward him. "Cornelius!" the angel said.

4 Cornelius stared at him in terror. "What is it, sir?" he asked the angel.

And the angel replied, "Your prayers and gifts to the poor have been received by God as an offering! 5 Now send some men to Joppa, and summon a man named Simon Peter. 6 He is staying with Simon, a tanner who lives near the seashore."

7 As soon as the angel was gone, Cornelius called two of his household servants and a devout soldier, one of his personal attendants. 8 He told them what had happened and sent them off to Joppa.

9 The next day as Cornelius's messengers were nearing the town, Peter went up on the flat roof to pray. It was about noon, 10 and he was hungry. But while a meal was being prepared, he fell into a trance. 11 He saw the sky open, and something like a large sheet was let down by its four corners. 12 In the sheet were all sorts of animals, reptiles, and birds. 13 Then a voice said to him, "Get up, Peter; kill and eat them."

14 "No, Lord," Peter declared. "I have never eaten anything that our Jewish laws have declared impure and unclean.*"

15 But the voice spoke again: "Do not call something unclean if God

consider ªunholy." ¹⁶This happened three times, and immediately the ªobject was taken up into the ᵇsky.

¹⁷Now while Peter was greatly perplexed in ªmind as to what the vision which he had seen might be, behold, the men who had been sent by Cornelius, having asked directions for Simon's house, appeared at the gate; ¹⁸and calling out, they were asking whether Simon, who was also called Peter, was staying there. ¹⁹While Peter was reflecting on the vision, the Spirit said to him, "Behold, ªthree men are looking for you. ²⁰But get up, go downstairs and accompany them ªwithout misgivings, for I have sent them Myself." ²¹Peter went down to the men and said, "Behold, I am the one you are looking for; what is the reason for which you have come?" ²²They said, "Cornelius, a centurion, a righteous and God-fearing man well spoken of by the entire nation of the Jews, was *divinely* directed by a holy angel to send for you *to come* to his house and hear ªa message from you." ²³So he invited them in and gave them lodging.

And on the next day he got up and went away with them, and some of the brethren from Joppa accompanied him.

10:1 ªOr *battalion*   10:2 ªOr *gifts of charity*
10:3 ªI.e. 3 p.m.   10:4 ªOr *deeds of charity*
10:7 ªOr *household slaves*   10:9 ªI.e. noon
10:11 ªOr *heaven* ᵇOr *vessel*   10:12 ªOr *reptiles*
ᵇOr *heaven*   10:13 ªOr *sacrifice*   10:14 ªOr
profane; lit *common*   10:15 ªLit *make common*
10:16 ªOr *vessel* ᵇOr *heaven*   10:17 ªLit *himself*
10:19 ªOne early ms reads *two*   10:20 ªLit
doubting nothing   10:22 ªLit *words*

has made it clean." ¹⁶The same vision was repeated three times. Then the sheet was suddenly pulled up to heaven.

¹⁷Peter was very perplexed. What could the vision mean? Just then the men sent by Cornelius found Simon's house. Standing outside the gate, ¹⁸they asked if a man named Simon Peter was staying there.

¹⁹Meanwhile, as Peter was puzzling over the vision, the Holy Spirit said to him, "Three men have come looking for you. ²⁰Get up, go downstairs, and go with them without hesitation. Don't worry, for I have sent them."

²¹So Peter went down and said, "I'm the man you are looking for. Why have you come?"

²²They said, "We were sent by Cornelius, a Roman officer. He is a devout and God-fearing man, well respected by all the Jews. A holy angel instructed him to summon you to his house so that he can hear your message." ²³So Peter invited the men to stay for the night. The next day he went with them, accompanied by some of the brothers from Joppa.

10:1 Greek *a centurion;* similarly in 10:22.
10:14 Greek *anything common and unclean.*

For all our many differences, such as race, creed, culture, gender, and nationality, people all over the world have at least one thing in common: prejudice. It's a stubborn, thorny weed that grows in every heart and draws nourishment from the rotting compost of our fallen, sinful nature. Cut it to the ground, poison its leaves, or pull it out by the roots . . . and it'll be back before you know it.

The creeping infestation of prejudice can happen so gradually it goes unnoticed. And it takes hold in unexpected ways. We're familiar with the most common variety, racial prejudice. Some nurture a secret bigotry against people with certain colors of skin, specific nationalities, different cultures, or even particular accents. Other types of prejudice take more subtle forms: political affiliation, economic stratum, marital status, religious background, the presence of tattoos, style of clothes or hair, or even the use of cosmetics. It's a universal problem. Your prejudice might not be my prejudice, but some form of it tries to grow in every heart. Even so, some people do a better job of weeding than others.

Peter, the hero of the Jerusalem congregation and arguably the most courageous Christian in the first two decades of the church, struggled with prejudice. Fortunately for Peter and the church, the Lord would not let that sinful attitude remain; He would soon uproot it.

— 10:1-2 —

As Acts 10 opens, the church is perhaps five or six years old. The gospel had swept through Judea, drawing many Jewish converts into the church. Philip had conducted an extremely effective ministry among the Samaritans, and—to his credit—Peter had embraced as brothers and sisters people that he and his fellow Jews considered half-breed religious compromisers. Having traveled to the seaport town of Joppa, he had accepted the hospitality of a tanner named Simon (9:43). This is also to Peter's credit—Jews considered tanners unclean because their trade required them to handle the skins of dead animals. Even so, despite Peter's impressively open-minded attitude concerning Samaritans and "unclean" Jews, he never would have considered a visit to Caesarea Maritima, about 30 miles north. The reader's curiosity is therefore piqued as Luke now introduces Cornelius, a Roman officer living in Caesarea.

Every faithful Jew regarded Caesarea with religious and national disdain. Herod the Great had rebuilt this dilapidated trading outpost into a new, thoroughly modern seaport and named it in honor of Caesar Augustus. It was an engineering marvel and quickly became the preferred harbor for merchant and military vessels.[26] Gentiles loved Caesarea for the same reasons Jews hated it. Herod had built it to rival Greek cities, complete with elaborate palaces, public buildings, a large amphitheater, a temple dedicated to Caesar and Rome, and statues of the emperor surrounding the harbor entrance. Consequently, Caesarea Maritima became the capital of the Roman occupation in Israel, where procurators and governors maintained their year-round residence and where Gentiles congregated.

To a faithful Jew, the city represented everything that was wrong with Israel—Roman domination and Gentile occupation aided by compromising Hellenistic Jews.

Barry Beitzel

The Ruins of the Harbor Built by Herod the Great. The ancient city of Caesarea Maritima surrounded the harbor. The ruins of the amphitheater and the hippodrome still stand.

Cornelius was a very common Roman name. This man is described as a centurion of the Italian cohort. A Roman cohort was a military unit consisting of at least six hundred fighting men, plus support personnel. Auxiliary cohorts sometimes added 240 cavalry. A centurion commanded one hundred of these men.[27] The name "Italian cohort" likely indicated that the original soldiers of this auxiliary were Roman-born troops, not conscripts from occupied territories.[28] Putting all of Luke's clues together, it becomes clear that Cornelius was about as Roman as a man could be outside of Rome. Even so, this Roman commander worshiped God and gave generously to the Jewish people. During the Lord's ministry in Galilee, Peter had probably met a man very much like him (Luke 7:1-10).

Luke's term for the centurion's "praying" (*deomai* [1189]) is an uncommon word that means "to beg," "to plead earnestly," or "to request." The man "continually" sought something specific from God, but we're not told what (Acts 10:2).

— 10:3-8 —

The "ninth hour" (10:3), or 3:00 p.m., was the designated time for afternoon prayer in the temple (cf. 3:1). Luke is thus suggesting that

Cornelius was following this observance in the privacy of his quarters when an angel interrupted his prayers. The commander addressed the heavenly messenger as "lord," but he was using this in the same sense as one would say "sir"—as a term showing respect. The angel assured the soldier that his actions had been received by God with the same regard as the sacrifices of Hebrew worshipers; the image created by "ascended" hints at smoke rising from an altar (10:4; cf. Gen. 8:21; Exod. 29:18, 25; Lev. 8:28).

The angel gave the centurion orders with military precision, telling him the name and location of the man he should request (Acts 10:5-6). And Cornelius immediately obeyed the command to the letter, sending two household servants and a trusted, God-fearing member of his staff (10:7-8).

— 10:9 —

Cornelius's messengers made good time, completing the 30-mile journey in considerably less than the normal day and a half; they had left the evening before and were approaching Joppa around the "sixth hour," noon by our reckoning of time. Either Cornelius provided them with horses or they left immediately and pressed on through the night. Either way, it was an urgent matter for the Roman commander.

Meanwhile, the Lord prepared Peter for an unexpected visit. A twenty-first-century, Western Gentile can hardly appreciate the difficulty of the Lord's task in preparing Peter, a devout Jew. When God chose Abraham, and through him his Hebrew descendants, He set His heart on the nation of Israel. Not because they were greater in number than any other nation, not because they were more righteous, not because they deserved His heart of love, but—again—because of His grace. In an act of sovereign choice, He decided to make the Hebrew people His unique instrument in bringing the world into a relationship with Himself.

In this way, the nation of Israel became God's chosen race. By the first century, however, pride had convinced many Jews that because they were a chosen nation, they were superior to all other nations. Perhaps they began to believe that they had been chosen because no other people group could have carried the burden of following God's Law. As time passed and tradition built upon tradition, prejudice took root in the Jewish heart. Jews had begun to think of the Gentiles as unclean dogs, and pious Jews avoided all contact with Gentiles, much as we would keep our distance from a pack of stray dogs in the street. Keep all this in mind as the Lord does a work in Peter's heart.

At noon—"the sixth hour"—the day after Cornelius's vision, Peter retreated from everyone else to pray in solitude.

— 10:10-14 —

Peter was hungry, and the Lord used it as an opportunity to change his theological perspective. While praying, he drifted into an altered state of mind (*ekstasis* [1611]), which the Lord used as a canvas for a vivid illustration. In a trance, Peter saw a "vessel like a giant linen cloth" (literally rendered) descend from beyond the sky. In terms of imagery, he understood the source to be heaven and that God had sent the object to earth. This object appeared to be a microcosm of the animal world, containing representatives of many species, including reptiles and birds (10:10-12).

A voice of heavenly origin—either God's or that of an angel—invited Peter to do something completely repulsive to a devout Jew: "kill and eat" these unclean animals (10:13). God had forbidden the Israelites to eat such animals under the old covenant (Lev. 11). But during Jesus' earthly ministry, He had declared all food "clean." The Old Testament ban on certain foods had served its ceremonial and educational purpose and was no longer needed (Mark 7:14-19; Luke 11:39-41; cf. Rom. 14:14). Still, as a matter of preference deeply rooted in his Jewish upbringing, Peter resisted in the strongest terms.

Though grace abounds, prejudice dies hard.

To be fair, this would be like asking a sincere, lifelong teetotaler to have a beer. Unsurprisingly, Peter's objection goes beyond personal preference to imply that his choice had moral value. He said, in effect, "No sir! I continue to maintain the high moral standard set for all Hebrews by Moses! I won't touch anything 'unholy and unclean'" (Acts 10:14, *koinos* [2839] and *akathartos* [169]). Legalists always seem to take pride in negatives, the things they would *never* do. Alexander Whyte offers a penetrating analysis of Peter's prejudice—and our own.

> All mankind, indeed, except Peter and a few of his friends, were bound up together in one abominable bundle. And Peter was standing above them, scouting at and spitting on them all. All so like ourselves. For, how we also bundle up whole nations of men and throw them into that same unclean sheet. Whole churches that we know nothing about but their bad names that we have given them, are in our sheet of excommunication also. All the other denominations of Christians in our land are common and unclean to us. Every party outside of our own party in the political state also. We have no language contemptuous enough

wherewith to describe their wicked ways and their self-seeking schemes. They are four-footed beasts and creeping things. Indeed, there are very few men alive, and especially those who live near us, who are not sometimes in the sheet of our scorn; unless it is one here and one there of our own family, or school, or party. And they also come under our scorn and our contempt the moment they have a mind of their own, and interests of their own, and affections and ambitions of their own.[29]

— 10:15-16 —

The heavenly voice instructed Peter that the opinions or preferences of people can never supersede the declaration of God (10:15).[30] The voice commanded him, "What God has cleansed"—*katharizō* [2511]—"no longer consider unholy"—*koinos* [2839]. The latter is an adjective for things that are common, profane, or defiled. In the ceremonial sense, this word describes something that is the opposite of pure, sacred, and holy. In time, the church would come to love the related noun *koinōnia* [2842], which described their unique bond in Christ in terms of fellowship, close association, communion, and mutual sharing. This would be the beginning of fellowship between Jewish and Gentile believers. In the words of one expositor, "It would be a short step from recognizing that Gentile food was clean to realizing that Gentiles themselves were 'clean' also."[31]

The lesson didn't come easily, however. The voice had to command Peter three times! Notably, Peter never did "kill and eat" in the dream— though he responded obediently to the dream's *purpose* (10:23).

— 10:17-20 —

Peter understood the words spoken by the voice, but he didn't comprehend their meaning or application. So what if he preferred kosher food? As he pondered the meaning, the answer to his question arrived at the gate (10:17-18). The Holy Spirit spoke to Peter, either audibly or from within, to help him make the connection between the vision and the messengers from Caesarea. He commanded the apostle to follow these Gentile men without second-guessing or wavering. He should do as they asked, with confident resolve and without hesitations related to becoming ceremonially unclean (10:19-20).

— 10:21-22 —

Everything about the messengers communicates humility and respect. They knew Jews considered Gentiles unclean, so they called out from the gate. Clearly, Simon the tanner didn't invite them in. The three men didn't know that the Lord had prepared Peter for their arrival, so they prefaced their request with a long introduction praising the Gentile centurion's worthiness (10:22). The phrase "righteous and God-fearing" set him apart from most Romans. This let Peter know he would not be disparaged by his Jewish peers for accepting the invitation. And they made it clear that the invitation to preach came not simply from Cornelius, but at the direction of God.

— 10:23 —

The journey would require two days of walking. The messengers were undoubtedly tired, and it was late in the afternoon, so Peter determined to set out the next morning. Normally, Jews didn't feed and lodge Gentiles, but the Lord's vivid illustration and direct command had its effect on the apostle. He extended the same hospitality he would have offered a fellow Jew. But one can only wonder how hard it was for him. A lifetime of prejudice doesn't go away in a single afternoon.

By the end of writing this segment, Luke had accomplished several objectives. First, he had acknowledged the difficult cultural adjustments made by the first Christians as they began to accept Gentile believers. Second, he had established the Lord's divine purpose as the cause of Gentile conversion, so that the church could not regard Gentiles as an inferior brand of Christian. Third, he shows that even before Paul had begun to evangelize the Gentile world, the church had already embraced Gentile evangelism as the will of God.

APPLICATION: ACTS 10:1-23

Pulling Weeds

Just as every garden has weeds, so every heart harbors prejudice of one kind or another. So, it's not a matter of whether you struggle with prejudice, but how you choose to deal with it. Like a gardener must diligently pull weeds to stay ahead of infestation, we must seek out and eliminate every form of bigotry and chauvinism.

To eliminate prejudice, we must first know what we're looking for. I define "prejudice" as any preconceived judgment or irrational attitude of hostility directed against any individual or group. Prejudice is simply making judgments about someone in advance, forming opinions strictly on the basis of preconceived ideas and assumptions. So, as I observe Peter's struggle with prejudice and periodically search my own heart, I observe three principles at work.

Principle 1: *The root of prejudice is pride.* Pride can't be satisfied with an honest assessment of oneself; pride thrives on comparisons. It's deeply ingrained in human nature to find a scapegoat rather than accept responsibility for our own failures. We also delight to find someone more pathetic than ourselves when we become uncomfortable with our own shortcomings. When those two strategies fail, we can feed our pride by associating with one group—literally or through the power of imagination—while disparaging another as inferior.

Pride is called a "deadly sin" because it spawns so many others. Prejudice grows out of pride.

Principle 2: *The rationalization for prejudice is tradition.* Prejudice thrives on tradition. In fact, most people inherit their bigoted attitudes from generations of institutionalized pride. People behave certain ways and harbor certain attitudes because "it has always been that way."

When I was a young boy growing up in rural Texas in the 1930s, I remember that my maternal grandfather, Judge Lundy, didn't much care for "the way it's always been." At a time when unemployment for white men topped 25 percent, my granddad hired a black man named Mr. Coats and kept him employed for many years. When it came time for the man's wife to deliver a child, my granddad used his influence to make sure that it was in the hospital—probably the first black patients in that maternity ward and undoubtedly the last for quite some time. I learned from his example to honor authority but to question tradition. As it turned out, most of the hospital staff didn't have a problem with black people; they had just never thought to change what had always been.

Even when people want to set aside prejudice, they often have to battle their own culture and the inertia of tradition. It's a tough battle. Nothing will make it easier. So, we simply have to do what's difficult in order to accomplish what's right.

Principle 3: *The rehabilitation from prejudice is painful.* Honest self-examination is an uncomfortable process. There's no way to get around it. Acknowledging sin is painful because there's no one to blame but ourselves. Facing the sin of prejudice, therefore, can feel downright agonizing. By the time you discover prejudice in your own life, you realize it's been a part of your thinking for as long as you can remember. The feelings of shame can be overwhelming as you trace your own history of chauvinism and find its tentacles wrapped around many decisions and actions.

The truth hurts, but Jesus promised that truth leads to freedom. Every change I've had to face in my life has been painful. No exaggeration—every single one. And the older I get, the more difficult change becomes. Still, I wouldn't trade anything for the freedom I enjoy when I choose to fight through the pain and do what is right.

God Is Not Partial
ACTS 10:24-48

NASB

24On the following day he entered Caesarea. Now Cornelius was waiting for them and had called together his relatives and close friends. 25When Peter entered, Cornelius met him, and fell at his feet and aworshiped him. 26But Peter raised him up, saying, "Stand up; I too am just a man." 27As he talked with him, he entered and found many people assembled. 28And he said to them, "You yourselves know how unlawful it is for a man who is a Jew to associate with a foreigner or to visit him; and yet God has shown me that I should not call any man aunholy or unclean. 29That is why I came without even raising any objection when I was sent for. So I ask for what reason you have sent for me."

30Cornelius said, "Four days ago to this hour, I was praying in my house during the aninth hour; and behold, a man stood before me in shining garments, 31and he said, 'Cornelius, your prayer has been heard and your aalms have been remembered before God. 32Therefore send to Joppa and invite Simon, who is also called Peter, to come to you; he is staying at the house of Simon the tanner by the sea.' 33So I sent for you immediately, and you have abeen kind

NLT

24They arrived in Caesarea the following day. Cornelius was waiting for them and had called together his relatives and close friends. 25As Peter entered his home, Cornelius fell at his feet and worshiped him. 26But Peter pulled him up and said, "Stand up! I'm a human being just like you!" 27So they talked together and went inside, where many others were assembled.

28Peter told them, "You know it is against our laws for a Jewish man to enter a Gentile home like this or to associate with you. But God has shown me that I should no longer think of anyone as impure or unclean. 29So I came without objection as soon as I was sent for. Now tell me why you sent for me."

30Cornelius replied, "Four days ago I was praying in my house about this same time, three o'clock in the afternoon. Suddenly, a man in dazzling clothes was standing in front of me. 31He told me, 'Cornelius, your prayer has been heard, and your gifts to the poor have been noticed by God! 32Now send messengers to Joppa, and summon a man named Simon Peter. He is staying in the home of Simon, a tanner who lives near the seashore.' 33So I sent for enough to come. Now then, we are all here present before God to hear all that you have been commanded by the Lord."

34 Opening his mouth, Peter said:

"I most certainly understand *now* that God is not one to show partiality, 35 but in every nation the man who ªfears Him and ᵇdoes what is right is welcome to Him. 36 The word which He sent to the sons of Israel, preaching ªpeace through Jesus Christ (He is Lord of all)— 37 you yourselves know the thing which took place throughout all Judea, starting from Galilee, after the baptism which John proclaimed. 38ª *You know of* Jesus of Nazareth, how God anointed Him with the Holy Spirit and with power, ᵇand *how* He went about doing good and healing all who were oppressed by the devil, for God was with Him. 39 We are witnesses of all the things He did both in the ªland of the Jews and in Jerusalem. They also put Him to death by hanging Him on a ᵇcross. 40 God raised Him up on the third day and granted that He become visible, 41 not to all the people, but to witnesses who were chosen beforehand by God, *that is,* to us who ate and drank with Him after He arose from the dead. 42 And He ordered us to ªpreach to the people, and solemnly to testify that this is the One who has been appointed by God as Judge of the living and the dead. 43 Of Him all the prophets bear witness that through His name everyone who believes in Him receives forgiveness of sins."

44 While Peter was still speaking these words, the Holy Spirit fell upon all those who were listening to the ªmessage. 45 All the ªcircumcised believers who came with Peter were amazed, because the gift of the Holy Spirit had been poured out on the Gentiles also. 46 For they were hearing them speaking with tongues and

you at once, and it was good of you to come. Now we are all here, waiting before God to hear the message the Lord has given you."

34 Then Peter replied, "I see very clearly that God shows no favoritism. 35 In every nation he accepts those who fear him and do what is right. 36 This is the message of Good News for the people of Israel—that there is peace with God through Jesus Christ, who is Lord of all. 37 You know what happened throughout Judea, beginning in Galilee, after John began preaching his message of baptism. 38 And you know that God anointed Jesus of Nazareth with the Holy Spirit and with power. Then Jesus went around doing good and healing all who were oppressed by the devil, for God was with him.

39 "And we apostles are witnesses of all he did throughout Judea and in Jerusalem. They put him to death by hanging him on a cross,* 40 but God raised him to life on the third day. Then God allowed him to appear, 41 not to the general public,* but to us whom God had chosen in advance to be his witnesses. We were those who ate and drank with him after he rose from the dead. 42 And he ordered us to preach everywhere and to testify that Jesus is the one appointed by God to be the judge of all—the living and the dead. 43 He is the one all the prophets testified about, saying that everyone who believes in him will have their sins forgiven through his name."

44 Even as Peter was saying these things, the Holy Spirit fell upon all who were listening to the message. 45 The Jewish believers* who came with Peter were amazed that the gift of the Holy Spirit had been poured out on the Gentiles, too. 46 For they heard them speaking in other tongues* and praising God.

Then Peter asked, 47 "Can anyone

exalting God. Then Peter answered, [47] "Surely no one can refuse the water for these to be baptized who have received the Holy Spirit just as we *did*, can he?" [48] And he ordered them to be baptized in the name of Jesus Christ. Then they asked him to stay on for a few days.

object to their being baptized, now that they have received the Holy Spirit just as we did?" [48] So he gave orders for them to be baptized in the name of Jesus Christ. Afterward Cornelius asked him to stay with them for several days.

10:25 ªOr *prostrated himself in reverence* 10:28 ªOr *profane;* lit *common* 10:30 ªI.e. 3 to 4 p.m. 10:31 ªOr *deeds of charity* 10:33 ªLit *done well in coming* 10:35 ªOr *reverences* ᵇLit *works righteousness* 10:36 ªOr *the gospel of peace* 10:38 ªOr *How God anointed Jesus of Nazareth* ᵇLit *who went* 10:39 ªOr *countryside* ᵇLit *wood* 10:42 ªOr *proclaim* 10:44 ªLit *word* 10:45 ªLit *believers from among the circumcision;* i.e. Jewish Christians

10:39 Greek *on a tree.* 10:41 Greek *the people.* 10:45 Greek *The faithful ones of the circumcision.* 10:46 Or *in other languages.*

Back in the 1970s, Ronald Sider wrote a book that bothered me from the first page to the last—for all the right reasons. Many consider *Rich Christians in an Age of Hunger* one of the most influential books ever written up to that time on the subject of Christian responsibility. I cried through some parts and ground my teeth in others. I squirmed as he probed the issue of prejudice and exposed examples of blatant partiality. By the end, I had to face the facts and accept my responsibility as a Christian—middle-class by American standards, yet affluent with respect to a world in which more than one billion people continue to starve.

At the beginning of the third chapter, Sider asks a penetrating question: "Is God biased?" We embrace a biblical theology that says no. Our behavior, on the other hand, suggests we believe otherwise. What we say we believe matters less than what we declare by our actions.

The Lord confronted Peter's prejudice in a similar way—except in his case it was through a disturbing vision that left the apostle "greatly perplexed in mind" (10:17). A. T. Robertson has paraphrased the Greek phrase as "to be completely at a loss to know what road to take."[32] Peter didn't have long to deliberate. Within an hour or two, three Gentiles stood at the gate with an invitation to visit Cornelius in Caesarea Maritima and to preach the gospel in his household. What a great opportunity for the gospel! Still, the request challenged everything Peter understood about Jews, Gentiles, and how the Messiah would establish the kingdom of God on earth. Based on his incomplete understanding, Gentiles would come into the kingdom first through the gate of a reformed and revitalized Judaism and then embrace Jesus as High Priest and King. In other words, it would likely have seemed unthinkable for

Gentiles to be united to the new covenant community of the Jewish Messiah without first converting to Judaism!

With three Gentiles standing at the gate of Simon the tanner's house, Peter had a decision to make. Whose vision of the kingdom would he pursue? The Lord's or his own? Peter couldn't overcome a lifetime of prejudice in a matter of hours, so when put to the test, what would he do?

To the Hebrew mind, what a person *did* revealed their true beliefs, regardless of the emotions involved. According to 10:23, Peter responded by committing two great cultural transgressions: he extended hospitality to Gentiles, and he agreed to accept the hospitality of Gentiles in the despised city of Caesarea.

— 10:24-25 —

The 30-mile journey took Peter and his Jewish brothers at least a day and a half to travel on foot. Like most people, they could cover 15 to 20 miles in daylight hours. The group left Joppa the next morning; then, sometime in the afternoon of the following day, they entered Caesarea Maritima, the headquarters of Roman occupation in Israel.

From the perspective of a devout Jew, Peter had entered enemy territory to consort with the enemy. From Cornelius's point of view, God had agreed to bless his household after years of pleading. So, when God's chief representative entered his home, the commander fell down and worshiped Peter (10:25). The Greek term translated "worshiped" (*proskyneō* [4352]) doesn't presume to say what's on the heart of the person worshiping; it merely describes his or her posture. It means "to prostrate oneself" or "to bow down." In pagan religions, a man or woman representing a deity was venerated as semidivine, even more so if he or she could work miracles (14:11; 28:6).[33] Pagan worshipers offered obeisance to the gods by falling down at the feet of their priests. While Cornelius "feared God," "gave many alms to the Jewish people," and "prayed to God continually" (10:2), he was nonetheless ignorant. In the presence of someone he considered a holy man, the Roman behaved as he had been taught from childhood.

— 10:26-27 —

The gesture undoubtedly embarrassed Peter. Devout Jews scrupulously avoided giving or receiving from anyone the veneration that God alone deserves. They didn't strike coins with anyone's image, and they didn't erect statues or paint portraits or memorialize any human being in any tangible way; they wanted to avoid anything remotely close to man

"Act Medium"

ACTS 10:26

When Peter saw the centurion bowing down and worshiping him, he said, "Stand up; I too am just a man." Wasn't that a beautiful response? He didn't say, "Here, my son, kiss the ring of the big fisherman."

As fallen creatures, we tend to worship the people we highly respect. If you hold a position of authority or respect, you have a duty to discourage inordinate admiration and any form of over-the-top reverence. Do everything you can to keep people from putting you on a pedestal. It's a precarious position for you and a long fall when you eventually topple. You don't want to block their vision of God, and you don't want to be responsible for their disillusionment with Him when they finally do see your clay feet.

If God uses you significantly in a particular sphere of influence, it is your responsibility to keep the eyes of the people on the Lord. Meanwhile, let them see the cracks in your own life. Let them know that you're one with them, that you struggle with many of the same issues as they do, and that you have no corner on spiritual truth.

Be like the kids who built a summertime clubhouse in the backyard and established three rules of conduct:

#1: Nobody act big.

#2: Nobody act small.

#3: Everybody act medium.

worship. So, when Peter saw Cornelius prostrated before him, he probably shuddered at the challenge of evangelizing Gentiles. With Hebrews and even Samaritans, the gospel was being built upon a relatively solid foundation of biblical and theological knowledge. Not so with non-Jews. Lesson #1: Worship God alone.

As Peter raised the centurion to his feet, he saw a houseful of Gentiles—ignorant, yet eager to hear about Jesus, the Son of God.

— 10:28-29 —

I have always appreciated Peter's transparency. He entered the household of a Gentile, which was difficult enough. He had to stop the man from worshiping him, which felt awkward, to say the least. Then he stood before a gathered crowd of Gentiles who wanted to know how the Hebrew God could save them. Rather than ignore the great cultural and theological divide that stood between them, Peter acknowledged it. Everyone there knew Jews were not supposed to associate with Gentiles.

The term translated "unlawful" (10:28; *athemitos* [111]) is better rendered "forbidden" or "illicit." Old Testament Law didn't prohibit Hebrews from associating with Gentiles. They were not to marry outside the covenant community, but Gentiles who converted were acceptable as mates. The people of Israel were encouraged to welcome traveling strangers into their homes and to socialize freely with Gentiles, so long as they didn't compromise their moral standards in the process. After returning from the Exile, rabbis became increasingly xenophobic in their interpretation of the Law.

Peter acknowledged that his coming to Caesarea violated the sensibilities of his fellow Jews, but that it was, in fact, an act of obedience to God (10:28). Contrary to some first-century Jews, God does not—and He *never* did—consider Gentiles unworthy of salvation. From the beginning, it had been the Lord's intention for Israel to be His instrument in bringing all nations into a relationship with Himself (Isa. 43:10; 44:8). Where the Hebrews had failed, Jesus would succeed. Where Israel had abdicated its role as God's priestly nation (Exod. 19:6; Isa. 61:6), the church would fulfill its mission. Peter, as the visible leader of the church standing in the home of Cornelius, represented the church's obedience to God's call to "be My witnesses" to everyone in the world (Acts 1:8).

Having acknowledged the great cultural divide and theological chasm separating them, Peter asked the assembled Gentiles to explain why they had sent for him (10:29). He, of course, knew the answer already (10:22). This was a courteous way of asking, "How may I serve you now that I'm here?"

— 10:30-33 —

Cornelius noted that Peter was standing in his home exactly four days to the hour from when he received his vision (10:30; cf. 10:9). (Eastern cultures reckon the passing of days differently than we do in the West. They include the present day in the total, whereas we start counting with yesterday.) He briefly recounted the angel's message and his immediate obedience, and he acknowledged Peter's arrival in obedience to his instructions. His short speech highlights the Lord's central role in bringing the meeting together.

— 10:34-36 —

Peter's message can be divided into two parts:

1. God is the God of all nations (10:34-36).
2. Jesus Christ offers salvation for all people (10:37-43).

Peter's opening line acknowledges a truth that he himself did not fully appreciate until the Lord intervened. The NASB inserts the italicized word "now" (10:34) because it's not in the Greek text yet could be supported by the context. Still, it seems best to leave it out. Peter undoubtedly accepted the scriptural doctrine that God shows no partiality (see Deut. 10:17; 2 Chr. 19:7), but only in theory; only recently had he taken the doctrine seriously enough to act upon it. Either way, it's a transparent admission. He stood in the Gentile home because he himself had changed.

The phrases "fears Him" and "does what is right" (Acts 10:35) do not suggest that people can be good enough to earn God's favor or to gain salvation for themselves. Peter merely acknowledges that God welcomes all who want a relationship with Him. "Fear Him" describes an attitude of belief; "does what is right" refers to the outward evidence of genuine faith.

Jesus is indeed the Jewish Messiah sent to Israel, but He came to redeem the whole world so that all might have "peace with God" (Rom. 5:1). The title "Lord of all" (Acts 10:36) was significant to everyone in the room, but for different reasons. Romans sometimes conferred deity upon their emperors, whom they saw as rulers of the world even beyond their borders. Pagan worshipers used the title in reference to their mythical gods. And Peter gained a new appreciation for the title

"Lord of all"—not just the Lord of the Jews—as a result of his recent experience.

— 10:37-43 —

God is the God of all, and Jesus Christ is the Savior of all. To support his claim, Peter recounted several facts about Jesus that were common knowledge in the region. Luke's synopsis of Jesus' life roughly follows the outline presented by Mark in his Gospel account:

- Baptism by John (10:37)
- Ministry in Galilee (10:37-38)
- Ministry in Judea (10:39)
- Ministry in Jerusalem (10:39)
- Crucifixion (10:39)
- Resurrection (10:40-41)
- Commissioning of the Disciples (10:42)

Peter declared himself and the other apostles to be eyewitnesses to these facts and then stressed the universal nature of Christ's work. The ministry of Jesus affects the whole world, leading all people to one of two destinies: judgment (10:42) or forgiveness of sins (10:43). The prophets of the Old Testament didn't promise salvation to Israel alone but to the whole world, to "everyone who believes in Him" (10:43).

— 10:44-46 —

Like many preachers, Peter never actually finished his sermon. "While Peter was still speaking," and even before he had a chance to urge his audience to place their trust in Jesus Christ, they believed (10:44)! They didn't have the biblical and theological knowledge of most Jews in Israel, but they believed with their whole selves. That was good enough for God, who knows the heart perfectly. In response to their belief, they immediately received the gift of the Holy Spirit. As a result, these Gentile believers behaved exactly like the original Jewish followers of Jesus on the Day of Pentecost, who had praised God in languages not their own (2:4, 11).

Luke doesn't refer to Peter and his companions in terms of their ethnicity; not all of them were Hebrew. Instead, he calls them "circumcised believers" (10:45), that is, Christians who came into the kingdom of God by first becoming Jews. Hebrews were natural-born "sons of the covenant," circumcised on the eighth day and reared in the temple. Gentile converts became "God-fearers," studied Hebrew and the Law, passed an exam, submitted to water baptism, were circumcised, and then received the designation "sons of the covenant."

By sending His Spirit upon the new Gentile believers—ignorant and uncircumcised though they were—and giving them power identical to that of the first Christians at Pentecost, God sent a clear message to all who witnessed the event: Salvation is by grace alone through faith alone in Christ alone. Nothing other than complete, authentic belief is required. Knowledge of the Law is good, but not necessary. Circumcision is good, but not required. Biblical and theological knowledge is good, but not essential. Only trusting in Christ brings forgiveness of sins.

— 10:47-48 —

Peter got the point. He acknowledged the obvious. The power of the Holy Spirit flowed through these Gentile believers, validating them as equal to Jewish believers, so he affirmed them as brothers and sisters in Christ. He baptized them in water immediately and stayed with them several days, undoubtedly to answer their questions, teach them the basics of living in grace, and encourage them to become witnesses. What a memorable experience for Peter!

APPLICATION: ACTS 10:24-48
Theology in Action

The Lord didn't blame Peter for his faulty theology or the attitude of prejudice his theology encouraged. The Jewish fisherman came by his bigotry honestly; that is, he inherited a long tradition of chauvinism from his parents and generations of rabbis gone wrong. As the most visible leader of the church, however, Peter couldn't remain as he had been; he needed radical, spiritual heart surgery.

In Acts 10:1-23, the Lord prepared Peter's heart by correcting his theology. The dietary Laws God gave to Moses and the Israelites had served their purpose. The restrictions taught the Hebrews that they are a sanctified race, a priestly nation, designated by God to be His representatives to all the nations. But the time had come for change. A new era had dawned, a new dispensation—the era of the church. Believers, whether Jewish or Gentile, no longer have to come to the temple to meet God; they now have Christ. Believers no longer need to express their faith through sacrifices with the aid of a priest; they now have direct access to the ultimate High Priest, the Son of God. To be saved, all people alike must believe in Christ with all their hearts, and the One who knows every heart will respond.

Peter understood the Lord's message theologically, but he failed to see how it applied to the process of conversion. That's when God gave Peter an opportunity to act upon what he had learned. He obeyed the Lord's command to go with the Gentiles and to preach the gospel among them, and in the process, he gained a more complete understanding. In other words, God changed Peter's mind in a vision on the rooftop and then changed Peter's heart through his obedience in the home of Cornelius. All of this suggests a principle and an imperative.

The principle: *What you do is more important than how you feel.* The Lord is so gracious. He knows how difficult it is for us to change, yet He can't allow us to remain as we are, saddled with harmful ways of thinking and shackled to habitual sin. Prejudice is only one of our many problems! So He shows us the truth and then challenges us to apply what He has taught. It would be nice if He would give us time to adjust to this new, heavenly way of thinking and behaving, but He doesn't. He expects obedience. He expects a faith response to His commands. It feels rushed. Uncomfortable. Sometimes even impossible. But the Lord is not concerned about how we feel about His commands, only that we act on them.

The imperative: *Do what is right and let God change your heart.* Peter knew what to do, and it's doubtful his obedience made him feel comfortable, but he did what was right. In the end, the apostle grew, the Gentiles received salvation, and the church began a new chapter of expansion. In fact, Peter's obedience set the stage for Paul's future ministry.

Our Maker knows that our discomfort is only temporary. When we set aside our discomfort to do what He has commanded, He knows the experience will accomplish its task and we will be changed. If you know you should do something because God says it's right, don't wait for your feelings to give you the go-ahead. Trust Him. Respond in faith. Do what is right and let your feelings follow your obedience.

Getting Out of God's Way
ACTS 11:1-18

¹Now the apostles and the brethren who were throughout Judea heard that the Gentiles also had received the word of God. ²And when Peter came up to Jerusalem, ᵃthose who were circumcised took issue with him, ³saying, "You ᵃwent to uncircumcised men and ate with them." ⁴But Peter began *speaking* ᵃand *proceeded* to explain to them in orderly sequence, saying, ⁵"I was in the city of Joppa praying; and in a trance I saw a vision, an ᵃobject coming down like a great sheet lowered by four corners from ᵇthe sky; and it came right down to me, ⁶and when I had fixed my gaze on it and was observing it ᵃI saw the four-footed animals of the earth and the wild beasts and the ᵇcrawling creatures and the birds of the ᶜair. ⁷I also heard a voice saying to me, 'Get up, Peter; ᵃkill and eat.' ⁸But I said, 'By no means, Lord, for nothing ᵃunholy or unclean has ever entered my mouth.' ⁹But a voice from heaven answered a second time, 'What God has cleansed, no longer ᵃconsider unholy.' ¹⁰This happened three times, and everything was drawn back up into ᵃthe sky. ¹¹And behold, at that moment three men appeared at the house in which we were *staying,* having been sent to me from Caesarea. ¹²The Spirit told me to go with them ᵃwithout misgivings. These six brethren also went with me and we entered the man's house. ¹³And he reported to us how he had seen the angel ᵃstanding in his house, and saying, 'Send to Joppa and have Simon, who is also called Peter, brought here; ¹⁴and he will speak words to you by which you will be saved, you and all your household.' ¹⁵And as I began

¹Soon the news reached the apostles and other believers* in Judea that the Gentiles had received the word of God. ²But when Peter arrived back in Jerusalem, the Jewish believers* criticized him. ³"You entered the home of Gentiles* and even ate with them!" they said.

⁴Then Peter told them exactly what had happened. ⁵"I was in the town of Joppa," he said, "and while I was praying, I went into a trance and saw a vision. Something like a large sheet was let down by its four corners from the sky. And it came right down to me. ⁶When I looked inside the sheet, I saw all sorts of tame and wild animals, reptiles, and birds. ⁷And I heard a voice say, 'Get up, Peter; kill and eat them.'

⁸"'No, Lord,' I replied. 'I have never eaten anything that our Jewish laws have declared impure or unclean.*'

⁹"But the voice from heaven spoke again: 'Do not call something unclean if God has made it clean.' ¹⁰This happened three times before the sheet and all it contained was pulled back up to heaven.

¹¹"Just then three men who had been sent from Caesarea arrived at the house where we were staying. ¹²The Holy Spirit told me to go with them and not to worry that they were Gentiles. These six brothers here accompanied me, and we soon entered the home of the man who had sent for us. ¹³He told us how an angel had appeared to him in his home and had told him, 'Send messengers to Joppa, and summon a man named Simon Peter. ¹⁴He will tell you how you and everyone in your household can be saved!'

¹⁵"As I began to speak," Peter

NASB

to speak, the Holy Spirit fell upon them just as *He did* upon us at the beginning. ¹⁶And I remembered the word of the Lord, how He used to say, 'John baptized with water, but you will be baptized ᵃwith the Holy Spirit.' ¹⁷Therefore if God gave to them the same gift as *He gave* to us also after believing in the Lord Jesus Christ, who was I that I could ᵃstand in God's way?" ¹⁸When they heard this, they ᵃquieted down and glorified God, saying, "Well then, God has granted to the Gentiles also the repentance *that leads* to life."

11:2 ᵃLit *those of the circumcision;* i.e. Jewish Christians   11:3 ᵃOr *entered the house of*
11:4 ᵃLit *and was explaining*   11:5 ᵃOr *vessel* ᵇOr *heaven*   11:6 ᵃLit *and I saw* ᵇOr *reptiles* ᶜOr *heaven*   11:7 ᵃOr *sacrifice*   11:8 ᵃOr *profane;* lit *common*   11:9 ᵃLit *make common*   11:10 ᵃOr *heaven*   11:12 ᵃOr *without making any distinction* 11:13 ᵃOr *after he had stood in his house and said* 11:16 ᵃOr *in*   11:17 ᵃLit *prevent God*   11:18 ᵃLit *became silent*

NLT

continued, "the Holy Spirit fell on them, just as he fell on us at the beginning. ¹⁶Then I thought of the Lord's words when he said, 'John baptized with* water, but you will be baptized with the Holy Spirit.' ¹⁷And since God gave these Gentiles the same gift he gave us when we believed in the Lord Jesus Christ, who was I to stand in God's way?"

¹⁸When the others heard this, they stopped objecting and began praising God. They said, "We can see that God has also given the Gentiles the privilege of repenting of their sins and receiving eternal life."

11:1 Greek *brothers.*   11:2 Greek *those of the circumcision.*   11:3 Greek *of uncircumcised men.* 11:8 Greek *anything common or unclean.* 11:16 Or *in;* also in 11:16b.

A good leader must know when it's time to make changes and when to stay the course. He or she must then communicate with others and convince them to follow. Those are the basics of Leadership 101, and they hold true no matter what kind of organization you lead. Spiritual leadership, however, requires at least one additional skill: knowing when to get out of God's way.

Every spiritual leader must come to terms with the fact that the church is *God's* organization to lead. It's easy to forget that. In our desire to keep the church on course amid shifting currents and prevailing winds, we tend to regard all change as unfavorable. Pastors, teachers, elders, and leaders must stand firm against constant pressure from the world to compromise divine truth in favor of popular opinion. So, when the Lord wants to alter course or adapt His church to meet new challenges, we're often the last to see it.

That's unfortunate. As spiritual leaders, we should be the first to sense His direction and be ready to change when we feel confident of His leading. After all, we serve a contemporary God! He's never surprised by the future, He's never out of date, and He's never threatened by technological advancement or evolving cultures. Our message never changes, but our methods often do. Consequently, He's kept the church cutting edge and relevant for more than two thousand years. He didn't do that by keeping things perpetually the same. As difficult as this may be for some to believe, change has always been part of His ministry strategy.

Peter would soon discover this for himself. As he went up to the rooftop to pray at his friend's house in Joppa, he had no idea things were about to change so dramatically. Up to that point, the church had been growing steadily as a result of the gospel being preached to communities of Jews. Successful evangelism among the Samaritans required church leaders to stretch their vision of ministry a bit—most Jews found Samaritans unsavory—but they worshiped the same God, believed and studied the same Law, and anticipated the same Messiah (see John 4:25), so they shared a great deal in common. Despite several significant challenges, everything was moving along comfortably—that is, until the Lord's encounter with Peter's prejudice signaled a major change.

The good news: Peter got the message and obeyed. That's an important first step for a leader, spiritual or otherwise. Then came the greater task of leadership. It was his responsibility to communicate the new direction and to convince others to follow. Fortunately, the Lord had armed the apostle with everything he needed to deliver a simple, clear message: *Get out of the Lord's way!*

— 11:1-3 —

News about the conversion of Cornelius and his household spread quickly throughout the region of Judea. That's not surprising, considering the importance of Caesarea to government and commerce as well as the controversial content of the news. So, when Peter arrived in Jerusalem—perhaps with his first taste of ham or shellfish still on his breath—some of his colleagues weren't eager to celebrate. Luke identifies the critics as "those who were circumcised" (11:2; see 10:45). He uses this expression for two reasons: First, to denote both kinds of Jewish believer—natural-born Hebrews and Gentile converts to Judaism prior to trusting in Christ. Second, to keep the basis of their objection in mind. Jews typically looked down on Gentiles as unclean and ignorant, but they also believed Gentiles could be made acceptable by teaching them to follow the Law. The rite of circumcision validated a male as one who knew and followed the Old Testament statutes.

The phrase rendered "took issue with him" (11:2) appears weak in English. The Greek verb used is *diakrinō* [1252], which literally means "to separate" and is most often translated "judge" or "decide." Followed by "with him" or "against him,"[34] it indicates that they disputed with him. To put it in context: They retained the very misgivings that Peter had just overcome (cf. *diakrinō* in 10:20; 11:12). They said, "You entered the home and company of uncircumcised men and ate with them" (11:3, my translation). The literal Greek is "You *went in to*," meaning "you associated with" or "you received the hospitality of" or "you shared fellowship with." This came as an accusation, not merely a statement of fact. They might well have asked, "How could you?!"

Many commentators have noted that the Jewish believers didn't object to Peter's preaching the gospel or baptizing the Gentiles, only that he mingled with them and ate their food. But this, I think, misses the point. The circumcised Christians objected to his having *anything* to do with the Gentiles, including evangelism. Remember, their understanding of New Testament evangelism followed the Old Testament pattern, which expected proselytes to seek God in the temple. Apparently, they didn't comprehend the full extent of the Lord's commissioning in 1:8. Furthermore, they couldn't fathom how anyone could come to the Messiah without at least some biblical and theological training.

To be fair, Peter himself would have held to the same opinion just a few days earlier. The believers in Jerusalem didn't receive a vision. They didn't hear God's direct command to visit Caesarea. They hadn't experienced anything like what Peter had.

— 11:4-6 —

The leading apostle immediately recognized the problem. He didn't berate his colleagues or flout his progressive attitude or shame them for being prejudiced and backward. He met them where they were so he could vicariously walk them through the transforming process he had experienced. He said, in effect, "A short time ago, I saw things as you do. Let me tell you what changed my mind."

When God wants to make a change within the church or a Christian organization, He rarely communicates it to the masses. More often, He prompts an individual—most often the leader—to become His agent of change. Depending upon the health of the organization, this individual receives either respect or ridicule—rarely anything in between. Truth be told, change is always challenging. If the vision for change comes from God, the proposal will not contradict Scripture; on the contrary, the new direction will help the organization become more obedient to the Word of God. Whether or not others recognize it, the future of that organization will depend upon its response to the Lord's agent of change.

Peter recounted his experience on the rooftop in Joppa "in orderly sequence" (11:4), and a comparison between his recollection (11:5-11) and the event (10:9-20) shows he left out no detail.

— 11:7-17 —

Throughout his account, Peter highlighted the Lord's prompting:

"Get up, Peter; kill and eat." (11:7)

"What God has cleansed, no longer consider unholy." (11:9)

"The Spirit told me to go with them without misgivings." (11:12)

"The Holy Spirit fell upon them just as He did upon us at the beginning." (11:15)

"God gave to them the same gift as He gave to us." (11:17)

Peter added the detail that when he traveled to Caesarea, six of the men in the room had accompanied him and had witnessed everything. There may have been others (10:23), but these six were among the group from Joppa. He undoubtedly asked them to come along not only for moral support but also to witness what God would do among the Gentiles. He didn't know what to expect, but his vision hinted that it would be something big!

He didn't bother to recount the details of his sermon; the specifics of his eloquence or sound reasoning weren't important. In fact, he admitted that he said relatively little compared to all he had planned. According to 10:34-43, he said a lot in a short space, so "began to speak" (11:15) suggests he had only gotten started on a lengthy sermon before the Holy Spirit interrupted. Peter explicitly tied the falling of the Holy Spirit in Caesarea to the events of Pentecost. "At the beginning" points to the beginning of the church (2:4). He also recalled the Lord's promise of Holy Spirit baptism (11:16; cf. 1:5). It was a well-crafted presentation.

John the Baptizer first uttered the promise of baptism in the Holy Spirit to the Jews he called to repentance (Matt. 3:11; Mark 1:8; Luke 3:16; John 1:33). Naturally, they applied the promise to themselves without much thought of anyone else. Jesus affirmed the promise just before His ascension, and the 120 or so gathered disciples who awaited its fulfillment (Acts 1:15) applied the words to themselves, without considering that it might apply to others beyond their community. Then they saw the Holy Spirit fill the three thousand converts after Peter's first sermon (2:37-41) and the five thousand after his second (4:4). Then several apostles watched as the Spirit fell on the Samaritan converts (8:14-17). At each stage of growth, the Lord's promise applied to more and more people.

Just in case they missed the point, Peter underscored it for them

(11:17). When God poured out His Spirit on the Gentiles, He validated them as authentically Christian, just like all the others who had believed and were baptized. Peter said, in effect, "Gentlemen, it doesn't matter what you or I think; God has spoken, and that puts an end to the debate." When Peter saw the power of the Holy Spirit fill the Gentiles, he knew enough to get out of the Lord's way.

— 11:18 —

Luke writes that the critics "quieted down," obviously referring to their arguments. The Lord had spoken; what more was there to say? They broke their silence only to give praise to God.

By this time in church history, the term "repentance" (*metanoia* [3341]) had taken on a technical meaning. "Repentance" encapsulates the response of Cornelius and his household to the gospel. The word literally means "a change of mind," but it clearly means more than that when used of new believers. "Faith" or "belief" (*pistis* [4102]) describes the attitude of a person who trusts in Christ alone for salvation. "Repentance" is the process of turning away from one's own ability to be good enough to earn salvation and turning toward Christ in an attitude of faith. The full expression of this special "change of mind" is repentance resulting in life.

This was a momentous occasion in the development of the church. Just as Peter didn't understand all the implications of his rooftop vision in Joppa, so these Jewish Christians didn't comprehend all this meant for the church as a movement or for them personally. Their acceptance of the Gentile converts gave them greater affinity with Gentiles—good for church unity—but would drive a permanent wedge between themselves and the temple. Up to this point, the Jesus followers in Jerusalem were considered a peculiar sect of Judaism. Embracing Gentiles as brothers and sisters would put an end to the goodwill they enjoyed among ordinary Jews in the temple.

APPLICATION: ACTS 11:1-18

Time to Face the Changes

As Peter recounted his encounter with the Lord in prayer, his obedience to the Lord's command, and his experience with the Gentiles, those listening must have grappled with the change that was imminent. They ultimately recognized that this change was of God. Through this process, the leaders of the early church learned at least three lessons we would do well to remember.

First, *some changes are inevitable.* Again, that might seem obvious, especially in our technological culture in which change is the only constant. The Lord taught Peter that the church can change with the culture without becoming tainted by it. For a thousand generations—and counting—the Lord has appointed human leaders to adapt His church to meet the stylistic bents of each region, race, language, and philosophy, yet without altering the core message of the gospel. Methods must change; the message must not.

Second, *any change requires adjustment.* For some reason, we perpetually think the most recent spiritual lesson we learned was the last leg of our spiritual journey—not consciously, only when someone proposes an uncomfortable change. Then we dig our heels in: "I finally have a firm grasp on how things should be." Then we become rigid and resistant instead of adaptable and accommodating. That's because we don't like big changes when the status quo meets our personal needs. Consequently, we'll use any means necessary to justify keeping things the way they are—even the misuse of Scripture and nonsensical theology.

The Lord continues to change His church to keep us in touch, flexible, and cutting edge. Peter is a wonderful model of how we must adapt to keep in step with God's program.

Third, *every change must be examined in light of Scripture.* When evaluating potential change, we must remember that some things are absolutes and some things are flexible. That might seem like good ol' common sense, but for some reason we have to be reminded of it when potential changes affect the church. Even the most successful risk takers in business suddenly revert to tradition and nostalgia when making decisions about how their local fellowship should conduct ministry. On the other hand, some people respond to changes in society impulsively without considering the long-term impact on the church or whether the truths of Scripture would be compromised. So, it's helpful for a local body to define what must remain absolute, such as the fundamentals of the faith. For any church I serve, that list must include these essentials:

- the inerrancy of Scripture
- the deity of Jesus Christ
- His virgin birth
- His sinlessness
- His atonement on the cross for the sin of humanity

- His bodily resurrection from the grave
- His literal return to this earth
- the fulfillment of His promises
- the assignment of those without Christ to hell and the assignment of those in Christ to heaven

Those are fundamentals of the faith we must not compromise in any decision. In regard to *how* we express those truths and *how* we conduct ministry, on the other hand, we have a duty to be creative and to remain current. Forgive me if it sounds unorthodox, but I think if Jesus Christ had come to earth in our day, His message would not change one bit, but His style would reach people where they are in the manner they can best hear. His people, therefore, should be no less flexible.

Operation Comeback
ACTS 11:19-30

NASB

19 So then those who were scattered because of the ᵃpersecution that occurred in connection with Stephen made their way ᵇto Phoenicia and Cyprus and Antioch, speaking the word to no one except to Jews alone. 20 But there were some of them, men of Cyprus and Cyrene, who came to Antioch and *began* speaking to the ᵃGreeks also, ᵇpreaching the Lord Jesus. 21 And the hand of the Lord was with them, and a large number who believed turned to the Lord. 22 The ᵃnews about them ᵇreached the ears of the church at Jerusalem, and they sent Barnabas off ᶜto Antioch. 23 Then when he arrived and ᵃwitnessed the grace of God, he rejoiced and *began* to encourage them all with ᵇresolute heart to remain *true* to the Lord; 24 for he was a good man, and full of the Holy Spirit and of faith. And considerable ᵃnumbers were ᵇbrought to the Lord. 25 And he left for Tarsus to look for Saul; 26 and when he had found him, he brought

NLT

19 Meanwhile, the believers who had been scattered during the persecution after Stephen's death traveled as far as Phoenicia, Cyprus, and Antioch of Syria. They preached the word of God, but only to Jews. 20 However, some of the believers who went to Antioch from Cyprus and Cyrene began preaching to the Gentiles* about the Lord Jesus. 21 The power of the Lord was with them, and a large number of these Gentiles believed and turned to the Lord.

22 When the church at Jerusalem heard what had happened, they sent Barnabas to Antioch. 23 When he arrived and saw this evidence of God's blessing, he was filled with joy, and he encouraged the believers to stay true to the Lord. 24 Barnabas was a good man, full of the Holy Spirit and strong in faith. And many people were brought to the Lord.

25 Then Barnabas went on to Tarsus to look for Saul. 26 When he found him, he brought him back to

him to Antioch. And for an entire year they ᵃmet with the church and taught considerable ᵇnumbers; and the disciples were first called Christians in Antioch.

²⁷Now ᵃat this time some prophets came down from Jerusalem to Antioch. ²⁸One of them named Agabus stood up and *began* to indicate ᵃby the Spirit that there would certainly be a great famine all over the ᵇworld. ᶜAnd this took place in the *reign* of Claudius. ²⁹And in the proportion that any of the disciples had means, each of them determined to send *a contribution* for the ᵃrelief of the brethren living in Judea. ³⁰And this they did, sending it ᵃin charge of Barnabas and Saul to the elders.

11:19 ᵃLit *tribulation* ᵇLit *as far as* 11:20 ᵃLit *Hellenists;* people who lived by Greek customs and culture ᵇOr *bringing the good news of* 11:22 ᵃLit *word* ᵇLit *was heard in* ᶜLit *as far as* 11:23 ᵃLit *saw* ᵇLit *purpose of heart* 11:24 ᵃLit *crowd was* ᵇLit *added* 11:26 ᵃOr *were gathered together* ᵇLit *crowd* 11:27 ᵃLit *in these days* 11:28 ᵃOr *through* ᵇLit *inhabited earth* ᶜLit *which* 11:29 ᵃLit *service* 11:30 ᵃLit *by the hand of*

Antioch. Both of them stayed there with the church for a full year, teaching large crowds of people. (It was at Antioch that the believers* were first called Christians.)

²⁷During this time some prophets traveled from Jerusalem to Antioch. ²⁸One of them named Agabus stood up in one of the meetings and predicted by the Spirit that a great famine was coming upon the entire Roman world. (This was fulfilled during the reign of Claudius.) ²⁹So the believers in Antioch decided to send relief to the brothers and sisters* in Judea, everyone giving as much as they could. ³⁰This they did, entrusting their gifts to Barnabas and Saul to take to the elders of the church in Jerusalem.

11:20 Greek *the Hellenists* (i.e., those who speak Greek); other manuscripts read *the Greeks.* 11:26 Greek *disciples;* also in 11:29. 11:29 Greek *the brothers.*

Benched. Shelved. Set aside. Taken out of circulation. If we go by what Luke reveals about Paul's activity during Peter's historic evangelism among the Gentiles in Acts 10, we might get the impression that Paul was out of action for ten years after his dramatic conversion. The truth is, Paul was never inactive. He certainly wasn't in the limelight or in the mainstream of activity, but he was doing ministry like the vast majority of faithful servants of God throughout history—in the background, in obscurity. But why? Why would God send him to "small time" ministry in Tarsus for ten years after such an explosive conversion?

Think about it. No Christian had a more impressive résumé for ministry among the Jews. Yet in His wise providence and for His own purposes, God often places such people in small-scale, nonglamorous ministries for a season. He hones their theology, whittles at their character, rearranges their priorities, and teaches them the techniques of walking in the Spirit and not walking in the flesh. Not as rejection, but as refinement, God set Paul aside in this way.

Again, from a human perspective, Saul seemed the ideal candidate for fast-tracking into ministry to his fellow Hebrews. The Lord, however,

THE AUTOBIOGRAPHY OF PAUL OF TARSUS

ACTS 11:25

If Paul were to pen an autobiography, it might go something like this:

"I am a Jew of Tarsus in Cilicia, a citizen of no insignificant city" (Acts 21:39). "I was actually born a [Roman] citizen" (Acts 22:28). "I . . . am an Israelite, a descendant of Abraham" (Rom. 11:1), "circumcised the eighth day, of the nation of Israel, of the tribe of Benjamin, a Hebrew of Hebrews; as to the Law, a Pharisee; as to zeal, a persecutor of the church; as to the righteousness which is in the Law, found blameless" (Phil. 3:5-6). "I am a Jew, born in Tarsus of Cilicia, but brought up in [Jerusalem], educated under Gamaliel, strictly according to the law of our fathers, being zealous for God" (Acts 22:3).

"I used to persecute the church of God beyond measure and tried to destroy it; and I was advancing in Judaism beyond many of my contemporaries among my countrymen, being more extremely zealous for my ancestral traditions. But when God, who had set me apart even from my mother's womb and called me through His grace, was pleased to reveal His Son in me so that I might preach Him among the Gentiles, I did not immediately consult with flesh and blood, nor did I go up to Jerusalem to those who were apostles before me; but I went away to Arabia, and returned once more to Damascus.

"Then three years later I went up to Jerusalem to become acquainted with Cephas, and stayed with him fifteen days. But I did not see any other of the apostles except James, the Lord's brother. (Now in what I am writing to you, I assure you before God that I am not lying.) Then I went into the regions of Syria and Cilicia. I was still unknown by sight to the churches of Judea which were in Christ; but only, they kept hearing, 'He who once persecuted us is now preaching the faith which he once tried to destroy.' And they were glorifying God because of me" (Gal. 1:13-24).

"I thank Christ Jesus our Lord, who has strengthened me, because He considered me faithful, putting me into service, even though I was formerly a blasphemer and a persecutor and a violent aggressor. Yet I was shown mercy because I acted ignorantly in unbelief" (1 Tim. 1:12-13). "I am the least of the apostles, and not fit to be called an apostle, because I persecuted the church of God. But by the grace of God I am what I am, and His grace toward me did not prove vain; but I labored even more than all of them, yet not I, but the grace of God with me" (1 Cor. 15:9-10). "For if I preach the gospel, I have nothing to boast of, for I am under compulsion; for woe is me if I do not preach the gospel. For if I do this voluntarily, I have a reward; but if against my will, I have a stewardship entrusted to me. What then is my reward? That, when I preach the gospel, I may offer the gospel without charge, so as not to make full use of my right in the gospel" (1 Cor. 9:16-18).

"For though I am free from all men, I have made myself a slave to all, so that I may win more. To the Jews I became as a Jew, so that I might win Jews; to those who are under the Law, as under the Law though not being myself under the Law, so that I might win those who are under the Law; to those who are without law, as without law, though not being without the law of God but under the law of Christ, so that I might win those who are without law. To the weak I became weak, that I might win the weak; I have become all things to all men, so that I may by all means save some. I do all things for the sake of the gospel, so that I may become a fellow partaker of it" (1 Cor. 9:19-23). "I know how to get along with humble means, and I also know how to live in prosperity; in any and every circumstance I have learned the secret of being filled and going hungry, both of having abundance and suffering need. I can do all things through Him who strengthens me" (Phil. 4:12-13).

"I am already being poured out as a drink offering, and the time of my departure has come. I have fought the good fight, I have finished the course, I have kept the faith; in the future there is laid up for me the crown of righteousness, which the Lord, the righteous Judge, will award to me on that day; and not only to me, but also to all who have loved His appearing" (2 Tim. 4:6-8). "The Lord stood with me and strengthened me, so that through me the proclamation might be fully accomplished, and that all the Gentiles might hear; and I was rescued out of the lion's mouth. The Lord will rescue me from every evil deed, and will bring me safely to His heavenly kingdom; to Him be the glory forever and ever. Amen" (2 Tim. 4:17-18).

doesn't recruit like a corporate headhunter. He chooses people based on His own omniscient insight and prepares them through His own sovereign omnipotence. God selected Saul to become His witness among Gentiles. He made this clear in the beginning, telling the newly converted Pharisee,

> "For this purpose I have appeared to you, to appoint you a minister and a witness not only to the things which you have seen, but also to the things in which I will appear to you; rescuing you from the Jewish people and from the Gentiles, to whom I am sending you, to open their eyes so that they may turn from darkness to light and from the dominion of Satan to God, that they may receive forgiveness of sins and an inheritance among those who have been sanctified by faith in Me." (26:16-18)

For whatever reason, Saul didn't pursue ministry among the Gentiles immediately; he headed straight for the synagogues. Within a short time after his Damascus road encounter with the risen Messiah, Saul was expertly defending the identity of Jesus as the Messiah and masterfully demonstrating the truth of the gospel, but with little effect among his fellow Jews. After escaping assassination in Damascus, Saul fled to Jerusalem, where he lived like a man without a country until Barnabas, the "Son of Encouragement," became his advocate. At the insistence of Barnabas, Peter and the other church leaders accepted Saul, and he enjoyed the fellowship of believers—for a time.

Peter had not yet visited the home of Cornelius. One wonders why that had not been Saul's task, since he was supposed to be the apostle

TARSUS

ACTS 11:25

Saul, later known as Paul, proudly declared himself "a Jew of Tarsus in Cilicia, a citizen of no insignificant city" (21:39). Even though he was a product of Jewish education, having sat under Gamaliel in Jerusalem (22:3), his eager, young mind undoubtedly found Tarsus enriching.

In its heyday, Tarsus commanded a strategic spot on the navigable Cydnus River and was on the route to the famous Cilician Gates, a crucial engineered mountain pass.[35] Anyone traveling by land between Asia Minor and eastern destinations, including Syria, Mesopotamia, Judea, and Egypt, had to use this passage through the Taurus Mountains. Consequently, this strategic location made it a natural place for trading merchandise and exchanging ideas.

With so many people and such a wealth of resources, Tarsus became a center of learning. The academy in Tarsus strived to attain to the fame of the renowned schools in Athens and Alexandria.[36] But the chief downfall of the school was that "Tarsians who had studied in their own city were known for completing their education abroad, and then making their home in Rome or elsewhere rather than returning to Tarsus. Strabo lists many notable scholars from Tarsus."[37] Some have suggested that Saul was one who studied locally and then moved to Jerusalem. However, it's more likely that Saul left Tarsus around the age of twelve to study under Gamaliel.[38]

During his ten-year residency in Tarsus after his conversion, a scholar like Saul would have undoubtedly availed himself of the resources of the academy in Tarsus, which would further prepare him for a future ministry among the Gentiles. In fact, his quotation of the poets Epimenides of Crete and Aratus of Soli (a fellow Cilician) hints at some Greek education (Titus 1:12; Acts 17:28).

How fitting that Tarsus should prepare Saul for ministry among the Gentiles. As one scholar noted, "Tarsus has been described as 'the heart of the Greco-Roman world' and 'a meeting place of East and West.' From such an environment, a man like Saul of Tarsus, at home with Greek and Roman culture and educated at the feet of Gamaliel, was singularly equipped to bring the gospel to the Jew first and also to the Greek."[39]

to the Gentiles. From a human perspective, it seems backwards, but we know God had His reasons. Regardless, Saul headed straight for the synagogues again, but with little more success than in Damascus. After he inflamed the religious leaders of two major cities against him and survived two assassination plots, Saul headed home to Tarsus. A Gentile city. A faraway city. Let's face it—with Saul removed to his hometown, everyone was safer. As Luke records, "So the church throughout all Judea and Galilee and Samaria enjoyed peace, being built up; and going on in the fear of the Lord and in the comfort of the Holy Spirit, it continued to increase" (9:31).

Benched. Shelved. Set aside. Taken out of circulation. But not forsaken. Not by a long shot. The vision for ministry that God had given Saul in Damascus had not been forgotten. The Lord had always intended for the gospel to be preached to all the world, but the church wasn't ready for Gentile converts, and Saul wasn't ready to be God's spokesman. This thoroughgoing Jew needed to know more about Gentile culture. He also needed to learn how to walk in the Spirit rather than conduct ministry on his own terms. Ten years of small-scale ministry in Tarsus gave him the education and the spiritual seasoning he needed.

As Luke resumes his narrative, Saul has been tucked away in the region of Cilicia, far removed from the action, waiting for the right moment.

— 11:19-21 —

After the martyrdom of Stephen, Saul's persecution of the church had scattered the believers in all directions. For the most part, these Jewish Christians proclaimed the gospel to their Hebrew kinsmen only. Some, however, weren't as discriminating, sharing the news with any Gentile who would listen. Luke identifies the more broad-minded Jews as "men of Cyprus and Cyrene" (11:20). Cyprus, the homeland of Barnabas, is a sizable island in the Mediterranean off the coast of Syria. Cyrene lay on the coast of North Africa almost 500 miles west of Alexandria.

Syrian Antioch was a massive city at the time, the third-largest city in the Roman Empire, after Rome and Alexandria, and home to an extremely large community of Jews, Gentile converts to Judaism, and Gentile "God-fearers." As a result, the gospel found an eager audience there. With such a large Jewish influence, the Gentiles were already familiar with the curious monotheism of the people of Judea. Within a short time, a large number of Gentiles had become Christians (11:21).

— 11:22-24 —

By the time news of Gentile conversions filtered down into Judea and up the slopes of Jerusalem, the church had come to terms with the ministry of Peter in Caesarea. Instead of sending critics to scrutinize the work in Syrian Antioch, they sent the "Son of Encouragement," Barnabas, the perfect man for the job (11:22). He was from Cyprus, where many of the Jewish evangelists were from, and his temperament predisposed him to welcome the Gentiles as brothers. Luke says, "He was a good man, and full of the Holy Spirit and of faith" (11:24). Upon his arrival, he saw authentic Christians very much in need of organization and training. Antioch was, after all, known for being a pleasure seeker's den because of the famed "paradise of Daphne" just 5 miles away,[40] where visitors pursued moral depravity as if it were a virtue.

Barnabas rejoiced at the sight of God's grace taking over the city, and he encouraged the new believers (11:23). That's what new Christians need—lots of encouragement. He didn't draw out a list of dos and don'ts or mark up a local map with places to avoid around Antioch. He mainly "encouraged." The verb is *parakaleō* [3870], a multifaceted word that carries the idea of standing alongside someone in order to provide counsel, courage, comfort, hope, and positive perspective. Like an athletic coach, an encourager challenges without condemning, instructs without lecturing, inspires without condescending, and helps another toward excellence. Barnabas, like a coach encouraging and challenging an athlete to reach a particular goal, urged the new believers in Antioch to grow in grace while remaining true to their Savior.

— 11:25-26 —

Barnabas was mature and knowledgeable, more than capable in his own right; nonetheless, he also knew he needed help. The last part of Acts 11:24 connects with 11:25 to provide an explanation. I would translate the sentence, "And sufficient enough crowds were added to the Lord. So he went to Tarsus to search for Saul." Barnabas was humble and wise: humble enough to recognize his limitations and wise enough to seek the best man to assist him in these responsibilities. Note that he didn't send to Jerusalem for Hebrew scholars; he journeyed 100 miles in the opposite direction for the man God had set aside for a ministry to Gentiles. Saul agreed to come.

The two men harmoniously ministered together in Antioch with great success, not only evangelizing, but establishing the believers as a church (11:26). This is where Saul learned the basics of church formation, organization, and stabilization. They had as their goal an independent community, led by indigenous elders, sustained without outside help, and perpetuated by its own evangelistic efforts. If a church is a living organism, Barnabas and Saul wanted the congregation in Antioch to breathe, eat, grow, and live on its own.

Luke adds the side note that Syrian Antioch was the birthplace of the term "Christian" (*Christianos* [5546]). Of course, the central idea is "Christ." The suffix -*ianos* denotes partisanship or identity with the leader of a movement or community. For example, the Gospel writers used "Herodian" to denote someone who supported or worked for the dynasty of Herod the Great (e.g., Matt. 22:16).

— 11:27-28 —

"At this time" (11:27) is literally "in these days." Sometime during the yearlong ministry of Barnabas and Saul, "prophets" visited from Jerusalem. (The phrase "came down" refers to the change in elevation; ancient people didn't think of north and south in terms of "up" and "down.") These people had a supernatural, miraculous gift of prophetic speech. Much like the Old Testament prophets, they were human mouthpieces for God who announced new revelation (1 Cor. 12:10, 28; 14:3). God told them what to say, and they said it. During the apostolic era, before the New Testament had been written, the church needed to hear directly from God via prophets.

One of the prophets, named Agabus (see Acts 21:10-11), predicted that a "great famine" would afflict the world (11:28). The phrase "all over the world" doesn't necessarily mean "in every universal location," but rather "in many significant places." Luke, like other Greek writers, used the term "world" (*oikoumenē* [3625]) to mean the known world of the Roman Empire. Luke affirms that the prediction by Agabus occurred during the reign of Claudius, who ruled as emperor for almost fourteen years (AD 41–54),[41] after Caligula and before Nero. Secular historians note his having to deal with at least two severe grain shortages in Rome due to famines in several parts of the empire.[42]

— 11:29-30 —

These grain shortages affected Rome in AD 42 and 51. According to hints from Egyptian records of the time and Josephus's *Antiquities*, Judea felt the effects around AD 46.[43] That year, the church in Syrian Antioch took up a collection and sent it to Jerusalem in the care of Barnabas and Saul. This is noteworthy for a couple of reasons. First, the autonomous body of believers in Antioch viewed themselves as part of a greater whole and, therefore, responsible to care for their needy brothers and sisters in Jerusalem (cf. 4:34-37). Second, the Antioch church had grown strong enough to send tangible help to Jerusalem instead of requiring assistance themselves. This signaled a subtle shift. The Jerusalem church would become less vital while Antioch would grow more important.

They sent this offering "to the elders" in Jerusalem (11:30). This, by the way, is the first time Luke uses the term "elder" (*presbyteros* [4245]) in reference to the church. The apostles didn't remain in Jerusalem. According to tradition—not authoritative like Scripture, but useful for providing historical clues—most of the Twelve traveled to different parts of the world to be "witnesses." To fill the leadership vacuum, the Jerusalem church appointed "elders." The Greek term literally means "older one" but is used in the technical sense of an office. The Jerusalem church followed the pattern of the synagogues, which selected several mature men to provide spiritual and practical leadership to the local congregation.

At this point, Saul of Tarsus had more to learn before he would become the Paul we know from his letters, but he was well on his way. He was off the bench and back in the game; nevertheless, his training would continue. A few key lessons yet to be learned would equip him for the task God had laid out for him.

APPLICATION: ACTS 11:19-30

Set Aside for Good Works

No one likes to feel set aside. After Saul's dramatic conversion on the road to Damascus and then his "furlough" in Tarsus ministry, he undoubtedly felt bewildered and disillusioned during those "silent" years back in his hometown. Thankfully, he submitted to a humbling decade of soul-shaping preparation in the shadows of the church. His patience allowed him to emerge later as the most influential man in the history of the New Testament age.

As I observe the Lord's preparation of Saul, two principles emerge.

First, *only the Lord can prepare a person for ministry*. After the Lord confronted Saul personally (9:4-6) and then revealed his future role in ministry (26:15-18), Saul got to work right away, confronting his kindred Jews in the synagogues. When that failed, he wisely retreated to Arabia for nearly three years. Perhaps thinking his experience had sufficiently prepared him and feeling ready to engage in ministry again, he returned to Damascus—to disastrous results there and again in Jerusalem. Clearly, he wasn't ready. Ten years passed with the great Saul of Tarsus pushed to the sidelines in a pagan university city, far from the action in Jerusalem, a town he once owned. Then, when the time for Saul was right, and when Saul was right for the times, the Lord allowed this humbled Pharisee to step into the spotlight. He reentered, a wiser man with a clearer understanding of the work of the Spirit in his life and his ministry.

Almost every seasoned minister can relate. After I received my call to ministry, I knew immediately I needed to prepare. But when I enrolled in the four-year program at Dallas Theological Seminary, I had no idea that a large percentage of my preparation would occur outside the classroom! Certainly, the professors gave me crucial knowledge and insight, but it was the Lord who prepared *me*. During that time, He whittled and filed and chipped away at my character to shape me into a suitable vessel. Then, after my formal schooling, I spent another two years assisting an older pastor and another two years struggling in a ministry not suited to my personal style and bent. As I look back, I realize that nothing could have prepared me for my future role in ministry like the Lord's personal touch during those difficult years out of the limelight. At the time, it was unclear what the Lord was doing. Looking back, it all makes sense.

Second, *the Lord must prepare the ministry for the person.* During his face-to-face encounter with the Lord and his three-day fast, Saul learned that he would minister to the Gentiles. The Lord told him,

> "For this purpose I have appeared to you, to appoint you a minister and a witness not only to the things which you have seen, but also to the things in which I will appear to you; rescuing you from the Jewish people and from the Gentiles, to whom I am sending you, to open their eyes so that they may turn from darkness to light and from the dominion of Satan to God, that they may receive forgiveness of sins and an inheritance among those who have been sanctified by faith in Me." (26:16-18)

At the time, however, Peter had not yet visited Cornelius. The Gentiles were only beginning to consider this strange Jewish teaching from

Jerusalem, and the church leaders had not even considered evangelism outside the Jewish community. Simply put, the world was not yet ready for Saul's ministry with such a marked emphasis on grace.

While the Lord prepared Saul for evangelism and church planting among the Gentiles, He also prepared the Gentiles and the church for him. In ministry—like a lot of things—timing is everything.

More Powerful than Prison Bars
ACTS 12:1-17

NASB

[1] Now about that time [a]Herod the king laid hands on some who belonged to the church in order to mistreat them. [2] And he had James the brother of John put to death with a sword. [3] When he saw that it pleased the Jews, he proceeded to arrest Peter also. Now [a]it was during the days of Unleavened Bread. [4] When he had seized him, he put him in prison, delivering him to four [a]squads of soldiers to guard him, intending after the Passover to bring him out before the people. [5] So Peter was kept in the prison, but prayer for him was being made fervently by the church to God.

[6] On [a]the very night when Herod was about to bring him forward, Peter was sleeping between two soldiers, bound with two chains, and guards in front of the door were watching over the prison. [7] And behold, an angel of the Lord suddenly appeared and a light shone in the cell; and he struck Peter's side and woke him up, saying, "Get up quickly." And his chains fell off his hands. [8] And the angel said to him, "Gird yourself and [a]put on your sandals." And he did so. And he said to him, "Wrap your cloak around you and follow me." [9] And he went out and continued to follow, and he did not know that what was being done

NLT

[1] About that time King Herod Agrippa* began to persecute some believers in the church. [2] He had the apostle James (John's brother) killed with a sword. [3] When Herod saw how much this pleased the Jewish people, he also arrested Peter. (This took place during the Passover celebration.*) [4] Then he imprisoned him, placing him under the guard of four squads of four soldiers each. Herod intended to bring Peter out for public trial after the Passover. [5] But while Peter was in prison, the church prayed very earnestly for him.

[6] The night before Peter was to be placed on trial, he was asleep, fastened with two chains between two soldiers. Others stood guard at the prison gate. [7] Suddenly, there was a bright light in the cell, and an angel of the Lord stood before Peter. The angel struck him on the side to awaken him and said, "Quick! Get up!" And the chains fell off his wrists. [8] Then the angel told him, "Get dressed and put on your sandals." And he did. "Now put on your coat and follow me," the angel ordered.

[9] So Peter left the cell, following the angel. But all the time he thought it was a vision. He didn't realize it was actually happening. [10] They passed the first and second guard posts and

by the angel was real, but thought he was seeing a vision. ¹⁰When they had passed the first and second guard, they came to the iron gate that leads into the city, which opened for them by itself; and they went out and went along one street, and immediately the angel departed from him. ¹¹When Peter came ªto himself, he said, "Now I know for sure that the Lord has sent forth His angel and rescued me from the hand of Herod and from all ᵇthat the Jewish people were expecting." ¹²And when he realized *this*, he went to the house of Mary, the mother of John who was also called Mark, where many were gathered together and were praying. ¹³When he knocked at the door of the gate, a servant-girl named Rhoda came to answer. ¹⁴When she recognized Peter's voice, because of her joy she did not open the gate, but ran in and announced that Peter was standing in front of the gate. ¹⁵They said to her, "You are out of your mind!" But she kept insisting that it was so. They kept saying, "It is his angel." ¹⁶But Peter continued knocking; and when they had opened *the door*, they saw him and were amazed. ¹⁷But motioning to them with his hand to be silent, he described to them how the Lord had led him out of the prison. And he said, "Report these things to ªJames and the brethren." Then he left and went to another place.

12:1 ªI.e. Herod Agrippa I 12:3 ªLit *they were the days* 12:4 ªLit *quaternions;* a quaternion was composed of four soldiers 12:6 ªLit *that night* 12:8 ªLit *bind* 12:11 ªLit *in himself* ᵇLit *the expectation of the people of the Jews* 12:17 ªOr *Jacob*

came to the iron gate leading to the city, and this opened for them all by itself. So they passed through and started walking down the street, and then the angel suddenly left him.

¹¹Peter finally came to his senses. "It's really true!" he said. "The Lord has sent his angel and saved me from Herod and from what the Jewish leaders* had planned to do to me!"

¹²When he realized this, he went to the home of Mary, the mother of John Mark, where many were gathered for prayer. ¹³He knocked at the door in the gate, and a servant girl named Rhoda came to open it. ¹⁴When she recognized Peter's voice, she was so overjoyed that, instead of opening the door, she ran back inside and told everyone, "Peter is standing at the door!"

¹⁵"You're out of your mind!" they said. When she insisted, they decided, "It must be his angel."

¹⁶Meanwhile, Peter continued knocking. When they finally opened the door and saw him, they were amazed. ¹⁷He motioned for them to quiet down and told them how the Lord had led him out of prison. "Tell James and the other brothers what happened," he said. And then he went to another place.

12:1 Greek *Herod the king.* He was the nephew of Herod Antipas and a grandson of Herod the Great. 12:3 Greek *the days of unleavened bread.* 12:11 Or *the Jewish people.*

All followers of the Messiah have to maintain a difficult balance. We live in a natural world guided by natural laws, yet we serve a God who can—and sometimes does—overrule the laws of nature. For the most part, we must accept circumstances at face value. Good people get sick and die. Hardworking people go bankrupt. Honest businesses go under. Innocent people are mistreated, convicted, and punished. In many situations, God does not supernaturally intervene to prevent misfortune, yet we must not view life strictly from a human perspective. Miracles rarely occur. Whether or not the Lord chooses to intervene miraculously, He remains in control and has promised to work out all events and circumstances for our good and for His glory (Rom. 8:28).

In an age when miracles are exceedingly rare, maintaining this natural-supernatural perspective can be a challenge. One might be tempted to think that holding an eternal, spiritual perspective would be easier if miracles were more common. As Luke demonstrates in this segment of his narrative, however, people always have trouble seeing beyond the temporal realm, even when God is more visibly active in the world. The Christians in Jerusalem, despite their seeing some of the Lord's most amazing displays of miraculous power, also struggled to break out of their two-dimensional perspective. In this notable example, they placed limits on what God could or would do on their behalf.

— 12:1-2 —

Luke sets the time as during the persecution of "Herod"—Herod Agrippa I— which predates the "famine visit" of Barnabas and Paul (11:19-30). In other words, Luke has rewound the clock, taking us back in the chronology to the time before the narrative detour to Syrian Antioch, back to the time shortly after Peter's visit to Caesarea. In terms of chronology, 12:1 follows 11:18.[44]

Up to this time, the chief enemies of the church had been the Sanhedrin, the political and religious heavyweights associated with the temple—the high priest, the aristocrats, the Pharisees, and the former high priest and crime boss, Annas. This religious persecution reached its zenith with Saul of Tarsus leading the charge; but with Saul now following Jesus and living quietly, far from Jerusalem, pressure from the temple subsided. At least for a few years. In the meantime, the church expanded dramatically, sweeping through Judea and Samaria. Its influence remained religious and sectarian within Judaism for the most part, so few people outside the ranks of devout Hebrews took notice. Then Peter visited Caesarea. That's when Herod Agrippa I began to involve himself for political reasons.

By this time, the name "Herod" had become a title, much as the imperial designation "Caesar" that later evolved from the life and influence of Julius Caesar.[45] This particular Herod was Agrippa I. He had acquired land and titles by choosing the right political partnerships

THE CHAOS OF THE HERODIANS

ACTS 12:1-4

For many years after the death of Herod the Great in 4 BC, the Herodian dynasty continued to cast a great shadow over Judea, Samaria, Galilee, and regions beyond. His descendants divided up his realm: Archelaus took Judea and Samaria, Antipas took Galilee and Perea, and Philip took over several northeast provinces and, later, some of Syria.[46]

Within a few years, Archelaus self-destructed. He was responsible for the murder of many Jewish subjects (Matt. 2:20-23), which provoked a massive conspiracy to get rid of him. Delegations representing Jews and Samaritans—usually bitter enemies—as well as his brothers,

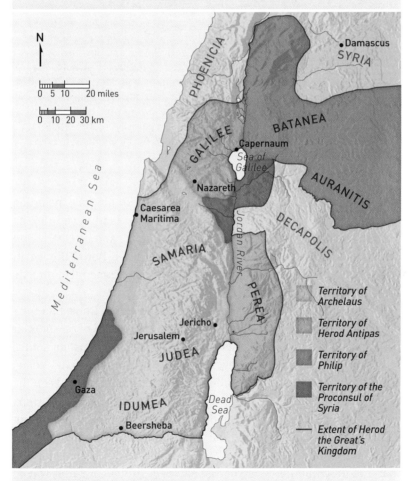

Israel after Herod the Great. After Herod the Great's death, his family divided his kingdom to rule.

Antipas and Philip, all converged on Rome to have him removed. Augustus heeded the chorus of voices against Archelaus, deposed him, banished him to Gaul in present-day France, and placed his land under Roman control. Thereafter, Roman procurators and governors ruled Judea.

Antipas proved more successful than Archelaus, although his dalliances eventually came back to destroy him. He drove his wife, the daughter of Nabataean King Aretas IV, into exile so he could marry his sister-in-law/niece, Herodias. He survived the consequent political and religious unrest by befriending Tiberius and by placating wealthy Hellenistic Jews. Eventually, however, his political calculations failed. Aretas attacked and seized some of his land—including the city of Damascus (2 Cor. 11:32-33)—and the death of Tiberius proved fatal to Antipas's reign. Here's how:

After the death of Herod the Great, Philip married his niece, Salome, the daughter of Herodias, whose sensual dance before Antipas led to the execution of John the Baptizer (Matt. 14:6-11; Mark 6:21-28). Philip lived quietly and maintained close ties with Rome, and upon his death in AD 34, his land reverted to Syrian control. But only for a short time. When Tiberius died, Caligula became emperor and gave Philip's land to Agrippa I, the brother of Herodias. He also gave Agrippa the coveted title of king. When Antipas and Herodias went to Rome to seek the same honor, Agrippa sent accusations against Antipas, resulting in Antipas's banishment to Gaul. Accordingly, Agrippa gained the land once ruled by Antipas.

at the right time, undercutting anyone who got in his way, including his own family. He had gained control of all the land once ruled by his uncles, Philip the Tetrarch and Herod Antipas, and he clearly had designs on eclipsing the power of his grandfather, Herod the Great. To do that, however, he would need Judea, which Rome ruled directly through procurators.[47]

To gain Judea, he needed to convince the powers of Rome that their interests were better served with him in control instead of one of their procurators. Gentile procurators, after all, had been a constant source of irritation to the Jews, and Jewish irritation always unnerved Rome. Local rulers had two primary, all-important responsibilities: keep the people from revolting and keep the money flowing to Rome. Agrippa could easily position himself as the best candidate. Who better than a Jew,[48] a descendant of Herod the Great, and a loyal friend of the emperor? If he could convince the Jews that he would be a better option than the procurators, he might just succeed. And what better way to curry favor with the Jews than to side with them against an insignificant, upstart, sectarian group following a dead Messiah?

His calculations proved successful, and timing worked in his favor. When Caligula died in AD 41, Agrippa was in Rome. He gave crucial advice to his childhood friend Claudius and interceded on his behalf with the Senate, ultimately helping him succeed Caligula as emperor. As a reward, Claudius gave Agrippa Judea and Samaria, helping him eclipse Herod the Great in terms of power and land.[49] He quickly moved his capital to Jerusalem and began to solidify his relations with Jews at all levels, from the populist Pharisees to the aristocratic Sadducees. He no doubt strengthened relations with them when he executed James, the brother of John, in the manner of the Romans: by beheading with a sword (12:2).

— 12:3-5 —

The designation "the Jews" in much of Luke's writings is a technical term for the religious and political leaders in Israel, usually brought up in references to their connection with the temple. This would include the high priest, along with his aristocratic associates and the members of the Sanhedrin. Throughout the Gospel of Luke and the first part of Acts, he doesn't mean "the Jews" in the racial sense. At the time, the vast majority of the church was comprised of ethnic Jews, who represented a significant part of the population in Judea. Increasingly, however, the Jewish rulers were able to turn more and more of the Jewish people against the followers of the Messiah—a program of propaganda that would become much easier when Jews saw how many Gentiles were joining the sect of the Christians. Therefore, at some point we can assume that Luke's use of the term "the Jews" begins to refer to more than just an elite group of rulers. A gradual parting of ways between Judaism and Christianity, synagogue and church, as distinct religious groups was taking place. Perhaps Peter's activity among Gentile converts in Caesarea proved too much.

Because Agrippa ruled Judea directly as a representative of Rome, he had the power to sentence people to death without needing anyone's permission. He had exercised that power by killing James, so he arrested Peter, intending to execute him as well (12:3). But first, he would "bring him out before the people" (12:4). Luke doesn't reveal why Agrippa wanted to do this, but the reason seems obvious. As the absolute sovereign of Judea with the conferred Roman ranks of praetor and consul, he didn't need to justify an execution. He didn't need to have Peter tried and convicted by the Sanhedrin, although that would not have been difficult. He intended to "bring him out before the *people*" to galvanize their hostility against the Christians by publicly accusing Peter of violating Jewish traditions. Peter enthusiastically associated with Gentiles, ate their food, and dared to call them his brothers.

Agrippa placed Peter in prison because the feasts of Passover and Unleavened Bread—celebrated back to back for eight days (Deut. 16:1-12)—prevented trials.[50] Naturally, the king posted a guard to prevent Peter's escape. The Greek term for "squad" is *tetradion* [5069], which is based on the number four. Normally, one *tetradion* would be sufficient to provide one soldier for each "watch" (three-hour shift) of the night. But Agrippa quadrupled the guard, assigning four squads to guard Peter, obviously worried that such a high-profile figure would have ample help for an attempted jailbreak. Furthermore, Peter had proven to be a slippery prisoner at least one other time (Acts 5:17-25).

Luke calls attention to the opposing forces involved. On the one side, Agrippa locks Peter behind bars and posts a quadrupled guard (12:4). On the other side, the church prays fervently on the apostle's behalf (12:5).

— 12:6-10 —

On the last night of the Passover, God intervened (12:7-8). Luke describes how the *tetradion* was arranged: one soldier chained to Peter's right arm, one chained to his left, and two posted at the entrance to his cell (12:6). If four squads guarded him around the clock, each took a shift of six hours before being relieved by the next. Given this arrangement, along with the heightened vigilance, it's doubtful the guards slept during the six hours they remained on duty. Peter, on the other hand, slept like a healthy baby!

Luke includes the detail that Peter slept in spite of circumstances that would keep most people on edge. Peter had been through similar situations before (4:1-3, 21; 5:17-25).

Luke's description of Peter's release highlights the supernatural, miraculous element involved. An angel appeared and filled Peter's cell with light. This was certainly more than a dreamlike vision within his mind. And yet, Peter's guards, all of whom undoubtedly remained awake during their six-hour shift, saw and heard nothing. Still, Peter was not aware of the angel's presence, so the angel "struck Peter's side and woke him up" (12:7). His chains dropped, and he heard the angel speak, which should have alerted the guards. It didn't. He got up, dressed himself, walked quietly out of his cell, and strode past the two outer guards, through the main gate of the prison, and out into the street (12:8-10). To Peter the experience seemed unreal, but there he stood outside on the street (12:9, 11). To the guards everything seemed normal. While Peter saw things as they were, the guards were deluded.

— 12:11-12 —

Luke describes Peter as coming out of a vision to full consciousness (12:11), yet he had seen things exactly as they were. That's because the whole experience felt unreal, perhaps because it was so extraordinary. Earlier, when an angel had released Peter and John (5:19-20), no guards were mentioned, suggesting the apostles simply walked out through open gates and a relatively deserted jail facility. This occasion was very different. Standing in the public street confirmed what had seemed surreal.

So Peter took off to find the believers, who were praying at "the house of Mary, the mother of John who was also called Mark" (12:12). Mark will become significant as the story of the church unfolds. John is a Hebrew name. Mark is a Greek name. He was the son of a woman named Mary, one of *many* Jewish women named for Miriam, the sister of Moses. She may have been a widow of some considerable means. No husband is ever mentioned, yet she had a home large enough to accommodate church meetings. John Mark was the cousin of Barnabas (Col. 4:10), so Mary must have been Barnabas's aunt.

The community of believers most likely met often in the home of Mary since that's where Peter immediately went.

— 12:13-15 —

Typical homes of the time—especially large homes—were encircled by a wall. The outer "gate" (12:13) was a solid door, large enough to allow carts drawn by animals to enter the courtyard. This large gate also had a smaller door cut into it to allow easier access to individuals. Like a phone call at three o'clock in the morning, a nighttime knock at this smaller "door of the gate" rarely brought good news. While the congregation prayed fervently for Peter, one of Mary's household servants, Rhoda, answered the knock. The Greek term translated "servant-girl" (*paidiskē* [3814]) suggests that the girl might have been quite young.[51] Unlike today, people wouldn't normally have opened the door to a nighttime knock—not without great risk of robbery. One opened the door only after confirming the identity of a friend. Rhoda recognized Peter's voice, but in her exuberance, failed to let him in! She couldn't wait to share the news. Meanwhile, Peter waited patiently.

I don't want to criticize the response of the praying congregation too harshly. They had just mourned the death of James, whom God did *not* deliver from the executioner's sword. Yet they should not have been completely surprised; this was, after all, Peter's second miraculous release from prison.

But they scolded little Rhoda: "You are out of your mind!" (12:15; *mainomai* [3105])—you're "raving mad," "no longer in control of your senses," "out of touch with reality." Each occurrence of this word in the New Testament (cf. John 10:20; Acts 26:24, 25; 1 Cor. 14:23) uses the term as hyperbole: "You must be stark raving mad!" When she insisted, the congregation tried to reason with her by offering a more plausible explanation. The statement "It is his angel" is troublesome for modern interpreters. Expositors suggest the following possible meanings:

- *"It is his ghost."*[52] Jewish superstition held that a person's spirit lurks around for a couple of days after death. This interpretation isn't likely for two reasons. First, they didn't expect Peter to be executed before the end of the festival week. Second, the term is *angelos* [32], which never means "spirit" or "ghost."
- *"It is his guardian angel."*[53] Based on Psalm 91:11 and Daniel 10:21 (along with Tobit 5:4-22 in the Apocrypha), the Talmud[54] teaches that a guardian angel assumes the appearance of the person he protects and can act on his or her behalf. If some of these Christians accepted this extrabiblical tradition, they may have jumped to this conclusion. This is possible, reflecting the state of denial they were in.
- *"It is his (human) messenger."* The term *angelos* literally means "messenger" or "envoy." The congregation may have insisted that Rhoda had heard Peter's assistant coming to them with a communiqué, perhaps conveying his dying wishes or last-minute instructions.

While either of the last two options is possible, I favor the last. It seems unlikely to me that these believers would to hold such poor theology, given the quality of teaching they had received from the apostles and the intense activity of the Holy Spirit. Regardless, two things are clear. First, they couldn't believe that Peter was standing safe and sound at the doorstep. The two verbs translated "she kept insisting" and "they kept saying" are in the imperfect tense, which describes ongoing or repetitive action, thus depicting Rhoda and the congregation in an ongoing, back-and-forth argument. Second, no one behaved rationally. Rhoda left Peter outside rather than let him in, the congregation suggested nothing helpful, and no one hurried to do the obvious thing: go to the door and find out!

— 12:16-17 —

Poor Peter, miraculously released from prison and having escaped certain death, couldn't wait to see his friends, but he was left standing out in the cold—literally—knocking repeatedly at the front door (12:16). He had supernaturally walked out of a high-security prison but couldn't get past the gate of his friend's house. He had casually walked past the king's guards to escape execution, but he couldn't get a little servant girl to let him in to join the prayer meeting held on his behalf.

When they finally opened the door and saw Peter, the gathered believers were beside themselves (*existēmi* [1839]). Finally, after gaining entrance, he related the story, giving all the credit to the Lord. He then instructed them to tell James, the Lord's brother, and "the brethren," the church elders in Jerusalem. He then departed to another location, either to visit others gathered for prayer or to remain out of public sight.

APPLICATION: ACTS 12:1-17

God Is in Control

I wish the application of this passage were simple. I wish I could say the enduring lesson is this: "The God of impossible circumstances will accomplish the impossible when you pray hard enough." But we all know that reality is more complicated than that. Even during this remarkable, unusual period when Holy Spirit miracles happened often, the church understood that Peter would most likely die by the sword before sunset the next day. They believed God, but they had seen their friend Stephen stoned to death, and they had just recently lost James the brother of John, one of the Twelve.

So, what do we learn from the incredulous believers who prayed and, to their shock, received a miraculous fulfillment of their greatest desires? How often have we prayed for the impossible, trusting God's ability, only to mourn our disappointment? While we live in a different time and our experiences will not necessarily duplicate theirs, I find two imperatives to apply.

First, *ask God for what you want—and be bold!* Too often we temper our requests—even good, godly requests like the healing of a friend or the restoration of a failing marriage—perhaps to protect ourselves from disappointment, or to pray responsibly, or to avoid presuming upon God, or to pray within the bounds of what we imagine the Lord's will might be: "Lord, if it be Your will, restore this failing marriage."

"If it be Your will . . . ?" *Really?* Pray boldly for what is good. Don't hold back. Don't qualify your requests. God's sovereignty isn't threatened and His goodness isn't compromised if you plead earnestly—supplicate shamelessly—for good to prevail. He may not choose to alter the circumstances. He may allow a Stephen to suffer unjustly. He may allow a wicked authority to deprive the church of a godly leader. Nevertheless, He will honor your earnest desires, if not in the manner you hope, then in some unexpected way you cannot foresee.

Second, *trust the sovereignty and goodness of God to prevail.* The people in the home of Mary gathered to pray for Peter. We don't know the content of their prayers, but some must have asked God for a miraculous release, just like the earlier release. Clearly, however, no one really expected to see Peter alive again, or they wouldn't have been so dubious when he knocked. Still, they trusted God.

We can't expect the Lord always to do as we ask or to give us exactly what we want. (In my own prayers, I stopped telling God how to fulfill my requests a long time ago.) Even so, we can be sure He will always do what is right and will always act in the long-term best interests of everyone involved. No matter how your circumstances turn out after earnest prayer, assure yourself with these words—repeat them as often as necessary: *The Lord is right in all His ways* (see Deut. 32:4 and Dan. 4:37).

Challenge . . . Triumph . . . Expansion
ACTS 12:18-25

NASB [18] Now when day came, there was no small disturbance among the soldiers *as to* ªwhat could have become of Peter. [19] When Herod had searched for him and had not found him, he examined the guards and ordered that

NLT [18] At dawn there was a great commotion among the soldiers about what had happened to Peter. [19] Herod Agrippa ordered a thorough search for him. When he couldn't be found, Herod interrogated the guards and

they be led away *to execution.* Then he went down from Judea to Caesarea and was spending time there.

²⁰ Now he was very angry with the people of Tyre and Sidon; and with one accord they came to him, and having won over Blastus the king's chamberlain, they were asking for peace, because their country was fed by the king's country. ²¹ On an appointed day Herod, having put on his royal apparel, took his seat on the ªrostrum and *began* delivering an address to them. ²² The people kept crying out, "The voice of a god and not of a man!" ²³ And immediately an angel of the Lord struck him because he did not give God the glory, and he was eaten by worms and ªdied.

²⁴ But the word of the Lord continued to grow and to be multiplied.

²⁵ And Barnabas and Saul returned ªfrom Jerusalem when they had fulfilled their ᵇmission, taking along with *them* John, who was also called Mark.

12:18 ªLit *what therefore had become* **12:21** ªOr *judgment seat* **12:23** ªLit *breathed his last breath* **12:25** ªTwo early mss read *to Jerusalem* ᵇLit *ministry*

sentenced them to death. Afterward Herod left Judea to stay in Caesarea for a while.

²⁰ Now Herod was very angry with the people of Tyre and Sidon. So they sent a delegation to make peace with him because their cities were dependent upon Herod's country for food. The delegates won the support of Blastus, Herod's personal assistant, ²¹ and an appointment with Herod was granted. When the day arrived, Herod put on his royal robes, sat on his throne, and made a speech to them. ²² The people gave him a great ovation, shouting, "It's the voice of a god, not of a man!"

²³ Instantly, an angel of the Lord struck Herod with a sickness, because he accepted the people's worship instead of giving the glory to God. So he was consumed with worms and died.

²⁴ Meanwhile, the word of God continued to spread, and there were many new believers.

²⁵ When Barnabas and Saul had finished their mission to Jerusalem, they returned,* taking John Mark with them.

12:25 Or *mission, they returned to Jerusalem.* Other manuscripts read *mission, they returned from Jerusalem;* still others read *mission, they returned from Jerusalem to Antioch.*

The book of Acts consists of a repeating cycle: challenge-triumph-expansion. At the *challenge,* a difficulty creates a crisis in the church, causing many to wonder, *Will the church survive? Will God's kingdom endure? Will God's plan of redemption succeed?* Through the *triumph,* the Lord resolves the crisis in a manner surprising to all, vindicating the righteous while sometimes judging the enemies of the church. (I say "sometimes" because the offer of grace remains open to all, so some are redeemed.) In the *expansion,* the gospel spreads farther and the church grows stronger, creating opportunities that would not have been possible had the crisis not occurred. Eventually, however, a new crisis challenges the church again.

As each cycle unfolds, we have an opportunity to examine the lives of the individuals involved and to consider how they respond to the work of God.

In Acts 4, Peter and John were arrested for proclaiming that Jesus the Messiah had been resurrected from the dead. After a night in jail, they stood before the Sanhedrin to give answer to the question "By what power, or in what name, have you done this?" (4:7). Bear in mind that undeniable evidence of the "power" and "name" stood in their midst: A man known to all as a beggar disabled from birth had danced around the temple just hours before (3:8-10). During the trial, he stood whole and sound in the courtroom. Instead of submitting to the obvious work of God and rather than heeding His call to repentance, "they began to confer with one another, saying, 'What shall we do with these men? For the fact that a noteworthy miracle has taken place through them is apparent to all who live in Jerusalem, and we cannot deny it. But so that it will not spread any further among the people, let us warn them to speak no longer to any man in this name'" (4:15-17).

In Acts 5, Peter and the other apostles continued to proclaim that Jesus the Messiah had risen from the grave. The miraculous healing power of God continued to validate the ministry of the church, "to such an extent that [people] even carried the sick out into the streets and laid them on cots and pallets, so that when Peter came by at least his shadow might fall on any one of them. Also the people from the cities in the vicinity of Jerusalem were coming together, bringing people who were sick or afflicted with unclean spirits, and they were all being healed" (5:15-16). How did the religious leaders of Israel respond? In belief? Did they submit to the message of God validated by the obvious, undeniable work of God? No, "the high priest rose up, along with all his associates (that is the sect of the Sadducees), and they were filled with jealousy. They laid hands on the apostles and put them in a public jail" (5:17-18).

The apostles' miraculous release from prison (5:19) led to more preaching in the temple (5:20-21), which led to yet another trial before the Sanhedrin (5:25-40). Gamaliel, a nonbelieving yet mature voice of reason among nonbelievers, clarified the issue for the religious leaders of Israel: "I say to you, stay away from these men and let them alone, for if this plan or action is of men, it will be overthrown; but if it is of God, you will not be able to overthrow them; or else you may even be found fighting against God" (5:38-39). Wise counsel. Bear in mind that the overwhelming evidence of God's power, attested to by the sheer multitude of miracles taking place in Jerusalem, left no room for any reasonable person to question whether "this plan or action is of men."

The temple leaders refused to acknowledge the message of the church, not because they *couldn't* believe, but because they *wouldn't* submit to the truths they could not deny.

There were more threats, more preaching, more persecution ... and more Christians pouring into the church.

Acts 12 documents the third and final round of Israel versus the church. In the years between Acts 5 and 12, much had changed. Judea had grown stronger. With Agrippa as their king, the temple rulers now had the backing of Rome; they wielded virtually unlimited political power to crush the church. Meanwhile, the church, with Peter as a prominent leader, had expanded beyond Jerusalem to reach all of Judea and Samaria. Moreover, Jews and Gentiles alike now called one another brothers and sisters because they followed the same King and swore allegiance to God's kingdom as fellow citizens. By Acts 12, both powers had grown to the point that a clash became inevitable. The land given to Abraham and his Hebrew descendants could no longer contain both groups.

Luke's story of Peter's three arrests and three triumphs documents the Lord's vindication of the gospel and care for the church, but we should also see three attempts to confront the leaders of Israel—three appeals attested by undeniably divine miracles for Israel to repent, believe, submit, and be saved. How the leaders of Israel responded to this third and final opportunity to embrace their Messiah would set the stage for how the kingdom of God would grow. Clearly, the Lord wanted His chosen nation, His beloved Israel, to be the means by which His kingdom would overtake the world. If the religious and political leaders of Israel wouldn't submit, however, God would complete His redemptive plan by another means.

Challenge: Agrippa arrested Peter (12:1-6). Triumph: God miraculously freed Peter (12:7-17). What would happen next?

— 12:18-19 —

When Peter visited the church after his miraculous release, he didn't say, "You'll never believe what great luck I had last night! By chance, both chains were loose, the guards just happened to be looking the other way at the right time, and somebody forgot to lock all the doors, so I was able to sneak out of that high-security prison without anybody happening to notice. What an amazing coincidence!" No, Peter gave God all the credit for his release. The people struggled to accept something so amazing at first, but when the truth stared them in the face, they couldn't deny the miracle. No rational explanation would suffice; only a supernatural act of God made sense. In response, the church spontaneously worshiped the Lord.

On the other side of town, however, the leaders of Israel viewed the situation in purely material terms. At daybreak, "there was no small disturbance among the soldiers" over their missing prisoner (12:18). The Greek word translated "disturbance" (*tarachos* [5017]) means "a state of acute distress, dismay, confusion, or tumult." When those guards came to their senses, when the morning light shown through the window and they saw the prison cell empty, it blew their minds. They didn't know what to do. With Peter reported missing, Herod initiated a manhunt.

When that failed, being unwilling to accept an explanation involving God's miraculous power, the king searched for a natural answer. He "examined" the guards (12:19). The Greek term for this is *anakrinō* [350]. The root word is *krinō* [2919], which carries the idea of sifting and dividing to arrive at an answer. *Anakrinō* applies this process to a person or persons. It was a judicial term meaning "to conduct an inquiry into facts and witnesses' testimonies." Herod didn't merely question the guards; he conducted a formal investigation using all his powers as a Roman and a king. His inquisition led him to suspect foul play on the part of the guards. All four must have colluded to release Peter; it was the only natural explanation that made sense. Certainly, Herod's investigation would have turned up Peter's arrest record. Somebody must have given him the whole story behind Peter's earlier release. Still, Herod accepted the natural explanation. So Herod had them "led away," which almost certainly implies execution and is reflected in English translations. "Led away" was a common idiom for being taken to trial, prison, or punishment, and the standard punishment for a lax jailer was execution. Prison guards would sooner kill all the prisoners— or themselves—than let any get away (see 16:27; 27:42).

After concluding the inquiries and assuring himself with a plausible explanation, the king went to Tiberius to hobnob with his Roman friends,[55] and then to Caesarea to attend a festival and administer his foreign policy.[56] By correlating Acts with the date from secular historians, we know Herod visited Caesarea in AD 44.

— 12:20-23 —

Although Luke's inspired description is definitive, information provided by Josephus adds more color to an already vivid story. According to this secular Jewish historian, Herod traveled to attend athletic games he had organized in honor of Claudius. While there, Luke notes that he received a delegation from Tyre and Sidon, two large coastal cities in the Roman province of Syria, a region very much on the king's mind. We read that Agrippa was "very angry" with these two cities, although Luke doesn't elaborate (12:20). Josephus offers some helpful background.

A few years earlier, the king attempted to rebuild and fortify the walls surrounding Jerusalem. The Roman governor of Syria, Gnaeus Vibius Marcus, objected in a letter to Emperor Claudius, who instructed Agrippa to stop construction. That became a source of irritation. Then, just before traveling to Caesarea, Agrippa spent time in Tiberius, a Hellenistic city by the Sea of Galilee, entertaining several kings from cities within and bordering Syria. When Marcus approached the city of Tiberius, Agrippa rode out to meet him in the company of all these kings. Naturally, Marcus suspected the worst: Powerful King Agrippa, friend of Claudius and consul of Rome, was colluding with the rulers of Syrian cities. When Marcus secretly urged each king to go home, Agrippa became angry and marked the governor of Syria as his enemy.

By the time Agrippa reached Caesarea, delegations from Tyre and Sidon—two Syrian cities—came asking for help with their food shortage. Apparently, Agrippa had restricted food exports to Syrian cities (see 12:20). On the second day of the festival, the king dressed in a tunic woven from silver strands that shimmered in the sunlight, and he sat at the judgment seat to address them, probably before going to the athletic games (12:21). Luke states that the people compared Agrippa to a god and summarizes their flattery: "The voice of a god and not of a man!" Luke further states that the people "kept crying out" using the imperfect tense, which indicates ongoing or repetitive action (12:22). According to Josephus, this occurred wherever Agrippa went, including the theater:

> On the second day of [the] shows he put on a garment made wholly of silver, and of a contexture truly wonderful, and came into the theatre early in the morning; at which time the silver of his garment being illuminated by the fresh reflection of the sun's rays upon it, shone out after a surprising manner, and was so resplendent as to spread a horror over those that looked intently upon him; and presently his flatterers cried out, one from one place, and another from another (though not for his good), that he was a god; and they added, "Be thou merciful to us; for

AGRIPPA, MESSIANIC HOPE OF THE SANHEDRIN

ACTS 12:22

In a way, Agrippa seems to have been positioning himself to become Israel's messiah. His power and land holdings eclipsed those of Herod the Great. In fact, he rivaled David and Solomon in terms of land and power. Given his rapid rise to power and his connections in Rome, one might even have suggested him as a successor to Claudius. Imagine, the "king of the Jews" ruling the Roman Empire, which in turn ruled much of the known world. Agrippa was the kind of messiah many Jews had been taught to anticipate. Regrettably, he believed his own press.

In AD 41, the Roman province of Judea was given to Agrippa, who already held Galilee, Perea, and Samaria. This effectively reunited the land once held by David and Solomon under a single king for the first time since the kingdom was divided a thousand years earlier. Agrippa also held the Roman title of consul and enjoyed close ties with emperors Caligula and Claudius.[57] If he managed his resources wisely and continued to build strong relations with other territorial rulers, he might one day become emperor himself.

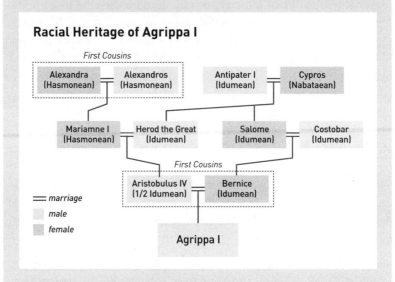

Racial Heritage of Agrippa I

First Cousins

| Alexandra (Hasmonean) — Alexandros (Hasmonean) | Antipater I (Idumean) — Cypros (Nabataean) |

Mariamne I (Hasmonean) — Herod the Great (Idumean)   Salome (Idumean) — Costobar (Idumean)

First Cousins

Aristobulus IV (1/2 Idumean) — Bernice (Idumean)

— marriage
male
female

Agrippa I

Agrippa was a hero to the religious and political elite in Jerusalem. Neither the aristocratic Sadducees nor the populist Pharisees seemed to mind the fact that he was not fully Jewish. His nearest Hebrew relative was his paternal grandmother, Mariamne I, the second wife of Herod the Great. He was, in fact, three-quarters Idumean, a race of people descended from Esau. Even so, when Agrippa moved his capital to Jerusalem to rule the reunited kingdom, the temple officials extended a great honor to the man they called king. At the Feast of Tabernacles in the Year of Jubilee, he read the Law in accordance with the instructions of Moses:

> "At the end of every seven years, at the time of the year of remission of debts, at the Feast of Booths, when all Israel comes to appear before the LORD your God at the place which He will choose, you shall read this law in front of all Israel in their hearing. Assemble the people, the men and the women and children and the alien who is in your town, so that they may hear and learn and fear the LORD your God, and be careful to observe all the words of this law. Their children, who have not known, will hear and learn to fear the LORD your God, as long as you live on the land which you are about to cross the Jordan to possess." (Deut. 31:10-13)

Jewish scholars interpreted this command to mean that the king of Israel should read the Law under the auspices of the high priest. So when Agrippa took the crown, the temple officials took steps to demonstrate their acceptance of Agrippa as their legitimate king. Here is how the Babylonian Talmud recalls the occasion:

> At the conclusion of the first day of the festival [of Tabernacles] in the eighth, i.e., the end of the seventh, they erect a wooden dais in the temple court, upon which he sits; as it is said, at the end of every seven years, in the set time etc. The synagogue-attendant takes a Torah-scroll and hands it to the synagogue president, and the synagogue-president hands it to the [high priest's] deputy. He hands it to the high priest who hands it to the king. The king stands and receives it, but reads sitting. King Agrippa stood and received it and read standing, for which act the sages praised him. When he reached, "Thou mayest not put a foreigner over thee," his eyes ran with tears.[58]

The passage that affected Agrippa so deeply appears midway through the reading:

> When you enter the land which the LORD your God gives you, and you possess it and live in it, and you say, "I will set a king over me like all the nations who are around me," you shall surely set a king over you whom the LORD your God chooses, one from among your countrymen you shall set as king over yourselves; you may not put a foreigner over yourselves who is not your countryman. (Deut. 17:14-15)

Agrippa knew his racial heritage. So did everyone else. Still, the temple authorities reassured the king, "Fear not, Agrippa, thou art our brother, thou art our brother!"[59]

although we have hitherto reverenced thee only as a man, yet shall we henceforth own thee as superior to mortal nature." Upon this the king did neither rebuke them, nor reject their impious flattery.[60]

Compare this response to Peter's when Cornelius bowed in worship: "Stand up; I too am just a man" (10:26).

When Agrippa accepted their worship and allowed himself to be regarded as a god, "an angel of the Lord struck him" (12:23). The expression translated "to strike," when used in this fashion, is known as a Hebraism. Luke intends for the reader to recall the Old Testament manner of describing divine wrath falling upon the wicked to protect the righteous (Exod. 9:15; 12:12-13; 2 Sam. 24:16-17; 2 Kgs. 19:35). Such a divinely sent "strike" is always a fatal blow.

Interestingly, Josephus states that Agrippa knew he was in trouble: "As he presently afterward looked up, he saw an owl sitting on a certain rope over his head, and immediately understood that this bird was the messenger of ill tidings, as it had once been the messenger of good tidings to him; and fell into the deepest sorrow."[61] Is it possible he saw a manifestation of the angel of the Lord? If so, the warning had no effect. He still had time to repent. Instead, he died suddenly and painfully, "eaten by worms" (Acts 12:23).

Agrippa didn't suddenly acquire the worms. He died suddenly because of them. How long had those worms been devouring the man from the inside? While he sat in haughty power over James before sentencing him to die? When he ordered the arrest of Peter and then played the pious king at Passover? When he laid plans to expand his holdings into Syria? No matter. His manner of death simply revealed his manner of living. A man eaten by worms presumed to sit in judgment over God's people, and he fell as quickly as he had risen.

— 12:24 —

Luke's parting comment on the episode is fitting: "He was eaten by worms and died. But the word of the Lord continued to grow and to be multiplied" (12:23-24). Since then, the word of the Lord has continued to grow and multiply for two thousand years. Agrippa's pathetic, three-year reign is a piece of lint on the scroll of church history.

Tragically, this also marked the nation of Israel's last hope of participation in God's redemptive plan—at least for now. He's not finished with His covenant people. He will fulfill all His Old Testament promises literally and completely in the future (Rom. 9–11). After the death of

Agrippa (AD 44), however, the nation grew even more estranged from the new covenant and increasingly hostile to the church. Then calamity destroyed the temple (AD 70) and scattered the people.

— 12:25 —

Acts 11:19-30 rewound the narrative clock to summarize the partnership of Barnabas and Saul in Antioch, but 12:25 takes us forward again to rejoin their ministry in progress. Agrippa died in AD 44; the famine took place two years later in AD 46.

Luke closes this section of the narrative with a transition statement. The focus will now shift away from Jerusalem to highlight the new center of Christianity in Antioch. The kingdom of God will expand chiefly among the Gentiles, not the Jews. Even though Peter will continue to minister effectively for many years to come, Paul will carry forward the word of God even more extensively. The baton has passed to new hands. Stage two of the plan, "Judea and Samaria," will now give way to stage three, "the remotest part of the earth" (1:8).

APPLICATION: ACTS 12:18-25

Contrasting Lives . . . A Compelling Lesson

Most symphonies have a major melody, a familiar strain that forms the main theme. You can hum it, or whistle it, or—in the case of Beethoven's Ninth—belt it out in German. It's the major melody you think of when that piece of music comes to your attention.

But behind the melody there are notes that nobody ever hums.

I remember playing in the Houston Youth Symphony years ago. I played oboe—the only oboist in the group. We were playing a piece called "The Caliph of Baghdad." At one point in that piece there's a counterpart by the oboe that backs up the melody. I have to admit, in an orchestra of sixty instruments—pounding percussion, screeching strings, blaring brass—I was afraid my little oboe wouldn't be heard. But the conductor assured me, "Young man, you just play that part quietly. That oboe pierces."

To prove his point, he recorded our performance. When we finished the piece, he played it back. Sure enough, behind the major melody was this subtle counterpart of the oboe, clear as could be . . . if you were listening for it. It wasn't the lyrical line everybody would be humming, but if you knew what to listen for, you'd know that was my oboe.

That's Acts 12:24-25. The omniscient Spirit of God knows how to arrange things in His inspired narrative to teach us profound truths. At the end of this section, He moved Luke to add two little verses that seem to stick out like mules in a shopping mall. From a human perspective you might think Luke didn't know where else to put these verses, but from a divine perspective we see a lesson in contrasts.

By flexing his political muscles and flaunting his eloquence, King Agrippa I drew great crowds of doting devotees. Their "messiah in the making" sounded to them like a god! Maybe, he thought, it was so—until an angel afflicted him with a downright disgusting disease. I'm sure everybody throughout Judea was distraught over that tragic turn of events.

But while the world fretted about worms, God focused on His word: "But the word of the Lord continued to grow and to be multiplied" (12:24). And while the world turned its attention to the fate of their false messiah, God pointed our attention to His faithful missionaries: "And Barnabas and Saul returned from Jerusalem when they had fulfilled their mission, taking along with them John, who was also called Mark" (12:25).

What contrasting lives . . . and opposing priorities!

Yet from this great divergence between the well known and the unknown, a compelling lesson emerges.

In life, the major melody always makes the headlines. It's what everybody is humming. And if we're not careful, those of us designed to "play oboe" will want to play that part, too. We'll want to be noticed. Don't do it! Play your part—the part God gave you to play. It may seem you're getting lost in the background, but never mind that. If God made you an oboist, just play the oboe. You never know what He may choose to do with your quiet, humble, barely noticeable contribution. Through your efforts—often unseen—God's doing His work. It's His symphony, after all.

THE EXPANSION OF THE CHURCH (ACTS 13:1–20:2)

The preceding section recounted how the church began to face the challenge of its own prejudice and to move into Samaria and beyond. The apostle Peter had personally seen the Holy Spirit fill Gentile Christians, and the Antioch church was readily sharing the gospel with Gentiles as well. It was evident that even uncircumcised Gentiles could enter the kingdom of God through faith in the Messiah (11:3, 18).

During this period, Saul of Tarsus had been confronted by the resurrected Messiah; he was rebuked for persecuting Jewish Christians and commissioned to evangelize the Gentiles. But it was only after the church's change of attitude toward the idea of Gentile conversions that the ministry of Paul could begin in earnest. Barnabas had come alongside Paul and brought him to the Antioch church. There, the Holy Spirit called the church to send these two men out on a missionary journey, further still from Jerusalem. Other similar journeys followed for Paul, and this section of Acts tells of the remarkably quick expansion of the church through Paul's ministry.

When we study the journeys of Paul in the book of Acts, we're not just reading the travel log of a man; we're observing the redemptive plan of God unfolding as He promised. Through the ministry of Saul of Tarsus, God's mission to reclaim His creation from the death grip of evil would move to its next stage. The plan of this mission was outlined in the Lord's promise at His ascension, where He said,

> "You will receive power when the Holy Spirit has come upon you; and you shall be My witnesses . . . in
>> Jerusalem [stage 1: Acts 2–7],
>> and in all Judea and Samaria [stage 2: Acts 8–12],
>> and even to the remotest part of the earth [stage 3: Acts 13–28]." (1:8)

God has neither forgotten nor forsaken His covenant people, the Hebrews, and He would carry His plan forward through the ministry of a Jew set aside by unmerited mercy and prepared by sovereign design.

A "Hebrew of Hebrews" (Phil. 3:5), Paul carried the gospel to the Gentiles who, in turn, became the stone and mortar of the kingdom for two thousand years and counting. Although the Lord used Paul's ministry to transform a localized sect of Judaism into a worldwide phenomenon, success didn't come easily or cheaply. Indeed, God had promised the newly converted persecutor that he would endure suffering himself (Acts 9:16). And the apostle indeed suffered every form of discomfort imaginable over the next ten to fifteen years as he pushed the boundaries of the kingdom across the eastern half of the Roman Empire from Jerusalem to Rome. This next phase of expansion occurred in three successive journeys, consequently called by scholars "the missionary journeys of Paul," each carrying the apostle farther from home for longer periods of time. Notably, Luke first begins to call Saul of Tarsus "Paul" with the first of these voyages into the Gentile world (13:9).

The major events of this section are the first missionary journey (13:1–14:28), the Jerusalem Council (15:1-35), the second missionary journey (15:36–18:22), and the third missionary journey (18:23–20:2). An overview of each is provided below.

Paul's First Missionary Journey (13:1–14:28)

Agrippa I died sometime after Passover in AD 44 (see 12:20-24). After this, Paul and Barnabas returned from Jerusalem to Antioch (12:25; cf. 11:28-30), then spent some time ministering there. After some time, the Holy Spirit selected Paul and Barnabas for special missionary work, so the pair departed Syrian Antioch for Cyprus (13:2-4), Barnabas's homeland, and crossed over to the Roman province of Pamphylia and then north to Pisidian Antioch (13:13-14; see map on page 256). They might have continued the circuit by traveling to Paul's hometown of Tarsus and then back home to Syrian Antioch, except for two considerations. First, the onset of winter would have made crossing the Taurus Mountains difficult. Second, spending the winter in Derbe would not have been the best use of their time. So they reversed course to shore up the communities they had already visited. They caught a ship in Attalia and sailed straight for Seleucia, the harbor town nearest Antioch (14:25-26).

The complete first missionary journey probably took the team eighteen months to complete—between the spring of AD 47 and fall of AD 48.

The Jerusalem Council (15:1-35)

As the church in Syrian Antioch flourished and the gospel continued to spread among Gentiles, a controversy arose over the question of circumcision. A group of Jewish Christians from the Jerusalem church again pressed the question of whether one could become a Christian without first converting to Judaism (15:1, 5; cf. 11:2-3). After all, Jesus is the Jewish Messiah and eventually will rule the world as a theocracy. This had been God's vision for Israel from the beginning. How could one embrace Jesus as the Messiah without first knowing the God of the Hebrews, His Old Testament Scriptures, and at least some Jewish theology? Unlike today, in which nearly two-thirds of the world's people—Jews, Christians, and Muslims—know "God" as the God of Abraham, first-century Gentiles were virtually ignorant of anything but their pagan pantheon of mythical caricatures.

On the other side of the issue stood Peter, James, Barnabas, Paul, and—of course—every Gentile believer. In their minds, Peter's experience in Caesarea settled the issue. God had given His Spirit to the uncircumcised Gentiles in the home of Cornelius, which the apostles and elders took as a divine declaration that salvation is by grace alone through faith alone in Christ alone. Even so, the controversy drove the Jerusalem church to distraction. A decision was made to call all of the church leaders—apostles and elders—to meet, debate, and then issue a declaration of the official church position. Most scholars place the date around AD 49 or 50.

Paul's Second Missionary Journey (15:36–18:22)

Luke sets the time for Paul's second journey as "after some days" following the Jerusalem Council (15:36). This could represent weeks or months, but not likely more than a year. Barnabas and Paul originally determined to revisit the cities of the first journey. They could not agree, however, on whether to take John Mark, who had left them midway through that first expedition. So, after a strong disagreement, Barnabas took John Mark with him to Cyprus and undoubtedly other destinations, and Paul chose Silas as a partner and headed north to Tarsus in Cilicia (15:40-41), through a pass in the Taurus Mountains, and into southern Galatia (16:1-2; see map on page 312). They would have continued west into Asia Minor, but the Holy Spirit prevented them (16:6). Instead, they turned north toward Bithynia but again were blocked by the Spirit (16:7). Turning west again, they found no entrance into Mysia, so they continued to the harbor city of Troas on the shore of the Aegean Sea (16:8).

With the whole of present-day Turkey closed off, they remained in Troas until Paul received a night vision of a man calling them to the vast province of Macedonia (16:9), which bordered the northwestern and western rim of the Aegean Sea. Paul's team visited each of the major cities along the coastline around the sea (16:10–17:14) and down toward Athens, where the apostle preached to the leading minds in Greek philosophy (17:15-34). From there, Paul traveled west to Corinth, where he ministered for at least eighteen months (18:1-11). There the Jews rose up against him and brought him before Gallio for trial, but Gallio objected that this was a Jewish argument and not a Roman concern (18:12-17). The mention of Gallio, the proconsul of Achaia, places the latter part of Paul's ministry there in AD 51, with his trial most likely taking place in the spring or summer.

When the time came for him to leave, his new friends Aquila and Priscilla traveled with him (18:2-3, 18). Landing in Ephesus, the principal city in Asia Minor, he preached in the synagogue to such a warm reception the leaders asked him to stay on. Instead, he left the Jewish couple he met in Corinth to minister in his place, expressing his desire to return soon (18:19-21). From there, he sailed to Caesarea and then returned home to Syrian Antioch (18:22).

Paul's Third Missionary Journey (18:23–20:2)

Luke's narrative suggests that Paul didn't remain in Antioch very long before he set out again to revisit the churches he had helped establish (see map on page 369). The narrative mentions "the Galatian region and Phrygia" (18:23), which would include cities along the route traveled in the second journey—Derbe, Lystra, and Iconium—and the northern part of Asia, perhaps with visits to Pisidian Antioch and Philadelphia along the way. "Upper country" (19:1) translates a Greek expression meaning "highlands," probably referring to a route over the Tmolus Mountains and then down into the Cayster valley leading to Ephesus. Paul undoubtedly selected this route to maximize the number of cities from his second journey he could visit while getting to Ephesus as soon as possible.

Paul spent two years using Ephesus as a base of operations in Asia (see 19:1-41, especially 19:10). His plan was to revisit the Macedonian cities—Philippi, Thessalonica, and Berea—and then Corinth before sailing directly back to visit Jerusalem. After one last time of worship in the temple, he would set out for Rome (19:21), where he planned to launch an expedition westward toward Spain (Rom. 15:24, 28).

He did visit Macedonia and then Greece, where he spent three months (Acts 20:1-3). This effectively ended his third missionary journey as he had planned it. Unfortunately, enemies among the Jewish leaders plotted to kill Paul, so his return home took a less direct route.

Perhaps to throw off the assassins, he instructed his traveling companions to sail from Greece as planned while he retraced his steps back through Macedonia to Philippi. He rendezvoused with the team in Troas shortly after Passover, and they sailed back to Caesarea, stopping at ports all along the way (20:1-8).

KEY TERMS IN ACTS 13:1–20:2

dialegomai (διαλέγομαι) [1256] "to dispute," "to reason," "to discuss"
Greek philosophers used this term in a technical sense, believing the use of logic and reason to be the means by which one may connect with the *logos*, the divine mind, the realm of pure idea. For example, "in Socrates, Plato and Aristotle there is developed the art of persuasion and demonstration either in the form of question and answer (Socrates), the establishment of the idea by pure thought (Plato), or the investigation of the ultimate foundations of demonstration and knowledge (Aristotle)."[1] Ancient Jews didn't "reason" in this technical sense, but they recognized disputation as a time-honored theological method. In the first century, however, Greek influence undoubtedly found its way into synagogues within predominantly Gentile cities. Acts uses the term *dialegomai* for Paul's practice of engaging unbelievers in apologetic and evangelistic encounters.[2]

katangellō (καταγγέλλω) [2605] "to proclaim," "to announce," "to make known widely"
The root word of this verb means simply "to announce." The prefix *kata-* [2596] usually functions as an intensifier, adding an emphasis of some kind. Outside the New Testament, writers used the term in reference to broadcasting official reports and announcing athletic games or religious festivals. The writings of Luke and Paul use the word with special theological meaning, describing the kind of "proclaiming" that eliminates excuses and produces a transformation. If there is widespread preaching and teaching, no one may claim ignorance as the reason for unbelief.

parakaleō (παρακαλέω) [3870] "to exhort," "to urge," "to encourage," "to comfort"
The primary idea of this verb is "to comfort," usually in reference to those grieving or dying. In the New Testament, the term takes on a specialized meaning, especially in the writings of Luke and Paul, for whom it's a multifaceted word that carries the idea of standing alongside someone in order to provide counsel, courage, comfort, hope, and positive perspective. The role of an athletic coach illustrates this expanded meaning well. A good coach challenges, instructs, inspires, and helps another toward excellence in reaching a specific goal.

parachrēma (παραχρῆμα) [3916] "suddenly,"
  "immediately," "at once"
Except for one notable exception (Matt. 21:19-20), this adverb appears
only in Luke (ten times) and Acts (six times). Luke uses the term to establish a clear cause-and-effect connection between one event and the
next, usually in the context of a supernatural event. Jesus, the apostles,
or God the Father acted, and "immediately" the results were seen (cf.
Acts 3:7; 12:23).

pistis (πίστις) [4102] "faith," "trust," "confidence,"
  "reliance"
This word denotes confidence in the reliability of a person or thing and
can describe one's trust in a person's word, a compact or treaty, or a deity
(or deities). The term implies both knowledge and action. One may receive
knowledge of a certain truth and may even offer verbal agreement, but
"trust" or "confidence" is not said to be present until one's behavior reflects
that truth. In the Hellenistic period, this word came to connote the conviction that gods do exist and are active. The Greeks worshiped and feared
their gods, but they did not have a relationship with them. Luke's readers, however, would also have known the word from the Septuagint (the
Greek translation of the Old Testament), where it—and related words, like
pisteuō [4100], "to believe," "to accept as truth," "to commit one's trust"—is
linked to the relationship with Israel's covenant-keeping God. For the Jew,
and therefore the Christian, *pistis* became a description of the means by
which someone relates to God—so much so that the participial form came
to designate members of the church as "believers" (e.g., 2:44; 4:32; 5:14).

When the Going Gets Tough
ACTS 13:1-13

NASB

¹Now there were at Antioch, in the church that was *there*, prophets and teachers: Barnabas, and Simeon who was called Niger, and Lucius of Cyrene, and Manaen who had been brought up with Herod the tetrarch, and Saul. ²While they were minister-ing to the Lord and fasting, the Holy Spirit said, "Set apart for Me Barn-abas and Saul for the work to which I have called them." ³Then, when they had fasted and prayed and laid their hands on them, they sent them away.

⁴So, being sent out by the Holy

NLT

¹Among the prophets and teachers of the church at Antioch of Syria were Barnabas, Simeon (called "the black man"*), Lucius (from Cyrene), Manaen (the childhood companion of King Herod Antipas*), and Saul. ²One day as these men were wor-shiping the Lord and fasting, the Holy Spirit said, "Appoint Barna-bas and Saul for the special work to which I have called them." ³So after more fasting and prayer, the men laid their hands on them and sent them on their way.

⁴So Barnabas and Saul were sent

Spirit, they went down to Seleucia and from there they sailed to Cyprus. ⁵When they reached Salamis, they *began* to proclaim the word of God in the synagogues of the Jews; and they also had John as their helper. ⁶When they had gone through the whole island as far as Paphos, they found a magician, a Jewish false prophet whose name was Bar-Jesus, ⁷who was with the proconsul, Sergius Paulus, a man of intelligence. This man summoned Barnabas and Saul and sought to hear the word of God. ⁸But Elymas the magician (for so his name is translated) was opposing them, seeking to turn the proconsul away from the faith. ⁹But Saul, who was also *known as* Paul, ᵃfilled with the Holy Spirit, fixed his gaze on him, ¹⁰and said, "You who are full of all deceit and fraud, you son of the devil, you enemy of all righteousness, will you not cease to make crooked the straight ways of the Lord? ¹¹Now, behold, the hand of the Lord is upon you, and you will be blind and not see the sun for a time." And immediately a mist and a darkness fell upon him, and he went about seeking those who would lead him by the hand. ¹²Then the proconsul believed when he saw what had happened, being amazed at the teaching of the Lord.

¹³Now Paul and his companions put out to sea from Paphos and came to Perga in Pamphylia; but John left them and returned to Jerusalem.

13:9 ᵃOr *having* just *been filled*

out by the Holy Spirit. They went down to the seaport of Seleucia and then sailed for the island of Cyprus. ⁵There, in the town of Salamis, they went to the Jewish synagogues and preached the word of God. John Mark went with them as their assistant.

⁶Afterward they traveled from town to town across the entire island until finally they reached Paphos, where they met a Jewish sorcerer, a false prophet named Bar-Jesus. ⁷He had attached himself to the governor, Sergius Paulus, who was an intelligent man. The governor invited Barnabas and Saul to visit him, for he wanted to hear the word of God. ⁸But Elymas, the sorcerer (as his name means in Greek), interfered and urged the governor to pay no attention to what Barnabas and Saul said. He was trying to keep the governor from believing.

⁹Saul, also known as Paul, was filled with the Holy Spirit, and he looked the sorcerer in the eye. ¹⁰Then he said, "You son of the devil, full of every sort of deceit and fraud, and enemy of all that is good! Will you never stop perverting the true ways of the Lord? ¹¹Watch now, for the Lord has laid his hand of punishment upon you, and you will be struck blind. You will not see the sunlight for some time." Instantly mist and darkness came over the man's eyes, and he began groping around begging for someone to take his hand and lead him.

¹²When the governor saw what had happened, he became a believer, for he was astonished at the teaching about the Lord.

¹³Paul and his companions then left Paphos by ship for Pamphylia, landing at the port town of Perga. There John Mark left them and returned to Jerusalem.

13:1a Greek *who was called Niger.* 13:1b Greek *Herod the tetrarch.*

Maintaining a balance between optimism and realism can be difficult anywhere, but especially in ministry. Idealism can't survive long in a world characterized by hardship, difficulty, and disappointment—not unless we live in denial, anyway. But even though we should forever remove from our minds the notion that once a person becomes a Christian hard times are over, we can't afford to live by Murphy's Law: "Anything that can go wrong, will go wrong." Christians—especially those in vocational Christian service—must maintain what might be called a healthy idealism.

Unhealthy idealism is what you commonly see in brides and grooms prior to the wedding day. They marry with great, high, beautiful, idealistic hopes about marriage, their mates, and the home, only to melt down at the first significant challenge. Men who plan to take large families on camping trips tend to be idealistic in an unhealthy way. Fresh-faced university graduates who descend the platform with degree in hand and a chest full of ambition often enter the workforce with unhealthy idealism, only to crash and burn after the first few rejections.

Healthy idealism, on the other hand, expects to achieve its goals even as it anticipates difficulties, challenges, and setbacks. This is not a Pollyanna kind of dreamy optimism; this is a confidence in the power and sovereignty of God to overcome *anything*. Jesus promised that His followers' path to glory would be strewn with heartache, suffering, persecution, and injustice; consequently, healthy idealism interprets difficulty as confirmation that the current path leads to victory. As the venerable F. B. Meyer wrote,

> Think it not strange, child of God, concerning the fiery trial that tries thee, as though some strange thing had happened. Rejoice! For it is a sure sign that thou art on the right track. If in an unknown country, I am informed that I must pass through a valley where the sun is hidden, or over a stony bit of road, to reach my abiding-place—when I come to it, each moment of shadow or jolt of the carriage tells me that I am on the right road. So when a child of God passes through affliction he is not surprised.[3]

The Lord did not promise to keep us *from* suffering (John 16:33); He promised to sustain us *through* suffering (Rom. 8:28-39), so that every experience will become God's means of creating in us a greater capacity for joy with each passing day. If you haven't discovered the Lord's supernatural use for suffering, you will continue to struggle with disillusionment, perhaps wondering who's at fault, you or God.

When Saul, Barnabas, and their team set out from Antioch, they had little idea of what they would confront. They knew only that they had been set apart for this work by the Holy Spirit. So, everyone departed home with a generous portion of optimism; the first leg of their journey, however, would reveal to everyone which kind of optimism each man possessed.

— 13:1-3 —

Luke begins this section of the narrative by calling attention to the leaders in the church of Antioch. Though great congregations can accomplish great things for the Lord, they need godly leaders to bring them together and to focus their efforts. Luke names five who were "prophets and teachers" (13:1)—two different gifts, two distinct offices working in

SYRIAN ANTIOCH

ACTS 13:1

Syrian Antioch (not to be confused with Pisidian Antioch) was the third largest city in the Roman Empire, after Rome and Alexandria, with close to one million residents at its peak. Seleucus I Nicator established the city around 300 BC to serve as the western capital of the Seleucid Empire.[4] To attract colonists, Seleucid generals granted land, titles, and citizenship to compensate Jewish mercenaries. By the time of Paul and Barnabas, Antioch had become a significant center of Jewish worship and culture.[5] As a result, the very large community of Jews attracted numerous Gentile converts to Judaism (known as proselytes), including Nicolas (6:5).

After the Romans conquered the region, Caesars Augustus and Tiberius invested in the city, with the help of Herod the Great, to make it the capital of the newly created province of Syria. Like Tarsus, it became an intersection of Eastern and Western civilization, but more in terms of commerce than education.[6] Unfortunately, the city also became a sometimes-turbulent intersection of good and bad influences. High art existed alongside brutal athletic games; monotheistic Judaism competed with numerous mystery religions. Worship of the Hebrew God attracted stable residents, while tourists came for orgiastic rites in the nearby attractive suburb of Daphne, the seat of a temple of Apollo.[7]

In this compost-like blend of East and West, good and bad, morality and depravity, the gospel germinated, took root, and flourished like a rose in a garbage dump. As the nation of Israel abdicated its privileged role in the divine plan, Syrian Antioch replaced Jerusalem as the center of church activity. It was from Antioch, not Jerusalem, that God raised up missionaries to push the boundaries of His kingdom westward across the Roman Empire.

harmony together to bring the word of God to the people and then to instruct them in how to apply it. God calls prophets to a ministry of "forth-telling," which in the first century, before the New Testament Scriptures were written and circulated, included "foretelling"—providing new divine revelation that includes predictions of the future (11:28). God calls teachers to help individuals turn truth into action.

These five prophets and teachers ministered faithfully in Antioch (13:1):

- Barnabas, a former priest of the temple who came from Cyprus
- Simeon, a Jew whose nickname, interestingly, means "black"
- Lucius, a Greek proselyte from the North African coastal city of Cyrene
- Manaen, an aristocratic, Hellenistic Jew (Sadducee) who grew up with Herod Antipas
- Saul of Tarsus, a Pharisee educated under the great rabbi Gamaliel

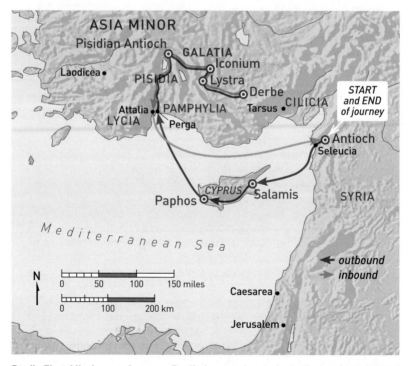

Paul's First Missionary Journey. Paul's journey began in Antioch, where he and Barnabas set off for the island of Cyprus. They traveled around Galatia through Antioch of Pisidia, Iconium, Lystra, and Derbe. From Derbe, they retraced their steps back to Antioch.

This diverse-yet-unified group of Christian leaders entered a season of fasting. During this time, they received instructions from the Lord to embark on an exciting new ministry (13:2). The Holy Spirit was specific enough to call Barnabas and Saul, but the task would be disclosed later. Not unlike the Lord's call of Abram, "Go forth from your country . . . to the land which I will show you" (Gen. 12:1), He gave the men enough information to take the first step. After they responded in obedience, God would reveal the information they needed next in due time.

The elders of this church "laid their hands" on the two men (Acts 13:3), like the Jerusalem church had laid hands on the seven (6:1-6). Through the "laying on of hands," the leaders said, in effect, "We endorse you and authorize you to carry out this mission on our behalf; we go with you in spirit as we pray for you here at home."

— 13:4-5 —

Luke deliberately ties the action of the church in the laying-on-of-hands ceremony to the commissioning of the Holy Spirit. They are, in fact, complementary acts; one goes with the other.

Saul and Barnabas traveled 14 miles down the Orontes River to catch a ship from Seleucia to Cyprus (13:4). Barnabas undoubtedly knew his island homeland like the back of his hand. Lush with crops and rich with minerals and precious metals, this became a favorite stopover for merchant ships sailing the Mediterranean Sea. Situated just 60 miles off the Syrian coast, it became a refuge for Jews hundreds of years before the birth of Christ. The Apocrypha notes settlements there during the Maccabean Revolt (1 Macc. 15:23), and when Caesar granted copper mines to Herod the Great, more people undoubtedly sought work there.[8] So, it comes as no surprise that several synagogues dotted the island. During the persecution that followed the martyrdom of Stephen, some Christians took refuge on Cyprus (Acts 11:19).

Barnabas and Saul didn't travel alone; they brought with them an unknown number of assistants. As a kind of "by the way" comment, Luke states that the group included John Mark, a cousin of Barnabas (Col. 4:10) and the son of Mary, in whose home the congregation in Jerusalem gathered to pray for Peter (Acts 12:12).

— 13:6-8 —

The team traveled from Salamis, a significant harbor city on the eastern end of the island, to Paphos on the western end, a journey of about 90 miles, encouraging congregations of believers and preaching in

PAUL'S TRAVELING COMPANIONS

ACTS 13:1

Paul rarely traveled or ministered alone. In fact, he almost always traveled with a fellow minister and a number of helpers, younger men we might today call interns. He did this for two important reasons. First, *no one* traveled between cities alone. Highway robberies were so common that even small groups of travelers would delay their itineraries to join larger caravans, which provided the greatest safety against bandits. Second, Paul—like all teachers of his era—selected and trained disciples to perpetuate his evangelistic and teaching ministry.

Luke's narrative style in Acts doesn't make the presence of fellow travelers obvious; he typically mentions specific names only when the narrative makes them necessary. For example, in 15:40, he begins his account of Paul's second missionary journey by stating that "Paul chose Silas and left." Then, because the narrative focuses on Paul, Luke refers to him in the third person singular as though he were alone. "And *he* was traveling through Syria and Cilicia, strengthening the churches" (15:41, emphasis mine). Luke does not mention Silas again until the two men are arrested in Philippi (16:19), even though Silas undoubtedly remained with Paul throughout the journey. The same is true of Timothy, who joined Paul in Galatia on his second journey but rarely appears in the narrative thereafter.

Most curious of all is the fact that Titus appears nowhere in Acts, even though this Gentile Christian appears to have been an aide to Paul from the very beginning. After Paul and Barnabas returned from the first missionary journey, they traveled to the Jerusalem Council with "some others" (15:2), a delegation that included both circumcised and uncircumcised believers. When describing the Jerusalem Council to the Galatians, Paul specifically mentioned Titus (Gal. 2:1, 3), strongly suggesting they knew him, perhaps as an unnamed helper on that expedition. This disciple also served as an envoy to Corinth during Paul's second journey. He most likely left from Ephesus (2 Cor. 12:18) when he went to reconnect with Paul somewhere in Macedonia (2 Cor. 2:13; 7:6, 13). Why Luke never mentions Titus remains a mystery.

Regardless, clues scattered throughout the New Testament reveal a growing entourage of disciples in addition to Timothy and Titus. The sudden appearance of Erastus of Corinth on Paul's third journey (Acts 19:22) implies that he joined the apostle on his second journey and had been with him ever since. In that same passage, Gaius and Aristarchus also emerge from the narrative chorus to receive brief mention. The phrase "Paul's traveling companions" (19:29) alludes to a group of men dedicated to serving as helpers. Apparently, Paul recruited these two while passing through Macedonia on his second journey and they had "ministered to him" ever since. Luke also names a sizable entourage returning with Paul to Jerusalem at the end of his third journey: "He was accompanied by Sopater of Berea, the son of Pyrrhus, and by Aristarchus and Secundus of the Thessalonians, and Gaius of Derbe, and Timothy, and Tychicus and Trophimus of Asia" (20:4).

We don't know when these other men joined Paul. He may have picked them up in their respective cities on his second and third journeys. We only know for certain they became his traveling companions before leaving Corinth, most likely recruited to help evangelize the western frontier as far as Spain (Rom. 15:24, 28) after visiting Jerusalem.

During Paul's first imprisonment in Rome, he would mention other men who had been his helpers for some time. These include Epaphroditus (Phil. 2:25; Col. 4:12; Phlm. 1:23), John Mark (Col. 4:10), and Demas (Col. 4:14; 2 Tim. 4:10; Phlm. 1:24). Of course, Paul added Luke on his return from the third missionary journey, the physician who most likely remained at the apostle's side until the end of his life in Rome roughly eight or nine years later (Acts 27:1–28:16; Col. 4:14; 2 Tim. 4:11; Phlm. 1:24).

synagogues along the way. Paphos first became famous when mythology set the city as the first home of Aphrodite, the goddess of love, after she was born from sea foam.[9] When the Romans annexed Cyprus in 58 BC and later made the island its own province, Paphos became the seat of the military government.[10] At the time of this visit by Saul and Barnabas, a proconsul by the name of Sergius Paulus governed (13:7).

A proconsul usually reported directly to those in the Senate, who endowed him with absolute military and judicial power over a province. Proconsuls usually served a limited term as part of their political climb up the ranks, the next level being consul.[11] In other words, Sergius Paulus was a high-ranking official in the Roman government.

While the proconsul was a "man of intelligence," he nevertheless kept a Jewish magician as an advisor (13:7-8). Being a "magician" (*magos* [3097]) didn't necessarily mean one dabbled in witchcraft or communicated with the dead. The Greek term *magos* is the same term Matthew uses of the men from the east ("magi") who came to worship the infant Christ (Matt. 2:1-12) and referred to a class of Persian priests who made Babylon their center of learning. Their education blended legitimate science with pagan superstition, so as experts in astronomy, they practiced astrology. They were not unlike medieval alchemists.

Unlike Simon of Samaria, who "was practicing magic (*mageuō* [3096]) in the city and astonishing the people" (Acts 8:9), Bar-Jesus appears to have been a highly educated man as well as an expert in astrology, interpretation of dreams, and divination using the occult. But this is hardly better than Simon Magus of Samaria; indeed, Luke calls him a false prophet (*pseudoprophētēs* [5578]), one who claims to speak for God yet has no divine connection.

His name is a mixture of influences. Bar-Jesus (*Bariēsous* [919]) blends the Aramaic prefix *bar* [H1247], which means "son of," and *Iesus* [2424], the Greek form of the Hebrew name Joshua [H3091]. The designation, Elymas (*Elymas* [1681]), appears to be an Arabic title meaning "sage" or "seer." All of this suggests he was widely traveled, having devoted much of his life to the study of the occult.

The proconsul had summoned Saul and Barnabas to preach, undoubtedly knowing something about their message. Given the company he kept, he may have been what we today call a "seeker," someone on a personal quest for spiritual truth. As the two men addressed the proconsul, however, Bar-Jesus argued against their teaching.

— 13:9-12 —

For the first time in this narrative, Luke calls Saul of Tarsus by the name we all know: Paul. The Greek name is *Paulos* [3972], a Roman surname that basically means "small." From this point on, Luke uses the name Paul, suggesting that in this confrontation with personified evil, the apostle came into his own. The scene is a fitting metaphor for Paul's ministry in the coming years: a Hebrew of Hebrews preaching the gospel to a quintessential Gentile, who desperately wanted to know divine truth—meanwhile, the voice of falsehood literally talking in his other ear.

Paul broke off the discussion to address the false prophet directly (13:10). The word translated "deceit" comes from a Greek term describing the work of a con artist, someone who takes advantage of others using underhanded schemes. The Greek word for "fraud" is actually less severe than the English term. In the words of one dictionary, the expression "suggests an easygoing approach to things in contrast to serious acceptance of responsibilities: 'frivolity' (the trickery of slaves is a common theme in Greek and Roman comedy)."[12] Taking all of these insults together, we see that Paul characterized the man as a villainous buffoon from a bad comedy. The charges "son of the devil" and "enemy of all righteousness," however, are much more serious. Bar-Jesus could be translated "son of salvation," so the epithet "son of the devil" is a deep, sarcastic dig at the man's identity. In terms of character, the man was a pathetic caricature of a "son of salvation"; in terms of morality, none could have represented evil more thoroughly.

Paul's question, "Will you not cease to make crooked the straight ways of the Lord?" draws from an old Hebrew expression to indicate a double meaning. The idea of making straight the way of the Lord recalls the exhortation of Isaiah to welcome the Messiah (Isa. 40:3; cf. Mal. 3:1). It was a cultural image the proconsul would have understood, though he would not likely have known the words of Isaiah. In ancient times, a city prepared for the arrival of a king or dignitary by upgrading the road leading into town. Obstacles and debris were cleared away, potholes filled in, landscaping completed. Whereas John the Baptizer had prophesied to prepare others for the arrival of the Messiah (Luke 3:4), Bar-Jesus created obstacles.

The expression also had a figurative element. The Hebrews often used "straight" and "crooked" to mean "righteous" and "unrighteous" or "moral" versus "immoral." God had sent Paul and Barnabas to clear the way for Christ to save the Gentiles, yet this Jewish false prophet littered His path with deception and unrighteousness.

Having indicted Bar-Jesus, Paul pronounced God's judgment upon him. The man who blinded others through his deceit became physically blind (Acts 13:11). This, believe it or not, was an act of grace on the part of the Lord on two counts. First, the false prophet deserved to die. As a Jew, he knew better. He had access to divine truth through the Scriptures, which he rejected in favor of pagan mysteries. Second, he was going blind only "for a time." To confront the wayward Hebrew seer, God struck him with the same affliction that had seized Saul of Tarsus on the road to Damascus. Saul had become Paul. How would Bar-Jesus respond?

Whatever the false prophet's response, Sergius Paulus believed! Seeing Bar-Jesus struck blind helped break the stalemate in his mind, and he embraced the gospel. Notably, he wasn't "amazed" by the supernatural event as much as the teaching Paul and Barnabas brought (13:12). After this incident, we hear nothing more of the Roman official.

— 13:13 —

Paul and the team departed Paphos to continue their journey. They sailed north to the coastal region known as Pamphylia, a traditional haunt for pirates who preyed on merchant ships bound for Syria and Phoenicia.[13] Before Pompey finally established control in 67 BC, piracy had become something of a cottage industry in Perga, creating a melting pot of cultural misfits and scoundrels. Even though Pamphylia no longer represented a significant threat to safety on the waters, land travel was another matter. A rim of high mountains isolated the coastal plain of Pamphylia from the interior. The plan of Paul and Barnabas to reach Pisidian Antioch presented the danger of robbery or a severe accident in the craggy terrain.[14] In addition, the hot, humid climate in Pamphylia would have been miserable in early summer.

All that to say: The honeymoon was over! The team had enjoyed great success on Cyprus, the very pleasant island known intimately by Barnabas. The large Jewish population had offered plenty of hospitality along the journey, which concluded with the dramatic conversion of a high-ranking Gentile. From Perga onward, the going would get tough. For reasons Luke doesn't reveal, John Mark abruptly abandoned the team and sailed for home (13:13). Perhaps the journey had proved too difficult or precarious. Maybe he dealt with some kind of illness or nursed an injury. Did he disagree with Paul's ministry methods? Did he get homesick and long for Jerusalem? To attempt to answer the question of why John Mark left would be pure speculation. In any case, Luke doesn't dwell on the matter. He merely includes Mark's departure before describing the team's ministry in Pisidian Antioch. Later in the narrative, John Mark's decision will prove to be a pivotal event in the ministries of Paul and Barnabas (15:36-40).

APPLICATION: ACTS 13:1-13

The Tough Get Going

Pardon the cliché, but it's true: "When the going gets tough, the tough get going." Not only is that classic halftime pep talk, it describes the reason some fail to survive ministry challenges while others thrive. Based on my observation of Paul's ministry, coupled with my own experience over the past fifty years of pulpit ministry, here are two principles to apply.

First, *there can be no accomplishment without determination.* It's a fact of life—and an even bigger fact of ministry. Standing between you and your objectives is a mountain range of obstacles, difficulties, dangers, and discouragement. Critics hide in the hollows of that treacherous land, waiting to steal your enthusiasm. Unhealthy idealism will set you up for utter disillusionment, which will make you believe that the reward isn't worth the risk. Healthy idealism never loses sight of the objective, even as it accounts for inevitable difficulties. To the healthy idealist, the goal makes any amount of suffering worthwhile.

David Livingston, the quintessential healthy idealist, famously said, "I determined never to stop until I had come to the end and achieved my purpose."[15]

Second, *there is no burden too heavy for Christ to carry.* That gives the Christian an edge that others can't claim. We do not bear our burdens or face our trials or endure our suffering alone. We have the Spirit of God within and the supernatural power of God at work in all circumstances. If God has called you to cross the foreboding peaks of Pamphylia, the valleys of which churn with danger, don't turn back. He doesn't send you alone. On the eve of His own suffering, Jesus prayed for us, saying,

> "Now I come to You; and these things I speak in the world so that they may have My joy made full in themselves. I have given them Your word; and the world has hated them, because they are not of the world, even as I am not of the world. I do not ask You to take them out of the world, but to keep them from the evil one. They are not of the world, even as I am not of the world. Sanctify them in the truth; Your word is truth. As You sent Me into the world, I also have sent them into the world. For their sakes I sanctify Myself, that they themselves also may be sanctified in truth.
>
> "I do not ask on behalf of these alone, but for those also who believe in Me through their word; that they may all be one; even as You, Father, are in Me and I in You, that they also may be in Us, so that the world may believe that You sent Me." (John 17:13-21)

A Hunger for the Truth
ACTS 13:14-52

NASB

[14]But going on from Perga, they arrived at Pisidian Antioch, and on the Sabbath day they went into the synagogue and sat down. [15]After the reading of the Law and the Prophets the synagogue officials sent to them, saying, "Brethren, if you have any word of exhortation for the people,

NLT

[14]But Paul and Barnabas traveled inland to Antioch of Pisidia.*

On the Sabbath they went to the synagogue for the services. [15]After the usual readings from the books of Moses* and the prophets, those in charge of the service sent them this message: "Brothers, if you have any word of encouragement for the people, come and give it."

say it." ¹⁶Paul stood up, and motioning with his hand said,

"Men of Israel, and you who fear God, listen: ¹⁷The God of this people Israel chose our fathers and ᵃmade the people great during their stay in the land of Egypt, and with an uplifted arm He led them out from it. ¹⁸For a period of about forty years He put up with them in the wilderness. ¹⁹When He had destroyed seven nations in the land of Canaan, He distributed their land as an inheritance—*all of which took* about four hundred and fifty years. ²⁰After these things He gave *them* judges until Samuel the prophet. ²¹Then they asked for a king, and God gave them Saul the son of Kish, a man of the tribe of Benjamin, for forty years. ²²After He had removed him, He raised up David to be their king, concerning whom He also testified and said, 'I HAVE FOUND DAVID the son of Jesse, A MAN AFTER MY HEART, who will do all My ᵃwill.' ²³From the descendants of this man, according to promise, God has brought to Israel a Savior, Jesus, ²⁴after John had proclaimed before ᵃHis coming a baptism of repentance to all the people of Israel. ²⁵And while John was completing his course, he kept saying, 'What do you suppose that I am? I am not *He*. But behold, one is coming after me the sandals of whose feet I am not worthy to untie.'

²⁶"Brethren, sons of Abraham's family, and those among you who fear God, to us the message of this salvation has been sent. ²⁷For those who live in Jerusalem, and their rulers, recognizing neither Him nor the ᵃutterances of the prophets which are read every Sabbath, fulfilled *these* by condemning *Him*. ²⁸And though they

¹⁶So Paul stood, lifted his hand to quiet them, and started speaking. "Men of Israel," he said, "and you God-fearing Gentiles, listen to me. ¹⁷"The God of this nation of Israel chose our ancestors and made them multiply and grow strong during their stay in Egypt. Then with a powerful arm he led them out of their slavery. ¹⁸He put up with them* through forty years of wandering in the wilderness. ¹⁹Then he destroyed seven nations in Canaan and gave their land to Israel as an inheritance. ²⁰All this took about 450 years.

"After that, God gave them judges to rule until the time of Samuel the prophet. ²¹Then the people begged for a king, and God gave them Saul son of Kish, a man of the tribe of Benjamin, who reigned for forty years. ²²But God removed Saul and replaced him with David, a man about whom God said, 'I have found David son of Jesse, a man after my own heart. He will do everything I want him to do.'*

²³"And it is one of King David's descendants, Jesus, who is God's promised Savior of Israel! ²⁴Before he came, John the Baptist preached that all the people of Israel needed to repent of their sins and turn to God and be baptized. ²⁵As John was finishing his ministry he asked, 'Do you think I am the Messiah? No, I am not! But he is coming soon—and I'm not even worthy to be his slave and untie the sandals on his feet.'

²⁶"Brothers—you sons of Abraham, and also you God-fearing Gentiles—this message of salvation has been sent to us! ²⁷The people in Jerusalem and their leaders did not recognize Jesus as the one the prophets had spoken about. Instead, they condemned him, and in doing this they fulfilled the prophets' words that are read every Sabbath. ²⁸They found no legal reason to

found no ground for *putting Him to death*, they asked Pilate that He be ᵃexecuted. ²⁹When they had carried out all that was written concerning Him, they took Him down from the ᵃcross and laid Him in a tomb. ³⁰But God raised Him from the dead; ³¹and for many days He appeared to those who came up with Him from Galilee to Jerusalem, the very ones who are now His witnesses to the people. ³²And we preach to you the good news of the promise made to the fathers, ³³that God has fulfilled this *promise* ᵃto our children in that He raised up Jesus, as it is also written in the second Psalm, 'YOU ARE MY SON; TODAY I HAVE BEGOTTEN YOU.' ³⁴*As for the fact* that He raised Him up from the dead, no longer to return to decay, He has spoken in this way: 'I WILL GIVE YOU THE HOLY *and* ᵃSURE *blessings* OF DAVID.' ³⁵Therefore He also says in another *Psalm,* 'YOU WILL NOT ᵃALLOW YOUR ᵇHOLY ONE TO ᶜUNDERGO DECAY.' ³⁶For David, after he had ᵃserved the purpose of God in his own generation, fell asleep, and was laid among his fathers and ᵇunderwent decay; ³⁷but He whom God raised did not ᵃundergo decay. ³⁸Therefore let it be known to you, brethren, that through ᵃHim forgiveness of sins is proclaimed to you, ³⁹and ᵃthrough Him everyone who believes is ᵇfreed ᶜfrom all things, from which you could not be ᵇfreed ᶜthrough the Law of Moses. ⁴⁰Therefore take heed, so that the thing spoken of in the Prophets may not come upon *you:*

⁴¹ 'BEHOLD, YOU SCOFFERS, AND
  MARVEL, AND ᵃPERISH;

execute him, but they asked Pilate to have him killed anyway.

²⁹"When they had done all that the prophecies said about him, they took him down from the cross★ and placed him in a tomb. ³⁰But God raised him from the dead! ³¹And over a period of many days he appeared to those who had gone with him from Galilee to Jerusalem. They are now his witnesses to the people of Israel.

³²"And now we are here to bring you this Good News. The promise was made to our ancestors, ³³and God has now fulfilled it for us, their descendants, by raising Jesus. This is what the second psalm says about Jesus:

'You are my Son.
 Today I have become your
  Father.★'

³⁴For God had promised to raise him from the dead, not leaving him to rot in the grave. He said, 'I will give you the sacred blessings I promised to David.'★ ³⁵Another psalm explains it more fully: 'You will not allow your Holy One to rot in the grave.'★ ³⁶This is not a reference to David, for after David had done the will of God in his own generation, he died and was buried with his ancestors, and his body decayed. ³⁷No, it was a reference to someone else—someone whom God raised and whose body did not decay.

³⁸★"Brothers, listen! We are here to proclaim that through this man Jesus there is forgiveness for your sins. ³⁹Everyone who believes in him is made right in God's sight— something the law of Moses could never do. ⁴⁰Be careful! Don't let the prophets' words apply to you. For they said,

⁴¹ 'Look, you mockers,
  be amazed and die!

NASB

For I am accomplishing a work
  in your days,
A work which you will never
  believe, though someone
  should describe it to
  you.'"

⁴²As ªPaul and Barnabas were going out, the people kept begging that these ᵇthings might be spoken to them the next Sabbath. ⁴³Now when *the meeting of* the synagogue had broken up, many of the Jews and of the God-fearing ªproselytes followed Paul and Barnabas, who, speaking to them, were urging them to continue in the grace of God.

⁴⁴The next Sabbath nearly the whole city assembled to hear the word of ªthe Lord. ⁴⁵But when the Jews saw the crowds, they were filled with jealousy and *began* contradicting the things spoken by Paul, and were ªblaspheming. ⁴⁶Paul and Barnabas spoke out boldly and said, "It was necessary that the word of God be spoken to you first; since you repudiate it and judge yourselves unworthy of eternal life, behold, we are turning to the Gentiles. ⁴⁷For so the Lord has commanded us,

'I have placed You as a light
  for the Gentiles,
That You may ªbring salvation
  to the end of the earth.'"

⁴⁸When the Gentiles heard this, they *began* rejoicing and glorifying the word of ªthe Lord; and as many as had been appointed to eternal life believed. ⁴⁹And the word of the Lord was being spread through the whole region. ⁵⁰But the Jews incited the ªdevout women of prominence and the leading men of the city, and instigated a persecution against Paul and Barnabas, and drove them out of their ᵇdistrict. ⁵¹But they shook off the dust of their feet *in protest* against them and went to Iconium.

NLT

For I am doing something in your
  own day,
something you wouldn't
  believe
even if someone told you
  about it.'*"

⁴²As Paul and Barnabas left the synagogue that day, the people begged them to speak about these things again the next week. ⁴³Many Jews and devout converts to Judaism followed Paul and Barnabas, and the two men urged them to continue to rely on the grace of God.

⁴⁴The following week almost the entire city turned out to hear them preach the word of the Lord. ⁴⁵But when some of the Jews saw the crowds, they were jealous; so they slandered Paul and argued against whatever he said.

⁴⁶Then Paul and Barnabas spoke out boldly and declared, "It was necessary that we first preach the word of God to you Jews. But since you have rejected it and judged yourselves unworthy of eternal life, we will offer it to the Gentiles. ⁴⁷For the Lord gave us this command when he said,

'I have made you a light to
  the Gentiles,
  to bring salvation to the
  farthest corners of the
  earth.'*"

⁴⁸When the Gentiles heard this, they were very glad and thanked the Lord for his message; and all who were chosen for eternal life became believers. ⁴⁹So the Lord's message spread throughout that region.

⁵⁰Then the Jews stirred up the influential religious women and the leaders of the city, and they incited a mob against Paul and Barnabas and ran them out of town. ⁵¹So they shook the dust from their feet as a sign of rejection and went to the

⁵²And the disciples were continu- ally filled with joy and with the Holy Spirit.

13:17 ᵃOr *exalted* **13:22** ᵃLit *wishes*
13:24 ᵃLit *the face of His entering* **13:27** ᵃLit
voices **13:28** ᵃLit *destroyed* **13:29** ᵃLit
wood **13:33** ᵃLate mss read *to us their children*
13:34 ᵃLit *trustworthy* **13:35** ᵃLit *give* ᵇOr *Devout*
or *Pious* ᶜLit *see corruption* **13:36** ᵃOr *served his*
own generation by the purpose of God ᵇLit *saw*
corruption **13:37** ᵃLit *see corruption* **13:38** ᵃLit
this One **13:39** ᵃLit *in* or *by* ᵇLit *justified* ᶜLit
by **13:41** ᵃLit *disappear* **13:42** ᵃLit *they* ᵇLit
words **13:43** ᵃI.e. Gentile converts to Judaism
13:44 ᵃOne early ms reads *God* **13:45** ᵃOr
slandering him **13:47** ᵃLit *be for salvation*
13:48 ᵃTwo early mss read *God* **13:50** ᵃOr
worshiping ᵇLit *boundaries*

town of Iconium. ⁵²And the believ- ers* were filled with joy and with the Holy Spirit.

13:13-14 *Pamphylia* and *Pisidia* were districts in what is now Turkey. **13:15** Greek *from the law.* **13:18** Some manuscripts read *He cared for them;* compare Deut 1:31. **13:22** 1 Sam 13:14. **13:29** Greek *from the tree.* **13:33** Or *Today I reveal you as my Son.* Ps 2:7. **13:34** Isa 55:3. **13:35** Ps 16:10. **13:38** English translations divide verses 38 and 39 in various ways. **13:41** Hab 1:5 (Greek version). **13:47** Isa 49:6. **13:52** Greek *the disciples.*

Tucked away in the Old Testament is the oracle of an unlikely, unconventional prophet named Amos. He wasn't a sophisticated man. Far from it. This weather-beaten, sunbaked, rugged man of God neither came from royal stock nor benefited from the formal education available to aristocrats. He learned to read and write, like all Hebrew boys, but he never claimed to be a philosopher or a theologian. In fact, when challenged by an apostate priest with impressive credentials, he simply said, "I am not a prophet, nor am I the son of a prophet; for I am a herdsman and a grower of sycamore figs. But the LORD took me from following the flock and the LORD said to me, 'Go prophesy to My people Israel'" (Amos 7:14-15).

Through Amos, the Lord warned Israel of a famine:

> "Not a famine for bread or a thirst for water,
> But rather for hearing the words of the LORD.
> People will stagger from sea to sea
> And from the north even to the east;
> They will go to and fro to seek the word of the LORD,
> But they will not find it." (Amos 8:11-12)

Eventually, the Lord's prediction came to pass, most notably after the postexilic prophet Malachi put down his pen four hundred years before the birth of Christ. Then, the Word of God became flesh in the person of Jesus. After His ascension (Acts 1:9), the Word of God came in the power of the Holy Spirit (2:4). But it was largely a localized event at first, limited to Judea, Samaria, and Galilee. Some urban centers around the empire began to hear the gospel proclaimed by scattered Christians escaping persecution, but for the most part, the world outside Israel remained in the dark. Vast stretches of territory remained under a severe famine—"not a famine for bread or a thirst for water, but rather for hearing the words of the LORD." As Paul, Barnabas, and their small support team set foot on the mainland of Pamphylia and began their trek across the mountain range into the interior, communities of Jews gathered for worship—all starving to hear the word of God. All around these obscure synagogues, Gentiles lived like sheep without a shepherd.

— 13:14-15 —

Having said farewell to John Mark, who had boarded a ship for home, Paul and Barnabas led their team 100 miles north, up 3,600 feet over the southern stretch of the Taurus Mountains, and into the region called Pisidia, which lay in the rugged southern half of the Roman province of Galatia. Paul's later letter to the Galatians indicated that he was not in good health (malaria?) after the trek (Gal. 4:13), and the defenseless team may have fallen victim to bandits who famously preyed on travelers in that area.

Pisidian Antioch—not to be confused with Paul's sending church in Syrian Antioch—had become a sizable city in the first century. To Romanize the area, Augustus had established several colonist cities and linked them with the Via Sebaste, an east–west highway leading from Ephesus, stretching across modern-day Turkey and through the Cilician Gates, and reaching all the way to the Euphrates.[16] Antioch already existed before Augustus, but it became a popular location for colonists and quickly grew into the most important city on this route.

According to Josephus, two thousand Jewish families were relocated to this area around 200 BC, and the existence of a synagogue in Antioch implies that many remained there by the time of Paul. They were Hellenized, spoke Greek, and were cut off from Jerusalem by both distance and terrain; only the most ardent Jews would have made the journey for the festivals, and they probably didn't receive a lot of visits from rabbis. Even so, this area attracted a significant number of Gentile "God-fearers."[17]

When Paul, Barnabas, and the others arrived in Antioch, they visited the synagogue, a logical place to start. As Jews, they would find a receptive community in the synagogue, which gave them easier access to the rest of the society. Besides, their first converts should be among fellow Jews who shared their monotheistic worldview. Paul and Barnabas could build upon a shared understanding of who God is and how the ministry of the Messiah should affect them personally.

Beginning their work among the Jews served another important purpose. Their association with the local synagogue identified the evangelists as representatives of the Hebrew God as opposed to some other, unknown deity. Gentile pagans may have worshiped their pantheon, but their association with Jews made them aware of the One Creator God worshiped in the synagogue. Paul and Barnabas wanted everyone to know that Jesus Christ had come to earth as *this* God—the Hebrew God—in human flesh.

For all these reasons, beginning their work among the Jews in any particular location became the paradigm for first contact in a new area.

The men entered the synagogue and sat in the congregation as fellow worshipers. They had introduced themselves earlier and had undoubtedly explained their association with the temple. Paul may have offered his services as a man schooled under the great rabbi and Pharisee Gamaliel. So, after the customary reading of the Scriptures, the officials invited Paul to preach to the congregation (Acts 13:15), a mixed group of natural-born Jews, proselytes, and "God-fearers," that is, Gentiles interested in Jewish thought.

— 13:16-18 —

This is one of several Pauline sermons described by Luke in the book of Acts (cf. 14:15-17; 17:22-31; 20:18-35). This is not a transcript of the apostle's address; it's an annotated outline summarizing his major points. Nevertheless, this discourse is the most detailed of all, providing a fairly complete look at his method of reasoning. He typically began by affirming points of agreement, creating intellectual and theological rapport with his audience. In this case, he alluded to no fewer than twelve Old Testament books as he recounted the story of the Lord's relationship with the nation of Israel, beginning with the patriarchs. Paul followed the Jewish custom of remembering God's faithfulness to Israel during difficult times.

In the first section of his sermon (13:16-22), Paul summarized Jewish history, acknowledging at least four points typically highlighted in Jewish confessions of faith:

- God chose the patriarchs by grace.
- God liberated the Israelites from Egypt.
- God gave the land to Israel.
- God gave the people a king.

Paul highlighted the fact that Israel's unfaithfulness had led to divine chastisement. The people's refusal to enter Canaan, fueled by fear of the inhabitants and distrust of God's promises, prompted a forty-year sojourn in the wilderness (Num. 14:34). The expression "put up with them in the wilderness" (Acts 13:18) reflects Moses' lament: "'In the wilderness where you saw how the LORD your God carried you, just as a man carries his son, in all the way which you have walked until you came to this place.' But for all this, you did not trust the LORD your God" (Deut. 1:31-32).

— 13:19-22 —

Paul then summarized Israel's governmental eras from the conquest of Canaan to the reign of David. He gave credit to the Lord for destroying her enemies in the land. God—not Joshua or his army—had defeated the seven nations and given the land to Israel's twelve tribes as He promised (13:19). The conquest led to the period of the judges, an especially shameful time in Hebrew history. During this time, the Israelites followed a downward spiral marked by a repeating pattern: disobedience earned affliction, affliction prompted repentance, repentance brought rescue, rescue inspired revival, and then revival dissolved into deeper disobedience. Finally, the moral decay became so acute that God appointed the prophet Samuel to lead the nation (13:20).

Eventually, the people rejected the Lord's administration-via-prophet, preferring to be like their neighbors who had kings. So, God gave them Saul (13:21), who started out well and then became a megalomaniac. After his forty-year reign ended in failure and suicide, the Lord put David on the throne, a man who loved Him and ruled righteously. To characterize David's rule, Paul noted that he was a man after God's heart (13:22; cf. Ps. 89:20; 1 Sam. 13:14).

Paul's short history of Israel highlighted three facts, each with an important implication:

- *Fact 1:* The Lord had been faithful to Israel despite the disobedience of the people.
- *Implication:* He would continue to be faithful to disobedient Jews.
- *Fact 2:* God's form of government over Israel had evolved over time, usually in response to Israel's disobedience.
- *Implication:* His administration of the nation would continue to evolve, and it was about to change again.
- *Fact 3:* The Lord had replaced a bad king, Saul, with a good king, David.
- *Implication:* The Lord was again about to present a new leader.

— 13:23-25 —

Paul immediately recalled what every Jew understood. Even though David was a good king—the best Israel ever had—he was not perfect. He fell short of being the kind of king God would have ruling His kingdom, and so did each of David's descendants. Even so, God had promised the nation that a worthy king would descend from David and ascend the throne of Israel (13:23). The Jews referred to this promised King as their Messiah—not merely *an* anointed one, but *the* Anointed One.

Paul boldly proclaimed Jesus as this Messiah, the Savior of the world. The people in Pisidian Antioch had undoubtedly heard of John the Baptizer. Paul's reference seems to assume their knowledge of his ministry (13:24-25). Everyone had revered John as a genuine prophet of God, the first since Malachi had stopped writing four hundred years earlier. Nevertheless, Paul quoted John's statement that the coming Messiah would far exceed him in every respect. This statement, "I am not He. But behold, one is coming after me the sandals of whose feet I am not worthy to untie," is attested in each of the four Gospels (13:25; cf. Matt. 3:11; Mark 1:7; Luke 3:16; and John 1:27). Consequently, everyone knew John as the forerunner of the Christ.

— 13:26-31 —

At last, Paul came to the crux of his message: the life, sacrificial death, and resurrection of Jesus. Addressing his audience as "brethren, sons of Abraham's family" (13:26), he identified himself as a Jew who shared their concerns as Jews. He said, in effect, "I am one of you, and I have great news concerning the Messiah we have all anticipated." He did, however, separate himself from the religious leaders in Jerusalem, accusing them of ignoring the very Scriptures the synagogue had just read aloud and of killing their Messiah (13:27-28). He noted that their actions in killing Jesus fulfilled predictions concerning the Messiah (13:29), further validating Jesus as the Christ. Furthermore, he referenced the eyewitness testimonies of Jesus' death, burial, and resurrection, obviously including himself (13:30-31).

— 13:32-37 —

Paul validated his claim of prophetic fulfillment by quoting several Old Testament passages concerning the Messiah:

> "I will surely tell of the decree of the LORD:
> He said to Me, 'You are My Son,

271

Today I have begotten You.'"
    (Ps. 2:7; cf. Acts 13:33)

"Incline your ear and come to Me.
Listen, that you may live;
And I will make an everlasting covenant with you,
According to the faithful mercies shown to David."
    (Isa. 55:3; cf. Acts 13:34)

For You will not abandon my soul to Sheol;
Nor will You allow Your Holy One to undergo decay.
    (Ps. 16:10; cf. Acts 13:35)

Those who expected the Christ to be a political and military leader naturally believed that death invalidated any claim to be the Messiah. Paul argued the contrary. Each messianic prophecy he quoted finds fulfillment in the resurrection of the Messiah. By that line of reasoning, only someone who died and rose from the grave could claim to be the Christ. To make his point clear, he compared King David with Jesus. King David, acknowledged by all to be a great king died after a long life of obedience, and then his body rotted in a grave. Clearly, his death didn't invalidate his life. Jesus, on the other hand, was bodily and miraculously resurrected by the Father and continues to live. Therefore, He must be greater than David.

Notably, Paul didn't claim that Jesus ruled over Israel. At the time, Israel had no king. The temple officials and Jewish aristocrats who rejected Jesus had seen in Herod Agrippa I everything they longed to see in the Messiah, but worms ate him from the inside and he died just three years into his reign (12:23). Nevertheless, Jesus did not rule as the King of the Jews. His position recalls the ordeal suffered by David, who endured a long period in the wilderness while Saul, no longer God's choice, continued to usurp the throne. Jesus is the legitimate King, but He does not yet rule Israel.

— 13:38–41 —

Paul concludes his sermon with an application based on the three facts and implications he had established earlier (13:19-22):

First, the Lord would continue to be faithful to Israel in spite of her disobedience; He sent the Messiah to grant forgiveness of sins. Second, God's form of government over Israel had evolved; Jesus had superseded the Law as Israel's rule of government. Third, the Lord had replaced a bad king, Saul, with a good king, David; Jesus should be embraced as the ultimate King. Quoting Habakkuk, who prophesied during the last days before Babylon carried Israel into exile, Paul warned the Jews not to reject Jesus as the Christ (13:41, quoting Hab. 1:5). He also encouraged them to find complete forgiveness of sins—justification—through faith in Jesus, in spite of their inability to fully obey the Law (Acts 13:38-39).

— 13:42-43 —

Paul's sermon was a lot for his hearers to take in. He called for the Jews of Pisidian Antioch to break with the religious leaders in Jerusalem and to embrace Jesus as the Messiah. Moreover, he preached that faith in the Messiah would result in the forgiveness of sins. Even so, the response was overwhelmingly positive; the synagogue members invited Paul and Barnabas to return the following Sabbath (13:42), and some members followed them that day to hear more immediately (13:43).

— 13:44-47 —

Luke's statement that "nearly the whole city assembled" (13:44) is most likely hyperbole, meaning that a massive crowd assembled to hear Paul. The population of the city and its environs at the time would have been around fifty thousand people;[18] excavations have revealed a theater large enough to hold perhaps five thousand people,[19] which would have been a significant gathering. Regardless, a large enough crowd gathered to anger "the Jews" (13:45).

Again, Luke uses the designation "the Jews" in a technical sense to denote religious leaders opposed to the gospel Paul had declared. The word translated "jealousy" connects this incident with the "jealousy" of the high priest and the Sanhedrin after the success of Peter's preaching in the temple (5:17). These local Jewish leaders argued against Paul's reasoning. They "began contradicting" (antilegō [483]) Paul, but this was no simple theological debate; the men also "were blaspheming" (blasphēmeō [987]) Paul. We often think of blasphemy only in religious contexts, but to blaspheme is to curse, slander, or treat someone with contempt. Blasphemy is any manner of speech that disregards or disrespects the value of another.

Paul and Barnabas refused to become embroiled in a lengthy verbal dispute. Rather than waste time on people who refused to believe, they responded with a sharp rebuke, vowing to carry the good news to those eager to believe. Paul declared that the Jews of Antioch had proven to "repudiate" (*apōtheō* [683]) the gospel, which describes a response of the will; by doing this, they "[judged themselves] unworthy of eternal life" (13:46). While God considered them worthy not only as "sons of the covenant," but also as individuals needing grace, they counted themselves out of salvation.

When Paul and Barnabas declared they would be "turning to the Gentiles"—that is, proclaiming the Messiah to non-Jews—they quoted Isaiah (13:47; cf. Isa. 42:6; 49:6). God always had intended for Israel to be His "light to the nations" so that Gentiles might hear and turn to the Lord. Paul and Barnabas said, in effect, "You continue your tradition of unfaithful disobedience; we, as faithful Jews, will fulfill our purpose as God's covenant people."

— 13:48 —

The response of the Gentiles is a stark contrast with that of the Jewish leaders. They "began rejoicing and glorifying the word of the Lord"! It's as though two sons of a king had listened to the reading of their father's will and the older refused his right of succession while the younger rejoiced to find that his father had thought him worthy to inherit anything. The Gentiles were hungry for this word from the Lord and rejoiced to receive it. Luke's description of the Gentile response to the gospel clearly highlights God's election, His sovereign predestination (see Rom. 8:28-30; Eph. 1:4-5, 11). The verb translated "appointed" is in the perfect tense in Greek, which is used to describe an action that was completed in the past with continuing results. The verb is in the passive voice, and scholars call this instance a "divine passive," indicating that God is the subject. Those who had been appointed believed. The great majority of them were Gentiles, which is ironic. The chosen people of God, the Jews, believed they were God's elect, destined by their heritage for salvation, yet they rejected their Messiah. Those who believed—most of them Gentiles—did so because they were appointed beforehand.

— 13:49-52 —

Luke closes the episode with another summary statement describing the ministry of Paul and Barnabas in the area. The gospel "spread through the whole region" (13:49). They followed through on their promise to proclaim Jesus the Messiah to Gentiles, and the positive response prompted the Jewish religious leaders to begin a campaign of persecution against them. They urged the aristocratic women—most of them Gentile converts to Judaism—to lobby their husbands for the expulsion of Paul and Barnabas. To convince the leading men of the city, the Jews would have to demonstrate that getting rid of the Christian evangelists was in the best interests of the city. They succeeded, and "drove them out of their district" (13:50).

So Paul and Barnabas "shook off the dust of their feet" and left for Iconium (13:51). The act of shaking dust off their feet recalls the instructions of Jesus (Luke 9:5) as well as a tradition among devout Jews, who used the gesture to illustrate their separation from unbelievers. Many did this when returning to Judea after a trip to pagan cities. They didn't want to mingle polluted dust with their own home soil or risk carrying pagan dust into the temple. Meanwhile, back in Pisidian Antioch, "the disciples were continually filled with joy and with the Holy Spirit" (Acts 13:52)!

APPLICATION: ACTS 13:14-52

How to Bring a Feast to a Famine

When Paul and Barnabas entered Pisidian Antioch, they found a city starved for the Word of God. The city had at least one synagogue and was perhaps dotted with several more, given the large Jewish population. These places of worship had apparently attracted a significant number of Gentile proselytes and "God-fearers," but for all its religion, the entire city lacked what it needed most—forgiveness of sins.

Paul told the people of Antioch something they had never heard: "Through [Jesus Christ] everyone who believes is freed from all things, from which you could not be freed through the Law of Moses" (13:39). Justification by grace through faith was not new teaching; that had always been the message of salvation. The prophet Isaiah illustrated the Lord's invitation to receive the forgiveness of sins through faith this way:

"Ho! Every one who thirsts, come to the waters;
And you who have no money come, buy and eat.
Come, buy wine and milk
Without money and without cost.

Why do you spend money for what is not bread,
And your wages for what does not satisfy?
Listen carefully to Me, and eat what is good,
And delight yourself in abundance. . . ."
Seek the LORD while He may be found;
Call upon Him while He is near.
Let the wicked forsake his way
And the unrighteous man his thoughts;
And let him return to the LORD,
And He will have compassion on him,
And to our God,
For He will abundantly pardon. (Isa. 55:1-2, 6-7)

To the starving people of Antioch, Paul and Barnabas had brought a feast! Strangely, though, the people gave a mixed response to the offer of spiritually nourishing food. Some rejoiced and ate; many rejected it and starved. How the apostles responded suggests two principles of evangelism.

First, *when there's a famine in the land, feed the hungry and ignore the rest.* That might sound harsh, but when there's a job to do, you must stay focused. Paul and Barnabas devoted their time to preaching to those hungry for the truth. When the synagogue leaders shut them down, they preached to the Gentiles. When the town became inhospitable, they shook the dust from their feet and sought more hungry people down the highway.

Second, *you can't feed people who don't want to eat.* Paul and Barnabas didn't try to talk fools out of their foolishness. They called rebellion what it was and looked for people starving for wisdom. They preached only to those who wanted to hear the word of God. By feeding only those who wanted to eat, they gave an opportunity for the hungry to respond to the call of God.

By following those two simple guidelines, Paul and Barnabas covered a lot of ground in a short time. They bore the great responsibility of proclaiming the gospel where it had not been heard, but they didn't take on the responsibility for how people responded. This gave them courage in the face of the unknown and resiliency in response to opposition.

Operation Yo-Yo
ACTS 14:1-20

NASB

¹In Iconium they entered the synagogue of the Jews together, and spoke in such a manner that a large number of people believed, both of Jews and of Greeks. ²But the Jews who ªdisbelieved stirred up the ᵇminds of the Gentiles and embittered them against the brethren. ³Therefore they spent a long time *there* speaking boldly *with reliance* upon the Lord, who was testifying to the word of His grace, granting that ªsigns and wonders be done by their hands. ⁴But the ªpeople of the city were divided; and some ᵇsided with the Jews, and some with the apostles. ⁵And when an attempt was made by both the Gentiles and the Jews with their rulers, to mistreat and to stone them, ⁶they became aware of it and fled to the cities of Lycaonia, Lystra and Derbe, and the surrounding region; ⁷and there they continued to preach the gospel.

⁸At Lystra a man was sitting who had no strength in his feet, lame from his mother's womb, who had never walked. ⁹This man was listening to Paul as he spoke, who, when he had fixed his gaze on him and had seen that he had faith to be ªmade well, ¹⁰said with a loud voice, "Stand upright on your feet." And he leaped up and *began* to walk. ¹¹When the crowds saw what Paul had done, they raised their voice, saying in the Lycaonian language, "The gods have become like men and have come down to us." ¹²And they *began* calling Barnabas, ªZeus, and Paul, ᵇHermes, because he was ᶜthe chief speaker. ¹³The priest of Zeus, whose *temple* was ªjust outside the city, brought oxen and garlands to

NLT

¹The same thing happened in Iconium.* Paul and Barnabas went to the Jewish synagogue and preached with such power that a great number of both Jews and Greeks became believers. ²Some of the Jews, however, spurned God's message and poisoned the minds of the Gentiles against Paul and Barnabas. ³But the apostles stayed there a long time, preaching boldly about the grace of the Lord. And the Lord proved their message was true by giving them power to do miraculous signs and wonders. ⁴But the people of the town were divided in their opinion about them. Some sided with the Jews, and some with the apostles.

⁵Then a mob of Gentiles and Jews, along with their leaders, decided to attack and stone them. ⁶When the apostles learned of it, they fled to the region of Lycaonia—to the towns of Lystra and Derbe and the surrounding area. ⁷And there they preached the Good News.

⁸While they were at Lystra, Paul and Barnabas came upon a man with crippled feet. He had been that way from birth, so he had never walked. He was sitting ⁹and listening as Paul preached. Looking straight at him, Paul realized he had faith to be healed. ¹⁰So Paul called to him in a loud voice, "Stand up!" And the man jumped to his feet and started walking.

¹¹When the crowd saw what Paul had done, they shouted in their local dialect, "These men are gods in human form!" ¹²They decided that Barnabas was the Greek god Zeus and that Paul was Hermes, since he was the chief speaker. ¹³Now the temple of Zeus was located just outside the town. So the priest of the

the gates, and wanted to offer sacrifice with the crowds. ¹⁴But when the apostles Barnabas and Paul heard of it, they tore their ᵃrobes and rushed out into the crowd, crying out ¹⁵and saying, "Men, why are you doing these things? We are also men of the same nature as you, and preach the gospel to you that you should turn from these ᵃvain things to a living God, WHO MADE THE HEAVEN AND THE EARTH AND THE SEA AND ALL THAT IS IN THEM. ¹⁶ᵃIn the generations gone by He permitted all the ᵇnations to go their own ways; ¹⁷and yet He did not leave Himself without witness, in that He did good and gave you rains from heaven and fruitful seasons, ᵃsatisfying your hearts with food and gladness." ¹⁸*Even* saying these things, with difficulty they restrained the crowds from offering sacrifice to them.

¹⁹But Jews came from Antioch and Iconium, and having won over the crowds, they stoned Paul and dragged him out of the city, supposing him to be dead. ²⁰But while the disciples stood around him, he got up and entered the city. The next day he went away with Barnabas to Derbe.

14:2 ᵃOr *disobeyed* ᵇLit *souls* 14:3 ᵃOr *attesting miracles* 14:4 ᵃLit *multitude* ᵇLit *were* 14:9 ᵃLit *saved* 14:12 ᵃLat *Jupiter*, the chief pagan god ᵇLat *Mercury*, considered the messenger or spokesman for the pagan gods of Greece and Rome ᶜLit *the leader of the speaking* 14:13 ᵃLit *in front of* 14:14 ᵃOr *outer garments* 14:15 ᵃI.e. idols 14:16 ᵃLit *Who in the generations gone by permitted* ᵇOr *Gentiles* 14:17 ᵃLit *filling*

temple and the crowd brought bulls and wreaths of flowers to the town gates, and they prepared to offer sacrifices to the apostles.

¹⁴But when the apostles Barnabas and Paul heard what was happening, they tore their clothing in dismay and ran out among the people, shouting, ¹⁵"Friends,* why are you doing this? We are merely human beings—just like you! We have come to bring you the Good News that you should turn from these worthless things and turn to the living God, who made heaven and earth, the sea, and everything in them. ¹⁶In the past he permitted all the nations to go their own ways, ¹⁷but he never left them without evidence of himself and his goodness. For instance, he sends you rain and good crops and gives you food and joyful hearts." ¹⁸But even with these words, Paul and Barnabas could scarcely restrain the people from sacrificing to them.

¹⁹Then some Jews arrived from Antioch and Iconium and won the crowds to their side. They stoned Paul and dragged him out of town, thinking he was dead. ²⁰But as the believers* gathered around him, he got up and went back into the town. The next day he left with Barnabas for Derbe.

14:1 *Iconium*, as well as *Lystra* and *Derbe* (14:6), were towns in what is now Turkey. 14:15 Greek *Men.* 14:20 Greek *disciples*; also in 14:22, 28.

Back in the 1970s, the Washington Redskins had a grizzled quarterback by the name of Sonny Jurgensen—as tough as an old boot on the field and off. In fact, he seemed to thrive on bearing the brunt of criticism when the team struggled through a long slump. At one point, someone asked Jurgensen if all the flak from the press was getting to him. He grinned and replied, "No, not really. I don't want to quit. I've been in this game long enough to know that every quarterback, every week of the season, spends his time either in the penthouse or in the outhouse."²⁰

Let me tell you as a pastor who's been on the field a long time: The same applies to anyone engaged in Christian ministry! While in Pisidian Antioch, Paul and Barnabas preached one Sabbath to rave reviews and then received an enthusiastic invitation to return and tell the people more. The next Sabbath, however, the synagogue leaders decided to run them out of town. As the two men led their team down the highway to Iconium and beyond, they were about to discover that the high-low cycle is not just *common* in ministry, it's the *norm*. In Iconium, large numbers believed, while others gathered stones, eventually forcing them to leave. In Lystra, like before, the men would be lifted to bizarre heights of acclaim only to fall fast and hard.

Along with the ups and downs that result from an audience's acceptance or rejection, Paul, Barnabas, and the team would also encounter the frustrations that come with making mistakes while learning to cope with new situations. In Lystra, they would encounter a population with a worldview so foreign to Jewish thought that Paul and Barnabas would themselves be mistaken for gods. Even so, they would discover that, through it all, God is faithful. He will fulfill His promises and He will accomplish His plan—no matter what.

— 14:1-4 —

Iconium lay about 80 miles east of Antioch along the Via Sebaste, an impressive highway linking all the Roman colonies from Comama in the west to Lystra, which lay south of Iconium. The origins of this city lay far back in the mists of history, so obscure that even the ancient Greeks were unable to determine who established the settlement or when.[21] In the first century AD, Iconium was an agricultural and trade center. While the Via Sebaste was the newest highway, five roads converged on the city to make it an important link in the routes between major regions of the Roman Empire.[22]

When Paul and Barnabas arrived, they went straight to the synagogue, eager to share the good news of the long-awaited Messiah among their countrymen and to proclaim the open arms of God's grace to the God-fearing Gentiles. As in Antioch, their message prompted a large number of people to believe, including God-fearing Gentiles who attended the synagogue service (14:1). And, as in Antioch, the Jews who rejected the gospel turned the town against the evangelists (14:2).

Although the team suffered opposition, the response appears to have been balanced: The people were divided (14:4). So, they continued preaching as they had been. In Pisidian Antioch Luke mentions nothing about miracles; in Iconium, however, God gave the men the ability to perform "signs and wonders" (14:3). As always, miracles served to validate their message as divine. This strongly suggests that miracles were not always a part of their ministry and were used only when rebellion was *not* the reason for unbelief.

— 14:5-7 —

Eventually, the unbelieving leaders of the synagogue managed to gather enough opposition against Paul and Barnabas to form a vigilante mob. That's when the team wisely decided to move on. If miracles didn't persuade the unbelievers, martyrdom would serve no purpose.

When sentiment grew too strong against them, Paul and Barnabas traveled roughly 20 miles south to the picturesque town of Lystra, which sat in an isolated valley at the convergence of two streams. Unlike Antioch and Iconium, Lystra did not warrant any major roads before Augustus designated it a colony and populated the town with military veterans. Then he routed the Via Sebaste through Lystra. Even so, Lystra never lost its remote, small-town identity.[23] Archaeologists have uncovered evidence to suggest that the town venerated Zeus and Hermes as patron gods: "One inscription records the dedication to Zeus on a statue of Hermes. Another records a dedication to 'Zeus before the town.'"[24]

— 14:8-10 —

Luke doesn't mention a synagogue, probably because there weren't enough Jews to warrant one. (Tradition held that at least ten Jewish males were required to form a local house of prayer.) Timothy hailed from Lystra, and his mother, Eunice, and grandmother Lois were Jews, but his father was a Gentile (16:1-2; cf. 2 Tim. 1:5). When no synagogue existed, Paul typically went to the marketplace (*agora* [58]), where Greeks gathered to socialize. This is also where traveling philosophers and entertainers attracted attention. Paul may have begun to speak in the marketplace when he noticed a man disabled from birth.

The man's condition was strikingly similar to that of the beggar by the temple gate in Acts 3:1-10. His feet were atrophied, perhaps from an injury at birth, and he had never walked (14:8). Everyone in Lystra undoubtedly knew him. Unlike the beggar outside the temple, however, the man's healing came after his belief. Whereas Peter had addressed the beggar with no prompting other than from the Holy Spirit, Paul saw on this man's face evidence of belief and then was moved to heal him

(14:9). Luke undoubtedly intends for the reader to associate this healing with Peter's; his use of similar terms, phrases, and imagery makes the connection unmistakable.

Paul commanded the disabled man to stand up (14:10). Notably, however, he didn't invoke the name of Jesus Christ as Peter did (3:6). Clearly, Luke chose to include this incident to show that Paul's apostleship equaled Peter's. But Paul's omitting the name of Christ in restoring the man's feet caused problems he didn't anticipate. Because no synagogue existed in the city, its citizens did not immediately identify the men as Jews, monotheistic worshipers of the God of Israel. Paul hadn't accounted for the cultural divide in this new missionary context.

— 14:11-13 —

As a result, Paul and Barnabas found themselves thrust into a local myth involving Zeus and Hermes, the patron gods of Lystra (14:11-12). The townspeople may have been influenced by a story from ancient folklore that has been preserved in Ovid's *Metamorphoses*.[25] The myth recounts a time when Zeus and Hermes (i.e., Jupiter and Mercury) found no hospitality in Phrygia until they came to the home of an elderly couple named Philemon and Baucis, who lived not far from Lystra. In return for their unselfish generosity, the married couple asked only two favors: to be caretakers of the temple and to die together so that neither would have to grieve the other. Their wishes were granted, and the two were transformed into a pair of trees adorning the steps of the temple.

The people of Lystra wanted to be generous like Philemon and Baucis, so they hastily prepared a sacrifice in honor of Paul and Barnabas, the supposed god-men (14:13). Unfortunately, they reverted to their local tongue, Lycaonian, so neither man could understand what was causing the people to become so animated. The origin of this language is a mystery. Some linguists say that Lycaonian evolved from Anatolian and Hittite tongues, while others suggest it was a special, regionalized dialect of Greek. Regardless, the people used their local language to deify Paul and Barnabas, so the two men could only watch in confused amazement as the local pagan priest made preparations for a sacrifice in their honor.

— 14:14-18 —

As my colleague Dr. Thomas Constable writes, "If Satan cannot derail Christian witness with persecution, he will try praise. Too much persecution has destroyed many preachers, and too much praise has ruined many others. One of the problems with miracles is that they often draw more attention to the miracle worker than to God."[26]

Paul and Barnabas, however, felt horrified when they finally understood what was happening. They rushed into the crowd as they "tore their robes" (14:14). Apparently, it didn't occur to anyone in Lystra that the gods in their midst didn't speak their native language! The gesture of tearing one's garments expressed overwhelming emotion, usually sorrow and grief.[27] Paul had healed the man through the power of Christ to authenticate the gospel as divine revelation, but he had not been prepared for the depth of the ignorance in Lystra. Therefore, to correct the misunderstanding, the men had to introduce the pagans of Lystra to the Creator God revealed in the Old Testament (14:15). They began by setting God apart from the king deity, Zeus, and the supposed creators of humanity, Prometheus and Athena.

The formula "the heaven and the earth and the sea" identified three realms of the Greek cosmos. The universe of Greek mythology thought of earth as a flat plane with air above, water around, and Hades below. Paul's statement comes from a Hebrew concept of the universe (cf. 4:24; Ps. 146:6). He wanted the pagans to understand that one God made all realms of the universe and created all the creatures therein, but he was still speaking from a foreign worldview. Meanwhile, the priests continued to slaughter the animals for sacrifice and the people stoked the fires of the altar (Acts 14:18).

Paul and Barnabas continued with an answer to the obvious question: "If this God is the one and only Creator, then why haven't we heard of Him before now?" Paul and Barnabas said that nations had been allowed "to go their own ways" but that the Hebrew God had revealed Himself by way of nature's bounty (14:16-17).

Eventually, the people called off the great sacrifice of oxen—the most productive beast a farmer could own—but it seems doubtful that Paul's crash course in biblical cosmology had convinced them. They probably halted the sacrifice because "Zeus" and "Hermes" insisted they stop.

— 14:19-20 —

Before long, the synagogue leaders from Antioch and Iconium tracked down Paul, Barnabas, and their helpers. They managed to sway the people of Lystra much as they had the city leaders in their own towns. Suddenly, the same people who had worshiped Paul and Barnabas as gods just days earlier rose up in anger to stone them as heretics (14:19). Execution by stoning was a distinctly Eastern, Semitic punishment, rarely heard of in Greek society. Clearly, the people of Lystra acted as a mob, following the lead of the Jewish instigators.

They stoned Paul, leaving Barnabas unharmed. Luke doesn't explain why. The mob may have looked for both men and, finding Paul alone, stoned him on the spot before carrying his body to the edge of the city. The mention of "the disciples" most likely refers to the men Paul and Barnabas had taken along as helpers (14:20; cf. 13:5), although they may have been new believers in Lystra whom Paul and Barnabas were nurturing, undoubtedly including Timothy. In either case, Luke writes that these "disciples" witnessed the stoning, suggesting that Barnabas did not because he was somewhere else.

Luke doesn't state whether Paul actually died, only that the mob "supposed" (*nomizō* [3543]) him dead. Regardless, he miraculously stood to his feet and walked back into Lystra in his own power (14:20). The mob had gone off in search of Barnabas, no doubt, but the rest of the town must have seen a bleeding and bruised Paul walking back from the dead, as it were. Over time, Paul would return to Lystra three more times (14:21; 16:1; 18:23). Doubtless, the memory of his ordeal helped to establish his authority as a genuine apostle among the believers.

This episode illustrates God's ability to fulfill His plan despite the weaknesses of all the people involved. The Jewish population in Lystra didn't warrant a synagogue, so these Gentiles were more ignorant than their peers in larger cities. As a result, their superstition ran deeper than other, more urban Greeks, who at least had the benefit of scientific and philosophical education. Furthermore, the people of Lystra proved to be exceedingly pliable, a trait that would cause Paul untold exasperation in the future (Gal. 3:1-4).

To be fair, however, this was not Paul and Barnabas's finest hour. While the men did their very best, they nonetheless came unprepared for the extreme superstition and profound ignorance in Lystra. Paul assumed the people would attribute the healing miracle to the one and only Creator God and then interpret the event as validation of their message. In making this assumption, he underestimated the power of their primitive worldview to shape their perception. He would not make this mistake again.

APPLICATION: ACTS 14:1-20

How *Not* to Proclaim the Gospel

This segment of Luke's narrative demonstrates that even the best ministers don't always get it right. In fact, this is a rare instance in which we can learn from Paul's example what *not* to do in ministry. I observe two glaring don'ts from this dark episode in the apostle's first journey into the mission field.

First, *don't assume your audience knows much about the God of the Bible.* Paul and Barnabas entered a pagan town that didn't have a synagogue. Without basic knowledge of the Hebrew God, the superstitious people of Lystra had every reason to misunderstand what they saw and heard. The evangelists should have started by introducing Lystra to the one and only God revealed in the Old Testament. Only then would they understand their need for what Jesus Christ offers. Don't assume people know much biblical truth. Ask questions. Listen carefully for gaps in their knowledge and for misinformation they might have picked up. Define your terms carefully. And follow up to be certain they understand what you have said.

Second, *don't underestimate the influence of one's worldview.* A worldview is how someone understands the universe—how it came into being, how it operates, and what purpose it has, if any. Primitive Greeks held to the old myths of a cosmos consisting of a flat earth surrounded by water and bounded by sky above and Hades below. Paul's explanation that God made "the heaven and the earth and the sea" (14:15) could have been misunderstood, perhaps even to suggest that Hades lay outside the Lord's control. Furthermore, the term "God" was not a name to the polytheistic Greeks, it was a noun that could apply to dozens of beings, some more powerful than others.

The same is true today. The word "god" means different things to different people. A Muslim will think of one being while a Buddhist will have a completely different idea in mind. An African pantheist will not hear the title "god" the same as a monotheistic Jew. Within Hinduism, there are dozens of different philosophies associated with the concept of divinity. Even within the United States, with its four-hundred-year-old Judeo-Christian heritage, you will find a dwindling population who thinks of God as the Bible describes Him. Consequently, the once-effective statement, "God loves you and has a wonderful plan for your life," may pose more problems than it solves.

Learn about the different worldviews people hold in the area you plan to evangelize. This will help you communicate effectively and decrease the potential for misunderstanding.

That said, don't fear that you will create a mess too big for the Lord to sort out. Despite the ignorance in Lystra, and even with the foibles of the apostles, many people believed and became strong disciples. Paul went on to have an effective ministry in the area, because God remained in control. He still is. He will use our most inept good-faith efforts to accomplish His plan. The important thing is to go and witness.

Wrapping Up a Memorable Trip
ACTS 14:21-28

NASB

21 After they had preached the gospel to that city and had made many disciples, they returned to Lystra and to Iconium and to Antioch, 22 strengthening the souls of the disciples, encouraging them to continue in the faith, and *saying,* "Through many tribulations we must enter the kingdom of God." 23 When they had appointed elders for them in every church, having prayed with fasting, they commended them to the Lord in whom they had believed.

24 They passed through Pisidia and came into Pamphylia. 25 When they had spoken the word in Perga, they went down to Attalia. 26 From there they sailed to Antioch, from which they had been commended to the grace of God for the work that they had ªaccomplished. 27 When they had arrived and gathered the church together, they *began* to report all things that God had done with them and ªhow He had opened a door of faith to the Gentiles. 28 And they spent ªa long time with the disciples.

14:26 ªLit *fulfilled*   14:27 ªLit *that*   14:28 ªLit *not a little*

NLT

21 After preaching the Good News in Derbe and making many disciples, Paul and Barnabas returned to Lystra, Iconium, and Antioch of Pisidia, 22 where they strengthened the believers. They encouraged them to continue in the faith, reminding them that we must suffer many hardships to enter the Kingdom of God. 23 Paul and Barnabas also appointed elders in every church. With prayer and fasting, they turned the elders over to the care of the Lord, in whom they had put their trust. 24 Then they traveled back through Pisidia to Pamphylia. 25 They preached the word in Perga, then went down to Attalia.

26 Finally, they returned by ship to Antioch of Syria, where their journey had begun. The believers there had entrusted them to the grace of God to do the work they had now completed. 27 Upon arriving in Antioch, they called the church together and reported everything God had done through them and how he had opened the door of faith to the Gentiles, too. 28 And they stayed there with the believers for a long time.

In the 1940s, virtually everyone in America knew the name Norman Rockwell. The illustrations he drew for the *Saturday Evening Post* reflected the best of the American spirit during some of the nation's most trying years. The words "heartwarming" and "nostalgic" come to mind when you see his work. For the May 26, 1945, issue, he released one of his most endearing illustrations: "Homecoming G.I." In this iconic scene, a soldier wearing faded green army fatigues stands in front of a brick tenement as excited family members and friends pour into the alley to welcome their hero home from the war. Everyone can find themselves somewhere in that painting: The weary returning soldier. The exuberant parents. The elated siblings. The joyous neighbors. The shy girlfriend-in-waiting.

A lot of emotion accompanies the return of a traveler after a long time away from home, especially if that journey involved trials and hardship, conflicts and struggle. Paul and Barnabas had left their homes in Syrian Antioch more than a year earlier to engage in an unusual kind of warfare. They battled supernatural forces on Cyprus and encountered spiritual enemies in the synagogues of Pisidia and Lycaonia. Paul's brush with death in Lystra may have left him with injuries that would affect him for the rest of his life; each scar would have reminded him and his associates that they had been to battle and would likely face the enemy again. Without a doubt, morale improved for Paul, Barnabas, and their team when their itinerary carried them ever closer to home. Still, they had a long way to go and a great deal to accomplish along the way.

— 14:21-23 —

After surviving the mob attack in Lystra, the team traveled 35 miles east to the city of Derbe, a relatively obscure town that was subsequently lost to history. This little town wasn't connected to Lystra by the paved Via Sebaste, so the team would have traversed 60 miles of rugged, unpaved road to reach Derbe.[28]

Paul and Barnabas preached there with great success, more than Luke reveals here. We learn later from Acts that a sizable community of believers formed a stable church and eventually supplied Paul with a helper named Gaius (20:4).

After completing their work in Derbe, the men retraced their steps rather than take a direct route through the mountains to Tarsus and then home. Luke doesn't explain their reasoning; he merely describes their activity on the way back. It appears winter may have been a factor in their decision. If they left home at the beginning of March, nine months of ministry would have put them in Derbe around November. The region is known today for its severe winters and heavy snowfalls, so the men had three options: risk a foolhardy trek through the mountains, spend the winter in Derbe before crossing over, or return the way they came. Of course, this third option presented some dangerous prospects; they would likely encounter the same people who had attempted to kill them earlier. But danger aside, the return route gave them an opportunity to further equip the new believers to survive and thrive on their own.

After completing the tasks of evangelism, preaching and making disciples (14:21), Paul and Barnabas accomplished the three primary objectives in church planting:

1. *"Strengthening the souls of the disciples, encouraging them to continue in the faith"* (14:22). Once we evangelize the lost and they believe, we have a duty to equip them for this new life. In this case, the believers continued to meet under difficult circumstances. The hostility shown to Paul and Barnabas would have attached to their disciples. The persecuted Christians needed reassurance. Paul's stoning and subsequent refusal to quit would have inspired the new believers to persevere. They needed training, which—in the absence of a written New Testament— was reliant upon verbal teaching and memorization as well as personal mentoring.

The new Christians also needed encouragement. Many had been polytheistic Gentiles. The Christian life required a radical departure from their former way of life, including how they maintained relationships with pagan family and friends. Their new beliefs also changed their participation in the community. Learning to be "in the world but not of the world" was a tall order, one that required lots of moral support.

2. *"Appoint[ing] elders"* (14:23). The practice of selecting elders came from centuries of tradition that went clear back to Israel's wilderness years, but it became especially prominent as the leadership structure in the Jewish synagogues, which was the immediate background for the establishment of elders in the first churches. These elders were always hand-selected by other mature leaders who were themselves qualified to recognize the necessary traits for leadership. The leaders were to be men of spiritual maturity, strong character, and good reputation in the community, regardless of their age, wealth, experience, power, or position. Paul later established the exact qualifications of elders, most likely as a result of the hard lessons learned in these early years (see Titus 1:5-16).

An elder holds a *spiritual* office; therefore, he must demonstrate that he lives under the control of the Holy Spirit. His qualities must include continual submission to the Spirit. He must show an example of loving leadership in his own home. He must display a humble and contrite heart that remains keenly sensitive to the presence of sin or any act of pride, stubbornness, or selfishness. He must be willing to confess his own wrongdoing. He must maintain a strong commitment to conform his behavior to the instruction of Scripture and maintain a humble vulnerability before the Lord.

3. *"Commend[ing] them to the Lord"* (14:23). This is perhaps the most difficult task of a church-planting ministry. After witnessing the birth of new believers, nurturing them from infancy, helping them stand on their own, and training them to lead others—all the while cultivating deep personal relationships—the time must come to leave. The word translated "commended" means "placed before." Literally, it's used in the sense of serving food. Greek writers use the term figuratively of teaching when a teacher sets before students a new concept to learn or evaluate. The literal and figurative senses come together when something is entrusted to the care of another, which is the meaning here. The apostles entrusted the people to the care of God.

Of course, Paul and Barnabas formally commended the disciples to God for their own peace of mind and not to signify a spiritual change. Nothing in heaven changed. The Lord didn't say, "Okay, thanks for getting these churches started. I'll take it from here." He had been taking care of these people since before the beginning of time!

— 14:24-26 —

The evangelistic team traveled roughly 90 miles south from Antioch, through the mountain range separating Pisidia from Pamphylia, down the Cestrus valley, and into Perga, where they had originally landed from Cyprus (13:13). They proclaimed the gospel there, as they did everywhere, but they didn't stay long. Attalia was a busier and more modern port, carrying the bulk of traffic between Ephesus and Syria. A ship carried them back to Seleucia, where they disembarked and walked 14 miles up the Orontes River to arrive home again, roughly eighteen months after leaving.

Luke sums up the mission using two significant terms:

1. "Commended" (*paradidōmi* [3860]). Here at the end of the mission, they remembered that the church in Syrian Antioch "commended [them] to the grace of God for the work" that they were

leaving to do (14:26; see 13:1-4). It's the same term used of Paul and Barnabas in entrusting the disciples to the Lord.

2. "Accomplished" (*plēroō* [4137]). Upon their return, they had "accomplished" all the work assigned to them. The term *plēroō* means "to make full" or "to fulfill." If the mission dossier were a glass, they filled it to overflowing.

— 14:27-28 —

The church had delegated a responsibility to Paul and Barnabas, equipped them with the necessary provisions, conferred its authority upon them, and sent them out. The missionaries owed the church accountability. They called the congregation together and gave a complete report of all that had occurred (14:27). While all the details interested the church, the bottom-line outcome thrilled them. They had "opened a door of faith" to the Gentiles. This was the first coordinated, organized effort to preach the gospel of Jesus Christ to Gentiles where not even a synagogue had existed. The ministry of Paul and Barnabas had shed light into the lives of the darkest pagans, and the Gentiles responded in belief. With the door of faith now open, they hoped to see innumerable Gentiles pour into the church.

Luke states that Paul and Barnabas spent "a long time" with their sending church in Syrian Antioch (14:28). This must have been a span of several months, perhaps the latter weeks of autumn and the winter of AD 48–49. Many scholars believe Paul wrote his letter to the Galatians during this time, just before attending the Council at Jerusalem (15:1-30). Although the theory raises some questions, it makes the best sense of the data we have concerning Paul's activities.

APPLICATION: ACTS 14:21-28

Heads Up!

When Paul and Barnabas left an area, they gave the newly established assemblies over to the Lord. They, of course, did this for their own peace of mind. By formally giving the people over to God, they consciously acknowledged their own limitations. This habit accomplished something else just as important. It helped the developing Christians look to God rather than men for their support, comfort, encouragement, and wisdom.

I have discovered that developing Christians go through three very definite stages: first, *eyes on people*; second, *eyes on self*; and finally, *eyes on the Lord*.

The first stage, *eyes on people*, is dangerous. The person who led you to Christ easily becomes your idol, your model. That's unfortunate. Many a pastor is somebody's model or idol. In some cases, he's virtually an object of worship. So, a pastor must remain faithful to help his admirers see that he is just one among a number of people who is being used by God. No one should ever allow others to focus their adoration or worship on any person.

Second, *eyes on self* is what we might call a Christian adolescence, during which we know just enough to be dangerous. Everything is all about us. We're impulsive, experimental, self-reliant, propelled through life with a sense of invincibility. As a result, we rely upon our own strength to overcome difficulties.

It's the minister's job to move Christians safely along to the third stage, *eyes on the Lord*. I appreciate the fact that Paul and Barnabas said to these assemblies, in effect, "Ladies and gentlemen, we turn your ministry over to the Lord. You're accountable to Him. Fix your hope and heart on Him, not on us." If you are a spiritual leader serving in any kind of Christian ministry, do your very best to keep believers' affection on Christ and their eyes heavenward.

Grace on Trial
ACTS 15:1-12

NASB

¹Some men came down from Judea and *began* teaching the brethren, "Unless you are circumcised according to the custom of Moses, you cannot be saved." ²And when Paul and Barnabas had ªgreat dissension and debate with them, *the brethren* determined that Paul and Barnabas and some others of them should go up to Jerusalem to the apostles and elders concerning this issue. ³Therefore, being sent on their way by the church, they were passing through both Phoenicia and

NLT

¹While Paul and Barnabas were at Antioch of Syria, some men from Judea arrived and began to teach the believers*: "Unless you are circumcised as required by the law of Moses, you cannot be saved." ²Paul and Barnabas disagreed with them, arguing vehemently. Finally, the church decided to send Paul and Barnabas to Jerusalem, accompanied by some local believers, to talk to the apostles and elders about this question. ³The church sent the delegates to Jerusalem, and they stopped along the way

Samaria, describing in detail the conversion of the Gentiles, and were bringing great joy to all the brethren. ⁴When they arrived at Jerusalem, they were received by the church and the apostles and the elders, and they reported all that God had done with them. ⁵But some of the sect of the Pharisees who had believed stood up, saying, "It is necessary to circumcise them and to direct them to observe the Law of Moses."

⁶The apostles and the elders came together to ᵃlook into this ᵇmatter. ⁷After there had been much debate, Peter stood up and said to them, "Brethren, you know that ᵃin the early days God made a choice among you, that by my mouth the Gentiles would hear the word of the gospel and believe. ⁸And God, who knows the heart, testified to them giving them the Holy Spirit, just as He also did to us; ⁹and He made no distinction between us and them, cleansing their hearts by faith. ¹⁰Now therefore why do you put God to the test by placing upon the neck of the disciples a yoke which neither our fathers nor we have been able to bear? ¹¹But we believe that we are saved through the grace of the Lord Jesus, in the same way as they also are."

¹²All the people kept silent, and they were listening to Barnabas and Paul as they were relating what signs and wonders God had done through them among the Gentiles.

15:2 ᵃLit *not a little* **15:6** ᵃLit *see about* ᵇLit *word*
15:7 ᵃLit *from days of old*

in Phoenicia and Samaria to visit the believers. They told them—much to everyone's joy—that the Gentiles, too, were being converted.

⁴When they arrived in Jerusalem, Barnabas and Paul were welcomed by the whole church, including the apostles and elders. They reported everything God had done through them. ⁵But then some of the believers who belonged to the sect of the Pharisees stood up and insisted, "The Gentile converts must be circumcised and required to follow the law of Moses."

⁶So the apostles and elders met together to resolve this issue. ⁷At the meeting, after a long discussion, Peter stood and addressed them as follows: "Brothers, you all know that God chose me from among you some time ago to preach to the Gentiles so that they could hear the Good News and believe. ⁸God knows people's hearts, and he confirmed that he accepts Gentiles by giving them the Holy Spirit, just as he did to us. ⁹He made no distinction between us and them, for he cleansed their hearts through faith. ¹⁰So why are you now challenging God by burdening the Gentile believers* with a yoke that neither we nor our ancestors were able to bear? ¹¹We believe that we are all saved the same way, by the undeserved grace of the Lord Jesus."

¹²Everyone listened quietly as Barnabas and Paul told about the miraculous signs and wonders God had done through them among the Gentiles.

15:1 Greek *brothers;* also in 15:3, 23, 32, 33, 36, 40.
15:10 Greek *disciples.*

Whenever you put people together, contention happens. Even in the church. Some might even say *especially* in the church. Poorly informed romantics like to talk about the glory days of the early church, as if the era of the apostles didn't have the same problems we face today . . . but an honest portrait of church history is a study in black and blue. Some of those places we have idealized—places we visit at ancient sites like Antioch, Corinth, Philippi, Thessalonica, and Ephesus—were, in reality, hotbeds of controversy in their time. The question is not *whether* a church will have contention, but *how* a church will move to resolve internal conflict.

Paul and Barnabas had just returned from their first missionary journey with amazing stories to tell of Gentiles coming to faith in Christ. With this bold initiative, the church had opened new territory and was poised to expand rapidly. Just as the momentum began to build, however, somebody threw a wrench into the machinery. An old controversy returned, bringing progress to a lurching halt and threatening to undermine the single most important doctrine of the church: salvation by grace.

How this first generation of believers resolved the conflict would not only affect generations of Christians, but it would also set the precedent for how earnest believers would resolve contention within their own communities.

— 15:1-2 —

Although Syrian Antioch had become increasingly important in terms of Christian expansion, Jerusalem remained the center of church authority. Prior to the writing and distribution of the New Testament Scriptures, the leaders in Jerusalem were the church's primary source of divine revelation and the ultimate authority on orthodox teaching. Consequently, a believer coming from Judea to teach was afforded great respect. Gentile churches especially regarded anyone coming from "headquarters" as authoritative.

Some of these teachers taught that anyone wanting to be saved must be circumcised (15:1). The issue ran deeper than merely submitting to a surgical procedure. How one understood the place of circumcision in the church defined how a person saw Israel and the Mosaic Law in relation to the new covenant. After all, God's covenants with Abraham (Gen. 12:1-3; 15:1-21), Israel (Deut. 28:1-68), and David (2 Sam. 7:8-16) had defined the meaning of "the kingdom of God" for generation upon generation of Hebrews.

Circumcision identified a male as a true "son of the covenant," heir to the promises of God to the descendants of Abraham and citizens of Israel. Anyone not born Jewish and circumcised on the eighth day had to learn Hebrew history and become sufficiently knowledgeable about the Mosaic Law. After a thorough examination of his knowledge, he would be baptized and then circumcised.[29] Only then would he be considered a true "son of the covenant," a real citizen of God's kingdom. Christians with this rich Hebrew background had a couple of valid concerns. How could someone appreciate the meaning of the new covenant without at least some knowledge of the old? How could someone become a citizen of God's kingdom so easily? And would this person truly be a good citizen without at least *some* demonstration of sincerity? And what of Israel? How do Gentiles factor into God's centuries-old plan?

Paul and Barnabas obviously took issue with such a teaching (Acts 15:2). The "circumcision group" posed valid questions, but their teaching contradicted the bottom-line teaching of Jesus Christ. Besides, hadn't this issue already been addressed adequately with the conversion of Cornelius and his household and the approval of the Holy Spirit a few years earlier (10:34-48; 11:17-18)? At that time, everyone in Jerusalem felt satisfied. Certainly, Peter didn't circumcise these Gentiles.

In response to the contention between believers, the leaders in Syrian Antioch appealed to their only source of divine authority, the apostles in Jerusalem. They formed a delegation consisting of Paul, Barnabas, and the circumcision teachers and sent them to the apostles and elders for a theological ruling. No threats of excommunication, no violence or threats of violence, no clandestine moves to split the church. They went together to seek the truth. Historians and theologians call this the Jerusalem Council.

— 15:3-5 —

The phrase "passing through" (15:3) indicates that the team traveled over land rather than by sea. Naturally, a ship would have been faster and less arduous. Instead, the men took the trouble to journey overland through Phoenicia and Samaria. This means they probably followed along the Orontes River valley south through Phoenicia, took the coastal road through Sidon, Tyre, and Acco, then turned inland to pick up the ancient trade route known as the International Coastal Highway or "great trunk route" (sometimes mislabeled as the Via Maris), which passed east–west through the Jezreel Valley and led them back out toward the coastline again.[30] This highway intersected a major road leading from Joppa to Jerusalem. It was quite a journey—more than 300 miles!

Luke's description implies that the two factions of the delegation didn't travel together, if the circumcision group bothered to go at all. Regardless, Paul and Barnabas made an effort to visit churches—predominantly Gentile—telling the story of their success among Gentile churches never before reached with the gospel (15:3). Whether or not they intended this as a campaign to create a grassroots movement, they gained huge anti-circumcision support among the churches outside Judea. When they finally arrived in Jerusalem, they were "received" (15:4). This word means "welcomed." The apostles and elders embraced the delegation, extending fellowship and hospitality to them as brothers.

At the council, both sides presented their cases to the apostles and elders. Luke's narrative highlights the fact that churches everywhere rejoiced at the news of Gentiles becoming Christians. Only a relatively small number of believers expressed any concern. Unfortunately, loud minority opinions can appear more significant than they really are. Luke describes the opposition as "Pharisees who had believed" (15:5; cf. John 19:38-39), a phrase that indicates that they were genuine believers. Some might say their faulty theology invalidated their faith in Christ because it interposed works as a condition of salvation. This charge is intriguing because it supposes one must have good theology in order to be saved—exactly the point made by the circumcision group. On the other hand, if someone believes that works contribute to salvation, what does that say about his or her understanding of the gospel and the purity of his trust in Christ? While it might seem that their theology casts doubt on their salvation, a plain reading of Luke supports their status as brothers in Christ.

— 15:6 —

The theological dispute was brought before "the apostles and the elders." By now, many of the Twelve had undertaken missionary journeys of their own. Church tradition, though not accurate in all respects, is probably correct in suggesting the majority of the Twelve left for various parts of the world and then died serving in these locations. Peter remained in Jerusalem to provide theological guidance, and John, who had been given the care of Jesus' mother, may have remained there as well. With many of the apostles gone, the responsibility for functional leadership and instruction passed to a number of elders led by James, the Lord's half brother. James the apostle, the brother of John, had been martyred by this time (12:2).

Divisive Devices

ACTS 15:5

When the status quo meets our personal needs, we will do anything to resist change. Anything.

One of my favorite professors told a story about something that occurred many years ago in a church in Midwestern America—a culture known for its love of tradition—in which a creative Sunday school teacher started using a flannelgraph to depict Bible stories. At the time, some considered her an innovator, others a radical. In those days, only businesses used flannelgraphs as a presentation tool, usually to graph out profit-loss trends or to map out future plans. To many, the woman had introduced a secular device into God's sacred house. Of course, many from my generation fondly remember the flannelgraph with a sense of childhood nostalgia.

Years later, a good friend of mine told me about a forward-thinking pastor who set up an overhead projector beside the pulpit. Some of the established members of the congregation wanted to know, "Why don't you just teach from the Bible? Why use all that 'worldly stuff'?"

Another friend remembered how a favorite youth minister in his hometown church decided to use a film to grab the attention of young people. So, he gathered the teens one evening at the church and ran the movie for a packed house. Mind you, it was a Christian film, a story from the mission field. Still, the leaders of the congregation called him into a private meeting for a confrontation.

"Why are you upset? What's wrong with showing a Christian film?" he asked. "We show slides of missionaries all the time. We have pictures all over the walls of this place."

One board member responded, "If it's still, it's fine. If it moves, it's sin."

— 15:7-9 —

Even though the issue had been discussed at length before and the church authorities in Jerusalem had already embraced the conversion of uncircumcised Gentiles (11:17-18), the apostles and elders committed to reexamining the issue. What a difference from the Sanhedrin! Rather than take a rigid, authoritarian position—"We've already made our decision, so shut up and fall into line, or else!"—these spiritually sensitive, wise men of God humbled themselves enough to reconsider their position. They also gave their Pharisaic Christian brothers the dignity of being heard. Rather than dismiss their Pharisaic colleagues outright, the apostles and elders listened carefully, considered seriously, debated thoroughly, and finally arrived at a conclusion. The way they handled the issue influenced Paul profoundly. Near the end of his life, he wrote to his younger colleague Timothy,

> The Lord's bond-servant must not be quarrelsome, but be kind to all, able to teach, patient when wronged, with gentleness correcting those who are in opposition, if perhaps God may grant them repentance leading to the knowledge of the truth, and they may come to their senses and escape from the snare of the devil, having been held captive by him to do his will. (2 Tim. 2:24-26)

Paul observed how the apostles and elders responded to their theologically wayward brothers, and he modeled their example throughout his own ministry.

Near the end of the deliberations, Peter took the floor to address the assembly. Luke doesn't reveal the theological points considered by both sides of the issue; none of that was important. Luke recounts only the speech by Peter, who rested his defense on the one important factor in the whole debate: What does God say concerning the Gentiles? He took his peers back several years to his experience in Joppa, where the Lord spoke to him directly, saying, "What God has cleansed, no longer consider unholy" (Acts 10:15). He reminded them that God had given these uncircumcised Gentiles His Spirit: "Therefore if God gave to them the same gift as He gave to us also after believing in the Lord Jesus Christ, who was I that I could stand in God's way?" (11:17). At the end of the day, God had spoken by giving His Spirit without requiring circumcision.

The key phrase in Peter's address is "cleansing their hearts by faith" (15:9; cf. 10:43). The concept of salvation by grace through faith was not new. God had always wanted His people to have "circumcised hearts" (see Deut. 10:16; 30:6), instructing them to "love the LORD your God with all your heart and with all your soul and with all your might" (Deut. 6:5). The concept of salvation through faith applied to their patriarch, Abraham, of whom the Scriptures say, "he believed in the LORD; and He reckoned it to him as righteousness" (Gen. 15:6). Besides, the outward symbol of circumcision applied to Abraham and his descendants as part of a specific kind of covenant. This was a new covenant, one with different terms and applicable to a broader group of people—with "no distinction" (Acts 15:9).

— 15:10-11 —

Peter then challenged the circumcision group to consider the implications of their demand. As with the circumcision of Jewish proselytes (see comments on 15:1-2), the outward symbol of circumcision was to reflect an inner commitment to obey every point of the Law (Gal. 5:3)—including sacrificial and purification rites, food prohibitions, and appointed festivals. Any Hebrew willing to be honest had to admit that even with the advantages of biblical training, theological knowledge, and a supportive culture, he had not kept that commitment—in a sense negating the value of the symbol itself (see Rom. 2:25-26). More importantly, as Peter would point out, observing the Law is not the basis of salvation.

Rather, as Peter reiterated, the basis of salvation is the grace of God alone received through faith alone, made possible by Jesus Christ alone (Acts 15:11). Grace plus works isn't grace!

— 15:12 —

Luke notes that by the end of the discussion, "all the people" were listening to Paul and Barnabas. The duo had been telling these stories since their return, and they told stories of Gentiles saved in the churches between Antioch and Jerusalem, and the believers had responded with rejoicing. Now, however, "all the people" listened. The presence of "signs and wonders" affirmed what God had declared earlier by giving His Spirit to the Gentile believers. Therefore, no one could deny the conclusion: Nothing, not even circumcision, can improve upon God's grace; He requires nothing more than trust in His Son.

APPLICATION: ACTS 15:1-12

The Blessings of Conflicts

My observation of this unpleasant episode in the life of the church yields three enduring lessons. I first examined this passage in depth back in the 1970s, soon after I became a senior pastor in Fullerton, California, and through the years, these lessons have influenced my selection of staff members and have guided how I conduct meetings.

First lesson: *Conflict is inevitable; expect it.* Issues that should have already been settled will resurface. People who should get along will knock heads every once in a while. Good-hearted, capable people will arrive at completely different conclusions. This is not a sign that something's wrong with your organization; it's normal. Your group shouldn't be characterized by contention; harmony should be the rule, not the exception. But if you never see disagreements, something has gone wrong. Communication has broken down or people have stopped being honest or the conflict has gone underground—or people have stopped caring.

Second lesson: *No conflict is ever easy; endure it.* Conflict is always unpleasant, always difficult. Contention brings out the worst in everybody. Consequently, many leaders try to end a disagreement by any means possible rather than let constructive conflict run its course. Difficult as it feels, maintain order and keep all contention within the bounds of mutual respect and unconditional love, but trust people enough to work through their difficulties.

Third lesson: *Any conflict can benefit the people involved; let it.* Chicago journalist Sydney J. Harris once wrote, "Agreement makes us soft and complacent; disagreement brings out our strength. Our real enemies are the people who make us feel so good that we are slowly, but inexorably, pulled down into the quicksand of smugness and self-satisfaction." If you're filling your staff positions only with yes-men, you have doomed your organization to failure and yourself to perpetual ignorance. You will soon become complacent and arrogant and obsolete. People who think, question, challenge, and evaluate are your benefactors. Encourage, praise, appreciate, and reward their respectful honesty. No conflict is easy. Contention with the right motives calls for honest appraisal, which rarely feels good but always creates an opportunity for improvement.

The Essentials
ACTS 15:13-35

NASB

[13] After they had stopped speaking, [a]James answered, saying, "Brethren, listen to me. [14]Simeon has related how God first concerned Himself about taking from among the Gentiles a people for His name. [15]With this the words of the Prophets agree, just as it is written,

[16] 'AFTER THESE THINGS I will return,
AND I WILL REBUILD THE [a]TABERNACLE OF DAVID WHICH HAS FALLEN,
AND I WILL REBUILD ITS RUINS,
AND I WILL RESTORE IT,
[17] SO THAT THE REST OF [a]MANKIND MAY SEEK THE LORD,
AND ALL THE GENTILES [b]WHO ARE CALLED BY MY NAME,'
[18] SAYS THE LORD, WHO [a]MAKES THESE THINGS KNOWN FROM LONG AGO.

[19]Therefore it is my judgment that we do not trouble those who are turning to God from among the Gentiles, [20]but that we write to them that they abstain from [a]things contaminated by idols and from fornication and from what is strangled and from blood. [21]For Moses from ancient generations has in every city those who preach him, since [a]he is read in the synagogues every Sabbath."

[22]Then it seemed good to the apostles and the elders, with the whole church, to choose men from among them to send to Antioch with Paul and Barnabas—Judas called Barsabbas, and Silas, leading men among the brethren, [23]and they [a]sent this letter by them,

"The apostles and the brethren who are elders, to the brethren in Antioch and Syria and Cilicia

NLT

[13]When they had finished, James stood and said, "Brothers, listen to me. [14]Peter* has told you about the time God first visited the Gentiles to take from them a people for himself. [15]And this conversion of Gentiles is exactly what the prophets predicted. As it is written:

[16] 'Afterward I will return
and restore the fallen house* of David.
I will rebuild its ruins
and restore it,
[17] so that the rest of humanity might seek the LORD,
including the Gentiles—
all those I have called to be mine.
The LORD has spoken—
[18] he who made these things known so long ago.'*

[19]"And so my judgment is that we should not make it difficult for the Gentiles who are turning to God. [20]Instead, we should write and tell them to abstain from eating food offered to idols, from sexual immorality, from eating the meat of strangled animals, and from consuming blood. [21]For these laws of Moses have been preached in Jewish synagogues in every city on every Sabbath for many generations."

[22]Then the apostles and elders together with the whole church in Jerusalem chose delegates, and they sent them to Antioch of Syria with Paul and Barnabas to report on this decision. The men chosen were two of the church leaders*—Judas (also called Barsabbas) and Silas. [23]This is the letter they took with them:

"This letter is from the apostles and elders, your brothers in who are from the Gentiles, greetings.

24 "Since we have heard that some ᵃof our number to whom we gave no instruction have disturbed you with *their* words, unsettling your souls,

25 it seemed good to us, having ᵃbecome of one mind, to select men to send to you with our beloved Barnabas and Paul,

26 men who have ᵃrisked their lives for the name of our Lord Jesus Christ.

27 "Therefore we have sent Judas and Silas, who themselves will also report the same things by word *of mouth.*

28 "For it seemed good to the Holy Spirit and to us to lay upon you no greater burden than these essentials:

29 that you abstain from things sacrificed to idols and from blood and from things strangled and from fornication; ᵃif you keep yourselves free from such things, you will do well. Farewell."

30 So when they were sent away, they went down to Antioch; and having gathered the ᵃcongregation together, they delivered the letter. 31 When they had read it, they rejoiced because of its ᵃencouragement. 32 Judas and Silas, also being prophets themselves, ᵃencouraged and strengthened the brethren with a lengthy message. 33 After they had spent time *there,* they were sent away from the brethren in peace to those who had sent them out. 34 [ᵃBut it seemed good to Silas to remain there.] 35 But Paul and Barnabas stayed in Antioch, teaching and preaching with many others also, the word of the Lord.

15:13 ᵃOr *Jacob* 15:16 ᵃOr *tent* 15:17 ᵃGr *anthropoi* ᵇLit *upon whom My name is called* 15:18 ᵃOr *does these things* which were *known* 15:20 ᵃLit *the pollutions of* 15:21 ᵃI.e. the books of Moses, Gen through Deut 15:23 ᵃLit *wrote*

Jerusalem. It is written to the Gentile believers in Antioch, Syria, and Cilicia. Greetings!

24 "We understand that some men from here have troubled you and upset you with their teaching, but we did not send them! 25 So we decided, having come to complete agreement, to send you official representatives, along with our beloved Barnabas and Paul, 26 who have risked their lives for the name of our Lord Jesus Christ. 27 We are sending Judas and Silas to confirm what we have decided concerning your question.

28 "For it seemed good to the Holy Spirit and to us to lay no greater burden on you than these few requirements: 29 You must abstain from eating food offered to idols, from consuming blood or the meat of strangled animals, and from sexual immorality. If you do this, you will do well. Farewell."

30 The messengers went at once to Antioch, where they called a general meeting of the believers and delivered the letter. 31 And there was great joy throughout the church that day as they read this encouraging message.

32 Then Judas and Silas, both being prophets, spoke at length to the believers, encouraging and strengthening their faith. 33 They stayed for a while, and then the believers sent them back to the church in Jerusalem with a blessing of peace.* 35 Paul and Barnabas stayed in Antioch. They and many others taught and preached the word of the Lord there.

15:14 Greek *Simeon.* 15:16 Or *kingdom;* Greek reads *tent.* 15:16-18 Amos 9:11-12 (Greek

by their hand   **15:24** ªLit *from us*   **15:25** ªOr
met together   **15:26** ªLit *given over*   **15:29** ªLit
from which keeping yourselves free   **15:30** ªOr
multitude   **15:31** ªOr *exhortation*   **15:32** ªOr
exhorted   **15:34** ªEarly mss do not contain this v

version); Isa 45:21.   **15:22** Greek *were leaders
among the brothers.*   **15:33** Some manuscripts
add verse 34, *But Silas decided to stay there.*

In 2003, a book hit the shelves that described a recent revolution in the historic game of baseball. *Moneyball: The Art of Winning an Unfair Game* tells the story of the Oakland Athletics and their revolutionary approach to selecting and fielding players.[31] While other teams evaluated players based on intangible qualities, such as confidence, physical potential, leadership, and intelligence, the team's front office ignored all subjective factors, choosing instead to evaluate players by their objective statistics. Baseball teams win by getting men on base and then home. When choosing players, recruiters asked the fundamental, bottom-line question, "Does the player get on base?" By focusing on this essential ability, the team started winning games. Lots of games.

It seems odd that recruiting players based solely on their ability to get on base would be considered revolutionary. After more than one hundred years of professional baseball, recruiters had become so sophisticated in their evaluations that they lost sight of the most basic requirement of success. But we shouldn't be too hard on them. It can happen to anyone. In fact, it happened to the church before the first generation of leaders had passed away. The Council at Jerusalem, unpleasant as it was, gave the apostles and the elders an opportunity to refocus the church on the essentials of the Christian life.

After much debate, Peter sealed the discussion with a sobering reminder. Theology is a necessary discipline. We should be biblical and logical in all our spiritual deliberations. When God speaks directly to an issue, however, all discussion ceases. By giving His Spirit to the uncircumcised Gentiles, authenticating them as genuine believers and citizens of His kingdom, God settled the matter. Clearly, eternal salvation is by grace alone through faith alone in Christ alone. With all in agreement, the leaders needed to inform the churches and to answer the question on everyone's mind: *What does God expect of Christians under the new covenant?*

— **15:13** —

By this time, James, the half brother of Jesus, had become the functional leader of the church in Jerusalem (12:17; 21:18; Gal. 2:9). Scripture regards him an apostle in the broader sense of the term (Gal. 1:19; cf. 1 Cor. 15:5-7).

According to church tradition, most of the Twelve had departed to carry the gospel to various parts of the world. Peter traveled around the region but didn't go far from Jerusalem. He (and perhaps John) remained close in order to provide spiritual guidance and instruction. He had been with Jesus from the beginning. He had received personalized instruction from the Lord for no fewer than three years, and he had been personally commissioned by Jesus to "tend My sheep" (John 21:17). He, with the other apostles, bore the oral teaching of the Master until the New Testament Scriptures were completed and distributed. James appears to have given leadership to the church in practical matters.

At the end of the discussion, he commented on Peter's defense of grace in preparation for a proposed course of action.

— 15:14-18 —

As the leader of the church in functional matters, James brought the deliberations to a conclusion and announced the council's official resolution on the matter. He first validated Peter's conclusion by citing Old Testament Scripture, proving that God had always planned to bring Gentiles into His kingdom. His support came from Amos 9:11-12, but the actual words recorded by Luke differ slightly from our Hebrew texts of this prophetic passage.

COMPARISON OF AMOS 9:11-12 IN ACTS 15:16-18		
Translated from Hebrew	**Translated from the Septuagint (NETS)**	**Luke's Account of James's Citation**
"In that day	"On that day	"After these things I will return,
I will raise up the fallen booth of David, and wall up its breaches;	I will raise up the tent of David that is fallen	and I will rebuild the tabernacle of David which has fallen,
I will also raise up its ruins and rebuild it as in the days of old;	and rebuild its ruins and raise up its destruction, and rebuild it as the days of old	and I will rebuild its ruins, and I will restore it,
that they may possess the remnant of Edom and all the nations who are called by My name,"	in order that those remaining of humans and all nations upon whom my name has been called might seek out me,"	so that the rest of mankind may seek the Lord, and all the Gentiles who are called by My name,"
declares the LORD who does this.	says the Lord who does these things.[32]	says the Lord.

James probably spoke in colloquial Hebrew or Aramaic at the council, Luke rendered his speech in Greek, and we have Luke's account translated into English. Beneath these layers of translation, we also have Amos 9:11-12 translated from Hebrew into Greek, a text we know as the Septuagint, produced around 200 BC.

Though similar in most respects, James's citation of Amos 9:11-12 differs slightly from our modern English translations from the Hebrew Old Testament, but it agrees with the ancient Greek translation known as the Septuagint. There the words "men," "mankind," and "humans" all presuppose the Hebrew word 'adam [H120]. In our modern translations from the Hebrew text of Amos 9:12, "Edom" presupposes the Hebrew word 'Edom [H123]. At the time of the Septuagint and in the first century, the Hebrew script didn't make consistent use of vowels, so the Hebrew words for "Edom" and "mankind" would have appeared the same. It depended on the reader to determine whether the original author meant to refer to the region of Edom or to humanity in general. Some ancient scribes who supplied vowel markings for the traditional Hebrew text upon which our English translations rest apparently understood the text as "remnant of Edom," while others, including the Septuagint translators and James, understood it as "remnant of mankind."

James's citation also agrees with the Septuagint on another point that differs from the traditional Hebrew text: Rather than reading "they may possess," it reads "[they] may seek," which reflects a difference of just one letter in Hebrew (a *daleth* in the Septuagint in place of a *yod*). Thus the remnant would "seek" the Lord.

James shared the scholarly opinion of the Septuagint translators that the text should be read as "the rest of mankind may seek" rather than "they may possess the remnant of Edom." The text, then, would show that God intends to use Israel as a means of reaching the Gentiles. James didn't, however, mean to imply that the church was fulfilling all that Amos prophesied. The oracle of Amos describes the restoration of Israel, which hasn't happened yet. James merely used the prophecy to demonstrate that the Lord had always intended to bring elect Gentiles into His kingdom.

— 15:19-21 —

James proposed that the council issue an official proclamation affirming grace (God's kindness alone, without works) as the only means of salvation. The expression "do not trouble those who are turning to God" is critical (15:19). The phrase identifies any addition of works (circumcision, baptism, Law keeping—any human activity other than simple belief, childlike trust, or genuine faith) as a man-made obstacle to God's agenda. He did, however, add a few practical principles to make the relationship between Jews and Gentiles in the church easier to maintain and to prevent unnecessary stumbling blocks to Jews outside the faith. These special commandments given in this particular historical situation don't necessarily imply that such rules need to be followed in perpetuity. They addressed a specific issue at a certain time.

James noted that the Law of Moses was widely read in synagogues throughout the Roman Empire (15:21). Many Jews in these locations would become Christians. Even though they would no longer try to obey the Law as a means of earning God's favor, they would still find repulsive anything associated with idol worship and sexual impurity. These Jewish believers would also shudder at the prospect of eating meat from a strangled animal that hadn't been properly bled (15:20). For the sake of unity, Gentile believers should voluntarily defer to the dietary sensibilities of their Jewish brothers and sisters. Moreover, this would remove dietary scruples as an obstacle when presenting the gospel to nonbelieving Jews.

— 15:22-27 —

The decision won unanimous agreement from "the apostles and the elders, with the whole church" (15:22). The council upheld the doctrine of grace alone while addressing some of the valid concerns presented by believing Pharisees. Theological truth won the day, but not at the expense of love. Indeed, grace leaves the believer free to set aside personal freedom for the sake of unity in the body. As the great Protestant motto states, "In essentials unity, in nonessentials liberty, in all things charity." As a unified body, the church in Jerusalem drafted a letter and placed it in the care of four men: Paul, Barnabas, Judas (also called Barsabbas), and Silas.

Paul and Barnabas were, of course, very public champions of grace in this matter, so the council sent along with them two witnesses to verify that the resolution was both authentic and unanimous. The names Judas and Barsabbas are the Greek renderings of the patently Jewish "Judah, the son of the Sabbath." He may have been the brother of Joseph (also called Barsabbas or Justus), who was one of the two candidates put forward to become the twelfth apostle (cf. 1:23). Silas, as a Roman citizen (cf. 16:37), could speak from the Hellenistic perspective.

Although the letter applied to all the churches, the council specifically addressed the resolution to the churches of the northwest Mediterranean: the lead church in Antioch and the churches in surrounding Syria, as well as in the region of Cilicia, where Paul's hometown of Tarsus was. It appears that by this time the churches in Galatia, where Paul and Barnabas had ministered on the first missionary journey, were struggling with this issue as well (cf. Gal. 1:6; 2:3-4), but Paul already had written a strong letter upholding the doctrine of grace. Furthermore, plans had not been laid for a visit to Galatia, at least not in the immediate future.

— 15:28-29 —

The council didn't offer a lengthy defense for the doctrine of salvation by grace through faith, it didn't recount its deliberations over the issue of circumcision, and it didn't issue a creed to uphold the original message of grace. The council recognized that the Gentiles came to Christianity by the true gospel of grace, and they labeled unauthorized teachers who taught otherwise disturbing and unsettling (15:24). In other words, the council effectively let the original message of the gospel stand.

The church leaders did, however, feel compelled by the Holy Spirit to "burden" the Gentile believers with two necessities: do not offend Jewish sensibilities—which find idols and blood-tainted meat especially repugnant—and abstain from sexual immorality (15:28-29). The word "fornication" (*porneia* [4202]) is an umbrella term for a broad range of sexual sin, not just adultery. The term, originally associated with prostitution, eventually grew to encompass a broad range of illicit sexual activities, including adultery, homosexuality, incest, bestiality, and child molestation.

Notably, the church leaders characterized these requests as "essential burdens." The Greek word for "burden" (*baros* [922]) pictures someone perpetually carrying an additional weight. Any decision to give up a freedom for the greater good of all is a burden. Nevertheless, the council, under the inspiration of the Holy Spirit, considered these burdens "essential" (*epanagkes* [1876]), something compulsory. The council felt compelled by the Holy Spirit and therefore felt led to exercise its authority to likewise compel the Gentile believers. Nevertheless, the provisions were not essential for salvation, but for unity; if you follow these directives, "you will do well" (15:29)—not "you will be saved." Grace is indeed freedom from the requirements of the

Law in terms of salvation, but grace does not declare moral standards wrong or even inferior. As Timothy Keller notes, "Luther so persistently expounded—'We are saved by faith alone, but not by faith which is alone.' That is, we are saved, not by anything we do, but by grace. Yet if we have truly understood and believed the gospel, it will *change* what we do and how we live."[33] Not the least of those changes will be an increasing hatred of idols and a deepening love for others.

— 15:30-35 —

In Greek, the expression translated as "sent away" (15:30; *apolyō* [630]) doesn't carry the same connotation of rejection as in English; here, it means "commissioned" or "sent with authority and blessing." The council sent the delegation to report the council's resolution to the affected churches. The church in Syrian Antioch was the hub of Christian communication and activity, and when they heard the letter, they rejoiced. Notably, they received the "burdens" with no less enthusiasm than the affirmation of grace; indeed, they considered it "encouragement" (15:31). Judas and Silas, sent as attesting witnesses to the authenticity of the letter and the unanimity of the council, preached messages that "encouraged" (*parakaleō* [3870]) and "strengthened" (*epistērizō* [1991]) the congregation (15:32). As for encouragement, the Lord used the related term "Helper" (*paraklētos* [3875]) to describe the Holy Spirit in His ministry of training, encouraging, correcting, comforting, cheering, and challenging believers (John 14:16, 26; 15:26; 16:7; see 1 Jn. 2:1). And Luke uses *epistērizō* several times to describe the apostles' work of strengthening both their converts and the churches they planted (Acts 14:22; 15:32, 41; 18:23).

After reading the letter in Antioch, the delegation was sent to the other churches in Syria and Cilicia, to whom the communiqué had been addressed (15:33).[34] Acts 15:35 is another of Luke's summary verses, in this case telling us that Paul and Barnabas returned to minister in Antioch after completing their task as emissaries. The Greek term translated "stayed" (*diatribō* [1304]) is a colorful expression meaning "to rub through." The idea is that someone remains in one place long enough to leave a mark or make an impression. More than simply describing sticking around, the word implies activity.

Paul and Barnabas continued their ministry of "teaching" and "preaching." The latter term is *euangelizō* [2097], "to announce good news" or in the Christian context, "to preach the gospel." They didn't do this alone; "many others" worked alongside them.

APPLICATION: ACTS 15:13-35

Liberty and Love

When the two opposing factions met in Jerusalem to discuss the issue of circumcision, make no mistake: Grace was on trial. The issue of circumcision merely stood as a symbol of obedience to the Law; the procedure itself produced an outward sign of an inner commitment to obey God. The proponents of circumcision asked a reasonable question: "Why not insist that Gentiles commit to obedience?" Luke calls them believers, so undoubtedly they understood the doctrine of grace. Nevertheless, they succumbed to a reasonable fear. Grace, if it is genuine, leaves open the possibility for abuse. Liberty from the demands of the Law can devolve into a license to sin. What's to keep people from becoming less moral instead of developing a stronger ethical conscience?

The letter written by the council to address this question of what God expects of Christians under the new covenant applied three principles concerning grace.

First, *legalism results in an emphasis on works*. The council recognized that any addition to grace, regardless of how small or seemingly insignificant, not only pollutes the gospel but also opens the door to the same kind of legalism that characterized the Pharisees in the temple. We see this today in denominations that insist, "Unless you are baptized, you cannot be saved" (cf. 15:1). This one slight stipulation in addition to simple belief leads to an obsessive focus on external behavior, such that the entire body becomes defined by its dos and don'ts.

A focus on the Law invariably leads to guilt. Once guilt has accomplished its purpose in driving the individual to repentance of sin and faith in Christ, it has served its purpose. At that point, another dynamic takes over. The Holy Spirit begins a process of transformation. Whereas legalism thrives on guilt and creates fear and hopelessness in the individual, grace thrives on love, which drives out fear and inspires hope — a confident expectation of future victory over sin and death.

Second, *license results in an emphasis on self*. License is the attitude that says, "Because of grace, I can do as I please without consequences." An attitude of license reveals the true object of one's love. People who truly understand the meaning of grace, however, cannot help but love the God who saved them (Luke 7:41-47). People who see grace as a license to sin merely reveal their deep love for sin rather than for God and neighbor. As the Lord stated, "No servant can serve two masters; for either he will hate the one and love the other, or else he will be devoted to one and despise the other. You cannot serve God and wealth" (Luke 16:13). The same is true of sin.

The impact of license is offense, not only against God, but against others as well. The inevitable result of license is division. Interpersonal wounds. Relationships that cannot be repaired until the person guilty of license repents of sin and seeks grace from his or her peers.

Third, *grace results in an emphasis on Christ*. If license reveals a love for sin and self, a true understanding of grace leads to ever-increasing love for the Lord and an ever-deepening commitment to His ways. The inevitable impact of grace is love for others. Fortunately, grace does not leave us alone to love and obey out of our own strength. The grace of God carries us beyond the moment of salvation to equip us for supernatural love and obedience. We bear the "burden" of restricting our own freedom for the sake of Christ and others, but we do not bear it without His Holy Spirit.

When Co-Workers Clash
ACTS 15:36-41

NASB

36 After some days Paul said to Barnabas, "Let us return and visit the brethren in every city in which we proclaimed the word of the Lord, *and see* how they are." 37 Barnabas wanted to take John, called Mark, along with them also. 38 But Paul kept insisting that they should not take him along who had deserted them ªin Pamphylia and had not gone with them to the work. 39 And there occurred such a sharp disagreement that they separated from one another, and Barnabas took Mark with him and sailed away to Cyprus. 40 But Paul chose Silas and left, being committed by the brethren to the grace of the Lord. 41 And he was traveling through Syria and Cilicia, strengthening the churches.

15:38 ªLit *from*

NLT

36 After some time Paul said to Barnabas, "Let's go back and visit each city where we previously preached the word of the Lord, to see how the new believers are doing." 37 Barnabas agreed and wanted to take along John Mark. 38 But Paul disagreed strongly, since John Mark had deserted them in Pamphylia and had not continued with them in their work. 39 Their disagreement was so sharp that they separated. Barnabas took John Mark with him and sailed for Cyprus. 40 Paul chose Silas, and as he left, the believers entrusted him to the Lord's gracious care. 41 Then he traveled throughout Syria and Cilicia, strengthening the churches there.

A disagreement is a collision, an ideological crash that occurs when two different personalities drive their agendas along the same issue from opposing directions. That's not to say that all disagreements occur because one person is wrong and the other right. Sometimes both parties of a conflict are correct yet cannot agree. Consequently, a resolution becomes especially difficult because both people see the issue correctly, just from different points of view.

The solution requires clear, objective, respectful, and patient communication and may result in compromise or an amicable separation. Yet, because we are fallen creatures, disagreements can be occasions for Christians to mistreat and hurt each other, even for pillars of the Christian faith such as Paul and Barnabas. Although there is evidence these two missionaries reconciled later, and the goals and methods of both were vindicated in church history, Luke indicates their clash was painful at the time.

— 15:36 —

This verse should be read in close connection with the one that comes before it. After their great victory at the Council at Jerusalem, and after proclaiming the triumph of grace throughout Syria and Cilicia, Paul and Barnabas returned to Antioch where they resumed their ministry of teaching and evangelism. These two men were more than partners in ministry; they had been close friends for many years, even before sharing the hardships of the first missionary journey. Barnabas became Paul's advocate during a time when no other Christian felt safe with the former persecutor. He determined him to be a true brother in the faith and then stood by him before the church leaders in Jerusalem (9:26-27). Because of Barnabas, the believers embraced Paul and even protected him from his former colleagues in the temple.

Threats and attempts on his life forced Paul to return to his childhood home in Tarsus, where he remained for nearly a decade. When Barnabas needed a partner to help organize and strengthen the church in Syrian Antioch, he traveled to Tarsus to recruit Paul, who may have been eager to engage in a broader ministry among the Gentiles after many years in Tarsus. Barnabas, the "Son of Encouragement," saw value in Paul, despite his earlier struggles, and engaged him in the difficult work of teaching and mentoring Gentiles (11:25-26). Because of Barnabas, at least in part, Paul came into his own as an apostle. Barnabas pulled Paul from obscurity to help him fulfill the word God had spoken earlier: "He is a chosen instrument of Mine, to bear My name before the Gentiles and kings and the sons of Israel" (9:15).

While the men ministered in Antioch, Paul suggested they follow up on their initial visit to check on the progress of the churches they had planted on the first journey.

— 15:37-38 —

When the time came to assemble their team, Barnabas suggested they add John Mark, his cousin (15:37; Col. 4:10), the same young man who joined the first journey as a "helper" (Acts 13:5) and then deserted Paul and Barnabas just when the going got tough. He had left the group soon after they landed in Perga (13:13), the historic pirate stronghold in Pamphylia, while the team prepared to cross the bandit-infested mountains into the unknown interior. The weather was oppressively hot and humid, such that some historians believe Paul contracted malaria there (cf. Gal. 4:13).

Having suffered even greater trials later—chased out of two towns (Acts 13:50; 14:5-6), stoned and left for dead in a third (14:19), worshiped as a god one day and condemned as a heretic the next (14:12-19), undoubtedly held up by robbers more than once—Paul knew more than ever that survival and success depended upon the solidarity of every member of the team (15:38). Returning to the churches of Lycaonia and Pisidia would have them facing the same hostile crowds they had narrowly escaped before. Maturity and stability were essential.

Paul and Barnabas considered the same question: Should a man who abandoned the mission at the first sign of trouble get a second chance? Unfortunately, they came to mutually exclusive answers on the issue. Whereas Paul said the stakes were too high to gamble on a former deserter, Barnabas believed in giving John Mark a second chance. After all, they were out on the road preaching a gospel of grace, calling people to repentance before the God of second chances. Paul himself was an example of someone who had failed twice before in his ministry to Jews; rather than bringing them to faith, he had incited them to murder (9:23-24, 29). Yet Barnabas sought Paul out to become his partner in Antioch.

Whereas Paul said the mission was too important to risk on undependable people, Barnabas said the mission was all about redeeming people after failure. Paul: "It's the mission!" Barnabas: "It's the people!" Both men had valid concerns, but their priorities and methods differed.

— 15:39-41 —

In Acts 15:37-38, the phrases "wanted to take" and "kept insisting" both use imperfect tense verbs, which indicates ongoing or repetitive action. Barnabas wanted to take John Mark and wouldn't let the issue go. Paul felt equally determined and refused to relent. Neither man would back down, which caused the argument to escalate to the point of "sharp disagreement" (*paroxysmos* [3948]). We derive our English word "paroxysm" from this Greek term, which the Septuagint uses in the context of God's wrath (Deut. 29:27) and "indignation" (Jer. 32:37). Classical Greek medical writers use the word to describe a sudden, violent spasm, such as a body-racking cough or an epileptic seizure. The air grew thick with passion as each man convulsed with fiery emotion in response to the other.

Both were right. Each could support his position with Bible verses. Neither behaved like the pillars of the church they had become. They had reached a complete impasse.

In the end, the two men formed independent teams and headed off in different directions. Barnabas took John Mark with him and "sailed away to Cyprus" (Acts 15:39). Either Barnabas departed for home, taking Mark with him, or he intended to follow the same itinerary as the first missionary journey. We don't know which for certain. Luke doesn't include anything more about Barnabas or his travels after this. Later, Paul wrote of Barnabas in positive, present-tense terms, suggesting that he continued to conduct a ministry well known enough for Paul to use him as an illustration with the Corinthian church (1 Cor. 9:6).

Paul chose Silas, whom he knew from the Jerusalem Council (Acts 15:40).[35] Silas was one of the "leading men among the brethren" in Jerusalem (15:22), a Hellenistic Jew before his conversion, and a Roman citizen like Paul (16:37). Luke states that Paul and Silas departed Antioch after they were "committed (*paradidōmi* [3860]) by the brethren to the grace of the Lord" (15:40). The term *paradidōmi* is the one used when Paul and Barnabas had been commissioned earlier (14:26). Though the inspired record remains silent on the point, we have no reason to assume the elders didn't do the same for Barnabas. Still, the parting of these two friends surely brought each man disappointment and caused their church untold heartache.

Paul wanted to follow up with the churches in Derbe, Lystra, Iconium, and Pisidian Antioch, especially after their scrape with the circumcision controversy. To get there, he traveled north through Syria and Cilicia to Tarsus, stopping to "strengthen" churches along the way

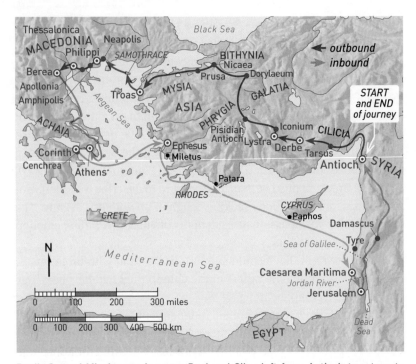

Paul's Second Missionary Journey. Paul and Silas left from Antioch to return to several of the cities where Paul had planted churches on his first missionary journey. They proceeded through Asia to Greece, all the way to Corinth. They returned by way of Ephesus and across the sea to Judea. Finally, they returned to Antioch.

(15:41). He then passed through the Taurus Mountains via the Cilician Gates, an engineered pass to Derbe on the high plateau of Anatolia.

Paul's team departed Antioch in the opposite direction from Barnabas for purely practical reasons; nevertheless, the image is compelling. As A. T. Robertson writes,

> No one can rightly blame Barnabas for giving his cousin John Mark a second chance nor Paul for fearing to risk him again. One's judgment may go with Paul, but one's heart goes with Barnabas. . . . Paul and Barnabas parted in anger and both in sorrow. Paul owed more to Barnabas than to any other man. Barnabas was leaving the greatest spirit of the time and of all times.[36]

That's the tragedy of an unreconciled argument or an unresolved conflict. Even when both sides are right, both sides lose! Paul, of course, put together a stellar team of missionaries and conducted a ministry so profound it changed the world. His letters comprise one third of the New Testament Scriptures. Barnabas, however, was right about John

Mark. The young man eventually won the trust of Peter (1 Pet. 5:13) and penned the Gospel bearing his name. Paul later added Mark to his evangelistic team (Col. 4:10) and even acknowledged him as "useful to me for service" (2 Tim. 4:11), a high compliment from the demanding apostle.

APPLICATION: ACTS 15:36-41

Relationship Rescue

My observation of the friendship shared by Paul and Barnabas and the dispute that ended their association suggests three guidelines for anyone hoping to avoid a similar fate.

First, *when involved in a dispute, pray for the ability to see both sides rather than just your own.* Good common sense says that seeing the other's point of view in a dispute will help tremendously. Unfortunately, in the heat of battle, common sense becomes a lot less common. What we want overshadows what we know to be right. Our rights have been violated and we want justice, or our viewpoint has been ignored and we want to be heard, or our standards have been compromised and we want excellence. When our own well-being is threatened, thinking about the welfare of another—especially our opponent—feels like self-destruction. Because our natural response is self-preservation, we need supernatural help to say, "I really want to see your point of view." Pray for this yourself and have others pray on your behalf.

Years after his partnership with Barnabas ended, Paul wrote to the church in Philippi, "Do nothing from selfishness or empty conceit, but with humility of mind regard one another as more important than yourselves; do not merely look out for your own personal interests, but also for the interests of others" (Phil. 2:3-4). I can't help but think Paul looked back on how he had responded to conflict and regretted his conduct.

Second, *when both sides of an issue have reasonable support, seek a wise compromise.* At one time in my own ministry, the word "compromise" bordered on heresy. As I grew older and wiser, I began to see more shades than pitch black and pristine white. I learned to distinguish between essential matters for which I would give my life and nonessentials that leave room for negotiation. Today, I see this passage very differently than I did as a younger man. As I examine the issues involved in the dispute between Paul and Barnabas, I don't see any doctrinal points at stake. Paul and Barnabas could have found a reasonable compromise, or even decided to part ways without a hint of bitterness or hard feelings, but neither would relent.

Third, *if a conflict persists, don't give up, stay at it.* We live in a fight-or-flight world. A broad range of choices, increased mobility, and declining value on relationships all have contributed to a society that says, "If you don't get your way, get out." Rather than doing the difficult work of seeing another's point of view, rather than bearing the discomfort of compromise, rather than seeking the greater good of all, we leave, hoping to find what we want somewhere else. Don't like the way things are done at church? Go to another. Don't like how your marriage turned out? Divorce and start over. Tragically, the choice to leave often occurs shortly before the solution God has prepared can present itself.

Stay at it. Don't give up on a resolution when the conflict goes on longer than you expected. Don't sacrifice the relationship when you've run out of options. That's when you need to trust the Lord to solve the problem on your behalf. Maintaining the relationship through the difficulty then becomes a matter of faith. If you stay at it and trust Him to accomplish what you cannot, He will be faithful. Even if the other party makes reconciliation impossible, God will honor your faithfulness.

Having said all that, I admit that times will come when a conflict simply refuses to be resolved, when no possible solution can be found and agreed upon. On such rare occasions, the best response is an amicable parting of ways.

What Opens When Doors Close?
ACTS 16:1-10

NASB

¹Paul came also to Derbe and to Lystra. And a disciple was there, named Timothy, the son of a Jewish woman who was a believer, but his father was a Greek, ²and he was well spoken of by the brethren who were in Lystra and Iconium. ³Paul wanted this man to ᵃgo with him;

NLT

¹Paul went first to Derbe and then to Lystra, where there was a young disciple named Timothy. His mother was a Jewish believer, but his father was a Greek. ²Timothy was well thought of by the believers* in Lystra and Iconium, ³so Paul wanted him to join them on their journey. In

and he took him and circumcised him because of the Jews who were in those parts, for they all knew that his father was a Greek. ⁴Now while they were passing through the cities, they were delivering the decrees which had been decided upon by the apostles and elders who were in Jerusalem, for them to observe. ⁵So the churches were being strengthened ᵃin the faith, and were increasing in number daily.

⁶They passed through the ᵃPhrygian and Galatian region, having been forbidden by the Holy Spirit to speak the word in ᵇAsia; ⁷and after they came to Mysia, they were trying to go into Bithynia, and the Spirit of Jesus did not permit them; ⁸and passing by Mysia, they came down to Troas. ⁹A vision appeared to Paul in the night: a man of Macedonia was standing and appealing to him, and saying, "Come over to Macedonia and help us." ¹⁰When he had seen the vision, immediately we sought to ᵃgo into Macedonia, concluding that God had called us to preach the gospel to them.

16:3 ᵃLit *go out*   16:5 ᵃOr *in faith*   16:6 ᵃOr *Phrygia and the Galatian region*   ᵇI.e. west coast province of Asia Minor   16:10 ᵃLit *go out*

deference to the Jews of the area, he arranged for Timothy to be circumcised before they left, for everyone knew that his father was a Greek. ⁴Then they went from town to town, instructing the believers to follow the decisions made by the apostles and elders in Jerusalem. ⁵So the churches were strengthened in their faith and grew larger every day.

⁶Next Paul and Silas traveled through the area of Phrygia and Galatia, because the Holy Spirit had prevented them from preaching the word in the province of Asia at that time. ⁷Then coming to the borders of Mysia, they headed north for the province of Bithynia,* but again the Spirit of Jesus did not allow them to go there. ⁸So instead, they went on through Mysia to the seaport of Troas.

⁹That night Paul had a vision: A man from Macedonia in northern Greece was standing there, pleading with him, "Come over to Macedonia and help us!" ¹⁰So we* decided to leave for Macedonia at once, having concluded that God was calling us to preach the Good News there.

16:2 Greek *brothers;* also in 16:40.
16:6-7 *Phrygia, Galatia, Asia, Mysia,* and *Bithynia* were all districts in what is now Turkey.
16:10 Luke, the writer of this book, here joined Paul and accompanied him on his journey.

It's hard to imagine how a closed door can be a gift from God. I'm not referring to personal tragedy, such as bankruptcy, divorce, the death of a loved one, terminal illness, or some other form of evil. God will use those events in your favor if you belong to Him (Rom. 8:28), but that's not what I mean by a "closed door." God *never* causes evil. He does, however, open and close opportunities to accomplish His purpose in individual lives and in the grand scheme of history. Jesus describes Himself as "He who is holy, who is true, who has the key of David, who opens and no one will shut, and who shuts and no one opens" (Rev. 3:7). Because closed opportunities keep us from achieving what we desire, the Lord's activity can feel like a curse. Life appears barren, wasted, hopeless. Emotionally, we feel set aside, forsaken, overlooked, even abused. Even so, a closed door can be a wonderful expression of God's love.

The first part of Paul's second missionary journey is a story of open doors. He had spent the last several months telling churches in Samaria, Phoenicia, and Syria about how the Lord had "opened a door of faith to the Gentiles" (Acts 14:27; cf. 15:3) on his first journey. The Council at Jerusalem had affirmed his ministry and given him written confirmation of the gospel of grace. His home church in Syrian Antioch enthusiastically commissioned him for another journey. The first leg of his voyage took him through the familiar territory of Syria and Cilicia, where people knew him and welcomed his teaching. After passing through the Taurus Mountains, he enjoyed reconnecting with the churches that he and Barnabas had previously planted in Derbe, Lystra, and Iconium. He even found a promising young student, Timothy, who was eager to learn about ministry. Then doors slammed shut.

Of all the challenges Paul had overcome—robbers, enemies, illness, rejection, stoning, idolatry—the hardship of closed doors would be his greatest to date.

— 16:1–3 —

Paul's route took him to familiar territory. He had been to Derbe and Lystra with Barnabas and their team earlier; he had suffered especially in Lystra when a posse of angry Jews from Iconium arrived, whipped up a mob, stoned him in the streets, dragged him to the edge of town, and left him for dead (14:19). Even so, Paul and Barnabas returned to encourage the stunned believers.

At this point, Luke introduces a man who would become Paul's student in ministry. Paul the apostle had and would continue to recruit and train a number of men, but he regarded Timothy as a son (1 Tim. 1:2). The young man may have come to faith through the ministry of Paul and Barnabas—if not, then certainly as a result of the churches they planted. He may have witnessed the aftermath of Paul's stoning; if not, he had certainly heard the stories. Luke states that Timothy had a Greek father (Acts 16:1), who is never mentioned elsewhere, perhaps because he had died by this time. As a Roman colony, Lystra had a significant population of retired soldiers. The city also served as a garrison for active troops who defended Galatia from the surrounding mountain tribes. Therefore, it is reasonable to surmise that Timothy's father had served in the Roman army as a soldier, married a Jewish woman, and taken up permanent residence in Lystra before he died.

Jewish blood ran through Timothy's veins, thanks to his mother, but he didn't receive a Hebrew upbringing in the synagogue. He received biblical and theological training from infancy (2 Tim. 3:14-15), but he never became a true "son of the covenant" through circumcision, most likely because his father objected to the rite. Paul mentions Timothy's godly upbringing by his mother, Eunice, and his grandmother Lois, whose influence helped prepare the young man for rapid spiritual growth after hearing the gospel (2 Tim. 1:5). By the time Paul and Silas arrived, Timothy had earned a solid reputation among the churches in Lystra and Iconium (Acts 16:2).

When Paul recruited Timothy for ministry, he circumcised the young man (16:3). This was not in obedience to the Law, and not just because Timothy was Jewish, but probably to allow him greater access to the synagogues that Paul and Silas planned to visit in the near future.

— 16:4-5 —

Luke's summary statement describes Paul's ministry in the region, both before and after picking up Timothy, which occurred just after his visit to Derbe. He read the official proclamation of the apostles and elders in Jerusalem, thus immediately shutting down any would-be teachers of the circumcision group (16:4). The churches had received authentic doctrine from the men who knew Jesus from the beginning and had been trained by Him. Because of the letter and through Paul's teaching, the churches were "strengthened" (16:5). A good mental image for the term *stepeoō* [4732] would be a preadolescent boy filling out as muscle replaces baby fat. As the churches grew stronger, they also grew larger.

Luke's repeated use of the imperfect tense—"were passing," "were delivering," "were being strengthened," "were increasing"—not only signals a summary passage, but the tense also implies that the effects of Paul's ministry continued after he moved on. Paul's team, which now included Timothy, solidified Christianity in southern Galatia and Phrygia as they moved east to west toward promising new territory in the Roman province of Asia.

Continuing into Asia made perfect sense. In 6 BC, the Romans had established a string of colonies across present-day Turkey and linked them with an impressive highway system. From Iconium and Pisidian Antioch, Paul could follow the Via Sebaste to Comama, where he could then follow the "Common Highway" all the way to Ephesus. These roads were broad (nearly 12 feet wide) and heavily traveled, making them relatively safe.[37] Most important, however, this gave them the best access to the greatest number of people in the interior of the land.

The Lord had other plans for Paul and Silas, however. Asia would have to wait.

— 16:6-8 —

Paul's team journeyed farther north in Phrygia and Galatia because the Lord had blocked their progress west into Asia. More closed doors. To the north, they kept attempting to enter Bithynia on the south shore of the Black Sea, but again the Lord barred their entry, keeping them south of Bithynia and north of Asia as they turned to the west, passing along the northern part of Mysia. Luke's use of verb tenses implies consistent, repeated attempts to enter Bithynia; they tried and tried until their westward progress ended. Eventually, they simply ran out of land at the coastal city of Troas.

Luke describes their experience as "forbidden by the Holy Spirit" when trying to enter Asia (16:6), and about turning north to Bithynia, he writes that "the Spirit of Jesus did not permit them" (16:7). "Forbidden" comes from a Greek term (kōlyō [2967]) that means "clipped," "snipped," or "cut off." Figuratively, it's a picturesque term meaning, "to prevent or hinder." Luke doesn't explain how the men perceived God's resistance. During the period of Acts, they could have heard audible instructions, but Luke doesn't indicate this. Perhaps instead certain circumstances—under God's sovereign control—kept Paul and Silas out of the forbidden areas. Rather than write off their unfortunate situations as coincidental, they recognized the sovereign hand of Christ guiding them where He wanted.

It takes a spirit sensitive to the Lord's leading to maintain this kind of perspective. We naturally tend to wonder what we did wrong or, if we know we did nothing wrong, play the victim. We compare ourselves to others for whom doors seem to open left and right. We try harder to go where the Lord has forbidden, or we give up and go home after a few doors slam shut. Paul and Silas did none of that. They persisted, never doubting their call. Simply stated, they submitted to the sovereign direction of God. They understood that the Lord has every right to open and close opportunities, to give and to take away. Through it all, however, they didn't doubt the Lord's goodness or kindness.

— 16:9-10 —

Troas was not a remarkable city, other than for its function as the gateway to Asia from Macedonia. Paul, Silas, and their team ended up there with nowhere else to go. From Phrygia, they simply followed the only course open to them, which carried them north of Asia, south of Bithynia, and westward until the Aegean Sea stopped them. Sometime after arriving—Luke doesn't state whether it took a matter of days, weeks, or months—Paul received a vision in his dreams, which he immediately recognized as divine in origin (16:9). In this vision, a man that Paul recognized as Macedonian was "appealing to" (*parakaleō* [3870]) him to "help us" (*boētheō* [997]). Suddenly, the past several weeks made sense. Paul had considered Asia the next logical choice for expansion of the gospel, but God had His heart set on Europe. The Lord would eventually bring Asia into the kingdom, but His timing differed from Paul's.

When you're following the plan of God, dead ends are never mistakes. The Lord maneuvered Paul and Silas to where He wanted them at a specific time. While in Troas, Paul met Luke, who seems to have lived in Philippi. This is the first of three "we" passages in which the writer switches from third-person pronouns to the first person. In other words, this is where Luke himself becomes a part of the story because he joins the team.

As we will discover soon, the city was a large Roman colony, but it didn't have a synagogue. Either the city leaders didn't want a Jewish house of prayer or, more likely, the population didn't include ten Jewish men, the minimum requirement to establish one. Paul preferred to preach in the local synagogue of a new city, not only for theological reasons, but also to find a way to break the ice with the Gentiles. Paul and Barnabas had preached to pagans in the marketplace without the benefit of a synagogue before, and the results could not have been worse. Their experience in Lystra demonstrated the clear benefits of having a contact on the inside of a community. By God's design, Luke fit the bill.

All the closed doors now made sense. The period of vague confusion suddenly came into focus to show that the Lord had them on a clear trajectory. The long weeks of frustrated ministry had prepared Paul, Silas, Timothy, and the others for new marching orders. Without hesitation, they set out for Macedonia (16:10).

APPLICATION: ACTS 16:1-10

Door Stops

Closed doors don't feel nearly so frustrating with the right perspective. When you trust in God's plan, knowing He's in control and always does what is right, anxiety melts into serene confidence, irritation yields to surrender, fear gives way to trust. Paul's closed-door experience offers some helpful truths to keep in mind when we have reached a dead end.

Number one: *Before the Lord can turn us, He often has to stop us.* Some of us are rolling along faster than ever in our lives. But you know how it is when you get stopped, when you find yourself at a dead end. Every door is shut. You try north; it doesn't open. South? Not any better. East? West? Equally closed off. You're stuck. He stopped you. That's the time to pause rather than panic. Find time to be alone so you can pay attention to what's going on within you and around you. God wants you to see something before moving on; there's some perspective you need or crucial information you lack.

Number two: *God never closes a door without a plan to open another.* That sounds like a platitude designed to inspire optimism, but there's more to this truth than saying "Everything will work out." This is a bold affirmation of God's sovereignty. No Christian has a right to feel hopeless. Quite the contrary: There's no such thing as a hopeless case for a Christian. Where the nonbeliever worries that a mistake or wrong turn has led to a dead end, the child of God knows that even his or her dead ends are part of God's design. In Paul's case, the Lord used circumstances to guide the apostle and his team, directing them like water down a chute, to Troas. At the end of this blind alley, they had little choice but to wait on the Lord for direction. Rather than despairing, they waited for direction, confident in their mission.

When facing a similar situation, resist the urge to fight your way out of the dead end. Instead, pull back and wait. Rather than search for escape, seek the Lord's direction.

Number three: *Doors open and close according to God's timing, which is perfect.* It appears that the Lord not only closed the door to Asia and opened the door to Europe, but He also arranged the timing so Paul could meet Dr. Luke, who would prove helpful in Philippi. If he was, indeed, a resident of that city, his personal contacts would have been invaluable in the absence of a synagogue. We tend to think of success in terms of destination and progress, but wise people have learned that it's also about timing. Paul waited on the Lord and didn't press on until he had clear direction. He understood that waiting is sometimes the best way to make progress.

A Foothold in Europe
ACTS 16:11-40

NASB

[11] So putting out to sea from Troas, we ran a straight course to Samothrace, and on the day following to Neapolis; [12] and from there to Philippi, which is a leading city of the district of Macedonia, a *Roman* colony; and we were staying in this city for some days. [13] And on the Sabbath day we went outside the gate to a riverside, where we were supposing that there would be a place of prayer; and we sat down and began speaking to the women who had assembled.

[14] A woman named Lydia, from the city of Thyatira, a seller of purple fabrics, a worshiper of God, was listening; [a]and the Lord opened her heart to respond to the things spoken by Paul. [15] And when she and her household had been baptized, she urged us, saying, "If you have judged me to be faithful to the Lord, come into my house and stay." And she prevailed upon us.

[16] It happened that as we were going to the place of prayer, a slave-girl having a spirit of divination met us, who was bringing her masters much profit by fortune-telling. [17] Following after Paul and us, she kept crying out, saying, "These men are bond-servants of the Most High God, who are proclaiming to you [a]the way of salvation." [18] She continued doing this for many days. But Paul was greatly annoyed, and turned and said to the spirit, "I command you in

NLT

[11] We boarded a boat at Troas and sailed straight across to the island of Samothrace, and the next day we landed at Neapolis. [12] From there we reached Philippi, a major city of that district of Macedonia and a Roman colony. And we stayed there several days.

[13] On the Sabbath we went a little way outside the city to a riverbank, where we thought people would be meeting for prayer, and we sat down to speak with some women who had gathered there. [14] One of them was Lydia from Thyatira, a merchant of expensive purple cloth, who worshiped God. As she listened to us, the Lord opened her heart, and she accepted what Paul was saying. [15] She and her household were baptized, and she asked us to be her guests. "If you agree that I am a true believer in the Lord," she said, "come and stay at my home." And she urged us until we agreed.

[16] One day as we were going down to the place of prayer, we met a slave girl who had a spirit that enabled her to tell the future. She earned a lot of money for her masters by telling fortunes. [17] She followed Paul and the rest of us, shouting, "These men are servants of the Most High God, and they have come to tell you how to be saved."

[18] This went on day after day until Paul got so exasperated that he

the name of Jesus Christ to come out of her!" And it came out at that very ᵃmoment.

¹⁹But when her masters saw that their hope of profit was ᵃgone, they seized Paul and Silas and dragged them into the market place before the authorities, ²⁰and when they had brought them to the chief magistrates, they said, "These men are throwing our city into confusion, being Jews, ²¹and are proclaiming customs which it is not lawful for us to accept or to observe, being Romans."

²²The crowd rose up together against them, and the chief magistrates tore their ᵃrobes off them and proceeded to order ᵇ*them* to be beaten with rods. ²³When they had struck them with many blows, they threw them into prison, commanding the jailer to guard them securely; ²⁴ᵃand he, having received such a command, threw them into the inner prison and fastened their feet in the ᵇstocks.

²⁵But about midnight Paul and Silas were praying and singing hymns of praise to God, and the prisoners were listening to them; ²⁶and suddenly there came a great earthquake, so that the foundations of the prison house were shaken; and immediately all the doors were opened and everyone's chains were unfastened. ²⁷When the jailer awoke and saw the prison doors opened, he drew his sword and was about to kill himself, supposing that the prisoners had escaped. ²⁸But Paul cried out with a loud voice, saying, "Do not harm yourself, for we are all here!" ²⁹And he called for lights and rushed in, and trembling with fear he fell down before Paul and Silas, ³⁰and after he brought them out, he said, "Sirs, what must I do to be saved?" ³¹They said, "Believe in the Lord Jesus, and you will be saved, you and your household." ³²And they spoke the word of ᵃthe Lord to him together

turned and said to the demon within her, "I command you in the name of Jesus Christ to come out of her." And instantly it left her.

¹⁹Her masters' hopes of wealth were now shattered, so they grabbed Paul and Silas and dragged them before the authorities at the marketplace. ²⁰"The whole city is in an uproar because of these Jews!" they shouted to the city officials. ²¹"They are teaching customs that are illegal for us Romans to practice."

²²A mob quickly formed against Paul and Silas, and the city officials ordered them stripped and beaten with wooden rods. ²³They were severely beaten, and then they were thrown into prison. The jailer was ordered to make sure they didn't escape. ²⁴So the jailer put them into the inner dungeon and clamped their feet in the stocks.

²⁵Around midnight Paul and Silas were praying and singing hymns to God, and the other prisoners were listening. ²⁶Suddenly, there was a massive earthquake, and the prison was shaken to its foundations. All the doors immediately flew open, and the chains of every prisoner fell off! ²⁷The jailer woke up to see the prison doors wide open. He assumed the prisoners had escaped, so he drew his sword to kill himself. ²⁸But Paul shouted to him, "Stop! Don't kill yourself! We are all here!"

²⁹The jailer called for lights and ran to the dungeon and fell down trembling before Paul and Silas. ³⁰Then he brought them out and asked, "Sirs, what must I do to be saved?"

³¹They replied, "Believe in the Lord Jesus and you will be saved, along with everyone in your household." ³²And they shared the word of the Lord with him and with all who

with all who were in his house. ³³And he took them that *very* hour of the night and washed their wounds, and immediately he was baptized, he and all his *household*. ³⁴And he brought them into his house and set ªfood before them, and rejoiced ᵇgreatly, having believed in God with his whole household.

³⁵Now when day came, the chief magistrates sent their policemen, saying, "Release those men." ³⁶And the jailer reported these words to Paul, *saying*, "The chief magistrates have sent to release you. Therefore come out now and go in peace." ³⁷But Paul said to them, "They have beaten us in public without trial, men who are Romans, and have thrown us into prison; and now are they sending us away secretly? No indeed! But let them come themselves and bring us out." ³⁸The policemen reported these words to the chief magistrates. They were afraid when they heard that they were Romans, ³⁹and they came and appealed to them, and when they had brought them out, they kept begging them to leave the city. ⁴⁰They went out of the prison and entered *the house of* Lydia, and when they saw the brethren, they ªencouraged them and departed.

16:14 ªLit *whose heart the Lord opened*
16:17 ªLit *a way* 16:18 ªLit *hour* 16:19 ªLit *gone out* 16:22 ªOr *outer garments* ᵇLit *to beat with rods* 16:24 ªLit *who* ᵇLit *wood* 16:32 ªTwo early mss read *God* 16:34 ªLit *a table* ᵇOr *greatly with his whole household, having believed in God* 16:40 ªOr *exhorted*

lived in his household. ³³Even at that hour of the night, the jailer cared for them and washed their wounds. Then he and everyone in his household were immediately baptized. ³⁴He brought them into his house and set a meal before them, and he and his entire household rejoiced because they all believed in God.

³⁵The next morning the city officials sent the police to tell the jailer, "Let those men go!" ³⁶So the jailer told Paul, "The city officials have said you and Silas are free to leave. Go in peace."

³⁷But Paul replied, "They have publicly beaten us without a trial and put us in prison—and we are Roman citizens. So now they want us to leave secretly? Certainly not! Let them come themselves to release us!"

³⁸When the police reported this, the city officials were alarmed to learn that Paul and Silas were Roman citizens. ³⁹So they came to the jail and apologized to them. Then they brought them out and begged them to leave the city. ⁴⁰When Paul and Silas left the prison, they returned to the home of Lydia. There they met with the believers and encouraged them once more. Then they left town.

An old Celtic benediction offers this delightful blessing: "And may the wind always be at your back." In the days of wind-powered travel, seafarers could hope for no greater fortune than a strong breeze filling their sails. Whatever else might go wrong, a stiff tailwind always felt like divine favor. Anyone who loves sailing can appreciate the metaphor. There's nothing more exhilarating than to have the full sail set and to have a strong, prevailing wind pushing the ship with ease. In smooth surf, the bow slips through the water without noise or resistance. The hearts of Paul and his men must have pounded with anticipation. Pardon the mixed metaphor, but having the wind at your back is the exact opposite of having to stop at closed doors.

So Paul, Silas, Timothy, Luke, and other unnamed helpers boarded a ship in Troas bound for Neapolis, the principal seaport serving Philippi, an important city in Macedonia (16:10-12). Imagine their feeling after several weeks of halting, frustrating, confusing attempts at progress. Luke describes their voyage as "a straight course" (16:11), meaning the winds favored their route, neither blowing them off course nor requiring the crew to tack against a headwind. They sailed, as it were, with the wind at their backs. Ahead of them: Europe. Uncharted territory brimming with potential. But even with fresh momentum, establishing a church in Europe would require tenacity and sacrifice in the face of new difficulties.

— 16:11-12 —

Paul's entourage departed Troas and ran "a straight course" (16:11) to Neapolis via the island of Samothrace. Draw a line on a map from Troas to Neapolis, and you will see that Samothrace is out of the way. The phrase "straight course" was a nautical expression meaning the ship sailed to its planned destination without having to tack (chart a zigzag course) against the wind. Luke states that the trip took two days, as opposed to five for the return trip (cf. 20:6). Ships didn't sail at night, so the captain dropped anchor off Samothrace.

Though Neapolis means "new city," it was founded more than five hundred years before Paul's visit, which occurred sometime around AD 50. Today, the modern city of Kavalla covers the site. This beautiful port served Philippi, which lay just 10 miles northwest, just over a small range of mountains surrounding the harbor.[38] After disembarking in Neapolis, the team went straightaway to Philippi, which Luke calls "a leading city of the district of Macedonia, a Roman colony" (16:12).

Philippi had been a small village, but was transformed into a military stronghold around 357 BC by Philip II of Macedon (the father of Alexander the Great), who used it to control nearby gold mines. The later Romans made it a colony, meaning it modeled the culture and economy of Rome in an effort to attract Roman citizens and military veterans. The seat of Roman government lay in Amphipolis, a little more than 35 miles southwest, so Philippi became known as a chief city because of its economy and influence.[39] It commanded a strategic location for both land and sea trade. In addition to robust agriculture and gold-mining industries, the city was the site of a famous school of medicine.[40]

— 16:13 —

In the absence of a synagogue, Jews typically gathered informally for teaching and prayer on the Sabbath. Philippi didn't have a synagogue, either because of hostility toward Jews[41] or because very few Jewish men lived in the area. Regardless, the team went outside the city gate to a spot on the riverbank customarily used as "a place of prayer," an informal synagogue.

"We were supposing" reflects the verb *nomizō* [3543] and gives the impression that Paul and his men made an educated guess about the location, as though they followed an assumption. *Nomizō* basically means "to think," "to believe," or "to consider" and can be more or less definite, but it's frequently used in the sense of "common knowledge." For example, it's common knowledge that movie theaters serve popcorn. It's not a rule, but everyone knows. In the same way, everyone knew where Jews in Philippi gathered for prayer each Sabbath. Of course, "everyone" included Luke, who knew the city well.

The men joined the gathering and began speaking to "the women who had assembled," a phrase implying the general absence of men. They would have welcomed a rabbi of Paul's stature; Timothy must have seen glimpses of his mother reflected on each face in the meeting, devout Jewish women without believing husbands.

— 16:14-15 —

It's possible that the people of Philippi knew this prominent woman not by her given name, but by a nickname, Lydia, because she came from Thyatira, a city founded by the Lydian kingdom in the region still known as Lydia. If so, she was using the designation to her advantage as a businesswoman importing the trade specialty of her hometown: purple cloth. Interestingly, Thyatira lies in the heart of the Roman province of Asia. The Lydian kingdom at its height covered the very territory Paul couldn't enter.

A hint from the narrative, "and her household" (16:15), suggests that Lydia was either single or widowed yet was wealthy in Philippi. A little history concerning her trade also shows her to be a brilliant and shrewd businesswoman. Romans incorporated purple cloth into clothing and tapestries to signify rank, so the demand for her product gave her a brisk business. Originally, the dye necessary to create the cloth came from Tyre in Phoenicia, where small amounts of murex dye were pains-takingly extracted from great quantities of mollusks.[42] The resulting cloth was worth its weight in gold. Lydia imported either the dye or the cloth and then sold it for much less than her Phoenician competitors.

Luke describes her as "a worshiper of God" (16:14), a common des-ignation for a Gentile who had formally embraced Judaism. She and her household came to faith in Christ as a result of Paul's teaching, and they were baptized. Luke gives God the credit for opening her heart to respond to the gospel. Her response included an outpouring of generosity, and she insisted she host Paul and his entourage. The word translated "urged" (*parakaleō* [3870]) is a potent term in its own right, meaning "to exhort, appeal, or encourage." To this Luke adds "prevailed" (*parabiazomai* [3849]), an almost violent Greek word that suggests the use of force. Factor in her rationale—"If you have judged me to be faithful to the Lord" (16:15)—and one can see why Lydia had become a rich merchant. No one said no to Lydia!

— 16:16-18 —

Paul and his companions continued to minister in Philippi, frequenting the "place of prayer" by the river outside the gates of the city (16:13). For whatever reason, a demon-possessed slave girl (*paidiskē* [3814]) began to endorse Paul's ministry. The term *paidiskē* refers to a maid or a slave girl, but her masters made lucrative use of her as a fortune-teller (16:16).

Luke describes the source of her "fortune-telling" (*manteuomai* [3132]) ability as a "spirit of divination" (*pneuma* [4151] of *pythōn* [4436]), referring to Python, the mythical serpent or dragon that guarded the oracle of Delphi, the renowned temple of priestesses who supposedly uttered prophecy while under a trance. The word eventually grew to include anyone thought to have a supernatural ability to see the future. Pagan generals throughout history have relied heavily on the services of shamans and fortune-tellers to indicate the best time for battle and to inspire their troops with favorable predictions. Someone with her abilities would have had a giant client base among the superstitious Romans in Philippi.

Whatever the designation, the text makes it clear that she was pos-sessed by a demon. Perhaps as a means of improving business, the spirit resorted to flattery (cf. Luke 4:34; 8:28), endorsing the men as prophets. Confronted by a rival the demon could not defeat, it cleverly exalted the girl's position by having her assume the role of community advisor: "I, your trusted seer, give my approval to these men." The demon probably hoped to secure enough goodwill to avoid a confrontation and maybe ride the coattails of Christianity: "They offer a way of salvation; I offer a way of salvation; we're together in the salvation business."

After several days of this, Paul reached the end of his tether. Unintimidated, he took control of the situation. Speaking to the demon, not the girl, he commanded the spirit to leave (Acts 16:18). He didn't rely upon his own authority; he commanded the demon "in the name of Jesus Christ," which meant "by the *authority* of Jesus Christ." Immediately, the demon released control of the girl and left, taking with it the ability to tell fortunes—and make money. Naturally, her masters deeply resented the loss of income (16:19). They obviously didn't see possession by an evil spirit as a drawback, so long as it brought money into the household.

— 16:19-24 —

In most ancient cities, the marketplace (*agora* [58]) was a public space not unlike a flea market. This large, open-air square, bounded by some permanent retail buildings and shelters, gave any paying vendor the opportunity to display his or her wares. The market also became the natural place to conduct public affairs and resolve disputes. In a Roman colony, the marketplace usually included a "judgment seat" (*bēma* [968]), a raised stone platform from which government officials tried cases and issued proclamations.

The slave girl's masters apprehended Paul and Silas, dragged them before the city officials, and issued a charge they thought would stick. Clearly, they couldn't tell the truth: "These men commanded a spirit to leave and now we have to work for a living." Not only would that make her masters look petty and foolish, but it was hardly a crime. If the spirit were evil, Paul should be commended. If the spirit were beneficial, as the girl's masters would claim, their accusation violated their own beliefs concerning spirits and gods. In Greco-Roman religion, spirits often did the commanding, not the obeying. Magic and occult practices attempted to fend off or appease the spirits or otherwise manipulate them, but everybody knew these superstitious practices weren't always effective. In the end, only gods could command spirits with any degree of authority. A face-value complaint against Paul and Silas would have validated their ministry publicly while discrediting Roman religious beliefs.

Although Judaism was a legally tolerated religion, Romans generally resented Jews as antisocial and regarded their belief in one God as antagonistic to Roman values, using terms like "superstitious" and "impious" to describe their practices.[43] So, unable to tell the truth about their actual grievance, the slave girl's owners instead branded Paul and Silas as particularly radical Jews bent on undermining the moral fabric of Philippi (16:20-21). To close their case, they accused the men of "throwing our city into confusion" (*ektarassō* [1613]), a verb that refers to causing a riot, disturbance, agitation, or disorder. And this affected the bottom-line concern of any empire-loving Roman. They prided themselves on the order they brought to the lands they conquered, brutal as their methods were.

This, of course, was not only a false charge, but it was hypocritical. The slave girl's masters successfully turned the city officials and court spectators into a mob. Considering recent events in Rome, they had a remarkably easy time. In AD 49–50, Emperor Claudius issued an edict expelling all Jews from Rome (18:2), though we are not sure why. Some have suggested that the intrusion of Christianity among the Jewish community in Rome had been causing unrest among Jews, Christians, and God-fearing Gentiles who were converting to Christianity.[44] In any case, because Romans did not yet distinguish mainline Judaism from the sect of the Christians, Rome's negative attitudes toward Jews at the time would have added fuel to the fire.

Certainly, a judge could exercise wide latitude in deciding a case, but he had an obligation to seek justice, which the Romans prized as a virtue. In this case, the accused were not given an opportunity to dispute the charges, no witnesses were presented to substantiate the accusation, and no time was given for cross-examination. In fact, they never discovered that Paul and Silas were both Roman citizens—which would have changed everything.

Instead, the magistrates summarily ordered Paul and Silas to be stripped and beaten and thrown into prison (16:22-24). Their ordered punishment reveals intense anger and fear. Being beaten with rods, locked in the most secure part of the prison, and put in stocks was an extreme reaction, even by Roman standards. Obviously, Paul and Silas had become outlets for a growing anti-Semitism in Philippi. The order to guard them securely also betrays the town's paranoia.

— 16:25-28 —

By midnight, Paul and Silas were bloodied and bruised, their feet in stocks, chained to a wall in the "inner prison," the deepest part of the prison (16:24). This would have taken the wind out of most people's sails, but Paul and Silas prayed and sang praise songs to God.

Luke highlights the evangelistic opportunity of the circumstance. Paul and Silas took their beatings without revealing their Roman citizenship (cf. 22:25). They could have proclaimed their innocence to the other prisoners; instead, they held a worship service (16:25). They didn't curse God for the injustice or worry that He had abandoned them; they prayed and praised. The other prisoners witnessed everything and observed their conduct. Then, for their benefit, the Lord shook the prison down to its foundations and set everyone free (16:26). Not just Paul and Silas. Everyone. Paul, Silas, and the entire prison population could have escaped, which would have been a fitting revenge against the city of Philippi! Even so, the evangelists elected to remain in their cell and apparently influenced everyone else to stay as well. (So much for undermining Roman order!)

Then Paul had to stop the jailer from killing himself (16:27-28). The jailer knew that if the prisoners had escaped, an excruciating death waited for him after a hasty trial.

— 16:29-34 —

The jailer lit up his ruined jailhouse and asked two of his prisoners, "What must I do to be saved?" (16:29-30). What he meant by being "saved" (*sōzō* [4982]) is debatable. He may have gained at least some prior knowledge of Paul and Silas's message, enough to understand that his soul was in some kind of peril. Some expositors claim he meant "How can I be saved from having offended two powerful magicians?" or something similar, which probably is closer to the truth. Regardless, Paul and Silas gave him a concise answer. Not sufficient for someone utterly lacking in knowledge of God or His Son or the concepts of sin, heaven, hell, and atonement, but clear enough to let him know that he needed to hear about Jesus Christ.

The jailer addressed Paul and Silas using *kyrios* [2962], which often means "sir," a title of respect. But the word *Kyrios* is also used in reference to God in the Greek translation of the Old Testament and is a common title for Jesus Christ, indicating His absolute lordship. If the jailer recognized Paul and Silas as representatives of God, their answer turned his attention to the proper object of fear and respect: "Believe the Lord—the true *Kyrios*—Jesus."

Sometimes Luke compresses the events of days or even weeks into a short description. Subtle clues, such as the use of the imperfect tense, signal when he is summarizing or compressing a span of time. None of those clues appear in this case. The fact is, a *lot* happened in a few short hours! Their concise answer, "Believe in the Lord Jesus, and you will be saved, you and your household" (16:31), set in motion a remarkable series of events. Paul and Silas—still bloodied, bruised, and stinking of prison—preached to the man's household (16:32). After they spoke, the jailer washed and dressed their wounds. In response to his faith, and that of his household, Paul and Silas baptized the new believers (16:33). Then the entire group sat down to share a meal as brothers and sisters (16:34)!

— 16:35-39 —

Apparently the sun rose on a new day for the city officials. Luke doesn't explain the reason for their sudden change of heart, but they said, "Release those men" (16:35). They may have received more information. Lydia may have interceded for Paul and Silas. The officials may simply have decided a sound beating and night in jail would temper the missionaries' rabble-rousing. Who knows?

The Greek term translated "policemen" (16:38; *rhabdouchos* [4465]) literally means "stick men"—that is, men who wield clubs. These were likely the same men who beat Paul and Silas with rods at the trial. When they came with the order of release, Paul turned the situation into an opportunity to accomplish two objectives (16:37). First, he confronted his offenders. He could have left quietly. In fact, that's how many Christians respond to personal injustice, mistaking passivity for forgiveness. Instead, Paul chose to confront his offenders with their outrageous mistreatment and their flagrant violation of their own laws. By demanding that the policemen come and release him personally, he forced the men to acknowledge their offense. This also sent a clear message to the magistrates, forcing them to acknowledge their wrongdoing, at least to themselves.

As a second objective, Paul wanted to give himself and the church enough political clout in Philippi to discourage bullying. Philippi was a Roman colony, and the magistrates were agents of Roman law. When they heard they violated the rights and privileges of two Roman citizens, they rightly feared reprisal from Rome (16:38). They also worried that the continued presence of Paul and Silas in Philippi might spark a severe public backlash when news of their mistreatment spread (16:39). The conduct of the city magistrates was a political scandal they desperately wanted covered up. Paul let them off the hook by withholding his complaint to Rome, but not without first letting the magistrates know he was no pushover.

He may have intended a third objective. Without a doubt, Paul's show of strength cultivated respect among those in the city government. Moreover, he did forgive their offense, and gratitude tends to soften hard hearts. Perhaps recognizing their close call would make the magistrates more open to the gospel.

— 16:40 —

Luke caps off the event concisely. Paul and Silas's return to the house of Lydia to encourage the believers—who were no doubt gathered for prayer—recalls Peter's release from prison (12:10-17). Luke demonstrates again that Paul's ministry to the Gentiles was in no way inferior to Peter's ministry to the Jews.

APPLICATION: ACTS 16:11-40
Principles for Success

After a long period of frustration trying to penetrate Asia with the gospel while one door after another closed, Paul and his team finally found an opening in Europe. Without hesitation, the group set sail for Macedonia. Their groundbreaking ministry in a brand-new area among people of a very different mindset highlights three practical principles regarding ministry—or any worthwhile effort.

Principle #1: *Beginning any worthwhile endeavor requires flexibility* (16:11-15). If you are set in concrete with a list of hard-and-fast rules and regulations, you're laying the groundwork for failure. One of the beautiful things about the Spirit of God is that He keeps us flexible. Paul's vision featured a man of Macedonia calling for help. His first convert? A woman from Asia, the region he had not been able to enter. Imagine if Paul had focused only on Macedonian men! When he found the customary place where Jews gathered for prayer, he found a group of women. They became the focus of his ministry.

It's a sign of maturity to stay flexible. Do your best as a growing Christian to flex with the scene. The message never changes, but we have a vast variety of methods available to meet an endless number of opportunities. What works when witnessing to one person might alienate another. So be sensitive. Stay flexible.

Principle #2: *Every major breakthrough is met with a corresponding resistance* (16:16-18). When you are involved in a unique ministry or a new kind of endeavor, or if your faithful efforts yield a sudden breakthrough, the devil has a way of bringing a unique kind of resistance. And he will meet you halfway or better. You will try one strategy and he will come with a counterattack. You will attempt one approach and he will be ready with another. And the resistance always feels overwhelming compared to the joy of progress.

This is normal. Expect Satan's counterattack. It is a backhanded compliment from the enemy that what you have done is effective. When you learn to see the resistance of evil in those terms, perseverance becomes easier. The last thing you want to do at this point is give up. Until you throw in the towel, Satan hasn't won. In the now-famous words of Winston Churchill, who rallied his country to fight Nazi Germany, "This is the lesson: never give in, never give in, never, never, never—in nothing, great or small, large or petty—never give in except to convictions of honour and good sense. Never yield to force; never yield to the apparently overwhelming might of the enemy."[45]

Principle #3: *Sowing praise in hard times reaps a harvest of joy* (16:19-34). It's so easy to praise God when the money's flowing in, the organization's humming along nicely, the wind's at your back, and the decisions are easy. It's natural to praise God after the earthquake has broken open the prison gates. But it's extremely difficult to praise God while you're still in the dungeon with your back against the wall and you see no natural reason to hope. When you have received mistreatment and misunderstanding for your best efforts, it's easy to wonder, *Is all this pain I'm suffering worth it?*

The longer I live, the more I believe that joy is a choice. Furthermore, God uses the joy of His servants to accomplish His plans. Not because He needs our power of positive thinking to make good things happen, but to encourage us to choose to find satisfaction in Him rather than in our circumstances. After all, He's permanent; circumstances change with the weather. Praising Him in the hard times will cause you to reap a harvest of joy, not only in the future, but in the present, where you are.

Neck Deep in Greece
ACTS 17:1-15

NASB

¹Now when they had traveled through Amphipolis and Apollonia, they came to Thessalonica, where there was a synagogue of the Jews. ²And according to Paul's custom, he went to them, and for three Sabbaths reasoned with them from the Scriptures, ³ᵃexplaining and ᵇgiving evidence that the ᶜChrist had to suffer and rise again from the dead, and *saying*, "This Jesus whom I am proclaiming to you is the ᶜChrist." ⁴And some of them were persuaded and joined Paul and Silas, ᵃalong with a large number of the God-fearing Greeks and ᵇa number of the leading women. ⁵But the Jews, becoming jealous and taking along some wicked men from the market place, formed a mob and set the city in an uproar; and attacking the house of Jason, they were seeking to bring them out to the people. ⁶When they did not find them, they *began* dragging Jason and some brethren before the city authorities, shouting, "These men who have upset ᵃthe world have come here also; ⁷ᵃand Jason has welcomed them, and they all act contrary to the decrees of Caesar, saying that there is another king, Jesus." ⁸They stirred up the crowd and the city authorities who heard these things. ⁹And when they had received a ᵃpledge from Jason and the others, they released them.

¹⁰The brethren immediately sent Paul and Silas away by night to Berea, ᵃand when they arrived, they went into the synagogue of the Jews. ¹¹Now these were more

NLT

¹Paul and Silas then traveled through the towns of Amphipolis and Apollonia and came to Thessalonica, where there was a Jewish synagogue. ²As was Paul's custom, he went to the synagogue service, and for three Sabbaths in a row he used the Scriptures to reason with the people. ³He explained the prophecies and proved that the Messiah must suffer and rise from the dead. He said, "This Jesus I'm telling you about is the Messiah." ⁴Some of the Jews who listened were persuaded and joined Paul and Silas, along with many God-fearing Greek men and quite a few prominent women.*

⁵But some of the Jews were jealous, so they gathered some troublemakers from the marketplace to form a mob and start a riot. They attacked the home of Jason, searching for Paul and Silas so they could drag them out to the crowd.* ⁶Not finding them there, they dragged out Jason and some of the other believers* instead and took them before the city council. "Paul and Silas have caused trouble all over the world," they shouted, "and now they are here disturbing our city, too. ⁷And Jason has welcomed them into his home. They are all guilty of treason against Caesar, for they profess allegiance to another king, named Jesus."

⁸The people of the city, as well as the city council, were thrown into turmoil by these reports. ⁹So the officials forced Jason and the other believers to post bond, and then they released them.

¹⁰That very night the believers sent Paul and Silas to Berea. When they arrived there, they went to the Jewish synagogue. ¹¹And the people

NASB

noble-minded than those in Thessalonica, ᵃfor they received the word with ᵇgreat eagerness, examining the Scriptures daily *to see* whether these things were so. ¹²Therefore many of them believed, ᵃalong with a number of prominent Greek women and men. ¹³But when the Jews of Thessalonica found out that the word of God had been proclaimed by Paul in Berea also, they came there as well, agitating and stirring up the crowds. ¹⁴Then immediately the brethren sent Paul out to go as far as the sea; and Silas and Timothy remained there. ¹⁵Now those who escorted Paul brought him as far as Athens; and receiving a command for Silas and Timothy to come to him as soon as possible, they left.

17:3 ᵃLit *opening* ᵇLit *placing before* ᶜI.e. Messiah
17:4 ᵃLit *and a large* ᵇLit *not a few* 17:6 ᵃLit
the inhabited earth 17:7 ᵃLit *whom Jason has
welcomed* 17:9 ᵃOr *bond* 17:10 ᵃLit *who when...
arrived went* 17:11 ᵃLit *who received* ᵇLit *all*
17:12 ᵃLit *and not a few*

NLT

of Berea were more open-minded than those in Thessalonica, and they listened eagerly to Paul's message. They searched the Scriptures day after day to see if Paul and Silas were teaching the truth. ¹²As a result, many Jews believed, as did many of the prominent Greek women and men.

¹³But when some Jews in Thessalonica learned that Paul was preaching the word of God in Berea, they went there and stirred up trouble. ¹⁴The believers acted at once, sending Paul on to the coast, while Silas and Timothy remained behind. ¹⁵Those escorting Paul went with him all the way to Athens; then they returned to Berea with instructions for Silas and Timothy to hurry and join him.

17:4 Some manuscripts read *quite a few of
the wives of the leading men.* 17:5 Or *the city
council.* 17:6 Greek *brothers;* also in 17:10, 14.

It's possible to live without being fully alive. It's possible to exist as a human being without being fully human. All of us go through periodic seasons of deadness; in fact, these winters are a necessary part of healthy growth. But we were not created merely to exist; God fashioned humanity for *living* (John 10:10). John Powell describes this kind of complete aliveness in his book *Fully Human, Fully Alive.*

> By way of a general description, fully alive people are those who are using all of their human faculties, powers, and talents. They are using them to the full. These individuals are fully functioning in their external and internal senses. . . . Such people are vibrantly alive in mind, heart, and will. . . .
>
> Fully alive human beings are alive in their external and internal *senses*. They see a beautiful world. They hear its music and poetry. They smell the fragrance of each new day and taste the deliciousness of every moment. . . .
>
> Fully alive people are also alive in their *minds*. They are very much aware of the wisdom in the statement of Socrates that "the unreflected life isn't worth living." Fully alive people are always

thoughtful and reflective. They are capable of asking the right questions of life and flexible enough to let life question them. They will not live an unreflected life in an unexamined world. Most of all, perhaps, these people are alive in *will* and *heart*. They love much. They truly love and sincerely respect themselves. All love begins here and builds on this. Fully alive people are glad to be alive and to be who they are.[46]

As the early church father Irenaeus once wrote, "The glory of God is a living man; and the life of man consists in beholding God."[47] Paul on his second missionary journey was a man fully alive. He accepted himself with all his own strengths and weaknesses, he knew his place in God's plan, he saw the needs before him, and he threw himself headlong into the mission God had prepared him to complete. He was "beholding God" as he lived out his divine purpose. So, by the time he departed Philippi, he was neck deep in the work of ministry. The trials and challenges he had endured did nothing to diminish his determination and confidence or temper his enthusiasm. With one city behind him, the rest of Greece lay before him like a field ready for harvest.

— 17:1 —

In the second century BC, the Romans built a highway called the Via Egnatia from Dyrrachium on the Adriatic Sea to Byzantium (now called Constantinople) near the Black Sea, a distance of almost 700 miles. Nearly 20 feet wide and paved with hand-laid stone slabs, it carried Roman troops to battle, taxes to the capital city, and merchandise everywhere.[48] And now it carried the gospel into Greece. Paul followed the Via Egnatia a little more than 35 miles from Philippi to Amphipolis, where the seat of Roman government administered its affairs in Macedonia. From there, he continued another 30 miles to Apollonia, and then to Thessalonica 33 miles away. Each leg of his journey required a long day's walk but put him in a major city by nightfall.

I offer this detail to make a point. Not long after his ordeal—a public beating with rods and a night in jail—Paul walked nearly 100 miles in three days! Emerson wrote, "Nothing great was ever achieved without enthusiasm."[49] Sir Edward Appleton, the Scottish physicist and Nobel Prize winner, said, "I rate enthusiasm even above professional skill." Paul's enthusiasm carried him beyond his own physical limitations to accomplish what God had set before him. I don't mean the enthusiasm of a cheerleader; I mean a throbbing, compelling, positive drive that can't be silenced until it is satisfied.

Notably, Luke's pronouns change back to third person. He had joined Paul in Troas and accompanied him to Philippi (Acts 16). When the team moved on, Luke remained, because he may have lived there. He would not see Paul again until the apostle returned on his third journey (20:2, 6).

Thessalonica was an unusual city in terms of politics. Cassander, a general of Alexander the Great, founded the city in 315 BC over the town of Therma, which was named for the nearby hot springs. Later, in 42 BC, when Antony and Octavian battled Brutus and Cassius (two of the leading conspirators against Julius Caesar) for control of Rome, Thessalonica sided with Octavian. As a reward, the city was declared free, meaning exempt from taxes, and autonomous, meaning they had the right to appoint their own magistrates, five men who bore the unusual title of "politarch" because the people had democratically selected their own city's rulers. When the province of Macedonia was divided into four districts, Thessalonica became the capital of the second.[50]

— 17:2-4 —

In keeping with his standard operating procedure, Paul entered the synagogue and "reasoned" (17:2; *dialegomai* [1256]) with his Jewish brethren. This is the first time Luke uses this term, but not the last. Paul would "reason" in Thessalonica (17:2), Athens (17:17), Corinth (18:4), Ephesus (18:19; 19:8, 9), Troas (20:7, 9), and finally, before the Roman governor, Felix, in Caesarea Maritima (24:25). In classical Greek, *dialegomai* meant "to converse, discuss, or argue" or, when delivering a lecture, "to instruct." Paul didn't "reason" in this technical sense used by Greek philosophers, but he recognized this as a style of communication he needed to master. He had entered a different culture, one he recognized from his study in the academy of Tarsus, and he adapted accordingly.

For three Sabbaths, he "reasoned" from the Old Testament Scriptures, proving that the Messiah had to die and rise again in order to fulfill the prophecies. Jewish theologians in the century before Christ and during the time of Paul struggled to understand how the Messiah could suffer death on behalf of His people (Isa. 53) and reign forever as their king (Dan. 7:13-14). They found it inconceivable that a true Messiah could die at the hands of his enemies. So, they postulated that perhaps the Messiah would really be two individuals, one who would die as the Suffering Servant and another who would resurrect the first and then reign as supreme King. But Paul reasoned that Christ is indeed one man

Clarity

ACTS 17:2–3

When Paul reasoned with the Jews at the synagogue in Thessalonica, he "explained" (dianoigō [1272]) the Old Testament Scriptures. The Greek word dianoigō means "to completely open up what before was closed." Obviously, the Jews in the synagogue had the Scriptures, but their true meaning remained closed until Paul "opened" those familiar passages by introducing Jesus as the Christ. Suddenly, for those who were willing, the meaning became clear for the first time.

I take Paul's example seriously. Consequently, I place a very high priority on making my teaching clear. I want to feel assured that anyone off the street can sit down in any worship service or any other gathering and understand most, if not all, of what I say. As a matter of fact, clarity is one of three priorities I try to maintain, along with accuracy and practicality.

Many years ago, very early in my ministry, a group of kids in Vacation Bible School taught me a valuable lesson I have never forgotten. I was teaching about the death of Christ and I said, "Now, kiddos, you understand, when Christ died on the cross, He shed His blood for our sins." A little girl in the back innocently asked, "What does 'shed' mean?" To her, a shed was a place you keep your pony. That's when something dawned on me. I never use the phrase "shed blood" in any other context besides church. It's jargon that can be inaccessible to many people.

If you throw the word "justification" around with lost people, they can't track with you. Or "redeem." They'll think about coupons. "Propitiation?" Forget it! They don't have the vocabulary, so it's our responsibility to use terms they know if we hope to communicate with clarity. Those who don't aren't effective—and usually they're the ones who complain that no one's interested in Christ. Those who work hard at speaking plainly and avoiding jargon have little trouble finding people willing to listen.

Keep it real and make it clear.

who is also God, who died to atone for sin and then rose from the grave to establish His kingdom. This is probably the same line of reasoning Jesus used with the two disciples on the road to Emmaus (Luke 24). To close his case, Paul spent time "giving evidence," validating the reasonableness of this theology by sharing about his personal encounter with the resurrected Jesus (Acts 17:3).

As in most cities, a number of Jews and Gentile proselytes believed the good news and then formed the nucleus of a church in Thessalonica (17:4).

— 17:5 —

As usual, not everyone found Paul's message to his or her liking. Luke describes the Jewish opposition with a Greek word that means "to be intensely interested in something" (*zēloō* [2206]), either positively or negatively. We derive our word "zealous" from this verb. In this case, the opposing Jews were zealous, but not for reasoning from the Scriptures. Finding little support in the synagogue, they rounded up some hoodlums from the marketplace and whipped the city into an anti-Paul frenzy. Unlike the mob in Philippi, which had been fueled by anti-Semitism, in Thessalonica the Jews led the attack.

— 17:6-9 —

The mob surrounded the house of Jason, who hosted Paul and his men much like Lydia had in Philippi. Apparently, the evangelists were busy somewhere else. So, they hauled their neighbor before the "city authorities" (17:6; *politarchēs* [4173]), the democratically elected magistrates of the city. They couldn't lodge their actual complaint: "These men teach a theology we don't like, so we want them beaten and, if it's not too much trouble, killed." Instead, they tried to characterize the Christians as treasonous and therefore a threat to city order.

Luke highlights the irony of their charge, which they exaggerated to the point of absurdity. The riotous mob accused Paul, Silas, Timothy, and the others of having already destabilized the world. Contrast that with the previous significant threat to stability, which was the revolt of Spartacus, who failed to "upset the world" with his army of perhaps seventy thousand men before his defeat in 71 BC.[51] Paul's Jewish accusers capped off their charge with an unexpected political concern for Rome. They accused the men of undermining the decrees of Caesar and supporting a rival king (17:7). Of course, their charges were absolutely true in the strictest sense. Paul and his men *were* in the process of upsetting the world, though not in the sense of inspiring revolt. And they did indeed proclaim allegiance to Jesus as King.

Again, the magistrates failed to do their due diligence in the matter. If they had simply asked, "Who is this rival king, Jesus?" the entire case would have come unraveled. The Romans didn't care if people supported a dead king, and if they claimed Jesus was alive, they would have to affirm His resurrection. Even so, the discussion ended when the city authorities determined what ruling would please their constituents.

Because the accused weren't present for trial, the magistrates compelled Jason, their host, to post a bond (17:9). Most likely, this bond insured that Paul wouldn't cause any trouble for the city; if he did, they would collect against Jason as a penalty.

— 17:10-12 —

Paul had completed his work in Thessalonica. He saw nothing to gain and much to lose by remaining. Further antagonism would only make things harder for the church. Besides, the believers had formed a church and could carry the work forward themselves. Therefore, Paul led his men out of town that night to begin their 45-mile walk to Berea. Only now, they didn't have the benefit of a highway. Cicero, who had been banished to Thessalonica for a time, called Berea an "off-the-road town."[52]

Luke's narrative draws a close comparison between Thessalonica and Berea. As in Thessalonica, Paul taught in the "synagogue of the Jews" (17:10), but in Berea he found a more "noble-minded" (17:11; *eugenēs* [2104]) audience. The term *eugenēs* means "well born, cultured, and high class." The aristocracy used this word as a description of themselves in comparison to what they perceived as the ignorant, mentally dull rabble. Luke intended this as a compliment to the Bereans, who carefully cross-checked Paul's evidence with the Scriptures. As before, many Jews and Gentile proselytes believed and then formed a sizable church (17:12).

— 17:13-15 —

Unfortunately, Paul's Jewish opposers from Thessalonica tracked him down and stirred up trouble in Berea, too (17:13), perhaps hoping to arrest Paul and bring him back for trial. The apostle again saw little to gain by staying; the new church was sufficiently equipped to thrive without him. To protect their teacher, the new believers proposed a brilliant plan. While Silas and Timothy remained in town, apparently to give the impression that Paul had not left, they sent the apostle "as far as the sea" (17:14). If people learned Paul had gone east toward the coast, they would not know whether he took a ship or followed a coastal road south toward Athens. Unfortunately, Luke doesn't tell us, either!

The preposition rendered "as far as" denotes the end of something. Luke uses the same preposition to state that the escorts took Paul "as far as Athens" (17:15), and we know he actually went into the city (17:16) and stayed there. For these reasons, and the practical need to spirit Paul away quickly, I lean toward his taking a ship. When Paul arrived in Athens with the help of some Berean believers, he sent his escorts back with instructions for Silas and Timothy (and others?) to join him as soon as possible (17:15).

APPLICATION: ACTS 17:1-15

Reality Checks for a Full Life

By the time Paul arrived in Thessalonica (17:1), he had hit his stride as an evangelist and church planter. He was in his element; the hardships merely formed part of the landscape. His experiences those first months in Greece illustrate at least three principles anyone in ministry would do well to remember.

First, *determination is at the heart of any great achievement*. There's nothing magical about Paul or any of the other biblical characters. They were people who knew their callings and pursued their divine purposes with determination. Paul was beaten and jailed in Philippi, he was mobbed and forced out of Thessalonica, his steps were dogged in Berea where he was hurried out of town, then he was dropped and left in Athens all alone—but he stayed strong. He saw each hardship as a small price to pay for the impact he would make in each city. They kept running off the apostle, but he kept leaving churches in his wake, whole communities of reproducing Christians.

Second, *rejection is to be expected when you share the truth*. Don't be surprised when people reject the truth. I know it doesn't make sense. Why reject what is true? But people regularly reject truth. They'll tell lies about you and then call you a liar. Unfortunately, truth rarely attracts large numbers of people. Proclaiming truth draws a remnant who will give their lives for the Lord while drawing enemies like a pack of angry dogs. That's why godly leadership requires courage, tenacity, resiliency, and most of all, humility. A proclaimer of God's truth isn't a politician and can't worry about image or applause, polls or popularity; rather, the proclaimer must be content to present the truth, recognizing that personal rejection is the most likely outcome.

If Paul got rejected while sharing truth, you can be certain it will be no different for you. When you accept this fact of ministry, personal rejection loses its sting.

Third, *appreciation is seldom expressed at the right time.* You will never find Paul cornered by a group of people from Thessalonica or Philippi or Berea saying, "Hey, man. Thanks. That was great stuff you said back there. And thanks for taking that beating. Thanks for upholding the gospel. Thanks for standing firm when everybody else was walking away." If you're waiting for that, then forget about becoming a good leader. You'll fold. Your reward will rarely come in the form of appreciation. Instead, you will feel a closer connection with your Master, who suffered and knows all about your suffering. You will also experience life more fully because you'll be living your purpose. And when you persevere and stand before your Creator, the reward for your faithfulness will be great.

Areopagus Eggheads vs. a Seed Picker
ACTS 17:16-34

NASB

[16] Now while Paul was waiting for them at Athens, his spirit was being provoked within him as he was observing the city full of idols. [17] So he was reasoning in the synagogue with the Jews and the God-fearing *Gentiles,* and in the market place every day with those who happened to be present. [18] And also some of the Epicurean and Stoic philosophers were [a]conversing with him. Some were saying, "What would this [b]idle babbler wish to say?" Others, "He

NLT

[16] While Paul was waiting for them in Athens, he was deeply troubled by all the idols he saw everywhere in the city. [17] He went to the synagogue to reason with the Jews and the God-fearing Gentiles, and he spoke daily in the public square to all who happened to be there.

[18] He also had a debate with some of the Epicurean and Stoic philosophers. When he told them about Jesus and his resurrection, they said, "What's this babbler trying to say

NASB

seems to be a proclaimer of strange deities,"—because he was preaching Jesus and the resurrection. [19]And they took him and brought him [a]to the [b]Areopagus, saying, "May we know what this new teaching is [c]which you are proclaiming? [20]For you are bringing some strange things to our ears; so we want to know what these things mean." [21](Now all the Athenians and the strangers visiting there used to spend their time in nothing other than telling or hearing something new.)

[22]So Paul stood in the midst of the [a]Areopagus and said, "Men of Athens, I observe that you are very religious in all respects. [23]For while I was passing through and examining the objects of your worship, I also found an altar with this inscription, 'TO AN UNKNOWN GOD.' Therefore what you worship in ignorance, this I proclaim to you. [24]The God who made the world and all things in it, since He is Lord of heaven and earth, does not dwell in temples made with hands; [25]nor is He served by human hands, as though He needed anything, since He Himself gives to all *people* life and breath and all things; [26]and He made from one *man* every nation of mankind to live on all the face of the earth, having determined *their* appointed times and the boundaries of their habitation, [27]that they would seek God, if perhaps they might grope for Him and find Him, though He is not far from each one of us; [28]for in Him we live and move and [a]exist, as even some of your own poets have said, 'For we also are His children.' [29]Being then the children of God, we ought not to think that the Divine Nature is like gold or silver or stone, an image formed by the art and thought of man. [30]Therefore having overlooked the times of ignorance, God is now declaring to men

NLT

with these strange ideas he's picked up?" Others said, "He seems to be preaching about some foreign gods."

[19]Then they took him to the high council of the city.* "Come and tell us about this new teaching," they said. [20]"You are saying some rather strange things, and we want to know what it's all about." [21](It should be explained that all the Athenians as well as the foreigners in Athens seemed to spend all their time discussing the latest ideas.)

[22]So Paul, standing before the council,* addressed them as follows: "Men of Athens, I notice that you are very religious in every way, [23]for as I was walking along I saw your many shrines. And one of your altars had this inscription on it: 'To an Unknown God.' This God, whom you worship without knowing, is the one I'm telling you about.

[24]"He is the God who made the world and everything in it. Since he is Lord of heaven and earth, he doesn't live in man-made temples, [25]and human hands can't serve his needs—for he has no needs. He himself gives life and breath to everything, and he satisfies every need. [26]From one man* he created all the nations throughout the whole earth. He decided beforehand when they should rise and fall, and he determined their boundaries.

[27]"His purpose was for the nations to seek after God and perhaps feel their way toward him and find him—though he is not far from any one of us. [28]For in him we live and move and exist. As some of your* own poets have said, 'We are his offspring.' [29]And since this is true, we shouldn't think of God as an idol designed by craftsmen from gold or silver or stone.

[30]"God overlooked people's ignorance about these things in earlier times, but now he commands

that all *people* everywhere should repent, [31] because He has fixed a day in which He will judge [a] the world in righteousness [b] through a Man whom He has appointed, having furnished proof to all men [c] by raising Him from the dead."

[32] Now when they heard of the resurrection of the dead, some *began* to sneer, but others said, "We shall hear you [a] again concerning this." [33] So Paul went out of their midst. [34] But some men joined him and believed, among whom also were Dionysius the Areopagite and a woman named Damaris and others with them.

17:18 [a] Or *disputing* [b] I.e. one who makes his living by picking up scraps 17:19 [a] Or *before* [b] Or *Hill of Ares*, god of war [c] Lit *which is being spoken by you* 17:22 [a] Or *the Council of the Areopagus* 17:28 [a] Lit *are* 17:31 [a] Lit *the inhabited earth* [b] Lit *by* or *in* [c] Or *when He raised* 17:32 [a] Lit *also again*

everyone everywhere to repent of their sins and turn to him. [31] For he has set a day for judging the world with justice by the man he has appointed, and he proved to everyone who this is by raising him from the dead."

[32] When they heard Paul speak about the resurrection of the dead, some laughed in contempt, but others said, "We want to hear more about this later." [33] That ended Paul's discussion with them, [34] but some joined him and became believers. Among them were Dionysius, a member of the council,* a woman named Damaris, and others with them.

17:19 Or *the most learned society of philosophers in the city.* Greek reads *the Areopagus.*
17:22 Traditionally rendered *standing in the middle of Mars Hill;* Greek reads *standing in the middle of the Areopagus.* 17:26 Greek *From one;* other manuscripts read *From one blood.*
17:28 Some manuscripts read *our.* 17:34 Greek *an Areopagite.*

I've never had an easier time saying no than when I first received a call in 1995 from Jack Turpin, then chairman of the Dallas Seminary Board, and Dr. Don Campbell, the president. They were asking me to consider becoming the next president of the school, and never had I felt so unqualified for a position. Ministry I knew. Shepherding a church, I had done. Leading a collection of world-class theological academics, on the other hand, was not something I saw in my future. After a series of encouraging events and a lot of affirmation from family and trusted advisors, however, I began to accept the possibility that maybe I had something to offer these brilliant theologians, most of whom had an alphabet trailing after their names. I moved to Dallas with a simple objective: remain who I was, give them the best I had, and let God make it good enough. During those first few days, I had never felt so displaced from familiar territory!

So, I can easily imagine what Paul must have felt when he first saw Athens sprawled across the Attica Basin. For as long as anyone could remember, this city had been the epicenter of a culture that covered much of the known world and shaped its thinking. Most people in the Roman Empire spoke at least two languages: their own native tongue and Koine Greek. They worshiped Greek gods, appreciated Greek art, read Greek literature, and witnessed Greek drama. They even changed the way they looked at the universe because of this extraordinary city. Even as Paul looked across the basin to the Acropolis presiding over the capital of Western thought, he saw buildings already five hundred years old, testifying to the genius of a people who had taught the world to think. Paul would tailor his message to this new crowd without compromising the gospel in any way, and as a result he would meet with three common responses: rejection, acceptance, and tentative contemplation.

The Acropolis of Athens is the peak of this ancient city. The most famous building still standing is the Parthenon, seen in the center of this photo.

On a smaller outcropping of a massive rock just 100 yards northwest of the Acropolis, philosophers met to debate, discuss, and discover truth. The Areopagus had a long history of oratory and debate. Since 500 BC—and perhaps even before—the Areopagus had been the site for political administration and judicial proceedings. Athenian democracy was born and nurtured there. In the centuries prior to Paul, some of the most venerated names in Greek history may have stood in that same place to speak. Themistocles, Aristides, Pericles, Socrates, perhaps even Aristotle and Plato could have addressed the political powers of their day on the rock. How many speeches were given? How much history was shaped? How many luminaries were privileged enough to address the historic council of the Areopagus? Thousands. Some of them we know as the greatest figures of western history. Yet today, when we hear the name "Mars Hill" (another name for the Areopagus), we immediately think of the words of a rabbi from Tarsus, a Jew of Jerusalem bearing good news from the east.

— 17:16-17 —

Luke doesn't state whether Paul arrived by land or by sea. If by sea, he would have landed at the nearby port of Piraeus, about 5 miles away. In more ancient times, the Athenians fortified Piraeus and then enclosed the road to their own city with two massive walls 50 feet high. He would have walked a well-traveled road that led through the western Dipylon Gate and continued straight to the marketplace (*agora* [58]).[53] He certainly found lodging first, either with the help of his escorts or on his own. Naturally, Paul explored the ancient city, but not with the eye of an admiring tourist; what he saw sickened him. What we now regard as relics were, in Paul's day, actively used for pagan worship. Tourists today visit Athens to appreciate the artwork, but those buildings were the implements of idolatry in the first century. Therefore, Athens represented a culture pulled in opposite directions.

On the one hand, "it was said that there were more statues of the gods in Athens than in all the rest of Greece put together, and that in Athens it was easier to meet a god than another person."[54] The Greek gods became the principal deities of a thousand cultures, including that of Rome. Superstition kept the common man and woman in the dark and ruled their lives with fear; meanwhile, the extended tribe of Rome considered their worship synonymous with civil virtue and loyalty to the state.

On the other hand, the great philosophers of Greece had been arguing against the existence of gods for centuries. They favored a cosmology ruled by some other guiding force. They couldn't agree on the exact nature of that spiritual entity—personal or nonpersonal, singular or plural, material or spiritual, good or ambiguous—but they did agree that it imposed on the world a set of laws and principles that could be studied, understood, predicted, and exploited. They rejected superstition, mythology, and sympathetic magic in favor of a rational scientific model. To avoid persecution, however, they gave a certain lip service to the gods, saying they existed and should be venerated but that they didn't participate in human affairs.

The tension between the traditional pagans and the freethinking academics continued into Paul's day. At the grassroots level, they met in the *agora*, where common people traded merchandise and exchanged ideas. That's where Paul spent many of his days while waiting for Silas and Timothy to join him. At other times, he could be found in the syna-gogue reasoning with the Jews and Gentile proselytes.

— 17:18 —

Two major schools of Greek philosophy, the Epicureans and the Stoics, used similar vocabulary, but saw the universe very differently. Each derived its teachings from the two major divisions of Greek thought first conceived by Plato and Aristotle. The Epicureans, who tended to follow Aristotle's ideas, believed that the universe consisted of atoms and that all of reality is essentially material, including the so-called spirit realm. Life begins when atoms come together and ends when they break apart; therefore, no afterlife exists. Because life is a random, orderless, chaotic collision of atoms, humans must use their free will to shape the world to suit themselves. While Epicureans didn't advocate licentious living, they did believe pleasure should replace suffering be-cause human existence ends with the grave.

The Stoics, who tended to follow Plato's ideas, also believed the uni-verse consisted of atoms, but they didn't think this constituted all of reality. Like Plato, they pointed to the reality of love, logic, truth, and beauty to show that some things could exist apart from atoms and, in fact, transcend the material realm. For the Stoics, the mere fact that logic exists proved the existence of an overarching logic giving order to the universe. This *logos* was a cosmic, supernatural, nonpersonal mind that caused the universe to operate according to predictable laws. Human spirits were pieces of this divine mind trapped, as it were, in material bodies. Death reunited an individual's mind with the cosmic *logos*. In the meantime, humans could commune with this divine mind through logic, meditation, and by ridding themselves of disruptive pas-sions and distracting emotions.

These two factions debated endlessly, locked in a philosophical stalemate; both kept attracting new followers, but neither gained any ground against the other. They heard Paul preaching in the *agora* [58] and engaged him in debate; this is how they began conversing with him. The Greek word translated "conversing" (*symballō* [4820]) carries a back-and-forth idea—not exactly contentious, but not seeing eye to eye, either. In their style of Socratic question-and-answer dialogue, they showed a certain curiosity for his theology. Some called him an "idle babbler" (*spermologos* [4691]), a compound of two Greek terms, *sperma* ("seed" [4690]) and *logos* ("word," "matter," "idea" [3056]). It pictured a seed picker walking from place to place picking up seeds in order to plant them somewhere else. This person gathered ideas from various sources during his travels and then cobbled them together to form a new school of thought.

Others saw Paul's teaching as dangerous to social order because he taught "strange deities." Most philosophers dismissed the deities as too holy to be sullied by human interaction, effectively marginalizing the gods without actually denying their existence. Paul, on the other hand, taught a "strange" (*xenos* [3581]) new dogma, a foreign one about "Jesus and the resurrection," which denied the Greek and Roman gods while advocating God the Father, God the Son, and God the Holy Spirit as the only real God.

— 17:19-21 —

So they took him to the Areopagus, the "Hill (*pagos* [697]) of Ares," the Greek god of war. The equivalent Roman god is Mars, so we also call it Mars Hill.

Barry Beitzel

The Areopagus in Athens was where a council of Athenian poets and philosophers would meet with one another to discuss important issues.

The invitation to address the council of the Areopagus did not come merely out of benign curiosity. Luke comments that the people of Athens spent much of their time seeking something new to occupy their conversations (17:21). Still, at least one function of this council in ancient times was to pass judgment on a teaching to be certain it did not undermine the virtue and security of the state. Under Roman control, however, it's unlikely that this council served this function in an official capacity; rather, it wielded popular influence as the voice of the official experts in all things religious and philosophical.

— 17:22-23 —

The job of a philosopher is to present a simple concept incomprehensibly and then to convince you it's your fault for not understanding. Paul didn't play the philosopher before this august group of philosophers. Paul gave a clear, simple, orderly presentation of the Judeo-Christian worldview, and then he drove them straight toward the final judgment and our need for salvation through the resurrected Christ. Even so, we should not see this as a complete transcription of his actual message. Luke's rendering here spans only ten verses and takes fewer than three minutes to read— five if you speak slowly and allow for long, dramatic pauses.

Paul's address, condensed as it is here, employs four significant features we should study, memorize, and duplicate when presenting the gospel to any group.

First, *Paul approached his subject from the audience's perspective.* Paul's opening statement (17:22) isn't a compliment; it's a statement of fact. He knew better than to attempt flattery, which would get him nowhere, especially with the intensely logical Stoics. He said, in effect, "You Athenians are very dedicated in your pursuit of spiritual knowledge." It is ambiguous whether the term *deisidaimōnia* [1175] is good or bad. Depending upon the context, it could mean either "devout" or "superstitious."

Second, *Paul used the familiar to introduce the unfamiliar.* He supported this opening statement with another observation of fact. Among the objects of "your worship" (note the pronoun) he had found an altar inscribed *agnōstō theō*, "TO AN UNKNOWN GOD" (17:23). Of course, the phrase is based on the two words *agnōstos* ([57], "not known") and *theos* ([2316], "god"). The Athenians had an all-inclusive culture, accepting any and all gods. For fear of incurring the wrath of any god they overlooked, they erected an all-purpose, catchall shrine. Paul used this to build a bridge. He said, as it were, "Let me tell you about the one God you have overlooked in your quest for spiritual truth."

— 17:24-29 —

Third, *Paul developed his theme tactfully yet boldly and clearly.* He unveiled the Creator God of the Bible by establishing four points, each building on the one before it.

1. *As the Creator, God cannot be contained* (17:24). Many Greeks and Romans struggled with the idea of a god that cannot be seen or at least depicted. The Hebrew God transcends creation, so nothing material can represent Him. Furthermore, He is infinite, whereas all the Greek gods of popular mythology were finite. God is omnipresent; the Greek gods were more like superhumans—immensely powerful, but suffering the same limitations as the creatures of earth. Paul established the vast superiority of God to all the Greek deities combined.

2. *As the Originator, God has no needs* (17:25). The Greek gods were petty and vain; they could be bribed with enough flattery or sufficient sacrifices. Worship consisted of giving the gods enough of what they wanted in order to release their particular, specialized blessings. This made them merchants or hirelings of humanity. The trick for the worshiper was to discover a god's material weakness and exploit it to personal advantage. But God has no needs; He cannot be bribed or manipulated; He instead provides for the needs of people by His own choice.

3. *As the Sovereign of the universe, He has a purpose and He is accessible* (17:26-27). Even though His ultimate power and complete transcendence make God impervious to flattery, bribery, or manipulation, He is neither remote nor aloof. The sophisticated Epicureans and Stoics both regarded their gods as too holy and dignified to dirty their hands with the affairs of humanity. The Hebrew God, however, remains intimately involved with His creation, participating daily in its administration. In a way, this personal deity is like the Stoic concept of the *logos*, which guides creation with laws of nature according to a set plan toward a specific destiny. But unlike this impersonal force, God longs to be known. The goal to which He drives the universe is Himself. In Christianity, the ultimate destiny of the universe is to acknowledge God as King.

4. *As the Source of life, God does not depend upon us; we depend upon Him* (17:28-29). The Epicureans believed that humans were not created by a *logos* or any other overarching creator and that we certainly don't have a purpose. Each life is the result of atoms coming together, perhaps randomly, and if we have any purpose, it is one we make for ourselves.[55] Against this notion, Paul insisted that our existence comes out of God's existence. We exist because He said we should; therefore, each life has dignity and purpose and worth. At the end of physical life, we do not cease to exist, because we are more than atoms and the Creator is more powerful than mere material. We will continue to exist after death because the Creator wants us to.

To support the reasonableness of this last point, Paul quoted a legendary (literally) poet and philosopher whom the Athenians revered like the Hebrews venerated Moses. Epimenides wrote a poem about Zeus after supposedly receiving the gift of prophecy. In response to critics who claimed Zeus was a mere mortal, the poem declares "In him we live and move and exist."[56] Paul quoted this line, not to affirm the existence of Zeus or to equate God with Zeus, but to demonstrate the reasonableness of believing in a personal God, contrary to the Stoics and Epicureans, whose logic led them to conclude that the Greek gods remained aloof. He also quoted the words of the third century BC poet Aratus of Soli (in Cilicia, Paul's home province), who wrote of Zeus, "We are also his offspring."[57]

— 17:30 —

Fourth, *Paul applied his principles to the needs of his audience.* Whereas the pagan gods of Athens selfishly wanted to be served and would grant blessing in return for flattery or bribery, the God of the Old Testament wants people to repent so He can grant them unmerited favor. He wants to save all people from the terrible ordeal of the final judgment. This concept, of course, departed from the teachings of both the Epicureans and the Stoics. Epicureans didn't believe in an afterlife, so the question of judgment was nonsense. Stoics believed that rejoining the *logos* after death was its own reward; no judgment awaited anyone.

— 17:31 —

Paul's next point not only departed from the worldview of Greek philosophy, it shattered it. Paul dropped a bombshell into their concept of the universe: resurrection. The Epicureans and Stoics couldn't agree on many points, but they both declared the idea of resurrection absurd.

For the Epicureans, who believed death was the disassembly and dissemination of one's atoms—which became parts of a billion other things—resurrection required the destruction of those other things in order to be reassembled. For the Stoics, who embraced death as one's reunification with the *logos*, resurrection re-created the problem death had solved. Paul spoke no further.

— 17:32-34 —

The concept of resurrection split the group and brought the meeting to an abrupt, spontaneous close. While Paul's sermon didn't convince the majority, Luke nevertheless names two converts among "others" (17:32) who became disciples that day. The man designated as "the Areopagite" (17:34) was a member of the council of Areopagus, the governing body in charge of Mars Hill and responsible for passing judgment on religious ideas. A woman named Damaris who had attended, and perhaps participated actively in the meeting, also became a believer. Luke's abbreviated closure of the episode suggests Paul remained in Athens long enough to strengthen the new disciples and to establish a community to sustain them long term. That was, after all, Paul's procedure everywhere he went.

APPLICATION: ACTS 17:16-34

Mixed Audiences

Paul's message had accomplished its purpose. He didn't expect to change six hundred years of philosophy in one speech. He never made it his goal to supplant this ancient worldview with the gospel through one sermon. He would instead set inexorable change in motion while gathering a handful of God's elect in the process. The response to Paul's sermon is typical, so we should take note. His presentation prompted three common responses (17:18, 32-34).

First, *instant rejection* (17:18). It did not surprise Paul to see some dismiss him immediately as a kook; their worldview made no room for the truth. He had seen this response many times before, quite often in the synagogues. He would preach the gospel, reasoning with the Jews and Gentile proselytes from the Old Testament Scriptures, only to have his irrefutable logic provoke a violent response from a relatively small yet volatile segment. Not everyone present in religious services and lecture halls has a desire for truth. If it can happen to a Spirit-filled apostle with a brilliant mind and flawless delivery, it will happen to us.

Second, *immediate acceptance* (17:34). Luke states that some joined him and believed. I take this to mean they asked some follow-up questions, heard the rest of the gospel, and trusted in Christ for their salvation. No resistance. No hesitation. Like dry sponges, they soaked up the truth Paul offered and believed with little or no resistance. This was a response the apostles had encountered many times as well. Early in his ministry among the Gentiles in Antioch, Paul had learned that proclaiming the gospel is a culling process. Therefore, he didn't preach to convince skeptics as much as to sift the multitudes for God's elect and establish them in self-sustaining communities.

Third, *tentative contemplation* (17:32). Still others remained open to the radical new idea Paul called resurrection. They neither accepted immediately nor rejected instantly, and they intended to delve deeper and learn more. This is perhaps the most common response of all. Some people use contemplation as a means of polite rejection, but many earnestly desire to know more while struggling to overcome one or another issue. Like the man whose sight returned slowly (Mark 8:23-25), the truth comes into focus gradually, sometimes after repeated exposure to the gospel.

Dr. Mark Bailey, the president of Dallas Theological Seminary, used to conduct an informal experiment with large classes of students. He asked everyone in the room to raise a hand and hold it there. Then he said, "If you responded to the gospel the first time you heard it, lower your hand." Typically, very few hands would go down. "If you responded to the gospel the second time, lower your hand." A few more fell. "The third time." And so on.

Quite often, he would get to five or more before half the people would lower their hands. That's because tentative contemplation is quite often the most common response to the gospel.

Jesus commanded us to "be My witnesses" (Acts 1:8). He calls us merely to testify to what we know, not to be successful deal closers. That's not in our power. We have a duty to offer our best, to know our audiences, to prepare well when possible, to deliver the good news with conviction, and to communicate clearly—but success is God's responsibility. If we are faithful, the Lord will see to the success.

A Corinthian Impact
ACTS 18:1-22

NASB

¹After these things he left Athens and went to Corinth. ²And he found a Jew named Aquila, a native of Pontus, having recently come from Italy with his wife Priscilla, because Claudius had commanded all the Jews to leave Rome. He came to them, ³and because he was of the same trade, he stayed with them and they were working, for by trade they were

NLT

¹Then Paul left Athens and went to Corinth.* ²There he became acquainted with a Jew named Aquila, born in Pontus, who had recently arrived from Italy with his wife, Priscilla. They had left Italy when Claudius Caesar deported all Jews from Rome. ³Paul lived and worked with them, for they were tentmakers* just as he was.

tent-makers. 4And he was reasoning in the synagogue every Sabbath and trying to persuade Jews and Greeks.

5But when Silas and Timothy came down from Macedonia, Paul *began* devoting himself completely to the word, solemnly testifying to the Jews that Jesus was the ªChrist. 6But when they resisted and blasphemed, he shook out his garments and said to them, "Your blood *be* on your own heads! I am clean. From now on I will go to the Gentiles." 7Then he left there and went to the house of a man named ªTitius Justus, a worshiper of God, whose house was next to the synagogue. 8Crispus, the leader of the synagogue, believed in the Lord with all his household, and many of the Corinthians when they heard were believing and being baptized. 9And the Lord said to Paul in the night by a vision, "Do not be afraid *any longer,* but go on speaking and do not be silent; 10for I am with you, and no man will attack you in order to harm you, for I have many people in this city." 11And he settled *there* a year and six months, teaching the word of God among them.

12But while Gallio was proconsul of Achaia, the Jews with one accord rose up against Paul and brought him before the judgment seat, 13saying, "This man persuades men to worship God contrary to the law." 14But when Paul was about to open his mouth, Gallio said to the Jews, "If it were a matter of wrong or of vicious crime, O Jews, it would be reasonable for me to put up with you; 15but if there are questions about words and names and your own law, look after it yourselves; I am unwilling to be a judge of these matters." 16And he drove them away from the

4Each Sabbath found Paul at the synagogue, trying to convince the Jews and Greeks alike. 5And after Silas and Timothy came down from Macedonia, Paul spent all his time preaching the word. He testified to the Jews that Jesus was the Messiah. 6But when they opposed and insulted him, Paul shook the dust from his clothes and said, "Your blood is upon your own heads—I am innocent. From now on I will go preach to the Gentiles."

7Then he left and went to the home of Titius Justus, a Gentile who worshiped God and lived next door to the synagogue. 8Crispus, the leader of the synagogue, and everyone in his household believed in the Lord. Many others in Corinth also heard Paul, became believers, and were baptized.

9One night the Lord spoke to Paul in a vision and told him, "Don't be afraid! Speak out! Don't be silent! 10For I am with you, and no one will attack and harm you, for many people in this city belong to me." 11So Paul stayed there for the next year and a half, teaching the word of God.

12But when Gallio became governor of Achaia, some Jews rose up together against Paul and brought him before the governor for judgment. 13They accused Paul of "persuading people to worship God in ways that are contrary to our law."

14But just as Paul started to make his defense, Gallio turned to Paul's accusers and said, "Listen, you Jews, if this were a case involving some wrongdoing or a serious crime, I would have a reason to accept your case. 15But since it is merely a question of words and names and your Jewish law, take care of it yourselves. I refuse to judge such matters." 16And he threw them out of the courtroom.

NASB

judgment seat. ¹⁷And they all took hold of Sosthenes, the leader of the synagogue, and *began* beating him in front of the judgment seat. But Gallio was not concerned about any of these things.

¹⁸Paul, having remained many days longer, took leave of the brethren and put out to sea for Syria, and with him were Priscilla and Aquila. In Cenchrea ᵃhe had his hair cut, for he was keeping a vow. ¹⁹They came to Ephesus, and he left them there. Now he himself entered the synagogue and reasoned with the Jews. ²⁰When they asked him to stay for a longer time, he did not consent, ²¹but taking leave of them and saying, "I will return to you again if God wills," he set sail from Ephesus.

²²When he had landed at Caesarea, he went up and greeted the church, and went down to Antioch.

18:5 ᵃI.e. Messiah   18:7 ᵃOne early ms reads *Titus;* two other early mss omit the name
18:18 ᵃLit *having his hair cut*

NLT

¹⁷The crowd* then grabbed Sosthenes, the leader of the synagogue, and beat him right there in the courtroom. But Gallio paid no attention.

¹⁸Paul stayed in Corinth for some time after that, then said good-bye to the brothers and sisters* and went to nearby Cenchrea. There he shaved his head according to Jewish custom, marking the end of a vow. Then he set sail for Syria, taking Priscilla and Aquila with him.

¹⁹They stopped first at the port of Ephesus, where Paul left the others behind. While he was there, he went to the synagogue to reason with the Jews. ²⁰They asked him to stay longer, but he declined. ²¹As he left, however, he said, "I will come back later,* God willing." Then he set sail from Ephesus. ²²The next stop was at the port of Caesarea. From there he went up and visited the church at Jerusalem* and then went back to Antioch.

18:1 *Athens* and *Corinth* were major cities in Achaia, the region in the southern portion of the Greek peninsula.   18:3 Or *leatherworkers*.
18:17 Greek *Everyone;* other manuscripts read *All the Greeks.*   18:18 Greek *brothers;* also in 18:27.   18:21 Some manuscripts read *"I must by all means be at Jerusalem for the upcoming festival, but I will come back later."*
18:22 Greek *the church*.

Culture shock can make for a difficult adjustment when moving into a new environment. Everything you take for granted must be reexamined and reevaluated, and the simplest tasks become laborious because everything works differently. The electricity will fry your appliances, signs bear images you can't decipher, vehicles travel in the opposite direction, and before every meal you have to ask, "What is this?"

In January of 1958, I braced myself for culture shock as our troop ship headed for Yokohama, Japan. After a seventeen-day voyage on a troop ship, our Marine detachment would be granted a couple days of liberty. I looked forward to seeing a part of the world very few got to see in those days. Based on reading and what others told me, I had a sense of what to expect: a language and writing not even remotely similar to English, cuisine almost entirely based on seafood and rice, laws stemming from a completely different tradition, and forms of entertainment that a country boy from El Campo, Texas, couldn't imagine—Kabuki theater? Gagaku music?

When I stepped off that troop ship and emerged from the naval compound, I discovered a dimension of culture shock I hadn't expected—I encountered morality shock. Pornography and open prostitution were everywhere I turned. The first quarter mile in every direction outside the naval compound was a moral spider web designed to snag young military men. I had never seen such a cheap, carnal, relentless display of depravity as I saw in and around that Japanese seaport. Because I was firmly committed to my wife and had a strong Christian upbringing, I was able to view the scene a little more objectively than many of the younger, single fellows. By the time I returned to the ship, I felt like I had lived ten years in two days.

When Paul left Athens and arrived in Corinth, he would add to culture shock the sickening jolt of morality shock. In Athens, he had spent time at the pinnacle of religious devotion and philosophical learning. Vain as it all was, at least the people in the *agora* [58] and on the Areopagus aspired to nobility of thought and deed. In Corinth, however, commerce fueled city life, and sensuality ruled religion. For a monotheistic Jew and temple-trained Pharisee, Paul may not have been ready for what he would encounter. Even so, he was in it for the long haul. As long as there were ears to hear, Paul would preach and teach.

— 18:1 —

Corinth presided over the isthmus between the Gulf of Corinth and the Saronic Gulf, which gave this Roman colony incredible strategic importance. Rather than brave the dangerous journey around Cape Malea at the southernmost tip of Achaia, ship owners preferred to have their vessels dragged across this narrow strip of land. The city also controlled land travel between the mainland of Greece and the semi-attached mass of land known as the Peloponnesus, so ancient travelers called it "the bridge of Greece."[58] Therefore, whoever controlled Corinth also controlled the flow of trade between east and west by sea and all north–south traffic by land. As Rome swept the world into its empire, a Roman general destroyed the city, exterminated the males, and sold the women and children into slavery. The city lay in ruins for nearly a century until, in 46 BC, Julius Caesar resurrected Corinth as a colony for Roman freedmen and as a means of preserving the isthmus for Roman interests.[59]

By the time of Paul, this Roman colony of approximately eighty thousand beat with the heart of Rome and strongly resembled the capital city. Corinth worshiped the emperor, upheld Roman law, pulsated with international trade, hosted athletic games, beckoned pagan worshipers, and thrived on slavery. The city became a popular refuge for Jews fleeing the expulsion of Claudius in AD 49, so a synagogue of unknown size formed amid the sprawl of pagan settlers seeking an immediate fortune and unbridled pleasure.[60]

Eric Dugdale/Wikimedia

The Acrocorinth at Corinth is the tallest point in the city and home to a temple dedicated to Aphrodite.

The city also lay in the shadow of the temple of Aphrodite, which loomed 1,900 feet overhead at the summit of the Acrocorinth and where a thousand female temple prostitutes enticed worshipers from the farthest reaches of the Roman Empire. So infamous was this city's debauched reputation that Aristophanes coined the word "corinthianize" to mean "to practice immorality."[61] Perhaps no city on earth presented Paul a greater challenge than the Las Vegas–like city of Corinth.

— 18:2-4 —

While ministering in Athens, Silas and Timothy had joined Paul for a time, but they apparently heard disturbing reports about persecution of the fledgling church in Thessalonica. To check on their progress and to offer assistance, Paul and Silas sent Timothy (1 Thes. 3:1-2, 5). During his absence, Paul decided to move on to Corinth, leaving Silas in

Athens to wrap up their work and to wait for Timothy. It would be some time before Paul saw either of them again.

Because we think of Paul as a hero of the faith, we might think he confidently strode into Corinth, assessed the situation, and got down to business. But that's not the picture Paul paints when describing his first encounter with the people of Corinth:

> You'll remember, friends, that when I first came to you to let you in on God's master stroke, I didn't try to impress you with polished speeches and the latest philosophy. I deliberately kept it plain and simple: first Jesus and who he is; then Jesus and what he did—Jesus crucified. I was unsure of how to go about this, and felt totally inadequate—I was scared to death, if you want the truth of it—and so nothing I said could have impressed you or anyone else. But the Message came through anyway. God's Spirit and God's power did it, which made it clear that your life of faith is a response to God's power, not to some fancy mental or emotional footwork by me or anyone else. (1 Cor. 2:1-5, MSG)

When he first arrived, Paul knew no one. Macedonia had not been kind to him. The churches he planted in Philippi, Thessalonica, and Berea came at great personal cost to him physically and emotionally. He performed brilliantly in Athens, but it resulted in little fruit—only a handful of believers to show for his time there. Trouble in Macedonia weighed heavily on his mind. Now, as the apostle entered another cultural circus and felt the first tremors of morality shock, the stress undoubtedly caught up with him. He needed support. Fortunately, the Lord had prepared a married couple uniquely positioned to help meet his most pressing needs. He needed accountability and companionship; Aquila and Priscilla were Jews, expelled from Rome and new to Corinth like him. He needed income; they practiced the same trade, shared their business with him, and offered him a place to live. Luke mentions nothing about how, when, or where the couple first believed; they may have been Christians already or they came to Christ through Paul's preaching. Regardless, while waiting for Silas and Timothy to arrive, Paul recuperated in the care and affection of these new friends.

Paul didn't spend all his time earning a living; he kept the Sabbath, and on those days he "reasoned" (see comments on Acts 17:2-4) in the synagogue with the local Jews, in keeping with his normal procedure (18:4).

— 18:5-6 —

The arrival of Silas and Timothy from Macedonia must have been an overwhelming relief to Paul. In addition to their comfort as partners in ministry, they brought good news from the Thessalonian believers. Paul wrote to them from Corinth,

> Now that Timothy has come to us from you, and has brought us good news of your faith and love, and that you always think kindly of us, longing to see us just as we also long to see you, for this reason, brethren, in all our distress and affliction we were comforted about you through your faith; for now we really live, if you stand firm in the Lord. (1 Thes. 3:6-8)

Timothy also brought financial support from the believers in Philippi. He recalled in a later letter, "You yourselves also know, Philippians, that at the first preaching of the gospel, after I left Macedonia, no church shared with me in the matter of giving and receiving but you alone; for even in Thessalonica you sent a gift more than once for my needs" (Phil. 4:15-16). Paul no longer continued his trade but devoted himself exclusively to ministry in the synagogue, trying to persuade the Jews and Gentile proselytes. Luke states that they "resisted and blasphemed," rejecting his message in both passive and aggressive forms (Acts 18:6). We now reserve the word "blaspheme" for those who revile God, but the Greek term applies more generally to mean any speech that denigrates someone else. Indeed, they didn't blaspheme God (at least not directly)—they blasphemed Paul. As we learned earlier, to blaspheme is to curse, slander, or treat someone with contempt. Blasphemy is any manner of speech that disregards or disrespects the value of another.

Paul's gesture of shaking out his garments is highly symbolic and extremely offensive. People shook their garments to rid themselves of crumbs after a meal or dust after sitting for a period of time. Without words, this said, "You are now like crumbs to me; I'm shaking you off and leaving you behind." Nehemiah used the gesture when charging a group of men to honor their promises: "I also shook out the front of my garment and said, 'Thus may God shake out every man from his house and from his possessions who does not fulfill this promise; even thus may he be shaken out and emptied'" (Neh. 5:13). Paul accompanied the gesture with a warning that judgment would follow their rejection of the gospel. And with that, he pledged to take the Word of God to the Gentiles (cf. Acts 13:46).

— 18:7-11 —

When Paul left the Jews to preach to the Gentiles, he didn't go very far! Titius Justus was a Gentile proselyte in the synagogue who had become a believer, presumably through Paul's ministry (18:7). Some scholars believe he's the same person as Gaius, who is mentioned elsewhere (Rom. 16:23; 1 Cor. 1:14), reasoning that Gaius is a first name and Titius Justus is a family name. But the evidence is too scant to make a firm determination. Regardless, he allowed Paul the use of his house, which happened to be next door to the synagogue and of sufficient size to serve as a base for ministry. Luke's mention of the many Corinthians hearing, believing, and being baptized appears to include a number of Jews. It must have been an embarrassing sight to have the synagogue sit silent and empty as throngs filled the house next door to worship. It became even more embarrassing when the leader of the synagogue, Crispus, took his family next door as well (Acts 18:8)!

By now, Paul must have started worrying about a repeat of the painful experiences he had endured in Philippi, Thessalonica, and Berea. He was, after all, just a normal human. Extraordinary in many ways, but no less affected by the outrage of false accusations and the physical and emotional trauma of beatings and imprisonment. Any normal person would begin to shudder at the prospect of more suffering. But the Lord reassured him, promising that this time boldly proclaiming the gospel would *not* result in suffering. The difference? "I have many people in this city" (18:9-10).

The phrase "many people" has two possible meanings. The first is "I have sufficient people in high places to protect you." The second is "I have many elect in this city, so their conversion in great numbers will serve to protect you." The latter is more likely. Even though Gallio, a high-ranking Roman, would go on to side with Paul, he wasn't a believer. As it turns out, the church in Corinth would grow very quickly and add to their number several powerfully positioned Christians.

Luke states that Paul ministered in Corinth for a total of eighteen months—much longer than any other location thus far (18:11). This is probably because the sheer size of the city demanded that much time and because he met with relatively little opposition.

— 18:12-13 —

Gallio was born Marcus Annaeus Novatus, the son of the rhetorician Seneca the Elder, but he took the name of his adopted father, Lucius Junius Gallio. Gallio's brother was the philosopher Seneca the Younger.

Between AD 51 and 53, Gallio held the rank of proconsul in Achaia, a position reporting directly to the senate and endowed with absolute military and judicial power over the province. He eventually returned to Rome to serve as consul during the administration of Nero. His participation in a plot to kill the demented emperor cost him his life in AD 65.[62]

The unbelieving Jews who retained control of the synagogue responded much like their apostate brethren in Macedonia, Pisidia, and Galatia. They appealed to pagan government officials to destroy Paul because they couldn't refute the gospel. Asking the Romans to intervene demonstrated their lack of loyalty to their Jewish heritage despite their supposed devotion to the synagogue. They dragged Paul before the *bēma* [968], the "judgment seat" in the *agora* [58], and lodged a complaint with the proconsul (18:12). Note their charge against Paul: "This man persuades men to worship God contrary to the law" (18:13; cf. 16:21; 17:6-7, 13).

Barry Beitzel

The *Bēma* at Corinth.

Whose law? The Jewish leader must have appealed to the proconsul with Roman law in view. Though through Roman eyes the budding Christian movement would have likely been seen as a sect of Judaism, and therefore a legal religion under Roman law, the Jewish religious leaders were already taking steps to jettison the followers of Jesus from the synagogue. By asserting that the Christians worshiped God contrary to the law, they were saying, in effect, that Paul and the early believers were not part of the Jewish orthodoxy allowed by Rome. If the Jewish leaders could get a Roman proconsul to acknowledge the differences between Christianity and Judaism, between church and synagogue, perhaps they could stomp out the disciples of Jesus through Roman edict!

— 18:14-17 —

Paul had been in this position before. This was not his first *bēma*. And it rarely went well for him. On those other occasions, he had never received the opportunity to mount a defense, call witnesses, or even tell his side of the story. So, when he opened his mouth to speak and Gallio cut him off, I'm sure his stomach tightened just a little. To his delight, however, Gallio recognized the foolishness of the situation. Ironically, he pointed the Jews to their own law, as if to say, "Don't you worry about Roman law; I'll take care of that. You mind your own law, in which I have no interest" (18:14-16). Because the rulings of a proconsul were binding on his successors, Gallio's decision set a crucial legal precedent in Corinth.

This hard, humiliating slap didn't sit well with the disbelieving faction of Jews. After Crispus vacated his position as "the leader of the synagogue" (18:8), a man named Sosthenes apparently took his place and may have led the next charge against Paul. When Gallio dismissed the Jews' complaint with some disdain, the predominantly Gentile audience began beating the Jewish leader (18:17).

In Paul's letter to Corinth, he includes a Sosthenes in the greeting (1 Cor. 1:1). It's possible that this is the same man; if so, this incident may have been a catalyst in his conversion.

— 18:18 —

At last, the time had come to return home, give a report, rest, and then decide what should happen next. "Syria" refers to Syrian Antioch, Paul's sending church. He left the busy metropolis of Corinth for Cenchrea, the seaport for eastbound travelers located just 7 miles southeast. Aquila and Priscilla, Paul's loyal new friends, accompanied him, although the reason is unclear. It appears they planned to relocate to Ephesus, either for personal reasons or as part of Paul's ultimate plan to penetrate the province of Asia with the gospel.

Luke's reference to Paul's haircut indicates that he had taken a Nazirite vow (Num. 6:1-21). By this special vow, a Jewish man or woman pledged him- or herself to the Lord's exclusive use to accomplish a specific objective. During this time, the individual agreed to abstain from any product of the vine—wine, strong drink, grapes, raisins, juice—to avoid contact with the dead, and to allow his or her hair to go uncut. When Jews saw a fellow Jew with long hair, especially a man, they immediately recognized the sign of taking a vow. According to the custom, Paul was to deliver a special sacrifice to the temple upon the conclusion of his vow (Num. 6:13-21). As an animal was burned on the altar in this elaborate ritual, he was to present his cut hair to the priest, who would burn it on the altar as a peace offering. After this ritual, the Nazirite could again enjoy the fruit of the vine.

— 18:19-21 —

On the way to Syria, Paul's ship landed near Ephesus, where Aquila and Priscilla disembarked. He used the opportunity to visit the synagogue and "reason" (18:19; cf. 17:2-4) with the Jews and Gentile proselytes. Unlike in other locations, the people in the Ephesian synagogue received his message openly, even inviting him to stay longer (18:20). Paul must have agonized over the errands he had to run; how often he had hoped to see his kindred Jews respond to the gospel so openly. He left with a promise to return "if God wills" (18:21).

— 18:22 —

Luke concludes his account of Paul's second journey with a brief summary of his itinerary. He landed in Caesarea, the principal seaport for Jerusalem. The phrase "went up" identifies the mountaintop city of Jerusalem as his destination, where he connected with the apostles and elders and presumably completed his Nazirite ritual in the temple. Ultimately, his journey took him back "down" to Syrian Antioch, his sending church.

APPLICATION: ACTS 18:1-22

Good Living in a Godless World

Paul had ministered in some of the most diverse and extreme cultures in the ancient world. Many were like his hometown of Tarsus, offering the best in terms of education and culture alongside the very worst opportunities for avarice and sensuality. As he ventured farther from home and closer to Rome, the balance tipped heavily toward pagan dissipation as Jewish communities made up a very small minority of the population. In Athens, Paul found virtually no Jewish influence. And Corinth? Like finding a church in the red-light district of Amsterdam.

Luke never states why Paul took his Nazirite vow. As a young Marine stepping off a ship in Yokohama, I can imagine. He arrived in Corinth alone. He was a red-blooded male, and apostles weren't immune to temptation; in fact, they undoubtedly bore a greater share because of their work. As a young man away from home alone for the first time, I found myself surrounded by opportunities for anonymous sin, and I had a decision to make. Looking down at my wedding band made that choice easier. I had made a vow. Someone back at home was trusting in me. I would have to look her in the eye one day and tell the truth about where I had gone and what I had done. Perhaps Paul, alone and unaccountable in the cesspool of Corinth, made his vow too.

Like Paul in Corinth, we struggle to maintain high Christian standards in a world that cares less and less about morality. Paul's experience highlights three principles that will help us survive and thrive despite the downward drag of moral decline.

First, *the darker the scene, the greater the challenge.* If you find yourself in an area dominated by non-Christians, this can work to your advantage. It's easy to become lethargic and complacent in exclusively Christian environments. So use the challenge of your dark circumstances to buoy you rather than drag you down. You do that by declaring your identity early. Do it boldly, yet without being obnoxious. If you're a college student, wear a tastefully designed Christian T-shirt that identifies you as a believer. If you're on a new job, discreetly place a small Bible on your desk. Simply keep it handy and in plain view; don't wave flags or erect a shrine in your office. Establishing your Christian identity early gives you something to uphold when the opportunity for anonymous sin presents itself.

Second, *the weaker the spokesman, the stronger the message.* I'm encouraged to know that Paul struggled with insecurity, feeling intimidated and unsure. He didn't consider his personal limitations a liability to the gospel; on the contrary, he highlighted his weaknesses to validate the gospel message as God-ordained (1 Cor. 2:1-5). He became a successful instrument of God because he remained faithful; he kept himself away from sin.

The same can be true for us. Surrounded by all the wrong influences, we feel inadequate to address them. In fact, we *are* inadequate! Fortunately, God has not called us to fix the world singlehandedly, only to remain faithful to Him—to follow His promptings and to do what we can. As we obey, He will speak through us. Our weakness will exhibit His strength.

Third, *the greater the resistance, the less the fear.* Anybody can fight a weak opponent. Anyone can keep going when the going is easy. That requires no determination and no faith, and it results in no personal growth. When people and influences contrary to Christ surround you, however, the opportunity for closeness with the Lord grows exponentially. That's when you discover the immense power of the Holy Spirit. When you determine to stand firm, acknowledging your own weakness, His courage takes over. Gradually and yet supernaturally, you lose your fear of ridicule and rejection. You discover the Spirit within you speaking through you without hesitation or intimidation.

The Full Gospel
ACTS 18:23–19:7

NASB

23 And having spent some time *there*, he left and passed successively through the Galatian region and Phrygia, strengthening all the disciples.

24 Now a Jew named Apollos, an Alexandrian by birth, ᵃan eloquent man, came to Ephesus; and he was mighty in the Scriptures. 25 This man had been instructed in the way of the Lord; and being fervent in spirit, he was speaking and teaching accurately the things concerning Jesus, being acquainted only with the baptism of John; 26 and ᵃhe began to speak out boldly in the synagogue. But when Priscilla and Aquila heard him, they took him aside and explained to him the way of God more accurately. 27 And when he wanted to go across to Achaia, the brethren encouraged him and wrote to the disciples to welcome him; and when

NLT

23 After spending some time in Antioch, Paul went back through Galatia and Phrygia, visiting and strengthening all the believers.*

24 Meanwhile, a Jew named Apollos, an eloquent speaker who knew the Scriptures well, had arrived in Ephesus from Alexandria in Egypt. 25 He had been taught the way of the Lord, and he taught others about Jesus with an enthusiastic spirit* and with accuracy. However, he knew only about John's baptism. 26 When Priscilla and Aquila heard him preaching boldly in the synagogue, they took him aside and explained the way of God even more accurately.

27 Apollos had been thinking about going to Achaia, and the brothers and sisters in Ephesus encouraged him to go. They wrote to the believers in Achaia, asking them to welcome him. When he arrived there, he proved to be of great benefit to those

he had arrived, he greatly ᵃhelped those who had believed through grace, ²⁸for he powerfully refuted the Jews in public, demonstrating by the Scriptures that Jesus was the ᵃChrist.

19:1 It happened that while Apollos was at Corinth, Paul passed through the upper country and came to Ephesus, and found some disciples. ²He said to them, "Did you receive the Holy Spirit when you believed?" And they *said* to him, "No, we have not even heard whether ᵃthere is a Holy Spirit." ³And he said, "Into what then were you baptized?" And they said, "Into John's baptism." ⁴Paul said, "John baptized with the baptism of repentance, telling the people to believe in Him who was coming after him, that is, in Jesus." ⁵When they heard this, they were baptized ᵃin the name of the Lord Jesus. ⁶And when Paul had laid his hands upon them, the Holy Spirit came on them, and they *began* speaking with tongues and prophesying. ⁷There were in all about twelve men.

18:24 ᵃOr *a learned man*   18:26 ᵃLit *this man*
18:27 ᵃOr *helped greatly through grace those who had believed*   18:28 ᵃI.e. Messiah   19:2 ᵃOr *the Holy Spirit has been* given   19:5 ᵃLit *into*

who, by God's grace, had believed. ²⁸He refuted the Jews with powerful arguments in public debate. Using the Scriptures, he explained to them that Jesus was the Messiah.

19:1 While Apollos was in Corinth, Paul traveled through the interior regions until he reached Ephesus, on the coast, where he found several believers.* ²"Did you receive the Holy Spirit when you believed?" he asked them.

"No," they replied, "we haven't even heard that there is a Holy Spirit."

³"Then what baptism did you experience?" he asked.

And they replied, "The baptism of John."

⁴Paul said, "John's baptism called for repentance from sin. But John himself told the people to believe in the one who would come later, meaning Jesus."

⁵As soon as they heard this, they were baptized in the name of the Lord Jesus. ⁶Then when Paul laid his hands on them, the Holy Spirit came on them, and they spoke in other tongues* and prophesied. ⁷There were about twelve men in all.

18:23 Greek *disciples;* also in 18:27.   18:25 Or *with enthusiasm in the Spirit.*   19:1 Greek *disciples;* also in 19:9, 30.   19:6 Or *in other languages.*

In the 1970s, the term "Full Gospel"—a divisive and derisive term—became popular among some charismatic Christians. According to this particular strain of charismatic, one could become a believer and live for years without receiving the gift of the Holy Spirit. Some modified this heretical theology, saying one could become a Christian and receive the Holy Spirit yet not be "filled" to the extent of displaying supernatural abilities, such as healing, prophecy, speaking in tongues, or casting out demons. Many noncharismatic Christians took offense—and rightly so—because the designation "Full Gospel" implies that those who do not exhibit these supernatural gifts are incomplete, or "partial Christians."

These "Full Gospel" theologians propped up their teaching with Acts 19:1-7. As we shall see, however, they conveniently missed Luke's point. Attention to the near context, beginning with 18:23, shows that Luke inserted this interlude between Paul's second and third missionary journeys to show that one can no more become a "partial believer" than a woman can become "partially pregnant." Either there's another life inside or there isn't. Luke illustrates this truth by providing two before-and-after portraits, both occurring in or around Ephesus.

— 18:23 —

At the conclusion of his second missionary journey, Paul returned to Syrian Antioch, where he probably spent the winter of AD 51/52. Soon after the spring thaw, he set out again, following the same course as the second journey, up through Syria and into Cilicia, where he probably stopped off in his hometown of Tarsus for a brief visit. As soon as the weather permitted, he would have used the Cilician Gates to traverse the Taurus Mountains into Galatia, then Phrygia. The churches he planted in Derbe, Lystra, Iconium, and Pisidian Antioch must have felt thrilled to see him. Luke states that he strengthened the believers along the way. Paul probably didn't stay long in each location; he had wanted to return to Ephesus soon. He not only wanted to keep his word, but he also couldn't wait to minister in the region God had closed to him earlier.

— 18:24-26 —

Luke takes this opportunity to shift the scene to Ephesus, ahead of Paul. Two vignettes focus on individuals who had heard part of the good news, but still needed instruction for a fuller understanding of the faith.

Apollos was a Jew from Alexandria, Egypt, influenced by the ministry of John the Baptizer (perhaps personally, but more likely by reputation). John's ministry had profound and far-reaching implications in its own right, even before the arrival of the Messiah. He had become known for giving the Jewish rite of water baptism a new application. Normally, Gentile proselytes were baptized as the final stage of their conversion to Judaism, after intense training in the Hebrew language and the Law of Moses, a rigorous examination, and then circumcision.

Many desired to be right with God, so they came to John to be baptized. But John taught these people that the Messiah would come with a greater baptism. John promised, "As for me, I baptize you with water;

JOHN THE BAPTIZER

ACTS 18:25; 19:1-7

John the Baptizer is a shadowy figure in the minds of many Christians. Most could fit all they know about him on one side of a three-by-five card with plenty of room to spare. Clearly, he baptized people. Some know he lived in the desert and subsisted on a weird diet of locusts and honey. Those interested in theology know him as the forerunner of the Messiah. But that's about all most people know. Yet Jesus said of him, "Among those born of women there has not arisen anyone greater than John the Baptist!" (Matt. 11:11).

Dr. Luke, a physician by training, was interested in the humanity of the men and women surrounding Jesus. From him we learn that John was born an only child to an aging priest, Zacharias, and his postmenopausal wife, Elizabeth. His birth attracted the attention of everyone in the Judean hill country, not only because it was surrounded by miraculous occurrences, but also because he would be set aside from day one to live an ascetic lifestyle similar to that of a Nazirite. He was not to cut his hair, touch anything dead, or partake of any product of the vine—no wine, no grapes, no raisins (Luke 1:15; Num. 6:2-6). God had chosen him, even before his conception, to be the prophesied forerunner of the Messiah (Isa. 40:3-5; Luke 1:76).

He didn't grow to manhood in the court of a palace. Luke says, "The child continued to grow and to become strong in spirit, and he lived in the deserts until the day of his public appearance to Israel" (Luke 1:80). Don't misunderstand—this was not a desert like Palm Springs. John grew up among dust and rock and scrub bushes and intense heat and the scarcity of everything, including food and water. However, in the silence and solitude and simplicity of those difficult days, John communed with the Author of truth. The Holy Spirit filled him from his earliest years (Luke 1:15), and he lived by the foundational principle of God's kingdom—a standard Israel had failed to heed centuries before: "Man does not live by bread alone, but man lives by everything that proceeds out of the mouth of the LORD" (Deut. 8:3).

When John came out of the wilderness to confront and convict the nation of Israel, how different he was from the religious leaders people were used to hearing! The Gospel of Mark tells us he "was clothed with camel's hair and wore a leather belt around his waist, and his diet was locusts and wild honey" (Mark 1:6). While the Sadducees, Pharisees, chief priests, scribes, and Herodians were robed in finery and nourished with meat and too much wine, John stood gaunt from ascetic living and leathery from the sun. And his message was just as unadorned and unyielding as his appearance. When Sadducees and Pharisees, practitioners of hypocritical religion, came to him for a showy baptism of counterfeit repentance, he would have none of it—and he told them so! "You brood of vipers, who warned you to flee from the wrath to come? Therefore bear fruit in keeping with repentance; and do not suppose that you can say to yourselves, 'We have Abraham for our father'; for I say to you that from these stones God is able to raise up children to Abraham" (Matt. 3:7-9). Oh, how the religious elite hated him! And they would have killed him were he not protected by the wilderness and surrounded by growing multitudes of people who genuinely repented of their sin.

The prophet Malachi had predicted that an Elijah-like figure would announce the imminent arrival of the Messiah (Mal. 3:1; 4:5-6). Many took the prophet's words literally and expected the return of the actual Elijah—especially since Elijah had been taken up to heaven before death (2 Kgs. 2:9-12). Although John the Baptizer was indeed the fulfillment of Malachi's prophecy, he was not the revered seer of old.

John began preaching repentance and baptizing people in the wilderness. Jewish baptism was a rite in which a new convert to Judaism was ceremonially immersed in water as a symbol of once-for-all cleansing from sin before entering the Hebrew covenant community. It was intended for Gentile proselytes, not Jews already born into God's covenant with Abraham. So John gave the rite of proselyte baptism a new application when he called Jews to a baptism of repentance. In effect, he was saying, "Because of your sin, you are outside of Abraham's covenant with God. You must repent like a Gentile and come to God as if for the first time." As a result, earnest Jews came in droves! Nevertheless, John admitted that his baptism was merely symbolic and quickly turned the discussion away from water baptism—which itself pointed to the Messiah—toward the One he had come to announce. After all, he was merely a witness to the truth, not the source of truth. He was only the lampstand, not the light.[63]

but One is coming who is mightier than I, and I am not fit to untie the thong of His sandals; He will baptize you with the Holy Spirit and fire" (Luke 3:16).

In Ephesus, Paul's companions Priscilla and Aquila came upon Apollos, an earnest Jew who proclaimed the Messiah while extending the ministry of John. Luke describes him as "an eloquent man" who was "mighty in the Scriptures" (Acts 18:24). The "Scriptures" in this case would have likely included the Old Testament translated into Greek, a work now known as the Septuagint. The word translated "eloquent" (*logios* [3052]) means "learned," "cultured," or "able to articulate what one has learned"—qualities the world had come to expect from Alexandria, the political and intellectual capital city of Egypt and, besides Rome, the most important city in the ancient world. Along with its other leading features, Alexandria was a center of learning and hosted the world's largest library where seven hundred thousand Greek texts were stored before the library's partial destruction by the army of Julius Caesar. In fact, the Septuagint books from Genesis to Deuteronomy had been translated in Alexandria during the third century BC. Consequently, a teacher from Alexandria would have carried considerable influence, not unlike a PhD from Harvard, Yale, Stanford, or Oxford.

Apollos had heard about Jesus and the arrival of the Holy Spirit from Jews returning from Pentecost, but he did not have the complete story; he had learned about "the way of the Lord," but he was "acquainted only with the baptism of John" (18:25). His teaching was good and right insofar as it proved from the Old Testament that Jesus is the Christ, but he missed key elements. Christian baptism differs from the baptism of John in that it symbolizes the believer's union with Christ in His death, burial, resurrection, new life, and unity in the kingdom of God (Rom. 6:3-10; 1 Cor. 12:13; Gal. 3:27; Col. 2:12). This deficiency prompted Aquila and Priscilla to instruct Apollos privately, to give him a more full and accurate picture of "the way of God" (Acts 18:26).

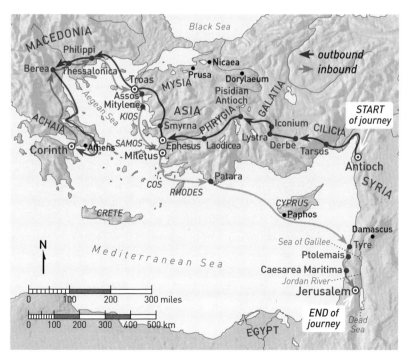

Paul's Third Missionary Journey. Paul and his companions set out once again from Antioch and journeyed across Asia and Greece to Corinth. Paul returned through the same cities of Greece; he then boated around the western coast of Asia and sailed across the Mediterranean to return to Jerusalem.

— 18:27-28 —

Notably, Luke doesn't describe a conversion experience for Apollos (cf. 9:1-7), most likely because he had already believed and had already received the Holy Spirit but did not display miraculous abilities. He received a more thorough explanation of Christian theology from Paul's friends, which made him a more effective teacher and evangelist, but he didn't experience a radical change. His credentials as a genuine believer and a learned teacher impressed the brothers in Ephesus enough that they wrote letters of introduction on his behalf, so he could minister effectively in Corinth with their endorsement.

— 19:1-2 —

Luke juxtaposes the experience of Apollos with that of twelve men near Ephesus.

Paul had been ministering to the churches he and Barnabas had established in Galatia and Pisidia, in the cities of Derbe, Lystra, Iconium, and Antioch, as he traveled east on the Via Sebaste. From Antioch, Paul passed through the "upper country," a Greek expression referring to highlands. The ancients didn't think of "up" and "down" as north and south, the way we do, but rather in terms of elevation. One went "up" to Jerusalem, a mountaintop city, and came "down" when leaving. So he probably did not visit Colossae and Laodicea (cf. Col. 2:1) but took a more direct route through Philadelphia, perhaps Sardis, and then through the Cayster River valley into Ephesus.

Luke's grammar can indicate that Paul "found some disciples" along the way to Ephesus or in Ephesus. A literal rendering would be, "Paul traveled through the upper parts to arrive in Ephesus and discovered some disciples." This could explain why the ministry of Apollos, Aquila, and Priscilla in the Ephesian synagogue had not affected these people. The transition to Acts 19:8, however, favors the idea that Paul found the disciples upon his arrival in Ephesus; it says that he entered the synagogue after his encounter with the disciples, implying that he had already arrived in the city of Ephesus.

Luke typically uses the Greek term for "disciple" (*mathētēs* [3101]) to refer to believers, but in this case it denotes Christians-in-waiting—Jews who had responded positively to John the Baptist's ministry but who had not yet received a complete articulation of the person and work of Jesus Christ. They had only partial information and had not received the Holy Spirit. Paul probed their understanding to diagnose their need—to determine whether they were ignorant or rebellious. He neither questioned nor denied their sincerity. He didn't probe their theology, examine their deeds, or measure their piety. He instead inquired about whether they had received the Holy Spirit. God the Father responds to genuine trust in Jesus Christ by giving the gift of His Spirit—always. In this case, He delayed this gift only to grant the apostles in Jerusalem an opportunity to witness the event; He wanted to assure the Jewish Christians that Samaritan and Gentile believers were fully accepted by Him (8:14-17).

— 19:3-7 —

When the disciples revealed their ignorance about the Holy Spirit, Paul recognized that they had not even heard about the events of Pentecost (19:2; see 2:1-12). Like Apollos, they had responded to the repentance invitation of John the Baptizer (19:3), and they anticipated the Messiah as John had indicated; but while Apollos had been instructed in "the Way" (18:25; cf. 9:2), these people knew nothing about Jesus Christ. Whereas Apollos was "teaching accurately the things concerning Jesus" (18:25) and then was instructed "more accurately" (18:26), Paul introduced Christ to these disciples for the first time. He began with the Baptizer's teaching, which pointed to the Messiah, and then he declared Jesus to be the Christ (19:4). In response, the disciples believed and then received Christian baptism (19:5).

In an unusual act, Paul laid hands on the new believers and they received the Holy Spirit. This parallels an earlier episode in which Peter and John (the apostle, not the Baptizer) did something similar. They had heard about the success of the gospel among the Samaritans, who were despised by Jews as half-breeds and Gentile compromisers. The possibility that the Samaritans could become genuine believers stretched the bounds of credibility for Jewish believers. So the two apostles traveled to Samaria to see for themselves. When they arrived, they laid hands on the new believers and the Holy Spirit filled the Samaritans (8:14-17). This proved conclusively, to the Jews and to the Samaritans, that God had accepted these new believers as full-fledged citizens of His kingdom. Paul's gesture in 19:6 accomplished a similar purpose. God authenticated these disciples by giving them supernatural evidence of His Spirit.

The miraculous evidence of the Holy Spirit also duplicates the effect at Pentecost. God allowed the newly empowered Jewish believers to speak in tongues and to prophesy in order to validate the Old Testament promise concerning God's Spirit (Joel 2:28-32). Similarly, these Jewish believers in Ephesus were given miraculous abilities to authenticate the reality of the Holy Spirit, about whom they had not heard, and to

INSTANCES OF MIRACULOUS EVIDENCE OF THE HOLY SPIRIT			
Passage	**Subjects**	**Observers**	**Purpose**
2:1-4	Jewish believers	Jewish nonbelievers	To authenticate the fulfillment of Old Testament prophecy concerning the Holy Spirit (Joel 2:28-32)
8:14-17	Samaritan believers	Jewish believers	To authenticate God's acceptance of Samaritans as Christians
10:44-47	Gentile believers	Jewish believers	To authenticate God's acceptance of Gentiles as Christians
19:1-7	Jewish disciples of John the Baptist	Jewish believers	To authenticate the gospel among the Jews in Ephesus

validate the gospel within the Jewish community (cf. 1 Cor. 14:22). The imperfect tense of "speaking" and "prophesying" is what grammarians call "ingressive," meaning that the new believers began and then continued to exhibit these miraculous abilities. The number twelve (Acts 19:7) would have been highly significant to the Jews because of its correspondence to the twelve tribes of Israel.

God allowed believers to demonstrate miraculous Holy Spirit power for one reason: to authenticate their acceptance as God's representatives. As Dr. Stanley Toussaint points out, not every instance of salvation is accompanied by a miraculous display, and "the reception of the Holy Spirit in Acts does not follow any set pattern. He came into believers before baptism (10:44), at the time of or after baptism (8:12-16; 19:6), and by the laying on of apostolic hands (8:17; 19:6)."[64]

APPLICATION: ACTS 18:23–19:7

The Spirit of Salvation

Apollos and the other incomplete disciples shared one similarity: They knew only about the baptism associated with John the Baptizer's ministry. Before Jesus emerged as the Messiah, John prepared Israel for His arrival while offering a baptism of repentance. Christian baptism builds upon John's, but it symbolizes much more. Christian baptism illustrates the believer's identification with Christ in His death, burial, resurrection (Rom. 6:3-5), new life, and unity with all other believers (1 Cor. 12:13). Neither Apollos nor the incomplete disciples knew about Christian baptism.

Beyond this similarity, however, Apollos and the incomplete disciples exhibit some helpful contrasts.

- Apollos had heard about Jesus (Acts 18:25); the disciples had not.
- Apollos had undoubtedly heard about Pentecost and the arrival of the Holy Spirit; the disciples had "not even heard whether there is a Holy Spirit" (19:2).
- The ministry of Apollos improved, but did not change; the disciples experienced a radical change.

Luke mentions nothing about miraculous evidence of the Holy Spirit in Apollos; the disciples did not hear of the Holy Spirit and then upon belief begin to speak in tongues and prophesy. These important differences highlight four important conclusions.

First, *repentance is not enough without trust in Christ.* Repentance is a necessary beginning, but repentance does not, by itself, save an individual from the eternal consequences of sin. One must believe in the atoning sacrifice of Jesus Christ and accept God's forgiveness as a free gift apart from good deeds.

Second, *the presence of the Holy Spirit indicates genuine belief, or what might be called "saving faith."* Christians receive the Holy Spirit as a gift at the moment of salvation; those who do not have the Spirit are not saved.

Third, *the Holy Spirit may or may not reveal Himself through miraculous abilities.* He will speak in other languages or prophesy through believers at His discretion to meet the needs of the time. Believers have no say in the matter. Miraculous ability is neither learned nor acquired, but solely a work of God.

Fourth, *while miraculous ability validates the presence of the Holy Spirit, we cannot interpret the absence of miracles as the absence of the Spirit.* In the Old and New Testaments, the effects of the Spirit's work in the lives of God's people take a variety of forms. For example, the Spirit's presence results in wisdom, understanding, strength, and fear of God (see Isa. 11:2). And His sanctifying work in the believer yields fruit of love, joy, peace, patience, kindness, goodness, faithfulness, gentleness, and self-control (Gal. 5:22–23).

God's Extraordinary Power
ACTS 19:8-20

NASB

[8] And he entered the synagogue and continued speaking out boldly for three months, reasoning and persuading *them* about the kingdom of God. [9] But when some were becoming hardened and disobedient, speaking evil of the Way before the ªpeople, he withdrew from them and took away the disciples, reasoning daily in the school of Tyrannus. [10] This took place for two years, so that all who lived in ªAsia heard the word of the Lord, both Jews and Greeks.

[11] God was performing extraordinary ªmiracles by the hands of Paul, [12] so that handkerchiefs or aprons were even carried from his body to the sick, and the diseases left them and the evil spirits went out. [13] But also some of the Jewish exorcists, who went from place to place, attempted to name over those who had the evil spirits the name of the Lord Jesus, saying, "I adjure you by Jesus whom Paul preaches." [14] Seven sons of one Sceva, a Jewish chief priest, were doing this. [15] And the evil spirit answered and said to them, "I recognize Jesus, and I know about Paul, but who are you?" [16] And the man, in whom was the evil spirit, leaped on them and subdued all of them and overpowered them, so that they fled out of that house naked and wounded. [17] This became known to all, both Jews and Greeks, who lived in Ephesus; and fear fell upon them all and the name of the Lord Jesus was being magnified. [18] Many also of those who had believed kept coming, confessing and disclosing their practices. [19] And many of those who practiced magic brought their books together and *began* burning them in the sight of everyone; and they

NLT

[8] Then Paul went to the synagogue and preached boldly for the next three months, arguing persuasively about the Kingdom of God. [9] But some became stubborn, rejecting his message and publicly speaking against the Way. So Paul left the synagogue and took the believers with him. Then he held daily discussions at the lecture hall of Tyrannus. [10] This went on for the next two years, so that people throughout the province of Asia—both Jews and Greeks—heard the word of the Lord.

[11] God gave Paul the power to perform unusual miracles. [12] When handkerchiefs or aprons that had merely touched his skin were placed on sick people, they were healed of their diseases, and evil spirits were expelled.

[13] A group of Jews was traveling from town to town casting out evil spirits. They tried to use the name of the Lord Jesus in their incantation, saying, "I command you in the name of Jesus, whom Paul preaches, to come out!" [14] Seven sons of Sceva, a leading priest, were doing this. [15] But one time when they tried it, the evil spirit replied, "I know Jesus, and I know Paul, but who are you?" [16] Then the man with the evil spirit leaped on them, overpowered them, and attacked them with such violence that they fled from the house, naked and battered.

[17] The story of what happened spread quickly all through Ephesus, to Jews and Greeks alike. A solemn fear descended on the city, and the name of the Lord Jesus was greatly honored. [18] Many who became believers confessed their sinful practices. [19] A number of them who had been practicing sorcery brought

counted up the price of them and found it ᵃfifty thousand pieces of silver. ²⁰So ᵃthe word of the Lord was growing mightily and prevailing.

19:9 ᵃLit *multitude* 19:10 ᵃI.e. west coast province of Asia Minor 19:11 ᵃOr *works of power* 19:19 ᵃProbably fifty thousand Greek drachmas; a drachma approximated a day's wage. 19:20 ᵃOr *according to the power of the Lord the word was growing*

their incantation books and burned them at a public bonfire. The value of the books was several million dollars.* ²⁰So the message about the Lord spread widely and had a powerful effect.

19:19 Greek *50,000 pieces of silver,* each of which was the equivalent of a day's wage.

On the border between Arizona and Nevada, a massive wall of concrete stands silent watch over just a little more than one trillion gallons of water.[65] There's enough water behind Hoover Dam to transform the state of Pennsylvania into a wading pool one foot deep. In the heart of this massive concrete wall, seventy stories high and more than a fifth of a mile across the top, seventeen turbines turn the high-pressure flow of water out of Lake Mead into 2,080 megawatts of electricity. To stand at the top is to see incredible potential power; to see the machinery transforming water flow into energy is amazing. But it's still hard to appreciate the power of this engineering marvel. Perhaps the best way to gauge the power of Hoover Dam is to look down from an orbiting space station at night to see more than two million tiny dots spread across Nevada, Arizona, and Southern California, each light representing a home all lit up. And yet, Hoover Dam represents more than just the energy to turn on lights and operate appliances. Its real power might better be measured in terms of change. Since its completion in 1936, the project has supplied vast stretches of uninhabitable land with power and water for eight million people.[66]

Of course, the power of Hoover Dam is nothing compared to the power of God, who is omnipotent, "all-powerful." We cannot measure His power; we can only appreciate His ability to accomplish change wherever and whenever He chooses. While the universe, in all its enormity and complexity, testifies to the immense power of the Creator, the cosmos is too vast to comprehend. We can gain a better appreciation of His omnipotence by observing the changes He brings to otherwise-hopeless lives.

By the time Paul reached Ephesus, much of the known world had been changed by the rapid spread of Holy Spirit power, following the pathways of the gospel as it radiated outward from Pentecost. But many places, like the province of Asia, had yet to be delivered from the death grip of evil. Now, during Paul's two-year stay in Ephesus, the Lord's power would be especially manifest, accompanying the gospel through miraculous signs and successful confrontations with demonic activity in ways that would begin the transformation of hardened hearts throughout Asia.

— 19:8-10 —

Luke introduces the ministry of Paul in Ephesus with a summary, using the imperfect tense (indicating ongoing, repetitive, or customary action) and painting the scene in broad strokes. As always, Paul began his work in Ephesus by speaking in the synagogue (19:8), which must have been sizable for a city of two hundred fifty thousand or more.[67] For three months, Paul "reasoned" with the Jews, building on the solid teaching of Apollos (18:24-26) and having the testimony of twelve new disciples in the area (19:1-7). He had enjoyed initial success during his first visit, receiving an enthusiastic invitation to stay (18:19-21). Now, however, the pattern began to follow that of other cities. Some Jewish leaders and a number of people from the congregation believed, but the majority turned against Paul and became resolutely opposed to his message, even resorting to slander. So, as in other cities, the apostle turned from the Jews to focus on the Gentiles.

When Paul withdrew and took the disciples away from the synagogue, he moved to "the school of Tyrannus" (19:9). The Greek word for "school" or "lecture hall" (scholē [4981]) originally referred to "leisure," because that was the luxury considered necessary for the scholarly pursuits of discussion, study, and contemplation. Typically located within the city, the architectural design of a lecture hall followed the function of teaching, taking full advantage of both lecture and the Socratic method of dialogue. This particular facility belonged to Tyrannus. Unfortunately, the significance of his name has been lost to history. Tyrannus was a very common name among Romans, so he could have been a wealthy disciple who allowed Paul to use his facility, or the leader of a school of philosophy who rented the space to Paul, or a businessman who lent the space to any paying customer. Regardless, Paul used the scholē effectively for two years (19:10). Ephesus became Paul's base of operations and the lecture hall of Tyrannus his headquarters, where he taught daily when he wasn't on a trip into the interior of Asia.

— 19:11-12 —

Throughout Acts, Luke highlights the fact that God accomplished similar things through Peter and Paul. Both healed a disabled man (3:2-12;

EPHESUS, THE MOTHER OF COMMERCE IN ASIA

ACTS 19:1-41

Ephesus was a city built of marble. Marble paved the streets, lined the foundations, supported the monuments, and channeled rainwater to the sea. Even the public toilets were constructed from polished marble. The city gleamed with white iridescence, as if to say to the world, "This city will shine forever." And of all the cities in the Roman Empire, Ephesus would have been one of the most difficult places in which to establish an orderly church. The city of Corinth struggled with rampant immorality, and that enemy was easy to spot. But a church in Ephesus also had to be on guard against two insidious killers of congregations: enticing prosperity and distracting philosophy.

This port city sat alongside the Aegean Sea at the mouth of the Cayster River and near the intersection of two important mountain passes. Ephesus, therefore, commanded a strategic position offering access in all directions from the sea, making the city an unusually busy and affluent economic hub for the Roman province of Asia. Materials and knowledge flowed into the city from all over the world, feeding its voracious appetite for more wealth and new ideas.

Ephesus was renowned for its paganism—as many as fifty different gods and goddesses were worshiped there.[68] None, however, challenged the economic and mystical power of the towering temple of Artemis, one of the seven wonders of the ancient world. Worship of the "earth mother" had become a huge attraction, combining tourism and sensual idolatry with such success that it fueled the city's core economy, even without its already burgeoning import/export trade. City officials set aside one month of every year to honor the goddess with a grand celebration, during which all work ceased. The stadium hosted athletic games, the theater produced plays, the odeum held concerts, and people flocked from every corner of Asia and beyond to make offerings in the sacred grove, the mythical birthplace of Artemis. Worship of the goddess brought such enormous sums of money into the temple that it became an important banking institution, perhaps the first of its kind in Asia. Moreover, the city of Ephesus became a sanctuary for debtors,[69] a place of refuge for anyone seeking to avoid a creditor's demands.

If the lure of money and magic didn't create enough chaos, the city of Ephesus also attracted schools of philosophy. Around 500 BC, Heraclitus, a Greek noble of Ephesus, taught that the universe operates according to a unified ordering principle, which he called the *logos*, that is, "the word."[70] Later philosophers built upon this theory, claiming that all the laws of physics, mathematics, reason, and even morality can be traced back to an impersonal divine mind. By the time of Paul, Ephesus had become a veritable cauldron of competing philosophies and a celebrated repository of texts on Greek philosophy.

Despite all its temptations and challenges, Ephesus was a perfect location for Paul's base of operations in Asia because "roads from

Ephesus radiated in every direction along the coast and through the interior of the province."[71] To ensure that the church would remain morally clean, doctrinally pure, and spiritually vibrant, Paul spent more time in Ephesus than in any other Gentile city. Moreover, he nurtured the congregation from afar, sending envoys to check on its members' well-being, writing at least one letter, and—perhaps most significant of all—placing them in the hands of his beloved disciple Timothy.

14:8-18). Both cast out demons (5:16; 16:16-18). Both confronted magicians (8:18-24; 13:6-11). Both raised the dead (9:36-40; 20:9-10). Both were dramatically and miraculously released from prison (12:7-10; 16:25-26). Luke didn't write this for the purpose of encouraging factions—the ministry of the gospel isn't a competition—but to accomplish at least one implied purpose of his narrative: to validate the expansion of the church among the Gentiles while explaining the relative lack of Jewish Christians. In this regard, Luke supplied the data while Paul articulated the theology (see Rom. 9–11).

While in Ephesus, Paul served as God's conduit of power much like Peter had in Jerusalem (Acts 5:15-16). The phrase translated "performing extraordinary miracles" (19:11) is especially curious in Greek. Literally rendered, it's "works of power, not the ordinary ones." By definition, *all* miracles are beyond normal; the fact that anything miraculous occurs is extraordinary. Luke means to say that the miracles God "was performing" differed from what Timothy and other disciples had seen before. In the words of A. T. Robertson, "In Samaria Philip wrought miracles to deliver the people from the influence of Simon Magus. Here in Ephesus exorcists and other magicians had built an enormous vogue of a false spiritualism and Paul faces unseen forces of evil."[72] G. Campbell Morgan described Ephesus this way: "The atmosphere of the city was electric with sorcery and incantations, with exorcists, with all kinds of magical impostors."[73] In other words, evil held the city of Ephesus and the region of Asia so tightly that the Lord had to exercise even greater and more unusual divine power to break its grip.

Now, as we look back, it becomes clear why the Lord sent Paul to Europe first. He set the gospel in motion there before returning Paul to Ephesus to begin a long, difficult battle against the powers of darkness. Paul thought in terms of geography; God knew that success depended upon timing. Before the apostle arrived to begin his work in earnest, Aquila and Priscilla began laying a foundation for ministry and Apollos expertly taught in the synagogue, using the Old Testament Scriptures to establish Jesus as the Christ.

Luke states that the power of God worked so extraordinarily and so often that people began to associate the power with Paul. They used the cloths he touched like talismans to ward off evil or to cure diseases (19:12). While Luke does not record that Paul sanctioned their use in this way, and Paul most likely discouraged the practice, the Lord nevertheless used the people's superstition to validate Paul's message (cf. Luke 8:44; Acts 5:15). That's the Lord's prerogative, however, not anyone else's. Modern-day charlatans should tremble at the consequences of their fraud.

— 19:13-16 —

Some in Paul's day did indeed try to cash in. Luke records an incident that serves three purposes in his narrative. First, to demonstrate that even earnest efforts to combat evil apart from the Spirit of God are dangerous. Second, to show that the power flowing through Paul came directly from God; Paul neither controlled nor directed the miracle activity. Third, comic relief. While the episode deals with a deadly serious matter, it's humorous!

Luke notes that seven sons of a chief priest attempted an exorcism. The number seven (19:14) should have been a good omen; Hebrew numerology associated seven with God's perfection. Their being the sons of a chief priest (whether or not that was true is open for debate) should have given them some clout in the spiritual realm. Furthermore, they had a foolproof incantation against evil spirits. In the ancient world, one invoked the authority of a higher power to command lower spirit beings. In this case, the men invoked the name of Jesus, whom they knew to be a wonder worker, and they tossed in Paul's name for good measure (19:13).

They moved from town to town, playing their confidence game wherever they could find people frightened enough to part with their money. Then they came to Ephesus, where evil didn't play games. In response to the seven schemers, the demon acknowledged Jesus (19:15). The second verb, translated "know about" (*epistamai* [1987]), denotes a cursory acquaintance that's even less formal than the first "know" (*ginōskō* [1097]). Regardless, the demon didn't wait for an answer; he pounced on the men and nearly tore them to pieces (19:16). (The sight of the seven con artists flying through the door naked must have been hilarious.) Luke further describes their state using a Greek word we transliterate to get the English term "traumatized."

— 19:17-19 —

The defeat of these seven false representatives of God sent shockwaves through the region, prompting the people to revere the Lord, and the reputation of Jesus Christ spread farther and faster. People who had been practicing magic or dabbling in the spirit realm confessed and repented.

The measure of this turn from the occult was a bonfire worth "fifty thousand pieces of silver" (19:19). If the pieces of silver were *drachmas*, each coin represented one day's wages for a common laborer (cf. Luke 15:8). Fifty thousand pieces represented more than 136 years of continuous labor with no days off! For a conservative estimate of the value today, use this formula:

50,000 days × 8 hours/day = 400,000 work hours
400,000 hours × [hourly wage] = _____

Luke offers this tangible measurement to help his readers gauge the impact of the Holy Spirit on Ephesus, the surrounding territory, and the Roman province of Asia at large. This figure represents a dramatic shift in the values of the people; they had invested heavily in written volumes containing incantations. Magicians and mediums voluntarily gave up their sources of income, which meant the people spent less money and time seeking help from the powers of darkness and, instead, turned toward the light. This monetary figure also speaks the language of Ephesus. Perhaps more than any other place in the world, money and dark powers enjoyed a symbiotic relationship that kept Asia in Satan's stranglehold.

— 19:20 —

Two years of ministry resulted in a growing success. As people broke free from their fear and bondage, even the economy of Ephesus began to shift. Luke concludes this summary of Paul's work with a Greek sentence that could be rendered, literally, "In this way, according to the mighty deeds of the Lord, the Word was growing and prevailing." The tide had begun to turn. Great news for the church, great news for the people of Ephesus. But this was no time to rest. When the balance of power shifts away from the dark toward the light, Satan fights harder than ever.

APPLICATION: ACTS 19:8-20

Breaking Free

By the time Paul arrived in Ephesus, the province of Asia had become a hard nut to crack. His church-planting efforts in other places came at the cost of suffering, but the response had always been fairly rapid. In each case, a few weeks of teaching and organizing established a small but thriving community that inevitably flourished for many years after Paul's departure. But Ephesus was different. Slavery to the occult and the oppression of demonism rendered the people so spiritually hardened that few could respond to the good news when they heard it. This required more intense miracles, more consistent teaching, more sustained persistence, and more patient optimism than anywhere else. After two years, Paul finally saw signs of hope.

What occurred in Ephesus can happen to an individual, and the occult doesn't have to be involved. The hardening of a heart occurs gradually and silently, usually in a subtle, imperceptible manner. Sometimes it begins when we're children; given no spiritual guidance, we develop methods of coping with guilt and shame in ways that create distance from God. If the pattern continues through adolescence and into the young adult years, we can develop a lifestyle of coping that deepens the hardening and may even cultivate destructive habits. Meanwhile, the Spirit of God continues to point out secret faults while we steadfastly resist. The result is a hardening of the heart and a whole lifestyle of futility. The truth may confront us daily, but it glances off our hard hearts like flint off steel. It flashes and it sparks but it does not penetrate.

Becoming pliable calls for a willingness to surrender, a willingness to abandon everything we've used as a substitute for an authentic, personal relationship with Jesus Christ. It's different for everyone. Money. Possessions. Self-reliance. Power. Relationships. Alcohol. Drugs. Sex. Achievement. Religion. Recognition. The list could go on for pages. You know yours. It's what you would most fear to lose if the Lord sat you down for a heart-to-heart talk. As long as you look to that replacement god for your safety, fulfillment, happiness, relief—whatever it is you crave—you will continue to harden. The first step is surrender. Then, with your arms empty and open, turn to your Creator.

Leading in the Midst of Conflict
ACTS 19:21–20:2

21 Now after these things were finished, Paul purposed in the ªSpirit to go to Jerusalem after he had passed through Macedonia and Achaia, saying, "After I have been there, I must also see Rome." 22 And having sent into Macedonia two of those who ministered to him, Timothy and Erastus, he himself stayed in ªAsia for a while.

23 About that time there occurred no small disturbance concerning the Way. 24 For a man named Demetrius, a silversmith, who made silver shrines of ªArtemis, was bringing no little ᵇbusiness to the craftsmen; 25 these he gathered together with the workmen of similar *trades,* and said, "Men, you know that our prosperity ªdepends upon this business. 26 You see and hear that not only in Ephesus, but in almost all of ªAsia, this Paul has persuaded and turned away a considerable number of people, saying that ᵇgods made with hands are no gods *at all.* 27 Not only is there danger that this trade of ours fall into disrepute, but also that the temple of the great goddess ªArtemis be regarded as worthless and that she whom all of ᵇAsia and the ᶜworld worship will even be dethroned from her magnificence."

28 When they heard *this* and were filled with rage, they *began* crying out, saying, "Great is ªArtemis of the Ephesians!" 29 The city was filled with the confusion, and they rushed ªwith one accord into the theater, dragging along Gaius and Aristarchus, Paul's traveling companions from Macedonia. 30 And when Paul wanted to go into the ªassembly, the disciples would not let him. 31 Also some of the ªAsiarchs who were friends of

21 Afterward Paul felt compelled by the Spirit* to go over to Macedonia and Achaia before going to Jerusalem. "And after that," he said, "I must go on to Rome!" 22 He sent his two assistants, Timothy and Erastus, ahead to Macedonia while he stayed awhile longer in the province of Asia.

23 About that time, serious trouble developed in Ephesus concerning the Way. 24 It began with Demetrius, a silversmith who had a large business manufacturing silver shrines of the Greek goddess Artemis.* He kept many craftsmen busy. 25 He called them together, along with others employed in similar trades, and addressed them as follows:

"Gentlemen, you know that our wealth comes from this business. 26 But as you have seen and heard, this man Paul has persuaded many people that handmade gods aren't really gods at all. And he's done this not only here in Ephesus but throughout the entire province! 27 Of course, I'm not just talking about the loss of public respect for our business. I'm also concerned that the temple of the great goddess Artemis will lose its influence and that Artemis—this magnificent goddess worshiped throughout the province of Asia and all around the world—will be robbed of her great prestige!"

28 At this their anger boiled, and they began shouting, "Great is Artemis of the Ephesians!" 29 Soon the whole city was filled with confusion. Everyone rushed to the amphitheater, dragging along Gaius and Aristarchus, who were Paul's traveling companions from Macedonia. 30 Paul wanted to go in, too, but the believers wouldn't let him. 31 Some of the officials of the province, friends of

his sent to him and repeatedly urged him not to ᵇventure into the theater. ³²So then, some were shouting one thing and some another, for the ªassembly was in confusion and the majority did not know ᵇfor what reason they had come together. ³³Some of the crowd ªconcluded *it was* Alexander, since the Jews had put him forward; and having motioned with his hand, Alexander was intending to make a defense to the ᵇassembly. ³⁴But when they recognized that he was a Jew, a *single* outcry arose from them all as they shouted for about two hours, "Great is ªArtemis of the Ephesians!" ³⁵After quieting the crowd, the town clerk said, "Men of Ephesus, what man is there after all who does not know that the city of the Ephesians is guardian of the temple of the great ªArtemis and of the *image* which fell down from ᵇheaven? ³⁶So, since these are undeniable facts, you ought to keep calm and to do nothing rash. ³⁷For you have brought these men *here* who are neither robbers of temples nor blasphemers of our goddess. ³⁸So then, if Demetrius and the craftsmen who are with him have a complaint against any man, the courts are in session and ªproconsuls are *available;* let them bring charges against one another. ³⁹But if you want anything beyond this, it shall be settled in the ªlawful ᵇassembly. ⁴⁰For indeed we are in danger of being accused of a riot in connection with today's events, since there is no *real* cause *for it,* and in this connection we will be unable to account for this disorderly gathering." ⁴¹After saying this he dismissed the ªassembly.

20:1 After the uproar had ceased, Paul sent for the disciples, and when he had exhorted them and taken his leave of them, he left to go to Macedonia. ²When he had gone through

Paul, also sent a message to him, begging him not to risk his life by entering the amphitheater. ³²Inside, the people were all shouting, some one thing and some another. Everything was in confusion. In fact, most of them didn't even know why they were there. ³³The Jews in the crowd pushed Alexander forward and told him to explain the situation. He motioned for silence and tried to speak. ³⁴But when the crowd realized he was a Jew, they started shouting again and kept it up for about two hours: "Great is Artemis of the Ephesians! Great is Artemis of the Ephesians!"

³⁵At last the mayor was able to quiet them down enough to speak. "Citizens of Ephesus," he said. "Everyone knows that Ephesus is the official guardian of the temple of the great Artemis, whose image fell down to us from heaven. ³⁶Since this is an undeniable fact, you should stay calm and not do anything rash. ³⁷You have brought these men here, but they have stolen nothing from the temple and have not spoken against our goddess.

³⁸"If Demetrius and the craftsmen have a case against them, the courts are in session and the officials can hear the case at once. Let them make formal charges. ³⁹And if there are complaints about other matters, they can be settled in a legal assembly. ⁴⁰I am afraid we are in danger of being charged with rioting by the Roman government, since there is no cause for all this commotion. And if Rome demands an explanation, we won't know what to say." ⁴¹*Then he dismissed them, and they dispersed.

20:1 When the uproar was over, Paul sent for the believers* and encouraged them. Then he said good-bye and left for Macedonia. ²While there, he encouraged the believers in all

NASB

those districts and had given them much exhortation, he came to Greece.

NLT

the towns he passed through. Then he traveled down to Greece,

19:21 aOr *spirit*   **19:22** aI.e. west coast province of Asia Minor   **19:24** aLat *Diana* bOr *profit*   **19:25** aLit *is from*   **19:26** aV 22, note 1 bLit *those*   **19:27** aLat *Diana* bV 22, note 1 cLit *the inhabited earth*   **19:28** aLat *Diana*   **19:29** aOr *together*   **19:30** aLit *people*   **19:31** aI.e. political or religious officials of the province of Asia bLit *give himself*   **19:32** aGr *ekklesia* bOr *on whose account*   **19:33** aOr *advised Alexander* bLit *people*   **19:34** aLat *Diana*   **19:35** aLat *Diana* bLit *Zeus; Lat Jupiter*   **19:38** aOr *provincial governors*   **19:39** aOr *regular* bGr *ekklesia*   **19:41** aGr *ekklesia*

19:21 Or *decided in his spirit.*   **19:24** *Artemis* is otherwise known as Diana.   **19:41** Some translations include verse 41 as part of verse 40.   **20:1** Greek *disciples.*

Great leaders never stop planning for the future. They dream on a grand scale, look further into the future than their peers, and imagine possibilities no one else thinks reasonable. They never let others sully their plans with too much realism, and they never scale back their goals because of difficult circumstances. After all, conditions change from day to day, but a great dream can sustain a leader for decades. Even so, visionaries learn to keep much of their long-range thinking to themselves because they grow weary of explaining what cannot be seen. Consequently, they share only what can be justified to those outside their inner circle but never enough to give naysayers fodder for dissent.

Paul had a dream. It was a vision so grand it would have overwhelmed most of his companions. After planting churches around the eastern half of the Roman Empire and ensuring their long-term sustainability, Paul imagined himself carrying the gospel to the vast stretches of frontier west of Rome, even as far as Spain (Rom. 15:24). It was an outrageous ambition. He had endured hunger, thirst, exposure, slander, rejection, beatings, imprisonment, and stonings in his effort to evangelize present-day Turkey and Greece, but the landmass he envisioned in the west more than tripled the area he had covered thus far. So he wisely kept this to himself, revealing only what he planned to do in the coming months.

While great leaders chart their courses far in advance, they also keep a close eye on the ground in front of them. Paul saw the work coming to a close in Ephesus; he would soon turn the ministry over to someone capable and trustworthy. Before setting out on his next journey, Paul sent assistants ahead of him. Luke doesn't specify why Paul stayed, but I suspect the Holy Spirit guided his choice to remain a little longer in Asia. As it turned out, he would need to see the fledgling church through a crisis that had been building for months.

— 19:21-22 —

Although Paul's long-range goals would have overburdened his companions, he could reveal his immediate plans. He intended to follow the course he had taken on his second journey so he could strengthen the churches in Philippi, Thessalonica, and Berea (the province of Macedonia) before turning south for Corinth (in Achaia). He also wanted to visit Jerusalem, very likely for the last time, before setting out for Rome.

To get a jump start on the ministry to Macedonia, Paul sent two trusted assistants, Timothy and Erastus. Timothy, of course, had joined Paul early in his second journey. Erastus was a very common nickname among freed slaves who no longer wished to be called by a number (e.g., Tertius, "third," or Quartus, "fourth"). Erastus means "beloved." He may have been the same Erastus who served as the city treasurer in Corinth (Rom. 16:23), but the likelihood is just as high that he wasn't. Regardless, these two men became Paul's choice to go ahead of him.

For whatever reason, Luke never mentions another key assistant to Paul: Titus. Paul's second letter to the Corinthians indicates he sent Titus—who had undoubtedly been with the apostle from the beginning—to minister to the troubled church. He most likely departed from Ephesus (2 Cor. 12:18), completed his mission, and then reconnected with Paul somewhere in Macedonia (2 Cor. 2:13; 7:6, 13).

— 19:23-27 —

Paul's ministry had undermined the occult economy of Ephesus, and this stirred up "no small disturbance" (19:23). The resulting commotion was large enough to potentially cause a response from outside the city (19:40), perhaps even as far away as Rome. The last thing anybody wanted was for Rome to get involved; they usually responded to disturbances with no small amount of force! The disorder concerned the Christian movement, which first-century believers referred to as "the Way" (19:23). Ephesians were turning away from the occult in large enough numbers to affect the local economy. Luke noted earlier that the burned texts alone exceeded the value of fifty thousand silver coins (19:19). In addition, people stopped buying trinkets from the talisman shops, stopped seeking the help of mediums, stopped asking the help of priests in the temple of Artemis, stopped bringing money to bribe the gods. Worse than that, they also told neighbors and tourists that Artemis had no power and did not, in fact, exist.

Demetrius, a local craftsman whose livelihood began to dry up when Paul came to town, began to organize the merchants in protest of the

commons.wikimedia.org

The people of Ephesus worshiped **Artemis** (also known as Diana), the mother goddess, depicted here with multiple breasts to signify fertility. Her value to the city was more than religious. Much of the city's economy depended upon the influx of worshipers' money.

new religion (19:24). A quick examination of his rationale shows him to be absolutely correct in his indictment (19:25-27). The issue was money, first and foremost. He didn't object to "the Way" on religious grounds. He didn't dispute the existence of God or even defend the reality of Artemis. In fact, he probably wouldn't have objected to any religion that wanted to relocate its headquarters to Ephesus, because the many schools of philosophy grew the economy. As a good businessman, he did a sales forecast and saw disaster looming, not just for the trades, but for the city itself. People who stop buying trinkets and charms also stop worshiping Artemis. The magnificent temple of Artemis, one of the seven wonders of the ancient world, drew many thousands of pilgrims from all over the empire. These pilgrims brought money to Ephesus—lots of it. So much cash, in fact, that the temple had become one of the largest banking institutions in the world.[74]

Demetrius did not start a religious riot; he sparked an economic panic.

— 19:28-31 —

"Great is Artemis of the Ephesians!" became the rallying cry for the riot (19:28). This sounded better than "Great is the income from the tourists!" The word rendered "confusion" (*synchysis* [4799]) means simply "tumult." In other words, Demetrius provoked a furious uproar. There was no confusion about the issue or what the riot instigators wanted.

They acted with unity of mind when they sought Paul in the school of Tyrannus, but found only two of his traveling companions, Gaius and Aristarchus (19:29). They dragged the two men to the theater, although the purpose is not clear. They may have intended to put them on trial.

The theater in Ephesus could comfortably seat twenty-five thousand people.

When the instigators dragged Gaius and Aristarchus through the streets, they attracted a large following. Before long, the theater was filled with protesting Ephesians. Paul wanted to address the crowd; he had undoubtedly seen this coming for a long time. But two groups urged him to stay away (19:30-31). "The disciples" didn't want to see their leader torn to pieces. He also received word from the "Asiarchs," provincial authorities who watched after Rome's interests in Asia Minor. Luke calls them "friends of his," which is no small detail. If any complaint about the riot were to reach Rome, the Asiarchs knew the truth of the matter and who should bear responsibility for the unrest.

— 19:32-34 —

Although the original instigators of the riot understood their purpose, the majority of the crowd "did not know for what reason they had come together" (19:32). Luke highlights the irony of the mob using the theater for their demonstration. As one commentator notes, "Greek comedy frequently parodied people's stupidity; Luke's readers would laugh at the crowd not knowing the purpose of their rioting."[75] The phrase rendered "for what reason" could be translated "on whose account." Maybe they were gathered for Demetrius, or maybe it was for Alexander, since the Jews in Ephesus put him forward to offer their "defense," most likely to distance the synagogue from Paul (19:33). The crowd, however, didn't see a distinction between Jews and Christians; they knew both groups opposed idolatry. So Alexander accomplished nothing more than whipping the mob into a sustained frenzy. For about two hours, the mob shouted and chanted, "Great is Artemis of the Ephesians!" (19:34). Of course, most of them didn't understand why they were chanting the name of their deity; they simply moved with the crowd, fueled by mob excitement.

— 19:35-40 —

Eventually, the "town clerk" (*grammateus* [1122]) got them quieted down (19:35). The title sounds menial compared to the man's true position in the political life of Ephesus. He was essentially the president of the city, a locally elected official responsible for management of the city, including its business affairs. There's nothing to suggest he was either a Christian or even sympathetic to Paul. He just wanted to be able to report to Rome that he had things well in hand. He merely analyzed the matter with a cool, rational disposition and then urged the Ephesians to do the same. His speech makes four points in favor of quietly going home.

First, he countered the assertion that Artemis was "made with hands" (19:26), an expression identifying something as man-made instead of having supernatural origins. The town clerk claimed that the statue of Artemis actually had supernatural origins. The phrase translated "the image which fell down from heaven" comes from a single term that can be rendered literally "that which fell from Zeus" (*diopetēs* [1356]).

Second, Rome recognized Ephesus with the official designation "guardian of the temple," a great honor from the imperial capital. As long as Rome favored Ephesus with the upkeep and protection of the magnificent temple, people would still come to see it—and continue to spend their money. Anger Rome with a senseless riot, however, and the economy would be sure to suffer (19:40).

Third, if you're confident in the truth of your beliefs, then you have no need of violence to defend them (19:36). The town clerk wisely understood that violent anger is the last refuge of the pathetic.

Fourth, Gaius and Aristarchus were not guilty of a crime (19:37); they just happened to be convenient for the crowd, who really wanted Paul anyway. Regardless, they had not robbed or desecrated or damaged or blasphemed. If they were guilty of a crime, trial by mob was not the way to go; the city had a proconsul supplied by Rome for just such an occasion (19:38-39).

— 19:41 —

Luke concludes his narrative of the episode with an appropriately succinct statement. You can almost feel the energy dissipate in the theater as the town clerk's wise, calming words bring reason and order to the frenzied crowd. He had addressed each of their concerns, showing their fear to be unjustified and demonstrating that a violent response would be counterproductive. After "he dismissed the assembly," you can almost sense the mood of the crowd shift from agitated outrage to sheepish contentment, like a child who suddenly discovers that asking politely works better than throwing tantrums.

— 20:1-2 —

The crisis and threat of violence and persecution had passed. The church would be safe from significant opposition. Other dangers lurked in the darkness surrounding Ephesus, and it would come in different forms, but the people no longer faced systematic or widespread persecution. As a result, it seems Paul felt confident enough in the sustainability of the church to resume his travel plans and leave them on their own. He summoned the believers in Ephesus, exhorted them (*parakaleō* [3870]) to remain faithful, and expressed his confidence in the Spirit to nurture them. Then he boarded a ship bound for Macedonia.

In Macedonia, Paul followed the itinerary of the second missionary journey, expecting to rendezvous with Timothy and Erastus somewhere along the route. He spent his time "exhorting" (*parakaleō*) the churches in Philippi, Thessalonica, and Berea before heading south to Corinth. Although he had most likely traveled by sea earlier while escaping the mob in Berea, he may have chosen an overland route for this journey, taking the opportunity to visit communities along the way. Regardless, he intended to conclude his journey in Corinth, from which he would sail home, just as he had before.

This effectively ends Luke's account of Paul's third missionary journey. The apostle had completed the work he planned. He would spend three months in Corinth, perhaps waiting for spring before beginning his journey home. He planned to visit Jerusalem and perhaps his home church in Syrian Antioch, and then embark for Rome on his way to the western frontier of the empire.

APPLICATION: ACTS 19:21–20:2

Peace in the Place of Panic

After a long and fruitful stay in Ephesus during which "the word of the Lord was growing mightily and prevailing" (19:20), a disturbance broke out that caused things to unravel for Paul's ministry (19:23). Throughout this uproar and upheaval, Paul kept his head, able to stay calm in spite of the panic of difficult circumstances. His attitude and actions of peace and calm in the midst of panic and confusion are worth pondering as we consider how we ought to respond to disturbing events in our life that threaten to undo us.

If you're facing an uncertain future or uncontrollable situation, remember that God knows the future and He's always in control. Not for a second did Paul wonder whether the world somehow got away from God's sovereign grip. Though he desired to enter the crowded theater to come to the aid of his companions and perhaps proclaim the gospel to such a large crowd, it became clear that this wasn't the wisest course of action (19:30-31). Instead of panicking and pushing his own will, Paul stepped back and let the circumstances unfold.

I'm sure a few wondered what was wrong with Paul. Why wasn't he losing his mind? Why didn't he try manipulating the situation from behind the scenes? How could he be at peace in the place of panic? Instead of asking what was *wrong* with Paul for letting go of the situation, maybe we should be asking what was *right* with him that he could find such peace in its midst.

The fact is, Paul had his spiritual feet planted firmly on the rock of Christ. He knew what the Lord would have said in that situation, when the tempests of controversy were breaking loose on the city of Ephesus, where his close friends were at the brink of suffering severely for the cause of Christ at the hands of jealous idolaters. The Lord would have said, "You can't stand on your own? Lean on Me. You can't control the situation? Depend on Me. You can't manipulate things? Wait on Me. Relax. I've got this under control."

And He did, too. Rather than making a way for Paul to slip in and save the day, God orchestrated circumstances so that an unnamed town clerk single-handedly calmed the crowd and dismissed them (19:35-41). Clearly, God is bigger than a crowd of thousands, and He's greater than a wealthy idolater. Learn to focus on people and circumstances through God's eyes. No mob is out of His control. Even if you can't handle the situation, He can.

This is why Paul could have peace in the place of panic.

And so can you.

THE CHALLENGES OF THE CHURCH (ACTS 20:3–28:31)

The church had experienced more than its share of difficulties and set-backs, but everything had gone according to God's plan. The third stage of that plan, taking the gospel "even to the remotest part of the earth" (1:8), began in the missionary journeys recounted in the preceding section and continues in this portion of Acts—but with new obstacles and stresses creating unsought yet valuable opportunities for the Lord's witnesses. In fact, challenges had already proven opportune for the church, and these would be no different. Not long after His resurrection, the Lord met with His followers—no fewer than 120 of them—and made a solemn promise: "You will receive power when the Holy Spirit has come upon you; and you shall be My witnesses both in Jerusalem, and in all Judea and Samaria, and even to the remotest part of the earth" (1:8). He not only promised power, but He also predicted victory. During His earthly ministry, Jesus told the Twelve, "I will build My church; and the gates of Hades will not overpower it" (Matt. 16:18). Within days of His ascension, the believers received the first part of His promise: The Holy Spirit filled every believer, granting each individual the power to fulfill his or her role in God's redemptive plan. Initial persecution did little to curb the church's growth until the martyrdom of Stephen dealt the community of believers its first significant blow.

Rather than curtailing church expansion, this challenge became—under the Lord's power—a catalyst for explosive growth. The believers scattered into the surrounding territories, carrying the gospel with them to Samaritans and Gentiles alike, just as Jesus had said: "You shall be My witnesses both in Jerusalem, and in all Judea and Samaria" (Acts 1:8).

The challenge of persecution gave way to the challenge of prejudice. Paul had been called to proclaim the gospel among the Gentiles and was in God's crucible, preparing for ministry, but he could not advance until the church had overcome its chauvinism. Then Peter became the Lord's anti-prejudice project.

After a profound vision and the experience of seeing the Holy Spirit fill Gentile believers in a quintessentially "unclean" home, Peter and the Jerusalem church could not deny the brotherhood of Gentiles in the kingdom of God.

With this change of perspective, the ministry of Paul to Gentiles all over the Roman Empire could begin in earnest. The challenge of prejudice had affirmed grace (cf. 15:11) and propelled the church into a new era. Jesus had said, "You shall be My witnesses . . . even to the remotest part of the earth" (1:8), and that, too, came to pass.

As Paul's third missionary journey concluded in Corinth, the plan of God had progressed remarkably quickly. Even so, the apostle found little reason to rest or even to slow down. Even though thriving churches dotted the eastern empire and inevitably would replicate themselves, little if anything had been done for the province of Gallia and the frontier of Hispania, the territories now known as France and Spain. Paul dreamed of carrying the gospel where few in the east dared to go. He would visit Jerusalem (20:22) to deliver a gift from the Gentile churches (Rom. 15:25-28; cf. Acts 24:17), maybe bid farewell in Antioch, and then sail for Rome, from where he would launch a fourth missionary journey. He had no way of knowing, of course, that the plan of God would ride on the wings of yet another challenge. Humanly speaking, it would appear that the rest of Paul's life was spent in continual frustration of a dream. By now we know differently. God has His own agenda, He is always right, and obstacles become divine catapults to success.

Rather than proclaiming the gospel to people in synagogues and marketplaces far to the west, Paul's divinely appointed itinerary would see him testify in places of power, before social and political leaders, beginning again from Jerusalem and proceeding to Rome, the very capital of the empire. As Paul and those around him faced swirling changes and unforeseen challenges, they would learn to adapt, accept God's plan, and trust in Him more than ever. So also today's believers must trust God amid challenges in the continuing story of the gospel's unhindered growth.

KEY TERMS IN ACTS 20:3–28:31

diōkō (διώκω) [1377] "to persecute," "to pursue,"
"to hasten," "to strive for"

This Greek term carries the idea of "forcing," "pressing," "impelling," "pursuing," or "zealously engaging," usually for the sake of a particular cause. Unlike the English term "persecute," its connotations are not always negative and do not necessarily imply a violation of human rights. For example, the Septuagint uses this word to render Hosea 6:3: "We will press on (*diōkō*, translating the Hebrew *radap* [H7291]) to know the Lord" (NETS). In Acts, most instances refer to the persecution of the church and therefore bear a negative connotation, but at key points that I will highlight, Luke makes use of the neutral nuances of the Greek term.

diamartyromai (διαμαρτύρομαι) [1263] "to solemnly
testify," "to bear witness," "to urge"

Based on the verb *martyreō* [3140], "to bear witness" or "to testify," this emphatic verb carries the idea of stating something firmly or with absolute assurance. Outside the Bible, this kind of testifying usually accompanied swearing an oath or calling down divine curses from the gods. This verb also describes the act of standing up in court to present the absolute truth, knowing that perjury would result in severe penalties.

eutheōs (εὐθέως) [2112] "immediately," "at once," "as soon
as," "then"

The adjective *euthys* ("straight" [2117]) came to be used as an adverb in both its adjectival form and later in the regular adverbial form *eutheōs*. Luke's use of the latter form marks his Greek style as different from that of Mark, for example, who uses *euthys*. Furthermore, ancient authors used these adverbs to connect points and events in a variety of ways. While John uses *eutheōs* to denote a short lapse of time between events, Luke uses *eutheōs* to establish a sequence of certain events while declaring others unrelated or incidental to the story.

katēgoreō (κατηγορέω) [2723] "to accuse," "to bring
charges against," "to denounce"

This term almost always appears in a legal context where one party brings another before a mutual authority for the purpose of obtaining justice through restitution, censure, or punishment. This term is used as a source of irony in Acts. Beginning with Paul's arrest, enemies of the gospel continually bring charges against Paul that create a legal dilemma for the Romans, who cannot release the apostle yet cannot find a charge. Thus, Paul becomes a prisoner of divine truth.

keleuō (κελεύω) [2753] "to command," "to issue
  a legal order"
The voice of official authority carried great weight in the Roman Empire.
The ability to give a command and have the world respond was the definition of power and status. Other matters, such as truth, fairness, kindness, and intelligence would be of concern only to historians who would
judge a person in posterity. In the present, none of those things mattered
without power. In Acts, the issue of power becomes a source of irony. Beginning with Paul's journeys, the commands and orders of secular rulers
appear to control the apostle; however, Luke shows that the Lord remains
in command throughout.

Adaptation
ACTS 20:3-12

NASB

³And *there* he spent three months, and when a plot was formed against him by the Jews as he was about to set sail for Syria, he decided to return through Macedonia. ⁴And ªhe was accompanied by Sopater of Berea, *the son* of Pyrrhus, and by Aristarchus and Secundus of the Thessalonians, and Gaius of Derbe, and Timothy, and Tychicus and Trophimus of ᵇAsia. ⁵But these had gone on ahead and were waiting for us at Troas. ⁶We sailed from Philippi after the days of Unleavened Bread, and came to them at Troas within five days; and there we stayed seven days.

⁷On the first day of the week, when we were gathered together to break bread, Paul *began* talking to them, intending to leave the next day, and he prolonged his ªmessage until midnight. ⁸There were many lamps in the upper room where we were gathered together. ⁹And there was a young man named ªEutychus sitting ᵇon the window sill, sinking into a deep sleep; and as Paul kept on talking, he was overcome by sleep and fell down from the third floor and was picked up dead. ¹⁰But

NLT

³where he stayed for three months. He was preparing to sail back to Syria when he discovered a plot by some Jews against his life, so he decided to return through Macedonia.

⁴Several men were traveling with him. They were Sopater son of Pyrrhus from Berea; Aristarchus and Secundus from Thessalonica; Gaius from Derbe; Timothy; and Tychicus and Trophimus from the province of Asia. ⁵They went on ahead and waited for us at Troas. ⁶After the Passover* ended, we boarded a ship at Philippi in Macedonia and five days later joined them in Troas, where we stayed a week.

⁷On the first day of the week, we gathered with the local believers to share in the Lord's Supper.* Paul was preaching to them, and since he was leaving the next day, he kept talking until midnight. ⁸The upstairs room where we met was lighted with many flickering lamps. ⁹As Paul spoke on and on, a young man named Eutychus, sitting on the windowsill, became very drowsy. Finally, he fell sound asleep and dropped three stories to his death below. ¹⁰Paul went

Paul went down and fell upon him,
and after embracing him, he said,
"ᵃDo not be troubled, for his life is
in him." ¹¹When he had gone *back*
up and had broken the bread and
ᵃeaten, he talked with them a long
while until daybreak, and then left.
¹²They took away the boy alive, and
were ᵃgreatly comforted.

20:4 ᵃLit *there accompanied him* ᵇI.e. west coast
province of Asia Minor   20:7 ᵃLit *word, speech*
20:9 ᵃ*Eutychus* means *Good fortune*, i.e. `Lucky'
ᵇOr *at the window*   20:10 ᵃOr *Stop being troubled*
20:11 ᵃLit *tasted*   20:12 ᵃLit *not moderately*

down, bent over him, and took him
into his arms. "Don't worry," he said,
"he's alive!" ¹¹Then they all went
back upstairs, shared in the Lord's
Supper,* and ate together. Paul continued talking to them until dawn,
and then he left. ¹²Meanwhile, the
young man was taken home alive
and well, and everyone was greatly
relieved.

20:6 Greek *the days of unleavened bread.*
20:7 Greek *to break bread.*   20:11 Greek *broke
the bread.*

While Luke didn't set out to write a biography of Paul, the Holy Spirit
nevertheless directed him to use the apostle's experiences to tell this
part of the story of the church. By observing Paul's three missionary
journeys, we learn about the church's extraordinary period of expansion. As he proclaimed the gospel, established new believers in communities, and then strengthened these churches, we discover how the
world was changed at a grassroots level so quickly by so few. By the end
of his third journey, Paul had honed his ministry method and planned
to apply it in the west; however, his time in Achaia, the region where
Corinth was situated, marks a transition. It is not obvious at first, but
his leaving Corinth began a new phase in the life of the church as the
Lord initiated a new strategy.

Paul would no longer travel the highways and byways of the empire;
the Lord had prepared others to do that now. Instead, the apostle would
scale the heights of power to preach Christ among kings and emperors.
Luke's narrative reflects this shift by focusing more on Paul, the man,
and less on his work.

In writing about most of the events up to this point, Luke functioned
like a typical historian. He researched, gathered facts, interviewed witnesses, double-checked his sources, and then compiled an accurate
account of how the church formed, grew, survived, and expanded.
Then, the Lord increasingly brought the storyteller into the story; the
physician/evangelist/historian became a constant companion to Paul.
As with the events of Acts 16:11-17, Luke would personally observe the
historical events Paul shaped and, more importantly, witness firsthand
the thoughts and choices of the man himself. Consequently, the book
of Acts now begins to read like a travelogue or a diary, especially in
the "we" passages of 20:5–21:18 and 27:1–28:16. Seemingly mundane

details serve the important purpose of bringing us into the story with Luke to observe from the inside how God began to change the world at the highest levels of government.

— 20:3-5 —

Paul spent three months in Corinth, probably the winter of AD 56/57. During this time he lived in the home of a man named Gaius (Rom. 16:23), where he wrote his letter to the church in Rome (cf. Rom. 15:23–16:2). If Gaius was the same man as Titius Justus (Acts 18:7), which is possible, Paul lived next door to the synagogue and continued to lead church services there. Earlier, in Paul's ministry in Ephesus, Crispus the synagogue leader had converted, along with a good portion of the synagogue's members. Later, it appears that the successor to Crispus, a man named Sosthenes, also converted (cf. 18:17; 1 Cor. 1:1). As a result, there were nonbelieving Jews in Corinth who hated Paul. Unable to defeat him and the church politically, they turned to violence, hatching a plot to kill him. He planned to board a ship for Syria and then visit the temple for Passover (Acts 20:6), a journey many Jews would take around that time. His enemies could easily blend in with the other pilgrims and make certain the apostle disappeared somewhere in the Mediterranean.

The evil intentions of his enemies forced a difficult decision. Paul had hoped to reach Jerusalem in time to celebrate Passover in the temple one last time, but he couldn't set sail from Corinth or any other nearby port without being discovered. The only other major harbor he could reach by land would take at least a week to get to on foot. The apostle had learned the crucial difference between trusting God and taking foolish chances, so he adapted his plan to meet his changing circumstances. This would be only the first adjustment of many.

Luke describes a sizable entourage, mentioning several people for the first time. In fact, he had never before mentioned other individuals traveling with Paul unless they played a direct part in the narrative. But it appears the group had been steadily growing throughout Paul's travels. Timothy had joined Paul in Lystra during his second journey. Gaius of Derbe came from Timothy's region, perhaps joining earlier, in Paul's third journey. Paul picked up Tychicus and Trophimus in Asia while ministering from Ephesus. When he passed through Thessalonica, Aristarchus and Secundus followed. The same would be true of Sopater from Berea, just down the road.

This entourage included representatives from each of the Roman provinces touched by the gospel through Paul's ministry: Galatia, Asia, and Macedonia. The churches in these provinces contributed sizable sums to help the impoverished believers in Judea, which was a significant concern of Paul's third expedition. Although Paul had originally hoped to reach Jerusalem in time for Passover, and he had undoubtedly looked forward to one last visit before evangelizing the western frontier, his primary purpose was to deliver the funds. His collection was as much symbolic as practical. As a Jewish apostle to the Gentiles, he longed to see the church unified, and he knew that grace is the glue that bonds the people of Christ together. What greater way to demonstrate the common bond Jews and Gentiles share than to have representatives of the Gentile churches present tokens of their love in Jerusalem?

Clearly, however, these men didn't join Paul merely to deliver the funds in person; all remained with him many years after this departure from Corinth. Aristarchus accompanied Paul to Rome and remained with him there even as a fellow prisoner (27:2; Col. 4:10). Sopater (also called Sosipater) attended to Paul in Rome as well (Rom. 16:21). Tychicus became an oft-used envoy of Paul and may have relieved Titus after his organization of the churches on Crete (Eph. 6:21; Col. 4:7; 2 Tim. 4:12; Titus 3:12). Trophimus traveled with Paul after his release from Rome (Acts 21:29) but fell ill and remained in Miletus to recover (2 Tim. 4:20).

When the time came for Paul to board his ship for Syria, it appears his entourage played the decoy. If Paul's enemies saw these seven companions on the docks in Cenchrea, they would have suspected nothing while he took an overland route back through Macedonia. Instead of sailing for home, however, they crossed over to Troas and waited to rendezvous (Acts 20:5) before resuming their journey to Syria.

Paul wisely backtracked through Berea, Thessalonica, Apollonia, Amphipolis, and then Philippi, where he celebrated the Passover feast. "The days of Unleavened Bread" (20:6) refers to the week following the Passover meal, which occurred in late March or early April. While in Philippi, Paul picked up Luke. From this point onward, Luke uses the pronoun "we."

One wonders how church history would have unfolded differently if Paul had followed his original itinerary and sailed directly for Syria from Corinth. Paul would not have bumped into Luke in Philippi; Luke would not have traveled with Paul to Jerusalem and had the opportunity to interview Peter, John, Mary, John Mark, and other eyewitnesses; perhaps he would not even have written the Gospel bearing his name or this account of the church. It's pointless to speculate how God would have arranged to give us these treasures by some other means; as always, His plan unfolded like He wanted! The evil intended by Paul's enemies merely advanced the Lord's agenda.

Paul adapted; God prevailed.

— 20:6-7 —

On the second missionary journey, Paul and his companions had the wind at their backs and made the trip from Troas to Neapolis in two days (16:11). The reverse course took five (20:6). (Paul was starting to sail against the wind in more ways than one.) He caught up with his companions and they remained in Troas another week. Either they found no suitable transport or they saw a need to strengthen the church before leaving. Luke never mentions their establishing a church in Troas, but it's conceivable that Paul, Silas, and Timothy evangelized the city while waiting for the Lord's instructions (16:8-11).

In Troas, the church assembled "on the first day of the week" (20:7). This is the first indication in Scripture that Sunday had become the customary day for Christian worship. It's very likely the practice goes all the way back to the first believers in Jerusalem, who observed the Sabbath and then met for fellowship and Christian teaching the following day, which, for Jews, began at sundown Saturday evening. Paul may have had a hand in exporting the Jerusalem tradition to other communities, especially where large synagogues existed. In keeping with the new custom, the Troas believers gathered and "broke bread." The idiom could mean either "shared a meal" or "observed communion." In the beginning, the two meanings were combined. Christians gathered for a weekly banquet they termed a "love feast" (Jude 1:12), during which they used bread and wine to celebrate the Lord's Supper.

After the meal and communion, churches sang hymns, read Scripture, and listened to teaching (Eph. 5:19; Col. 3:16, cf. Matt. 26:30). Because Paul didn't expect to visit Troas again, he extended his teaching late into the night.

— 20:8-9 —

Several factors conspired to put Paul's audience to sleep, even with an engaging speaker. A full stomach, a warm room, and the late hour were reasons enough to nod off. Add to those factors a lowered oxygen content because of the many lamps burning, and a "deep sleep" is inevitable. The Greek term rendered "young man" indicates a boy of about ten to seventeen years of age. Writers frequently use the word to describe those who exhibit behavior characteristic of a teenager: impetuous, active, spirited, willful.

The gathering met in the upper room of a home, three stories up, which meant he fell approximately 20 feet, maybe more. Dr. Luke pronounced him dead on the spot, but the young man's name, Eutychus, would prove to be prophetic. It means "good fortune" or "lucky."

— 20:10-11 —

Paul went out and "fell upon" the young man (20:10). Luke's description of Paul's behavior deliberately echoes that of Elijah and Elisha (1 Kgs. 17:21-22; 2 Kgs. 4:34-35). Elijah stretched himself across the son of his hostess three times, begging the Lord to raise the boy. When the boy's life returned, the prophet presented him to his mother: "See, your son is alive" (1 Kgs. 17:23). She responded, "Now I know that you are a man of God and that the word of the LORD in your mouth is truth" (1 Kgs. 17:24). Similarly, Elisha stretched himself across the dead son of a woman from Shunem who had shown him extraordinary hospitality. When the boy woke, the prophet returned him to his mother (2 Kgs. 4:36). In both cases, the miracle validated the man as an authentic prophet and affirmed the word of God spoken through him.

The incident with Eutychus put Paul on the same plane of authority as Elijah and Elisha, two of Israel's most revered prophets. Theologically, this established a continuity from the Old Testament to the New Testament, affirming the church as an instrument of God just as powerful as Israel. In terms of the narrative, this miraculous display of divine power through Paul anticipated his visit to the temple, where he would be accused of preaching against the Law of Moses (Acts 21:20-21).

After the boy's life had been restored, Paul and the gathered believers returned to the upper room and resumed their meeting. "Broken the bread and eaten" (20:11), in this case, refers to a regular meal. They enjoyed more conversation over a twilight breakfast before Paul would leave, never expecting to see them again.

— 20:12 —

Luke concludes the episode with the reassurance that the boy suffered no lingering effects from his ordeal. He wasn't merely "lucky" to be alive; the power of God had restored him to complete health. The church in Troas had in their congregation a living reminder of God's mercy. And if anyone doubted the authenticity of Paul as God's spokesman, they need only talk to the boy who fell asleep in church.

APPLICATION: ACTS 20:3-12

No "Plan B"

Luke's accounts of Paul's hampered journey to Troas and his miraculous restoration of Eutychus's life serve a literary and theological purpose. The rest of Paul's life would be a series of adaptations to challenges presented by unfortunate circumstances, and his flexibility would become the means by which God would advance His agenda. Although Paul was prevented from spending Passover in Jerusalem, we have the Gospel of Luke and the book of Acts because he adapted his itinerary to avoid danger and picked up Luke in Philippi. Although a boy fell to his death during Paul's teaching at Troas, Paul's compassionate response gave the Lord an opportunity to miraculously affirm the apostle's authority, validating his ministry.

The Lord didn't stop working in the first century. He still has a plan and He will continue to see it through. Therefore, we would be wise to observe Paul's experience to find principles we can apply today.

First, *hold all personal plans loosely*. If anyone in the world could claim a direct line to heaven, it was Paul. He was fulfilling his calling and accomplishing his divine purpose. God used the apostle as His mouthpiece and He channeled His power through this servant to heal illnesses, cast out demons, and even raise the dead. Yet Paul encountered circumstances he could not change. He established noble plans to carry out his mission with selfless abandon, yet enemies forced him to adjust. If Paul had to remain flexible and adaptable, we shouldn't be surprised when our plans come unraveled. Make detailed plans and follow them when you can. But hold them loosely. Expect changes.

Second, *don't waste time lamenting a ruined plan*. I've served in ministry long enough to remember multiple occasions when a busted plan turned out to be a gift in disguise. I look back on those episodes and I shudder to think what might have happened if my plans—as good and as well thought-out as they seemed—had not been preempted by some unforeseen difficulty. I also recall how upset I was when my plans got dashed. On one occasion, I remember feeling like my life had been completely ruined. Today, as I reflect on the past, I see God's loving, gracious hand steering me toward a future I could not have imagined. Having so many of these gifts of broken plans in my past, today I accept much more easily what I cannot change.

Third, *be prepared to adapt your plans when circumstances change.* The Marines never engage the enemy without a clear objective and a detailed plan. More than 235 years of combat experience have taught them that the first moments of battle can change everything—except the *objective.* So, they drill a mantra into each combat-ready warrior, from fresh recruits all the way up to the commandant: "Improvise. Adapt. Overcome."

Keep your eye on the objective, but learn to flex with the changes to get the job done.

Fourth, *never forget that your adaptation was always God's "Plan A."* From Paul's perspective, the plot to kill him required a shift to "Plan B." From our perspective—graciously provided by Providence—we can see that God had always wanted Paul to pick up Luke in Philippi. The same can be said of each instance in which the church had to adapt in response to a difficulty. Time eventually revealed that each "adaptation" resulted in their following the path God had set before them.

God doesn't have a "Plan B." When plans fall apart, look for how the Lord might use the situation to advance His redemptive plan, and then join Him.

A Touching Farewell
ACTS 20:13-38

NASB

13 But we, going ahead to the ship, set sail for Assos, intending from there to take Paul on board; for so he had arranged it, intending himself to go ªby land. 14 And when he met us at Assos, we took him on board and came to Mitylene. 15 Sailing from there, we arrived the following day opposite Chios; and the next day we crossed over to Samos; and the day following we came to Miletus. 16 For Paul had decided to sail past Ephesus so that he would not have to spend time in ªAsia; for he was hurrying to be in Jerusalem, if possible, on the day of Pentecost.

17 From Miletus he sent to Ephesus and called to him the elders of the

NLT

13 Paul went by land to Assos, where he had arranged for us to join him, while we traveled by ship. 14 He joined us there, and we sailed together to Mitylene. 15 The next day we sailed past the island of Kios. The following day we crossed to the island of Samos, and* a day later we arrived at Miletus.

16 Paul had decided to sail on past Ephesus, for he didn't want to spend any more time in the province of Asia. He was hurrying to get to Jerusalem, if possible, in time for the Festival of Pentecost. 17 But when we landed at Miletus, he sent a message to the elders of the church at Ephesus, asking them to come and meet him.

church. ¹⁸And when they had come to him, he said to them,

"You yourselves know, from the first day that I set foot in ªAsia, how I was with you the whole time, ¹⁹serving the Lord with all humility and with tears and with trials which came upon me ªthrough the plots of the Jews; ²⁰how I did not shrink from declaring to you anything that was profitable, and teaching you publicly and ªfrom house to house, ²¹solemnly testifying to both Jews and Greeks of repentance toward God and faith in our Lord Jesus Christ. ²²And now, behold, bound by the ªSpirit, I am on my way to Jerusalem, not knowing what will happen to me there, ²³except that the Holy Spirit solemnly testifies to me in every city, saying that bonds and afflictions await me. ²⁴But I do not consider my life of any account as dear to myself, so that I may finish my course and the ministry which I received from the Lord Jesus, to testify solemnly of the gospel of the grace of God.

²⁵"And now, behold, I know that all of you, among whom I went about preaching the kingdom, will no longer see my face. ²⁶Therefore, I ªtestify to you this day that I am ᵇinnocent of the blood of all men. ²⁷For I did not shrink from declaring to you the whole purpose of God. ²⁸Be on guard for yourselves and for all the flock, among which the Holy Spirit has made you ªoverseers, to shepherd the church of God which He ᵇpurchased ᶜwith His own blood. ²⁹I know that after my departure savage wolves will come in among you, not sparing the flock; ³⁰and from among your own selves men will arise, speaking perverse things, to draw away the disciples after them. ³¹Therefore be on the alert, remembering that night and day for a period of three years I did not cease to admonish each one with tears. ³²And now I commend you

¹⁸When they arrived he declared, "You know that from the day I set foot in the province of Asia until now ¹⁹I have done the Lord's work humbly and with many tears. I have endured the trials that came to me from the plots of the Jews. ²⁰I never shrank back from telling you what you needed to hear, either publicly or in your homes. ²¹I have had one message for Jews and Greeks alike—the necessity of repenting from sin and turning to God, and of having faith in our Lord Jesus.

²²"And now I am bound by the Spirit* to go to Jerusalem. I don't know what awaits me, ²³except that the Holy Spirit tells me in city after city that jail and suffering lie ahead. ²⁴But my life is worth nothing to me unless I use it for finishing the work assigned me by the Lord Jesus—the work of telling others the Good News about the wonderful grace of God.

²⁵"And now I know that none of you to whom I have preached the Kingdom will ever see me again. ²⁶I declare today that I have been faithful. If anyone suffers eternal death, it's not my fault,* ²⁷for I didn't shrink from declaring all that God wants you to know.

²⁸"So guard yourselves and God's people. Feed and shepherd God's flock—his church, purchased with his own blood*—over which the Holy Spirit has appointed you as leaders.* ²⁹I know that false teachers, like vicious wolves, will come in among you after I leave, not sparing the flock. ³⁰Even some men from your own group will rise up and distort the truth in order to draw a following. ³¹Watch out! Remember the three years I was with you—my constant watch and care over you night and day, and my many tears for you.

³²"And now I entrust you to God and the message of his grace that is able to build you up and give you an

NASB

to God and to the word of His grace, which is able to build *you* up and to give *you* the inheritance among all those who are sanctified. ³³I have coveted no one's silver or gold or clothes. ³⁴You yourselves know that these hands ministered to my *own* needs and to the men who were with me. ³⁵In everything I showed you that by working hard in this manner you must help the weak and remember the words of the Lord Jesus, that He Himself said, 'It is more blessed to give than to receive.'"

³⁶When he had said these things, he knelt down and prayed with them all. ³⁷And ªthey *began* to weep aloud and ᵇembraced Paul, and repeatedly kissed him, ³⁸ªgrieving especially over the word which he had spoken, that they would not see his face again. And they were accompanying him to the ship.

20:13 ªOr *on foot*   20:16 ªI.e. west coast province of Asia Minor   20:18 ªV 16, note 1   20:19 ªLit *by*   20:20 ªOr *in the various private homes*   20:22 ªOr *in spirit*   20:26 ªOr *call you to witness*   ᵇLit *pure from*   20:28 ªOr *bishops*   ᵇLit *acquired*   ᶜLit *through*   20:37 ªLit *a considerable weeping of all occurred*   ᵇLit *threw themselves on Paul's neck*   20:38 ªLit *suffering pain*

inheritance with all those he has set apart for himself.

³³"I have never coveted anyone's silver or gold or fine clothes. ³⁴You know that these hands of mine have worked to supply my own needs and even the needs of those who were with me. ³⁵And I have been a constant example of how you can help those in need by working hard. You should remember the words of the Lord Jesus: 'It is more blessed to give than to receive.'"

³⁶When he had finished speaking, he knelt and prayed with them. ³⁷They all cried as they embraced and kissed him good-bye. ³⁸They were sad most of all because he had said that they would never see him again. Then they escorted him down to the ship.

20:15 Some manuscripts read *and having stayed at Trogyllium.*   20:22 Or *by my spirit,* or *by an inner compulsion;* Greek reads *by the spirit.*   20:26 Greek *I am innocent of the blood of all.*   20:28a Or *with the blood of his own [Son].*   20:28b Or *overseers,* or *bishops.*

NLT

On March 11, 1942, Japanese imperial forces bore down on Corregidor Island in the Philippines. President Roosevelt recognized the brilliance of General Douglas MacArthur and the absolute necessity of having him as the Pacific Theater of War Commander, so he ordered the general to relinquish command of Corregidor, leave his troops, and relocate to Australia. In his book, *Reminiscences*, MacArthur describes his difficult farewell:

> It was 7:15 on the evening of March 11th [1942] when I walked across the porch to my wife. "Jean," I said gently, "it is time to go." We drove in silence to the South Dock, where Bulkeley and PT-41 were waiting; the rest of the party was already aboard. Shelling of the waterfront had continued intermittently all day. I put Jean, [our son] Arthur, and Ah Cheu on board, and then turned slowly to look back.

On the dock I could see the men staring at me. I had lost 25 pounds living on the same diet as the soldiers, and I must have looked gaunt and ghastly standing there in my old war-stained clothes—no bemedaled commander of inspiring presence. . . .

Darkness had now fallen, and the waters were beginning to ripple from the faint night breeze. The enemy firing had ceased and a muttering silence had fallen. It was as though the dead were passing by the stench of destruction. The smell of filth thickened the night air. I raised my cap in farewell salute, and I could feel my face go white, feel a sudden, convulsive twitch in the muscles of my face. I heard someone ask, "What's his chance, Sarge, of getting through?" and the gruff reply, "Dunno. He's lucky. Maybe one in five."

I stepped aboard PT-41. "You may cast off, Buck," I said, "when you are ready."[1]

When reporters pressed for a statement, he explained the president's reasoning and then promised, "I came through and I shall return."[2]

Goodbyes are never easy, especially under difficult circumstances, and they are never more difficult than when the farewell is likely to be the last. As Paul made his way back to Syria, he couldn't bypass Ephesus without saying a final farewell. Unlike General MacArthur, however, he did not intend to return. A quick report to his sending church in Syrian Antioch, a final visit to the temple in Jerusalem, and then off to the western frontier, where he planned to serve during all his remaining years.

— 20:13-15 —

After meeting with the Troas church through the night, Paul and his team departed the city. In those days, ships usually kept land within sight for the sake of navigation and typically sailed only during daylight hours, seeking safe harbor each night. For reasons Luke doesn't state, Paul decided to walk the 20-mile journey across the peninsula to Assos while the rest of the men boarded the ship that would carry them toward Syria. That evening, Paul came aboard and they went to Mitylene, a city on the leeward side of Lesbos Island (20:13-14).

Over the next three days, the ship weaved through the islands off the west coast of Asia until they arrived in Miletus, a once-important seaport at the mouth of the Meander River (20:15). Although it was still impressive in Paul's day, the glory days of Miletus were mostly in the past. It made an ideal location for him to meet with the elders of the

Ephesus church: large enough for comfort and convenience, yet isolated from the bustle and traffic of the big city.

— 20:16-17 —

Paul had missed his opportunity to reach Jerusalem by Passover (20:6). Pentecost, another major festival for Jews, was still within reach if he didn't delay. Meeting in Miletus presented less risk of local entanglements. Luke's description of their itinerary suggests that Paul could determine the route and ports of call, which would not be the case if they had purchased transit on a merchant ship. Apparently, they had chartered a vessel for their exclusive use.

When they arrived in Miletus, Paul sent one of the interns to Ephesus to summon the church elders. When the elders arrived, Paul gathered them for what we might call a one-day "pastors' conference." Of all his letters and his declarations recorded by Luke, none is more intimate or emotional than this final farewell. He looked into the faces of some of his closest friends, realizing he had to leave them to stand or fall on their own; he would no longer be available to help them.

Of course, Luke didn't provide a transcription of Paul's message, which probably took the form of several addresses throughout the day. Instead, he summarized the apostle's parting words, which can be divided into three main sections:

1. Paul's Ministry in Ephesus (20:18-21)
2. Paul's Immediate Future (20:22-27)
3. The Future of the Church in Ephesus (20:28-35)

— 20:18-21 —

Paul began his address by remembering his own personal history with the people of Ephesus, especially his faithfulness regarding several tests. I observe in his words five pitfalls he avoided.

1. *He overcame the test of laziness:* "From the first day that I set foot in Asia . . . I was with you the whole time" (20:18). He devoted himself to proclaiming the gospel and then nurturing those who believed. He didn't leave them to fend for themselves; he diligently taught them each day, using the *scholē* of Tyrannus as a meeting place.

2. *He overcame the test of pride:* "serving the Lord with all humility and with tears" (20:19). He wasn't bragging; he was remembering. He didn't say this to dote on himself but to inspire the elders. The Greek word translated "humility" (*tapeinophrosunē* [5012a]) carries the idea

of lowliness of mind. It means he didn't talk down to the Ephesians like they were ignorant or stupid. He spoke peer to peer, simply sharing information they lacked.

3. *He overcame the test of discouragement:* "and with trials which came upon me through the plots of the Jews" (20:19). Ministers who avoid sexual immorality, greed, and pride still must struggle with unfair criticism. The Ephesians didn't respond to the gospel as quickly as other groups Paul had preached to; the spiritual darkness covering Asia took a long time to penetrate. If that weren't difficult enough, Paul endured personal rejection so acute his enemies wanted to see him dead. It's hard not to take that personally, but he didn't succumb to discouragement.

4. *He overcame the test of fear:* "I did not shrink from declaring to you" (20:20). The Greek word rendered "shrink" (*hypostellō* [5288]) means "to hold oneself back" or "to draw away." Ministers often struggle with intimidation. Certain people—most often those who are seen as successes in the secular arena—can easily intimidate God's servants who have left all to serve God full-time. Frankly, we're almost always caught off guard because we find it confusing. It's a perplexing, exasperating waste of time and energy that has no place in Christian work. Effective ministers learn not to back down.

5. *He overcame the test of inefficiency:* "anything that was profitable, and teaching you publicly and from house to house" (20:20). The word translated "profitable" (*sympherō* [4851]) refers to anything that helps, creates an advantage, or confers a benefit. Paul measured his every decision and action by how it would help the Ephesians. He was willing to try anything that would help them learn and grow: teaching in groups, in homes, one on one, publicly, privately—he overlooked no promising method.

While Paul ministered effectively and efficiently, avoiding any hint of favoritism, he always gave priority to sound doctrinal teaching. The basic formula "repentance toward God and faith in our Lord Jesus Christ" is the bedrock message upon which everything else in Christian theology and practice builds (20:21).

— 20:22-27 —

Paul turned from describing his personal history with the church, recounting how he had invested himself so personally in the Ephesians, to discussing his immediate plans. He became very transparent with the elders. He no longer spoke to them like pupils; he regarded them as equal partners. Having ministered to them, he made himself vulnerable and allowed them the opportunity to offer comfort and encouragement.

We discovered earlier that Paul had wanted to be in Jerusalem for Passover; then, after a change of plans, he hoped to reach the city in time for Pentecost. Somewhere along his journey, Paul learned that his own desire was, in fact, a prompting by the Holy Spirit (20:22). A desire became a need; the need grew into a passion; now the passion had become an obsession. (I mean "obsession" in the best way. People who have experienced a clear call of the Spirit experience His leading as a single-minded compulsion to do as He directs.) He openly discussed the dilemma the Lord's leading presented him. In each city along the way, Paul had been given the same message: "Bonds and afflictions await" (20:23). Paul usually sidestepped danger. He didn't shrink from threats, but he wisely avoided suffering when possible. In this case, however, the Spirit directed him to walk toward affliction rather than turn away from it.

Paul had been told earlier that his ministry would include suffering. Jesus said, "He is a chosen instrument of Mine, to bear My name before the Gentiles and kings and the sons of Israel; for I will show him how much he must suffer for My name's sake" (9:15-16). Perhaps Paul thought he had suffered enough during his three missionary journeys! As he got closer to Jerusalem, it became clear that more affliction awaited him, although he couldn't anticipate specifically what would happen. Even so, he couldn't shrink from his duty.

Although he didn't know what would happen to him in Jerusalem, Paul followed two convictions that had been with him from the beginning. First, he had deserved to die on the road to Damascus, but the Lord extended mercy; each day he lived after that was a gift of grace. Second, he had to preach Christ with every day given to him. Very little mattered to Paul beyond those two convictions. If the path before him led to his death, he could follow it no less enthusiastically.

He acknowledged that, in all likelihood, they would not see him again, either because he would die or because he would be somewhere in Gallia or Hispania.

Paul's declaration of innocence is curious, like the confession of a dying man (20:26). He was, of course, guilty of persecuting the innocent Christians, which led to their arrest and sometimes execution, before his encounter with Christ (7:58; 8:1, 3; 9:1; 1 Cor. 15:9). Nevertheless, he was "innocent of the blood of all men" in two respects. First, his crimes had been erased from his account by the sacrificial death of

Jesus Christ. Second, wherever he went, he proclaimed the same opportunity to everyone within earshot; any who died in their sins could not blame Paul. No one in the cities he visited could claim ignorance as an excuse, and that included Ephesus. Even in the face of certain danger, Paul didn't "shrink."

— 20:28-30 —

In the last section of his address (20:28-35), Paul looked to the future of the church in Ephesus, warning them of three specific dangers (20:28-30) that form a basis for his final admonition to them (20:31-35).

First, he warned them of *the danger of personal compromise* (20:28). Paul admonished the leaders to "be on guard." The Greek word for this, *prosechō* [4337], could be used to give a similar charge to a soldier or sentry, whose first responsibility was to stay awake; if he failed at that, all would be lost. If he remained awake, he had to continually scan his area for intruders in order to protect himself and others. If a trespasser overwhelmed the guard, the entire stronghold would become compromised. Paul reminded them that as leaders, God had entrusted them with a priceless treasure, and like sentries at their posts, they must be vigilant and diligent.

The Greek word translated "overseers" (*episkopos* [1985]) means literally "*over*-seers," that is, protective "watchers." Athenians used the term for state officials, those who watched over an institution or a territory. Athens called its state officials *episkopoi*, the plural form of the word. In the Septuagint (the Greek translation of the Old Testament), an *episkopos* was one who served as judge, as treasurer, or as supervisor of the priests and the Levites serving in the temple. Elsewhere in the New Testament, Peter calls Jesus the *episkopos* of our souls (1 Pet. 2:25). In this sense, the church official designated by this term is someone charged to "shepherd" (*poimainō* [4165]) the church, to serve as an undershepherd to the Lord, leading His flock on His behalf and under His authority. Paul listed the qualifications of an "overseer" in his letter to Timothy, who was serving in Ephesus at the time (1 Tim. 3:2-7).

Second, Paul prepared them for *the danger of external attack by false teachers* (20:29). He warned the elders with a palpable image of wolves among sheep. Ephesus had become famous for its schools of philosophy, some of which would eventually mingle their ideas with Christianity and even adopt Christian vocabulary and then corrupt the gospel while sounding orthodox. So-called teachers from other cities would arrive in Ephesus, announcing themselves as emissaries of the apostles, looking for occasions to address the church members. Paul saw them as wolves slinking among the sheep, looking for opportunities to carry the weaker ones off to their deaths.

Third, he cautioned the Ephesian church about *the danger of internal corruption by apostasy* (20:30). Theological corruption could creep in from the outside in the form of false teachers, or it could arise from within as leaders drifted from the teaching of the apostles and Scripture. The term rendered "perverse" (*diastrephō* [1294]) means "deformed," "distorted," "perverted," or "corrupted." Church leaders must keep one another accountable so that when one begins to teach doctrines that do not conform to the Bible, his or her friends can gently correct the errors (see Gal. 6:1-2).

— 20:31-35 —

"Therefore" introduces these verses and marks Paul's admonition to "be on the alert" as the needed response to the three dangers he highlighted. To make the concept more concrete, Paul used himself as an example of how the elders should guard their churches from personal compromise, false teachers, and apostasy. He noted his tireless devotion to teaching, using every opportunity—"night and day"—for three years to help the Ephesian Christians become mature believers (20:31). He had carried the burden faithfully and now he transferred the responsibility of leadership to the elders (20:32).

Paul also highlighted the selfless nature of his service, which he considered a major factor in remaining alert. He worked around many rich people in Ephesus; some were high-ranking officials who would have delighted to give Paul money, clothes, a large home—anything he wished. But he accepted no bribes, no perks—nothing (20:33). His reference to "these hands" suggests he used his trade or some other means of earning income to pay his own expenses (20:34). Paul again turned his example into a solemn charge to care for the sheep rather than expect the flock to support the shepherd (20:35).

To summarize his argument, Paul quoted Jesus, although these words do not appear in any of the Gospels. Obviously, the apostles—the men who were with Jesus and had followed Him from the beginning—saw and heard much more than could be documented in the Gospel accounts (John 21:25). Paul had spent time with more than one apostle and remembered this statement, which he applied this way: The blessings of ministry must never be taken from the flock; the Lord will reward the giver with a greater measure of blessing than he or she surrenders.

— 20:36-38 —

Paul undoubtedly spent the entire day with the Ephesian elders, developing and applying each point, answering questions, discussing specific situations, and anticipating future scenarios and how to handle them. Then at the end of his time, he knelt and prayed for them (20:36). Imagine the impact of hearing this faithful apostle interceding for you just before departing for the last time. "They began to weep aloud and embraced Paul, and repeatedly kissed him" (20:37). They were "grieving" (20:38; *odunaō* [3600]), suffering mental pain and distress, over their mentor—the man who had guided them out of darkness and into a life of freedom and hope—who was departing to certain suffering and potential death. This caused them deep anguish, and they did not attempt to hide it.

This scene follows Paul to the ship, where he and his entourage set sail.

APPLICATION: ACTS 20:13-38

How to Look Back Before Moving Forward

When Paul stopped off in Miletus, he could have used the time to relax, collect his thoughts, and enjoy some much-needed solitude. He could have regarded the absence of a church there as an opportunity to prepare himself for what lay ahead. Instead, he decided to call the Ephesus church leaders together to engage them in an exercise that can benefit anyone on the threshold of a significant transition. He knew that it's often helpful to take a lingering look backward before moving forward. This would prepare them for the transition to carrying on the work of ministry without his help.

Paul's daylong address offers two principles worth remembering when we prepare to leave one ministry and begin another.

First, *reflecting on the past calls for honesty*. Few lies do more damage than the ones we tell ourselves. Ignoring past failures won't make them any less embarrassing, only more likely to occur again. So, to eliminate the threat of repeating our failures, we must embrace them as teachers, learn from them what we can, make them our friends, and keep them close. But we need not dwell on faults and foibles exclusively. An honest assessment of the past includes not only remembering our regrets but also celebrating successes and analyzing what we did right so we can determine how to establish a pattern of triumphs.

Second, *enjoying success demands a constant awareness of peril.* All of us would do well to remember that success today offers no guarantee of success tomorrow. The blessings we enjoy right now can be maintained only as we remain aware of potential threats and then prepare to meet them. That doesn't mean we let paranoia steal our joy. In fact, we must take care not to fixate on dangers that might never occur; our focus must remain on Christ and His promise that nothing—not even the fearsome powers of hell—will defeat His church. Nevertheless, maintaining a realistic awareness of the perils looming in the darkness will help safeguard the flock.

Human Advice vs. Divine Direction
ACTS 21:1-17

NASB

¹When we had parted from them and had set sail, we ran a straight course to Cos and the next day to Rhodes and from there to Patara; ²and having found a ship crossing over to Phoenicia, we went aboard and set sail. ³When we came in sight of Cyprus, leaving it on the left, we kept sailing to Syria and landed at Tyre; for there the ship was to unload its cargo. ⁴After looking up the disciples, we stayed there seven days; and they kept telling Paul ᵃthrough the Spirit not to set foot in Jerusalem. ⁵When ᵃour days there were ended, we left and started on our journey, while they all, with wives and children, escorted us until *we were* out of the city. After kneeling down on the beach and praying, we said farewell to one another. ⁶Then we went on board the ship, and they returned home again.

⁷When we had finished the voyage from Tyre, we arrived at Ptolemais, and after greeting the brethren, we stayed with them for a day. ⁸On the

NLT

¹After saying farewell to the Ephesian elders, we sailed straight to the island of Cos. The next day we reached Rhodes and then went to Patara. ²There we boarded a ship sailing for Phoenicia. ³We sighted the island of Cyprus, passed it on our left, and landed at the harbor of Tyre, in Syria, where the ship was to unload its cargo.

⁴We went ashore, found the local believers,* and stayed with them a week. These believers prophesied through the Holy Spirit that Paul should not go on to Jerusalem. ⁵When we returned to the ship at the end of the week, the entire congregation, including women* and children, left the city and came down to the shore with us. There we knelt, prayed, ⁶and said our farewells. Then we went aboard, and they returned home.

⁷The next stop after leaving Tyre was Ptolemais, where we greeted the brothers and sisters* and stayed for one day. ⁸The next day we went on

next day we left and came to Caesarea, and entering the house of Philip the evangelist, who was one of the seven, we stayed with him. ⁹Now this man had four virgin daughters who were prophetesses. ¹⁰As we were staying there for some days, a prophet named Agabus came down from Judea. ¹¹And coming to us, he took Paul's belt and bound his own feet and hands, and said, "This is what the Holy Spirit says: 'In this way the Jews at Jerusalem will bind the man who owns this belt and deliver him into the hands of the Gentiles.'" ¹²When we had heard this, we as well as the local residents *began* begging him not to go up to Jerusalem. ¹³Then Paul answered, "What are you doing, weeping and breaking my heart? For I am ready not only to be bound, but even to die at Jerusalem for the name of the Lord Jesus." ¹⁴And since he would not be persuaded, we fell silent, remarking, "The will of the Lord be done!"

¹⁵After these days we got ready and started on our way up to Jerusalem. ¹⁶*Some* of the disciples from Caesarea also came with us, taking us to Mnason of Cyprus, a disciple of long standing with whom we were to lodge.

¹⁷After we arrived in Jerusalem, the brethren received us gladly.

21:4 ªI.e. because of impressions made by the Spirit   21:5 ªLit *we had completed the days*

to Caesarea and stayed at the home of Philip the Evangelist, one of the seven men who had been chosen to distribute food. ⁹He had four unmarried daughters who had the gift of prophecy. ¹⁰Several days later a man named Agabus, who also had the gift of prophecy, arrived from Judea. ¹¹He came over, took Paul's belt, and bound his own feet and hands with it. Then he said, "The Holy Spirit declares, 'So shall the owner of this belt be bound by the Jewish leaders in Jerusalem and turned over to the Gentiles.'" ¹²When we heard this, we and the local believers all begged Paul not to go on to Jerusalem.

¹³But he said, "Why all this weeping? You are breaking my heart! I am ready not only to be jailed at Jerusalem but even to die for the sake of the Lord Jesus." ¹⁴When it was clear that we couldn't persuade him, we gave up and said, "The Lord's will be done."

¹⁵After this we packed our things and left for Jerusalem. ¹⁶Some believers from Caesarea accompanied us, and they took us to the home of Mnason, a man originally from Cyprus and one of the early believers. ¹⁷When we arrived, the brothers and sisters in Jerusalem welcomed us warmly.

21:4 Greek *disciples;* also in 21:16.   21:5 Or *wives.*   21:7 Greek *brothers;* also in 21:17.

The longer I live, the more I wish it were easier to determine the will of God. I usually have less difficulty following God's instructions than determining exactly what He wants. To be candid, I've found that receiving counsel from others often creates more confusion than clarity. Paul, too, faced this tension in following the Spirit's direction.

At times I long for God to speak as He did before the Bible was complete. Joshua stood before the walls of Jericho, knowing that he had to invade and that God had guaranteed success. He knew exactly what to do because the historical account specifically says, "The LORD said to Joshua . . ." (Josh. 6:2). Joshua followed the Lord's instructions without hesitation, and of course, it worked!

Elijah stood before King Ahab, the wimpy, weak-willed ruler of Israel who had a habit of issuing rash, violent edicts. After the prophet delivered the Lord's condemnation, he received clear instructions: "Go away from here and turn eastward, and hide yourself by the brook Cherith, which is east of the Jordan" (1 Kgs. 17:3). How's that for specific? No need to ponder his next move; Elijah went where he was told, did as he was instructed, and his ministry continued as God intended.

In the New Testament era, which continues today, God doesn't typically communicate this way. Even during the apostolic period, when God spoke miraculously through apostles and prophets, He rarely issued specific instructions. On the Day of Pentecost, He began to administer His kingdom differently. Jesus hinted at this in the upper room on the eve of His crucifixion, saying, "No longer do I call you slaves, for the slave does not know what his master is doing; but I have called you friends, for all things that I have heard from My Father I have made known to you" (John 15:15). A little later, Jesus continued, "But when He, the Spirit of truth, comes, He will guide you into all the truth; for He will not speak on His own initiative, but whatever He hears, He will speak; and He will disclose to you what is to come. He will glorify Me, for He will take of Mine and will disclose it to you. All things that the Father has are Mine; therefore I said that He takes of Mine and will disclose it to you" (John 16:13-15).

In the Old Testament era, God administered His kingdom by speaking His instructions audibly and issuing His commandments in writing. Unfortunately, this only revealed the depths of our depravity; even when humanity knows the will of God for certain, we still struggle to obey it. The Lord used the old covenant to prove that *hearing* the word of God isn't our primary problem; *heeding* the word of God is our constant challenge. With the inauguration of the new covenant (Jer. 31:31-34; Acts 1:8), our Master has taken a different approach. Instead of standing before us to issue orders, He now lives within us to transform our minds (Rom. 12:1-2) so that we begin to think His thoughts. As the Spirit gradually takes over, defeating our old, selfish, vain, foolish manner of life, we begin to cherish what God cherishes, make decisions according to His values, and view life from His eternal perspective.

As Paul continued his journey, steadily closing the distance between himself and Jerusalem, this new covenant dynamic became ever more evident. He began to experience a growing tension between the leading of the Spirit and the advice offered by godly people who cared deeply for him. His experience, therefore, is worth close scrutiny.

— 21:1-2 —

After his tearful departure from Miletus, Paul and his team "ran a straight course" to the island of Cos (21:1), meaning the wind was at their back and they made good time. The following day, their ship threaded the islands off the southwestern coast of present-day Turkey to reach Patara by the end of their third day at sea. This seaport in the Roman province of Lycia (on the southern coast of the Turkish mainland) was one of the largest and most prosperous in the region.[3] The winds favored ships departing for the eastern part of the Mediterranean. Here Paul and his men changed ships.

The region known as Phoenicia was a narrow strip of land along the coast northwest of Galilee, surrounded by the province of Syria. Paul had originally intended to visit Syria, specifically his adopted hometown of Antioch (20:3), but time was running short. He hoped to be in Jerusalem in time to celebrate Pentecost. He also carried a large sum of money donated by the Gentile churches he had visited in Macedonia and Achaia (Rom. 15:26). Having found a ship bound for Tyre, the men set sail.

— 21:3-6 —

Luke explains that their ship avoided the dangerous lane between Cyprus and Pamphylia, running a course south of the island straight for Tyre. The vessel had to unload its cargo before carrying Paul south to his disembarkation at Caesarea Maritima. Apparently, unloading the ship took a full seven days. Paul used this time to summon the nearby believers for a conference and undoubtedly strengthened the churches as he had in Miletus.

Throughout his time with them, however, the Christians kept telling him to avoid Jerusalem. The phrase "through the Spirit" (21:4) is troublesome, because it appears Paul received conflicting instructions from the Holy Spirit. Acts 20:22 and 21:14 both suggest Paul went to Jerusalem in obedience to God's command. Luke's grammar here doesn't solve the problem; throughout his narrative, he uses this phrase[4] to indicate authentic communication from God (cf. 1:2; 4:25; 11:28).

Though some may dispute this interpretation, I don't think Paul made a mistake going to Jerusalem; Acts 20:22 and 21:14 cannot be discounted. Paul had earlier demonstrated his willingness to avoid unnecessary suffering and to escape imminent danger, especially when he saw little to be gained. On a few occasions, he faced certain affliction head-on when he thought his suffering might accomplish greater good than self-preservation. In other words, Paul demonstrated uncommon bravery in the face of hardship, but he was no fool. This was an unusual situation. By the Spirit's revelation, Paul knew that suffering awaited him in Jerusalem (20:23), but he couldn't deny the prompting of the Spirit to go forth and face the danger.

So, how should we interpret the warning of the believers in Tyre? Like the many concerned voices before them (20:23), they accurately saw Paul's future as revealed by the Spirit—persecution and suffering in Jerusalem—but then they gave him advice based on their own desires. They faithfully foretold Paul's suffering, but they advised him "not to set foot in Jerusalem" (21:4), where Paul, by the Spirit, felt compelled to go. I don't think I've ever made a major decision in my adult life that some individuals did not say was wrong. That makes tough decisions even tougher, but I've learned to expect some poor advice given in love; our closest family members and friends mean well and want the best for us. Still, we need people who will look out for *God's* good, people who will say to us, "Let God be God."

Paul listened to the believers' warnings but continued his journey to Jerusalem undeterred. As in Miletus, the believers in Tyre accompanied Paul to his ship, prayed with him, and said goodbye, never expecting to see him again.

— 21:7-9 —

Ptolemais, also known as Acco, was a short, 25-mile trip down the Phoenician coast. Paul and his men didn't have to stop, but they chose to spend a day with Christians in the area. The next day, they sailed another 30 miles south to the port of Caesarea Maritima, where Peter had first learned to accept Gentile believers as brothers. It's fitting that the last leg of Paul's missionary journeys should take him from Caesarea to Jerusalem.

Sometime after the Jerusalem Council, Philip the evangelist, one of the first seven deacons (6:5) and the first to carry the gospel into Samaria (8:5), moved to the Roman stronghold of Caesarea and made his home there. Luke states that he had "four virgin daughters who were prophetesses" (21:9). The fact that they had not yet married has nothing to do with their prophetic gifts; Luke merely indicates that they were present in Philip's home while Paul and his companions stayed in

Tough Love

ACTS 21:4

I remember when the Lord called me to move from a pastorate in Texas to one in California. When the day came for us to depart Irving and drive to Fullerton, some people came by to say a final farewell. We exchanged tears and hugs and promises to stay in touch as Cynthia, the children, and I took our places in the car. Just before we pulled out of the driveway, one woman bent down, looked through Cynthia's window at the four kids, then Cynthia, and then me. "You keep saying the Lord is in this," she said. "But the Lord gets blamed for a lot of things He has nothing to do with." She held my confused gaze for a moment, and then walked away. Tough words to hear.

As I pulled out of the driveway, I said, "That's a rough final memory." Cynthia didn't say anything; she just cried as we drove down Finley Road. One of the children asked, "What does that mean?" I replied, "Oh, it doesn't matter." But the woman's words rang in my ears all the way to Abilene. Not because I doubted our decision. I had asked the Lord to grant a few other requests on behalf of the church and He had fulfilled them in remarkable fashion. Any doubts I had were washed away by these tangible assurances that the Lord would take care of Irving Bible Church. The woman's words stung because I didn't want to leave with anyone thinking anything but the best. But that's unrealistic. I've learned that when people lose a pastor, they often say things they later regret. I refused to let those words cloud the four great years of ministry in Irving.[5]

Caesarea. It is likely that they gave Paul more of the same warnings he had received since leaving Corinth.

— 21:10-12 —

Sometime during their stay, the prophet Agabus visited from Judea (21:10). He had earlier predicted the famine that took place around AD 46 during the reign of Emperor Claudius (11:28), and he had ample opportunity to observe the political climate in Jerusalem; no one could offer clearer information concerning Paul's safety than this man. In a dramatic gesture reminiscent of the great Old Testament prophets (e.g., 1 Kgs. 11:29-31), he bound his own hands and feet with Paul's belt, which was not a leather strap with a buckle like modern belts, but a long cloth sash that would have been wrapped several times around the midsection and tied in a knot to hold the outer garment in place.

During his demonstration, the prophet made it clear that he spoke on behalf of God. "This is what the Holy Spirit says . . ." (Acts 21:11) leaves little room for misunderstanding. He stated unequivocally that Paul would be arrested and handed over to the Gentiles. His choice of words closely resembles the Lord's prediction of His own arrest (Luke 18:31-32).

A natural response to all the warnings might have been for Paul to board a ship and sail for Spain immediately. From a purely human standpoint, that would be the implied message from God: "Danger awaits you in Jerusalem; don't go there!" But Paul couldn't ignore the divine compulsion within, even when Luke himself and others in Paul's company joined in urging him to avoid Jerusalem (Acts 21:12). Paul knew he had been called to Jerusalem to accomplish a yet-unknown divine purpose. The warnings merely gave him the opportunity to count the cost of obedience before his ordeal began and to prepare himself mentally for what he would face. If he had gone to Jerusalem and his arrest took him by surprise, he might have responded differently to the injustice and failed to see opportunities for ministry.

Luke had at least three reasons to document the many warnings about Paul's visit to Jerusalem: (1) to establish Paul's ordeal as a grave injustice, (2) to characterize Paul's ministry as following in the Lord's footsteps, and (3) to show that God was in control of His plan. Luke had earlier asserted Paul's innocence of any wrongdoing (20:26) and would later refute the allegations against him (21:29). The false accusations were simply the culmination of a long-running plot by unbelieving Jews to silence their former colleague.

— 21:13-14 —

The response of Paul's friends caused him to feel hurt and misunderstood. He undoubtedly felt isolated, even betrayed, by the very people who should have appreciated better than anyone why he had to go to Jerusalem. He had a destiny to fulfill that required his walking into certain danger. Just like Jesus, he walked his path without his companions understanding his purpose (cf. Luke 18:34). He wasn't the last to do such a thing!

As on every occasion when Paul suffered, the Lord would use the situation to accomplish His plan. In fact, Luke's narrative demonstrates that every circumstance, from the ascension of Christ to the imprisonment of Paul in Rome, had unfolded according to God's design.

The final statement of the people in Acts 21:14 shows them submitting to the Lord's agenda, just like their leader, Paul.

— 21:15-17 —

With everyone in sync with the Lord's plan, Paul and his helpers began their march toward Jerusalem, joined by some of the believers living in Caesarea. The procession therefore must have been sizable, not unlike the Lord's final ascent from Jericho to Jerusalem. Upon their arrival, they got settled in the home of Mnason, a Christian from Cyprus, and they met with the leaders of the Jerusalem church.

APPLICATION: ACTS 21:1-17

Offering and Receiving Wise Counsel

Although some New Testament instructions for believers are as straightforward as the Ten Commandments (e.g., Rom. 12:19; 1 Thes. 5:14), in many matters there are no specific instructions. Rather, we have the Spirit of God living within us, transforming us to think and behave like Christ. He has given us a great privilege that comes with immense responsibility. How do we know the difference between the prompting of the Spirit and our own slanted manner of thinking? Obviously we need to check everything against Scripture, but our own reading can become skewed by wishful thinking, personal blind spots, pet issues, or hidden fears. Therefore, we need wise advice from godly counselors.

Paul's experience suggests three guidelines for seeking and giving advice.

Guideline 1: *When you seek advice, be discerning.* If you're seeking the mind of God, choose your counselors wisely. You need the perspective of mature Christians who have demonstrated a pattern of good decision making. They should be people whom you admire, who show signs of having their priorities straight, and who always put the will of God before their own. These counselors should be experienced in the spiritual life, know their Bible well, and have a good reputation within their Christian communities as well as among nonbelievers.

Seek out several counselors in order to gain a well-rounded perspective, and find them early so you have as much time as possible to think, discuss, pray, and weigh options. Take time away from your normal routine to spend time in solitude, to pray, and to discuss the decision multiple times with your advisors.

Guideline 2: *If you give advice, be restrained.* God gave you two ears and one mouth. That suggests a good ratio when counseling someone making a significant decision! Listen twice as much as you talk. We never learn while talking, but we always do while listening. But don't simply take in facts; force yourself into the shoes of the person so you can understand the issue from his or her perspective. Then, before you offer a response, ask for some time to think, if that's possible. Use that time to think about the issue from God's point of view, thinking of what He values. Draw some principles of your counsel from Scripture. That'll never lead you astray. God never contradicts His Word. So, when you seek to counsel a friend, base everything on biblical insights. In *Knowing God's Will and Doing It!*, J. Grant Howard writes, "When we give Word-oriented counsel, it will be instructive. When we give experience-centered counsel, it may be nothing more than opinion."[6]

Guideline 3: *Whether you give or receive advice, remember that humans are fallible.* That's obvious, I know. Even so, when the desire for clear direction becomes intense, we seem to expect that if we find the right person or listen to enough advice, a message from God will come through. Unfortunately, we rarely get the kind of certainty we want most. It's possible for wise people to give bad counsel with the best of motives. (I know; I've done it.) And it's possible to make a decision based on a broad consensus of wise advisors, only to discover they were mistaken. (I've been on that end of the dilemma as well.) The fact is, people are fallible, so expecting 100 percent accuracy isn't realistic. In the end, we simply have to make the best decisions we can with the information we have available, accepting the possibility that we might make a wrong move.

Rather than become paralyzed with indecision, use the time you have available to determine the best course of action, commit it to the Lord, and then move ahead. If you make a bad move in good faith, the Lord will honor your trust in Him, and as always, He'll use the circumstance for your good. Regardless, remember that there's no such thing as a decision without a downside, and sometimes, the tradeoff is significant no matter what you do.

When Misunderstanding Takes Over
ACTS 21:18-39

NASB

18 And the following day Paul went in with us to ªJames, and all the elders were present. 19 After he had greeted them, he *began* to relate one by one the things which God had done among the Gentiles through his ministry. 20 And when they heard it they *began* glorifying God; and they said to him, "You see, brother, how many ªthousands there are among the Jews of those who have believed, and they are all zealous for the Law; 21 and they have been told about you, that you are teaching all the Jews who are among the Gentiles to forsake Moses, telling them not to circumcise their children nor to ªwalk according to the customs. 22 What, then, is *to be done?* They will certainly hear that you have come. 23 Therefore do this that we tell you. We have four men who ªare under a vow; 24 take them and purify yourself along with them, and ªpay their expenses so that they may shave their ᵇheads; and all will know that there is nothing to the things which they have been told about you, but that you yourself also walk orderly, keeping the Law. 25 But concerning the Gentiles who have

NLT

18 The next day Paul went with us to meet with James, and all the elders of the Jerusalem church were present. 19 After greeting them, Paul gave a detailed account of the things God had accomplished among the Gentiles through his ministry.

20 After hearing this, they praised God. And then they said, "You know, dear brother, how many thousands of Jews have also believed, and they all follow the law of Moses very seriously. 21 But the Jewish believers here in Jerusalem have been told that you are teaching all the Jews who live among the Gentiles to turn their backs on the laws of Moses. They've heard that you teach them not to circumcise their children or follow other Jewish customs. 22 What should we do? They will certainly hear that you have come.

23 "Here's what we want you to do. We have four men here who have completed their vow. 24 Go with them to the Temple and join them in the purification ceremony, paying for them to have their heads ritually shaved. Then everyone will know that the rumors are all false and that you yourself observe the Jewish laws.

25 "As for the Gentile believers, they

believed, we wrote, having decided that they should abstain from ªmeat sacrificed to idols and from blood and from what is strangled and from fornication." 26Then Paul ªtook the men, and the next day, purifying himself along with them, went into the temple giving notice of the completion of the days of purification, until the sacrifice was offered for each one of them.

27When the seven days were almost over, the Jews from ªAsia, upon seeing him in the temple, *began* to stir up all the crowd and laid hands on him, 28crying out, "Men of Israel, come to our aid! This is the man who preaches to all men everywhere against our people and the Law and this place; and besides he has even brought Greeks into the temple and has defiled this holy place." 29For they had previously seen Trophimus the Ephesian in the city with him, and they supposed that Paul had brought him into the temple. 30Then all the city was provoked, and ªthe people rushed together, and taking hold of Paul they dragged him out of the temple, and immediately the doors were shut. 31While they were seeking to kill him, a report came up to the ªcommander of the *Roman* ᵇcohort that all Jerusalem was in confusion. 32At once he took along *some* soldiers and centurions and ran down to them; and when they saw the ªcommander and the soldiers, they stopped beating Paul. 33Then the ªcommander came up and took hold of him, and ordered him to be bound with two chains; and he *began* asking who he was and what he had done. 34But among the crowd some were shouting one thing *and* some another, and when he could not find out the ªfacts because of the uproar, he ordered him to be brought

should do what we already told them in a letter: They should abstain from eating food offered to idols, from consuming blood or the meat of strangled animals, and from sexual immorality."

26So Paul went to the Temple the next day with the other men. They had already started the purification ritual, so he publicly announced the date when their vows would end and sacrifices would be offered for each of them.

27The seven days were almost ended when some Jews from the province of Asia saw Paul in the Temple and roused a mob against him. They grabbed him, 28yelling, "Men of Israel, help us! This is the man who preaches against our people everywhere and tells everybody to disobey the Jewish laws. He speaks against the Temple—and even defiles this holy place by bringing in Gentiles.*" 29(For earlier that day they had seen him in the city with Trophimus, a Gentile from Ephesus,* and they assumed Paul had taken him into the Temple.)

30The whole city was rocked by these accusations, and a great riot followed. Paul was grabbed and dragged out of the Temple, and immediately the gates were closed behind him. 31As they were trying to kill him, word reached the commander of the Roman regiment that all Jerusalem was in an uproar. 32He immediately called out his soldiers and officers* and ran down among the crowd. When the mob saw the commander and the troops coming, they stopped beating Paul.

33Then the commander arrested him and ordered him bound with two chains. He asked the crowd who he was and what he had done. 34Some shouted one thing and some another. Since he couldn't find out the truth in all the uproar and into the barracks. ³⁵When he got to the stairs, he was carried by the soldiers because of the violence of the ᵃmob; ³⁶for the multitude of the people kept following them, shouting, "Away with him!"

³⁷As Paul was about to be brought into the barracks, he said to the ᵃcommander, "May I say something to you?" And he said, "Do you know Greek? ³⁸Then you are not the Egyptian who some ᵃtime ago stirred up a revolt and led the four thousand men of the Assassins out into the wilderness?" ³⁹But Paul said, "I am a Jew of Tarsus in Cilicia, a citizen of no insignificant city; and I beg you, allow me to speak to the people."

21:18 ᵃOr *Jacob* 21:20 ᵃLit *ten thousands*
21:21 ᵃI.e. observe or live by 21:23 ᵃLit *have a vow on them* 21:24 ᵃLit *spend on them* ᵇLit *head*
21:25 ᵃLit *the thing* 21:26 ᵃOr *took the men the next day, and purifying himself* 21:27 ᵃI.e. west coast province of Asia Minor 21:30 ᵃLit *a running together of the people occurred* 21:31 ᵃI.e. chiliarch, in command of one thousand troops ᵇOr *battalion* 21:32 ᵃV 31, note 1 21:33 ᵃV 31, note 1 21:34 ᵃLit *certainty* 21:35 ᵃLit *crowd* 21:37 ᵃV 31, note 1 21:38 ᵃLit *days*

confusion, he ordered that Paul be taken to the fortress. ³⁵As Paul reached the stairs, the mob grew so violent the soldiers had to lift him to their shoulders to protect him. ³⁶And the crowd followed behind, shouting, "Kill him, kill him!"

³⁷As Paul was about to be taken inside, he said to the commander, "May I have a word with you?"

"Do you know Greek?" the commander asked, surprised. ³⁸"Aren't you the Egyptian who led a rebellion some time ago and took 4,000 members of the Assassins out into the desert?"

³⁹"No," Paul replied, "I am a Jew and a citizen of Tarsus in Cilicia, which is an important city. Please, let me talk to these people."

21:28 Greek *Greeks*. 21:29 Greek *Trophimus, the Ephesian*. 21:32 Greek *centurions*.

Ralph Waldo Emerson declared, "To be great is to be misunderstood."[7] Writer, artist, philosopher, and free spirit Elbert Hubbard expressed this thought more eloquently in his book *Love, Life and Work*: "The man who is anybody and who does anything is surely going to be criticised, vilified and misunderstood. This is a part of the penalty for greatness, and every great man understands it; and understands too that it is no proof of greatness. The final proof of greatness lies in being able to endure [derision] without resentment."[8]

The great difficulty of being misunderstood is that the more you work at revealing facts in your favor, the guiltier you appear. Yet doing nothing seems to concede defeat. To accept this no-win scenario without suffering personal anguish requires almost supernatural self-assurance—or at least confidence in God's approval against a chorus of criticism.

No one worked harder than Paul at the art of communication. He described his complete commitment to making the gospel understood this way:

For though I am free from all men, I have made myself a slave to all, so that I may win more. To the Jews I became as a Jew, so that I might win Jews; to those who are under the Law, as under the Law though not being myself under the Law, so that I might win those who are under the Law; to those who are without law, as without law, though not being without the law of God but under the law of Christ, so that I might win those who are without law. To the weak I became weak, that I might win the weak; I have become all things to all men, so that I may by all means save some. I do all things for the sake of the gospel, so that I may become a fellow partaker of it. (1 Cor. 9:19-23)

So, imagine Paul's frustration when his fellow Jews twisted his message to characterize him as a blasphemer and an enemy of the Mosaic Law. Paul had impacted the community of the Gentiles in a never-to-be-forgotten manner over the course of three great journeys. But back home, back among the squint-eyed, narrow-minded, petty guardians of a closed society, a vindictive few took advantage of a simple misunderstanding to inflame a mob. Paul's response would become his most challenging test of greatness.

— 21:18-21 —

Luke's narrative stops using the pronouns "we" and "us" after 21:18, but there's no reason to believe Luke left. At this point, the entourage fades into the background as the events of the story center on Paul. As a Gentile, Luke could move about freely in Jerusalem, but he wisely kept a low profile in the temple and around unbelieving Jews. Meanwhile, Paul's experiences would isolate him from the group, leaving very few contexts in which "we" would be relevant. Luke could personally witness Paul's experiences, even visit the apostle throughout the events, but he would not participate in them.

Paul's visit to Jerusalem started pleasantly enough. He met with the elders of the Jerusalem church and James, the brother of Jesus, who had become their functional leader. In deference to their authority, Paul gave a full account of his three missionary journeys and the results. Dozens of churches thrived in major cities across the eastern half of the empire, and already they were beginning to grow and replicate themselves. Notably, he gave God the credit for the rapid spread of the gospel among the Gentiles. The elders appropriately glorified God as Paul told of each success (21:19-20). They warned, however, that not everyone in Jerusalem would be as pleased with his efforts. Rumors

CIRCUMCISION: A RIGHT OR A RITE?

ACTS 21:21
When the Lord confirmed His covenant with Abraham for the third and final time (Gen. 17), He commanded that each male living in the covenant community was to be circumcised as a symbol of his participation (cf. Lev. 12:3; Luke 1:59). Refusing circumcision (for oneself or, more often, one's male children) was tantamount to divorcing oneself from the community and rejecting God. Therefore, such a rebel and his family were to be removed from Hebrew society and regarded as outsiders. Such a rejection of God and His covenant was a mark of condemnation. The faithful observance of circumcision, on the other hand, allowed one's male offspring access to all the rights and privileges of Hebrew society once he came of age.

With such emphasis placed on this intimate rite of participation in God's covenant, it's easy to see why many Jews enlarged its significance. Many reasoned that if refusing circumcision condemned a man, then circumcision must save him. Participation in the covenant and obedience to the Law came to be seen as the exclusive path to salvation, an attitude that some Jewish Christians attempted to carry over to the church (Acts 15:1; Gal. 2:3-4).

This was, of course, a perversion of the rite as God had established it. Justification by faith had always been the cornerstone of Hebrew doctrine. As Paul noted, "Abraham believed God, and it was reckoned to him as righteousness" (Gal. 3:6; cf. Gen. 15:6). The rite of circumcision did nothing to save a man from sin or credit him with righteousness. Paul called it a "seal" (Rom. 4:11), a notary stamp authenticating the Hebrew male's participation by faith in Abraham's covenant with God. Although this covenant with Abraham was unilateral and unconditional—God gave an oath to do what He promised, regardless of the people's response—the Lord intended Hebrew participation to include both this private physical sign and a plainly visible godly character.

had been circulating among the *myrias* [3461], the "tens of thousands" of Christian Jews, concerning Paul's teaching.

These tens of thousands of believing Jews were enthusiastic about keeping the Law of Moses (21:20). In fact, it seems that the believing Jews, saved by grace alone through faith alone in Christ alone, had a renewed joy in the Law—not as a means of salvation, but as a means of demonstrating their love for God and for others within their unique Jewish cultural and religious context. This doesn't necessarily identify them as legalistic. Their decision to keep the Law was an authentic act of worship and devotion, not a way to please God, and not something to force upon Gentile converts as their legalistic, Judaizing counterparts were eager to do.

Unfortunately, rumors flowed into Jerusalem stating that Paul lambasted Jews who wanted to keep the Law, even to the point of forsaking the rite of circumcision (21:21). Even though the church agreed that Gentiles should not be required to submit to circumcision, they never forbade Jews from continuing the ancient ceremony, which even predated the giving of the Law.

Of course, the rumors were false. Paul didn't object to circumcision unless someone assigned value to the ritual as a means of salvation. In fact, he circumcised Timothy for the sake of expediency (16:3). The elders most likely knew this before Paul arrived. After his visit, any and all doubts were wiped away.

— 21:22-24 —

The church elders believed Paul immediately. Having affirmed him and his ministry, they turned to the question of vindicating his work among those who did not have an opportunity to interview the apostle in person. For the sake of unity and order, they needed to reassure tens of thousands of believing Jews without the aid of mass media. So they decided to use the same grapevine that had spread the rumors.

The "vow" (21:23) refers to the Nazirite vow, one of Israel's most ancient customs (Num. 6:1-21). This special oath set a Jew apart from normal life, often to be used by God to accomplish a specific objective. While he or she was dedicated to this task, the individual agreed to three stipulations: abstain from any product of the vine (wine, strong drink, grapes, vinegar, raisins, juice), avoid all contact with the dead, and allow his or her hair to grow uncut. In recorded Hebrew history, we know of only two men who took the oath of the Nazirite for life— Samson (Judg. 13:7; 16:17) and John the Baptizer (Luke 1:15). In most cases during Paul's time, the vow was temporary. At the end of this special season, the Nazirite would deliver a special sacrifice to the temple:

> one male lamb a year old without defect for a burnt offering and one ewe-lamb a year old without defect for a sin offering and one ram without defect for a peace offering, and a basket of unleavened cakes of fine flour mixed with oil and unleavened wafers spread with oil, along with their grain offering and their drink offering. (Num. 6:14-15)

During the ceremony, the Nazirite shaved his or her head and presented the cut hair to the priest, who burned it on the altar. After this ritual, the Nazirite received a portion of the sacrificial meal to eat and could again enjoy the fruit of the vine.

Naturally, ending a vow cost the Nazirite a large sum; the animals alone could serve a hundred people at a banquet. Because Jews regarded Nazirites so highly, the community considered any assistance given to them a great honor. Moreover, the vow provided the ideal opportunity for Paul to illustrate his disposition toward Old Testament Law. Unlike circumcision, which Jews confused with the means of gaining salvation, people placed themselves under the Nazirite vow voluntarily. Paul could show his support for Jewish law without compromising his stand on grace. So, the elders suggested he sponsor these four Christian Jews as they consummated their vows. As a patron, he would go through the purification ritual with them and pay for their offerings. Funding one Nazirite ritual demonstrated a high regard for Jewish tradition; funding four would have made front-page news.

This gesture would not only mollify Jewish Christians, but it should also have gone a long way to pacify angry nonbelieving Jews. When Agrippa I received the crown of Judea from Claudius, "he also came to Jerusalem and offered all the sacrifices that belonged to him, and omitted nothing which the law required; on which account he ordained that many of the Nazirites should have their heads shorn,"[9] meaning he sponsored their sacrifices. Paul was much more Jewish than Agrippa in terms of ethnicity, culture, education, and customs. No conscientious Jew could accuse Paul of denigrating Judaism. Or so the elders thought.

— 21:25-26 —

Although the elders hoped to reassure Jewish Christians that Paul had not blasphemed or declared the Law obsolete, they nevertheless affirmed their earlier resolution concerning Gentiles and the old covenant (cf. 15:20, 29). While the Law is good, God never intended it to become a means of salvation; while the Law benefits any who follow it, God has written His law on the hearts of believers and will personally see to their conduct of life. For the sake of unity, however, the Council at Jerusalem had requested that Gentiles limit their freedom in deference to their Jewish brothers who detested meat contaminated with blood or defiled by association with idols. And they should avoid all *porneia* [4202], the Greek word for all forms of sexual sin.

Paul followed through with the gesture (21:26). By that time, the temple had embellished the ritual described in Numbers 6:13-21—as they had done with every point of the Law—making a great show of the purification, which took seven days to complete. Of course, the church elders hoped that the Jews' love of conspicuous piety would work in Paul's favor. Over a period of several days, Paul came and went from the temple with each of the four Nazirites, meticulously following protocol and shelling out a small fortune for the sacrifices.

— 21:27-29 —

Regrettably, but not surprisingly, Paul's gesture wasn't enough to offset the hatred of his enemies from Ephesus. Several recognized him and "laid hands on him" (21:27), meaning they seized him in a citizen's arrest the same way a crowd in a shopping mall might subdue an infamous felon.

They publicly accused Paul of preaching against the Jews and the Law of Moses and of defiling the temple. In a twist of historical irony, they accused Paul of the same crimes for which they—with his affirmation—had stoned Stephen (6:11-14). Their charge immediately should have been seen as a blatant lie. Paul had come to the temple in support of four Jews under the Nazirite vow, in honor of the Law, to sacrifice on the temple altar! The liars from Ephesus topped their slander

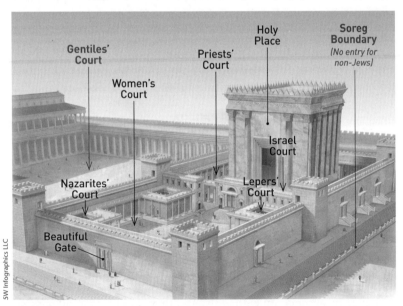

This illustration of **Herod's temple complex** features the courts surrounding the holy place (or most holy place). The low gate, or soreg boundary, marked the perimeter that Gentiles were not allowed to cross.

with the allegation that Paul had defiled the temple by escorting un-circumcised Gentiles beyond the wall separating the court of Gentiles from the court of Israel, where no Gentiles were allowed. This wall was referred to in Hebrew as the soreg (Mishnah *Middot* 2:3).

Archaeologists have discovered inscriptions warning Gentiles not to pass the wall. The Ephesian Jews recognized Paul and had seen him around Jerusalem with a confirmed Gentile, Trophimus, whom they knew from Ephesus (21:29). Luke states that they did not actually see Trophimus within the balustrade; they only "supposed" (*nomizō* [3543]), which means they made an educated assumption based on what they thought they knew about Paul.

Suddenly, the assumption was treated as a fact, which they used to incite a crowd in the temple. These men had apparently studied in the school of Demetrius the silversmith (19:24-27) and become experts in the art of stirring crowds into a frenzy with little or no factual support. As in Ephesus, the mob didn't know why they had formed.

— 21:30-32 —

The mob dragged Paul from the court of Israel out to the court of Gen-tiles, and temple officials closed the doors to ensure that no other Gentiles entered during the melee. They intended to kill Paul, which would have encroached on a Roman prerogative; the Romans reserved use of the death penalty for themselves. Furthermore, vigilante justice undermined Roman authority and could mushroom into outright in-surrection. Suddenly, a sectarian religious matter became a political matter.

When Herod the Great built the massive temple structure, it is likely that some people in Rome worried that it could double as a fortress of the Jews. To ease tensions, he refurbished a garrison directly adjacent to the temple, which the Romans used to house a cohort of soldiers.[10] Upon completion, he named it Antonia in honor of his patron, Mark Antony. The Fortress of Antonia sat just outside the northwest corner of the wall and rose high enough for sentries to keep watch over the courtyard.

The "report" (21:31) probably came from one of the sentries. The commander, later identified as Claudius Lysias (23:26), led as many as two hundred fighting men into the temple courtyard to restore order. (A centurion commanded one hundred soldiers; the commander took "soldiers and centurions," which means there were at least two cen-turions.) The Romans generally gave the Jews wide latitude, but they gave none for civil disorder. In the chaos, soldiers would focus on anyone engaged in violence and stop them using any means they deemed appropriate, including death. Naturally, the mob backed away from Paul as soon as the soldiers arrived.

— 21:33-36 —

The commander arrested Paul not because he considered the apostle guilty but to secure the object of the mob's anger. His priorities were to restore order first, then sort out the details. His binding Paul with two chains probably means that he secured each arm to a soldier. He tried to get some answers from Paul, but the commotion began to escalate again. Luke's description here resembles his description of the mob of pagan merchants in the theater of Ephesus (19:32). When the commander finally decided to remove Paul to the garrison, the crush of people followed after him, shouting "Away with him!" (21:36), just like the enemies of Christ had done (Luke 23:18).

The "stairs" (Acts 21:35) most likely led down to a paved pathway running between the temple exit and the Fortress of Antonia.

— 21:37-39 —

When Paul had been taken far enough away from the tumult in the temple courtyard, he respectfully asked to speak with the commander. The Jews in Jerusalem, like most people around the empire, spoke at least two languages, their own and Greek. Many even spoke Latin. So it should not have surprised the man that Paul spoke fluent Greek (21:37). The commander revealed the reason for his confusion: He had mistaken the apostle for a returning Egyptian false prophet, who had gathered a small army on the Mount of Olives, promising to overtake the Fortress of Antonia and then rule over Jerusalem (21:38). Josephus places this during the rule of Roman procurator Marcus Antonius Felix (AD 52–60), who "met him with his Roman soldiers, while all the people assisted him in his attack upon them, insomuch that, when it came to a battle, the Egyptian ran away, with a few others, while the greatest part of those that were with him were either destroyed or taken alive."[11] Apparently, this had occurred in the recent past, making the commander's assumption plausible.

Paul corrected the commander, providing an impressive résumé of Roman civility. He was a Jew, not an Egyptian. He came from Tarsus, a large city known for its education and culture. He was a Roman citizen, not a thug. Based on these qualifications, he asked permission to address the mob, hoping that a rational response to the false allegations lodged by the Jews from Ephesus would set everything straight (21:39). He had been sorely misunderstood and he felt certain that once he had presented the facts, the case against him would unravel and the city of Jerusalem would come to its senses. However, the people instigating the mob against him didn't care about facts or the truth; their motivation came from a dark place in the human soul. They were driven by jealousy and an obsessive need to destroy anyone they could not dominate.

For all his wisdom, Paul suffered from the same naïveté common to most decent, rational people: He couldn't imagine anyone not wanting to know the truth and then live by it. Paul had faced a misunderstanding within the church, but his confrontation with the temple leadership was a flat-out war of ideas and agendas that could not be abated.

APPLICATION: ACTS 21:18-39

Understanding Misunderstanding

No one likes to be misunderstood. It's lonely. It's frustrating. It leaves us feeling helpless, and then hopeless, and if we're not careful, resentful toward others. Bitterness can easily set in. As I observe Paul's experience with misunderstanding, three truths emerge.

First, *the reality of misunderstanding is inescapable.* If you want to have any kind of meaningful impact or cultivate significant relationships, you will be misunderstood. If you want to drift through this life, do what everyone else does, go along with the majority opinion, and avoid saying or doing anything of significance, then you'll never have to worry about being misunderstood. If, however, you expect to be different from the run-of-the-mill crowd, if you hope to achieve something that hasn't been attempted, if you try to improve upon the status quo, I repeat: You *will* be misunderstood. Count on it.

Noah? That whole boat scene must have been unbelievable. Moses? He expected his people to understand God's purpose for his life, but they didn't. Joseph? He maintained the highest level of integrity and purity, yet Potiphar sided with his wife, who accused Joseph of attempted rape. In spite of his honesty, he landed in prison. And the Old Testament prophets? Ignored, marginalized, accused of disloyalty, mercilessly criticized, openly hated, often killed as enemies of Israel.

John the Baptizer? Hailed as a prophet, ignored as a madman. The Protestant Reformers? Treated like heretics, cursed like devils, and hunted like animals. Anyone who has ever done anything worthwhile has been misunderstood.

Second, *the reasons for misunderstanding are unpredictable.* Misunderstandings occur for many reasons, so we cannot anticipate how or when they will occur. Furthermore, most of them lie beyond our control. Snap judgments, pride, fear, prejudice, slander, pettiness, ambition, vainglory—the causes are too numerous and diverse to count. And when misunderstandings occur, we can do very little to resolve them. Most could be settled in a matter of minutes with a simple conversation, but only if the other party wants to listen. You can be responsible only to communicate clearly; the response of others isn't up to you.

Recognizing your helplessness in these situations can be incredibly freeing, giving you permission to step away and leave the matter in God's hands.

Third, *the reaction to misunderstanding is yours to decide.* Typically, people respond to misunderstandings in three ways. Some work themselves into a frenzy trying to get the other party to hear and acknowledge the truth. They scream, they plead, they repeat themselves endlessly, they live in anguished desperation to be heard. Others turn inward, sulkily determined to play the martyr and allow the acid of bitterness to eat away at them. I don't recommend either of these two responses. The best response to misunderstanding is to extend an invitation to discuss the matter, and then get on with life. Accept your helplessness, pray for strength to go on, allow God to handle the difficulty, expend no more energy to resolve it, and then devote yourself to fulfilling your purpose in life. These are true marks of greatness.

An Unanswerable Argument
ACTS 21:40–22:30

NASB

40 When he had given him permission, Paul, standing on the stairs, motioned to the people with his hand; and when there ªwas a great hush, he spoke to them in the ᵇHebrew dialect, saying,

NLT

40 The commander agreed, so Paul stood on the stairs and motioned to the people to be quiet. Soon a deep silence enveloped the crowd, and he addressed them in their own language, Aramaic.*

22:1 "Brethren and fathers, hear my defense which I now *offer* to you." ²And when they heard that he was addressing them in the ªHebrew dialect, they became even more quiet; and he said, ³"I am a Jew, born in Tarsus of Cilicia, but brought up in this city, educated ªunder Gamaliel, ᵇstrictly according to the law of our fathers, being zealous for God just as you all are today. ⁴I persecuted this Way to the death, binding and putting both men and women into prisons, ⁵as also the high priest and all the Council of the elders ªcan testify. From them I also received letters to the brethren, and started off for Damascus in order to bring even those who were there to Jerusalem ᵇas prisoners to be punished.

⁶"But it happened that as I was on my way, approaching Damascus about noontime, a very bright light suddenly flashed from heaven all around me, ⁷and I fell to the ground and heard a voice saying to me, 'Saul, Saul, why are you persecuting Me?' ⁸And I answered, 'Who are You, Lord?' And He said to me, 'I am Jesus the Nazarene, whom you are persecuting.' ⁹And those who were with me saw the light, to be sure, but did not ªunderstand the voice of the One who was speaking to me. ¹⁰And I said, 'What shall I do, Lord?' And the Lord said to me, 'Get up and go on into Damascus, and there you will be told of all that has been appointed for you to do.' ¹¹But since I could not see because of the ªbrightness of that light, I was led by the hand by those who were with me and came into Damascus.

¹²"A certain Ananias, a man who was devout by the standard of the Law, *and* well spoken of by all the Jews who lived there, ¹³came to me, and standing near said to me, 'Brother Saul, receive your sight!'

22:1 "Brothers and esteemed fathers," Paul said, "listen to me as I offer my defense." ²When they heard him speaking in their own language,* the silence was even greater.

³Then Paul said, "I am a Jew, born in Tarsus, a city in Cilicia, and I was brought up and educated here in Jerusalem under Gamaliel. As his student, I was carefully trained in our Jewish laws and customs. I became very zealous to honor God in everything I did, just like all of you today. ⁴And I persecuted the followers of the Way, hounding some to death, arresting both men and women and throwing them in prison. ⁵The high priest and the whole council of elders can testify that this is so. For I received letters from them to our Jewish brothers in Damascus, authorizing me to bring the followers of the Way from there to Jerusalem, in chains, to be punished.

⁶"As I was on the road, approaching Damascus about noon, a very bright light from heaven suddenly shone down around me. ⁷I fell to the ground and heard a voice saying to me, 'Saul, Saul, why are you persecuting me?'

⁸"'Who are you, lord?' I asked.

"And the voice replied, 'I am Jesus the Nazarene,* the one you are persecuting.' ⁹The people with me saw the light but didn't understand the voice speaking to me.

¹⁰"I asked, 'What should I do, Lord?'

"And the Lord told me, 'Get up and go into Damascus, and there you will be told everything you are to do.'

¹¹"I was blinded by the intense light and had to be led by the hand to Damascus by my companions. ¹²A man named Ananias lived there. He was a godly man, deeply devoted to the law, and well regarded by all the Jews of Damascus. ¹³He came and stood beside me and said, 'Brother

And ªat that very time I looked up at him. ¹⁴And he said, 'The God of our fathers has appointed you to know His will and to see the Righteous One and to hear an ªutterance from His mouth. ¹⁵For you will be a witness for Him to all men of what you have seen and heard. ¹⁶Now why do you delay? Get up and be baptized, and wash away your sins, calling on His name.'

¹⁷"It happened when I returned to Jerusalem and was praying in the temple, that I fell into a trance, ¹⁸and I saw Him saying to me, 'Make haste, and get out of Jerusalem quickly, because they will not accept your testimony about Me.' ¹⁹And I said, 'Lord, they themselves understand that in one synagogue after another I used to imprison and beat those who believed in You. ²⁰And when the blood of Your witness Stephen was being shed, I also was standing by approving, and watching out for the coats of those who were slaying him.' ²¹And He said to me, 'Go! For I will send you far away to the Gentiles.'"

²²They listened to him up to this statement, and *then* they raised their voices and said, "Away with such a fellow from the earth, for he should not be allowed to live!" ²³And as they were crying out and throwing off their cloaks and tossing dust into the air, ²⁴the ªcommander ordered him to be brought into the barracks, stating that he should be examined by scourging so that he might find out the reason why they were shouting against him that way. ²⁵But when they stretched him out ªwith thongs, Paul said to the centurion who was standing by, "Is it ᵇlawful for you to scourge a man who is a Roman and uncondemned?" ²⁶When the centurion heard *this,* he went to the ªcommander and told him, saying, "What are you about to do? For this man is a Roman." ²⁷The ªcommander came

Saul, regain your sight.' And that very moment I could see him!

¹⁴"Then he told me, 'The God of our ancestors has chosen you to know his will and to see the Righteous One and hear him speak. ¹⁵For you are to be his witness, telling everyone what you have seen and heard. ¹⁶What are you waiting for? Get up and be baptized. Have your sins washed away by calling on the name of the Lord.'

¹⁷"After I returned to Jerusalem, I was praying in the Temple and fell into a trance. ¹⁸I saw a vision of Jesus* saying to me, 'Hurry! Leave Jerusalem, for the people here won't accept your testimony about me.'

¹⁹"'But Lord,' I argued, 'they certainly know that in every synagogue I imprisoned and beat those who believed in you. ²⁰And I was in complete agreement when your witness Stephen was killed. I stood by and kept the coats they took off when they stoned him.'

²¹"But the Lord said to me, 'Go, for I will send you far away to the Gentiles!'"

²²The crowd listened until Paul said that word. Then they all began to shout, "Away with such a fellow! He isn't fit to live!" ²³They yelled, threw off their coats, and tossed handfuls of dust into the air.

²⁴The commander brought Paul inside and ordered him lashed with whips to make him confess his crime. He wanted to find out why the crowd had become so furious. ²⁵When they tied Paul down to lash him, Paul said to the officer* standing there, "Is it legal for you to whip a Roman citizen who hasn't even been tried?"

²⁶When the officer heard this, he went to the commander and asked, "What are you doing? This man is a Roman citizen!"

²⁷So the commander went over

and said to him, "Tell me, are you a Roman?" And he said, "Yes." ²⁸The ᵃcommander answered, "I acquired this citizenship with a large sum of money." And Paul said, "But I was actually born *a citizen*." ²⁹Therefore those who were about to examine him immediately ᵃlet go of him; and the ᵇcommander also was afraid when he found out that he was a Roman, and because he had ᶜput him in chains.

³⁰But on the next day, wishing to know for certain why he had been accused by the Jews, he released him and ordered the chief priests and all the ᵃCouncil to assemble, and brought Paul down and set him before them.

and asked Paul, "Tell me, are you a Roman citizen?"

"Yes, I certainly am," Paul replied.

²⁸"I am, too," the commander muttered, "and it cost me plenty!"

Paul answered, "But I am a citizen by birth!"

²⁹The soldiers who were about to interrogate Paul quickly withdrew when they heard he was a Roman citizen, and the commander was frightened because he had ordered him bound and whipped.

³⁰The next day the commander ordered the leading priests into session with the Jewish high council.* He wanted to find out what the trouble was all about, so he released Paul to have him stand before them.

21:40 ᵃLit *occurred* ᵇI.e. Jewish Aramaic 22:2 ᵃI.e. Jewish Aramaic 22:3 ᵃLit *at the feet of* ᵇLit *according to the strictness of the ancestral law* 22:5 ᵃLit *testifies for me* ᵇLit *having been bound* 22:9 ᵃOr *hear* (with comprehension) 22:11 ᵃLit *glory* 22:13 ᵃOr *instantly;* lit *at the very hour* 22:14 ᵃOr *message;* lit *voice* 22:24 ᵃI.e. chiliarch, in command of one thousand troops 22:25 ᵃOr *for the whip* ᵇInterrogation by torture was a procedure used with slaves 22:26 ᵃV 24, note 1 22:27 ᵃV 24, note 1 22:28 ᵃV 24, note 1 22:29 ᵃLit *withdrew from* ᵇV 24, note 1 ᶜLit *bound him* 22:30 ᵃOr *Sanhedrin*

21:40 Or *Hebrew.* 22:2 Greek *in Aramaic,* or *in Hebrew.* 22:8 Or *Jesus of Nazareth.* 22:18 Greek *him.* 22:25 Greek *the centurion;* also in 22:26. 22:30 Greek *Sanhedrin.*

Around AD 57, Paul entered the temple to participate in one of Israel's most treasured and revered traditions. Four men were concluding a Nazirite vow with a complicated and expensive ritual involving sacrifices. The apostle had concluded a vow of his own during his second missionary journey (18:18), and he now stood with four Jewish believers to undergo purification rites along with them and to fund their sacrifices. No gesture could have better proven his loyalty to Jewish traditions or shown higher regard for the temple. Yet his enemies, Jewish nonbelievers from Ephesus, seized the opportunity to accuse him of blasphemy, of preaching against Jews, and of desecrating the temple by bringing a Gentile into the court of Israel.

In that moment, Paul saw an opportunity to give his unanswerable argument—the story of his life and his miraculous encounter with the risen Lord Jesus. Such events and personal testimonies about them form unanswerable arguments for the gospel. An example from the

Gospels is seen in John 9: When Jesus healed a blind man on the Sabbath, the Pharisees couldn't argue with the facts of the man's life—he had been blind and now could see. Instead, they slandered Jesus and excommunicated the man who had been healed.

Now it was Paul's turn. He had been struck blind when he persecuted the church and then received his sight when He believed in Jesus Christ (Acts 9). Now, he would testify before his brothers in the temple, saying, as it were, "Though I was blind, now I see." The question remained whether the self-appointed guardians of the temple would choose continued blindness or find the light and the truth through his unanswerable argument.

— 21:40 —

The riot Paul's enemies sparked escalated so dramatically that the commander of the Roman troops in the Fortress of Antonia had to restore order with the help of at least two hundred fighting men. He bound Paul in chains, and the soldiers carried the apostle out of the temple complex toward the fortress. At the entrance, he asked the commander for permission to address the people, most of whom had acted upon false information. He felt certain that, given the facts, they would respond reasonably.

Standing on the stairs above the outer court of the temple, Paul silenced the crowd and addressed them in a dialect of the Hebrew people, which was probably Aramaic. His defense can be divided into three sections:

- Paul's Life before Christ (22:1-5)
- Paul's Encounter with Christ (22:6-16)
- Paul's Ministry in Christ (22:17-21)

— 22:1-3 —

Paul's opening statement identified him as a kindred Jew. Of course, most knew him by reputation, if not personally. He had once been a rising star in the religious and political sphere of Judaism and a leading opponent of the church. Some in the Sanhedrin may have recognized his first words, "Brethren and fathers" (22:1), from Stephen's defense (7:2).

He had been accused of denigrating the temple, preaching against the Law of Moses, and discouraging circumcision among Jews, so he established his impeccable Hebrew pedigree immediately. "I am a Jew" (22:3) was straightforward enough, but some might identify him as a

Hellenistic Jew because he came from Tarsus, a Gentile city in Cilicia. He hastened to note that he had been reared in Jerusalem and taught in the renowned school of Gamaliel, who once sat on the Sanhedrin as one of its most respected members (5:34). Paul's teacher was the grandson of the legendary rabbi Hillel, a Pharisee of the first order—literally. The Pharisees interpreted the Scriptures loosely and amplified God's instruction with a host of traditions. They became theologically innovative to enhance their appearance of piety and to sanctify their strict separation from anything not Jewish. The teachings of Hillel virtually defined Pharisaism during the time of Jesus and Paul.

Paul declared that he had been schooled "strictly according to the law of our fathers" (22:3). The word rendered "strictly" is from a Greek word (*akribeia* [195]) that describes precise conformity to an authoritative standard, as in the case of mathematical accuracy. Paul added that he was as zealous for the Law as his audience and then proved it with a brief recounting of his own career as a Pharisee.

— 22:4-5 —

Paul recounted how he had "persecuted this Way to the death" (22:4). Although Saul's reference to "persecution" might sound to us like an implicit admission of wrongdoing, he presented it to the Jewish leaders as a positive point of commonality. He illustrated his genuine zeal for the Law by recalling his methods, which included throwing Christians into prison and even killing some. If any doubted his dedication to the Law, they could consult the high priest and the Sanhedrin for corroboration. After all, they had commissioned him to stamp out "the Way" and even authorized his journey to Damascus to arrest fleeing Christians.

The term translated "persecuted" (*diōkō* [1377], possibly reflecting *radap* [H7291]) refers to pursuit, but not necessarily with hostile intent. This stands in contrast to our word "persecute," which bears an entirely negative connotation. For example, Romans 12:13-14 uses the term both positively ("*practicing* hospitality") and negatively ("Bless those who *persecute* you").

— 22:6-10 —

Paul recounted his dramatic encounter with the risen Christ, highlighting facts that would have interested his audience while accomplishing his purpose. For example, Jesus was "the Nazarene" (22:8), a detail with negative connotations among the Pharisees. They denied that the Messiah could come from Galilee, much less the despised town of Nazareth. Paul called attention to his Hebrew name, Saul, which strengthened his claim of being a loyal Jew. And he stressed that God had initiated the encounter to stop him from completing his mission. He reminded those who knew him from years past that witnesses— some undoubtedly still alive—could corroborate details of his story. They saw the light, and while they failed to understand what Jesus said, they heard the voice. They also saw Paul's immediate transformation.

His description of the encounter with Christ conspicuously assigned God the responsibility for his subsequent actions. He included a crucial part of his dialogue: "What shall I do, Lord?" (22:10). Christ's answer would issue a divine call: "The God of our fathers has appointed you" (22:14). This supernatural encounter should have reminded Paul's Jewish audience of several Old Testament prophets who had received visions and were compelled to heed the divine call. This subtly implied, "If you don't like what I'm doing, take it up with God!"

— 22:11-16 —

Paul's testimony includes an extended account of his time with Ananias, "a man who was devout by the standard of the Law, and well spoken of by all the Jews" in Damascus (22:12). This highly regarded Jew also received a divine message regarding Paul's ministry. If anyone doubted the apostle's sincerity or sanity, they could contact Ananias for corroboration. This prophet gave Paul specific instructions concerning his ministry among the Gentiles. Note that Paul identified the presence he had encountered as "Jesus the Nazarene" (22:8) and Ananias heard from "the God of our fathers" (22:14), a distinctly Jewish description of God. All of this works together to vindicate Paul's ministry as God-ordained and entirely consistent with the way He had worked through prophets in the past.

— 22:17-21 —

If Paul had merely wanted to clear his name and vindicate his ministry among the Gentiles, he could have concluded his defense with 22:16. This would have sent the message, "God said to do something and I did it. Case closed. The defense rests." But Paul had another agenda. He recognized this occasion as an opportunity to confront his countrymen with their sin. Though not politically smart, the final section of his message remained faithful to his calling.

Paul returned to Jerusalem to find that the city and his old peers had turned against him. According to Luke's earlier account (9:29-30), the Jerusalem church leaders had sent him to Tarsus for his safety; Paul declared that the Lord had affirmed the plan in a vision. God stated that the reason for his leaving was that the temple leaders would not accept Paul's testimony about Him (22:18). And with that statement, Paul lost all sympathy with his audience. This declaration put them on the wrong side of God's revelation. While Paul had obeyed God in his ministry to Gentiles, the nonbelieving Jews had disobeyed by opposing him. Furthermore, in his "before and after" testimony, he declared his persecution of the Christians to be sinful, which implied that his audience continued in the sin from which he had repented.

His "standing by approving" recalls his role in the murder of this first Christian martyr (22:20). The temple leaders had led a mob of zealous Jews as they dragged Stephen to the outskirts of the city and stoned him. Paul implied that the people had sinned along with him and should repent. This also bore the subtle suggestion that they were seeking to do the same to him, forcing his flight from Jerusalem. God's instructions to Paul contained a dig against the Jews. The implied message was, "They continue in their sin and will not heed your testimony, so I am sending My Word to the Gentiles through you" (see 22:18, 21).

The notion that Israel was no longer God's light to the Gentiles angered the mob. Paul's claim that God would use the church instead—spearheaded by his own ministry—caused the religious leaders to seethe with murderous rage.

— 22:22-24 —

The enraged audience called for Paul's execution (22:22). They didn't object to his evangelizing the Gentiles; Jews had attracted proselytes for centuries. Even the Pharisees traveled around the empire preaching to Gentiles (Matt. 23:15). Paul's method, however, offended them on two counts. First, he refused to bring Gentiles into the kingdom of God through the door of Judaism, implying that Gentiles and Jews stood on an equal plane before God. Second, his notice that he had turned to the Gentiles sent the message that God had set aside the Jews.

The crowd's throwing off their cloaks and tossing dust into the air has no symbolic or cultural meaning. They simply felt so enraged that they literally didn't know what to do with themselves. They couldn't get at Paul, or they would have torn him to pieces.

The phrase "shouting against him" (Acts 22:24) is better translated, "shouting at him" or "shouting to him." The verb *epiphōneō*

[2019] means simply "to cry out loudly" or "to shout." The preposition "against" is an interpretation by the translators. The commander didn't know what the people shouted or what motivated them because Paul and the Jews had been speaking "the Hebrew dialect" (probably Aramaic) throughout the incident (21:40). He had simply heard Paul address the people and observed their angry response. For all he knew, the apostle had just rallied the multitude in the temple for an insurrection. He needed to discern what had just happened, but the only bilingual witnesses were all Jewish. Everyone he might ask had a motive for lying if Paul and the mob had formed a conspiracy against Rome. So, he decided to use a method familiar to Romans—torture.

Paul was set to "be examined by scourging" (22:24), to be whipped until he confessed to something. The commander had full authority to beat the truth out of Paul if it served the emperor's interests. The noun translated "scourging" (*mastix* [3148]) indicates the use of a different instrument than soldiers used on Jesus before His crucifixion. A more accurate translation would be "examined by the whip." Paul asked, "Is it lawful for you to scourge" (*mastizō* [3147]) a Roman citizen (22:25)? That term is different from the "scourging" (*mastigoō* [3146]) Jesus suffered. The verbs are similar, but *mastigoō* inflicted the "halfway death" Jesus endured, which involved the use of a *flagrum*, a leather thong with bits of metal and sheep bone braided along its length. Romans didn't use that type of scourging to obtain information, because victims of this procedure went into shock and struggled to remain conscious. *Mastizō*, using a *mastix*, on the other hand, could inflict intense pain for hours, leaving the victim lucid enough to feel every lash and still communicate clearly.

— 22:25-29 —

Roman citizens enjoyed extraordinary privileges compared to other subjects of the empire. They received the kind of civil protections most people in Western countries today take for granted. A Roman could not be punished without due process, and Paul was "uncondemned" (22:25). He was given the benefit of the doubt until proven guilty. Punishments for Roman citizens were never humiliating; even when sentenced to death, the manner of execution was swift and private. And they could appeal a charge to a higher authority, all the way up to the emperor himself.

Paul waited until he had been taken down to the dungeon, tied to leather straps, and stretched out for the whipping before announcing his status as a Roman citizen. He did this for the same reason as in Philippi (16:37), for the sake of legal strategy. He brought his captors to the brink of committing a crime in order to leverage their fear to his advantage. When the commander discovered how close he had come to beating a citizen, he felt grateful and probably more accommodating with Paul. Furthermore, his interview with the apostle revealed that Paul held a higher social status. A freeborn citizen was an aristocrat compared to someone who obtained the privilege through bribes. The practice of selling citizenship had become a common form of corruption during the reign of Emperor Claudius.

— 22:30 —

The commander still had a duty to determine what had occurred in the temple. He had apparently determined—probably during his conversation with the apostle—that the Jews had accused Paul of something. He refused to let a mob manipulate him or the Roman government, but to encourage order, he called a hearing with the chief priests and the Sanhedrin so they could lodge any complaints they might have in a civilized manner.

Based on the council's findings, he would determine whether to charge Paul with a crime. If their charges did not impact Roman interests, he would leave the matter in the Jewish leaders' hands. If he determined that Paul had broken a Roman statute, he would refer the case to the procurator.

APPLICATION: ACTS 21:40–22:30
A Witness worth Hearing

Paul believed evangelism to be his sole purpose for living, so he viewed every circumstance as an opportunity to be a witness or to create more opportunities for witnessing. When a mob tried to kill him and a contingent of Roman soldiers carried him to safety, he saw another opportunity to testify. His example highlights three principles worth remembering.

First, *a factually based personal testimony is unanswerable; internal experience alone is questionable.* The most compelling case for Christianity is a personal testimony. It follows a simple outline:

1. Before Christ
2. Encounter with Christ
3. After Christ

No one can argue with your personal experience. Subjective experience alone, however, doesn't convince others to believe. Paul laced his personal testimony with verifiable facts. He highlighted the parts of his life that many had observed before his salvation, during his experience with Christ on the road to Damascus, and then after. And he referred to objective witnesses the audience could respect and trust.

So if you're going to prepare a testimony, think through the wording. In fact, write it down and limit it to two pages. Include only relevant details that others have observed and could affirm. Read it through a few times, not to memorize it, but to become comfortable with what you would like to say. Then let the opportunities and the Holy Spirit be your guide as you testify from the heart.

Second, *humility is one thing; indignity is something entirely different.* When the soldiers stretched out Paul for an unjust whipping, he looked into the face of the officer and declared his citizenship in order to avoid unnecessary suffering. In Philippi, Paul had taken his undeserved beating because it served his purpose. He had used the illegal punishment as leverage to secure greater safety for the church in Philippi. In Jerusalem, however, his suffering would serve no constructive purpose, so he put an end to it.

A strange trend in Christian teaching has twisted the doctrine of submission into something grotesque and tragically unlike anything Jesus taught. It's the idea that Christians should submit to any kind of abuse that happens to come their way. Consequently, wives endure battering while churches shout, "Submit!" Children suffer bizarre forms of neglect and mistreatment in the name of submission and discipline. Christians everywhere seem to believe that accepting abuse and humiliation is part and parcel of the Christian life and, therefore, that they should take their beatings when they could otherwise avoid injustice. But that's not biblical teaching.

Paul suffered when he saw something greater to be gained. He accepted—submitted, if you will—to the unalterable will of God when it called for suffering. When escape was not an option, he bore his mistreatment with dignity. *That* is quintessentially Christian. Volunteering for mistreatment and injustice is a perversion of the doctrine of submission. God created humans for dignity. Evil has been tearing down

God's creation from the moment of the first sin. We, as Christians, are called to suffer with Christ in the war against Satan and sin, but God never calls us to lay down human dignity when we have the option to see justice prevail.

Third, *an honest testimony is our responsibility; a positive response is not.* In terms of positive response, Paul's testimony was a massive crash-and-burn failure. His defense of the gospel and his ministry to the Gentiles didn't convince the audience to change their opinion and decide to fund a fourth missionary journey. He merely told the truth of his own experience with Jesus Christ: his life of sin before, his conversion, and his ministry after. The audience saw themselves in his "before" picture and they didn't like what they saw. The audience saw themselves in contrast to Paul's "after" picture and they liked the reflection even less. The apostle didn't set out to convince the Jews to convert; he only determined to tell the truth. What they did with the truth, he left to the Holy Spirit.

People won't like what we have to say. Our job is not to change their minds; our responsibility is to proclaim the truth. Nothing more. Nothing less.

When Pressure Mounts
ACTS 23:1-22

NASB

¹Paul, looking intently at the ªCouncil, said, "Brethren, I have ᵇlived my life with a perfectly good conscience before God up to this day." ²The high priest Ananias commanded those standing beside him to strike him on the mouth. ³Then Paul said to him, "God is going to strike you, you whitewashed wall! Do you sit to try me according to the Law, and in violation of the Law order me to be struck?" ⁴But the bystanders said, "Do you revile God's high priest?" ⁵And Paul said, "I was not aware, brethren, that he was high priest; for it is written, 'YOU SHALL NOT SPEAK EVIL OF A RULER OF YOUR PEOPLE.'"

NLT

¹Gazing intently at the high council,* Paul began: "Brothers, I have always lived before God with a clear conscience!"

²Instantly Ananias the high priest commanded those close to Paul to slap him on the mouth. ³But Paul said to him, "God will slap you, you corrupt hypocrite!* What kind of judge are you to break the law yourself by ordering me struck like that?"

⁴Those standing near Paul said to him, "Do you dare to insult God's high priest?"

⁵"I'm sorry, brothers. I didn't realize he was the high priest," Paul replied, "for the Scriptures say, 'You

NASB

6But perceiving that one group were Sadducees and the other Pharisees, Paul *began* crying out in the ªCouncil, "Brethren, I am a Pharisee, a son of Pharisees; I am on trial for the hope and resurrection of the dead!" 7As he said this, there occurred a dissension between the Pharisees and Sadducees, and the assembly was divided. 8For the Sadducees say that there is no resurrection, nor an angel, nor a spirit, but the Pharisees acknowledge them all. 9And there occurred a great uproar; and some of the scribes of the Pharisaic party stood up and *began* to argue heatedly, saying, "We find nothing wrong with this man; suppose a spirit or an angel has spoken to him?" 10And as a great dissension was developing, the ªcommander was afraid Paul would be torn to pieces by them and ordered the troops to go down and take him away from them by force, and bring him into the barracks.

11But on the night *immediately* following, the Lord stood at his side and said, "Take courage; for as you have solemnly witnessed to My cause at Jerusalem, so you must witness at Rome also."

12When it was day, the Jews formed a ªconspiracy and bound themselves under an oath, saying that they would neither eat nor drink until they had killed Paul. 13There were more than forty who formed this plot. 14They came to the chief priests and the elders and said, "We have bound ourselves under a solemn oath to taste nothing until we have killed Paul. 15Now therefore, you ªand the bCouncil notify the ccommander to bring him down to you, as though you were going to determine his case by a more thorough investigation; and we for our part are ready to slay him before he comes near *the place*."

NLT

must not speak evil of any of your rulers.'*"

6Paul realized that some members of the high council were Sadducees and some were Pharisees, so he shouted, "Brothers, I am a Pharisee, as were my ancestors! And I am on trial because my hope is in the resurrection of the dead!"

7This divided the council— the Pharisees against the Sadducees—8for the Sadducees say there is no resurrection or angels or spirits, but the Pharisees believe in all of these. 9So there was a great uproar. Some of the teachers of religious law who were Pharisees jumped up and began to argue forcefully. "We see nothing wrong with him," they shouted. "Perhaps a spirit or an angel spoke to him." 10As the conflict grew more violent, the commander was afraid they would tear Paul apart. So he ordered his soldiers to go and rescue him by force and take him back to the fortress.

11That night the Lord appeared to Paul and said, "Be encouraged, Paul. Just as you have been a witness to me here in Jerusalem, you must preach the Good News in Rome as well."

12The next morning a group of Jews* got together and bound themselves with an oath not to eat or drink until they had killed Paul. 13There were more than forty of them in the conspiracy. 14They went to the leading priests and elders and told them, "We have bound ourselves with an oath to eat nothing until we have killed Paul. 15So you and the high council should ask the commander to bring Paul back to the council again. Pretend you want to examine his case more fully. We will kill him on the way."

¹⁶But the son of Paul's sister heard of their ambush, ᵃand he came and entered the barracks and told Paul. ¹⁷Paul called one of the centurions to him and said, "Lead this young man to the ᵃcommander, for he has something to report to him." ¹⁸So he took him and led him to the ᵃcommander and said, "Paul the prisoner called me to him and asked me to lead this young man to you since he has something to tell you." ¹⁹The ᵃcommander took him by the hand and stepping aside, *began* to inquire of him privately, "What is it that you have to report to me?" ²⁰And he said, "The Jews have agreed to ask you to bring Paul down tomorrow to the ᵃCouncil, as though they were going to inquire somewhat more thoroughly about him. ²¹So do not ᵃlisten to them, for more than forty of them are lying in wait for him who have bound themselves under a curse not to eat or drink until they slay him; and now they are ready and waiting for the promise from you." ²²So the ᵃcommander let the young man go, instructing him, "Tell no one that you have notified me of these things."

23:1 ᵃOr *Sanhedrin* ᵇOr *conducted myself as a citizen* 23:6 ᵃOr *Sanhedrin* 23:10 ᵃI.e. chiliarch, in command of one thousand troops 23:12 ᵃOr *mob* 23:15 ᵃLit *with* ᵇOr *Sanhedrin* ᶜV 10, note 1 23:16 ᵃOr *having been present with them, and he entered* 23:17 ᵃV 10, note 1 23:18 ᵃV 10, note 1 23:19 ᵃV 10, note 1 23:20 ᵃOr *Sanhedrin* 23:21 ᵃLit *be persuaded by them* 23:22 ᵃV 10, note 1

¹⁶But Paul's nephew—his sister's son—heard of their plan and went to the fortress and told Paul. ¹⁷Paul called for one of the Roman officers* and said, "Take this young man to the commander. He has something important to tell him."

¹⁸So the officer did, explaining, "Paul, the prisoner, called me over and asked me to bring this young man to you because he has something to tell you."

¹⁹The commander took his hand, led him aside, and asked, "What is it you want to tell me?"

²⁰Paul's nephew told him, "Some Jews are going to ask you to bring Paul before the high council tomorrow, pretending they want to get some more information. ²¹But don't do it! There are more than forty men hiding along the way ready to ambush him. They have vowed not to eat or drink anything until they have killed him. They are ready now, just waiting for your consent."

²²"Don't let anyone know you told me this," the commander warned the young man.

23:1 Greek *Sanhedrin;* also in 23:6, 15, 20, 28. 23:3 Greek *you whitewashed wall.* 23:5 Exod 22:28. 23:12 Greek *the Jews.* 23:17 Greek *centurions;* also in 23:23.

In 1865, the year America found peace after four years of civil war, a baby boy was born on the other side of the world in Bombay, India—just one of thousands in a region few people knew or cared to know about. Born to wealth and privilege, he never suffered poverty except vicariously by living alongside the millions inhabiting Punjab, where his father had moved the family when he took a job as curator of the eminent Lahore Museum. His family's privileged position in British society surrounded him with elegance and nobility.

His father, an artist in his own right, recognized the boy's artistic genius early and made sure he received the finest education England could provide, both in the British Isles and in India. By and by, the world began to recognize the literary genius of this boy, Rudyard Kipling, and would award him the Nobel Prize for literature at the age of forty-one. Despite his acclaim among sophisticates, he never lost his earthy connection with the common people. If he was criticized for anything, it was his affection for those less fortunate than he; many of his wealthy peers disparaged him and delighted to cut him down with sarcasm. Nevertheless, he endured with dignity and never turned from his convictions.

Perhaps while enduring a particularly stinging assault, he wrote these words to his son:

> If you can keep your head when all about you
> Are losing theirs and blaming it on you;
> If you can trust yourself when all men doubt you,
> But make allowance for their doubting too:
> If you can wait and not be tired by waiting,
> Or being lied about, don't deal in lies,
> Or being hated don't give way to hating,
> And yet don't look too good, nor talk too wise;
>
> If you can dream—and not make dreams your master;
> If you can think—and not make thoughts your aim,
> If you can meet with Triumph and Disaster
> And treat those two impostors just the same:
> If you can bear to hear the truth you've spoken
> Twisted by knaves to make a trap for fools,
> Or watch the things you gave your life to, broken,
> And stoop and build 'em up with worn-out tools;
>
> If you can make one heap of all your winnings
> And risk it on one turn of pitch-and-toss,
> And lose, and start again at your beginnings
> And never breathe a word about your loss:
> If you can force your heart and nerve and sinew
> To serve your turn long after they are gone,
> And so hold on when there is nothing in you
> Except the Will which says to them: 'Hold on!'

If you can talk with crowds and keep your virtue,
Or walk with Kings—nor lose the common touch,
If neither foes nor loving friends can hurt you,
If all men count with you, but none too much:
If you can fill the unforgiving minute
With sixty seconds' worth of distance run,
Yours is the Earth and everything that's in it,
And—which is more—you'll be a Man, my son![12]

Eighteen and a half centuries before Kipling released those poignant words, there lived a man who also was misunderstood. He also was a genius. He also was honored. As best we can tell, he was hailed among the temple elite as a rising star in Jewish culture and government. Then his theology changed. He no longer preached the Law as the way to salvation; he now proclaimed a gospel of grace, authenticated by the resurrection of Jesus, whom he accepted as the Messiah of Israel and of his own life. The great Saul of Tarsus became Paul the Small, an apostle of Jesus Christ. When hated, he did not hate in return. When he saw the truths he preached twisted against him, he stood firm and resolutely gave himself to them all the more. But even Paul had his tough days. Having survived a riot in the temple and arrest by the Roman guard, he stood to face his former colleagues in the Sanhedrin, now graying with age and wrinkled with time after some twenty years, but all the more powerful in the realm of religion and politics.

The commander of the Roman guard arranged for this hearing, but Paul didn't see this as a trial to determine the future course of his life; he left that to God. Instead, he saw yet another opportunity to confront his countrymen with their sin and, hopefully, call them to repentance.

— 23:1 —

Acts 23:10 implies that the commander observed the hearing along with several troops. On the other hand, if Paul was standing in the chamber, he would have known that the high priest had addressed him (23:5), if not by sight then by the location of the voice. Therefore, I'm inclined to believe that the Sanhedrin assembled somewhere in the common area of the temple to accommodate the commander's request without compromising sacred tradition.

Paul began his address with a bold declaration both the Sadducees and the Pharisees should have appreciated. He lived with a "perfectly good conscience before God" (23:1), not because he had never sinned, but because he had earnestly devoted himself to pleasing God and because Christ had justified him by grace through faith in His sacrificial atonement for sin on the cross.

— 23:2-3 —

Paul's claim to have a "perfectly good conscience before God" (23:1) did not please the high priest, who broke with Sanhedrin protocol to have an attendant punch the apostle in the mouth. Notably, Jesus experienced the same treatment during his hearing before Annas (John 18:22). Whereas the Lord had rebuked the high priest gently, Paul condemned the man sharply, calling him a "whitewashed wall" (Acts 23:3). The metaphor could have two references. The first pictures the whitewashed front of a burial cave, the implication being that the high priest only appeared pure on the outside but was full of dead men's bones within (see Matt. 23:27). The other reference alludes to an image used by Ezekiel in which the Lord condemned false prophets for speaking lies in His name (Ezek. 13:10-16). The high priest's hypocrisy enraged Paul. They had gathered to examine the accusation against the apostle that he had escorted a Gentile into the court of Israel, among other charges, yet the high priest violated the rules of the Sanhedrin in front of everyone.

— 23:4-5 —

The comment by someone observing the hearing illustrates the twisted logic at work in the Sanhedrin. Paul objected to the high priest's violation of the Law, and he was rebuked for being disrespectful of the office! The apostle's response is difficult to interpret. Some see this as evidence, along with Galatians 6:11, that he suffered from failing eyesight, but "looking intently" in Acts 23:1 argues against this. There are two reasonable explanations: (1) He in fact didn't recognize the high priest because he wasn't wearing his traditional vestments for this hearing and the office had been occupied by several men since Paul last visited Jerusalem; or (2) he responded sarcastically, saying, in effect, "He wasn't acting like God's high priest, so I didn't recognize him."

Paul's quoting Exodus 22:28 (Acts 23:5) favors the latter explanation. He highlighted the irony of his situation: He stood before the council voluntarily, in deference to their authority, to hear their complaint about his supposed denigration of the temple and flouting of God's Law. Meanwhile, God's high priest broke the law in the first moments of his appearance. Or, as one commentator states, "Paul's quotation from Exodus 22:28 showed that he was in subjection to God's revealed will that he was on trial for repudiating."[13]

— 23:6-8 —

Paul had appeared before the Sanhedrin as a courtesy to the Roman commander, to listen to and then respond to any complaints the temple officials had against him. He immediately saw that he would never get a hearing with the council, so he decided to show his Roman audience that the religious officials were pathetically irrational and hopelessly corrupt. It occurred to Paul that he could use the polarized views of the Sadducees and Pharisees to make his point. Probably looking at the Pharisee majority, he suddenly cried out, in effect, "I'm not on trial for denigrating the Law. I'm a Pharisee. I'm on trial because the Sadducees don't like our theology, brothers!" (see 23:6). And with that, the trial ended. The council turned on themselves, some defending Paul as a fellow Pharisee, all of them compulsively drawn into their never-ending theological debate (23:7-8).

— 23:9-10 —

Again, I maintain that the hearing took place informally in the common area of the temple complex, where the commander and his troops could observe. If so, the audience extended beyond just the council: Common Jewish worshipers heard the great "dissension" (*stasis* [4714b]) developing, and dangerous arguments rippled among the general public. Such dissension often degenerated into dangerous public mayhem, and therefore the commander began to worry that "Paul would be torn to pieces" (23:10). To restore order and rescue a Roman citizen from danger, he motioned to the Fortress of Antonia, and troops poured in to extract Paul and return him to the garrison.

Josephus didn't refer to this incident in his chronicle, but he describes the political tone in Jerusalem leading up to the end of Felix's term, a time period coinciding with Paul's trial and subsequent imprisonment in Caesarea:

> And now arose a sedition between the high priests and the principal men of the multitude of Jerusalem; each of whom got them a company of the boldest sort of men, and of those that loved innovations, about them, and became leaders to them; and when they struggled together, they did it by casting reproachful words against one another, and by throwing stones also. And there was

nobody to reprove them; but these disorders were done after a licentious manner in the city, as if it had no government over it.[14]

Evidently, the dissension between the Sadducees ("the high priests") and the Pharisees (who represented "the principal men of the multitude") grew steadily worse after Paul's hearing.

— 23:11 —

When the commander had realized Paul was a Roman citizen, he released him from custody (22:30), so Paul didn't stay in the barracks against his will. He had most likely spent the previous several nights under the protection of the commander, and this night would be no different. Ironically, Peter had spent the night in this same structure under very different circumstances. Agrippa I had locked him up intending to execute him upon the conclusion of Passover. On the eve of his execution, an angel visited Peter, released him from his chains, and led him out of the fortress (12:1-11).

This time, Paul had a very different experience. As darkness fell over the garrison and the soldiers slept, Jesus appeared to the apostle to provide comfort and reassurance. He told Paul that he would not be walking out of the prison that night, and then He revealed the purpose of Paul's arrest and what lay in the future. Paul had hoped to visit Rome; Jesus assured him that he would, just under different circumstances than he had planned. Notably, Jesus stood by Paul's side as if to say, "I'm right beside you all the way."

— 23:12-15 —

Josephus reports that under the procurator, Felix, people routinely hired the Sicarii, "dagger men," to assassinate their enemies. Originally, the Sicarii were an extremist faction of zealots who used cloak-and-dagger methods to rid Israel of those they considered enemies of an independent state: Gentiles, Roman sympathizers, Hellenistic Jews, Herodians, and so forth. They degenerated into nothing more than blades for hire. Josephus records,

> The robbers went up with the greatest security at the festivals after this time; and having weapons concealed in like manner as before, and mingling themselves among the multitude, they slew certain of their own enemies, and were subservient to other men for money; and slew others, not only in remote parts of the city, but in the temple itself also; for they had the boldness to

murder men there, without thinking of the impiety of which they were guilty.[15]

A cadre of more than forty men, probably aligned with the Sadducees, approached the high priest and his cronies with a plan. The chief priests would call another meeting of the Sanhedrin on the pretext of giving Paul a fair hearing, only they would ensure that he never made it across the temple courtyard (23:15). They bound themselves to the plot with an unusually severe oath (*anathematizō* [332]) even more extreme than the Nazirite vow (23:12, 14). The *anathematizō* describes a pagan vow that calls down divine curses upon oneself if one should renege or fail to fulfill the commitment. They promised not to eat or drink until they had assassinated Paul. Of course, Paul lived for several more years after this. Either the murderous enemies starved to death—not likely!—or they found clever lawyers to wheedle their way through a loophole.

— 23:16-22 —

Paul's nephew by his sister discovered the plan. Paul referred to him as a *neanias* [3494] (23:17), the same term used of Eutychus in Troas (20:9), indicating that he was an adolescent perhaps ten to seventeen years of age. The centurion called him a *neaniskos* [3495], which Philo reports that Hippocrates described as "a boy till his beard begins to grow, and that time is the end of a third period of seven years"[16]—between fourteen and twenty-one. He may have been devoted to temple service, not unlike an altar boy in the Catholic Church, and overheard talk among the temple leaders.

Paul was not a "prisoner" (23:18) in the sense that he was detained; rather, he remained in protective custody. Moreover, as a citizen, he could request the cooperation of a Roman commander. Rather than deliver the warning himself, he let the commander hear of the plot directly from his nephew. The way Luke describes the scene suggests he was there in the barracks with Paul at the time—visitors were commonly allowed, especially under circumstances like Paul's.

The commander took the boy's report seriously. He knew exactly what to do. This was his realm of expertise.

APPLICATION: ACTS 23:1-22

Facing the Past, Planning the Future

As I observe this passage with a little imagination, two truths emerge.

First, *the grace of God can overshadow any guilt within us.* When Paul stood to face the Sanhedrin, he had come full circle. He had not interacted with these men, his former colleagues, since leaving for Damascus on his deadly errand more than twenty years earlier. The last time he spoke with a high priest, he had received letters authorizing him to deputize Jews in the synagogue of Damascus, round up Christian Jews, and return them to Jerusalem to face trial. On this day, he was the defendant. By the time of his original departure, he had amassed an impressive record of arrests and convictions, resulting in the deaths of many innocent people. Even so, he stood before the council of Israel and declared, "Brethren, I have lived my life with a perfectly good conscience before God up to this day" (23:1).

The grace of God gave him permission to make that claim. That same grace frees us to say the same. Perhaps you need to stop listening to the condemnation of other people and take your stand on grace with Paul. It is amazing how Christians heed the voices that continually underscore guilt and wrong and failure and inadequacy and incompetence! But it is remarkable how the reassurance of God comes in grace and says to you, "All is forgiven. I have Rome in My sights. If I didn't have a plan for you," says the Father, "I would take you out of this world. Because you are alive, I am still at work, barracks or not, mistreatment or not. I know what I'm doing." You see, God specializes in imperfect people. The grace of God can overshadow any guilt within us.

The second truth I've found here is that *the power of God can overcome any plot against us.* If you have placed your trust in Jesus Christ, you stand before God as His child, justified, declared righteous, destined for a greater purpose than anyone—including you—can possibly imagine. It is an invincible, unalterable, irrefutable plan! And God will get you there! He's *committed* to it, failure and mistakes and sin notwithstanding. He knows you, He knows what He wants to accomplish, He sees beforehand what threatens to undermine His plan, and nothing can stand in His way.

Stay focused on what the Lord wants to accomplish through you and let Him take care of potential dangers. The power of God can overcome any plot against us, even those hatched by Satan himself.

Between the Frying Pan and the Fire
ACTS 23:23–24:9

NASB

23 And he called to him two of the centurions and said, "Get two hundred soldiers ready by ªthe third hour of the night to proceed to Caesarea, ᵇwith seventy horsemen and two hundred ᶜspearmen." 24 *They were* also to provide mounts to put Paul on and bring him safely to Felix the governor. 25 And he wrote a letter having this form:

26 "Claudius Lysias, to the most excellent governor Felix, greetings.

27 "When this man was arrested by the Jews and was about to be slain by them, I came up to them with the troops and rescued him, having learned that he was a Roman.

28 "And wanting to ascertain the charge for which they were accusing him, I brought him down to their ªCouncil;

29 and I found him to be accused over questions about their Law, but ªunder no accusation deserving death or ᵇimprisonment.

30 "When I was informed that there would be a plot against the man, I sent him to you at once, also instructing his accusers to ªbring charges against him before you."

31 So the soldiers, in accordance with their orders, took Paul and brought him by night to Antipatris. 32 But the next day, leaving the horsemen to go on with him, they returned to the barracks. 33 When these had come to Caesarea and delivered the letter to the governor, they also presented Paul to him. 34 When he had read it, he asked from what province he was, and when he learned that

NLT

23 Then the commander called two of his officers and ordered, "Get 200 soldiers ready to leave for Caesarea at nine o'clock tonight. Also take 200 spearmen and 70 mounted troops. 24 Provide horses for Paul to ride, and get him safely to Governor Felix." 25 Then he wrote this letter to the governor:

26 "From Claudius Lysias, to his Excellency, Governor Felix: Greetings!

27 "This man was seized by some Jews, and they were about to kill him when I arrived with the troops. When I learned that he was a Roman citizen, I removed him to safety. 28 Then I took him to their high council to try to learn the basis of the accusations against him. 29 I soon discovered the charge was something regarding their religious law—certainly nothing worthy of imprisonment or death. 30 But when I was informed of a plot to kill him, I immediately sent him on to you. I have told his accusers to bring their charges before you."

31 So that night, as ordered, the soldiers took Paul as far as Antipatris. 32 They returned to the fortress the next morning, while the mounted troops took him on to Caesarea. 33 When they arrived in Caesarea, they presented Paul and the letter to Governor Felix. 34 He read it and then asked Paul what province he was from. "Cilicia," Paul answered.

he was from Cilicia, ³⁵he said, "I will give you a hearing after your accusers arrive also," giving orders for him to be kept in Herod's ªPraetorium.

²⁴:¹After five days the high priest Ananias came down with some elders, ªwith an ᵇattorney *named* Tertullus, and they ꟲbrought charges to the governor against Paul. ²After *Paul* had been summoned, Tertullus began to accuse him, saying *to the governor,*

"Since we have through you attained much peace, and since by your providence reforms are being carried out for this nation, ³we acknowledge *this* in every way and everywhere, most excellent Felix, with all thankfulness. ⁴But, that I may not weary you any further, I beg you ªto grant us, by your kindness, a brief hearing. ⁵For we have found this man a real pest and a fellow who stirs up dissension among all the Jews throughout ªthe world, and a ringleader of the sect of the Nazarenes. ⁶And he even tried to desecrate the temple; and ªthen we arrested him. [ᵇWe wanted to judge him according to our own Law. ⁷But Lysias the commander came along, and with much violence took him out of our hands, ⁸ordering his accusers to come before you.] By examining him yourself concerning all these matters you will be able to ascertain the things of which we accuse him." ⁹The Jews also joined in the attack, asserting that these things were so.

23:23 ªI.e. 9 p.m. ᵇLit *and* ꟲOr *slingers* or *bowmen* 23:28 ªOr *Sanhedrin* 23:29 ªLit *having* ᵇLit *bonds* 23:30 ªLit *speak against him* 23:35 ªI.e. governor's official residence 24:1 ªLit *and* ᵇLit *orator* ꟲOr *presented their evidence* or *case* 24:4 ªLit *to hear...briefly* 24:5 ªLit *the inhabited earth* 24:6 ªLit *also* ᵇThe early mss do not contain the remainder of v 6, v 7, nor the first part of v 8

³⁵"I will hear your case myself when your accusers arrive," the governor told him. Then the governor ordered him kept in the prison at Herod's headquarters.*

²⁴:¹Five days later Ananias, the high priest, arrived with some of the Jewish elders and the lawyer* Tertullus, to present their case against Paul to the governor. ²When Paul was called in, Tertullus presented the charges against Paul in the following address to the governor:

"You have provided a long period of peace for us Jews and with foresight have enacted reforms for us. ³For all of this, Your Excellency, we are very grateful to you. ⁴But I don't want to bore you, so please give me your attention for only a moment. ⁵We have found this man to be a troublemaker who is constantly stirring up riots among the Jews all over the world. He is a ringleader of the cult known as the Nazarenes. ⁶Furthermore, he was trying to desecrate the Temple when we arrested him.* ⁸You can find out the truth of our accusations by examining him yourself." ⁹Then the other Jews chimed in, declaring that everything Tertullus said was true.

23:35 Greek *Herod's Praetorium.* 24:1 Greek *some elders and an orator.* 24:6 Some manuscripts add an expanded conclusion to verse 6, all of verse 7, and an additional phrase in verse 8: *We would have judged him by our law, ⁷but Lysias, the commander of the garrison, came and violently took him away from us, ⁸commanding his accusers to come before you.*

Let's face it; we feel more secure when we're in control. Researchers have confirmed this as a fact while studying medical patients. Those who know about their illness and understand the reasons for prescribed therapies respond better to treatment, cooperate more with orders, suffer less depression, and recover more consistently. Patients who know less about their conditions or why they should do this or that experience the highest levels of stress and struggle to heal. As a result, the best physicians have changed their bedside manner. Gone are the days when a doctor says simply, "Do this because I'm the medical professional and I know what's best for you." The best physicians now see patient education as a critical tool in the course of treatment. They take time to explain the ailment, the options and consequences of possible treatment, how each procedure or therapy works, what the patient will likely experience, and the probable results. They recruit the patient as an ally in defeating the physical problem because people who feel in control of their own destinies do better in life.

All of us have times when we feel utterly powerless. I remember a horrible Thursday afternoon when a voice on the phone said, "Pastor Swindoll, your daughter Charissa has been injured, and the paramedics are here. We need to know which hospital you prefer." She had been practicing with the cheerleaders, fell from the top of the pyramid, and landed on her head. When I arrived at her school, she lay on a gurney, strapped to a board with her head immobilized. With tears streaming from her eyes, she said, "Daddy, I can't feel anything." While the trauma team at the hospital examined X-rays and conducted neurological tests, time stopped for her mother and me in the waiting room. Without information from the doctors, fear consumed our minds. We fought off images of our good friend Joni Eareckson Tada, whose tragic diving accident left her paralyzed from her shoulders down. We held each other, cried, and prayed the desperate groanings of desperate parents: "Oh, God, no . . . no, no, no . . . please, Lord, no . . . please help us, please . . ."

The attending physicians finally called us back late in the evening. One of them pointed to the X-ray images—which I could never make sense of—and confirmed that Charissa showed no signs of permanent damage. My head swam and I felt weak in the knees. Waves of relief and gratitude washed over Cynthia and me as we cried.

In times like these, we would do *anything* to gain at least some measure of control. That's when we have no choice but to trust others and, to a much greater degree, trust our Savior. When we feel utterly powerless—completely unable to alter the slightest detail of the future—we actually experience life as it is. In truth, we *are* powerless. We always have been powerless. Our well-being is like a piece of dust in a whirlwind. To avoid living in constant terror, we construct an elaborate illusion that says we control our own destinies—until some circumstance brings us back to reality.

God has a better way. He wants to replace our delusions of autonomy with the truth of His sovereign care for His people.

Paul's trial (22:30–23:10) had ended badly, from a purely human perspective. He didn't stand a chance going into the hearing, but he didn't realize this at first. He had entertained a small hope that the leaders of Israel might listen, heed the truth, repent of their rebellion, and embrace the Messiah. Just before leaving Corinth on his journey to Jerusalem, he confessed to the church in Rome,

> I am telling the truth in Christ, I am not lying, my conscience testifies with me in the Holy Spirit, that I have great sorrow and unceasing grief in my heart. For I could wish that I myself were accursed, separated from Christ for the sake of my brethren, my kinsmen according to the flesh, who are Israelites, to whom belongs the adoption as sons, and the glory and the covenants and the giving of the Law and the temple service and the promises, whose are the fathers, and from whom is the Christ according to the flesh, who is over all, God blessed forever. Amen. (Rom. 9:1-5)

After his opening statement earned him a punch in the mouth (Acts 23:2), however, Paul realized that the heart of Israel had turned to stone. He could say nothing that would turn the people from their rebellion. The temple should have been a sanctuary for this faithful Jew; from that day forward, however, the Lord would use the Gentiles to protect His apostle, to preserve His Word, and to carry His gospel to the rest of humanity. Ironically, the nation He had ordained to be a light to the nations would become the dark backdrop against which the Gentiles would see the gleaming hope of the gospel. Paul would spend the next five years presenting his case (Acts 24–28)—the case for the good news—before powerful Gentiles in response to Israel's false accusations.

Beginning with a nighttime departure from Jerusalem for Caesarea (23:23), Paul's fate lay in the hands of others. No longer able to travel freely or determine what should be done next to advance the gospel, he had to wait for others to act and then respond, moment by moment, to opportunities as they arose. He was powerless and helpless, yet never more composed. While others appeared to control his destiny, he trusted the Savior who had directed his steps from Damascus, three times around the empire, and now toward Rome.

— 23:23-24 —

When the commander learned of the Jewish plot to lure Paul into the temple on the pretext of a fair hearing and then stab him to death, he summoned two centurions and assembled a transport detail. Each centurion held the equivalent rank of a captain or major today and commanded approximately one hundred men, which included support staff, such as junior officers and armor bearers. Upper-level centurions also filled staff positions in support of more senior officers or commanded special details, such as guarding dignitaries, managing prisons, or carrying out punishment, including crucifixion.

The commander clearly believed in the "overwhelming force doctrine." To ensure the safety of his own men, he surrounded Paul with such a dominant display of military power that no one dared attempt an assassination. He called for two hundred soldiers to be ready by nine o'clock that night. And the total number of men could have climbed to 270 or 470, depending upon how one interprets the commander's order for "seventy horsemen and two hundred spearmen" (23:23). The conjunction translated "and" (*kai* [2532]) normally means "in addition to" in a context like this. Along with the two hundred foot soldiers, he added seventy cavalry and two hundred spearmen (*dexiolabos* [1187]), which is variously translated "slinger," "bowman," or "spearman." They all have in common their role of launching missiles, whether rocks from slings, arrows from bows, or spears thrown by hand.

They placed Paul on an animal, most likely a horse, and sent him to Caesarea, the Roman headquarters in Judea. The commander recognized that Paul's case rose above his pay grade and that he had a duty to safeguard the rights of a Roman citizen against local vigilantes. Allowing a mob to kill a citizen would give Rome a black eye, and the longer he kept Paul in Jerusalem, the more likely his enemies would succeed.

— 23:25-30 —

The commander sent Paul with a letter to Felix, a Roman procurator appointed to act as governor. His letter highlights three crucial points. First, Paul was a Roman citizen, which obligated Felix to fulfill his duty

FELIX

ACTS 23:24

Around AD 50, Felix's predecessor, Cumanus, had made himself an enemy of the Jews. His dispute with the high priest, Ananias, son of Nebedeus, led to a hearing in Rome, where each accused the other of sedition against the empire. Meanwhile, back in Judea, Jonathan, the son of Annas, served as the interim high priest. When Claudius found Cumanus guilty and banished him, Jonathan requested the appointment of Marcus Antonius Felix as procurator.[17]

Felix was a freedman, originally a slave with his brother, Pallas, under the daughter of Mark Antony. Both men rose to prominence after gaining their freedom, with Pallas becoming a secretary of the treasury for both Claudius and Nero.[18] Felix used his family connections and wily politics to skim the surface of scandals without actually getting wet. He somehow managed to make an impression on Jonathan, who now led the Annas crime family in Jerusalem. As a result, he became the only governor on record to have been a former slave.

At first, Felix worked hard to control the growing numbers of brigands in the region, outlaws who used robbery and assassination as tools against Roman occupation. He captured and executed many of them, but not all. Some he kept for his own use. After two years of listening to Jonathan's constant criticism, he arranged to have the interim high priest murdered by the Sicarii,[19] "dagger men," an extremist faction of zealots. Soon, however, the plan backfired. Having done the deed, the robbers used their underworld ties to the procurator to take over the city. One of their leaders was a certain Egyptian false prophet who "stirred up a revolt and led the four thousand men of the Assassins out into the wilderness" (21:38). Felix cleverly used this revolt as an opportunity to clean up the city, make himself a hero to the Romans, and eliminate the witnesses to his earlier crime. While the Egyptian escaped and was never seen again, Felix killed four hundred of the robbers.

Felix was an opportunist without a conscience. Tacitus described him as one who "practiced every kind of cruelty and lust, wielding the power of [a] king with all the instincts of a slave."[20] He used people and circumstances to accomplish his own agenda, which was to gain greater power and accumulate more wealth. He used Jonathan to get his appointment in Judea, only to have him assassinated. He used brigands to carry out his dirty work and then prosecuted them to vindicate himself. He took bribes and decided disputes based on political expediency instead of justice. He allowed the high priest, Ananias, son of Nebedeus, to carry out his corruption and extortion without interference, and then he used his corruption to fuel the Jews' dispute with Syria for his own political gain.

For unknown reasons, Felix returned to Rome around AD 59, where Jewish delegates brought a complaint against him in court. He would have been convicted if not for another opportune connection. His brother, Pallas, enjoyed the favor of Nero at the time and successfully pleaded for his acquittal.[21]

as a representative of Rome. Second, Paul was not guilty of violating any Roman law (18:14-15; 23:9); otherwise, Lysias could have handled the matter on his own. Third, the Jewish subjects were angry enough to murder Paul, which made their dispute a state matter with significant political implications.

Lysias carefully crafted the letter to make himself appear valiant and wise. His taking Paul into custody and away from the violent mob (21:30-32) had the effect of "rescuing him" (see 23:27), but that had not been his intent, and he had not known that Paul was a Roman citizen. He merely seized and removed the focus of the riot, intending to sort out the truth afterward, by torture if necessary.

The commander made a wise decision in sending Paul to Caesarea. He didn't have the authority to rule in a dispute between a citizen and the local government. After his attempt to help them settle the matter locally, he sent Paul to the appropriate authority and invited the temple leaders to press their complaint legally before the procurator.

— 23:31-35 —

Antipatris was a town about 40 miles from Jerusalem in the coastal plain of Samaria. The military escort stayed the night, after which the centurions decided the most dangerous part of the journey lay behind them and so sent the foot soldiers back to Jerusalem. The cavalry could cover the remaining 25 miles to Caesarea before noon. Felix received the apostle, read the letter, and began to assess the situation. If Paul had been Judean, jurisdiction would have remained entirely under Felix. But because Paul came from Cilicia, at that time a part of the Syrian province, the case affected his relationship with Quadratus, the governor of Syria responsible for deposing Felix's predecessor, Cumanus.

Felix decided to accept the case, promising to hear from Paul when his accusers arrived from Jerusalem. Paul was a citizen and had not yet been charged with a crime. Furthermore, Lysias had made it clear that Paul was under protective custody. Therefore, the apostle remained under guard in Herod's palace in relative comfort. (The verb translated "kept" is *phylassō* [5442], which means "to watch," "to guard closely," or "to protect," but not necessarily to place in a cell under lock and key.)

— 24:1 —

Five days later, Ananias arrived with several elders—handpicked from among the Sadducees, no doubt—and an "attorney" (*rhētōr* [4489]), someone who was not an expert in Roman law as much as a professional speaker. Legal precedence and knowing the finer points of the legal code didn't mean nearly as much in those days as convincing a ruler to act in one's favor. In this case, the law was only one factor among many, and none was more important than what Felix deemed best for himself. So, an able rhetorician would know how to flatter without being obvious and subtly suggest a resolution that favored the temple officials while advancing Felix's interests—power and money.

— 24:2-4 —

Tertullus was a common name among Romans, but this man may have been a Jew. He opened his case with some carefully crafted flattery, common for the time. The content of his compliments affirmed Felix as a keeper of the peace and champion of justice. The "reforms" (24:2) referred to Felix's crackdown on brigands and the Sicarii. Ananias, a notorious extortionist himself, undoubtedly knew that Felix operated on both sides of the fence regarding robbers and assassins. In fact, Ananias may have played a tangential role in getting the interim high priest killed.

— 24:5-6 —

Tertullus's statement of the accusations against Paul involved three charges:

1. *Paul was a world-renowned troublemaker* (24:5a). The Romans hated unrest and charged governors with the responsibility of maintaining civil order. The emperor would appreciate any action taken to fulfill this mandate; even if it involved a miscarriage of justice, the offense would be forgiven in light of the motive. Tertullus subtly suggested that disposing of Paul, even with his citizenship, could be justified as a means of keeping the peace. After all, the Jews of at least three major cities—Corinth, Ephesus, and Jerusalem—would back him up with testimonies.

2. *Paul was a leader of a dangerous, anti-Roman cult* (24:5b). Romans

tolerated other religions, but they also expected all subjects of the empire to adopt the gods of Rome. To worship a Roman god was like saluting a flag; failing to do so expressed contempt for the state. Paul not only led others to reject Roman religion, but he also proclaimed a King other than Caesar.

3. *Paul even tried to desecrate the Jewish temple* (24:6). Tertullus barely touched on this issue, not because Felix, a Roman, didn't find it relevant, but because he would immediately understand the political implications. His predecessor had been in Rome in a dispute with Ananias—who at that moment stood beside the attorney—and *lost*. Moreover, Felix owed his current position to the interim high priest. The implied statement was, "Paul defiled the temple, and the temple has the power to change your future, Felix."

— 24:7-9 —

Tertullus closed his legal précis with the implication that Lysias had behaved improperly when intervening in what the temple considered an internal matter among Jews. In this way, he alluded to the indiscretions of Felix's predecessor, Cumanus. During Passover one year, the former procurator had posted Roman troops on the roof around the perimeter of the temple complex. According to Josephus, "One of the soldiers pulled back his garment, and cowering down after an indecent manner, turned his breech to the Jews, and spoke such words as you might expect upon such a posture."[22] The act sparked a riot that led to the deaths of many worshipers and began a long-running feud between the Jews and Felix's predecessor. That eventually led to the former procurator's conviction and banishment.[23]

At that point, the other temple officials—likely all Sadducees—joined the complaint. Felix saw many influential voices urging him to rule in their favor, all of them potential witnesses in Rome, either for him or against him.

At the conclusion of his opening statement, Paul must have seen what he was up against. His hearing in Jerusalem had ended before it began; now, in Caesarea, he faced a trial before a corrupt ruler. He also knew that this path led to Rome, not to freedom. He was not in control of his future, but thankfully, neither were these powerful men.

APPLICATION: ACTS 23:23–24:9

How to Make the Most of Your Powerlessness

From Paul's time in protective custody in Jerusalem throughout his transport to Caesarea and during his stay in the Praetorium, he surrendered to his powerless position, sandwiched between two unchangeable circumstances. His response to his powerlessness offers two lessons worth remembering.

First, *refuse to wrestle and learn to rest*. When you wrestle, you don't think clearly. When you wrestle, you talk much and pray little. When you wrestle, you panic rather than trust. When you wrestle, you think only about your way, your rights, your plan, your well-being. I'm not saying there's never a time to fight. When fighting can achieve a clear objective without committing a sin, then fight for all you're worth. If struggling against your circumstances could make things worse, or when any choice causes more problems than it solves, then it's time to take control of yourself and let God have control of your future.

Second, *release your pressure and claim God's peace*. In the book *Your Churning Place*, Robert Wise says that everyone has a place where we feel the physical effects of pressure, tension, anxiety, and frustration.

> You discover [the churning place] in the early years of your life. It seems to be located either near the pit of your stomach or at the base of your neck, where every muscle tightens. When it begins to turn and pump like an old washing machine, you find that every other area of your life marches to its lumbering, dull, paralyzing beat. . . .
>
> Nothing exempts us from the relentless process created by haunting memories and bankrupt expectancies. As universal as the human heart and head, the existence of the churning place cannot be denied.
>
> And it is not a constructive place. Positive thoughts lead to action and results, but the churning place is a tank that fills with anxieties that just settle into a stagnant infection.[24]

God never asked us to meet life's pressures and demands on our own terms or by relying upon our own strength. This self-reliance produces only an anxious, turbulent existence in which we become increasingly hardened and insensitive to God's leading. Earlier in his ministry, Paul had learned the secret to powerlessness—surrender. When Paul stopped wrestling against an issue over which he had no control, he learned to find strength in God's peace.

> And He has said to me, "My grace is sufficient for you, for power is perfected in weakness." Most gladly, therefore, I will rather boast about my weaknesses, so that the power of Christ may dwell in me. Therefore I am well content with weaknesses, with insults, with distresses, with persecutions, with difficulties, for Christ's sake; for when I am weak, then I am strong. (2 Cor. 12:9-10)

By releasing control into the hands of God, Paul found greater strength than he had ever imagined could be his.

The Peril of Procrastination
ACTS 24:10-27

NASB

10 When the governor had nodded for him to speak, Paul responded:

"Knowing that for many years you have been a judge to this nation, I cheerfully make my defense, 11 since you can take note of the fact that no more than twelve days ago I went up to Jerusalem to worship. 12 Neither in the temple, nor in the synagogues, nor in the city *itself* did they find me carrying on a discussion with anyone or causing a a riot. 13 Nor can they prove to you *the charges* of which they now accuse me. 14 But this I admit to you, that according to the Way which they call a sect I do serve a the God of our fathers, believing everything that is in accordance with the Law and that is written in the Prophets; 15 having a hope in God, which these men cherish themselves, that there shall certainly be a resurrection of both the righteous and the wicked. 16 In view of this, I also a do my best to maintain always

NLT

10 The governor then motioned for Paul to speak. Paul said, "I know, sir, that you have been a judge of Jewish affairs for many years, so I gladly present my defense before you. 11 You can quickly discover that I arrived in Jerusalem no more than twelve days ago to worship at the Temple. 12 My accusers never found me arguing with anyone in the Temple, nor stirring up a riot in any synagogue or on the streets of the city. 13 These men cannot prove the things they accuse me of doing.

14 "But I admit that I follow the Way, which they call a cult. I worship the God of our ancestors, and I firmly believe the Jewish law and everything written in the prophets. 15 I have the same hope in God that these men have, that he will raise both the righteous and the unrighteous. 16 Because of this, I always try to maintain a clear conscience before God and all people.

a blameless conscience *both* before God and before men. [17] Now after several years I came to bring [a]alms to my nation and to present offerings; [18] in which they found me *occupied* in the temple, having been purified, without *any* crowd or uproar. But *there were* some Jews from [a]Asia— [19] who ought to have been present before you and to make accusation, if they should have anything against me. [20] Or else let these men themselves tell what misdeed they found when I stood before the [a]Council, [21] other than for this one statement which I shouted out while standing among them, 'For the resurrection of the dead I am on trial before you today.'"

[22] But Felix, [a]having a more exact knowledge about the Way, put them off, saying, "When Lysias the [b]commander comes down, I will decide your case." [23] Then he gave orders to the centurion for him to be kept in custody and *yet* have *some* freedom, and not to prevent any of his friends from ministering to him.

[24] But some days later Felix arrived with Drusilla, his [a]wife who was a Jewess, and sent for Paul and heard him *speak* about faith in Christ Jesus. [25] But as he was discussing righteousness, self-control and the judgment to come, Felix became frightened and said, "Go away for the present, and when I find time I will summon you." [26] At the same time too, he was hoping that money would be given him by Paul; therefore he also used to send for him quite often and converse with him. [27] But after two years had passed, Felix [a]was succeeded by Porcius Festus, and wishing to do the Jews a favor, Felix left Paul imprisoned.

24:12 [a]Lit *an attack of a mob* 24:14 [a]Lit *the ancestral God* 24:16 [a]Lit *practice myself* 24:17 [a]Or *gifts to charity* 24:18 [a]I.e. west coast province of Asia Minor 24:20 [a]Or *Sanhedrin* 24:22 [a]Lit *knowing more accurately* [b]I.e. chiliarch, in command of one thousand troops 24:24 [a]Lit *own wife* 24:27 [a]Lit *received a successor, Porcius Festus*

[17] "After several years away, I returned to Jerusalem with money to aid my people and to offer sacrifices to God. [18] My accusers saw me in the Temple as I was completing a purification ceremony. There was no crowd around me and no rioting. [19] But some Jews from the province of Asia were there—and they ought to be here to bring charges if they have anything against me! [20] Ask these men here what crime the Jewish high council* found me guilty of, [21] except for the one time I shouted out, 'I am on trial before you today because I believe in the resurrection of the dead!'"

[22] At that point Felix, who was quite familiar with the Way, adjourned the hearing and said, "Wait until Lysias, the garrison commander, arrives. Then I will decide the case." [23] He ordered an officer* to keep Paul in custody but to give him some freedom and allow his friends to visit him and take care of his needs.

[24] A few days later Felix came back with his wife, Drusilla, who was Jewish. Sending for Paul, they listened as he told them about faith in Christ Jesus. [25] As he reasoned with them about righteousness and self-control and the coming day of judgment, Felix became frightened. "Go away for now," he replied. "When it is more convenient, I'll call for you again." [26] He also hoped that Paul would bribe him, so he sent for him quite often and talked with him.

[27] After two years went by in this way, Felix was succeeded by Porcius Festus. And because Felix wanted to gain favor with the Jewish people, he left Paul in prison.

24:20 Greek *Sanhedrin*. 24:23 Greek *a centurion*.

There once lived a man who was transported into the black abyss inside the earth, surrounded by the evil spirits and their ruler, Satan himself. He watched as a discussion unfolded between Satan and his spirits. He saw that the ruler held a scepter of wickedness in his hand, and he heard him as he said with a loud voice, "Who will go to earth for me and persuade people that I may accomplish the ruin of their souls? What message will you use? How will you say what you want to say so that men and women, boys and girls, will turn away from the things of God?"

A spirit responded, "I will go for you, and I will tell people that there is no heaven." The ruler frowned and replied, "No, that will not do. For too many centuries humanity has been told that there is a heaven. And our enemy, God, has given the Christians a book that talks about heaven and promises that it is a place where there will no longer be death and tears and sorrow and pain and affliction and tragedy."

A second spirit glided forward and said, "I will go, and I will tell men and women that there is no hell." Again, the ruler responded negatively: "That will not do either. The conscience, if nothing else, convinces people that someday there must be a day of reckoning and a place where men and women will come to terms with their lives. In fact, that book I mentioned, the Christian's handbook, has more to say about hell than about heaven. You could never convince them there's no hell."

There was a pause. The ruler added, "I need someone who will make an appeal to all classes, all ages, and all cultures in all the countries around the planet where men and women live."

One dark spirit stepped up and said, "I have the answer. I will go for you. I will not tell people there is no hell. I will not tell them there is no heaven. I will simply tell them there is no hurry."

They sent him.[25]

The word used for that destroyer of souls is "procrastination."

— 24:10 —

Paul had accepted his role in the plan of God. Several nights earlier, Jesus had stood by his side to reassure him: "Take courage; for as you have solemnly witnessed to My cause at Jerusalem, so you must witness at Rome also" (23:11). So Paul knew he didn't stand before Marcus Antonius Felix to win an acquittal. His purpose hadn't changed from the day Jesus called him to be "a minister and a witness not only to the things which you have seen, but also to the things in which I will appear to you" (26:16). He had but one duty: to tell the truth simply and plainly.

The orator for the temple officials seeking his execution had finished his legal précis after asserting three charges. Paul would address each accusation—and more. He would have begun with the customary flattery, but he found little he could compliment in good conscience. He didn't call Felix "excellent" (cf. 24:3). He didn't praise him as a great reformer. He didn't even use the opening to position his response. "You have been a judge to this nation" was like saying to the mother of an ugly infant, "My, isn't that a baby!"

— 24:11-13 —

Paul offered three facts in response to the first charge, that he was a world-renowned troublemaker (24:5a). First, he had not been in Jerusalem much more than a week when he was arrested. The past several days had been spent in custody (24:11).

Paul was seized in the temple "when the seven days were almost over" (21:27). He stood before the Sanhedrin the following day (22:30). He spent that night in the barracks (23:11). At nine o'clock the next evening (23:23) he was taken to Antipatris, where he spent the night (23:31-32), and he arrived in Caesarea the following day (23:33). After a short interview, he waited five days for his accusers to show up (24:1). He could not have accomplished much to "stir up dissension" in Jerusalem in about a week's time!

Second, he had not been seen "carrying on a discussion" (literally, "reasoning with") anyone in the temple or synagogues (24:12). He had not attempted to proselytize, much less incite others to riot. In fact, his only activity in the temple had been to support four men in the conclusion of their Nazirite vows (21:23-26).

Third, his accusers had absolutely no evidence to support their claim. He could produce a dozen witnesses to counter each perjurer they might pay to lie in court (24:13).

— 24:14-16 —

He then answered their second charge, that he was a leader of a dangerous, anti-Roman cult (24:5b). He said, in effect, "I am innocent of leading a cult, but I am devoted to spiritual truth." He supported this with four points:

- I serve the God of the Hebrews.
- I believe everything in the Hebrew Scriptures.

- I hope in the God of the Hebrews.
- I anticipate a resurrection and final judgment before this God.

On the first three points, he and his accusers (the Sadducees) agreed completely. The Sadducees did not, however, share his view on the fourth point. Even so, the majority of Jewish theologians were Pharisees, who did hold this point of view. Therefore, this charge hardly made him the purveyor of a dangerous cult. Paul didn't attempt to preach Christ at this hearing. He merely laid the groundwork for demonstrating the reasonableness of Christianity. It was no bizarre mystery religion or antigovernment sect. If Rome had no objection to Jews, Rome should have no objection to Christians. Whereas Tertullus had tried to claim that their differences were political, Paul demonstrated that the real issue was theological.

He concluded this part of his defense with a declaration every reasonable person should affirm, no matter what philosophy or religion they claimed: "In view of this, I also do my best to maintain always a blameless conscience both before God and before men" (24:16). Unfortunately, neither Felix nor Ananias could say this along with Paul. Not by a long shot!

— 24:17-21 —

Paul turned to their third charge, that he had tried to defile the Jewish temple (24:6). A person who wants to defile a temple doesn't donate money to it first. He had entered the temple to pay large sums of money in support of the four Nazirites (24:17). Besides this, Paul had arrived in Jerusalem with a load of money given by the believers in Corinth and Philippi to ease the suffering of Jewish Christians (Rom. 15:25-26; 1 Cor. 16:1-4; 2 Cor. 8:1-4). Furthermore, when he was seized, he had gone through a rite of purification along with the four devout men—not the actions of a defiler (Acts 21:26; 24:18).

He then turned to the group of accusers from Jerusalem and noted that the men who had actually started the commotion, the nonbelieving Jews from Ephesus (21:27), were not present to testify for the prosecution (24:19). The letter from Lysias to Felix had indicated that the actual complainants would present their charges in person (23:30). Where were they? They did not show up, so Paul challenged the temple officials to charge him with anything they had personally witnessed (24:20).

Paul closed his remarks with a frank admission. When standing before the Sanhedrin, he declared his belief in the resurrection of all humanity to face a final judgment before God, and it was this conviction for which he was on trial (24:21). He accomplished two objectives with this final statement. First, he reinforced the true nature of the high priest's dispute with him, which was entirely theological and not a matter for Roman interference. Second, he wanted Felix to think about his life and the eternal consequences of his sin. He hoped to establish the context for a future discussion concerning salvation.

— 24:22-23 —

Luke states that Felix had "a more exact knowledge about the Way" (24:22). There are two primary ways to interpret this editorial comment by Luke: (1) Felix already had a more exact knowledge about the Way, and so he put them off; or (2) Felix, now having gained a more exact knowledge about the Way, put them off.

The first option is possible. Felix's wife, Drusilla, was the daughter of Herod Agrippa I and, according to Luke, "a Jewess" (24:24). She may have had extended contact with Christians, especially in Caesarea, where many Jewish and Gentile believers lived. Felix could not have been procurator very long in Judea without at least some contact with Christians. Luke may have intended this to mean that Felix was not fooled by the temple leaders but could not ignore their thinly veiled political threats. I believe the second option is more probable, however. As a result of Paul's testimony, Felix gained a better understanding of the issues, which concerned Jewish theology, not Roman law. Nevertheless, the delegation from Jerusalem had him between a rock and a hard place.

Either way, Felix wasn't about to decide the case on its own merits or make a ruling based on justice. Perhaps not knowing exactly what to do, he procrastinated. He put off a decision on the pretext of getting more information from the commander in Jerusalem, Claudius Lysias. Of course, he never intended to do anything further with the case, at least in the immediate future. This can be seen in the orders he gave the centurion who served as his chief of security.

The phrase "to be kept in custody" (24:23) renders a Greek word meaning simply "to watch or guard." The term translated "freedom" means "liberty" or "relief." I would translate the command as "guard him so that he has liberty."[26] Paul was still in protective custody and had still not been charged with any wrongdoing. The hearing with the temple officials had been an arraignment upon which Felix had yet to rule. He really didn't care if Paul escaped; in fact, it might have solved his political problem.

— 24:24-25 —

"Some days later" (24:24) offers no clue about the length of time. Other occurrences of "some days" in Acts appear to designate a length of time shorter than a month (9:19; 10:48; 16:12). Felix apparently took a trip, perhaps to where his wife, Drusilla, had been staying, and then returned to Caesarea with her. She was his second wife. According to Tacitus, Felix had first married the great-granddaughter of Mark Antony and Cleopatra (also named Drusilla).[27] Not long after assuming power in Judea (AD 52), he met Drusilla, the daughter of Agrippa I and sister of Agrippa II. She would have been about fourteen at the time. He divorced his first wife and set out to break up the young Drusilla's marriage.[28] According to Josephus,

> He sent to her a person whose name was Simon, one of his friends; a Jew he was, and by birth a Cypriot, and one who pretended to be a magician, and endeavored to persuade her to forsake her present husband, and marry him; and promised, that if she would not refuse him, he would make her a happy woman. Accordingly she acted ill, and because she was desirous to avoid her sister Bernice's envy, for she was very ill treated by her on account of her beauty, was prevailed upon to transgress the laws of her forefathers, and to marry Felix.[29]

In any case, the illicitly married couple sent for Paul to hear him preach. It appears that Felix was earnest enough to give the apostle an open-minded hearing; I don't think he used Paul for entertainment. If so, he didn't like what he heard. Paul's message discussed tender subjects with the couple; neither had been paragons of righteousness and self-control. When he began to talk about the last judgment, Felix recoiled and fell back on his standard response—procrastination (24:25). He sent Paul away just like he had sent the temple officials home with a promise to revisit the issue later.

Note Felix's key phrase, the battle cry of the procrastinator: "when I find time."

— 24:26-27 —

We often refer to this period as "Paul's Caesarean imprisonment," but there are worse places to be held captive than the governor's palace. Paul had free rein within the Praetorian grounds. He could receive visitors and move freely among the palace guard. He undoubtedly took the opportunity to interact with Felix's high-level visitors. This went on for two years as the procurator conversed with Paul, hoping to wheedle a bribe from Paul's rich friends. Although he was curious about Paul's faith, he showed no signs of making a decision or trusting Christ. Eventually he returned to Rome, although history does not tell us why. Tacitus and others report that he narrowly escaped punishment for plundering the Jews during his rule. This explains why he detained Paul for so long: He needed the goodwill of his subjects to balance his cruelty.

After two years of waiting for a decision from Felix regarding either the case against him or the case he had made for Christ—*nothing*. Felix left for Rome and Festus took his place. As Dr. Tom Constable states so well, "The apostle had become a political pawn in the will of God."[30]

APPLICATION: ACTS 24:10-27

Wait No More

Even though Felix gave Paul a hearing, he failed to act on the message that had been pricking his conscience. History shows that his attitude toward Paul and spiritual things continued to harden. As far as we can tell, Felix died in his sins.

Procrastination never pays. The more you believe there is no hurry, the less concern you have for the consequences of inaction. God sent His Holy Spirit, in part, to bring fear, to make lost people aware of their guilt before their Creator. The experience of Felix—and countless procrastinators throughout history—highlights a couple of lingering lessons.

First, *delay hardens the heart against the edge of the sword of the Spirit*. The truth of God never dulls, never loses its edge; still, the heart can grow callous so the sword no longer causes discomfort. It's possible to become a scholarly authority on Scripture and lose the ability to be affected by the Word of God. Failing to heed its warnings and delaying necessary responses create this insensitivity. And it's deadly! Would-be saints go to their graves without concern for what comes later. Even those who believe can harden their hearts, sometimes becoming shining-knight examples of Christianity on the outside yet completely corrupt within.

Don't put off important decisions, especially when confronted by

Scripture and convicted by the Holy Spirit. Heed your concerns when they first upset your conscience. Take them to God and let Him do whatever is necessary to settle the issue.

Second, *delay distracts the mind with less important issues.* Felix came face to face with his sin and his need for Christ, but he backed away and put off the necessary decision. He then became interested in advancing his personal agenda, increasing his power, and making money. There was suddenly a materialistic motivation for this whole religious discussion. He met with Paul for two years. He interacted personally with the most articulate spokesman for Jesus Christ in the first century—for two years! Imagine the dialogues they must have had. Yet he maintained a consistent preoccupation with the horizontal realm.

This is unbelievably common in religious circles: intellectual discussions, materialistic motivation, horizontal preoccupation. People feel good about raising money for good causes, discussing deep subjects, and pleasing people, yet they never plan to say, "Before God, I am guilty. I open my life. I bow before Him. I ask Him to do radical things in my life, my home, my business, and my social contacts, because I want to be a disciple of Jesus Christ."

One day will be your last to heed the gospel of Jesus Christ. If you have not, don't delay. There is a heaven. There is a hell. And there is a hurry.

Disciplines that Cultivate Maturity
ACTS 25:1-22

NASB

¹Festus then, having arrived in the province, three days later went up to Jerusalem from Caesarea. ²And the chief priests and the leading men of the Jews brought charges against Paul, and they were urging him, ³requesting a ᵃconcession against ᵇPaul, that he might ᶜhave him brought to Jerusalem (*at the same time,* setting an ambush to kill him on the way). ⁴Festus then answered that Paul was being kept in custody at Caesarea and that he himself was about to leave shortly. ⁵"Therefore,"

NLT

¹Three days after Festus arrived in Caesarea to take over his new responsibilities, he left for Jerusalem, ²where the leading priests and other Jewish leaders met with him and made their accusations against Paul. ³They asked Festus as a favor to transfer Paul to Jerusalem (planning to ambush and kill him on the way). ⁴But Festus replied that Paul was at Caesarea and he himself would be returning there soon. ⁵So he said, "Those of you in authority

he said, "let the influential men among you ᵃgo there with me, and if there is anything wrong ᵇabout the man, let them ᶜprosecute him."

⁶After he had spent not more than eight or ten days among them, he went down to Caesarea, and on the next day he took his seat on the tribunal and ordered Paul to be brought. ⁷After Paul arrived, the Jews who had come down from Jerusalem stood around him, bringing many and serious charges against him which they could not prove, ⁸while Paul said in his own defense, "I have committed no offense either against the Law of the Jews or against the temple or against Caesar." ⁹But Festus, wishing to do the Jews a favor, answered Paul and said, "Are you willing to go up to Jerusalem and ᵃstand trial before me on these *charges*?" ¹⁰But Paul said, "I am standing before Caesar's tribunal, where I ought to be tried. I have done no wrong to *the* Jews, as you also very well know. ¹¹If, then, I am a wrongdoer and have committed anything worthy of death, I do not refuse to die; but if none of those things is *true* of which these men accuse me, no one can hand me over to them. I appeal to Caesar." ¹²Then when Festus had conferred with ᵃhis council, he answered, "You have appealed to Caesar, to Caesar you shall go."

¹³Now when several days had elapsed, King Agrippa and Bernice arrived at Caesarea ᵃand paid their respects to Festus. ¹⁴While they were spending many days there, Festus laid Paul's case before the king, saying, "There is a man who was left as a prisoner by Felix; ¹⁵and when I was at Jerusalem, the chief priests and the elders of the Jews brought charges against him, asking for a sentence of condemnation against him. ¹⁶I answered them that it is not the custom of the Romans to hand over any man before the accused

can return with me. If Paul has done anything wrong, you can make your accusations."

⁶About eight or ten days later Festus returned to Caesarea, and on the following day he took his seat in court and ordered that Paul be brought in. ⁷When Paul arrived, the Jewish leaders from Jerusalem gathered around and made many serious accusations they couldn't prove.

⁸Paul denied the charges. "I am not guilty of any crime against the Jewish laws or the Temple or the Roman government," he said.

⁹Then Festus, wanting to please the Jews, asked him, "Are you willing to go to Jerusalem and stand trial before me there?"

¹⁰But Paul replied, "No! This is the official Roman court, so I ought to be tried right here. You know very well I am not guilty of harming the Jews. ¹¹If I have done something worthy of death, I don't refuse to die. But if I am innocent, no one has a right to turn me over to these men to kill me. I appeal to Caesar!"

¹²Festus conferred with his advisers and then replied, "Very well! You have appealed to Caesar, and to Caesar you will go!"

¹³A few days later King Agrippa arrived with his sister, Bernice,* to pay their respects to Festus. ¹⁴During their stay of several days, Festus discussed Paul's case with the king. "There is a prisoner here," he told him, "whose case was left for me by Felix. ¹⁵When I was in Jerusalem, the leading priests and Jewish elders pressed charges against him and asked me to condemn him. ¹⁶I pointed out to them that Roman law does not convict people without a trial. They must be given an

meets his accusers face to face and has an opportunity to make his defense against the charges. ¹⁷So after they had assembled here, I did not delay, but on the next day took my seat on the tribunal and ordered the man to be brought before me. ¹⁸When the accusers stood up, they *began* bringing charges against him not of such crimes as I was expecting, ¹⁹but they *simply* had some points of disagreement with him about their own ᵃreligion and about a dead man, Jesus, whom Paul asserted to be alive. ²⁰Being at a loss how to investigate ᵃsuch matters, I asked whether he was willing to go to Jerusalem and there stand trial on these matters. ²¹But when Paul appealed to be held in custody for ᵃthe Emperor's decision, I ordered him to be kept in custody until I send him to Caesar." ²²Then Agrippa *said* to Festus, "I also would like to hear the man myself." "Tomorrow," he said, "you shall hear him."

25:3 ᵃOr *favor* ᵇLit *him* ᶜLit *send for him to Jerusalem* 25:5 ᵃLit *go down* ᵇLit *in* ᶜOr *accuse* 25:9 ᵃLit *be judged* 25:12 ᵃA different group from that mentioned in Acts 4:15 and 24:20 25:13 ᵃLit *greeting Festus* 25:19 ᵃOr *superstition* 25:20 ᵃLit *these* 25:21 ᵃLit *the Augustus's* (in this case Nero)

opportunity to confront their accusers and defend themselves.

¹⁷"When his accusers came here for the trial, I didn't delay. I called the case the very next day and ordered Paul brought in. ¹⁸But the accusations made against him weren't any of the crimes I expected. ¹⁹Instead, it was something about their religion and a dead man named Jesus, who Paul insists is alive. ²⁰I was at a loss to know how to investigate these things, so I asked him whether he would be willing to stand trial on these charges in Jerusalem. ²¹But Paul appealed to have his case decided by the emperor. So I ordered that he be held in custody until I could arrange to send him to Caesar."

²²"I'd like to hear the man myself," Agrippa said.

And Festus replied, "You will—tomorrow!"

25:13 Greek *Agrippa the king and Bernice arrived.*

Any worthwhile spiritual journey must include discipline. In the Christian life, we often think of spiritual disciplines in terms of prayer, reading Scripture, self-control, sacrifice, worship—activities that help us "know [Jesus Christ] and the power of His resurrection and the fellowship of His sufferings" (Phil. 3:10). These behaviors might be termed "active disciplines" because we voluntarily choose to engage ourselves in them. The Lord has not left us alone in our spiritual journey; in fact, He has taken responsibility for transforming us when we either can't or won't do it ourselves. This is His ongoing grace. Paul declared to his disciples in Philippi, "I am confident of this very thing, that He who began a good work in you will perfect it until the day of Christ Jesus" (Phil. 1:6). Consequently, some disciplines of the spiritual life God initiates without our permission, and He will use these times of training to mold us into the likeness of His Son.

These disciplines often come in unexpected forms. While Paul waited two years for Felix to make a decision—any decision!—Nero made a change. Suddenly another man took up residence in the Praetorium, and this promised to alter the course of Paul's life. The following four situations recounted during this period were opportunities for discipline in Paul's life:

1. Prolonged Delay (24:27)
2. False Accusations (25:6-8)
3. Unfair Exploitation (25:9-12)
4. Ongoing Uncertainty (25:13-22)

God initiates some disciplines, and He will be faithful to accomplish His divine purpose within believers; nevertheless, we have a stake in the process of transformation. We may choose how to respond: We can resist His discipline by fighting our circumstances, we can ignore His lessons through destructive coping, or we can submit to His leading by trusting Him. The choice is ours, but He will accomplish His purpose regardless. Paul's responses provide a worthy example to follow.

— 25:1-5 —

Porcius Festus arrived in Judea to find the province a tangled mess, political intrigue at the top levels of government, and the streets infested with bandits and roving gangs of Sicarii who savaged villages for the purpose of advancing their political agenda. Almost nothing is known about Festus except that he shrewdly handled the problem of robbers by making use of an impostor. This person held himself out as a leader of bandits, promising to organize and lead them if they would meet him in the wilderness. Festus had forces waiting, and he put all the robbers to the sword. In one fell swoop, he solved the Sicarii problem.[31]

The tangled politics, however, proved infinitely more difficult. Within three days of arriving, he traveled to Jerusalem to meet with the political and religious leaders of Judea. In the absence of a king, this was the high priest and the chief priests, all of them Sadducees. By this time, Agrippa II had removed Ananias and installed Ishmael, son of Fabi, in his place;[32] however, Ananias remained very much a power behind the scenes, just like Annas during Jesus' trials.[33]

Festus discovered that after two years the religious leaders had not, in fact, lost interest in Paul's case. They were secretly hoping to create an opportunity to kill Paul. Among the many issues they had discussed

Sidelined

ACTS 24:27

Felix had allowed the dispute between the temple leaders and Paul to go unresolved for two years, perhaps hoping the chief priests would lose interest or Paul would escape or they would patch things up on their own—anything that would save him from having to take a stand. Paul spent those two years in a frustrating legal limbo, neither captive nor free, able to receive visitors but unable to minister at his full potential. Two years in Macedonia and Achaia had established half a dozen thriving churches—perhaps more. Two years in Asia had laid the foundation for a church that would lead the region in Christian theology. Who knows what two years in the western frontier might have accomplished? Instead, Paul remained a prisoner of God's sovereign design. Remarkably, the apostle didn't attempt a jailbreak from his divinely constructed cell. He patiently allowed the Lord's plan to unfold. God had promised Rome; Paul waited on the Lord.

When I left the near-ideal and exciting ministry of our church in Fullerton, California, for the unfamiliar culture of academia at Dallas Seminary, I began a two-year spiritual journey I did not anticipate. This move not only required a change in our living address, but also that we relocate the entire ministry of Insight for Living, which proved to be a lengthy, monumental, and financially stretching undertaking that amounted to starting over virtually from scratch. During that time, Cynthia and I had to spend many of our weeks apart. She managed the transition from California while I fulfilled my responsibilities in Dallas. Maintaining two homes, therefore, was out of the question. So, I took up residence in an apartment over the garage of a board member's house for the next two years.

After settling in, the truth began to sink in. I had left the pleasant weather of California for the searing summers, bleak winters, and turbulent skies of Texas. I had left a home filled with twenty-three years of our fondest memories, where all four of our children had grown to adulthood, to a space the size of which I hadn't squeezed into since attending Dallas Seminary as a student. But most difficult of all, I was a pastor without a church—a shepherd without a flock. Nevertheless, in terms of ministry, I was exactly where God wanted

(continued on next page)

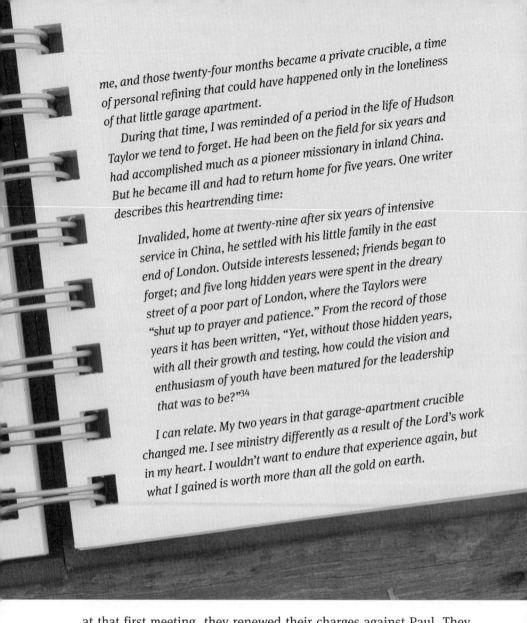

me, and those twenty-four months became a private crucible, a time of personal refining that could have happened only in the loneliness of that little garage apartment.

During that time, I was reminded of a period in the life of Hudson Taylor we tend to forget. He had been on the field for six years and had accomplished much as a pioneer missionary in inland China. But he became ill and had to return home for five years. One writer describes this heartrending time:

Invalided, home at twenty-nine after six years of intensive service in China, he settled with his little family in the east end of London. Outside interests lessened; friends began to forget; and five long hidden years were spent in the dreary street of a poor part of London, where the Taylors were "shut up to prayer and patience." From the record of those years it has been written, "Yet, without those hidden years, with all their growth and testing, how could the vision and enthusiasm of youth have been matured for the leadership that was to be?"[34]

I can relate. My two years in that garage-apartment crucible changed me. I see ministry differently as a result of the Lord's work in my heart. I wouldn't want to endure that experience again, but what I gained is worth more than all the gold on earth.

at that first meeting, they renewed their charges against Paul. They made what appeared to be a reasonable request (25:3). The term rendered "concession" is *charis* [5485], which we frequently translate as "grace," "favor," or "act of goodwill." They politely asked Festus for a small indulgence as a gesture of goodwill: "have him brought to Jerusalem" to stand trial.

Festus needed a little goodwill from the temple leaders. We saw earlier that his two immediate predecessors, Cumanus (AD 48–52) and Felix (AD 52–59), had not managed their relationships with the Jews well and had suffered as a result. Festus would have recognized the need to have a much better relationship with the Jews if he were to survive politically as procurator. So in his interactions with the priests, he needed to tread lightly. Instead of granting their request, he subtly reminded them that Paul remained in protective custody for a reason; besides, he had not planned to be in Jerusalem long. As a concession, he returned the invitation to join him in Caesarea and hold the trial there.

It was a shrewd move on his part; he avoided giving the priests what they wanted without leaving a reason to take offense.

— 25:6-8 —

After his introductory conference with the high priest and the Sanhedrin, Festus returned to Caesarea and convened a tribunal to deal with Paul. Whereas Felix had held an informal hearing to determine whether charges should be made official, Festus proved more decisive. He took his place on the "tribunal" (*bēma* [968]), which was the ancient equivalent of donning the judge's vestments and taking a seat on the bench with gavel in hand. He committed himself to resolving the issue officially and for the record. The charges presented were numerous and serious. The accusations came from the Jewish nation's most respected institution, presumably from men deserving of such high positions of religious authority. Festus sat on the *bēma* formulating opinions about the man Felix had detained as one lie after another tumbled from the group of men surrounding the lone apostle.

The affliction of false accusations can be another soul-refining experience. They force the accused to take honest stock of his or her deeds, to sift nuggets of truth from the fiction, and to take responsibility for wrongdoing and discard the rest. The falsely accused learn who they are in Christ, independent of their peers' opinions, and then emerge from that particular flame purified of both grandiosity and self-recrimination.

The temple officials had two years to develop a strategy. Even so, they could offer no proof of their claims. Festus respected the Jews' power, but he held the fate of a citizen in his hands, which had far-reaching implications as well. Paul offered a succinct defense, recognizing that without a solid case against him, he had nothing to rebut. His three denials (25:8) exempted him from trial in Jerusalem ("against the Law of the Jews") or in a Roman court ("against Caesar"). He offered a simple, measured, factual response, the kind that only a confident, innocent defendant can give.

— 25:9-12 —

Luke stated earlier the reason Paul's case had not been resolved for two years: "Wishing to do the Jews a favor, Felix left Paul imprisoned" (24:27). The procurator had changed, but the motive to use the apostle like a pawn remained the same. Festus, too, hoped to gain the goodwill of the temple leaders (25:9), but he couldn't set aside justice, and he couldn't compel Paul to stand trial in Jerusalem; therefore, he hoped Paul would be naive enough to agree to a change of venue. Clearly, he underestimated Paul, who clarified the situation for the record. He had not yet been charged with any crime against Rome, so the court had no jurisdiction to compel him to do anything. Furthermore, the crimes alleged by the Jews had no evidence to support them, so the empire had a duty to protect its citizen.

To borrow from Dr. Tom Constable's earlier comment: The apostle had become a political pawn of men in a chess game run by God.[35] Unfair exploitation refines the soul by clarifying the issue of submission. Not submission to people—submission to God. It must have cut Paul to the core when everyone in the courtroom treated him like a *thing*. All the same, he recognized that God could have stopped the proceedings; He could have intervened to help Paul. He submitted to the will of God, but he refused to be treated unjustly by the enemies of God. That gave him the courage to state the truth boldly and without apology, ready to accept the consequences of his stand.

He recognized the trap beginning to form in front of him. Rather than risk a ruling in favor of the high priest out of expediency, Paul preempted the procurator's next move by requesting a privilege available to all citizens. He requested to have his case heard by the emperor himself (25:11). Some dispute whether he had this automatic right; Festus may not have been compelled by Roman law to grant Paul's request. He consulted with his *consilium*, the panel of legal advisors kept on hand for procurators who may not have expertise in law. While Festus may not have been legally bound to comply, the appeal solved his problem. Passing the apostle up to a higher court removed him from the middle of a no-win scenario (25:12).

— 25:13 —

Uncertainty has a way of wearing down even the strongest personalities. Paul had endured more than two years of ambiguity. Humanly speaking, his future lay in the hands of people who played by no set of rules except their own, who viewed him as no more valuable than a pawn to push around in the interests of self. With the trial in Caesarea over, Paul waited to be transferred to Rome, just as Jesus had promised (23:11). All the same, the apostle's immediate future remained uncertain. A lot of time and many miles lay between Caesarea and Rome, and the Lord's reassurance didn't reveal the outcome of his testimony in Rome, only that he would testify there. All the same, Paul submitted to the plan of God. Where his certainty in people and circumstances failed, he looked to his Master for reassurance.

It's a good thing Paul kept his eyes on Christ during this time; the characters about to walk into this theater of the absurd would top all who had come before. And that's saying a lot! Ananias was a ravenously evil high priest whose talent for crime rivaled the legendary Annas. Felix, the Teflon procurator, had the uncanny ability to immerse himself in corruption, including wife stealing, bribery, extortion, double-dealing politics, and murder, yet rise higher in society without so much as a spot. Festus, the least dysfunctional character of all, still sailed rudderless through life, more than willing to sacrifice justice for selfish gain and serve up an innocent man for expediency. Now, enter Agrippa II and Bernice.

If you read Acts 25:13–26:32 and come away with the impression that Agrippa and Bernice were husband and wife, you would have seen them as others did in the first century. Many who didn't know any better assumed they were a married couple. They traveled together, appeared together at public functions, and neither spent much time with a spouse. Historians don't mention a wife for Agrippa; Bernice was married only a short time to her uncle, Herod of Chalcis, before he died. She didn't stay long with her second husband before leaving him to be with Agrippa.[36] By most accounts the two were very much in love but couldn't legally marry. Even in the pagan culture of the Romans, *a brother could not marry his sister!*

— 25:14-22 —

Luke records this visit from Agrippa and Bernice for two reasons. His first purpose can be found in the explanation provided by Festus in which he summarized and clarified the legal issues involved. Before moving the story forward, the reading audience needs to understand the situation.

Second, Luke intends to further vindicate Paul of any crime. The king would eventually declare him innocent (26:31-32), which is significant. Despite his utter immorality, no other figure could speak more objectively. Agrippa had no quarrel with either Festus or the high priest. In fact, upon the death of Bernice's husband, he received the authority to appoint the high priest at his own whim, and he already had done so by this meeting. Furthermore, as a Jew (Luke called his other sister, Drusilla, a Jewess; 24:24), he was familiar with Hebrew law, and as a client king, he understood Roman politics and law. Therefore, he could speak objectively and knowledgeably.

Festus told Agrippa about Paul's case, but he wasn't seeking any real advice; he pretended to need Agrippa's help in order to win him as an ally—one with the power to appoint the high priest. Once again, "the apostle had become a political pawn in the will of God."[37]

APPLICATION: ACTS 25:1-22

Let Us Grow Up, Not Just Old

Maturity is one of those qualities we all desire. It's not simply a matter of growing old in the Lord but growing up in Him. We have a wonderful example in the life of the apostle Paul, especially as we see him under the stress of one trial after another in our study of the book of Acts. As the Lord continues His transformation process, applying divine discipline as needed, I feel reassured by three truths.

First, *the disciplines God applies assure us of His love* (see Heb. 12:5-11). An athlete knows that when a coach stops riding his or her case, it's not a good sign. That means the coach considers other players more promising and, therefore, a better investment of time. We have God's assurance that He will never give up on us; He will always invest Himself in our continued growth and maturity. Regrettably, not many opportunities for growth are easy, brief, or pleasant. Nevertheless, they offer tangible evidence that the Holy Spirit remains committed and involved.

Second, *the reproofs they bring carry God's message*. At the conclusion of a crucible experience, something amazing happens. A part of our spirit has been transformed. A place deep within us that once responded to temptation now resonates in perfect tune with a truth from Scripture. A biblical truth we once accepted intellectually, but never completely assimilated, now enlightens every aspect of our lives. We see the world more clearly. We experience relationships more fully. We make decisions more wisely. We work, love, serve, create, learn, and discern more effectively. With each reproof, we incrementally think and behave more like Christ.

Third, *the results of both disciplines and reproofs make us invaluable for His use.* The Lord doesn't lift believers out of the world when they first begin to trust Him. He has us here for a reason. When Jesus prayed on our behalf, He said, "As You sent Me into the world, I also have sent them into the world. For their sakes I sanctify Myself, that they themselves also may be sanctified in truth" (John 17:18-19). Just before He departed physically, He said to His followers, "You will receive power when the Holy Spirit has come upon you; and you shall be My witnesses both in Jerusalem, and in all Judea and Samaria, and even to the remotest part of the earth" (Acts 1:8). He encourages us and equips us through disciplines from the outside and by His Spirit on the inside so that we might fulfill our purposes more effectively.

God has a plan for you. He made you with a specific purpose in mind, not because He needs you—He can achieve all things on His own—but to let you join Him in accomplishing something wonderful and then share the joy of victory with Him. His disciplines help prepare you to fulfill your unique role in His plan to redeem the world from evil.

Almost Persuaded
ACTS 25:23-26:32

NASB

23 So, on the next day when Agrippa came ᵃtogether with Bernice amid great pomp, and entered the auditorium ᵇaccompanied by the ᶜcommanders and the prominent men of the city, at the command of Festus, Paul was brought in. 24 Festus said, "King Agrippa, and all you gentlemen here present with us, you see this man about whom all the people of the Jews appealed to me, both at Jerusalem and here, loudly declaring that he ought not to live any longer. 25 But I found that he had committed nothing worthy of death; and since he himself appealed to ᵃthe Emperor, I decided to send him. 26 ᵃYet I have nothing definite about him to write to my lord. Therefore I have brought him before you *all* and especially

NLT

23 So the next day Agrippa and Bernice arrived at the auditorium with great pomp, accompanied by military officers and prominent men of the city. Festus ordered that Paul be brought in. 24 Then Festus said, "King Agrippa and all who are here, this is the man whose death is demanded by all the Jews, both here and in Jerusalem. 25 But in my opinion he has done nothing deserving death. However, since he appealed his case to the emperor, I have decided to send him to Rome.

26 "But what shall I write the emperor? For there is no clear charge against him. So I have brought him before all of you, and especially you,

481

NASB

before you, King Agrippa, so that after the investigation has taken place, I may have something to write. [27] For it seems absurd to me in sending a prisoner, not to indicate also the charges against him."

[26:1] Agrippa said to Paul, "You are permitted to speak for yourself." Then Paul stretched out his hand and *proceeded* to make his defense:

[2] "In regard to all the things of which I am accused by the Jews, I consider myself fortunate, King Agrippa, that I am about to make my defense before you today; [3a] especially because you are an expert in all customs and [b] questions among *the* Jews; therefore I beg you to listen to me patiently.

[4] "So then, all Jews know my manner of life from my youth up, which from the beginning was spent among my *own* nation and at Jerusalem; [5] since they have known about me for a long time, if they are willing to testify, that I lived *as* a Pharisee according to the strictest sect of our religion. [6] And now I am [a] standing trial for the hope of the promise made by God to our fathers; [7] *the promise* to which our twelve tribes hope to attain, as they earnestly serve *God* night and day. And for this hope, O King, I am being accused by Jews. [8] Why is it considered incredible among you *people* if God does raise the dead?

[9] "So then, I thought to myself that I had to do many things hostile to the name of Jesus of Nazareth. [10] And this is [a] just what I did in Jerusalem; not only did I lock up many of the [b] saints in prisons, having received authority from the chief priests, but also when they were being put to death I cast my vote against them. [11] And as I punished them often in all the synagogues, I tried to force them to blaspheme; and being furiously

NLT

King Agrippa, so that after we examine him, I might have something to write. [27] For it makes no sense to send a prisoner to the emperor without specifying the charges against him!"

[26:1] Then Agrippa said to Paul, "You may speak in your defense."

So Paul, gesturing with his hand, started his defense: [2] "I am fortunate, King Agrippa, that you are the one hearing my defense today against all these accusations made by the Jewish leaders, [3] for I know you are an expert on all Jewish customs and controversies. Now please listen to me patiently!

[4] "As the Jewish leaders are well aware, I was given a thorough Jewish training from my earliest childhood among my own people and in Jerusalem. [5] If they would admit it, they know that I have been a member of the Pharisees, the strictest sect of our religion. [6] Now I am on trial because of my hope in the fulfillment of God's promise made to our ancestors. [7] In fact, that is why the twelve tribes of Israel zealously worship God night and day, and they share the same hope I have. Yet, Your Majesty, they accuse me for having this hope! [8] Why does it seem incredible to any of you that God can raise the dead?

[9] "I used to believe that I ought to do everything I could to oppose the very name of Jesus the Nazarene.* [10] Indeed, I did just that in Jerusalem. Authorized by the leading priests, I caused many believers* there to be sent to prison. And I cast my vote against them when they were condemned to death. [11] Many times I had them punished in the synagogues to get them to curse Jesus.* I was so violently opposed to

enraged at them, I kept pursuing them even to ªforeign cities.

12 "ªWhile so engaged as I was journeying to Damascus with the authority and commission of the chief priests, 13 at midday, O King, I saw on the way a light from heaven, ªbrighter than the sun, shining all around me and those who were journeying with me. 14 And when we had all fallen to the ground, I heard a voice saying to me in the ªHebrew dialect, 'Saul, Saul, why are you persecuting Me? ᵇIt is hard for you to kick against the goads.' 15 And I said, 'Who are You, Lord?' And the Lord said, 'I am Jesus whom you are persecuting. 16 But get up and stand on your feet; for this purpose I have appeared to you, to appoint you a minister and a witness not only to the things which you have ªseen, but also to the things in which I will appear to you; 17 rescuing you from the *Jewish* people and from the Gentiles, to whom I am sending you, 18 to open their eyes so that they may turn from darkness to light and from the dominion of Satan to God, that they may receive forgiveness of sins and an inheritance among those who have been sanctified by faith in Me.'

19 "So, King Agrippa, I did not prove disobedient to the heavenly vision, 20 but *kept* declaring both to those of Damascus first, and *also* at Jerusalem and *then* throughout all the region of Judea, and *even* to the Gentiles, that they should repent and turn to God, performing deeds appropriate to repentance. 21 For this reason *some* Jews seized me in the temple and tried to put me to death. 22 So, having obtained help from God, I stand to this day testifying both to small and great, stating nothing but what the Prophets and Moses said was going to take place; 23ª that ᵇthe Christ was ᶜto suffer, *and* ªthat by reason of *His* resurrection

them that I even chased them down in foreign cities.

12 "One day I was on such a mission to Damascus, armed with the authority and commission of the leading priests. 13 About noon, Your Majesty, as I was on the road, a light from heaven brighter than the sun shone down on me and my companions. 14 We all fell down, and I heard a voice saying to me in Aramaic,* 'Saul, Saul, why are you persecuting me? It is useless for you to fight against my will.*'

15 "'Who are you, lord?' I asked.

"And the Lord replied, 'I am Jesus, the one you are persecuting. 16 Now get to your feet! For I have appeared to you to appoint you as my servant and witness. Tell people that you have seen me, and tell them what I will show you in the future. 17 And I will rescue you from both your own people and the Gentiles. Yes, I am sending you to the Gentiles 18 to open their eyes, so they may turn from darkness to light and from the power of Satan to God. Then they will receive forgiveness for their sins and be given a place among God's people, who are set apart by faith in me.'

19 "And so, King Agrippa, I obeyed that vision from heaven. 20 I preached first to those in Damascus, then in Jerusalem and throughout all Judea, and also to the Gentiles, that all must repent of their sins and turn to God—and prove they have changed by the good things they do. 21 Some Jews arrested me in the Temple for preaching this, and they tried to kill me. 22 But God has protected me right up to this present time so I can testify to everyone, from the least to the greatest. I teach nothing except what the prophets and Moses said would happen—23 that the Messiah would suffer and be the first to rise

NASB

from the dead He would be the first to proclaim light both to the *Jewish* people and to the Gentiles."

²⁴While *Paul* was saying this in his defense, Festus said in a loud voice, "Paul, you are out of your mind! ᵃ*Your* great learning is ᵇdriving you mad." ²⁵But Paul said, "I am not out of my mind, most excellent Festus, but I utter words ᵃof sober truth. ²⁶For the king ᵃknows about these matters, and I speak to him also with confidence, since I am persuaded that none of these things escape his notice; for this has not been done in a ᵇcorner. ²⁷King Agrippa, do you believe the Prophets? I know that you ᵃdo." ²⁸Agrippa *replied* to Paul, "ᵃIn a short time you ᵇwill persuade me to ᶜbecome a Christian." ²⁹And Paul *said*, "ᵃI would wish to God, that whether ᵇin a short or long time, not only you, but also all who hear me this day, might become such as I am, except for these chains."

³⁰The king stood up and the governor and Bernice, and those who were sitting with them, ³¹and when they had gone aside, they *began* talking to one another, saying, "This man is not doing anything worthy of death or ᵃimprisonment." ³²And Agrippa said to Festus, "This man might have been set free if he had not appealed to Caesar."

25:23 ᵃLit *and Bernice* ᵇLit *and with* ᶜI.e. chiliarchs, in command of one thousand troops 25:25 ᵃV 21, note 1 25:26 ᵃLit *About whom I have nothing definite* 26:3 ᵃOr *because you are especially expert* ᵇOr *controversial issues* 26:6 ᵃLit *being tried* 26:10 ᵃLit *also* ᵇOr *holy ones* 26:11 ᵃOr *outlying* 26:12 ᵃLit *In which things* 26:13 ᵃLit *above the brightness of* 26:14 ᵃI.e. Jewish Aramaic ᵇAn idiom referring to an animal's futile resistance to being prodded with goads 26:16 ᵃTwo early mss read *seen Me* 26:23 ᵃLit *whether* ᵇI.e. the Messiah ᶜLit *subject to suffering* 26:24 ᵃLit *The many letters* ᵇLit *turning you to madness* 26:25 ᵃLit *of truth and rationality* 26:26 ᵃOr *understands* ᵇI.e. a hidden or secret place 26:27 ᵃLit *believe* 26:28 ᵃOr *With a little* ᵇOr *are trying to convince* ᶜLit *make* 26:29 ᵃOr *I would pray to* ᵇOr *with a little or with much* 26:31 ᵃLit *bonds*

NLT

from the dead, and in this way announce God's light to Jews and Gentiles alike."

²⁴Suddenly, Festus shouted, "Paul, you are insane. Too much study has made you crazy!"

²⁵But Paul replied, "I am not insane, Most Excellent Festus. What I am saying is the sober truth. ²⁶And King Agrippa knows about these things. I speak boldly, for I am sure these events are all familiar to him, for they were not done in a corner! ²⁷King Agrippa, do you believe the prophets? I know you do—"

²⁸Agrippa interrupted him. "Do you think you can persuade me to become a Christian so quickly?"*

²⁹Paul replied, "Whether quickly or not, I pray to God that both you and everyone here in this audience might become the same as I am, except for these chains."

³⁰Then the king, the governor, Bernice, and all the others stood and left. ³¹As they went out, they talked it over and agreed, "This man hasn't done anything to deserve death or imprisonment."

³²And Agrippa said to Festus, "He could have been set free if he hadn't appealed to Caesar."

26:9 Or *Jesus of Nazareth.* 26:10 Greek *many of God's holy people.* 26:11 Greek *to blaspheme.* 26:14a Or *Hebrew.* 26:14b Greek *It is hard for you to kick against the oxgoads.* 26:28 Or *"A little more, and your arguments would make me a Christian."*

In the early years of the church, many Roman rulers thought nothing of exterminating Christians. Around AD 100, Pliny the Younger wrote to the emperor, Trajan, explaining his process for identifying and slaughtering Christians in Bithynia-Pontus, where he had been appointed governor:

> The method I have observed towards those who have been brought before me as Christians is this: I asked them whether they were Christians; if they admitted it, I repeated the question twice, and threatened them with punishment; if they persisted, I ordered them to be at once punished: for I was persuaded, whatever the nature of their opinions might be, a contumacious and inflexible obstinacy certainly deserved correction. There were others also brought before me possessed with the same infatuation, but being Roman citizens, I directed them to be sent to Rome. But this crime spreading (as is usually the case) while it was actually under prosecution, several instances of the same nature. An anonymous information was laid before me containing a charge against several persons, who upon examination denied they were Christians, or had ever been so. They repeated after me an invocation to the gods, and offered religious rites with wine and incense before your statue (which for that purpose I had ordered to be brought, together with those of the gods), and even reviled the name of Christ: whereas there is no forcing, it is said, those who are really Christians into any of these compliances: I thought it proper, therefore, to discharge them. Some among those who were accused by a witness in person at first confessed themselves Christians, but immediately after denied it; the rest owned indeed that they had been of that number formerly, but had now (some above three, others more, and a few above twenty years ago) renounced that error. They all worshipped your statue and the images of the gods, uttering imprecations at the same time against the name of Christ. They affirmed the whole of their guilt, or their error, was, that they met on a stated day before it was light, and addressed a form of prayer to Christ, as to a divinity, binding themselves by a solemn oath, not for the purposes of any wicked design, but never to commit any fraud, theft, or adultery, never to falsify their word, nor deny a trust when they should be called upon to deliver it up; after which it was their custom to separate, and then reassemble, to eat in common a harmless meal.[38]

Times have changed for Christians over the past twenty centuries, and no more so than in Western countries where the culture rests on a long heritage of Christendom. Even though the tide has begun to turn against Christianity in the West in recent years, we don't suffer the kind of wholesale slaughter that many of our forebears came to accept as the price of discipleship. (God forbid that it should ever occur again.) Consequently, it's difficult for us to imagine what Paul faced when he stood before the most powerful men in the world. His journey began with a mock trial in Jerusalem, where the high priest and the temple officials demanded his execution for no reason other than their own jealousy and hatred. That led to his protective custody in Caesarea and two more trials in which godless men used Paul like a pawn in their bid for more power and money. Each appearance before the *bēma* [968] raised the stakes as each judge wielded more authority than the one before.

Roman persecution of the Christians had not yet begun, but Paul didn't know whether it might not start with him. He likely saw the church and Rome on a collision course, for two reasons. First, the church had been growing exponentially around the empire and would soon become a force the Romans could not ignore. Second, the Christian worldview could not have been more antithetical to everything Rome treasured—Jesus, not the emperor, was Lord; Christianity was the only true religion, not one of many options in a pluralistic society; and God's laws, not the laws of Rome, had the final say in the life of the follower of Christ. So each trial increased the probability of Paul's death.

Paul's next stop on the road to Rome was Agrippa II, whose influence in Rome towered above both Festus and the high priest. Only Paul's Roman citizenship could protect him from instant execution at the whim of an angered Agrippa II, but with a wave of his hand or nod of his head, he could still make Paul's life miserable. Even so, Paul had to declare the truth and leave his fate in the hands of God.

Although the truth of Paul's innocence would become clear to Agrippa (26:32), and Paul's reasoning in support of the gospel would receive a hearing, the king would not be persuaded to act in any way. Even so, Paul's actions would set the pattern for all faithful believers standing before earthly powers to give account for their beliefs.

— 25:23-27 —

Luke highlights the vast difference between Agrippa and Paul by describing Agrippa's entry with great "pomp" (25:23; *phantasia* [5325]), a term that emphasizes the concept of appearance. One lexicon notes that the term implies "a cheap display of high status."[39] Agrippa entered the hall with attention to pageantry; Paul entered in chains (26:29). A company of high-ranking commanders[40] and influential city leaders surrounded Agrippa; Paul stood alone. Agrippa wielded great human power; Paul carried divine truth. This encounter, with all its contrasts, would become the first of many between Rome and Christendom.

Festus had arranged for the meeting, which could have been held privately. Instead, he invited everyone connected with Rome so he could make them witnesses to his political dilemma and perhaps create accomplices in his decision. With enough support among the elite in Caesarea, he could silence any objections raised by the temple. To accomplish this, he turned his political dilemma into a parlor game. He said, in effect, "I need your help in solving a puzzle. Those irrational Jews in Jerusalem have put me in a bad position, demanding that I hand over a Roman citizen for execution when they don't even have a case against him. He has appealed to Rome, which is his right, but it's ridiculous to send him without a credible charge. So, here's your assignment: Help me draft a reasonable charge for the letter to Caesar."

Politically, it was a brilliant move. He put all of Caesarea, including Agrippa, in his shoes so they could appreciate his quandary, and he made them allies against the temple officials.

— 26:1-3 —

Paul heard the speech given by Festus. He had an excellent view of the political landscape; he understood the complex interactions, he knew exactly what each party wanted, and he saw what the procurator was doing. Even though he had little time to arrange his presentation—Luke offers no indication of advance notice—Paul's lifetime of experiences had prepared him for this moment. He had spoken at length before audiences of all kinds: Jewish and Gentile, superstitious and philosophical, Hellenized and primitive, ignorant and academic—the whole gamut of humanity. And he had had two years to assess his situation.

The gesture of raising his hand (26:1) put him in a class of orator that cultured people were used to hearing. His opening remarks included compliments, which also followed the conventions of good speech. He didn't say anything untrue, but he found a way to affirm Agrippa. The king had not distinguished himself as a practicing Jew like his father, but he nevertheless understood the "customs and questions among the Jews" (26:3). The term translated "questions" (*zētēma* [2213]) refers to complex issues or matters of dispute. The king had a working knowledge of the theological matters creating tension between the different factions of Judaism.

— 26:4-7 —

The main body of his speech began with the expression "so then" (*men* [3303] + *oun* [3767]), which connected what he was about to say with what he had just stated. He affirmed that Agrippa knew the theological disputes that kept Jews continually fighting among themselves, "so then," he should appreciate why Paul's opponents hated him so passionately. Paul positioned the dispute as just one more "question" among many (cf. 26:3).

Paul admitted that the story of their disagreement went back many years to a time when he had been a shining example of their theological position, which included a great anticipation of the Messiah. The trouble had begun when he broke ranks and accepted Jesus Christ as "the hope" that all Hebrews had longed for since Moses (26:6). The men of the temple had tried to accuse him of other infractions, such as blaspheming the Law and desecrating the temple, but Paul exposed their hidden agenda. They had killed their Messiah, and they wanted to kill anyone who believed in Jesus Christ (26:7).

— 26:8 —

Paul's rhetorical question appears to disrupt the flow of his argument. The Pharisees, who represented the majority of Jews, believed in resurrection. The Sadducees, who had led the campaign to kill Jesus, had rejected Him before his followers claimed He had risen. Moreover, Jewish beliefs aside, the issue of resurrection could only alienate his audience. Believing in resurrection defied the predominant worldview in the empire, and Paul's assertion was not unlike preaching a round globe to a flat-earth audience. In terms of mounting a legal defense, the question of resurrection didn't fit here. It did, however, serve his greater purpose. Rather than use the occasion to win acquittal, he looked around the room and saw a fulfillment of a prophecy given about him long ago. Jesus had said, "He is a chosen instrument of Mine, to bear My name before the Gentiles and kings and the sons of Israel" (9:15).

Resurrection had nothing to do with Paul's defense, but it's central to the gospel. All of Christian theology hangs from this core issue.

— 26:9-11 —

His argument resumed with another "so then" (*men* [3303] + *oun* [3767]) connecting his next statement to his opening thought and saying, in essence, "I was in full agreement with the Pharisees, so then I did many things hostile to the name of Jesus" (see 26:9). Paul confessed to having stood with the temple authorities against those who believed in Jesus as the Christ and proclaimed His resurrection (26:10-11). His hatred for Christians also put him in good company with Herod's father, Agrippa I, who had killed the apostle James and tried to kill Peter. Paul had led the persecution that killed the Jesus-following sect of Jews and had set out for Damascus as their representative on an errand to round up Christians (26:12). He made this confession to explain how and why he made a 180-degree theological turn.

He had believed and behaved as he did because he thought he understood God and His plan. He didn't change to spite his former colleagues or to advance a political agenda or to increase his own power or wealth. His present circumstances should have been proof of that! If he had any selfish motive for breaking ranks with the temple, he could have solved his problem long ago by recanting his belief in Jesus. He changed his theology because a direct encounter with the risen Christ had revealed the truth about God and His plan.

— 26:12-18 —

Paul related the details of his conversion experience to explain how he could make so dramatic a change so suddenly and with such certainty. A personal, direct confrontation with the risen Christ had proven that the resurrection stories were true and that God had a plan Paul had not comprehended. In this recounting of the event, he revealed some new details. Jesus had spoken to him in "the Hebrew dialect" (possibly a Jewish dialect of Aramaic) to remove any doubt about the identity of the voice (26:14). He also revealed that the Lord had chastised him for resisting God's plan. The expression "kick against the goads" pictures a herd animal kicking the shepherd's stick. Like the modern image of "banging your head against a wall," it conveys the ideas of futility and hurting yourself while resisting the inevitable. Paul's audience would have recognized it from Greek literature as a common metaphor for opposing a god.

Paul also compressed the message he had received over several days into one extended conversation. Twenty-first-century Western historians might object to what they perceive as an inaccuracy, but Eastern storytellers did this frequently, and their audiences didn't interpret the timing as necessarily literal. They cared more about relationships and conversations; when people talked, and for how long, were secondary concerns. Some members of this audience would have been delighted to hear that the Hebrew God had repudiated what they considered Jewish arrogance and had approved Paul's ministry to Gentiles. They might have thought, *Ah, no wonder the Jews in Jerusalem hate this man so much.*

Paul concluded his quotation of Jesus with a clear statement of the gospel (26:18). The assembled "Gentiles and kings and the sons of Israel" (9:15) heard the offer of salvation from the lips of Christ as recounted by His apostle.

— 26:19-23 —

Paul told the story of his encounter with Jesus to establish an important point. His devotion and obedience was to a person, not a sectarian idea. He didn't risk his life merely for the sake of a theological point of view; God had established a relationship with him and had called him to become part of a plan heralded by all the prophets, which had been in motion since Moses. He had been given a crucial role in the plan of redemption, in which he would tell Jews and Gentiles alike about Christ's atoning sacrifice and the destruction of evil (26:18).

Paul's description of his ministry should not be viewed strictly in terms of chronology, but rather as one of priority. In this speech, he literally said, "To those in Damascus first and to Jerusalem and to the district of Judea and to the Gentiles, I was declaring repentance and turning to God" (my translation). Some see an apparent discrepancy in his letter to the Galatians, where he stated that after his time in Tarsus and Syrian Antioch, "I was still unknown by sight to the churches of Judea which were in Christ" (Gal. 1:22). But I don't see a discrepancy. After Paul returned from Arabia (Gal. 1:17) and had to escape from Damascus (Acts 9:23-25), he came to Jerusalem and was "speaking out boldly in the name of the Lord" (9:28) before another plot formed against him. To preserve his life, the disciples relocated him to Tarsus. So Paul did indeed attempt to evangelize Judea, though not for very long. Even so, the chronology of his ministry was not his point. He intended to show that his own people had always been a priority to him throughout his ministry to the Gentiles. He turned to the Gentiles out of necessity because the Jews, for the most part, rejected the gospel. In every city he visited, he spoke in the synagogues first and then, when rejected, turned to the Gentiles.

Paul's priority on ministry to Jews further invalidated the charges against him. He had not forsaken his own people; they had forsaken him by rejecting the truth of their own Scriptures concerning the death and resurrection of their Messiah. Contained within this last statement in 26:23 was a countercharge. The temple had forsaken its duty to proclaim the "light" God had given them to steward (cf. Isa. 42:6; 49:6).

— 26:24-29 —

If these verses represented the apostle's verbatim address, this speech would have taken fewer than five minutes to deliver; however, we must remember that Luke recorded a summary of Paul's address, not a transcript. This is implicit when Festus expresses his admiration for the extent of Paul's knowledge, commenting on his "great learning" (26:24). This suggests that Paul had supported all of his statements with logic and Scripture. Indeed, Paul affirmed, "I have declared words of truth and rationality" (26:25; my literal translation).

Festus suggested that the apostle's great knowledge was "driving [him] mad" (*mania* [3130]) because, in the Greek worldview, resurrection was a logical impossibility. Paul's response suggested that Agrippa held a broader perspective than the Greeks. Paul also presumed knowledge of the Scriptures on the part of Agrippa, suggesting that he had prior knowledge of the king's theological leanings. The apostle pressed Agrippa to affirm in public what he perhaps believed privately concerning "the Prophets" (26:26-27). If the king affirmed the Old Testament Prophets as Scripture, he would have aligned himself with the Pharisees—while his aristocratic peers were mostly Sadducees—and his belief in resurrection would have made him a laughingstock among his Gentile colleagues. Moreover, if Agrippa affirmed the writings of the Old Testament, he would affirm the basis for Paul's reasoning, and to affirm Paul's reasoning would be to affirm belief in the gospel.

Paul used the insult from Festus to lead Agrippa down a theological path he did not want to travel. He apparently held out the possibility of resurrection and had at least some respect for the Old Testament prophets, but he didn't like where the logical trail led. So he responded with a joke. The original Greek manuscripts did not contain punctuation corresponding to the modern question mark, but it's best to see Agrippa's response as sarcasm: "So, in a short time you will persuade me to become a Christian?" Regardless, Agrippa ended his part in the hearing.

The apostle responded with a reaffirmation of his commitment to the gospel, his God, and his ministry. His mention of "chains" is most likely literal, which indicates that his status had changed. When he first came to Caesarea under Felix, he lived in relative comfort in the

Praetorium, able to receive guests, guarded loosely, perhaps even able to move about the compound freely. Somewhere along the way, however, his status had changed. After Festus heard the charges against Paul, he may have feared the apostle's escape. Furthermore, when Paul appealed his case to Caesar, he effectively turned his case into a criminal matter (yet without formal charges, hence the hearing before Agrippa). Consequently, his custody was no longer a matter of his own protection; Festus had a duty to deliver him to Rome.

— 26:30-32 —

Luke includes this final conversation between Festus and Agrippa to vindicate Paul of any wrongdoing. The Pharisees (23:9), the commander in Jerusalem (23:29), the procurator, Felix (24:27; by his inaction), and Festus (25:25) all agreed that the apostle had committed no crime and did not deserve his circumstances. Now Agrippa added his opinion to the rest, stating that Paul might have been set free except for his appeal to Rome. Of course, the king spoke purely in legal terms. Felix and Festus both struggled with a political problem that prevented them from ignoring the temple. Besides that, Paul's release would almost certainly result in his death unless he spent the rest of his life on the run in the wilderness.

APPLICATION: ACTS 25:23-26:32

The Limits of the Gospel

Paul's powerful defense of Christian truth before the social and political leaders of Caesarea prompts two observations concerning the good news and what it will *not* accomplish for humanity.

First, *hearing about Christ doesn't automatically bring internal changes.* Some hear the good news of Christ all their lives yet never respond in belief. They go from Sunday to Sunday and Bible study to Bible study without making a decision concerning their eternal destiny. Each time, they close the Bible and say, "Well, we'll meet again." They apparently think that if they spend enough time in church they will become Christian enough to deserve heaven. It is true that spiritual awakening can be a journey. But for those who die on the way—that is, before making a decision to trust Christ—hell awaits, not heaven.

The grace of God presents us with an opportunity for salvation from sin, and He requires nothing more than trust in His Son; but without a response, the truth accomplishes nothing in the unbeliever.

Second, *responding to Christ doesn't instantly remove external chains.* Despite what many religious hucksters may tell you, becoming a child of God doesn't release the powers of good fortune from heaven to exempt us from the evils of earth. Some would have you believe that it's God's will for His people to live lives that are healthy, wealthy, and free from troubles, and if you do struggle with difficulties, it's because you don't have enough faith. A brief review of Paul's life should be enough to dispel that bit of heresy. In Caesarea, he stood in chains, alone, and poor as dirt because he believed in Jesus as the Messiah and faithfully followed God's plan for his life. Difficult as it is to understand, God's plan for His people might *not* lead to our living in comfort and privilege, but to endure difficulties just like His own Son and the apostles who followed Him.

Responding to Christ doesn't remove our chains of affliction—in *this* life. Our health, wealth, and freedom from troubles will come in the life to come, when our lives in the fallen realm of evil and sin have ended. He has promised victory at the end of our strife. He has promised to carry us through our difficulties in the here and now to give us a hope and a future beyond anything we can imagine. *That* is the promise of the good news.

How to Enjoy a Shipwreck
ACTS 27:1-44

NASB

¹When it was decided that we would sail for Italy, they proceeded to deliver Paul and some other prisoners to a centurion of the Augustan ᵃcohort named Julius. ²And embarking in an Adramyttian ship, which was about to sail to the regions along the coast of ᵃAsia, we put out to sea accompanied by Aristarchus, a Macedonian of Thessalonica. ³The next day we put in at Sidon; and Julius

NLT

¹When the time came, we set sail for Italy. Paul and several other prisoners were placed in the custody of a Roman officer* named Julius, a captain of the Imperial Regiment. ²Aristarchus, a Macedonian from Thessalonica, was also with us. We left on a ship whose home port was Adramyttium on the northwest coast of the province of Asia;* it was scheduled to make several stops at ports along the coast of the province. ³The next day when we docked at

treated Paul with consideration and allowed him to go to his friends and receive care. ⁴From there we put out to sea and sailed under the shelter of Cyprus because the winds were contrary. ⁵When we had sailed through the sea along the coast of Cilicia and Pamphylia, we landed at Myra in Lycia. ⁶There the centurion found an Alexandrian ship sailing for Italy, and he put us aboard it. ⁷When we had sailed slowly for a good many days, and with difficulty had arrived off Cnidus, since the wind did not permit us *to go* farther, we sailed under the shelter of Crete, off Salmone; ⁸and with difficulty sailing past it we came to a place called Fair Havens, near which was the city of Lasea.

⁹When considerable time had passed and the voyage was now dangerous, since even the ªfast was already over, Paul *began* to admonish them, ¹⁰and said to them, "Men, I perceive that the voyage will certainly be with damage and great loss, not only of the cargo and the ship, but also of our lives." ¹¹But the centurion was more persuaded by the pilot and the ªcaptain of the ship than by what was being said by Paul. ¹²Because the harbor was not suitable for wintering, the majority reached a decision to put out to sea from there, if somehow they could reach Phoenix, a harbor of Crete, facing southwest and northwest, and spend the winter *there.*

¹³ªWhen a moderate south wind came up, supposing that they had attained their purpose, they weighed anchor and *began* sailing along Crete, close *inshore.*

¹⁴But before very long there rushed down from ªthe land a violent

Sidon, Julius was very kind to Paul and let him go ashore to visit with friends so they could provide for his needs. ⁴Putting out to sea from there, we encountered strong headwinds that made it difficult to keep the ship on course, so we sailed north of Cyprus between the island and the mainland. ⁵Keeping to the open sea, we passed along the coast of Cilicia and Pamphylia, landing at Myra, in the province of Lycia. ⁶There the commanding officer found an Egyptian ship from Alexandria that was bound for Italy, and he put us on board.

⁷We had several days of slow sailing, and after great difficulty we finally neared Cnidus. But the wind was against us, so we sailed across to Crete and along the sheltered coast of the island, past the cape of Salmone. ⁸We struggled along the coast with great difficulty and finally arrived at Fair Havens, near the town of Lasea. ⁹We had lost a lot of time. The weather was becoming dangerous for sea travel because it was so late in the fall,* and Paul spoke to the ship's officers about it.

¹⁰"Men," he said, "I believe there is trouble ahead if we go on—shipwreck, loss of cargo, and danger to our lives as well." ¹¹But the officer in charge of the prisoners listened more to the ship's captain and the owner than to Paul. ¹²And since Fair Havens was an exposed harbor—a poor place to spend the winter—most of the crew wanted to go on to Phoenix, farther up the coast of Crete, and spend the winter there. Phoenix was a good harbor with only a southwest and northwest exposure.

¹³When a light wind began blowing from the south, the sailors thought they could make it. So they pulled up anchor and sailed close to the shore of Crete. ¹⁴But the weather changed abruptly, and a wind of typhoon strength (called a

wind, called ᵇEuraquilo; ¹⁵and when the ship was caught *in it* and could not face the wind, we gave way *to it* and let ourselves be driven along. ¹⁶Running under the shelter of a small island called Clauda, we were scarcely able to get the *ship's* ᵃboat under control. ¹⁷After they had hoisted it up, they used ᵃsupporting cables in undergirding the ship; and fearing that they might run aground on *the shallows* of Syrtis, they let down the ᵇsea anchor and in this way let themselves be driven along. ¹⁸The next day as we were being violently storm-tossed, ᵃthey began to jettison the cargo; ¹⁹and on the third day they threw the ship's tackle overboard with their own hands. ²⁰Since neither sun nor stars appeared for many days, and no small storm was assailing *us,* from then on all hope of our being saved was gradually abandoned.

²¹ᵃWhen they had gone a long time without food, then Paul stood up in their midst and said, "Men, you ought to have ᵇfollowed my advice and not to have set sail from Crete and ᶜincurred this damage and loss. ²²*Yet* now I urge you to keep up your courage, for there will be no loss of life among you, but *only* of the ship. ²³For this very night an angel of the God to whom I belong and whom I serve stood before me, ²⁴saying, 'Do not be afraid, Paul; you must stand before Caesar; and behold, God has granted you all those who are sailing with you.' ²⁵Therefore, keep up your courage, men, for I believe God that ᵃit will turn out exactly as I have been told. ²⁶But we must run aground on a certain island."

²⁷But when the fourteenth night came, as we were being driven about in the Adriatic Sea, about midnight the sailors *began* to surmise that ᵃthey were approaching some land. ²⁸They took soundings and found *it*

"northeaster") burst across the island and blew us out to sea. ¹⁵The sailors couldn't turn the ship into the wind, so they gave up and let it run before the gale.

¹⁶We sailed along the sheltered side of a small island named Cauda,* where with great difficulty we hoisted aboard the lifeboat being towed behind us. ¹⁷Then the sailors bound ropes around the hull of the ship to strengthen it. They were afraid of being driven across to the sandbars of Syrtis off the African coast, so they lowered the sea anchor to slow the ship and were driven before the wind.

¹⁸The next day, as gale-force winds continued to batter the ship, the crew began throwing the cargo overboard. ¹⁹The following day they even took some of the ship's gear and threw it overboard. ²⁰The terrible storm raged for many days, blotting out the sun and the stars, until at last all hope was gone.

²¹No one had eaten for a long time. Finally, Paul called the crew together and said, "Men, you should have listened to me in the first place and not left Crete. You would have avoided all this damage and loss. ²²But take courage! None of you will lose your lives, even though the ship will go down. ²³For last night an angel of the God to whom I belong and whom I serve stood beside me, ²⁴and he said, 'Don't be afraid, Paul, for you will surely stand trial before Caesar! What's more, God in his goodness has granted safety to everyone sailing with you.' ²⁵So take courage! For I believe God. It will be just as he said. ²⁶But we will be shipwrecked on an island."

²⁷About midnight on the fourteenth night of the storm, as we were being driven across the Sea of Adria,* the sailors sensed land was near. ²⁸They dropped a weighted line

NASB

to be twenty fathoms; and a little farther on they took another sounding and found *it to be* fifteen fathoms. ²⁹Fearing that we might run aground somewhere on the ªrocks, they cast four anchors from the stern and ᵇwished for daybreak. ³⁰But as the sailors were trying to escape from the ship and had let down the *ship's* boat into the sea, on the pretense of intending to lay out anchors from the bow, ³¹Paul said to the centurion and to the soldiers, "Unless these men remain in the ship, you yourselves cannot be saved." ³²Then the soldiers cut away the ropes of the *ship's* boat and let it fall away.

³³Until the day was about to dawn, Paul was encouraging them all to take some food, saying, "Today is the fourteenth day that you have been constantly watching and going without eating, having taken nothing. ³⁴Therefore I encourage you to take some food, for this is for your preservation, for not a hair from the head of any of you will perish." ³⁵Having said this, he took bread and gave thanks to God in the presence of all, and he broke it and began to eat. ³⁶All of them ªwere encouraged and they themselves also took food. ³⁷All of us in the ship were two hundred and seventy-six ªpersons. ³⁸When they had eaten enough, they *began* to lighten the ship by throwing out the wheat into the sea.

³⁹When day came, they ªcould not recognize the land; but they did observe a bay with a beach, and they resolved to drive the ship onto it if they could. ⁴⁰And casting off the anchors, they left them in the sea while at the same time they were loosening the ropes of the rudders; and hoisting the foresail to the wind, they were heading for the beach. ⁴¹But striking a ªreef where two seas met, they ran the vessel aground; and the prow stuck fast and remained immovable,

NLT

and found that the water was 120 feet deep. But a little later they measured again and found it was only 90 feet deep.* ²⁹At this rate they were afraid we would soon be driven against the rocks along the shore, so they threw out four anchors from the back of the ship and prayed for daylight.

³⁰Then the sailors tried to abandon the ship; they lowered the lifeboat as though they were going to put out anchors from the front of the ship. ³¹But Paul said to the commanding officer and the soldiers, "You will all die unless the sailors stay aboard." ³²So the soldiers cut the ropes to the lifeboat and let it drift away.

³³Just as day was dawning, Paul urged everyone to eat. "You have been so worried that you haven't touched food for two weeks," he said. ³⁴"Please eat something now for your own good. For not a hair of your heads will perish." ³⁵Then he took some bread, gave thanks to God before them all, and broke off a piece and ate it. ³⁶Then everyone was encouraged and began to eat—³⁷all 276 of us who were on board. ³⁸After eating, the crew lightened the ship further by throwing the cargo of wheat overboard.

³⁹When morning dawned, they didn't recognize the coastline, but they saw a bay with a beach and wondered if they could get to shore by running the ship aground. ⁴⁰So they cut off the anchors and left them in the sea. Then they lowered the rudders, raised the foresail, and headed toward shore. ⁴¹But they hit a shoal and ran the ship aground too soon. The bow of the ship stuck fast, while the stern was repeatedly

but the stern *began* to be broken up by the force *of the waves.* ⁴²The soldiers' plan was to kill the prisoners, so that none *of them* would swim away and escape; ⁴³but the centurion, wanting to bring Paul safely through, kept them from their intention, and commanded that those who could swim should ^ajump overboard first and get to land, ⁴⁴and the rest *should follow,* some on planks, and others on various things from the ship. And so it happened that they all were brought safely to land.

27:1 ^aOr *battalion* 27:2 ^aI.e. west coast province of Asia Minor 27:9 ^aI.e. Day of Atonement in September or October, which was a dangerous time of year for navigation 27:11 ^aOr *owner* 27:13 ^aLit *a south wind having gently blown* 27:14 ^aLit *it* ^bI.e. a northeaster 27:16 ^aOr *skiff:* a small boat in tow or carried on board for emergency use, transportation to and from shore, etc. 27:17 ^aLit *helps* ^bOr *gear* 27:18 ^aLit *they were doing a throwing out* 27:21 ^aLit *there being much abstinence from food* ^bLit *obeyed me* ^cLit *gained* 27:25 ^aLit *it will be* 27:27 ^aLit *some land was approaching them* 27:29 ^aLit *rough places* ^bLit *they were praying for it to become day* 27:36 ^aLit *became cheerful* 27:37 ^aLit *souls* 27:39 ^aLit *were not recognizing* 27:41 ^aLit *place* 27:43 ^aLit *throw themselves*

smashed by the force of the waves and began to break apart.

⁴²The soldiers wanted to kill the prisoners to make sure they didn't swim ashore and escape. ⁴³But the commanding officer wanted to spare Paul, so he didn't let them carry out their plan. Then he ordered all who could swim to jump overboard first and make for land. ⁴⁴The others held on to planks or debris from the broken ship.* So everyone escaped safely to shore.

27:1 Greek *centurion;* similarly in 27:6, 11, 31, 43. 27:2 *Asia* was a Roman province in what is now western Turkey. 27:9 Greek *because the fast was now already gone by.* This fast was associated with the Day of Atonement (*Yom Kippur*), which occurred in late September or early October. 27:16 Some manuscripts read *Clauda.* 27:27 The *Sea of Adria* includes the central portion of the Mediterranean. 27:28 Greek *20 fathoms . . . 15 fathoms* [37 meters . . . 27 meters]. 27:44 Or *or were helped by members of the ship's crew.*

I've seen a number of bumper stickers that read, "I'd rather be sailing." That's understandable. Sea lovers can't resist the exhilaration of skimming the water in a beautiful sailing vessel pushed along by the silent power of the wind. Captains tell me they love the challenge of harnessing nature's energy and equally enjoy the calm, peaceful isolation of the open water. To hear them talk, I want to purchase a thirty-six-foot sailing yacht, take lessons, and chart a course for leisure on the sea. Then I recall my first sea voyage, which began in San Diego aboard a troop ship. The first several hours felt like a pleasure cruise, but two days later, forty-foot swells tossed our ship like a toothpick and our commander ordered each man to tie himself to his bunk.

I never see bumper stickers that read, "I'd rather be shipwrecked." No one sets sail with the hope of running aground somewhere, but experienced sailors have learned to accept certain risks in exchange for their love of the sea. You have to take the bad with the good. Likewise, Paul learned to accept suffering and difficulties as a natural part of the remarkable life God had planned for him. This extraordinary man of God described the downside of greatness this way:

Five times I received from the Jews thirty-nine lashes. Three times I was beaten with rods, once I was stoned, three times I was shipwrecked, a night and a day I have spent in the deep. I have been on frequent journeys, in dangers from rivers, dangers from robbers, dangers from my countrymen, dangers from the Gentiles, dangers in the city, dangers in the wilderness, dangers on the sea, dangers among false brethren; I have been in labor and hardship, through many sleepless nights, in hunger and thirst, often without food, in cold and exposure. Apart from such external things, there is the daily pressure on me of concern for all the churches. (2 Cor. 11:24-28)

I'll admit that sometimes I would like to be a man like Paul; then I think about some of his experiences, and I feel more content with who I am and what God has for me instead. If that is the price of greatness, I'm tempted to be content with mediocrity!

Of course, Paul didn't see the future laid before him as a path to glory. His ministry had carried him far, now the will of God led him upward. If any ambition drew him, it was the opportunity to carry the good news of Jesus Christ to the pinnacle of Roman power in the hope that it might trickle down. With the decree of Festus, the Lord's promise (Acts 23:11) began to be fulfilled. Paul would finally carry the gospel to Rome—courtesy of the government. But his journey would not be a pleasure cruise. As God so often does, He took His follower through hardship on the way to his destiny. Fortunately, Paul had by now learned to take each circumstance as an opportunity to point others toward Jesus Christ. The terrifying ordeal in front of him would be no exception.

— 27:1-2 —

No one knows for certain the identity of the unit in which Julius served. The identifier "Augustan cohort" (27:1) was an honorary title, so the unit may have been one stationed in Syria that had distinguished itself in battle. Paul joined an unknown number of other prisoners to be taken to Rome via ship based in Adramyttium, a city on the coast of Mysia, southeast of Troas. It may have been on its last voyage of the season before returning to its home port when it received the good fortune of a government commission. Pirates would not attack a vessel carrying Roman soldiers, so the journey past Pamphylia on the way to the southern coast of Asia would be less hazardous.

Luke resumes the use of the first-person pronouns "we" and "us."

He most likely attended to Paul's needs during his two-year wait in Caesarea and did not leave his side until the apostle's death. Luke remained with Paul on this journey and while he waited for trial in Rome. Paul also mentions Luke during his second imprisonment in Rome just before his execution (2 Tim. 4:11).

Luke mentions only one of Paul's many traveling companions who came to Jerusalem with him after the third missionary journey (cf. Acts 20:4-5). It appears that several men had accompanied Paul throughout his journeys, yet Luke rarely if ever mentions them. Timothy joined Paul early in his second missionary journey (16:1-5) but almost never appears in Luke's narrative, even when others are named. Titus had been with Paul and Barnabas for the Jerusalem Council (Gal. 2:1), and he served on the second missionary journey (2 Cor. 2:13), yet his name never appears in Acts. Therefore, others may have been—and I would argue most likely were—aboard the ship with Paul, but they are not mentioned. We know from Paul's letters from Rome that John Mark (Col. 4:10) and Demas (Phlm. 1:24) were with him there, although they may have joined him later. Regardless, why Luke names Aristarchus of Thessalonica is a mystery.

— 27:3-5 —

Before departing for Asia, the merchant ship stopped at Sidon to take on cargo. The unloading process in Tyre took another ship seven days (21:3-4), so they may have been in Sidon a week or more. Paul was not a typical prisoner—his journey to Rome served his own interests, and escape was not a concern. The centurion may have known Paul from his twenty-four months in Caesarea and held him in high enough regard to treat him with "consideration" (27:3; *philanthrōpōs* [5364]) and grant him unusual freedom.

The winds blew west to east in the fall, so upon leaving Sidon, the ship sailed on the leeward side of Cyprus (27:4). The better sailing conditions came at the risk of piracy in the dangerous alley between Cyprus and Pamphylia, but with a centurion aboard, the ship's captain could breathe a little easier. They arrived in Myra without incident (27:5). The ancient remains in this port indicate a significant trade in the purple dye made from murex shells, a principal export of Tyre.

— 27:6-12 —

The centurion put Paul, his traveling companions, and the other prisoners aboard a large Alexandrian ship capable of carrying grain (27:38) and at least 276 passengers (27:37). Ancient documents from the period mention medium-sized merchant galleys that were 70 feet long,[41] with the largest running 150 feet.[42] Ships rarely sailed in open water far from land; captains usually navigated by sight. In this case, the captain tried to turn north after passing Rhodes, most likely trying to reach Ephesus. From there, he might follow a straight east–west course across the Aegean to Piraeus using islands for navigation. The ship would be portaged across the Isthmus of Corinth via the Diolkos and then across the Ionian Sea to Italy.

The fall winds didn't cooperate with the planned route. Unable to sail north, they made for Crete, hoping to run along the leeward side, then perhaps turn north toward Achaia. They put in at the harbor of Fair Havens, where they spent "considerable time" (27:7-9). Without a doubt, Paul used that time to determine the state of the church on Crete and found the communities of Christians disorganized and struggling. He would eventually return to the island and delegate the responsibility of strengthening and organizing the church to his assistant, Titus (Titus 1:5).

The "fast" Luke references is the Day of Atonement, which occurs in September or October, a late time in the year to be at sea. Paul advised spending the winter in Fair Havens; the ship's crew favored a harbor near the western end of the island (27:9-12). The centurion had the final say and sided with the captain, which proved to be a mistake.

— 27:13-20 —

As they worked their way down the island, a south wind pushed them toward the island, so they didn't have to worry about being blown out to sea. So they pulled up the anchor to allow the ship to sail faster. Then a nor'easter (*Eurakylōn* [2146b]) took over and blew them out to sea. They hoped that a tiny island about 25 miles off the southern coast of Crete would provide refuge, but the wind proved too strong. The crew had to perform several emergency procedures to save the ship. The "ship's boat" (27:16) was a smaller craft held in tow that was used for transporting people from ship to shore when no harbor was available. It either became waterlogged or battered by the wind, so they had to pull it aboard. They used ropes drawn under the hull to reinforce the structure. They dropped anchor to slow their southerly drift, worried they might run aground near the North African coast. They jettisoned cargo so the ship would ride higher and take on less water. They even started throwing the ship's equipment overboard. Neither sun nor stars could be seen, so navigation became impossible; they may have used soundings and charts to determine how close to Africa they had drifted.

— 27:21-26 —

The crew had not eaten for some time, perhaps for a number of reasons. Perhaps they didn't know how long they would have to stretch their food supply, stress killed their appetites, seasickness overwhelmed them, or they fasted to please the gods. Regardless, they had begun to lose all hope of making it to shore alive. That's when Paul took command of the situation. He reminded them of his earlier warning and chided them for not heeding his advice—not to say "I told you so," but to encourage them to heed him now (27:21). He used the occasion to encourage them with a vision he had received assuring him that all would survive the ordeal. Paul said, "Keep up your courage" (*euthymeō* [2114])—essentially, "Take heart and be brave!"

The apostle had received his own supernatural reassurance before (18:9-10; 23:11), but this time the Lord gave him a message for the benefit of his shipmates. God promised to preserve everyone on board for the sake of His messenger, which gave Paul added credibility when talking to the others about Jesus Christ. He expressed his belief in the word of God and encouraged the others to believe with him (27:22-25).

He concluded his speech with a piece of practical advice: They needed to run aground on the next suitable island they saw (27:26). The Greek word rendered "a certain" (*tis* [5100]) in the NASB means "any" or "some." The Lord had promised that all would be preserved through the crisis, but they needed to act wisely. They needed to forget about their destination or preserving the ship and make survival their first priority. God's assurance of survival was not a license to take foolish chances; if anything, their promise of salvation from the sea gave them greater reason to use wisdom.

— 27:27-32 —

Luke identifies their location as somewhere in the "Adriatic Sea" (27:27), which is the ancient designation. Today, we know the Adriatic as the sea between the "boot" of Italy and the coast of Croatia. In modern terms, they floated somewhere in the southern Ionian Sea between Crete and Malta.

After two full weeks adrift, hopelessly lost and helpless against the winds and currents, the crew surmised that they were close to land. The term "surmise" (*uponoeō* [5282]) means "to conjecture" or "to form an opinion based on scant evidence." At night, they couldn't see birds or clouds indicating land, so they must have heard surf crashing in the distance or even caught the scent of land, which experienced sailors are known to do. They could also take soundings (measuring depth using a lead weight) and compare the results to depth charts. In the fourth century BC, Herodotus noted, "This is the nature of the land of Egypt: in the first place, when you approach it from the sea and are still a day's sail from land, if you let down a sounding line you will bring up mud from a depth of eleven fathoms."[43] When they took soundings, they found that the depth had changed from twenty fathoms to fifteen (27:28). The fathom (*orguia* [3712]) measured the length of a man's outstretched arms, so at approximately 6 feet per fathom, they were in about 90 feet of water.

To keep the ship under control, they dragged four anchors (27:29). Several of the crew thought they stood a better chance of making it to shore alive in the ship's dinghy rather than crashing on the rocks in the main vessel (27:30). They lowered the smaller boat on the pretext of using it to drop anchors, but Paul knew their plan. He had been through three previous shipwrecks, so he knew all the tricks and how people would behave. They couldn't afford to let any of the crew abandon ship; the other passengers didn't have the sailing experience required to guide the vessel close to land without crashing (27:31).

The centurion had by this time learned to trust Paul's advice, so he ordered the dinghy cut loose (27:32).

— 27:33-38 —

After all they had endured, Paul emerged as the clear leader of the group. The sound of surf and the soundings confirmed they were close to land, so the next few hours would be physically demanding for everyone, especially the crew. Paul spoke with divine authority to reassure each person he or she would survive the grounding. Because most of the people aboard had not eaten in the past several days, Paul led them in a meal (27:33-36). He used the opportunity to thank God for their continued safety.

In anticipation of the grounding, they threw the grain overboard (27:38). The captain had kept the grain for financial reasons, of course, but also for ballast during the storm. At this point, however, every pound of cargo translated into precious inches between the hull and the sea floor. The lighter the ship, the closer to land they could get before running aground.

— 27:39-44 —

No one aboard recognized the land by sight, but they had no other choice but to get the ship as close as possible (27:39-40). When the bow struck a reef, the surf began to pound the stern, threatening to tear the ship apart (27:41). The soldiers could not afford to let their prisoners escape in the chaos of abandoning ship, so they planned to kill them instead, the standard procedure. The centurion, however, had learned to trust Paul's word, so he determined to get everyone to shore alive (27:42-43).

Some swam, others clung to anything that would float, and all made it to dry land, just as the Lord had promised through Paul (27:44).

APPLICATION: ACTS 27:1-44

Three Spiritual Anchors

When 276 people boarded the grain ship to leave Fair Havens, they expected to sail no more than 40 miles down the coast of Crete to Phoenix, a more suitable harbor for spending the winter. But, as often happens, nature turned their simple plan into a terrifying ordeal. A half-day jaunt became two weeks at sea, forcing them to fight for survival through a long series of life-threatening events. As their situation worsened, each leader aboard grew silent and faded from the narrative, leaving Paul as the standout leader. While the crew threw out anchors to regain control of the ship, Paul cast three spiritual anchors to help the people cling to hope.

Spiritual Anchor #1: *Assurance of God's Presence* (27:22-26). The Lord reassured Paul that he and everyone aboard would survive their distress at sea. Paul passed this along to the people, letting them know that God saw their trouble and had not forsaken them. In fact, he urged them to celebrate like they already had been rescued, because the Lord had, in fact, saved them. It was only a matter of time before His rescue plan played out. Paul trusted God's word and he encouraged others to do the same.

Imagine yourself traveling back in time to stand on the deck of this ship as one of the passengers, knowing the end of the story as you do now. How would your behavior differ from the others aboard? The unpleasant conditions would affect you no less, the wind and rain would chill you just the same, but anxiety would have no effect on your outlook. So it is with your circumstances now. Struggles and difficulties will always be a part of life this side of the grave, and your life in this realm will someday end, but we have been assured of God's presence in the person of His Holy Spirit within us. And He has promised to save all who trust in Him. Furthermore, every experience—pleasure cruises and shipwrecks—will be used for our good.

Spiritual Anchor #2: *Practical Encouragement* (27:33-38). After many days at sea, the people had forgotten God's promise to preserve everyone alive. Some of the crew tried to get into the dinghy and abandon the ship and its passengers, but Paul intervened. As they appeared to be close to land, Paul urged the people to eat. He gave thanks to God for the food and His assurance of their safety, and he passed the bread. They had not yet spotted land, but they tossed the cargo overboard to prepare for a run toward a coast.

Paul's encouragement took physical, tangible form. Words were fine two weeks earlier; deeds made the promise of God concrete. His behavior reflected his belief that they would step onto dry land soon.

Spiritual Anchor #3: *Absolute Faith* (27:39-44). Throughout the ordeal, Paul demonstrated a calm, assured belief in the promise of God, and his faith became contagious. When the soldiers prepared to kill the prisoners, the centurion stopped them. His primary motivation was to preserve Paul's life, but he made his decision with confidence. The people followed Paul's lead and never gave up hope of survival.

How you face ordeals affects how others regard the Word of God. Your verbal testimony will help reveal the promises of God, but it is your personal demonstration of trust that adds validation to the message. People need to hear the gospel, but seeing the good news have its effect will do more to encourage their faith than anything you say.

Time to Heal
ACTS 28:1-11

NASB

¹When they had been brought safely through, then we found out that the island was called ªMalta. ²The ªnatives showed us extraordinary kindness; for because of the rain that had set in and because of the cold,

NLT

¹Once we were safe on shore, we learned that we were on the island of Malta. ²The people of the island were very kind to us. It was cold and rainy, so they built a fire on the shore to welcome us.

they kindled a fire and received us all. ³But when Paul had gathered a bundle of sticks and laid them on the fire, a viper came out ªbecause of the heat and fastened itself on his hand. ⁴When the ªnatives saw the creature hanging from his hand, they *began* saying to one another, "Undoubtedly this man is a murderer, and though he has been saved from the sea, ᵇjustice has not allowed him to live." ⁵However he shook the creature off into the fire and suffered no harm. ⁶But they were expecting that he was about to swell up or suddenly fall down dead. But after they had waited a long time and had seen nothing unusual happen to him, they changed their minds and *began* to say that he was a god.

⁷Now in the neighborhood of that place were lands belonging to the leading man of the island, named Publius, who welcomed us and entertained us courteously three days. ⁸And it happened that the father of Publius was lying *in bed* afflicted with *recurrent* fever and dysentery; and Paul went in *to see* him and after he had prayed, he laid his hands on him and healed him. ⁹After this had happened, the rest of the people on the island who had diseases were coming to him and getting cured. ¹⁰They also honored us with many ªmarks of respect; and when we were setting sail, they ᵇsupplied *us* with ᶜall we needed.

¹¹At the end of three months we set sail on an Alexandrian ship which had wintered at the island, and which had ªthe Twin Brothers for its figurehead.

28:1 ªOr *Melita*　28:2 ªLit *barbarians*　28:3 ªOr *from the heat*　28:4 ªLit *barbarians*　ᵇOr *Justice,* i.e. the personification of a goddess　28:10 ªLit *honors*　ᵇOr *put on board*　ᶜLit *the things pertaining to the needs*　28:11 ªGr *Dioscuri*; i.e. Castor and Pollux, twin sons of Zeus

³As Paul gathered an armful of sticks and was laying them on the fire, a poisonous snake, driven out by the heat, bit him on the hand. ⁴The people of the island saw it hanging from his hand and said to each other, "A murderer, no doubt! Though he escaped the sea, justice will not permit him to live." ⁵But Paul shook off the snake into the fire and was unharmed. ⁶The people waited for him to swell up or suddenly drop dead. But when they had waited a long time and saw that he wasn't harmed, they changed their minds and decided he was a god.

⁷Near the shore where we landed was an estate belonging to Publius, the chief official of the island. He welcomed us and treated us kindly for three days. ⁸As it happened, Publius's father was ill with fever and dysentery. Paul went in and prayed for him, and laying his hands on him, he healed him. ⁹Then all the other sick people on the island came and were healed. ¹⁰As a result we were showered with honors, and when the time came to sail, people supplied us with everything we would need for the trip.

¹¹It was three months after the shipwreck that we set sail on another ship that had wintered at the island—an Alexandrian ship with the twin gods* as its figurehead.

28:11 The *twin gods* were the Roman gods Castor and Pollux.

Around 400 BC, a Greek physician rose above his peers to become what many consider to be "the father of modern medicine." Hippocrates became the first medicine man to declare publicly that diseases occur from natural causes, not because of evil spirits or punishment from the gods, and he spent twenty years in prison for separating medicine from religion. He also resisted the philosophy of his contemporaries, who aggressively diagnosed and treated diseases, often causing more harm than good. He believed in the body's ability to heal itself, so he prescribed immobilization, cleanliness, soothing balms, and plenty of rest. He opens his work *Precepts* with this simple bit of wisdom: "Healing is a matter of time, but it is sometimes also a matter of opportunity."[44] Therefore, he believed in giving the body both time and opportunity to heal.

Four centuries after Hippocrates passed on, another physician accompanied Paul on his harrowing journey across the Mediterranean. As an intellectual successor to Hippocrates, Luke undoubtedly approved of the time his patient would spend on their island refuge. As King Solomon wrote a thousand years earlier, "There is an appointed time for everything. And there is a time for every event under heaven" (Eccl. 3:1). Among these appointed times is "a time to heal" (Eccl. 3:3).

I find it strange that in our modern, "enlightened" era, when medicine has advanced light-years beyond the knowledge of Luke and Hippocrates, we have so little room in our theology for rest or the biblical concept of "time to heal." We want people to "get over it." If you have spent much time trying to recover from an ailment that cannot be explained by an X-ray, if you have been trapped in the dregs of depression, if you have grieved deeply the loss of a loved one and you can't seem to recover, you've undoubtedly heard from someone "Snap out of it!" or "Get with it!" Hippocrates was right. Healing *is* a matter of time. It is, indeed, a matter of opportunity, which few today want to offer.

After a long ordeal in Caesarea and this two-week crisis at sea, Paul undoubtedly enjoyed this three-month rest before pushing on to Rome. But more than his personal rest and health would be affected in Malta— God would bear witness through the apostle by healing many on the island. Times of physical, mental, and emotional healing, whether miraculous or the result of normal processes, offer an opportunity to express and reflect on the compassionate and redeeming power of the gospel in one's spiritual life. This same power would ready Paul for the next stage of his journey.

— 28:1-2 —

Soon after arriving, Luke learned the island was named *Melitē* [3194] (now known as Malta). The term rendered "natives" (28:2; *barbaros* [915]) is a reference to foreigners that derives from the sound of foreign speech, which seems like babbling. Greeks and Romans looked down on any who did not speak their "civilized" language as culturally and intellectually inferior. The people of Malta descended from the Phoenicians, who had colonized the island as far back as 500 BC and, despite occupation by the Romans in 218 BC, remained a fixture on the island.

The people of Malta showed the shipwrecked travelers "extraordinary kindness" (*philanthrōpia* [5363]), warming them with a fire and extending hospitality.

— 28:3-6 —

Luke illustrates the character of the natives with a story about Paul suffering a snakebite. Paul threw a bundle of sticks on the fire and a snake latched onto his hand (28:3). The natives were familiar with their wildlife and knew the serpent to be poisonous, so they expected the apostle to swell up and die. Their superstition led them to believe that justice had caught up with Paul, supposing him to be a murderer, since he was obviously one of several prisoners (28:4). Their words personify justice (*dikē* [1349]) as a Greek goddess, "Justice herself" (NET). The inhabitants, though Phoenician in culture and descent, probably attached their superstitions to Greek deities. They thought unseen forces were punishing Paul, but when he didn't suffer any ill effects, they supposed him to be a god himself (28:5-6)!

By now the apostle had seen a lot and had been worshiped as a god before (14:11). Luke doesn't conclude the story to show Paul's response. By now his readers could guess. Instead, he transitions to another incident the apostle used for evangelism.

— 28:7-10 —

An inscription found on the island refers to the chief magistrate as bearing the title of *prōtos*.[45] Luke refers to a "leading man" (*prōtos* [4413]) named Publius, which was a popular name among the Romans; this suggests that he was a Roman who owned an estate on Malta. He extended hospitality to the group over a three-day period (28:7). The father of Publius was laid up with "fever and dysentery" (28:8; *dysenterion* [1420]). Some described the malady as "bloody flux" because the intense diarrhea contained blood and mucus. Today, we know the cause to be a parasitic bacteria or amoeba; in Paul's day, superstition still attributed many ailments to evil spirits or angry gods. Patients usually contracted this ailment by contacting the fluids of infected people, so epidemics were not uncommon. Those who did not recover usually died from dehydration. Dr. Luke notes the presence of a fever as well, which suggests a bacterial form known as Marlow syndrome, which can be particularly difficult to treat.

Paul prayed over the man, and God healed him. The context suggests an instantaneous healing, which explains why so many others came to see Paul. Everyone on Malta suffering from various diseases came to be cured as well (28:9). Luke doesn't state how Paul used this opportunity for the gospel, but we can surmise based on his character throughout Acts that he did. After a generous and gracious farewell from the locals, Paul and his men boarded an Alexandrian ship bound for Rome.

— 28:11 —

In this verse, Luke offers a couple of clues which, combined with other historical records, help establish a fairly reliable date for their departure. According to Pliny the Elder, the sailing season opened "on the sixth day before the Ides of February,"[46] which corresponds to February 8 on our calendar. If they were on Malta for three months, they crashed on the shores in early November, which means they had earlier left Crete after the fast of Yom Kippur in late October. Therefore, this would suggest a late date for the fast that year. In AD 59, "the Fast fell on or about 5th October, much later than in any neighboring year."[47]

They boarded an Alexandrian ship that featured the twin sons of Zeus (*Dioskouroi* [1359]), Castor and Pollux, the patron gods of sailors. As Paul and his men boarded the ship, one wonders if they felt a sense of irony. Whose deity saved the crew and passengers from almost certain death three months earlier?

Paul might have had the opportunity to recuperate on Crete during the three-month wait for the passing of winter if the ship's captain and the centurion had heeded his advice (27:10-11). The apostle had been through a lot in the past couple of years, and his time in Rome would be just as intense. Regrettably, Paul's advice went unheeded, so they ended up enduring a harrowing, two-week odyssey at sea that resulted in the loss of the captain's ship and its valuable cargo. Only by the grace of God did all 276 people wade onto the shores of Malta. The centurion's poor decision notwithstanding, the Lord would prevail. He would make sure Paul got his much-needed respite—if not on Crete, then on Malta, with its mild winter months and abundant sunshine.

APPLICATION: ACTS 28:1-11

For Those Who Heal

Very few people in the world have experienced the kind of instantaneous healing the people of Malta received from God through Paul. One touch, and a moment later their symptoms had vanished and full strength had returned. Usually, however, healing is a process. It takes time. Occasional setbacks punctuate a patient's progress toward a full recovery. Sometimes during long periods nothing happens—no progress, no regression. Then suddenly a dramatic improvement surprises everyone. Hippocrates was right: "Healing is a matter of time, but it is sometimes also a matter of opportunity."

With that in mind, let me offer two principles that may encourage those who are healing. They apply to physical recovery, but they're just as valid for those healing from other kinds of wounds: Tragedy. Divorce. Unemployment. Infertility. Bankruptcy. Depression. Death of a loved one.

Here's the first principle: *The one who takes time to heal should be respected, not resented.* Those who are healing often struggle to express themselves because they lack the energy to communicate. Inside, they're screaming for compassion: "I'm trying to find myself. I'm trying to put it together. Stay with me. Love me through it. Accept me in it. Don't write me off." Many feel guilty for being a burden to others during their recovery, and they suffer more when family or friends grow impatient with their pain. No one hates the healing process more than the one who's going through it. So give those who are healing a lot of grace. And tell them how much you respect them for continuing the healing process without giving up.

The second principle: *The one who is healed will be better equipped to help others.* While suffering the utter privation of Auschwitz during World War II, the psychologist Victor Frankl found relief when thinking about how his present suffering might be used in the future. He wrote,

> Suddenly I saw myself standing on the platform of a well-lit, warm and pleasant lecture room. In front of me sat an attentive audience on comfortable upholstered seats. I was giving a lecture on the psychology of the concentration camp! All that oppressed me at that moment became objective, seen and described from the remote viewpoint of science. By this method I succeeded

somehow in rising above the situation, above the sufferings of the moment, and I observed them as if they were already of the past.⁴⁸

No one will understand the loss of a baby like a parent who's suffered the death of a child. Who else but a former psychiatric patient will understand what it means to go through intensive therapy, emerge whole, and then recover self-respect? Divorce care is run by people who have been divorced. Recovering addicts know how to lead others out of addiction. The difficulties and tragedies we survive make us real to people suffering what we once suffered. I have found this principle to be incredibly valuable when I'm in the process of healing. It helps to think about how we might use today's painful experiences to help others in the future.

The End of the Beginning
ACTS 28:12-31

NASB

¹²After we put in at Syracuse, we stayed there for three days. ¹³From there we sailed around and arrived at Rhegium, and a day later a south wind sprang up, and on the second day we came to Puteoli. ¹⁴ᵃThere we found *some* brethren, and were invited to stay with them for seven days; and thus we came to Rome. ¹⁵And the brethren, when they heard about us, came from there as far as the ᵃMarket of Appius and ᵇThree Inns to meet us; and when Paul saw them, he thanked God and took courage.

¹⁶When we entered Rome, Paul was allowed to stay by himself, with the soldier who was guarding him.

¹⁷After three days ᵃPaul called together those who were the leading men of the Jews, and when they came together, he *began* saying to them, "Brethren, though I had done nothing against our people or the customs of our ᵇfathers, yet I was delivered as

NLT

¹²Our first stop was Syracuse,* where we stayed three days. ¹³From there we sailed across to Rhegium.* A day later a south wind began blowing, so the following day we sailed up the coast to Puteoli. ¹⁴There we found some believers,* who invited us to spend a week with them. And so we came to Rome.

¹⁵The brothers and sisters* in Rome had heard we were coming, and they came to meet us at the Forum* on the Appian Way. Others joined us at The Three Taverns.* When Paul saw them, he was encouraged and thanked God.

¹⁶When we arrived in Rome, Paul was permitted to have his own private lodging, though he was guarded by a soldier.

¹⁷Three days after Paul's arrival, he called together the local Jewish leaders. He said to them, "Brothers, I was arrested in Jerusalem and handed over to the Roman government, even though I had done

a prisoner from Jerusalem into the hands of the Romans. ¹⁸And when they had examined me, they were willing to release me because there was no ground ᵃfor putting me to death. ¹⁹But when the Jews ᵃobjected, I was forced to appeal to Caesar, not that I had any accusation against my nation. ²⁰For this reason, therefore, I ᵃrequested to see you and to speak with you, for I am wearing this chain for the sake of the hope of Israel." ²¹They said to him, "We have neither received letters from Judea concerning you, nor have any of the brethren come here and reported or spoken anything bad about you. ²²But we desire to hear from you what ᵃyour views are; for concerning this sect, it is known to us that it is spoken against everywhere."

²³When they had set a day for Paul, they came to him at his lodging in large numbers; and he was explaining to them by solemnly testifying about the kingdom of God and trying to persuade them concerning Jesus, from both the Law of Moses and from the Prophets, from morning until evening. ²⁴Some were being persuaded by the things spoken, but others would not believe. ²⁵And when they did not agree with one another, they *began* leaving after Paul had spoken one *parting* word, "The Holy Spirit rightly spoke through Isaiah the prophet to your fathers, ²⁶saying,

'GO TO THIS PEOPLE AND SAY,
"ᵃYOU WILL KEEP ON HEARING,
   ᵇBUT WILL NOT UNDERSTAND;
AND ᶜYOU WILL KEEP ON SEEING,
   BUT WILL NOT PERCEIVE;
²⁷ FOR THE HEART OF THIS PEOPLE
   HAS BECOME DULL,
AND WITH THEIR EARS THEY
   SCARCELY HEAR,
AND THEY HAVE CLOSED THEIR
   EYES;

nothing against our people or the customs of our ancestors. ¹⁸The Romans tried me and wanted to release me, because they found no cause for the death sentence. ¹⁹But when the Jewish leaders protested the decision, I felt it necessary to appeal to Caesar, even though I had no desire to press charges against my own people. ²⁰I asked you to come here today so we could get acquainted and so I could explain to you that I am bound with this chain because I believe that the hope of Israel—the Messiah—has already come."

²¹They replied, "We have had no letters from Judea or reports against you from anyone who has come here. ²²But we want to hear what you believe, for the only thing we know about this movement is that it is denounced everywhere."

²³So a time was set, and on that day a large number of people came to Paul's lodging. He explained and testified about the Kingdom of God and tried to persuade them about Jesus from the Scriptures. Using the law of Moses and the books of the prophets, he spoke to them from morning until evening. ²⁴Some were persuaded by the things he said, but others did not believe. ²⁵And after they had argued back and forth among themselves, they left with this final word from Paul: "The Holy Spirit was right when he said to your ancestors through Isaiah the prophet,

²⁶ 'Go and say to this people:
   When you hear what I say,
      you will not understand.
   When you see what I do,
      you will not comprehend.
²⁷ For the hearts of these people are
      hardened,
   and their ears cannot hear,
   and they have closed their
      eyes—

NASB

OTHERWISE THEY MIGHT SEE WITH
  THEIR EYES,
AND HEAR WITH THEIR EARS,
AND UNDERSTAND WITH THEIR
  HEART AND RETURN,
AND I WOULD HEAL THEM.'"

[28] Therefore let it be known to you that this salvation of God has been sent to the Gentiles; they will also listen." [29] [ᵃWhen he had spoken these words, the Jews departed, having a great dispute among themselves.]

[30] And he stayed two full years ᵃin his own rented quarters and was welcoming all who came to him, [31] ᵃpreaching the kingdom of God and teaching concerning the Lord Jesus Christ with all openness, unhindered.

28:14 ᵃLit *Where*   28:15 ᵃLat *Appii Forum*, a station about 43 miles from Rome   ᵇLat *Tres Tabernae*, a station about 33 miles from Rome   28:17 ᵃLit *he*   ᵇOr *forefathers*   28:18 ᵃLit *of death in me*   28:19 ᵃLit *spoke against*   28:20 ᵃOr *invited you to see me and speak with me*   28:22 ᵃLit *you think*   28:26 ᵃLit *with a hearing*   ᵇLit *and*   ᶜLit *seeing you will see*   28:29 ᵃEarly mss do not contain this v   28:30 ᵃOr *at his own expense*   28:31 ᵃOr *proclaiming*

NLT

so their eyes cannot see,
  and their ears cannot hear,
  and their hearts cannot
    understand,
and they cannot turn to me
  and let me heal them.'*

[28] So I want you to know that this salvation from God has also been offered to the Gentiles, and they will accept it."*

[30] For the next two years, Paul lived in Rome at his own expense.* He welcomed all who visited him, [31] boldly proclaiming the Kingdom of God and teaching about the Lord Jesus Christ. And no one tried to stop him.

28:12 *Syracuse* was on the island of Sicily.   28:13 *Rhegium* was on the southern tip of Italy.   28:14 Greek *brothers*.   28:15a Greek *brothers*.   28:15b *The Forum* was about 43 miles (70 kilometers) from Rome.   28:15c *The Three Taverns* was about 35 miles (57 kilometers) from Rome.   28:26-27 Isa 6:9-10 (Greek version).   28:28 Some manuscripts add verse 29, *And when he had said these words, the Jews departed, greatly disagreeing with each other.*   28:30 Or *in his own rented quarters.*

It was a dark day in London on November 10, 1942. Perhaps it had never been darker. Debris lay in piles along the streets after two years of relentless bombing attacks by the Luftwaffe. The buildings that remained were caked with the dust of those who had fallen. The church bells no longer rang in celebration; the city reserved them for warning citizens each time German bombers darkened their skies. Still, the Brits stood firm against the menace of the Third Reich. For years, while the rest of Europe appeased the Nazis, England defied the demented little corporal from Germany and paid dearly with the lives of its citizens. Lately, however, the news from the various battlefronts had appeared promising. The United States had finally joined the conflict, and others began to rally against Germany.

On November 9, city dignitaries had gathered as they had for more than seven hundred years to present the Lord Mayor of London to the Lord Chief Justice for formal approval. Naturally, the long conflict with Germany tempered the normally festive occasion. Still, the city officials carried on with tradition and, on the following day, gathered from all over the city—perhaps stepping over the debris of war on their way—to attend the Lord Mayor's Luncheon at the Mansion House, where Prime Minister Winston Churchill was scheduled to speak.

Despite their recent victories and the addition of several allies, the fight for freedom had a long way to go. The bombings continued and morale teetered on the brink of despair, but Churchill declared, "We mean to hold our own. I have not become the King's First Minister in order to preside over the liquidation of the British Empire."[49] His own determination became a symbol of British resolve during the darkest years of the war—which were yet to come. Fearing that complacency might weaken his countrymen, the British bulldog warned, "Now this is not the end. It is not even the beginning of the end. But it is, perhaps, the end of the beginning."[50]

Churchill's words ring in my ears as we come to the end of Luke's history of the first Christians. The infant church started strong and almost immediately became the target of systematic abuse—beaten black and blue before it ever crawled out of the crib, as it were. Kicked, struggling, bleeding, the community of believers survived those early days nurtured by men like Peter, Barnabas, John, and James (the brother of Jesus), good men who devoted their lives to helping the church mature into a world-changing force. Persecution pushed the people of God out of Jerusalem to carry the good news throughout Judea and Samaria. Then God transformed an enemy of the church into the apostle who would make the greatest impact. Through Paul's ministry, the kingdom of God spanned the empire between Jerusalem and Rome. He had scored crucial victories in the war against evil, but the struggle had only begun. He now would take the fight to the seat of world power.

Paul originally intended to use Rome as a launching pad for the western frontier, where he hoped to continue the ministry he had conducted in the East. But the Lord had other plans. The apostle had carried the gospel far and wide; now the time had come to carry it high, up the political ladder to the pinnacle of power, where the good news might influence entire regions as rulers submitted to King Jesus. If Paul had arrived in Rome as a free man, no politician with any kind of power would give him an audience. But, thanks to the jealousy of the temple officials and the petty maneuvering of local procurators, Paul had an audience with the emperor himself.

— 28:12-14 —

After a much-needed, three-month rest on Malta, Paul and his men boarded another Alexandrian grain transport bound for Syracuse, the capital city of the Roman province of Sicily. Cicero called Syracuse "the most beautiful and highly decorated of all."[51] After a three-day layover, the ship sailed against the wind, tacking its way to Rhegium where its passengers waited for a south wind. Three days later, they arrived in Puteoli, a seaport on the Bay of Naples famous for its odorous sulfur springs.[52] Despite the odor, the port had become the principal port of Rome and a popular resort for rich Romans.

The centurion allowed Paul to visit Christians in the area before departing a week later for the capital city of the empire. The missionaries most likely walked to Capua and then followed the famous Appian Way 143 miles into Rome.

— 28:15-16 —

News of Paul's arrival reached the believers in Rome well in advance. He had not been to Rome before, but several Christians knew him from their travels in Greece and Ephesus, including Aquila and Priscilla (Rom. 16:3-15), and they of course revered his teaching in his letter to the Romans. Some came out to meet him (Acts 28:15). The Greek word for "meet" here, *apantēsis* [529], describes the custom of an entourage coming out of a city to meet a dignitary and then escorting him back, usually in celebration.

The Market of Appius or Forum of Appius was a marketplace and staging post along the Appian Way about 40 miles south of Rome, infamous for its rough setting. The Roman satirist Horace wrote that the station was "stuffed with sailors and surly landlords."[53] He continued, "Here I, on account of the water, which was most vile, proclaim war against my belly. . . . The cursed gnats, and frogs of the fens, drive off repose. While the waterman and a passenger, well-soaked with plenty of thick wine, vie with one another in singing the praises of their absent mistresses."[54] Paul and his growing entourage traveled farther to another post called Three Taverns about 30 miles short of Rome. Several more believers from Rome met him, and this filled him with confidence. The Greek term translated "took courage" in 28:15 is frequently used in the Septuagint to describe the courage given to people in distress (cf. Isa. 41:10-14; 43:1; 44:2).

Luke's narrative reaches a climax with Paul's arrival in Rome. Jesus predicted that His disciples would "be My witnesses both in Jerusalem, and in all Judea and Samaria, and even to the remotest part of the earth" (Acts 1:8). For Luke's purposes, Rome was sufficiently "remote" to fulfill Christ's promise.

Paul still had not been formally charged with a crime. (We can only speculate about what Festus finally wrote in his letter to the emperor.) Yet he wasn't a free man either. Rather than wait for trial in a prison like those suspected of a crime, he found rented quarters and waited under house arrest with only one soldier to guard him (28:16). He could, of course, attempt escape, but he would no longer have the protection of citizenship. This legal protection would be even more valuable in the less stable cities west of Rome.

— 28:17-20 —

While Paul enjoyed far better accommodations than the imperial prison system, he was not permitted to move about freely. Apparently confined to his apartment, he welcomed visitors and his assistants ran errands. He couldn't go to the synagogue, so he invited the Jewish elders to his home (28:17). He had two reasons to speak with them. First, he wanted to gauge their hostility in the event news from the temple officials had reached Rome. Surprisingly, they knew nothing of his dispute (28:21). Second, he always preached to the Jews before turning to the Gentiles.

His address began with a brief summary of his legal history to explain why he had come to Rome and why he was forced to stand before Gentiles for judgment. He wanted them to know that the temple hated him, not the other way around, and that he had done nothing immoral to earn their hostility. His innocence had been affirmed by everyone in Judea except the temple leaders (28:18-19). He concluded with a statement clearly intended to pique their interest. He remained in chains not because of anything he had done, but for his proclaiming "the hope of Israel," an unmistakable reference to the Hebrew Messiah, who promised to fulfill all the prophecies concerning Israel (28:20).

— 28:21-22 —

The Jewish leaders didn't want a dispute coming to Rome. According to Suetonius, Claudius "banished from Rome all the Jews, who were continually making disturbances at the instigation of one Chrestus."[55] External dating points to this occurring ten years earlier, around AD 49 or 50 (cf. 18:2).[56] In the intervening time, Nero had become emperor and Jews had returned. The Jewish elders claimed to have received no communication concerning Paul's charges or anything painting him in a poor light (28:21).

On the one hand, this is surprising. The Jews in Judea were tireless in trying to have Paul either assassinated or executed; why they would not try to involve the synagogues of Rome is a mystery. Of course, the Jews in Rome probably remained purposefully and blissfully ignorant rather than risk upsetting the Romans again. On the other hand, the Jews in Judea may have recognized the hopelessness of pressing a case against Paul in a city where they had no political clout. They could intimidate a procurator; no one intimidates the emperor.

The Roman Jews expressed interest in hearing Paul's views (28:22). They knew enough about Christianity to recognize his reference to "the hope of Israel" (28:20) as related to Jesus. Again, they claimed ignorance of any specific details, perhaps as a way to avoid conflict.

— 28:23-24 —

On the appointed day, the elders of the Jewish synagogues in Rome came to Paul's residence, which was apparently large enough to accommodate a great many visitors at once (28:23). These were the "leading men of the Jews" (28:17), and a large number of Jews lived in Rome at the time. History suggests that at the beginning of the Christian era, as many as sixty thousand Jews lived in and around Rome.[57] Each of these leading men had the ability to influence hundreds, if not thousands, of Jews under their teaching.

Paul focused on the kingdom of God, evoking the very core of Hebrew identity, encompassing their history, culture, cosmology, and government. The kingdom of God is where the covenants of God with Abraham (Gen. 12:1-3; 15:1-21; 17:1-27), Israel (Deut. 28), and David (2 Sam. 7:8-17) all intersect with the promises of the Messiah. And for centuries, Jewish theologians thought they had it all worked out; they thought they understood God's mind and how He would carry out His plan. Paul began "explaining" and "testifying" and "trying to persuade" the Jewish elders to surrender their faulty paradigm and see the kingdom of God as the Father had revealed it through His Son.

For Luke, the kingdom of God is central to the gospel, which affects the entire world on a cosmic, supernatural level that transcends the realm of the physical world. Theologians call his emphasis "eschatological" because it concerns "last things"—the end of time, the days when Christ will physically return to end the world as we know it. His death, burial, and resurrection were essential precursors to His return, when He will end the reign of evil and replace it with His own kingdom. Consequently, we see Luke reference the kingdom of God throughout both his Gospel and Acts.[58] Indeed, Luke highlights the connection between God's kingdom and the church in the very opening of the book (Acts 1:6-8).

The verb translated "explaining" (*ektithēmi* [1620]) means "to elaborate, explain, or expound." Today we might say, "Let me strip this down to its essence."

The verb rendered "solemnly testifying" (*diamartyromai* [1263]) is an intensive form of *martyromai* [3143], which means "to solemnly declare the truth," as one might do under oath. In general, a witness can testify only to what he or she has seen personally, so Paul must have testified to his personal encounter with Christ. He didn't come by his theology on his own through reason; he received it directly from God in the same manner the Old Testament prophets were given divine revelation to pass on to God's people.

"Persuade," or "convince" (*peithō* [3982]), pictures someone using every means possible to get the other party to do something. In the negative sense, it means "to seduce or mislead." In the positive sense, it means "to win over." In this case, Paul wanted the men to believe what he saw as plainly obvious.

Paul used reason and his own personal encounter with Jesus, but he based everything on a clear exposition of the Old Testament Scriptures. He devoted himself to these Jewish leaders all day long—with partial success. Some allowed themselves to consider Paul's evidence; others refused outright (28:24).

— 28:25-28 —

Throughout the book of Acts, Luke has established a consistent pattern (13:46; 18:6; cf. Rom. 11:7-10):

- Someone preaches the gospel to Jews.
- A remnant believes while the majority rejects the good news.
- The Lord turns away from the Jews to focus on Gentiles.
- The nonbelieving Jews persecute the church.

In Rome, Paul saw the pattern beginning to repeat itself. The Jewish leaders began arguing with one another, very few if any professing belief. As they began to leave, Paul quoted Isaiah 6:9-10 (Acts 28:26-27). He most likely quoted the Hebrew text for his Jewish brothers; Luke inserts the verses verbatim from the Septuagint. Paul attributed the words to the Holy Spirit so there was no mistake (28:25). This was not Isaiah's estimation of his Hebrew brothers; these were the words of God. Similarly, Paul's quoting the verses didn't reflect his own opinion; he merely observed the Lord's prophecy coming to pass.

The apostle warned that the Gentiles would gladly receive what

God's covenant people had rejected (28:28). This was a repudiation of the worst kind. This statement brings Luke's narrative to a climax. The age of the church had begun. The Jews have been set aside for a time and will remain sidelined until one day in the future when once again God brings them front and center (Rom. 11:11-29).

— 28:29 —

Early manuscripts don't contain this verse, and it is probably not part of the original work. While this seems to accurately describe the reaction of the synagogue leaders in Rome, Luke probably intended his narrative to end abruptly with Paul's warning and then transition to a brief postscript.

— 28:30-31 —

Luke closes volume two of his history with another summary statement. Paul ministered from his "rental," which appears to have been more substantial than one of the small apartment rooms common in first-century Rome (28:23). From here, the apostle wrote what scholars call the "prison epistles," which include Ephesians, Colossians, Philemon, and Philippians. He freely interacted with the church in Rome, receiving visitors, teaching during the week like he did in the *scholē* [4981] in Ephesus, and preaching to any who darkened his door, Jew or Gentile (28:30). Undoubtedly, Paul had the opportunity to meet more than one Roman dignitary who heard about the famous Jew who couldn't stop talking about a resurrected man named Jesus.

Just as Jesus promised, nothing could or will overpower His church (Matt. 16:18). From Paul's rented home in the capital city of a worldwide empire, the gospel continued to go forth "unhindered" (Acts 28:31).

Almost every scholar agrees that Paul eventually got his hearing and that the overblown nonissue resulted in his anticlimactic release. I don't think it's implausible to suggest that the whole matter annoyed Emperor Nero and only contributed to his growing anti-Semitism. At this point, one hypothesis is as good as another. Some believe Paul launched a mission to the western frontier and did indeed make it to Spain and back. I happen to think Paul embarked on one last farewell tour of the churches around the Aegean Sea: Crete, Miletus, Troas, Philippi, Thessalonica, Berea, Ephesus, and Corinth. (See my extended discussion in the introduction to 1 Timothy in *Insights on 1 & 2 Timothy, Titus*.[59]) After this last visit, Paul finally intended to launch his mission west from Rome. By then, however, Nero's persecution had taken over. Paul couldn't leave the church during its most desperate time, and he became one of many thousands of martyrs before the death of the madman.

Paul's final letter from prison, written just a few months before his execution, mentions Luke by his side (2 Tim. 4:11). The physician doubtless traveled with Paul after his release from house arrest and remained with him until his death. He could have written a brilliant and treasured first-person account of this entire period—but he didn't. The Holy Spirit didn't inspire him to write. The story God wanted written was completed. But not because it was the end of the story—or even the beginning of the end. On the contrary, the story continues today with you and me and a gospel that needs sharing. When Luke laid down his pen, it was merely the end of the beginning.

APPLICATION: ACTS 28:12-31

Guidelines for Evangelism

Those earliest apostles, prophets, and evangelists like Peter, Paul, Barnabas, Silas, and Timothy were true pioneers. Called by God, equipped by the Spirit, and motivated by the gospel of Jesus Christ, they set out to do what no one had attempted before. They left the comforts of the familiar to carry the gospel to unfamiliar people in foreign lands with alien cultures—from Jerusalem to Judea and Samaria and even to the ends of the earth (1:8). Not knowing what to expect or how to prepare, they muddled their way through the first missionary journeys. In the end, they established a paradigm for evangelism and missions many follow today.

From their example of evangelism and missions throughout the book of Acts, I want to conclude this study with three guidelines for disciple-making ministries.

Guideline 1: *Start with the people most familiar to you.* When entering a new area, the apostles usually approached their fellow Jews in the synagogues first. This was not simply for theological reasons—"to the Jew first and also to the Greek" (Rom. 1:16; cf. Acts 3:26; 13:46)—but for practical reasons as well. Their kindred bond in Abraham established an immediate trust. Their shared Hebrew culture made communication easier. Their shared worldview gave them fewer theological obstacles to overcome. Most importantly, converts from this familiar group could facilitate communication with the less familiar groups in their community and help Paul and Barnabas establish trust more effectively.

Today, all of us have circles of family, friends, colleagues, or neighbors who are like us in many ways. We share similar language, culture, values, and even daily routines. When it comes to evangelism and missions—carrying out the great commission—we may not be able to cross the world, but all of us can cross the street. Start in your own "Jerusalem and Judea." Share the love of Christ and the message of the gospel with those you know and those who know you.

Guideline 2: *Learn everything you can about the people you intend to reach.* When the apostles had been cast out of the synagogues, or if they entered a place where there was no Jewish population, they tried to communicate with the Gentile population as best they could. In doing so, they drew on knowledge learned through open interaction with people they would normally not understand, overcoming prejudices and setting aside cultural obstacles.

Paul's sermon on Mars Hill during his second missionary journey shows how he could use this knowledge of many cultures, religions, and values to his advantage (17:22-34). He got to know his audience to better understand their worldview. He began his address by establishing rapport, commending them for their interest in spiritual matters, and affirming points of agreement. He then drove his message straight for the gospel. Many still rejected his preaching, but not because he was unprepared or unclear.

When we step out beyond our own "Jerusalem and Judea," we enter uncomfortable territory. But it need not be insurmountable or unreachable. Like Peter and Paul, we too can learn how to minister cross-culturally. To do so, we need to learn how others think, what they think, and why. We need to find points of contact, connections that give us a platform to share our story and to introduce them to the great story—the saving work of Jesus Christ. Only when we learn to listen well will we be able to speak well.

Guideline 3: *Go as far as God will lead you.* It's often said that "where the Lord guides, He provides." It may sound cliché, but it's true. We've seen God's guidance and provision in the ministries of Peter and Paul, Barnabas and Silvanus—from Jerusalem and Judea, throughout Samaria, even to Rome and beyond. This divine provision didn't always come as material support in the form of cash or supplies. In fact, Paul often had to work for his own support as a tentmaker. However, God always provided opportunities, opening doors for evangelism before crowds and kings. He steered the missionaries into places they would never have gone on their own. And He provided them with the right ministry partners at the right times in the right places.

As we seek to serve the Lord beyond our own Jerusalem, Judea, and Samaria, and even in the remotest parts of the earth, we should step out in faith as God leads, trusting that He will never lead us astray and knowing that, like those earliest missionaries in the book of Acts, where He guides, He also provides. Whether you're the one going or the one sending, never lose sight of God's own vision for reaching those at the ends of the earth.

ENDNOTES

INTRODUCTION

1   William A. Sunday, "Billy Sunday's Bible," *The Christian Advocate*, vol. 91 (New York: Hunt & Eaton, 1916), 890.
2   F. F. Bruce, *The Book of the Acts*, rev. ed., The New International Commentary on the New Testament, ed. Gordon D. Fee (Grand Rapids: Eerdmans, 1988), 13.
3   William Barclay, *The Acts of the Apostles* (Philadelphia: Westminster John Knox Press, 1966), xvii.
4   Though neither the Gospel nor the book of Acts explicitly identifies Luke as the author, he is identified as such in a second-century description of the New Testament canon. See Bruce M. Metzger, "The Muratorian Fragment," in *The Canon of the New Testament: Its Origin, Development, and Significance* (Oxford: Clarendon Press, 1987), 305.
5   Charles R. Swindoll, *Insights on Luke* (Grand Rapids: Zondervan, 2012).
6   Luke included himself in three sections of Acts, in which he used the first-person "we" instead of the third-person "they."

THE BIRTH OF THE CHURCH (ACTS 1:1–7:60)

1   Gerhard Kittel and Gerhard Friedrich, eds., *Theological Dictionary of the New Testament: Abridged in One Volume*, trans. and ed. Geoffrey W. Bromiley (Grand Rapids: Eerdmans, 1985), 316.
2   William Arndt, Frederick W. Danker, and Walter Bauer, eds., *A Greek-English Lexicon of the New Testament and Other Early Christian Literature*, 3rd ed. (Chicago: University of Chicago Press, 2000), s.v. μαρτυρία.
3   Carmine Gallo, *The Innovation Secrets of Steve Jobs: Insanely Different Principles for Breakthrough Success* (New York: McGraw-Hill, 2010), 1.
4   See Everett Ferguson, *Baptism in the Early Church: History, Theology, and Liturgy in the First Five Centuries* (Grand Rapids: Eerdmans, 2009), 33.
5   There is some dispute about whether the rabbinical sources describing "proselyte baptism" reflect a later post-Christian development or a practice that was current at the time of Christ and the founding of the church. For a discussion, see ibid., 76–82.
6   Harry A. Ironside, *Acts*, Ironside Expository Commentaries (Grand Rapids: Kregel Publications, 2007), 18.
7   Cf. Josephus, *Wars of the Jews* 1.621; 2.171; *Antiquities* 18.59; 19.349; *Life* 138; Euripides, *Rhesus*, line 797; Hesiod, *Shield of Heracles*, line 365; Homer, *Iliad* 2.418; 4.544; 5.58; Philo, *On the Creation* 157; *On Husbandry* 113; *On Dreams* 2.269.
8   This story is found in 1 Maccabees 2, a chapter from a deuterocanonical book recording intertestamental Jewish history.
9   Robert L. Wise, *Your Churning Place* (Glendale, CA: Regal Books, 1977), 66.
10 Kittel and Friedrich, eds., *Dictionary: Abridged*, 75.

[11] Richard N. Longenecker, "The Acts of the Apostles," in *The Expositor's Bible Commentary*, ed. Frank E. Gaebelein and J. D. Douglas, vol. 9, *John—Acts* (Grand Rapids: Zondervan, 1981), 272.

[12] Some would add Acts 19:2-7, but in this case, the men had not heard the complete gospel; they had merely submitted to the baptism of John the Baptizer—a baptism of repentance in expectation of the coming Messiah.

[13] W. E. Vine, Merrill F. Unger, and William White Jr., *Vine's Complete Expository Dictionary of Old and New Testament Words* (Nashville: Thomas Nelson, 1996), 2:636.

[14] Henry Jacobsen, *The Acts: Then and Now* (Wheaton, IL: Victor Books, 1973), 20.

[15] E. M. Blaiklock, *The Acts of the Apostles: An Historical Commentary*, reprint ed., Tyndale New Testament Commentaries 5 (Grand Rapids: Eerdmans, 1979), 58.

[16] Lazarus doesn't qualify; he was resurrected in his corruptible body, so he eventually died again. Jesus was raised to a new kind of life that cannot suffer disease, injury, deprivation, or death.

[17] Kittel and Friedrich, eds., *Dictionary: Abridged*, 641–642.

[18] Daniel B. Wallace, *Greek Grammar Beyond the Basics: An Exegetical Syntax of the New Testament* (Grand Rapids: Zondervan, 1996), 369–371.

[19] A. T. Robertson, *Word Pictures in the New Testament* (Oak Harbor, WA: Logos Research Systems, 1997), Acts 2:38.

[20] Arndt, Danker, and Bauer, eds., *Lexicon*, 552.

[21] Geoffrey W. Bromiley, ed., *The International Standard Bible Encyclopedia*, rev. ed. (Grand Rapids: Eerdmans, 1979), 1:66.

[22] Millard J. Erickson, *Christian Theology* (Grand Rapids: Baker, 1985), 1057. Emphasis mine.

[23] Meir Ben-Dov, *In the Shadow of the Temple: The Discovery of Ancient Jerusalem*, trans. I. Friedman (Jerusalem: Keter, 1982), 77; cited in *The Anchor Bible Dictionary*, 6:365.

[24] Flavius Josephus, *Wars of the Jews*, in *The Works of Josephus: Complete and Unabridged*, trans. William Whiston (Peabody, MA: Hendrickson, 1996), 5:201.

[25] Temple officials only allowed people to beg if they had no other means of obtaining money. Vocational rehabilitation didn't really exist in ancient times.

[26] Karl Marx, *Critique of Hegel's "Philosophy of Right,"* ed. Joseph O'Malley (Cambridge: Cambridge University Press, 1970), 131.

[27] Josephus, *Wars of the Jews* 2.162–166.

[28] Bromiley, *International Standard Bible Encyclopedia*, 1:128.

[29] Johannes Weiss, *Earliest Christianity: A History of the Period A.D. 30–150* (Gloucester, MA: Peter Smith, 1970), 1:42–43.

[30] In Greek, "son of *paraklēsis*" [3874].

[31] Adapted from Charles R. Swindoll, *Jesus: The Greatest Life of All* (Nashville: Thomas Nelson, 2007), 80–81.

[32] Elton Trueblood, *The Incendiary Fellowship* (New York: Harper & Row, 1967).

[33] F. F. Bruce, *The Spreading Flame* (Grand Rapids: Eerdmans, 1953).

[34] For other summary statements, see Acts 2:42, 47; 4:4; 5:14; 6:1; 9:31; 12:24; 16:5; 19:20; and 28:31.

[35] Jerusalem Talmud, *Megillah* 3 [*Daf* 23a].

[36] L. L. Grabbe, "Synagogues in Pre-70 Palestine: A Re-Assessment," in *Ancient Synagogues: Historical Analysis and Archaeological Discovery*, ed. Dan Urman and Paul V. M. Flesher, vol. 1 (Leiden: Brill, 1995), 22.

[37] James D. G. Dunn, *Christianity in the Making*, vol. 2, *Beginning from Jerusalem* (Grand Rapids: Eerdmans, 2009), 247.

[38] Z. Safrai, "The Communal Functions of the Synagogue in the Land of Israel in the Rabbinic Period," in *Ancient Synagogues*, ed. Urman and Flesher, vol. 1, 200.

39 Michael William Holmes, *The Apostolic Fathers in English* (Grand Rapids: Baker, 2006), 151.

40 Laurna L. Berg, "The Illegalities of Jesus' Religious and Civil Trials," *Bibliotheca Sacra*, 161, no. 643 (July–September, 2004), 330–342; citing the Mishnah *Sanhedrin* 3:3-4.

41 Darrell L. Bock, "Jesus v. Sanhedrin: Why Jesus 'Lost' His Trial," *Christianity Today* 42, no. 4 (April 6, 1998): 49.

42 See Acts 7:2, 11, 12, 15, 19, 32, 38, 39, 44, 45 (two times).

43 See Exod. 32:9; 33:3, 5; Lev. 26:41; Deut. 30:6; Jer. 4:4; 9:25-26; and Ezek. 44:7-9.

44 Stephen had been using "our fathers" (Acts 7:11-12, 15, 19, 38-39, 44-45) but switched to "your fathers" to denounce his opponents (7:51-52).

45 Berg, "Illegalities," 330–342.

46 Tertullian, *The Apology*, in *The Ante-Nicene Fathers: Translations of the Writings of the Fathers down to A.D. 325*, ed. Alexander Roberts, James Donaldson, and A. Cleveland Coxe, vol. 3 (Grand Rapids: Eerdmans, 1997), 3:55.

THE RISE OF THE CHURCH (ACTS 8:1–12:25)

1 Thomas Kuhn, *The Structure of Scientific Revolutions*, 3rd ed. (Chicago: University of Chicago Press, 1996).

2 J. Goetzmann, "Conversion, Penitence, Repentance, Proselyte," in *The New International Dictionary of New Testament Theology,* ed. Colin Brown (Grand Rapids: Zondervan, 1986), 1.357.

3 Josephus, *Antiquities* 13.254–256.

4 Ibid.

5 Fritz Graf, *Magic in the Ancient World*, trans. Franklin Philip, Revealing Antiquity 10 (Cambridge, MA: Harvard University Press, 1999), 1.

6 Ibid., 2.

7 At no other time does the New Testament imply that the Holy Spirit comes through the agency of man.

8 Irenaeus, *Against Heresies* 1.23.2, in *The Ante-Nicene Fathers*, ed. Roberts, Donaldson, and Coxe, 1:348.

9 Ibid., 1.27.1–2, 1:352.

10 Bromiley, *International Standard Bible Encyclopedia*, 1:591.

11 By the sixth century AD, some manuscripts had added, "And Philip said, 'If you believe with all your heart, you may.' And he answered and said, 'I believe that Jesus Christ is the Son of God'" (Acts 8:37, NASB).

12 The earliest New Testament manuscript evidence for the reading is in the sixth century AD; however, it's clear that the early church knew a tradition of this confession. Irenaeus (AD 130–202) wrote, "The believing eunuch . . . said, 'I believe Jesus Christ to be the Son of God'" (*Against Heresies* 3.12.8).

13 The term "snatched away" (*harpazō* [726]) can describe making off with loot (Matt. 12:29; 13:19), taking prey (John 10:12, 28, 29), taking a prisoner (John 6:15; Acts 23:10), being "caught up" in a visionary state (2 Cor. 12:2), or being caught up into heaven (1 Thes. 4:17; Rev. 12:5).

14 D. James Kennedy, *Evangelism Explosion*, 4th ed. (Carol Stream, IL: Tyndale, 1996), 56.

15 Everard Meynell, *The Life of Francis Thompson* (New York: Charles Scribner's Sons, 1913), 58.

16 Francis Thompson, *The Hound of Heaven* (New York: Dodd, Mead, 1934), 43–44.

17 Johannes P. Louw and Eugene Albert Nida, eds., *Greek-English Lexicon of the New Testament: Based on Semantic Domains*, electronic ed. of the 2nd ed. (New York: United Bible Societies, 1996), 1:360.

18 John F. Walvoord, Roy B. Zuck, and Dallas Theological Seminary, *The Bible Knowledge Commentary: An Exposition of the Scriptures* (Wheaton, IL: Victor Books, 1983), 377–378.

19 Obviously, this is not Judas Iscariot, who had committed suicide by this time. Judas (the Greek rendering of Judah), was an extremely popular name in the first century because it was the name of the patriarch for whom the tribe of Judah was named. Genesis 29:35 connects his name to the idea of praise (cf. Gen. 49:8).

20 Kenneth S. Wuest, *Wuest's Word Studies from the Greek New Testament: For the English Reader* (Grand Rapids: Eerdmans, 1997), Gal. 1:18.

21 A. W. Tozer, *The Root of the Righteous* (Camp Hill, PA: Christian Publications, 1986), 137.

22 Alan Redpath, in an unpublished sermon delivered in Chafer Chapel at Dallas Theological Seminary in 1959.

23 I. Howard Marshall, *The Acts of the Apostles: An Introduction and Commentary*, reprint ed., Tyndale New Testament Commentaries 5 (Grand Rapids: Eerdmans, 1980), 179.

24 A third might be 2 Kings 4:18-37, which tells of a woman who laid her dead son on Elisha's bed in the upper room of the family home, the prophet's guest quarters. She had complete trust that the boy would be returned to life because God had promised her a son. So she sent for Elisha. Through prayer, Elisha raised the boy to life.

25 John Walvoord, *The Holy Spirit* (Grand Rapids: Zondervan, 1991), 174.

26 Walter A. Elwell and Philip W. Comfort, *Tyndale Bible Dictionary*, Tyndale Reference Library (Wheaton, IL: Tyndale, 2001), 243–244.

27 See Darrell L. Bock, *Acts*, Baker Exegetical Commentary on the New Testament (Grand Rapids: Baker, 2007), 385–387.

28 See discussion in Alexander Kyrychenko, *The Roman Army and the Expansion of the Gospel* (Berlin: Walter de Gruyter, 2014), 38–39.

29 Alexander Whyte, *Bible Characters*, vol. 5, *Stephen to Timothy* (Edinburgh: Oliphant, Anderson & Ferrier, 1901), 36–37.

30 See Paul's perspective on clean and unclean foods in Romans 14:14; 1 Corinthians 10:19; Ephesians 2:11-22; and 1 Timothy 4:3-4.

31 I. Howard Marshall, *Acts*, 186.

32 Robertson, *Word Pictures*, Acts 10:17.

33 Many pagan temples hired men of science and paid them large sums to engineer illusions.

34 The preposition is *pros* [4314] with an accusative object, which is a marker of opposition.

35 Jack Finegan, *The Archaeology of the New Testament: The Mediterranean World of the Early Christian Apostles* (New York: Routledge, 1981), 52.

36 Richard Wallace and Wynne Williams, *The Three Worlds of Paul of Tarsus* (New York: Routledge, 1998), 181–182.

37 C. J. Hemer, "Tarsus," in *International Standard Bible Encyclopedia*, ed. Bromiley, 4:736.

38 See Finegan, *Archaeology of the New Testament*, 51–52.

39 Walter A. Elwell and Barry J. Beitzel, *Baker Encyclopedia of the Bible* (Grand Rapids: Baker, 1988), 2038.

40 See Edward Gibbon, *The History of the Decline and Fall of the Roman Empire* (New York: Harper & Brothers, 1898), 2:638–639.

41 He actually died in October of AD 54 as a victim of assassination: "Now Claudius Caesar died when he had reigned thirteen years, eight months, and twenty days; and a report went about that he was poisoned by his wife Agrippina" (Josephus, *Antiquities* 20.148).

42 Cassius Dio, *Roman History* 11.11; Suetonius, *Divus Claudius* 18.2; and Tacitus, *Annals* 12.43.

43 Josephus, *Antiquities* 20.51–53.

44 Herod Agrippa I (9 BC–AD 44) gained power over Galilee in AD 39 and over Judah and Samaria in AD 40, ruling until his death in AD 44. Claudius served as Roman emperor from AD 41–54. They had to deal with a series of famines during his reign, which explains Luke's "about that time" to refer to events that related to both Herod's and Claudius's reigns.

45 Ibid., 105–109.

46 For a detailed account of the life and legacy of Herod Antipas and the Herodian dynasty, see the magisterial work of Harold W. Hoehner, *Herod Antipas*, Society for New Testament Studies Monograph Series 17 (Cambridge: Cambridge University Press, 1972).

47 See Harold W. Hoehner, "Herodian Dynasty," in Bruce M. Metzger and Michael D. Coogan, eds., *The Oxford Companion to the Bible* (Oxford: Oxford University Press, 1993), 283.

48 In truth, Agrippa I was Jewish by the slimmest margin. His paternal grandmother was Jewish; his other three grandparents were Idumean, descendants of Esau.

49 Hoehner, "Herodian Dynasty," 283.

50 Mishnah *Sanhedrin* 4:1; see also Berg, "Illegalities," 330–342.

51 Very often, wealthy families adopted orphans, giving them a place to live in exchange for helping maintain the home. Technically "servants," they were really unofficial members of the household.

52 Tremper Longman III, ed. *The Baker Illustrated Bible Dictionary* (Grand Rapids: Baker, 2013), 69.

53 Bock, *Acts*, 428–429.

54 This particular portion of the Talmud was not completed until AD 500 at the earliest. It nevertheless reflects a fairly stable body of traditional teaching.

55 Josephus, *Antiquities* 19.8.1 (338).

56 Ibid., 19.8.2 (343).

57 Robyn Tracy, "Syria," in *Graeco-Roman Setting*, ed. David W. J. Gill and Conrad Gempf, The Book of Acts in Its First Century Setting 2 (Grand Rapids: Eerdmans, 1994), 246.

58 Babylonian Talmud, Tractate *Sotah*, Folio 41a, trans. Rev. A. Cohen, ed. Rabbi Dr. I. Epstein.

59 Ibid.

60 Josephus, *Antiquities* 19.8.2 (343–346).

61 Ibid., 19.8.2 (346)

THE EXPANSION OF THE CHURCH (ACTS 13:1–20:2)

1 Gerhard Kittel, Geoffrey W. Bromiley, and Gerhard Friedrich, eds., *Theological Dictionary of the New Testament* (Grand Rapids: Eerdmans, 1964), 2:93.

2 See Acts 17:2, 17; 18:4, 19; 19:8, 9; 20:7, 9; 24:12, 25.

3 F. B. Meyer, *Christ in Isaiah* (London: Morgan & Scott, 1917), 9.

4 Magnus Zetterholm, *The Formation of Christianity in Antioch: A Social-Scientific Approach to the Separation between Judaism and Christianity*, Routledge Early Church Monographs (New York: Routledge, 2003), 41.

5 Ibid., 42.

6 Glanville Downey, *A History of Antioch in Syria: From Seleucus to the Arab Conquest* (Princeton: Princeton University Press, 1961), 61.

7 Ibid., 19, 105.

8 Adam Kolman Marshak, *The Many Faces of Herod the Great* (Grand Rapids: Eerdmans, 2015), 145–146.

9   Trevor Bryce, *The Routledge Handbook of the Peoples and Places of Ancient Western Asia* (New York: Routledge, 2009), 524.

10 Vassos Karageorghis, *Cyprus: From the Stone Age to the Romans*, Ancient Peoples and Places 101 (New York: Thames & Hudson, 1982), 172.

11 William Smith, *A Concise Dictionary of Greek and Roman Antiquities*, ed. F. Warre Cornish (London: John Murray, 1898), 517.

12 Arndt, Danker, and Bauer, eds., *Lexicon*, 902.

13 Philip de Souza, *Piracy in the Graeco-Roman World* (Cambridge: Cambridge University Press, 1999), 97.

14 Mal Couch, ed., *A Bible Handbook to the Acts of the Apostles* (Grand Rapids: Kregel Publications, 1999), 307.

15 David Livingstone, quoted in *The Contagion of Character*, Newell Dwight Hillis (New York: Fleming H. Revell, 1911), 229.

16 G. Walter Hansen, "Galatia," in *Graeco-Roman Setting*, ed. Gill and Gempf, 384.

17 John B. Polhill, *Paul and His Letters* (Nashville: Broadman & Holman, 1999), 88.

18 Stephen Mitchell and Marc Waelkens, *Pisidian Antioch: The Site and Its Monuments* (London: Duckworth, 1998), 3, 15.

19 Alfred Hoerth and John McRay, *Bible Archaeology: An Exploration of the History and Culture of Early Civilizations* (Grand Rapids: Baker, 2005), 243.

20 See Charles R. Swindoll, *Hand Me Another Brick* (New York: Random House, 1983), 93.

21 Clyde E. Fant and Mitchell G. Reddish, *A Guide to Biblical Sites in Greece and Turkey* (Oxford: Oxford University Press, 2003), 228–229.

22 William J. Larkin Jr., *Acts*, The IVP New Testament Commentary Series, ed. Grant R. Osborne, vol. 5 (Downers Grove, IL: InterVarsity Press, 1995), 208.

23 Paul A. Hartog, "Lystra," in *Eerdmans Dictionary of the Bible*, ed. David Noel Freedman (Grand Rapids: Eerdmans, 2000), 834.

24 Elwell and Beitzel, *Encyclopedia*, 1370.

25 Ovid, *Metamorphoses* 8.970–1122.

26 Tom Constable, *Tom Constable's Expository Notes on the Bible* (Galaxie Software, 2003), Acts 14:11.

27 See Gen. 37:29, 34; Num. 14:6; Josh. 7:6; Judg. 11:35; 2 Sam. 1:2, 11. Second Temple Judaism did this to signal rejection of blasphemy (Matt. 26:65; Mark 14:63-64; Mishnah *Sanhedrin* 7.5; 1 Macc. 2:14; 3:47).

28 Craig S. Keener, *The IVP Bible Background Commentary: New Testament*, 2nd ed. (Downers Grove, IL: InterVarsity Press, 2014), 364.

29 For discussion on the Jewish practice of proselyte baptism, see Ferguson, *Baptism in the Early Church*, 76–82.

30 See Yohanan Aharoni, *The Land of the Bible: A Historical Geography*, rev. and enlarged ed., trans. A. F. Rainey (Philadelphia: Westminster John Knox Press, 1979), 45–54.

31 Michael Lewis, *Moneyball: The Art of Winning an Unfair Game* (New York: W. W. Norton, 2003).

32 Albert Pietersma and Benjamin Wright, eds., *A New English Translation of the Septuagint*, trans. George E. Howard (New York: Oxford University Press, 2009), Amos 9:11-12.

33 Timothy J. Keller, foreword to *Bonhoeffer: Pastor, Martyr, Prophet, Spy*, by Eric Metaxas (Nashville: Thomas Nelson, 2010), xv–xvi.

34 Early manuscripts lack the words "But it seemed good to Silas to remain there" (15:34); perhaps later copyists inserted them to explain the presence of Silas in Antioch later (15:40).

35 Silas was also known as Silvanus (2 Cor. 1:19; 1 Thes. 1:1; 2 Thes. 1:1).

36 Robertson, *Word Pictures*, Acts 15:39.

37 Jerome Murphy-O'Connor, *St. Paul's Ephesus: Texts and Archaeology* (Collegeville,

MN: Liturgical Press, 2008), 36–37; David French, "Acts and the Roman Roads of Asia Minor," in *Graeco-Roman Setting*, ed. Gill and Gempf, 52.

38 Konstantinos P. Moustakas, "Kavalla," in *Encyclopedia of Ancient Greece*, ed. Nigel Wilson (New York: Routledge, 2006), 403–404.

39 James S. Jeffers, *The Greco-Roman World of the New Testament Era: Exploring the Background of Early Christianity* (Downers Grove, IL: InterVarsity Press, 1999), 281–282.

40 Robert B. Hughes and J. Carl Laney, *Tyndale Concise Bible Commentary* (Wheaton, IL: Tyndale, 1990), 599.

41 This is quite likely in light of the expulsion of Jews from Rome that occurred around this time (c. AD 49) under Claudius (cf. Acts 18:2).

42 See Mark J. Olson, "Lydia," in Watson E. Mills et al., eds., *Mercer Dictionary of the Bible* (Macon, GA: Mercer University Press, 1990), 531–532.

43 Leonard Victor Rutgers, "Roman Policy toward the Jews: Expulsions from the City of Rome during the First Century C.E.," in *Judaism and Christianity in First-Century Rome*, ed. Karl P. Donfried and Peter Richardson (Grand Rapids: Eerdmans, 1998), 94, 107–108.

44 Ibid., 105–107.

45 Winston Churchill, in his speech to Harrow School, 29 October 1941.

46 John Powell, *Fully Human, Fully Alive: A New Life through a New Vision* (Thomas More Association, 1989), 11–12.

47 Roberts, Donaldson, and Coxe, eds., *The Ante-Nicene Fathers*, 1:490.

48 Yannis Lolos, "Via Egnatia after Egnatius: Imperial Policy and Inter-regional Contacts," in *Greek and Roman Networks in the Mediterranean*, ed. Irad Malkin, Christy Constantakopoulou, and Katerina Panagopoulou (New York: Routledge, 2009), 267–269.

49 Ralph Waldo Emerson, "Circles," in *Essays: First Series* (1841).

50 See Leon Morris, *The First and Second Epistles to the Thessalonians*, rev. ed. (Grand Rapids: Eerdmans, 1991), 2.

51 William E. Dunstan, *Ancient Rome* (Lanham, MD: Rowman & Littlefield, 2011), 159.

52 Cicero, *In Pisonem* 89.

53 David H. Conwell, *Connecting a City to the Sea: The History of the Athenian Long Walls* (Leiden: Brill, 2008), 13.

54 Barclay, *Acts*, 152.

55 Richard Wallace, "Epicurus 341–270 BC," in *Encyclopedia of Ancient Greece*, ed. Wilson, 263.

56 This also alludes to a poem titled "Hymn to Zeus," which was written by Cleanthes, a disciple of Zeno, the father of Stoicism. Paul demonstrated that the Stoics of Athens had drifted from their founder by claiming it was unreasonable to believe that a god would interact with creation.

57 Aratus, *Phaenomena* 5.

58 William Barclay, *A Beginner's Guide to the New Testament* (Louisville: Westminster John Knox Press, 1995), 30.

59 William Smith, ed., *Dictionary of Greek and Roman Geography* (Boston: Little, Brown, 1854), 1:678.

60 See a detailed description of Corinth in the first century in "The Scholarly Quest for Paul's Church at Corinth: A Critical Survey," in *Christianity at Corinth: The Quest for the Pauline Church*, ed. Edward Adams and David G. Horrell (Louisville: Westminster John Knox Press, 2004), 2–8.

61 Bromiley, *International Standard Bible Encyclopedia*, 1:773.

62 See Bruce, *The Book of the Acts*, 352.

63 Adapted from Charles R. Swindoll, *Insights on John* (Carol Stream, IL: Tyndale, 2014), 32–34.

64 Stanley D. Toussaint, "Acts," in *Bible Knowledge Commentary*, ed. Walvoord, Zuck, and Dallas, 409.

65 1,127,332,800,000 gallons.

66 For a detailed description of Hoover Dam, see Joseph E. Stevens, *Hoover Dam: An American Adventure* (Norman, OK: University of Oklahoma Press, 1988).

67 Craig S. Keener, *Acts: An Exegetical Commentary* (Grand Rapids: Baker Academic, 2014), 3:597.

68 Ralph P. Martin and Peter H. Davids, eds., *Dictionary of the Later New Testament and Its Developments*, The IVP Bible Dictionary Series 7 (Downers Grove, IL: InterVarsity Press, 1997), s.v. "Ephesus."

69 Plutarch, *Plutarch's Morals*, trans. William W. Goodwin (Boston: Little, Brown, 1878), 5:414.

70 Daniel W. Graham, "Heraclitus," in *Encyclopedia of Ancient Greece*, ed. Wilson, 346–347.

71 Martin and Davids, *Dictionary*, s.v. "Ephesus."

72 Robertson, *Word Pictures*, Acts 19:11.

73 G. Campbell Morgan, *The Acts of the Apostles*, reprint ed. (London: Pickering & Inglis, 1965), 350.

74 Everett Ferguson, *Backgrounds of Early Christianity*, 3rd ed. (Grand Rapids: Eerdmans, 2003), 198.

75 Keener, *IVP Bible Background Commentary*, Acts 19:32.

THE CHALLENGES OF THE CHURCH (ACTS 20:3–28:31)

1 Douglas MacArthur, *Reminiscences* (New York: Ishi Press, 2010), 142–143.

2 Ibid., 145.

3 Fant and Reddish, *A Guide to Biblical Sites in Greece and Turkey*, 259–260.

4 The preposition *dia* [1223] with the genitive form of *pneuma* [4151].

5 Adapted from Charles R. Swindoll, *Saying It Well: Touching Others with Your Words* (New York: Faith Words, 2012), 75.

6 J. Grant Howard Jr., *Knowing God's Will and Doing It!* (Grand Rapids: Zondervan, 1976), 66.

7 Ralph Waldo Emerson, "Self-Reliance," in *Self-Reliance and Other Essays* (Nashville: American Renaissance, 2010), 36.

8 Elbert Hubbard, *Love, Life and Work: Being a Book of Opinions Reasonably Good-Natured Concerning How to Attain the Highest Happiness for One's Self with the Least Possible Harm to Others* (self-published, 1906), 54.

9 Josephus, *Antiquities* 19.6.1 (293–294).

10 Lee I. Levine, *Jerusalem: Portrait of a City in the Second Temple Period (538 B.C.E.–70 C.E.)* (Philadelphia: The Jewish Publication Society, 2002), 194–196.

11 Josephus, *Wars of the Jews* 2.13.5 (263).

12 Rudyard Kipling, "If—," in *Rewards and Fairies* (New York: Doubleday, Page & Company, 1911), 181–182.

13 Constable, *Expository Notes*, Acts 23:4-5.

14 Josephus, *Antiquities* 20.180.

15 Ibid., 20.165.

16 Philo of Alexandria, *On the Creation* 105, in *The Works of Philo: Complete and Unabridged*, trans. Charles Duke Yonge (Peabody, MA: Hendrickson, 1996), 16.

17 Emil Schürer, *A History of the Jewish People in the Age of Jesus Christ*, rev. and ed. Geza Vermes, Fergus Millar, and Matthew Black (London: Bloomsbury, 2014), 1:459–460.

18 Rainer Riesner, *Paul's Early Period: Chronology, Mission Strategy, Theology*, trans. Doug Stott (Grand Rapids: Eerdmans, 1998), 104–105; Gerhard A. Krodel, *Acts*, Augsburg Commentary on the New Testament (Minneapolis: Augsburg, 1986), 434–435.

19 Josephus, *Antiquities* 20.162–164, 179.

20 Tacitus, *Histories* 5.9.

21 Josephus, *Antiquities* 20.182.

22 Josephus, *Wars of the Jews* 2.224.

23 Daniel R. Schwartz, *Studies in the Jewish Background of Christianity*, WUNT 60 (Tübingen: Mohr Siebeck, 1992), 226–227.

24 Wise, *Your Churning Place*, 9–10.

25 Adapted from "Origin of Procrastination," *New Cyclopaedia of Prose Illustrations*, ed. Elon Foster (New York: Thomas Y. Crowell, 1870), 1:527.

26 The infinitive *echō* [2192], "to have," acts adverbially to modify "to watch or guard." I take it to be an adverb of result (Wallace, *Grammar*, 592).

27 Tacitus, *Histories* 5.9.

28 Ironside, *Acts*, Ironside Expository Commentaries (Grand Rapids: Kregel, 2007), 323.

29 Josephus, *Antiquities* 20.142–143.

30 Constable, *Expository Notes*, Acts 24:27.

31 Josephus, *Antiquities* 20.185–188.

32 Ibid., 20.179.

33 Ibid., 20.205–207.

34 V. Raymond Edman, *The Disciplines of Life* (Eugene, OR: Harvest House Publishers, 1982), 82.

35 Constable, *Expository Notes*, Acts 24:27.

36 Josephus, *Antiquities* 20.145–147. Josephus became close friends with Agrippa II, who provided inside information for *Antiquities* and *Wars of the Jews*, praised him for his accuracy, and commissioned copies for himself.

37 Constable, *Expository Notes*, Acts 24:27.

38 Pliny the Younger, "Letter 97," in *The Selected Letters of Pliny: Pliny the Younger*, trans. William Melmoth, rev. F. C. T. Bosanquet (Lawrence, KS: Digireads Publishing, 2010), 136.

39 Louw and Nida, eds., *Lexicon*, 738.

40 The Greek word *chiliarchos* [5506] means "commander of a thousand."

41 Lionel Casson, *Ships and Seamanship in the Ancient World* (Baltimore: Johns Hopkins University Press, 1995), 164.

42 Ibid., 166.

43 Herodotus, *Histories* 2.5.2, in *Herodotus. With an English Translation by A. D. Godley*, ed. A. D. Godley (Medford, MA: Harvard University Press, 1920).

44 Hippocrates, *Precepts* 1, in *Hippocrates Collected Works I*, ed. W. H. S. Jones (Cambridge, MA: Harvard University Press, 1923), 313.

45 Larkin, *Acts*, 381.

46 Pliny the Elder, *The Natural History* 2.47, ed. John Bostock (Medford, MA: Taylor and Francis, Red Lion Court, Fleet Street, 1855), 1075.

47 Colin J. Hemer, "First Person Narrative in Acts 27–28," *Tyndale Bulletin* 36 (1985): 79–109.

48 Victor E. Frankl, *Man's Search for Meaning* (New York: Simon & Schuster, 1962), 73–74.

49 Winston S. Churchill, "A Speech at the Lord Mayor's Day Luncheon at the Mansion House, London, 10 November 1942," in *The End of the Beginning* (London: Cassell, 1943), 265–266.

50 Ibid.

51 Cicero, *In Verrem* 4.52, in *The Orations of M. Tullius Cicero*, trans. C. D. Yonge (London: George Bell & Sons, 1903).

52 H. F. Helmolt, *The World's History: A Survey of Man's Record*, vol. 4, *The Mediterranean Nations* (London: William Heinemann, 1902), 331.

53 Horace, *Satires* 1.5, in *The Works of Horace*, trans. C. Smart (Medford, MA: Harper & Brothers, 1863).

54 Ibid.

55 C. Suetonius Tranquillus, *Divus Claudius* 25, in *Suetonius: The Lives of the Twelve Caesars: An English Translation, Augmented with the Biographies of Contemporary Statesmen, Orators, Poets, and Other Associates*, ed. Alexander Thomson (Medford, MA: Gebbie, 1889). Some scholars consider "Chrestus" to be a misinformed reference to "Christos."

56 Brian Rapske, *Paul in Roman Custody*, The Book of Acts in Its First Century Setting 3 (Grand Rapids: Eerdmans, 1994), 161.

57 F. F. Bruce, *Paul: Apostle of the Heart Set Free* (Grand Rapids: Eerdmans, 1977), 30.

58 Luke 1:33; 4:43; 6:20; 7:28; 8:1, 10; 9:2, 11, 27, 60, 62; 10:9, 11; 11:2, 20; 12:31-32; 13:18, 20, 28-29; 14:15; 16:16; 17:20-21; 18:16-17, 24-25, 29-30; 19:11; 21:31; 22:16, 18, 29; 23:42, 51; Acts 1:3-6; 8:12; 14:22; 19:8; 20:25; 28:23, 31.

59 Charles R. Swindoll, *Insights on 1 & 2 Timothy, Titus* (Carol Stream, IL: Tyndale, 2014).